The College Game

The Coll

Game

Special Photography by Malcolm Emmons

A Rutledge Book
Bobbs-Merrill
Indianapolis/New York

Fred R. Sammis: *Director*
John Sammis: *Creative Director*
Doris Townsend: *Editor-in-Chief*
Allan Mogel: *Art Director*
Sally Andrews: *Managing Editor*
Jeremy Friedlander: *Associate Editor*
Mimi Koren: *Associate Editor*
Arthur Gubernick: *Production Consultant*
Annemarie Bosch: *Production Manager*
Elyse Shick: *Art Associate*
David Russell: *Art Associate*
Jay Hyams: *Editorial Assistant*

Bob Gutkowski: *Contributing Editor*

Contents

Saturday's Child

by Furman Bisher

ootball was not discovered; it had no clear beginning. Historians point to the 1869 Rutgers-Princeton match as the first football game, but long before it young men had found pleasure in scurrying about a field, seemingly detached from one another, only to collide in a writhing mass of limbs and bodies. Ever since, football has evolved—from the flying wedge to the basic T-formation and its sophisticated wishbone offspring; from bleak battles in the mud to festive affairs, accompanied by brightly uniformed brass bands and briefly skirted pompon girls; from a casually interested clump of spectators to 80,000 clamoring partisans thundering in unison, "We're number one!"

Football American Style

It is overcast in East Lansing, Michigan, a town whose very name suggests college football, but thousands mill about the Michigan State campus. With pennants, badges, buttons, jackets, and an occasional partisan outburst, the fans proclaim their allegiance for the big game to come. Already on this cold, soggy day, on a field not many yards from the Spartan Stadium gridiron, an NCAA soccer play-off game has begun. A handful of curious football fans, momentarily diverted, peer through the fence at the players romping about and at another handful of fans huddled in the jury box of stands along the sideline of the soccer field. To the goaltender's father or the center forward's girl friend, this match is the struggle of the day. But to the 78,000 fans who have come to Michigan State for football American style, the soccer game may as well be marbles.

They have traveled all distances to watch the match for the national championship of college football—an unofficial title to be accorded the winner of a fearsome match-up: undefeated Michigan State, coached by impish Duffy Dougherty, will battle equally impressive Notre Dame, directed by smooth Ara Parseghian, a car salesman on TV in his spare time. Unfortunately for the rabid crowd, the game decides nothing; it ends in a tie, and the once-fevered partisans depart disconsolately subdued.

In isolated northwest Arkansas, lines of cars grope through the November fog in search of Fayetteville, where the University of Arkansas Razorbacks are to defend their fortress against the invasion of damnable Texas Tech and their devilish leader, Donny Anderson. On the battlefield the two teams dispatch the lingering uncertainty as to who rules the Southwest Conference. That night the cars desert Fayetteville, a small town that seems barely large enough to accommodate the university, much less the warring teams and their legions of supporters. Like a long, hideous monster, the cars strangle the twisting Ozark highways, the headlights shining through the foggy darkness. Arkansas having prevailed that day, a hillbilly eulogist sings of the victory on the car radios, creating an instant folk hero in tribute to one of the boys of Arkansas.

"Jon Brittenum wuh-uh-uh-z a quarterbacking man. . . ."

On still another Saturday, Cajun accents flow gently across the hedges and the statuary of the campus at Notre Dame. "The Fighting Irish," hallowed, dominant, steeped in the tradition of Rockne, will meet the Bengal Tigers, from Lousiana State, gregariously indulgent, vociferously challenging the world in Baton Rouge, where there are Saturday nights like no others in the world. The two teams have never before come together on a football field. Today, to mark the inaugural game, Louisiana has followed its team en masse, drawn both by the auguries of the collision and by the chance to visit this citadel of Holy Church football.
"Hail Mary, full of grace . . .
Coach Rockne is in his place."

The southern fans flood the campus store in search of souvenirs. They pause and gaze in awe at the statue of Father Sorin, whose arm is raised, as if signaling, it has been said, for a fair catch. They look for a trace of Rockne's trail—surely there must be some mark preserved—before which to stand and be reverent. Or Leahy—they would settle for him. They are frustrated, and later even more so when defeat comes at the foot of a fat, unathletic field-goal kicker named Hempel, who accounts for the decisive, and the only, score.

Two Rural Scenes

The screen door screeched for oil as it opened. A boy, carrying his school books under his arm, let the door slam behind him. He approached the proprietor at the back of the general store, walking past the candy case and the shelves stacked with canned goods on one side and piles of Blue Bell overalls on the other. Judge of recorder court, township checkers champion, and father of the hell-raising star center on the high school basketball team and pitcher on the baseball team, proprietor Lineberry Hill straightened up from stoking the pot-bellied stove, turned to the boy, and said sorrowfully, "Knute Rockne's been killed in an airplane crash."

For a moment the man felt close to the boy, generally regarded, in spite of his youth, as the town's authority on sports records, history, and personalities. "Knute Rockne—dead," the man repeated, turning back to his stoking.

The village where they lived, tucked away in a grassy niche of the South, offered a few hills rising to the west, a small railroad that served the residents twice a day, a water tank on a hill, the imported daily newspaper that arrived each morning from Greensboro, and an unwavering attachment to football. The townspeople knew the game well. They knew that Albie Booth was "Little Boy Blue," who made Yale yell on Saturday, that Warburton of Southern California would surely be All-America that season, that Cagle would not be back at West Point because he had committed the crime of secret wedlock. By way of old Atwater Kent radios that sometimes belched, scratched, and squawked, but always delivered, the fans regularly tuned in the stentorian voice of Ted Husing, who described the Saturday football dramas.

This was college football before its epidemic popularity. Far from the playing fields, a fan could unleash his imagination and visualize a clean, pure game played by Galahads of the campuses. Only later would television deliver the game in full color and, with its intimacy, blemish that vision.

Forty years later, in another small town, deep in Mississippi, the only paved street is the highway that cuts between the town's few buildings—some houses, a church with an adjoining cemetery, a cotton gin, a popcorn-box post office, and the filling station, which is also a grocery store, a drugstore, and a farm-supply store. A motorist passing through stops for a fill-up and ventures to converse with the gas station attendant, an old man in khaki pants, denim shirt, and ageless hat.

"So this is the hometown of Buster Brewer?"

"Nope. Buster don't live in town. He lives out aways. Rode the school bus over here to the high school."

"Poor kid. Must have been tough on a boy trying to play football."

"Nope. Sometimes the coach would take him home after practice. Other times he'd walk, what times he didn't run. Wuzn't no more than two, three miles. Had to get home to hep with the stock. Got a younger brother now that's playin' but he'll never be like Buster. Got uhn old jalopy he rides in all the time. Comes from a good family. His daddy owns the house they live in and twenty-two acres of land he farms. Always pays right on time."

The Perfect Metaphor

Under the gun of a deadline in a chilled press box on a Saturday afternoon, newspapermen record the history of the game they have just witnessed. While the stadium empties and the cars in the parking lot laboriously disentangle themselves from a jam that dwarfs the most massive goal-line pileup, the writers peck at their typewriters, glance at the scarred turf below, and seek the inspiration of Grantland Rice, who looked down on the Polo Grounds battlefield in 1924 after Notre Dame had beaten Army, and wrote, "Outlined against a blue-gray October sky, the Four Horsemen rode again. In dramatic lore they are known as Famine, Pestilence, Destruction, and Death. These are only aliases. Their real names are Stuhldreher, Miller, Crowley, and Layden. They formed the crest of the South Bend cyclone before which another fighting Army team was swept over the precipice. . . ."

The source of such inspired prose was a Notre Dame student serving as the athletic department's information director. George Strickler, now retired as sports editor of the

Chicago Tribune, had attended a movie, "The Four Horsemen of the Apocalypse," the night before with the Notre Dame squad. The next day coach Knute Rockne raised false hope in the Cadets by starting mainly second stringers against them. Then he rushed on Stuhldreher, Miller, Crowley, and Layden. He watched the Irish roll up eight first downs to Army's none and take a 7-0 lead in the second quarter. At half-time Strickler moved through the press box, stopped at Rice's chair, and excitedly told the veteran sportswriter, "Our backfield reminds me of that movie we saw last night, Mr. Rice, 'The Four Horsemen.'"

Armed with this fragment, Rice's mind raced to the task after the game ended, and the memorable lead sprang from his typewriter. It had an explosive effect. By Monday four horses were rounded up and delivered to the Notre Dame practice field for what would prove to be one of the monumental publicity pictures of all times—Stuhldreher, Miller, Crowley, and Layden in the saddles.

Dinner and a Show

In the parking lots before the game, the high society of football gathers informally. Once these patrons arrived in buggies, which they often drew next to the field. Later they came by automobile to see their team play. Armed with a marvelous invention, the forward pass, and chastened by President Theodore Roosevelt's stern admonitions ("Brutality and foul play should receive the same summary punishment given to a man who cheats at cards"), football was no longer a simple campus diversion with which a few boys let off some steam and entertained a few hundred on the grounds. Football had moved from the province of the students to the hearts and pocketbooks of the old grads, who now made it a point to see that the old school kept up with other schools. Rivalries were born.

Today the parking lots fill with station wagons, mobile homes, campers, and sports cars. Where the weather permits, picnics have become an unofficial, and in some small towns a necessary, preface to the game. Football crowds used to overwhelm small college towns with demands for food until the prudent fan began to provide his own. Now the tailgate party is firmly a part of the Saturday afternoon ritual.

At Tiger Stadium in Baton Rouge, where Lousiana State plays its games at night to avoid the oppressive heat, the parking lots begin to fill as early as 4 P. M. Station wagons sit yawning, their tailgates flopped open, while families mill about like Scottish clans at the Highland games.

Years ago Duke University began to barbecue meat inside the stadium to provide for the hungry masses. The fires were started the night before, and early on Saturday morning, the succulent fragrance wafted across the field where the Blue Devils would meet the opposition later in the day.

At Stanford studied elegance prevails over the yard party. Families set up their tables and attempt to outdo their neighbors with the elaborateness of their centerpieces. Linen, candles, sometimes formal wear, silver buckets of iced champagne, and the other portable accoutrements of the country club are part of the Palo Alto scene.

Clemson, South Carolina, population 5,000, absorbs a near smothering invasion on football weekends. The football stadium, christened "Death Valley" by a former head coach, Frank Howard, who would try anything to intimidate the opposition, now accommodates 60,000. Without the picnicking tailgater and the athletic department's barbecue lunches, the little town would be overwhelmed by starving fans (and would find new meaning in its stadium's nickname).

Spectacle and its Censor

A town changes when a game is to be played there. Ribbons flutter from the lampposts, banners stretch across busy streets, shop windows display portraits of players, coaches, even mascots. The football teams may be weak, but the flavor of the day strengthens them. The University of South Carolina used to meet Clemson in Columbia, South Carolina, on "Big Thursday." Almost a sideshow to the annual state fair there, the game was played amidst prize cattle, popcorn and cotton candy vendors, home-canned vegetables, Ferris wheels, and shooting galleries. It was the only college football game in America on that day; it was a headline in Seattle as well as in Baltimore.

Like all college football crowds, the Big

Thursday throng saw its share of sophomoric pranks. Once a Clemson partisan ran the length of the field wringing the neck of a gamecock, symbol of the South Carolina team. Another year a band of South Carolina fraternity men raced onto the field dressed as the Clemson team. Their masquerade was flawless, and even the Clemson faithful applauded, noting that in the role of coach Frank Howard the fraternity men had not forgotten to cast a man with a properly protruding paunch.

Unfortunately, Clemson alumni in the state legislature eventually grew weary of coming to hostile Gamecock territory each year. They forced the transfer of the game to a Saturday on alternate campuses and so discontinued a tradition as bloodlessly as they had dispatched roosters in their college days. Similarly disgruntled legislators in Louisiana futilely tried to bar coach Paul Dietzel, a winner obviously, from leaving LSU for West Point. The college game, like collegians in general, bears the afflictions of overprotective parents.

Emigrants to the City

College football is found in towns so small they share their names with their schools—College Station, Texas; State College, Pennsylvania; Auburn, Alabama—and in cities that offer lucrative deals for staging the annual contest between out-of-town traditional rivals. The Texas-Oklahoma game belongs to Dallas, an insane city when the Sooners from the north and the Longhorns from the south converge like two armies of cowhands celebrating the end of a cattle drive.

Many years ago, the athletic departments at both Florida and Georgia universities needed money to supplement budgets that were as modest and as haphazard as the vest-pocket offices where they originated. Offering the services of local promotional agencies that neither Gainesville, Florida, nor Athens, Georgia, could match, Jacksonville inherited the Florida-Georgia game. Frequently called "the capital of South Georgia," Jacksonville was a neat geographical compromise. The game grew into a classic social sports event of the South long before the Gator Bowl, also staged in Jacksonville, became a gala holiday affair. Besides football, the Florida-Georgia game

boasts "the world's largest outdoor cocktail party," a dubiously honorary title that is nonetheless much borrowed. It's the only football game, someone once wrote of the Florida-Georgia match, that begins on Tuesday and doesn't end until Sunday night.

The Fans' Pastime

No one has yet devised a popularly accepted system of each year selecting the finest college football team in the nation. Neither the news services that poll member sportswriters, nor a board of coaches, nor any syndicated columnist can settle with the definitiveness of a Super Bowl or the World Series the disputes over who is number one. The issue is fiercely debated and invariably left unresolved wherever fans talk football. At local Touchdown, Quarterback, Morning After, or Fifth Quarter clubs, those who are willing to pay a membership fee and subject themselves to wan chicken and shriveled peas can find a congenial forum for their weekly discussions.

Perhaps in search of some official recognition, these clubs honor a variety of football personalities with plaques and citations. Some say this custom began at New York's Downtown Athletic Club, which each year chooses a most valuable player of college football and bestows upon him the Heisman Trophy. Southerners claim that Atlanta's Touchdown Club, which still shuns the pro game, was the first to honor the college stars.

Whether they meet in posh clubs or country stores, college football enthusiasts, like all sports fans, soothe themselves with reminiscences, of disastrous as well as triumphant moments. I remember the crushing blindside block of Alex Wojciechowicz, one of Fordham's "Seven Blocks of Granite," on Andy Bershak in Chapel Hill. When Bershak died a few years later, some of the old players dated his demise from Wojciechowicz's block.

Charlie ("Choo Choo") Justice was a sailor who got no closer to World War II than a training base in Maryland. When the war ended and he settled at North Carolina after rejecting offers from a host of other schools, his glowing reputation as a football player preceded him. "I understand Mr. Justice has entered school at North Carolina," remarked coach Carl Snavely

laconically. "I hope he comes out for football."
He did, of course, and fulfilled every expectation.

It's pleasant to remember too the names
almost everyone else has forgotten. Sons of the
Irish have memorialized the victory over Ohio
State in 1935, when with the final seconds
fleeing, Bill Shakespeare won the game with a
toss to Wayne Millner for Notre Dame's second
touchdown in three minutes. Jim McKenna was
part of that play. A sophomore quarterback from
St. Paul, Minnesota, who had not been chosen to
travel with the football squad, McKenna had
packed his uniform and boarded the student
train. He had no admission ticket, but in
Columbus he sought out coach Elmer Layden and
won permission to watch the game in uniform
from the bench.

The rules then allowed no player to leave the
game and return in the same quarter, and
Layden, who had been sending in plays with
substitutes, found himself without a messenger
when Andy Pilney was injured. He turned to
McKenna and gave him the play. The sophomore
raced on the field to call it, Shakespeare threw to
Millner, and McKenna returned to the bench. A
few weeks later he dropped out of school,
having played only one play for Notre Dame.
Except for the player who called it, the play was
unforgettable.

An Innocent Error
Roy Riegels made a glaring mistake in the most
important game of his era before the biggest
audience of the year, including millions at home
listening to the first coast-to-coast radio
broadcast of a football game. He ran the wrong
way with the ball against Georgia Tech in the
1929 Rose Bowl game. Fixated with the memory
of that wild boner, many football fans recall
Riegels only as a bungler, not as captain of his
team the next season nor as center on the
Associated Press second All-America team. Those
achievements have been buried.

Today, well-preserved and good natured, Roy
Riegels gracefully ages in a small town in central
California, where he is a seed and feed
wholesaler. From necessity he has learned to
laugh at himself and to live with his image. He
smiles easily, retains his dignity, and disarmingly
admits, "I still thought I was going the right
way."

The Eccentric and the Infamous
College football is not a game that successfully
preserves the distinction between spectator and
player. At or near the end of the game, football
fans, like other sports fans, invade the field and
unconsciously search for the real game, not fully
satisfied with having vicariously experienced it
from afar for two-and-a-half hours. On the field
you can examine the jagged wounds that a
halfback's sharp cutbacks have left in the grass,
or the deep ruts gouged by the foot of a stubborn
tackle who would not give ground.

The true zealot can't always keep himself off
the battlefield until the last shot has been fired
and the soldiers have moved on. I won't forget
the man in Berkeley, California, whom a
photographer caught running formlessly from
the stands, awkwardly attempting to tackle
youthful Tom Harmon of Michigan. Many years
later, when a curious reporter tracked him down,
the wayward pursuer admitted that on that day
he had stopped in a bar, had had a few too
many, and had accepted a companion's dare. I
can empathize with him, having been a lowly
student manager who stood on the sideline
barely restrained and watched Ace Parker pass
only a few feet away on a 107-yard trip to the
North Carolina end zone. What partisan has not
wanted to leap to the defense of his team?

The game has learned to tolerate these Walter
Mittys. The impulsive fan who rushed onto the
field is soon forgiven and largely forgotten. But
the player on the sideline who surrenders to that
mad inspiration is branded for life. Tommy Lewis's
unauthorized sally onto the Cotton Bowl field to
halt Dickie Moegle was born in the same frenzy
as the sloshed fan's. Lewis, however, made the
tackle, and for that will never be forgotten or
forgiven. He can still diagram the play.

"Everybody was standing up watching; all of
us along the sideline were. They ran a sweep
and turned our defensive end—a flip, I
remember that. And here came Moegle, doing
eighty or eighty-five, I suppose. As he got closer,
I turned to Corky Tharp, who was probably
our best runner, and said, 'He's going all
the way.'

"I turned back around, and there he was—
right in my line. Right in it. I don't know if it was
a conditioned reflex or not. I don't know why I

did what I did. I lowered my head, and I hit him; I hit him as hard as I could. I knew it wasn't premeditated. If it had been, I'd have put my helmet on."

That inglorious moment ruined Lewis's reputation as the wrong-way run destroyed Riegels's. Football fans no longer remember that Lewis scored Alabama's only touchdown in that 1954 game against Rice. Worse, Lewis found himself subjected to a reenactment some years later when a player on the high school team he coached leaped off the bench and tackled an opponent.

Lewis and his protégé were only continuing the tradition of one Hooks Autrey, who deviously conspired before a game to burst from the sidelines into a play. Ordered not to dress for the game but to position himself near the sideline after the kickoff, Autrey dashed on the field on the first play from scrimmage, caught a touchdown pass, and set off a riot. He was (by default) the best-dressed receiver in history.

A Few More Tales

College football is rich with such weird legends and traditions, many from schools with only modest prowess at football. After head coach Gordon Kirkland of Catawba College was stricken by a heart attack at the beginning of the 1945 season, his doctor ordered him to rest in bed. The war years had pared Kirkland's staff of assistants to one, clearly not enough manpower to efficiently oversee practice. So Kirkland rigged up a telephone line from his home to the football field and directed practice from his bed. On game days, however, the doctor ordered the line disconnected, leaving Kirkland to judge his team's progress only from the cries that floated through his window from the nearby field. Appraising his team by this haphazard method, susceptible as it was to wishful misinterpretation, Kirkland might recuperate better, felt the doctor, than if he were subjected to blunt, coldly realistic telephone reports.

The coach at Renssalaer Poly, Ed Jontos, could find no replacement large enough for the size 12 1/2 shoe ripped off the foot of Stanley Gorzelnic, who had decimated Buffalo until dispatched from the game for lack of footwear. Jontos ordered his players to remove their shoes and check the sizes, but no one's was large

enough. With Renssalaer deprived of Gorzelnic, Buffalo took advantage and won. Afterward Jontos undressed in the locker room, removed his shoes, and saw their size: 12 1/2.

A halfback at Appalachian State awoke in the middle of the night from a dream so portentous that he rushed to tell the school's publicity director. Drowsily the publicity man, who had been content with his own dreams, heard the halfback's vision of the next day's game against Catawba: reserve halfback Earl Henson would come in with a few seconds left and run 96 yards for the winning touchdown. Happily unburdened, the halfback went back to sleep, and the next day his prediction came true.

In the days when a timer on the sideline kept the official time and there were no big field clocks to keep spectators or participants informed, the coach at Greeley State in Colorado turned to a substitute near the end of the game and ordered, "Go check the time, son."

Returning from the timer's table a moment later, the sub breathlessly blurted, "It's a quarter to four, coach."

The Accoutrements Have Meaning

The life of the college game is found not only on the field but in the peripheral activities. The entreaties and the tricks of the cheerleading squad, the prettiness of the pompon girls, the stirring sounds of the bands, are all part of the flavor of the college game, but transfer them to a professional game and there is nothing more meaningless and unnecessary.

College football thrives on deep loyalty, tradition, the sight of a bell tower, and the sound of its bells. Staged in such an idealized setting, it is a game of inspired make-believe. Unlike pro football players, who are working—sometimes with the mundane cares of miners, desk clerks, or stockbrokers—college players are playing—heatedly but usually not with their careers at stake. Ninety-eight percent of them will never play the game again after they finish college. The game that seems all-important on Saturday night really isn't, nor should it be.

At times the most professional of amateur sports, college football still retains the freshness its professional counterpart may have lost. For the players as well as the fans, it is still a game, and perhaps that is why it continues to flourish.

To Uphold the H

eritage: the East
by Mervin D. Hyman

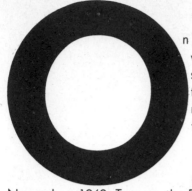

"On Saturday, November 6, Princeton sent 25 picked men to play our 25 a match game of football."

That sentence, the beginning of a routine story in the November, 1969, *Targum*, the Rutgers University paper, announced the birth of football. The infant was delivered in New Brunswick, New Jersey, by inventive young men from Rutgers University and nearby Princeton University, natural rivals at almost anything, from penny-pitching to billiards.

From a sluggish child, the game would mature to a dynamic adult—a big-time sport that today captures the fancy of millions. Each fall its fans overflow college and professional stadiums or spend their weekends watching on television, unaware for the most part of the game's humble origins.

That first football game attracted very little attention outside central New Jersey. The *Targum*, however, curious about this latest competition between Rutgers and Princeton, reported it in some detail.

The strangers came up in the 10 o'clock train, and brought a good number of backers with them. After dinner, and a stroll around the town, during which stroll billiards received a good deal of attention, the crowds began to assemble at the ball ground, which, for the benefit of the ignorant, we would say, is a lot about a hundred yards wide, extending from College Avenue to Sicard Street. Previous to calling the game, the ground presented an animated picture. Grim looking players were silently stripping, each one surrounded by sympathizing friends, while around each of the captains [William J. Leggett of Rutgers, who later became a distinguished clergyman of the Dutch Reformed Church, and William S. Gummere of Princeton, who served as chief justice of the Supreme Court of New Jersey for 31 years] *was a little crowd, intent upon giving advice, and saying as much as possible. The appearance of the Princeton men was very different from that of our own players. They were almost without exception tall and muscular, while the majority of our twenty-five are small and light, but possess the merit of being up to much more than they look.*

Very few were the preliminaries, and they were quickly agreed upon. The Princeton captain, for some reason or other, gave up every point to our men without contesting one. The only material points were that Princeton gave up "free kicks," whereby a player, when he catches the ball in the air is allowed to kick it without hindrance. On the other hand, our practice of "babying" [holding] *the ball on the start was discarded, and the ball was mounted, in every instance, by a vigorous "long kick"* [similar to today's kickoff.]

Princeton won the toss, and chose the first mount, rather oddly, since it had been agreed to start the ball against the wind. At 3 P.M., the game was called [begun]. *The Princetonians suffered from making a very bad 'mount' or*

THE FOOT-BALL MATCH.

On Saturday, November 6th, Princeton sent twenty-five picked men to play our twenty-five a match game of foot-ball. The strangers came up in the 10 o'clock train, and brought a good number of backers with them. After dinner, and a stroll around the town, during which stroll billiards received a good deal of attention, the crowds began to assemble at the ball ground, which, for the benefit of the ignorant, we would say, is a lot about a hundred yards wide, extending from College Avenue to Sicard-street. Previous to calling the game, the ground presented an animated picture. Grim-looking players were silently stripping, each one surrounded by sympathizing friends, while around each of the captains was a little crowd, intent upon giving advice, and saying as much as possible. The appearance of the Princeton men was very different from that of our own players. They were almost without exception tall and muscular, while the majority of our twenty-five are small and light, but possess the merit of being up to much more than they look.

Very few were the preliminaries, and they were quickly agreed upon. The Princeton captain, for some reason or other, gave up every point to our men without contesting one. The only material points were, that Princeton gave up "free kicks," whereby a player, when he catches the ball in the air is allowed to kick it without hindrance.

Preceding pages: *En route to annual battle with Navy, Army Cadets receive encouragement from classmates.*
Left: Rutgers's newspaper, The Targum reports on the first football game.
Opposite: Marshall Goldberg. Top: Rutgers plays Rensselaer in football game that more resembles rugby. Above: Rutgers versus Haverford, 1910.

*Two coaches with enviable records:
Lou Little of Columbia (top)
and Cornell's coach for 15 years,
Gilmour Dobie (above).
Opposite: Yale's Albie Booth.*

"buck" [kickoff] *as they call it; the effects of
which were not remedied before the sides closed,
and after a brief struggle, Rutgers drove it home
[between the goal posts] and won, amid great
applause from the crowd. The sides were
changed, Rutgers started the ball, and after a
somewhat longer fight, Princeton made it a tie
by a well directed kick, from a gentleman whose
name we don't know, but who did the best·
kicking on the Princeton side.*

*To describe the varying fortunes of the match,
game by game, would be a waste of labor, for
every game was like the one before. There was
the same headlong running, wild shouting and
frantic kicking. In every game the cool
goaltenders saved the Rutgers goal half a dozen
times; in every game the heavy charger of the
Princeton side overthrew everything he came in
contact with; and in every game, just when the
interest in one of those delightful rushes at the
fence was culminating, the persecuted ball
would fly for refuge into the next lot, and
produce·a cessation of hostilities until, after the
invariable "foul", it was put in straight.*

*Well, at last we won the match, having won
the 1st, 3rd, 5th, 6th, 9th, and 10th games;
leaving Princeton the 2nd, 4th, 7th, and 8th. The
seventh game probably would have been added
to our score, but for one of our players, who, in
his ardor, forgot which way he was kicking, a
mistake which he fully atoned for afterward.*

*To sum up. Princeton had the most muscle, but
didn't kick very well, and wanted organization.
They evidently don't like to kick the ball on the
ground. Our men, on the other hand, though
comparatively weak, ran well, and kicked well
throughout. But their great point was their
organization, for which great praise is due to the
Captain, Leggett '72. The right men were always
in the right place.*

*After the match, the players had an amicable
"feed" together, and at 8 o'clock our guests went
home, in high good spirits, but thirsting to beat
us next time, if they can.*

*The next time was the following Saturday at
the Princeton ball grounds, and Princeton did
win, 8-0. The* Targum *dutifully reported
Rutgers's defeat, graciously noting, "Their cheer
sounding as if they meant to explode, but for a
fortunate escape of air, followed by a grateful*

yell at the deliverance of such a catastrophe, still sounds in our ears as we thank them for their hospitality. If we must be beaten, we are glad to have such conquerors."

The occasion of the first football game was celebrated a century later, when Rutgers and Princeton met in 1969, for the sixtieth time in New Brunswick. Again, Rutgers triumphed, 29-0. Unhappily for the Scarlet, however, victories in this venerable series have been scarce. Through 1972, Princeton leads in games 52-11.

The Early Dynasties

From 1889 to 1923, except for an odd year, the East completely dominated college football. The region's Big Three—Harvard, Yale, and Princeton—annually provided the nation with its number-one team, as picked by the Helms Athletic Association. (The AP and UPI polls, generally regarded now as authoritative, didn't begin until 1936 and 1950, respectively.) Pennsylvania and later Cornell would occasionally wrest the top ranking from the older schools. Still, Yale, Harvard, and Princeton produced the fiercest rivalries and the most legendary heroes.

Harvard men still point with pride to Marshall Newell, a tackle who played from 1890-93, Charlie Daly, a star from 1898-1900 who later played for Army, Charley Brickley, the great drop-kicker in 1912 and 1913, Huntington ("Tack") Hardwick, a superb end, Eddie Mahan of the pre-World War I teams, and a little later, Eddie Casey, an elusive, hard-running back. Princeton had Edgar Allen Poe, a nephew of the famed poet, Knowlton ("Snake") Ames, Shep Homans, Langdon Lea, and later Jack Slagle.

Yale's list reads like a *Who's Who* of college football: Almos Alonzo Stagg, William ("Pudge") Heffelfinger, a guard who may have been the strongest man ever to play college football, the immortal Frank Hickey, a spectacular runner they called "the Disembodied Spirit," Tom Shevlin, a distinguished end, Ted Coy, who ran Eli opponents ragged from 1907-09, and Century Milstead, the best tackle in the country in 1923.

So intense was the rivalry among the Big Three that on December 1, 1883, it inspired the Reverend Henry Ward Beecher, the prestigious Brooklyn preacher, to thunder to his congregation, "I stood yesterday to see Yale and Princeton at football. I always did hate Princeton, but I took notice there was not a coward on either side, although I thank God that Yale beat."

Michigan's famed and powerful point-a-minute teams broke the Eastern dynasty in 1901 and 1902, and coach Amos Alonzo Stagg's Chicago club, which snapped the Wolverines' long winning streak with a 2-0 upset, was acclaimed the national champion in 1905. Otherwise, the only outlanders to surpass the Eastern football powers were Georgia Tech in 1917 and California in 1920. Army in 1914, Cornell in 1915, 1921, and 1922, and Pittsburgh in 1916 and 1918 wrested the national championship from the Big Three.

Under coach Gil Dobie, Cornell had the first unbeaten and untied team in its history in 1915 but only later reached its peak, with three straight undefeated clubs, (in 1921-23), led by quarterback George Pfann and halfback Eddie Kaw. Pfann, later a Rhodes scholar at Oxford, a member of the staff of General George S. Patton, Jr., during World War II, and an assistant United States Attorney, ran the team with the precision of a drill sergeant while Kaw perplexed opponents with his daring running. Swede Hanson and Sunny Sundstrom, a pair of superb tackles, and Charlie Cassidy at end led the charge up front.

Gloomy Gil Dobie, was a tall, spare, dour Scot who had earned his nickname with perennial, if unwarranted, pessimism. He had achieved unusual success as the head coach at the University of Washington, where he had nine unbeaten teams, and at Navy. He was a perfectionist and a demanding taskmaster who rarely flattered a player. Once, after his Washington team had trounced California 72-0, Dobie ordered his squad to run a couple of laps around the field to ensure that no one was out of shape after the easy victory.

Gloomy Gil compensated for his unwinning personality with success on the field. In 33 years of coaching, he established a sterling record of 180-45-15 and piloted 14 unbeaten teams. He developed the off-tackle smash, which operated with drill-like precision. It became one of the most dreaded power plays in football and has

been a model for many of today's coaches.

In 1923, as big-time football emerged in other sections of the country, the East lost its near monopoly on football powerhouses. Illinois, with wondrous Red Grange, began the breakthrough. But despite its dearth of championship teams since the twenties, Eastern football hasn't disappeared from the national scene. It has been the rare year when one or more teams from the East have not ranked among the top ten in either the AP or the UPI poll. And there have been a couple of years, such as 1968 and 1969, when the East has been barely (Penn State partisans say unjustly) deprived of a national crown.

Meehan's Violets

There was a new man at New York University in 1925, and he began to make his presence felt soon after he arrived. John ("Chick") Meehan, who had been a star player and later the successful head coach at Syracuse, was recruited by NYU to revive the Violets' sagging football fortunes. A flamboyant showman, Meehan began to gather a flock of high-powered stars. He instituted what he called "the military huddle" and "the shift" (both of which he had his team practice aboard the old *U.S.S. Illinois*, then moored in the Hudson River). The Violets,

who once had blushed at the mention of football, entered a golden era. Over a three-year period, 1926-28, NYU lost only four games. (Nebraska beat Chick Meehan's team in '26 and '27, and Georgetown and Oregon State defeated NYU in '28.) In 1928, the Violets upset Carnegie Tech 27-13 just a week after the Tartans, then something of a power in the East, had stunned Notre Dame.

NYU built its attack around Ken Strong, a solid 200-pounder who crashed through enemy lines or used his blinding speed to go around them. He ran, passed, punted, and kicked field goals and extra points. Later he brought his many talents to pro football's New York Giants. In addition to Strong, several other stars helped to forge those NYU teams into national contenders: Cowboy Ed Hill, Len Grant, Jack Connor, Frank Briante, and Al Lassman, a burly, tremendously strong tackle who also was the collegiate heavyweight boxing champion. Tragically, three of those stars met an untimely death. Lassman drowned trying to save a youngster; Hill was shot and killed in a scuffle; Grant was killed by lightning.

Yale's Bullet; Harvard's Rifle

Yale and Harvard hardly tore up the turf in the late 1920s and early 1930s, but they did produce

23

a pair of stars who dominated the Eastern scene. The brightest was Yale's Albie Booth, a 144-pound dynamo who exploded against a good Army team one Saturday afternoon in 1929. Early in the second quarter in the Yale Bowl, big, powerful Army led the Elis 13-0 on runs by Chris ("Red") Cagle and John Murrell. Confident of an easy romp, the Cadets could hardly have noticed when the spindly Booth trotted on the field. But within minutes, the inimitable Albie, inevitably nicknamed "Little Boy Blue," brought Yale back with one of the most memorable individual performances. Flitting like a wraith, he first led the Elis on a 32-yard march, scored the touchdown that culminated it, and drop-kicked the extra point. Then he took his team 35 yards for another touchdown and again drop-kicked the extra point. Suddenly, Yale led 14-13 in a game that every one of the 80,000 fans in the Yale Bowl had moments before given up for lost.

There was more to come. Booth took an Army punt on his 35-yard line and with spectacular open-field chicanery squirmed 65 yards through the Cadets' entire team for the final touchdown in Yale's 21-13 upset. After demoralizing the Cadets, Albie Booth continued to distinguish himself in his career at Yale. He was one of the school's all-time greats.

About the same time, Harvard introduced quarterback Barry Wood, a sharpshooting passer and devastating runner who later became a famous physician. Wood enthralled Harvard fans for three years, and in 1931 was named to the All-American team.

The Mighty Lions
Columbia struck one of the most telling blows for Eastern football in the 1934 Rose Bowl. Except for a humiliating 20-0 loss to Princeton, coach Lou Little's Lions had enjoyed huge success in the 1933 season, including solid victories over Penn State, Navy, and Syracuse—three very worthy opponents. But Eastern football, especially the Ivy League brand, was so lightly regarded by the rest of the nation that the prospect of Columbia meeting Stanford in the Rose Bowl evoked howls of derision, especially from Old Nassau. With a super backfield led by Bobby Grayson and Bones Hamilton and a powerful line anchored by Bob Reynolds at tackle, Stanford was a heavy favorite to trounce the upstarts from the East.

The experts speculated only on the margin of victory.

A torrential downpour the day and night before the game drenched the field. It was still raining when the teams lined up for kickoff. In this quagmire the Lions of Columbia played Stanford's mighty Indians to a standstill, repulsing the heralded Grayson and Hamilton whenever they threatened. Then, in the second quarter, the Lions reached Stanford's 17-yard line and played one of coach Little's specials.

Quarterback Cliff Montgomery took the ball from center, spun away from the line, and handed the ball to fullback Al Barabas. Barabas faked another handoff to a back crashing into the Stanford line and then, with the defense pulled off balance, bolted around his left end. Stanford hardly noticed until he crossed the goal line. That score and the subsequent extra point gave Columbia a 7-0 lead, which it held grimly to the end of the bitterly fought game. It was perhaps the greatest victory in Columbia's largely uninspiring football history and certainly a major triumph for Eastern football.

The Elis' Complementary Opposites
Yale added to its magnificent football lore in the mid-thirties through the efforts of Clint Frank and Larry Kelley, as disparate a pair as ever played for the Elis. An extraordinary runner and passer with a sharp football mind, Frank ran the Yale team from his left halfback position. On defense Clint was the team's best tackler, and he had an uncanny knack for diagnosing and breaking up enemy pass plays. For three seasons, 1936-38, he was the heart and soul of the triumphant Elis. Kelley, a superb pass-catching end, was glib, witty, and immodest. Once, after aborting a Harvard end sweep, he inquired boldly of the Crimson quarterback, "What kind of judgment do you call that, trying Kelley's end on fourth down?"

Another time, when Penn was leading Yale 20-6 (the Elis eventually won, 31-20), one of the Pennsylvanians chided Kelley, "I thought you were a gabby guy, Kelley. What's the matter, a little bashful today?"

Remembering that Penn's lineup included several names with more consonants than vowels, Larry retorted "Oh, do you fellows speak English?"

24

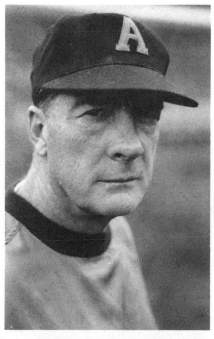

Old Elis still fondly remember his performances. Navy remembers him less kindly for a bit of trickery that turned the tide against the sailors in 1936. In that game Yale trailed 7-6 when the Elis' Tony Mott punted to Navy's Sneed Schmidt, who promptly fumbled on his 25. Rushing downfield to cover the kick, Kelley "accidentally" kicked the ball. It bounded to Navy's 2-yard line before Kelley recovered it. Two plays later, Frank pounded over for the touchdown that gave Yale a 12-7 victory.

Navy protested of course that Kelley had intentionally kicked the ball. Kelley insisted that he hadn't, but his disclaimer convinced no one but the officials. The argument raged for months until even the rules committee found itself debating the questionable play. Soon, the committee changed the rule so that all free balls that are kicked, deliberately or accidentally, are declared dead on the spot. In addition to his contribution to Yale football, Larry Kelley made his mark on the rules of the game.

Both Kelley and Frank received All-American recognition (Kelley's selection was unanimous), and both were Heisman Trophy winners, Kelley in 1936 and Frank in 1937.

Pitt versus Fordham

From 1935 to 1937, the Pitt teams of coach Jock Sutherland and the Fordham clubs of coach Jim Crowley clashed in some of the most bruising battles the East has seen. The two superb teams were able to beat almost everybody but each other; in those three years, the Panthers and Rams played three straight scoreless ties— "Much Ado About Nothing to Nothing," said Tim Cohane, the noted author who was then the sports information director at Fordham.

Neither Sutherland nor Crowley believed much in throwing the ball. Sutherland's teams completed an entire season having attempted no more passes than one of today's teams will throw in a single game. The style of the day was ground play and Sutherland had one of the finest backfields for it. Marshall Goldberg, Dick Cassiano, John Chickerneo, Harold ("Curly") Stebbins, Frank Patrick, John Michelosen, Bill Stapulis, Bobby LaRue, and Ben Kish alternated at the four positions, giving Pitt unbelievable depth. Up front, the Panthers had such stalwarts as Frank Souchak and Bill Daddio at the ends,

Tony Matisi at tackle, and Al Lezouski and Steve Petro at the guards. They were tough defenders, as well as great blockers.

Fordham's strength was its Seven Blocks of Granite, a collection of tough, hard-hitting, unyielding defensive linemen. In 1935 and 1936, this uncompromising crew was composed of Leo Paquin and Johnny Druze at the ends, Ed Franco and Al Babartsky at the tackles, Nat Pierce and Vince Lombardi at the guards, and Alex Wojciechowicz at center. In 1937, after Paquin, Pierce, and Lombardi had graduated, Harry Jacunski, Mike Kochel, and Joe Bernard replaced them. The backfield in '35 and '36 was quarterback Andy Palau, halfbacks Frank Mautte and Al Gurske, and fullback Johnny ("Bull") Locke. The 1937 ball-carrying corps was Bill Krywicki and Angelo ("Butch") Fortunato at quarterback, Joe Woitkowski, Steve Kazlo, and Joe Gransi at the halfbacks, and Dom Principe at fullback.

The Seven Blocks made football history. The 1936 unit didn't surrender a touchdown, even though they faced the potent offenses of schools such as Southern Methodist, St. Mary's, Purdue, and Pitt. The cry at Fordham that year was "From Rose Hill to the Rose Bowl." Unhappily, the Rams blew it when they lost their last game to old rival NYU 7-6. Pitt went west instead and beat Washington 21-0.

Pitt's 1937 team was Jock Sutherland's best. The austere, grim Scotsman was football's ultraperfectionist. His demeanor reflected his game plan—a simple, powerful, uncompromising ground game based on the finest blocking and determined running. Led by Goldberg, a thoroughly competent blocker as well as ball carrier who was equally dangerous at halfback or fullback, Pitt was frightening.

In temperament and personality, Jim Crowley was the direct opposite of Sutherland. One of Notre Dame's Four Horsemen and then coach at Michigan State before coming to Fordham, Crowley possessed a keen coaching mind. With the help of a dry, quick, ample sense of humor, Jim was expert at needling, coaxing, and inspiring his players.

All three Fordham-Pitt battles were bitterly fought. Pitt matched its overpowering running attack, maybe the best of all time, against the

impenetrable Fordham defensive line. The closest either team came to scoring was in the 1937 game. In the second quarter Pitt hammered away relentlessly at the Seven Blocks and reached Fordham's 5-yard line. Behind precise blocking, Goldberg then shot around left end on a reverse and into the end zone, but Matisi, the Pitt left tackle, had been detected holding on the 1-yard line. The Panthers were penalized back to the 16, and their threat died. Pitt argued strenuously over the holding penalty, but a picture in the next day's *New York Sunday News* clearly showed Matisi with a tight armlock on Al Gurske's leg. End of controversy.

That scoreless tie was the only blemish on either team's record in '37. Pitt was voted the national championship, and Fordham was ranked number three in the country.

The Master at BC

Frank Leahy, who as Jim Crowley's end coach at Fordham helped to construct the Seven Blocks of Granite, became a head coach in 1939 when Boston College summoned him. It was the start of a brilliant coaching career. A sound football tactician and proficient recruiter, Leahy had learned much under Knute Rockne at Notre Dame, including timely, uplifting invocations of the deity.

There was never a shortage of material for Leahy either at Boston College, where he started, or at Notre Dame, where he finished in a blaze of triumph. It took him merely two years to give the Eagles a winner. For the 1940 team, he had a galaxy of stars: quarterback Charlie O'Rourke, fullback Mike Holovak, end Gene Goodreault, and guards George Kerr and Joe Zabilski. Ten of BC's eleven starters would join the NFL after college. Individually they were stars; together they formed one of the best teams in the nation. The 1940 BC team went unbeaten in 10 games and climaxed the season with a stirring 19-13 win over Tennessee in the Sugar Bowl.

Only one opponent really threatened the Eagles. Georgetown, in the midst of a hot streak under coach Jack Hagerty, was undefeated in 23 straight games over three years when it met

Boston College and threatened to ground the high-flying, heavily favored Eagles. With two minutes left and BC clinging to a slender 19-16 lead, the Eagles were pinned deep in their territory. O'Rourke, the clever quarterback, took the ball from center, scrambled back into his end zone, and killed the clock for a full 30 seconds by dodging the onrushing Hoyas. Finally, they caught him for a safety, making the score 19-18, but the Eagles used the subsequent free kick from the 20-yard line to punt themselves out of danger and the gritty Hoyas out of the ball game. Old BC alums still cherish the memory of O'Rourke's ploy.

After the 1940 season, Leahy answered a call from his alma mater and left to coach Notre Dame through some of its most illustrious campaigns. Leahy's successor at BC, Denny Meyers, produced another superb Boston College team in 1942. In addition to Holovak, who was

still around, Meyers had center Fred Naumetz, tackle Gil Bouley, end Don Currivan, and quarterback Eddie Doherty, a slick passer and runner who was tabbed "the Brain."

With Holovak and Doherty supplying the firepower and Naumetz, Bouley, and Currivan sparking a superb defense, BC trampled its first eight opponents, amassing 249 points to a mere 19 for its opponents. Only Holy Cross, an old rival, remained before BC could complete an unbeaten season and meet Alabama in the Orange Bowl. The Crusaders, beaten four times and tied once, were far from an awe-inspiring challenge for the powerful Eagles. But led by two marvelous running backs, John Grigas and John Bezemes, the Crusaders crushed the Eagles 55-12 in one of football's most surprising upsets.

Smaller Powers' Interlude

After Fordham and Pitt vied for supremacy in the East but before Boston College's rise to the top,

Glenn Davis leads Army over Notre Dame in 1945.
Army team was called its greatest ever,
and Davis finished second in Heisman balloting.

Villanova, Cornell, and little Duquesne in Pittsburgh made their marks. Villanova had unbeaten seasons in 1937 and 1938, stretching its string to 29 games before losing to Texas A & M in 1939.

The 1939 Cornell team, perhaps the best coach Carl Snavely ever had at Ithaca, beat Syracuse 19-6, Princeton 27-0, and Penn State 47-0 in its first three games. Then the Big Red traveled to Columbus, Ohio, to meet Ohio State of the fearsome Big Ten Conference. Even three straight wins seemed inadequate credentials for challenging the Buckeyes, who quickly built a 14-0 lead. But with Hal McCullough, Mort Landsberg, and Pop Scholl, a skinny 159-pound tailback, darting behind the blocking of captain Walt Matusczak, and with tackle Nick Drahos raging on defense, Cornell surprised the Buckeyes 23-14. The Big Red then whipped its Eastern foes—Columbia, Colgate, Dartmouth,

and Penn—and completed an 8-0 season.

Duquesne built a mini-dynasty in 1939, 1940, and 1941. Under coach Buff Donelli, a former star player at the Pittsburgh school who would later coach at Columbia, the Dukes lost only once (to Mississippi) and tied once in three years. Alan Donelli, the coach's brother did much of the running, passing, and punt returning, and Carl Nery glittered at tackle.

The Soldiers

For years football at West Point had been a highly successful commodity. From 1914-16, Charlie Daly, the man who had been an All-American quarterback at Harvard and had then played a couple of seasons at the Point (there were no eligibility rules in those days), coached Army teams that were considered among the nation's finest. Under the coaches who followed Daly—John McEwan, Biff Jones, Ralph Sasse, Gar Davidson, and Bill Wood—the Cadets continued to rank consistently with the best. In this era too, the Army-Navy rivalry became the spectacle that captivates the football world each fall.

Players such as McEwan, Jones, Nig Prichard, Bob Neyland, Elmer Oliphant, Ed Garbisch, Walter French, and Earl ("Red") Blaik were cadets who shone among college football's greatest stars during the period through 1922. Later, there were others who captured the headlines and All-American honors: Lighthorse Harry Wilson, Moe Daly, Bud Sprague, Chuck Born, Bosco Schmidt, and the great Chris ("Red") Cagle, a spectacular runner who may have been the best of all. And Ray Stecker, Jack Price, Polly Humber, Milt Summerfelt, Jabbo Jablonsky, Jack Buckler, Joe Stancook, Monk Meyer, Bill Shuler, and Frank Hartline.

Army's football fortunes began to decline in the late thirties. A laxness in recruiting and more rigid limitations on the height and weight of entering cadets pushed the academy toward mediocrity in football. The most telling blow came in 1938 when President Franklin D. Roosevelt directed Army to limit its varsity players to three years of play. The three-years rule deprived Army of an unfair advantage it had enjoyed over all other colleges—including Navy—but there were Army men who couldn't help suspect that as a former assistant secretary

of the navy, Roosevelt may have had more than fairness in mind.

The Cadets slumped in '39 and '40, winning only four games, and the brass at West Point fell into unsoldierly consternation. Winning football was very important to the army. Brig. Gen. Robert K. Eichelberger, who had become the superintendent of the academy in mid-November, 1940, quickly recommended to the athletic board that it scrap the policy of appointing only graduate-officers as head coaches. That done, Eichelberger lured Earl ("Red") Blaik, a West Point graduate but a *retired*, and therefore previously overlooked colonel, down from the hills of Hanover, New Hampshire, where he had coached Dartmouth with spectacular success. For Blaik's wife, Merle, Eichelberger promised to build the Blaiks a large comfortable home. For Blaik he vowed to fight for liberalizing the restrictions on height and weight for entering cadets. Then he clinched his case with the assurance that the new coach would report only to the athletic board and to him, Eichelberger.

Blaik was a natural for West Point, having played there as a cadet and having served as an assistant under three Army coaches from 1927 to 1933. A stern uncompromising man who countenanced nothing less from his players than complete dedication to football, Blaik made the practice field a battleground. He had no patience with those who used injuries as an excuse for not participating in the rough drills.

Blaik recognized the advantage of coming to West Point when Army football fortunes were at a low ebb. "A coach who comes in at the bottom of a curve has a pronounced advantage over one who succeeds to a going or even a half-going operation," said Blaik later. "In 1941, there was no place to go at West Point but up. And we went up at a rate of speed that surprised a lot of people."

Army's resurrection was astonishing. After three successively better rebuilding years, Blaik moved his Cadets to three straight undefeated seasons and national championships in 1944 and 1945. Several factors contributed to Army's rapid comeback. One was World War II, which drained many college football programs when players enlisted or were drafted. But because the service

academies had the responsibility of training officers, they kept their players.

Perhaps the most important factors in Army's resurgence were two of West Point's greatest superstars: Felix ("Doc") Blanchard, a 6-foot 206-pound fullback who hit enemy lines like thundering artillery yet had the speed and deftness of a halfback, and Glenn Davis, a 5-foot 9-inch, 172-pound halfback who was Army's answer to Red Grange. They were to become known as "Mr. Inside and Mr. Outside," perhaps the most potent one-two punch ever to play college football. Davis and Blanchard each won All-American honors three times, and the Heisman Trophy.

Michigan's Fritz Crisler described the way Blanchard and Davis complemented each other. "If you tighten up your line to stop Blanchard's drives," said Crisler, "there goes Davis. If you extend your flanks to check Davis, there goes Blanchard."

With Blanchard and Davis spearheading its attack, the 1944 Army team overwhelmed its opposition in sweeping to a 9-0 season. The Cadets whomped North Carolina 46-0, Brown 59-7, Pitt 69-7, the Coast Guard Academy 76-0, Duke 27-7, Villanova 83-0, Notre Dame 59-0, Penn 62-7, and Navy 23-7. After the win over Navy, their first in seven years, the Cadets were acclaimed national champions.

The 1944 performance was difficult to surpass, but the 1945 club did. Blaik unequivocally called the '45 squad the best ever at West Point. Blanchard and Davis finished one-two in the voting for the Heisman Trophy. The other two

Opposite: *Doc Blanchard, "Mr. Inside," against Villanova. Army was undefeated in 1945.*
Top: *Andy Kerr on his return to Colgate in 1946.*

backs, quarterback Arnold Tucker and halfback Shorty McWilliams, joined the two stars behind one of college football's most formidable lines: ends Barney Poole and Hank Foldberg, tackles Tex Coulter and Al Nemetz, guards Johnny Green and Art Gerometta, and center Ug Fuson. These were still the days of single-platoon football, so these super players played both offense and defense, with equal proficiency.

No opponent even came close to the 1945 Army team. In addition to two easy wins over service teams, the freewheeling Cadets thrashed Wake Forest 54-0, Michigan 28-7, Duke 48-13, Villanova 54-0, Notre Dame 48-0, Penn 61-0, and Navy 32-13. Blanchard scored 19 touchdowns, Davis 18; but in most games they played little more than a half. Once again Army won the national championship, and Blanchard, Davis, Green, Coulter, Nemetz, Foldberg, Poole, and McWilliams won All-American honors.

Only a scoreless tie with Notre Dame marred a perfect season for Army in 1946. This time Army ranked number two, behind Notre Dame in the final AP poll. Blaik was voted Coach of the Year. In four years Davis had gained 4,129 yards and scored 59 touchdowns and 354 points; in three years, Blanchard had gained 1,666 yards and scored 38 touchdowns and 231 points.

Davis and Blanchard were gone in 1947, but Army continued winning early in the season, stretching its undefeated streak to 33 games. Then they encountered coach Lou Little's Columbia Lions eight years after the usually docile Lions had shredded Stanford in the 1934 Rose Bowl. This time the Lions' cubs, freshmen Gene Rossides and Lou Kusserow, led the team's resurgent ferocity. They ran and passed the Cadets silly, and Bill Swiacki, a splendid end, made acrobatic catches all over the field. Finally, midway in the fourth quarter, Swiacki capped the day with an amazing shoestring grab on the Army 3-yard line of a 26-yard Rossides pass. Two plays later, with Blaik still fuming that Swiacki had trapped, not caught the ball, Kusserow smashed over for the touchdown that upset the Cadets 21-20.

Notre Dame then clobbered Army, but the Cadets started another winning streak a week later—this one 28 games. Coach Eddie Erdelatz's Navy team ended it in the last game of the 1950

season, but despite the defeat, Army was ranked number two in the nation, behind Oklahoma. In seven seasons, 1944-50, coach Earl Blaik's Army teams had lost only twice.

Then disastrous scandal struck at West Point. Ninety students, including 60 athletes and 31 football players were dismissed from the academy for violating the honor code. One of the guilty was quarterback Bob Blaik, the coach's son. It seemed that Army football would never recover, but three years later, Blaik's Cadets were winning again.

The 1958 Army team contended for the national championship. Another pair of superstar backs, Bob Anderson and Pete Dawkins, revived the Cadets. Anderson, 6 feet 2 inches and 205 pounds, ran with power and long-distance speed. In 1957, as a sophomore, he ran for 983 yards, breaking Glenn Davis's one-season record, and scored 15 touchdowns. Dawkins, who first came to West Point as a left-handed quarterback, was a driving, determined runner and an outstanding pass receiver.

While vacationing at Key Biscayne, Florida, after the 1957 season, Blaik concocted a simple but weird formation for his offense. He flanked the end wider than ever before, some 20 to 30 yards from the ball, forcing defenses to spread wider to cover him. Not content with the substantive advantages of the new formation, Blaik dreamed up a gimmick to enhance it: the so-called "Lonely End" never entered the huddle. Instead he mysteriously received the signals—coach Blaik never revealed how—as he stood alone, the greatest diversion since cheerleaders.

Anderson and Dawkins ran freely against defenses weakened by the Lonely End formation, and tall, skinny 156-pound Joe Caldwell threw superbly to Bill Carpenter, the Lonely End himself. Army went unbeaten in its nine games, tied only by Pitt, 14-14. The Cadets won the Lambert Trophy and a number-six national ranking.

Following the 1958 season, Blaik abruptly retired, rankled by academy policy decisions that decreased the number of football appointments and prohibited the Cadets from going to the Cotton Bowl. Blaik left with one of the glossiest records in all football coaching 121-32-10, two national championships, and six unbeaten seasons in eighteen years. Under Blaik's successors, football at the Point has never recaptured the magic of the Blaik years, except for a brief flurry in 1966, when Tom Cahill became the head coach through a fortuitous set of circumstances, both for him and for West Point. Shortly before spring practice in 1966, Paul Dietzel resigned suddenly and moved to South Carolina. Army tried but failed to attract a name coach to replace him. Meanwhile, the quiet, unassuming, and very capable Cahill, who had been the plebe coach for seven years, handled the Cadets in spring practice. With no one else to turn to, the Army brass reluctantly named Tom the head coach for a year, intending to defer but not abandon their search for someone else. Cahill spared them the effort.

Under Cahill's low-key, efficient coaching, Army quite unexpectedly posted an 8-2 record, losing only to Notre Dame (the national champions) and Tennessee. Less reluctantly this time, Army hired Cahill for another year, sparing itself some embarrassment when Cahill was named Coach of the Year by his colleagues. Surprisingly, Army was 8-2 again in 1967 and 7-3 in 1968. But things haven't been the same for Cahill and West Point since then. The Vietnam War and increased postgraduate duty in the army for graduating cadets have made recruiting blue-chip athletes almost impossible.

In a recent interview with sportswriter Bob Gutkowski, Cahill detailed his problems with recruiting and how he deals with them. "Unlike most athletic programs at other universities and colleges where the football programs are heavily funded, I have a strict budget guideline," he explained. "But since I know the framework in which I have to function, it makes my job a little easier. We know beforehand what to expect from a boy who has seen other recruiters. Some may have promised him anything to get his letter of intent. When he declares himself for West Point, he knows he's going to be doing

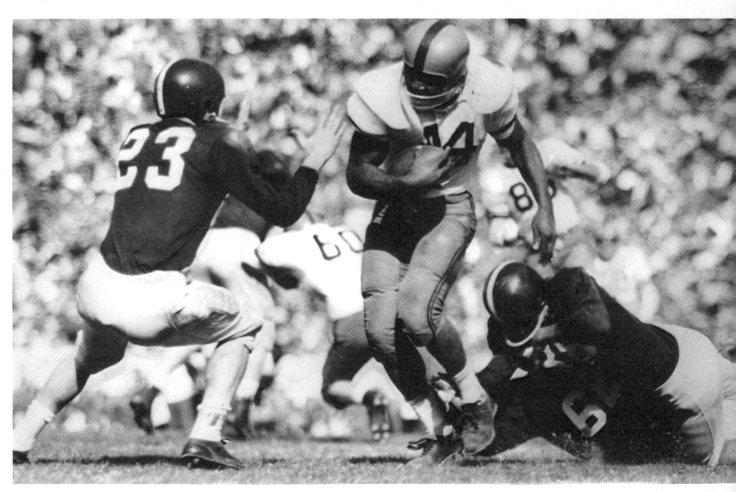

Jim Brown cracks TCU's right tackle for a long
gain in 1957 Cotton Bowl. Brown was the first
of great Syracuse runners who wore number 44.

everything largely on his own merit. About the only thing we can promise him is a shot at making the team; that's about it."

With its depleted ranks, Army plays as demanding a schedule—Stanford, Arkansas, Nebraska, Notre Dame, and Tennessee—as any independent. Tom Cahill faces the unpromising future resolutely and realistically. The glory of the Davis and Blanchard years may never return.

Princeton and Rutgers: Latter-day Triumphs
Princeton's older Tigers reverently remember the 1922 "Team of Destiny," the one that upset Chicago. For Tigers' alumni of more recent vintage, the memorable Princeton teams were the ones of 1950 and '51 under coach Charlie Caldwell, who had played on the 1922 team of blessed memory.

Dick Kazmaier, as good a triple threat halfback as college football has ever seen, led those mid-century teams. Kaz was a superb runner who combined speed with remarkable changes of pace. Perhaps the best passer of his time, he also did all the punting for the Tigers. He made the All-American team two years running and won the Heisman Trophy in 1951 over such notables as Babe Parilli of Kentucky, Johnny Bright of Drake, and Hugh McElhenny of Washington.

Kazmaier led Princeton through two undefeated and untied seasons in 1950 and 1951. In the latter year, he topped the nation in total offense with 1,827 yards rushing and in passing with 62.6 percent completions. In his three years of varsity football, Dick totaled 4,357 yards and threw 35 touchdown passes in an era when the pass was rarely any team's principal weapon, least of all Princeton's. Coach Caldwell used the single wing, a formation the Tigers would retain long after Caldwell had gone and the rest of the country had switched to the T.

The 1950 Princeton team played in its own Ivy backyard and for that reason alone did not receive the national recognition it deserved. Even after blasting Harvard 63-26 and Yale 47-12, the Tigers ranked no higher than sixth in the wire service polls.

Quarterback George Chandler, Kazmaier's principal aide, almost never handled the ball in the single-wing system, but he blocked with deadly efficiency. Frank McPhee, a brilliant end,

Holland Donan, Brad Glass, and Dave Hickok sparked the Tigers on defense.

Princeton almost didn't survive the second game the next year. After soundly whipping NYU, 54-20, the '51 Tigers encountered a combative Navy team that fiercely battled them before surrendering 24-20. Penn also frightened coach Caldwell's team, losing only 13-7. After that, it was relatively easy. The Tigers mastered Lafayette 60-7, Cornell 53-15, Brown 12-0, Harvard 54-13, Yale 27-0, and Dartmouth 13-0, extending their winning streak to 22 games. Penn finally throttled Princeton 13-7 for the Tigers' only loss in 1952 and an end to the string.

Although Princeton hasn't reached such lofty national heights since 1951, the Tigers have had their good years and their stars. Under coach Dick Colman, Princeton battled Dartmouth for the Ivy League championship in the fifties and sixties. The Tigers were unbeaten and untied in 1964.

On the fringe of the big time, Rutgers had one of its best seasons in 1958, when it lost only to the rugged Quantico Marines. That year Rutgers claimed its first All-American since Homer Hazel in 1923 and 1924. He was Billy Austin, a sure-footed runner and able blocker who scored 106 points. Then, after coach John Bateman's first Rutgers team, in 1960, lost only to Villanova, the '61 outfit survived close calls with Princeton (16-13) and Delaware (27-19) and finished with a 32-19 defeat of Columbia for the school's first unbeaten and untied season ever. With the unbeaten season, came All-American center Alex Kroll.

The Sailors
Perhaps Navy's 1954 club was its most memorable. Coach Eddie Erdelatz named his team "Desire," an apt description of a group of players who with more spirit than skill lifted the Middies out of the doldrums.

Navy was Erdelatz's first head coaching assignment. An outstanding end at St. Mary's in the mid-thirties under coach Slip Madigan, Eddie had served as an assistant at Annapolis for coaches Oscar Hagberg and Tom Hamilton from 1945-47. Then Erdelatz moved to the pro ranks as a line coach for the San Francisco 49ers, where Navy discovered him.

Any Navy coach knows what his principal

34

"He whirled through enemy teams like a giant top . . . ."
Navy's Joe Bellino, Heisman winner,
leaps over BC line for one of many substantial gains.

assignment is: beat Army. Erdelatz did little more in his first year, 1950. The Middies had won only two games all season and were a heavy underdog against unbeaten Army, but they stunned the Cadets 14-12 and broke their 28-game unbeaten streak.

The bellweather of the 1954 Navy team was quarterback George Welsh, a deft ball handler, a smart play caller, an able runner on the option play, and one of the sharpest passers ever to throw the ball for the Middies. His principal target was Ron Beagle, an All-American end.

This Navy team intrigued people precisely because it wasn't invincible. The Middies lost to Pitt 21-19, and to Notre Dame 6-0 after fumbling away the tying touchdown at the goal line. But they trounced Stanford (25-0) and Duke (40-7), supposedly two of the nation's prestige teams. Navy brought a 6-2 record into the Army game but hardly appeared to be the equal of the undefeated Cadets, who had one of their best offensive teams.

More than 100,000 screaming fans in Philadelphia's cavernous Municipal (now John F. Kennedy) Stadium in 1954 saw one of football's most exciting games that November afternoon. George Welsh played the finest game of his career and led Navy to a 27-20 victory. In addition to bedeviling the Cadets with his faking, ball handling, and running on keeper plays, Welsh threw three touchdown passes and set up a fourth score with another aerial.

In the Sugar Bowl against Mississippi, Navy blinded the Rebels with Welsh's faking and passing and fullback Joe Gattuso's 111 yards and four touchdowns. The Middies scored an easy 21-0 victory.

Erdelatz continued triumphant for the next few years, especially in 1957. Led by All-American quarterback Tom Forrestal and tackle

Bob Reifsnyder, Navy ranked fifth in the country. Then, Eddie suddenly fell into disfavor with the administration at the Naval Academy and resigned before the 1959 season. Wayne Hardin, who succeeded him, inherited one of the brightest stars in Navy's history. He was Joe Bellino, a stumpy 185-pound halfback who whirled through enemy teams like a giant top, darting and swerving toward the goal line.

In a game against Maryland in 1959, Navy found itself bogged down in a 14-14 tie with about six minutes to play. Then Maryland thoughtlessly punted directly to Bellino on the Navy 41-yard line. Assuming there was little chance for a long punt return, Hardin wanted a dead ball, which would permit him to send quarterback Joe Tranchini back into the game without a time out. Otherwise the substitution would violate the rule then in force and draw a 5-yard penalty. So as Bellino started up the sideline Hardin screamed at him to run out of bounds. Joe, however, blithely ignored Hardin's screams, evaded a horde of tacklers on the sideline, skittered toward midfield, and ran 59 yards for the winning touchdown. "I heard the coach," Joe confessed later, "but I thought I could find daylight, and if I did, we wouldn't need a quarterback, except to hold for the extra point."

Bellino enjoyed his biggest day of the '59 season, fittingly enough, against Army. With the game only seven minutes old, he burst through the Army line for 16 yards and a touchdown. Less than three minutes later, he burned the Cadets with a 46-yard scoring run. Before Army's long afternoon ended, Bellino had scored again, from the 1-yard line, becoming the first Middie to score three touchdowns in a single game against Army. He surprised the oddsmakers, who had made Army a touchdown favorite, as much as the Cadets in leading Navy to an easy 43-12 win.

After the season, the Washington, D. C., Touchdown Club honored Bellino as the outstanding service school player. In accepting a handsome trophy, Joe began graciously. "I want to thank the Touchdown Club, and I want to thank the Navy coaches and my great Navy teammates," he said. "I also want to thank the Army football team," he added.

In 1960, Bellino quickly began running toward

a banner year and led Navy to similar success. Joe's running carried the Middies to a 9-2 record, a number four national ranking, and another win over Army—this time by a 17-12 score, the fourth straight for Navy in the series. The squad lost only to Duke, and to Missouri in the Orange Bowl. Bellino rushed for 834 yards, a new Naval Academy one-season record, and completed his three years with 1,664, another record. In his football career at Navy, Joe had compiled 833 yards on kick returns and scored 198 points on 31 touchdowns and 12 extra points. A nearly unanimous choice for the All-American team, he won the Heisman Trophy as well.

Two years later, in 1962, Wayne Hardin and Navy were blessed with another superstar, a young quarterback named Roger Staubach. Tall and lean, Staubach ran as superbly as he passed. Staubach barely left the bench for Navy's first three games but barely sat down for the rest of the season.

Despite Hardin's extravagant preseason prediction, Navy opened its 1962 schedule by absorbing a 41-7 trouncing from Penn State, staggered past William and Mary 20-6, and took a 20-0 thumping from Minnesota. Hardin turned to Staubach, the raw sophomore quarterback who had played a total of six minutes in the first three games.

Passing and running like a veteran, Staubach led the Middies past Cornell 41-0 and permanently earned the starting job. Navy then whipped Boston College 26-6 and Pitt 32-9, but not even Staubach's expansive skills could salvage a victory for the overmatched Middies against Notre Dame, Syracuse, and USC. Navy brought an uninspiring 4-5 record into the Army game, but Staubach's individual statistics were impressive: 56 pass completions in 85 attempts for 778 yards and five touchdowns; 231 yards rushing and five more scores. Budd Thalman, the imaginative Navy sports information director at the time, dubbed him "Jolly Roger."

Army coach Paul Dietzel knew his team was in for trouble trying to stop Staubach, but little did he suspect how much. Before the usual 100,000 in Philadelphia's Municipal Stadium, the imperturbable Staubach almost single-handedly destroyed Army. When not coolly drilling passes through the Army secondary into his teammates'

Larry Csonka carries against UCLA. Csonka blasted his way to fame at Syracuse in 1966 and 1967, after which Orange football declined disastrously.

waiting arms, Roger carried the ball, darting and dancing elusively among the frantic Cadets. That wild afternoon Staubach threw two touchdown passes among 11 completions in 13 tries for 118 yards and scored twice himself, once on a 20-yard dash and again on a 2-yard run. Navy won 34-14.

Asked later if there was a turning point in the game, coach Hardin grinned and quipped, "Yep. When we showed up."

In 1963, with Staubach leading them, the Middies waltzed through their typically rough schedule, whipping Michigan 26-13, Pitt 24-12, Notre Dame 35-14, Maryland 42-7, Duke 38-25, and Army 21-15. They stumbled only against Southern Methodist, finally losing 38-28 after a spirited comeback attempt fell short. Staubach performed tremendously all season, confounding foes with his improbable scrambling and marvelously accurate passing. He became the last Eastern player to win the Heisman Trophy until 1973.

At the conclusion of the regular season, Navy ranked behind only unbeaten Texas in the national polls. The Middies had only to upset the favored Longhorns in the Cotton Bowl to win their first national championship. But Texas was simply too strong for Staubach and his teammates. The Longhorns won 28-6.

Staubach's senior year was an utter disaster, both for him personally and for Navy collectively. After the Middies beat Penn State 21-8 and William and Mary 35-6, they won only one more game the rest of the year—a 27-14 decision over Duke. They lost to Michigan, Georgia Tech, California, Notre Dame, Maryland, and Army. Beset by injuries most of the season, Staubach played well below his 1962 and 1963 form, and Navy sank to mediocrity. Nevertheless, Roger finished his career with a remarkable record: 292 pass completions in 463 attempts (a completion average of 63.1 percent) for 3,571 yards and 18 touchdowns; 682 yards rushing and 17 touchdowns; 4,253 yards in total offense.

After Staubach graduated, Navy was plagued by tough schedules and the same ills that affected Army, with similarly discouraging results.

The Orangemen of Syracuse

Back in 1948, Syracuse beat Niagara—the Orangemen's only win all season.

Opposite: *Pitt clashes with UCLA.* Top: *Dick Shiner rolls out for Maryland.* Above: *Tubby Raymond signals his Delaware team.*

(Coincidentally, perhaps, Niagara gave up football shortly thereafter.) The dismal '48 season prompted Syracuse, which had known more prosperous football days in the 1920s and 1930s, to take a drastic step. It fired coach Reaves Baysinger and hired Floyd ("Ben") Schwartzwalder, a tough former paratroop major who had achieved considerable success at Muhlenberg. A short man with light blue eyes, close cropped hair, and a strong jaw, Schwartzwalder looked more like a Dutch banker than a football coach.

He slowly rebuilt Syracuse, and in 1952, his team posted a 7-2 record, losing only to powerful Michigan State and Bolling Air Force Base. But disaster struck in the Orange Bowl when Alabama mauled the Easterners 61-6. Schwartzwalder went back to the drawing board; the blueprint he charted was wonderfully simple—Jimmy Brown. A power runner with the craft of a halfback, Brown exploded against unsuspecting opponents in 1956. Jimmy had languished in comparative obscurity before his senior year, but once given the chance, he proved to be the most devastating runner in college football. Against Colgate, Brown scored 43 points on six touchdowns and seven extra points.

Schwartzwalder and Syracuse finally hit the jackpot in 1959, winning Syracuse's only national championship. In 1958, the Orange had achieved a respectable 8-2 season (notwithstanding another Orange Bowl loss, this time to Oklahoma), but quarterback, Chuck Zimmerman had graduated, and his replacement, Bob Thomas, suffered a back injury that sidelined him for 1959. The only solution, it seemed, was to move Gerhard Schwedes, a halfback, to quarterback.

Convinced by Schwartzwalder's loud laments, the experts decided Syracuse would probably not survive Kansas on opening day of the '69 season. But after trailing 15-12 in the third quarter, the Orange suddenly came to life and won 35-21. Syracuse was on its way to a sensational season.

While wily old Ben was moaning, he also was quietly building a forbidding defense: Fred Mautino and Gerry Skonieczki at the ends, Maury Yoemans and Bob Yates at the tackles, Roger Davis and Bruce Tarbox at the guards, and Al Bemiller at center. They were a colorful, swashbuckling group that Val Pinchbeck, then the Syracuse sports information director, quickly dubbed "the Sizable Seven." Each of the merry crew had his own nickname, too. Davis was "Hound Dog," Skonieczki was "Hands," Tarbox was "Cinderella," Yoemans was "Yo Yo," Mautino was "Chief," Bemiller was "Tombstone" (for his ambition to be an undertaker), and Yates, who did the place kicking, was "Toe."

To a frolicking defense, Schwartzwalder added a reformed, potent offensive backfield. He entrusted the controls to a pair of sophomore quarterbacks, Dave Sarette and Dick Easterly, allowing Schwedes to remain at his natural halfback position where he teamed with another soph, Ernie Davis. Davis inherited Jim Brown's "44" and soon demonstrated that he was more than worthy of the honor. Art Baker was the fullback, and Mark Weber and Gary Fallon spelled the starters when they needed a breather.

Maryland was the first to feel the fury of the Syracuse team. The Terps went down 29-0 as the Orange defense held them to a mere 8 yards rushing and two first downs. Then, with Sarette and Easterly passing, Schwedes, Baker, and Davis running, and the Sizable Seven clubbing away, Syracuse rolled over Navy 32-6, Holy Cross 42-6, West Virginia 44-0, and Pitt 35-0. Those five largely uncontested victories prefaced the Orangemen's annual grudge match with Penn State. With both teams unbeaten and ranked in the nation's top ten, the struggle promised to decide which team ruled the East and maybe even the nation.

For Schwartzwalder, his longtime adversary, Penn State coach Rip Engle readied All-American quarterback Richie Lucas and Roger Kochman, a halfback who could outrun every player on both squads and proved it in the game.

Penn State took a 6-0 lead on a 17-yard burst by Kochman, but Syracuse soon bolted to a 20-6 advantage on a 6-yard run by Schwedes, Sarette's touchdown pass to Baker, Ernie Davis's 2-yard plunge, and two extra points by Yates. Syracuse seemed on the verge of another decisive victory, but suddenly Kochman took a kickoff on his goal line, sprinted upfield, and

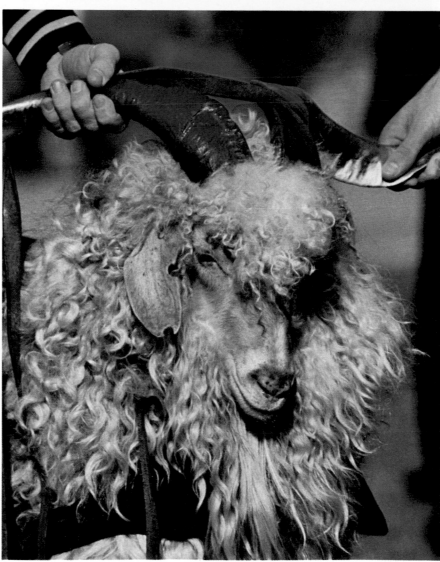

Preceding pages: Harvard braces for Dartmouth rush.
Clockwise from above: Navy goat, JFK
Stadium; Navy band; Army cadets; Ivy pennants

Opposite: *Penn State's Kwalick.* Below: *Princeton-Penn.*

broke into the clear with the aid of a crushing block by linebacker Earl Kohlhaas. Roger never stopped until he crossed the goal line, 100 yards from his starting point. Penn State failed in its bid for a two-point conversion when Lucas passed low to Don Hoak, but minutes later the inspired Nittany Lions, trailing only by 20-12 threatened again. Andy Stynchula led a Penn State charge that blocked Yates's attempted punt and sent the ball flying back to the Syracuse 1-yard line, where the Nittany Lions took over. Sam Sobczak hammered into the end zone, and the score was 20-18. Penn State partisans among the 32,800 at the school's old Beaver Field clamored for the tying points, but the Sizable Seven rose to foil Kochman's off-tackle smash. Then the Orangemen held on grimly until the end. As they left the field after the final gun, they showed visible relief.

With their flawless record preserved, the marauders from Syracuse clobbered Colgate 71-0 and Boston University 48-0. Against BU, the defense permitted minus 85 yards rushing, for which performance, the AP named the entire Syracuse line its "Lineman of the Week." In its last regular season game, against UCLA in the Los Angeles Memorial Coliseum, the visitors from the East solidified their number-one national ranking. While the defense held UCLA to 13 yards rushing, Syracuse won 36-8 for its tenth straight victory and its first national championship.

"We of the decadent East are very happy with our win in the West," said Ben dryly. Then, he admitted, "We made no effort to keep the score down."

There remained one more challenge to Syracuse in its role as defender of Eastern football: a Cotton Bowl clash with Texas. Coach Darrell Royal's Longhorns had completed a 9-1 season, losing only to Texas Christian and beating, among others, Nebraska, Maryland, California, Oklahoma, and Arkansas. Texas was ranked number four.

Syracuse more than upheld the prestige of the East. The Orange defeated Texas 23-14 in a bitterly fought, bruising battle marked by brawls and charges of racial insults. Ernie Davis was the star of the long afternoon, scoring on an 87-yard pass from Schwedes and on a 1-yard plunge. He

also set up the third touchdown with a pass interception and a 21-yard run. It was a satisfying close to a glorious season for the Orangemen from Piety Hill.

Although the only team that had threatened the Orange was its Eastern neighbor, Penn State, there remained some cynics who insisted on downgrading the Easterners. The abuse prompted Jesse Abramson to write in the *New York Herald Tribune:*

"Because it is an Eastern team, wrongly associated in the national mind with the Ivy League, Syracuse had to be super special in its season-long operations to be accepted, grudgingly no doubt in some powerhouse areas, as the true-blue and Orange king of the football hill. Because its schedule, a typically rugged schedule for Syracuse, didn't impress non-Easterners, the Orangemen had to win by pulverizing margins. And they did in every game except the 20-18 battle with formidable Penn State. . . ."

In addition to winning a national championship, the first for the East since Army won in 1945, Syracuse had led the nation in scoring (390 points to 59 for the opposition), total offense (451.5-yard average per game), rushing (313.6-yard average per game), rushing defense (permitting a 19.3-yard average per game), and touchdown passes (20). Ben Schwartzwalder was named Coach of the Year, Ernie Davis was proclaimed Rookie of the Year, and Roger Davis, Fred Mautino, Bob Yates, Maury Yoemans, Gerhard Schwedes, and Davis were picked for one or more All-American teams.

After that brilliant sophomore year, Ernie Davis continued virtually unstoppable in his junior and senior years, climaxing his college career by winning the Heisman Trophy in 1961. A modest unassuming young man, he was one of college football's greatest running backs. But he did not live to play pro football. Signed by the Cleveland Browns, Davis died of leukemia in the fall of 1962. All football mourned his death.

There were more glory years to come for Syracuse and Ben Schwartzwalder. In the early and mid-sixties, only rarely were the Orange not contenders for the Lambert Trophy. There were more superstars, too, such as Floyd Little, the third in the line of "44s," who ran his way to All-

American honors in 1965 and 1966; and Larry Csonka, the crunching fullback who blasted his way to fame in 1966 and 1967. Then, suddenly the flow of talent to Syracuse ebbed. Racial problems in 1970 added to Syracuse's troubles. Schwartzwalder announced he would retire after the 1973 season, at age 65, the compulsory retirement age at Syracuse. A disappointing finish has tarnished 25 impressive Schwartzwalder years at Syracuse.

The Ivy Still Thrives

While the big independents became the leading lights in the East in the 1960s, the Ivy League shone too. Yale started the decade by producing one of its finest teams, its first unbeaten eleven since 1923. Yale alumni in the Chicago area had done their recruiting homework well, providing coach Jordan Olivar with a 1960 team that was loaded with former Midwestern high school stars. One of the brightest was quarterback Tom Singleton, a good passer who also was extremely adept at running the rollout in coach Olivar's split T. His backfield mates, halfbacks

Kenny Wolfe and Lou Miller (publicist Charlie Loftus called them "the world's tallest elves") and fullback Tom Blanchard were all excellent runners and blockers.

Led by tackle Mike Pyle, who had been an all-Ivy center in 1959, guards Ben Balme and Paul Bursiek and center Hardy Will, the Eli line was big, strong, fast, and resourceful—perhaps the equal of any other forward wall in the country that year. Like any fine defensive front, it yielded least nearest the goal line.

Yale picked up momentum after barely subduing Connecticut 11-8 and Brown 9-0 in its first two games. The Elis swept past Columbia 30-8, Cornell 22-6, Colgate 36-14, Dartmouth 29-0, and Penn 34-9 and began to sense that not only the Ivy League championship but an undefeated season might be theirs. Only Princeton and Harvard remained to be beaten. Of the two old rivals, Princeton proved the toughest. It took all Singleton's passing skill to throttle the aroused Tigers. Following coach Olivar's conservative game plan, Singleton

Above: *Midshipmen form a sea of white hats at JFK Stadium. Opposite. Penn State's McNaughton flies past OSU's Spahr (82), Bugel (66), and Kelley (53).*

threw only seven passes but completed six of them, three for touchdowns, and Yale outscored the stubborn Tigers 43-32.

Harvard was a great deal easier. The first time the Elis got the ball, Wolfe charged 41 yards for a touchdown, beginning a 39-6 rout. Yale had its championship and its undefeated season, all the more impressive because only one other team—New Mexico State—went unbeaten that year.

There was only one sour note: Yale had to share the Lambert Trophy with Navy, which had finished the season with a 9-1 record. The selection committee argued that the Middies' schedule, which included Southern Methodist, Air Force, Notre Dame, Duke, Boston College, Villanova, and Army, was stronger than the Elis' Ivy League slate.

In 1968, under Carmen Cozza, Yale produced another unbeaten campaign, but this time the Elis had to share the Ivy championship with Harvard. Both teams had clean slates as they confronted one another in the season's final. The teams failed to resolve their impasse but not for lack of trying. Frank Champi, a balding 20-year-old substitute Harvard quarterback, threw two touchdown passes in the final 42 seconds, the last one as time ran out, and then passed for the two-point conversion that pulled the Cantabs into a 29-29 tie.

Meanwhile, Dartmouth had become the perennial team-to-beat in the Ivy League. Coach Bob Blackman came to Hanover in 1955 (after coaching at Pasadena City College and Denver University) and wasted little time before winning his first Ivy title. His Indians won it in 1957 and again in 1958.

The 1962 Dartmouth team was the school's first unbeaten and untied squad in 37 years. Quarterback Bill King and halfback Tom Spangenberg led the Indians, passing and running from coach Blackman's complex multi-formation offense. It included a touch of all versions of the T (slot, wing, and double wing) and what Bob called the V formation. The team's greatest strength, however, was its defense, led by center Don McKinnon, a big, quick fellow who liked to introduce himself to the enemy early in each game with an unforgettable, bone-shattering block or tackle.

Dartmouth coasted past its first seven opponents—Massachusetts, Penn, Brown, Holy Cross, Harvard, Yale, and Columbia—yielding only a single touchdown. Against Columbia, King completed 14 of 16 passes for 324 yards, including touchdown strikes of 31, 51, 36, and 48 yards. He scored a fifth on a 7-yard run and amassed 348 yards in total offense for the afternoon.

After all those easy pickings, Dartmouth encountered a tough Cornell team, but King rescued his team with three touchdowns, and Dartmouth won its eighth game, 28-21. Princeton, in the finale, was even tougher. Cosmo Iacavazzi, a nimble, hard-charging fullback, rocked the Indians with a 47-yard touchdown run in the first period, and the Tigers led 21-15 in the second quarter. But again King, with help from Spangenberg, revived the Indians. King scored three touchdowns, Spangenberg, who carried 29 times for 208 yards, countered twice more, and Dartmouth finally prevailed 38-27.

Three years later, in 1965, Dartmouth achieved another flawless record, this time with Mickey Beard at quarterback, Pete Walton at fullback, and Gene Ryzewicz, an exciting scatter-legged runner who was equally effective at quarterback or halfback. This team was more permissive on defense than its '62 predecessor, but the offense produced more points. The Indians survived threats from Pennsylvania and Yale (salvaging the game against the Elis with a touchdown in the last seven minutes) and once again found only Princeton standing between them and an unbeaten season. Also undefeated, the Tigers boasted tailback Ron Landeck and a 17-game winning streak when the two teams met in the last game of the season. Beard and Ryzewicz proved too much for Princeton. Although Landeck ripped the Dartmouth defense for 249 yards, the Indians won 28-14 and added the Lambert Trophy to their Ivy League crown. At the conclusion of the season, Iowa tried to lure coach Blackman, a native Iowan, from Hanover, but Bob remained in New Hampshire.

He had his best team of all in 1970. Offensive threats Jim Chasey at quarterback, John Short at halfback, and Stu Simms at fullback took full advantage of an explosive offensive line, led by tight end Darrel Gaule, tackle Bob Peters, and center Mark Stevenson. Linebacker Murray

Bowden, who won All-American honors, and safety Willie Bogan keyed the defense.

The Indians massacred their seven Ivy League rivals and added the scalps of Massachusetts and Holy Cross for their perfect season. Only Cornell, with All-American fullback Ed Marinaro, gave Dartmouth a mild fright. The Indians defense permitted Marinaro only 60 yards, but the Cornell defense was similarly stifling. After three quarters, the Big Red trailed only 3-0. Then in the final period Short and Chasey broke the game open and Dartmouth won 24-0.

Dartmouth again took the Lambert Trophy, over Penn State, which had a 7-3 season against tougher competition. The Nittany Lions' coach, Joe Paterno, drew a few headlines when he challenged the Indians to a postseason game, to which Blackman replied serenely, "If we could play a postseason game, I'd personally prefer to play someone with a better record."

After the season the Big Ten sought Blackman again, and this time Illinois landed him. In 16 years at Dartmouth, Blackman had a magnificent record: 104-37-3, three unbeaten and untied teams, four outright Ivy League titles, and a share in three others. The Indians, however, have continued their Ivy League success under coach Jake Crouthamel, one of Blackman's former backfield stars.

The Big Time Returns . . .

Despite his pointed rejoinder to Joe Paterno's challenge in 1970, even Blackman would probably admit that Penn State under Paterno has become the East's premier team and indeed one of the nation's powers.

Penn State's rise to national prominence has been less than sudden. As far back as 1947, led by coach Bob Higgins and All-American guard Steve Suhey, the Nittany Lions went unbeaten and played in the Cotton Bowl. Then in the 1950s and early 1960s under coach Rip Engle, Penn State accumulated a string of winning seasons while meeting such formidable intersectional foes as Nebraska, Purdue, Michigan State, Texas Christian, Illinois, Missouri, Oregon, California, Rice, Georgia Tech, UCLA, Houston, and Ohio State. Engle's teams beat Ohio State all three times they played the Buckeyes, including a 27-0 upset in 1964, one of the top reversals of the decade. The loss rankled Woody Hayes no

Above: *Pitt's Mike Ditka. Ditka enjoyed great success in the pros.*

*Penn and Princeton captains hurriedly
shake hands before
departing for their respective sidelines.*

end, although he and Engle were good friends.

Engle produced his two best teams in 1959 and 1962. The 1959 club lost twice, once only barely to national champion Syracuse. The 1962 team was even better, losing only to Army 9-6. Quarterback Pete Liske and halfback Roger Kochman led the offense, and Dave Robinson, a superb end, starred on the tough, talented defense.

Engle also developed a galaxy of bright stars: Jesse Arnell, Milt Plum, Sam Tamburo, Sam Valentine, Lenny Moore, Rosey Grier, Richie Lucas, Kochman, Liske, Bob Mitinger, Robinson, and Glenn Ressler, many of whom achieved All-American honors and then fame in the pros.

After the 1964 season, Engle retired and yielded the head coaching reins to Paterno, his longtime assistant. A quarterback under Engle at Brown University, Brooklyn-bred Paterno had developed a long line of outstanding Penn State quarterbacks to lead the offense, for which he was mainly responsible as assistant coach.

A personable, articulate man with a sharp sense of humor, he brought exciting and unorthodox attitudes to big-time college football. "There are other things in life besides football," he proclaimed unashamedly, while coaching traditionalists shuddered. Then Paterno compounded his heresy by suggesting that his players get involved in campus life, that athletic dormitories be abolished, and even that football scholarships be limited. A new generation of collegians, especially more socially aware black athletes, responded well to Paterno's nonconformist methods.

In just two seasons, Paterno returned Penn State to the top ten, and since 1967, the Nittany Lions have left the elite list only once. Twice Penn State has been the runner-up for the national championship.

The National Collegiate Sports Service recently released statistics that show Penn State second only to Texas in winning percentage over the five-year period from 1968. Texas's record is 45-4 for a .918 percentage; Penn State is 47-5 for .904. Counting postseason bowl games however, Penn State is 50-6-1 to Texas's 48-6-1, and in the 1972 Cotton Bowl, the Nittany Lions mauled the

Longhorns 30-6. It would be hard to deny that Penn State isn't actually number one for the five-year period.

Paterno began less than auspiciously as head coach. His team struggled to a 5-5 record in 1966 and lost two of its first three games in 1967, to Navy 23-22 and to UCLA 17-15. But then the Nittany Lions began a 31-game unbeaten streak, winning their last seven games in 1967, tying Florida State 17-17 in the Gator Bowl, and then enjoying consecutive 11-0 season in 1968 and '69. When Colorado finally ended the streak in the second game of 1970, Penn State had firmly established itself as one of the top football schools in the country.

More than an unorthodox coach in the way he handles his players, Joe Paterno is an innovative, imaginative tactician and strategist as well. After Joe concocted a gambling version of the standard 4-3 defense, his defensive team captured everyone's imagination with its penchant for blocking kicks, intercepting passes, and forcing fumbles. This alert roughhouse crew was composed of ends John Ebersole and Gary Hull, tackles Mike Reid and Steve Smear (two of the best), linebackers Dennis Onkotz, Jim Kates, and Jack Hamm, and in the secondary Pete Johnson, Paul Johnson, Neal Smith, and Mike Smith.

Paterno also had players who fit perfectly into his equally free-wheeling offense. On the 1968 team, quarterback Chuck Burkhart was just an average passer but a real money player who never started a losing game. Running backs Bill Campbell and Charlie Pittman could break open a game, and All-American Ted Kwalick, the tight end, was the best in the country at his position.

Except for a close game with Army, Penn State had little competition in 1968. The Lions hammered Navy, Kansas State, West Virginia, UCLA, and Boston College, but Army stoutly resisted before yielding 28-24. The difference was a freak play that backfired on the Cadets. Late in the game Army tried an onside kick that produced a pile of writhing bodies on Penn State's 47-yard line. About the only player who was not in the crowd groping for the ball was Penn State's Kwalick. Suddenly, the ball squirted out of the pack. Kwalick picked it up

and nonchalalantly sprinted 53 yards for the touchdown that gave the Lions victory.

Penn State sailed through the rest of the regular season, conquering Miami, Maryland, Pitt, and Syracuse. Then the Lions accepted an invitation to play Kansas, the once-beaten Big Eight champions, in the Orange Bowl. Favored Kansas led 14-7 with slightly more than a minute to play and Penn State in possession of the ball on the 50-yard line after a punt. It hardly seemed likely that the Lions would be able to salvage this one, but they did, with one of the most spectacular finishes the Orange Bowl has ever seen. On the first play, Burkhart survived a Kansas rush and hit Campbell with a perfect pass. The halfback raced to the 3-yard line before he was dragged down. Three plays later, Burkhart decided to keep the ball instead of handing off to Pittman, as the play he had called dictated, and lunged over for a touchdown as time ran out. In keeping with his style, coach Paterno went for two points and victory on the conversion instead of settling for a tie. When Burkhart's pass to Campbell was batted down, Kansas apparently had a 14-13 win, but an official had spotted an infraction. The Jayhawks had had 12 men on the field, an unusual goal-line defense that coach Pepper Rodgers, now at UCLA, is still trying to explain on the banquet circuit.

With the Kansas defense limited to 11 men and Penn State given another chance at the conversion, Campbell crashed into the end zone for the two points that gave the Lions a 15-14 triumph. Later, the game films showed that Kansas had had 12 men on the field for *four* straight plays, including the one on which Burkhart had scored. What, asked Joe Paterno, were his four assistant coaches (George Welsh, Joe McMullen, Bobby Phillips, and Frank Patrick) doing on the phones up in the press box while all this was going on?

"We were all busy cheering, Joe," they chorused happily.

Several weeks later, they cheered some more when Paterno was voted Coach of the Year by his peers in the American Football Coaches Association and then turned down a big money offer to coach the Pittsburgh Steelers.

With practically the same cast of characters,

except for the notable additions of Lydell Mitchell and Franco Harris, a pair of brilliant sophomore running backs, Penn State swept to another 11-0 season in 1969. Led by Onkotz, Reid, and Smith, all of whom were named All-Americans, the defense produced the devastating big plays time after time. Pittman had a big year running the ball and also was picked for the All-American team. And again the Lions were threatened only once during the regular season, this time by Syracuse. Navy, Colorado, Kansas State, and West Virginia all fell relatively easily, but it took another last-minute touchdown and another gamble on a two-point conversion for the Lions to overcome a 14-0 deficit against Syracuse and squeak past 15-14. With easy victories over Ohio University, Boston College, Maryland, Pitt, and North Carolina State, Penn State completed a second straight undefeated and untied season and stretched its unbeaten streak to 29 games.

A quirk of fate cost Penn State a chance at the national championship. When bowl invitations were extended in mid-November, three teams

ranked ahead of Penn State. Number-one Ohio State had only to beat underdog Michigan on November 22 to secure the top spot. Southwest Conference rivals Texas (number two) and Arkansas (number three) would meet each other on December 6. Penn State had already been invited to both the Cotton Bowl, where it would meet the Texas-Arkansas winner, and the Orange Bowl, where it would meet Missouri, the Big Eight champion. Unfortunately, the Lions had to decide by November 17 which invitation to accept: gamble on an Ohio State defeat, which seemed highly unlikely, and go to the Cotton Bowl with a chance for the national championship against Texas or Arkansas, or return to the pleasures of Miami and the Orange Bowl? The Lions' coaches and players opted for the Orange Bowl.

For once the Lions were too conservative. Michigan upset Ohio State, depriving the Buckeyes of the number-one spot. Texas succeeded to the throne, and President Nixon, presidential plaque in hand, journeyed to Fayetteville, Arkansas, to crown the winner of

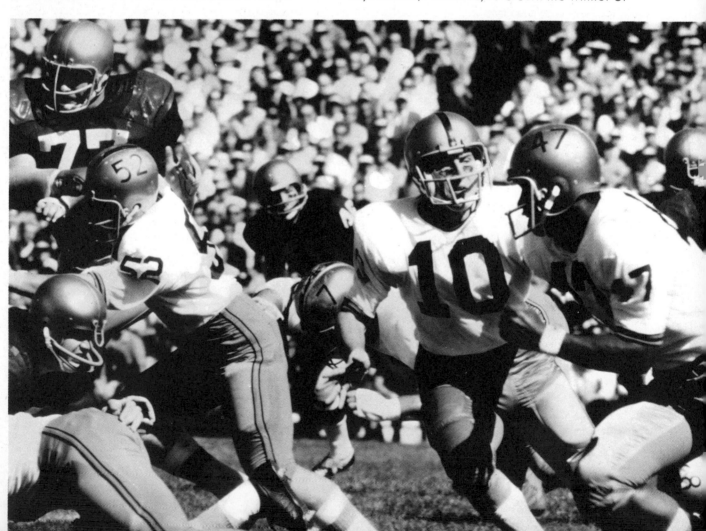

the Texas-Arkansas game. Texas won 15-14, and Nixon proclaimed Texas number one. An angry Joe Paterno promptly demonstrated his displeasure by publicly rejecting another presidential plaque, which Nixon planned to award to Penn State for its long unbeaten streak. The furor didn't diminish when Texas beat Notre Dame in the Cotton Bowl and defiant Penn State whipped Missouri 10-3 in the Orange Bowl. Penn State remained number two, behind the Longhorns, in the final AP poll and spent the off-season contemplating the vagaries of national rankings.

After considerable soul-searching, Paterno rejected a million-dollar offer to coach the Boston Patriots. Apparently, he was content to continue to produce top-flight teams at Penn State, which he did in '71 and '72, when the Lions were among the best teams in the country. They lost only once in the regular season each year, both times to Tennessee. The Lions trounced Texas in the Cotton Bowl after the 1971 season, gaining some retribution for what they considered a slight two years earlier, but lost to powerhouse Oklahoma in the Sugar Bowl after the '72 campaign. It was their only bowl loss in five tries under Paterno.

Winning breeds success in recruiting. Those blue-chip athletes (mostly Easterners, incidentally) continue to come to Penn State: All-Americans such as tackle Dave Joyner, linebacker Charlie Zapiec, halfback Lydell Mitchell, quarterback John Hufnagel, linebacker John Skoupan, and end Bruce Bannon. And there were more to come—Heisman winner John Cappalletti and linebacker Ed O'Neil of the 1973 team.

. . . While the Small Time Prospers
A host of small colleges also have contributed their share to Eastern football, past and present. Lafayette, which used to play some of the big schools, went unbeaten in 1921, 1926, 1937, and 1940 and produced such stars as Frank Schwab and Charlie Berry. A host of small Pennsylvania schools have crept into the national small-college rankings in recent years: Bucknell, West Chester State, California State, Juniata, Lock Haven State, Indiana, Franklin and Marshall, and Edinboro State. Alfred, Rochester, Bridgeport, Boston University, C. W. Post, Wagner, Hofstra,

Kings Point, Montclair State, and the Little Three—Amherst, Williams, and Wesleyan—all enjoy good but relatively low-pressure football. Massachusetts, a cut above these institutions but still a college-division school, flourished in the 1960s under coach Vic Fusia.

The current leading light is Delaware. The Mud Hens, first under Dave Nelson, the old Michigan teammate of Tom Harmon and Forrest Evashevski, and now under Tubby Raymond, have been bruising their small-college neighbors for years, and some folks claim that Delaware's recent teams could hold their own with a lot of the big-time teams.

Perhaps the limited resources and modest recruiting program are more help than hindrance at Delaware. Coach Raymond told Bob Gutkowski, "I feel that in many ways being from a small state has helped us develop an *esprit de corps*. The boy is a person, not a number, and it works just fine for us. I view Delaware football as a community rather than just a production. We have a lot of followers in this area, so we feel more like it's a home rather than a school. We have always recruited within a radius of a hundred miles because I have found that players are more content being closer to home and have a feeling of loyalty when they live nearby. A lot of boys have told me that they came here because out-of-state recruiting pressures turned them off. We have a minimal budget, and we're interested in the kids and their academic lives."

A Conclusion
Because Eastern football no longer dominates college football, some detractors insist that the game survives in the region on memories alone. They do the game as well as the region a disservice, for college football is an adaptable sport, which can and should be played on all levels. From mighty Penn State and small-time power Delaware, to the tradition-rich Ivies and the service academies, to the tiniest school in the foothills of New England, Eastern football offers the game in its many different settings. As recruiting scandals and drug problems at the big schools demonstrate that bigness in college football is not always best, perhaps the critics will realize that in its diversity Eastern football has once again stolen a lead on the rest of the country.

Army quarterback Bernie Wall (10) starts a roll-out against Notre Dame. The Notre Dame-Army rivalry can no longer produce a fair contest.

A Noble Du

y: the South
by Jesse Outlar

In the 1929 dedicatory game of Sanford Stadium in Athens, Georgia, end Vernon ("Catfish") Smith scored all the points as the University of Georgia stunned Albie Booth and highly favored Yale 15-0. While Georgians celebrated their greatest football triumph, the Yale players and their solemn followers were stranded at the railroad station; the Yale special, 10 Pullmans and two diners, had derailed departing Athens. The delay gave George Trevor ample time to reflect on the story he had filed for the Sunday edition of the *New York Sun*.

In one afternoon Trevor had seen that football in the South is much more than a game. He observed in his column, "This college spirit was refreshing to Eastern observers. Athens and Georgia University will remain delightfully unsophisticated and ingenuous in an era when it is smart to be blasé. The soft-voiced Georgians aren't ashamed to whoop it up over a football game.

"Football provides an escape valve for that adventurous urge; that martial ardor, which despite an outward appearance of languor is the heritage of every son of Dixie. Northerners may have orginated the American version of rugby, but the game is in the blood down here in the Deep South, and they play it for blood."

Football was first played in the Deep South in 1890, when Vanderbilt routed the University of Nashville 46-0.

An Atlanta Journal editorial, on the eve of the first game between the University of Georgia and Auburn in 1892 in Atlanta, reflected the warm response the game received.

"Players and all of the town men and town ladies are leaving everything else to talk of football and to encourage and enthuse the boys with their presence at the practice game every day."

Southerners were instantly attracted to the game, but it was several years before they were able to field teams on the level of the powers of the Ivy League and Midwest.

Dr. William L. Dudley, dean of Vanderbilt's medical college, took the lead in organizing football in Southern colleges. He and other educators met in Atlanta on December 22, 1894

and formed the Southern Intercollegiate Athletic Association. The charter stated, "The object shall be the development, regulation and purification of college athletics in the South."

The Southern, Southeastern, and Atlantic Coast Conferences are descendants of the Southern Intercollegiate Athletic Association. There were 7 charter members of the SIAA: Alabama, Auburn, Vanderbilt, Sewanee, Georgia, Georgia Tech, and North Carolina. By 1922, Dr. Dudley's conference had grown to an unwieldly family of 46 colleges. Larger colleges then withdrew and formed the Southern Intercollegiate Conference, which later became the Southern Conference with 23 members. The

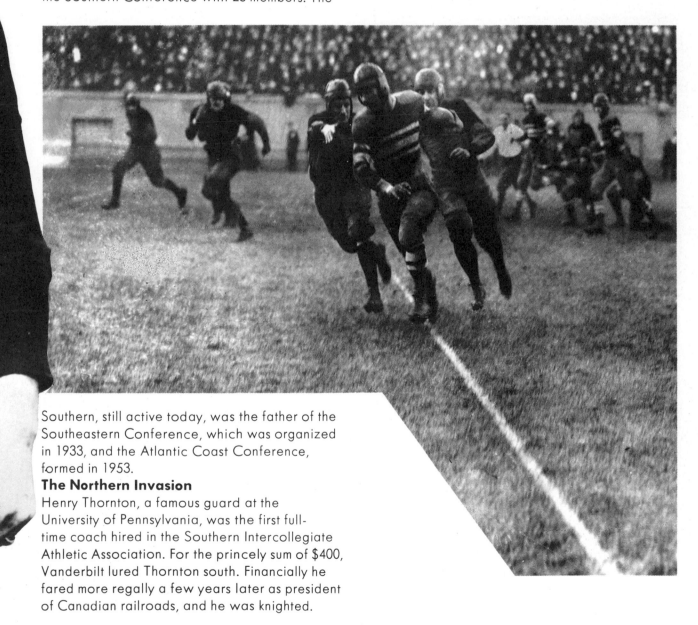

Southern, still active today, was the father of the Southeastern Conference, which was organized in 1933, and the Atlantic Coast Conference, formed in 1953.

The Northern Invasion

Henry Thornton, a famous guard at the University of Pennsylvania, was the first full-time coach hired in the Southern Intercollegiate Athletic Association. For the princely sum of $400, Vanderbilt lured Thornton south. Financially he fared more regally a few years later as president of Canadian railroads, and he was knighted.

Preceding pages: Ole Miss fans back their team. Left: John Heisman. Above: Bo McMillin makes his famous run, and Centre upsets mighty Harvard.

The University of Georgia wasn't as extravagant as Vandy. Glen ("Pop") Warner began his fabled coaching career in 1895 in Athens, Georgia, for $34 per game. The Bulldogs played only seven games, so coach Warner moonlighted by conducting preseason practice at Iowa State before coming to Georgia for the regular season. Despite Warner's 3-4 debut year, astute Georgia officials were impressed by the young man and boosted his salary to $40 per game, enabling him to resign at Iowa State.

"I prized that first contract more than any I signed in all the other years," Warner said later. "I got a lot of raises as a coach . . . but I never forgot that first six-dollar increase at Georgia."

When Warner's Georgia team met Auburn in 1895, he encountered another coach who would become a living legend. Auburn had induced John Heisman to leave Oberlin. The rival coaches in that game in Atlanta became two of football's most famous and widely traveled coaches. Warner coached Georgia, Cornell, Carlisle, Pittsburgh, Stanford, Temple, and San Jose State. Heisman coached Oberlin, Akron, Auburn, Clemson, Georgia Tech, Pennsylvania, Washington and Jefferson, and Rice.

A Lady Saves the Game

Then, as now, football had many critics. The Georgia-Virginia game in Atlanta on October 3, 1897, produced football's first crisis in the South. Richard Von Gammon, a Georgia linebacker, suffered a concussion in attempting a tackle, and he died the following morning in Henry Grady Hospital.

The Georgia Athletic Association issued a terse bulletin: "There will be no more football at the University." Other colleges announced that they were abolishing football, and headlines in Southern newspapers sounded "Death Knell of Football."

Georgia's General Assembly unanimously passed a bill outlawing the game in all schools that received state funds. But there were strong defenders of the sport, including Dr. Charles Herty, famed scientist and father of football at Georgia. In an open letter to newspapers, Dr. Herty wrote, "Instead of condemning sports, the lawmakers should make provisions for their proper development. Regret over the Von Gammon disaster is general and sincere, but the degree to which some critics go is unreasonable and unjust."

Von Gammon's mother read the published letter and promptly wrote to her state representative. "It would be the greatest favor to the family of Von Gammon if your influence could prevent his death from being used as an argument detrimental to the athletic cause and its advancement at the University," she pleaded. "His love for college and his interest in all manly sports, without which he deemed the highest type of manhood impossible, is well known by his classmates and friends, and it would be inexpressibly sad to have the cause he held so dear injured by his sacrifice.

"Grant me the right to request that my boy's death should not be used to defeat the most cherished objects of his life. Dr. Charles Herty's article in *The Constitution* of November 2 is timely, and authorities of the University can be trusted to make all changes for . . . the welfare of students. . . ."

Governor W. Y. Atkinson vetoed the bill abolishing football. A lady had saved the game in an area where it was then enjoying its most rapid growth.

The Iron Men of Sewanee

The first Southern team that attracted the nation's attention was Sewanee, a small Episcopal college of some 300 students nestled in the mountains of Tennessee. In 1899, in the span of six days, 21 Sewanee players traveled 3,000 miles and won five games.

Coach Herman Suter, a famous player at Princeton, directed the famous trip. It began in Austin, Texas. Sipping from the two barrels of special spring water they had brought from Tennessee, the Tigers of Sewanee tamed Texas 12-0 and then celebrated the victory at a dance in Austin. Shifting to Houston the next afternoon, the Tigers blanked Texas A & M 10-0 and then rode the night train to New Orleans. They had sufficient stamina to subdue Tulane 23-0. The next day, perhaps due to an oversight in scheduling, the players enjoyed an off day, during which coach Suter took them on a tour of the sugar plantations of Louisiana instead of the French Quarter. Rested the next afternoon, Sewanee ripped Louisiana State 23-0 in Baton

Clockwise from bottom: Herman Hickman, Tennessee's All-American in 1931; Frank Sinkwich of Georgia, all-decade; Dixie Howell of Alabama gets one away.

Clockwise from far left: *Beattie Feathers, Tennessee; Charley Conerly, Mississippi; George Cafego, Tennessee; Charlie Justice, North Carolina.*

Rouge and then caught a special train to Memphis. There, the Tigers beat Ole Miss 12-0 for their fifth triumph in six days. Finally the weary heroes headed home. Coach Suter had played only 15 of his 21 iron men on the trip.

McGugin of Vanderbilt

Sewanee continued to be the dominant power in Dixie football through the turn of the century, but a new era began in 1904, when Vanderbilt hired Daniel Earle McGugin. No coach has had more influence on Southern football than McGugin, who witnessed the transition from the Southern Intercollegiate Athletic Association to the Southeastern Conference in a fantastic 30-year career. During the McGugin regime, Vanderbilt won 13 titles and logged an overall record of 196-54-19. Frank Howard of Clemson was the only coach in the South to match McGugin's longevity record for a head coach at one school.

Dr. Dudley, the SIAA founder and the man for whom the Vanderbilt stadium is named, hired McGugin. Dan had learned his football as a star guard on Fielding ("Hurry Up") Yost's 1902-03 teams at Michigan. McGugin worked for Yost as an assistant after graduating and later became his brother-in-law. Of the several colleges that were interested in hiring him as a head coach, McGugin preferred Vanderbilt. He applied for the coaching job at the prestigious Nashville university, but due to a mix-up in communications, Dr. Dudley did not reply promptly, so McGugin decided to accept an offer from Western Reserve in Cleveland. Only minutes after he dispatched a telegram of acceptance to Cleveland, McGugin received word from Dudley that Vanderbilt wanted to hire him. McGugin intercepted his telegram before it was delivered to Western Reserve and took the Vandy job. Had Dudley's message come any later, McGugin would already have committed himself to Cleveland. Thus, McGugin came to Nashville instead of Cleveland and launched one of football's most famous dynasties.

The McGugin era began with shattering impact. Vanderbilt breezed to eight straight victories, outscoring its opponents 452 to 4. The Missouri School of Mines accounted for the lone score—a field goal than worth four points.

McGugin emulated Yost, clapping his hands and hollering "Hurry Up!" at practice sessions. He stressed speed instead of power, the trademark of early Southern teams. He pioneered intersectional games, scheduling Michigan and Ohio State, the only teams to defeat his Commodores during his first five years. Sewanee in 1909 earned the distinction of being the first Southern team to defeat McGugin.

McGugin's super success at Vanderbilt prompted a flurry of offers for his services from other colleges, including a lucrative bid from Alabama in 1923. Instead of accepting it himself, McGugin induced the Crimson Tide to hire his unknown assistant, Wallace Wade, who became a giant at Alabama and Duke.

In 1923, McGugin's Vanderbilt squad dedicated Dudley Field by playing to a scoreless tie with a powerful Michigan team. The Vandy captain and quarterback that day, Jess Neely, later became a famous coach at Clemson and Rice before returning to his alma mater as athletic director. Two other members of Vandy's team, end Lynn Bomar and Herk Wakefield, became members of the school's all-time team. And Michigan quarterback Harry Kipke would enjoy a fabulous coaching career at his alma mater.

Rival colleges accelerated their programs, but they could not compete with Vanderbilt. In 1905, John Heisman, who would win 100 games as coach at Georgia Tech, wrote, "Vanderbilt has grown out of the class of her sister colleges in the SIAA, and it is pertinent for someone to inquire if it wouldn't be for the best interest of Vandy and other SIAA teams for her to move into some larger or higher class league.

"That she is tending that way is shown by the arrangement of a game with Michigan. I am not arguing that Vandy should leave the SIAA, for surely no one is more welcome and no one has a better right to be in it."

In an overzealous effort to keep up with Vanderbilt, rivals resorted to fielding ineligible players, and a major scandal hit the campuses. "The colleges were desperate over their inability to cope with the Commodores," wrote football historian Fuzzy Woodruff. "Alumni decided that if Vanderbilt could not be beaten by fair means,

it must be beaten by foul. In their desire to raise some schools to the eminence of Vanderbilt, alumni lost sight of the plain facts in the case, which were that Vanderbilt had been elevated by the sheer genius of Dan McGugin, coupled with good material."

Not only a sound football tactician, McGugin was an orator—a practicing attorney who delivered pregame talks to arouse his teams. Fred Russell, sports editor of the *Nashville Banner*, made available a copy of the lecture that McGugin delivered before Vandy trounced a strong Texas team 20-0 in Dallas.

"You are about to be put to an ordeal which will show the stuff that is in you," McGugin began. "What a glorious chance you have! Every one of you is going to fix your status for all time in the minds and hearts of your teammates

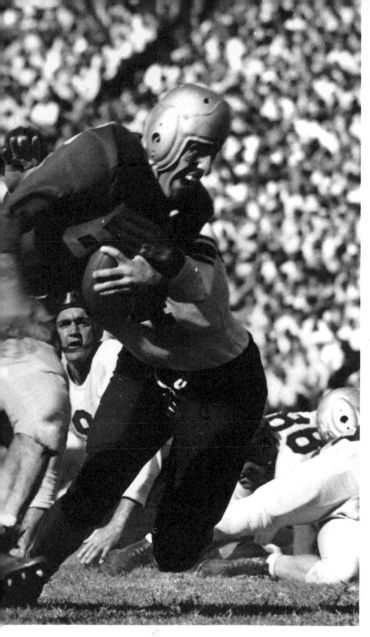

today. How you fight is what you will be remembered by. If anyone shirks, the Lord pity him. He will be degraded in the hearts of the rest of you as long as he lives.

"I heard repeatedly before we left Nashville that this team might win from Texas *if it would only fight.* Has anyone the right to imply such an insult? And if so, when before now could such a thing be said of men from Tennessee?

"Who the devil started all this bunk about the Texas team? Who thinks they are unbeatable? They say that they have the greatest team in history. They say Vanderbilt never had a team which could beat theirs this year, but that is not true. Texas has a shield like ours. We have some scars on it, but there are a lot of stars there. Texas has no such athletic tradition and history.

"Now is there any man here who will not

fight every inch of the way? Will any man here disgrace himself and live in the contempt of his teammates the rest of his days? Are you going to establish yourselves in your own self-respect and in the eyes of thousands watching you? Are you going to make your own record and leave memories for others to live by?"

To coach McGugin and the men of Vanderbilt, football was a noble duty not lightly spurned.

Heisman and Donahue

Vanderbilt had won six straight SIAA championships when Auburn snapped the skein in 1908. Mike Donahue, an Irishman born in Kerry County, came to Auburn the same year that McGugin started at Vanderbilt. Only 5 feet 4 inches, Donahue had been a star back at Yale. He was a scholar in Latin, Greek, and English, but he had such a brogue that his players frequently had difficulty understanding him. An inspirational man, Donahue introduced the famed "War Eagle" spirit at Auburn, and in 19 seasons he gave the alumni plenty to shout about. When Donahue went to LSU, he left a record of 101-37-5 at Auburn. He and Heisman were among the first coaches to favor wide-open offenses, in which the forward pass was a prime weapon.

John Heisman, for whom the Heisman Trophy is named, ended the McGugin monopoly in the SIAA. From 1915-18, Heisman's Georgia Tech teams won four straight titles, and in 16 seasons in Atlanta, Heisman never had a team with a losing record. The first of three Georgia Tech coaches to win more than 100 games (Bill Alexander and Bobby Dodd were the others), Heisman established an overall record of 102-29-6.

Heisman's 1916 champions beat Cumberland University 222-0, setting the record for most points scored in a college football game. The massacre occurred in Atlanta on October 7, 1916, before 11,000 fans, who saw Georgia Tech score 32 touchdowns and 30 extra points in less than 50 minutes. Heisman, a Shakespearean actor during the off season, eloquently explained why Tech had slaughtered Cumberland.

"We at Tech determined this year, at the start of the season, to show folks that it was no very difficult thing to run up a score in one easy game, from which it might perhaps be seen that

it could also be done in other easy games as well. Accordingly, in the Cumberland game, the Jackets set all their sails to make a record run, and for the first time in our football career, we turned loose all we had in the way of scoring stuff. The result was a world's record; two hundred and twenty-two points rolled up in forty-five minutes of play.

"Now we find a lot of people and papers all over the country once more making much of it and printing our name in big type at the top of columns of flub-dub. My, my, but it is easy to fool some folks."

Old-timers related that on the first day of practice at Tech, Heisman would greet his squad, hold up a football, and rhetorically inquire, "What is it? It is a prolate spheriod—that is, an elongated sphere—in which the outer leathern casing is drawn tightly over a somewhat small rubber tubing. Better to have died as a small boy than for any of you to fumble it."

After 16 seasons at Tech, Heisman and his wife were divorced. He agreed to leave Atlanta if she elected to stay. She did, and Heisman took his trophies, his volumes of Shakespeare, and his

enviable record to the University of Pennsylvania. Donahue had departed Auburn for LSU, so as the twenties began, McGugin was the last of the old guard still operating at his accustomed post.

The Upset of the Century

Molding the South's new powerhouse teams were young men such as Wallace Wade of Alabama, Bob Neyland of Tennessee, Bill Alexander of Georgia Tech, Clark Shaughnessy of Tulane, and Bernie Bierman of Mississippi State, Tulane, and later Minnesota. But the most famous team of the era was little Centre College of Danville, Kentucky, the team that shook the football world by beating mighty Harvard 6-0 on October 29, 1921. When the Associated Press conducted a poll 29 years later to determine "the upset of the century," sportswriters nominated Centre College's victory over Harvard.

Bo McMillin scored the lone touchdown of the game on a 32-yard run one minute into the third quarter. McMillin continued on the road to fame as the coach of Indiana's first Big Ten champion years later and concluded an illustrious career as head coach of the Detroit Lions. He frequently related the early chapters of his touching football career, which started in Fort Worth, Texas, and reached its climax when Centre beat Harvard and became the national champion. Robert ("Chief") Myers coached North Side High in Fort Worth, and when he moved to Centre as head coach, he took McMillin, center Red Weaver, end Matty Bell, and several other players with him. Myers forecast that his Texans would form the nucleus of a championship team at Centre. To achieve the feat, however, he decided that the college needed a different head coach, so Myers became athletic director and brought in Uncle Charley Moran, a shrewd coach who had attracted more attention as a major league baseball umpire than as a football coach.

Myers's dream quickly came true. A small college in the Kentucky wilderness, Centre had only 300 students, but Moran and the Texans needed no more. The 1919 Centre team went undefeated, beating highly regarded West Virginia and Indiana in games that put Danville, Kentucky, on America's football map.

Boston sportswriters suggested that a game between Harvard, undefeated king of college football, and Centre, the little giant of the South, would fill the Cantabs' stadium and attract national attention. Harvard officials concurred, and a game was scheduled in 1920.

Hardly anyone rated the Praying Colonels a chance. Harvard had started the year by defeating Oregon in the Rose Bowl, thereby extending its victory skein to 28 straight games. When Centre staged its historic upset, the Praying Colonels joined the legendary teams of sport.

Red Smith, renowned New York sports columnist, relates a story about Bill Crowell, a raconteur himself, who officiated in the memorable game. Centre players had earned the nickname of Praying Colonels the previous season for praying before games, but when Crowell strolled past the Centre dressing quarters and heard the prayers, he was startled. He rushed down the corridor and got the other officials. They listened and then watched as the Centre players, tears streaming down their faces, rushed out of the room. McMillin, the last one out the the door, paused and said to the officials, "Mistah, out there on that field today

you're gonna see the blankety blankest gang of fightin' such and suches you eva saw in your unexpurgated Yankee life."

The Tide Rises

As the McGugin dynasty faded at Vanderbilt, his former assistant, Wallace Wade, moved Alabama into Dixie's football penthouse, and in ensuing years the Tide has remained near the top. The first and last Southern team to play in the Rose Bowl, Alabama made six trips to Pasadena, more than all its neighbors combined. The school has gone to the other bowls even more often. Wade, Frank Thomas, Red Drew, and Bear Bryant produced 23 bowl teams and 16 championships through the 1973 season.

McGugin's most successful pupil, Wade fashioned a record of 61-13-3 at Alabama and a mark of 110-36-7 at Duke. Alabama football historians generally agree that Wade's 1927 Rose Bowl champions played the most important game in the Tide's proud football history. Trailing the University of Washington 12-0 in the third quarter, the Tide struck for three touchdowns in six minutes and won 20-19. Johnny Mack Brown, who became a cowboy movie star, Pooley Hubert, and Grant Gillis sparked the comeback that gave the South the national exposure it had been seeking since McGugin's early days.

Wade and his Tide returned to the Rose Bowl the following New Year's Day and tied Pop Warner's highly esteemed Stanford Indians. In 1931, in Wade's last trip to Pasadena as Alabama coach, soph back Johnny Cain and tackle Fred Sington led the Tide to a 24-0 triumph over Washington State.

When Wade moved to Duke in 1931, he recommended as his successor Frank Thomas, a former Notre Dame quarterback who had played for Rockne and roomed with George Gipp. Fortunately for Alabama football, Dr. George H. Denny took Wade's advice. Thomas gave alumni little reason to bemoan the loss of Wade to Duke.

"Material is ninety percent and coaching ability is ten percent," Dr. Denny told the young Thomas. "You will be provided with the ninety percent, and you will be held to strict accounting for delivering the remaining ten percent."

Thomas responded nobly, and his Alabama teams rolled up a fantastic 115-24-7 record before ill health in 1947 forced his retirement at the peak of his career. Thomas's teams played in the Rose, Cotton, Orange, and Sugar bowls. The team that upset Stanford 29-13 in the 1935 Rose Bowl was his most memorable. That outfit featured the famous battery of tailback Dixie Howell and end Don Hutson, who became an all-pro at Green Bay. The other end on the '34 team also became well known. He was Paul ("Bear") Bryant.

Longtime Tide assistant and former athletic director Hank Crisp noted, "Players like Hutson, Howell, Riley Smith, and guard Bill Marr would have made any college team any time."

Like Wade, Thomas bowed out of the Rose Bowl victoriously. Harry Gilmer, a soph and the last of Thomas's great backs, pitched the Tide to a 34-14 victory over Southern Cal on New Year's Day, 1946. When Thomas's ill health forced him to step down the next year, Harold ("Red") Drew took over. After 24 years as a Tide assistant, Drew would be the head man for the next 7. Quarterback Ed Salem was Drew's only All-American back but not his best remembered. That honor must be awarded to Tommy Lewis, who attained lasting notoriety with one tackle in the 1954 Cotton Bowl. When Dickie Moegle of Rice raced past the Alabama bench, Lewis jumped from the sidelines and made his famous "twelfth man tackle." Officials awarded Moegle a touchdown, one of three he scored during the 28-6 victory. In a prophetic statement, the crestfallen Lewis said, "I'm just too full of Alabama. I know I'll hear about this the rest of my life."

Some of Drew's chargers shone more as alumni than as members of his team. As an Alabama freshman, Bart Starr quarterbacked Drew's 1952 Orange Bowl team to the most lopsided victory in bowl annals, a 61-6 humiliation of Syracuse. However, after such an illustrious start, Starr failed to make all-conference at Alabama, although he later was a consistent all-pro at Green Bay.

In the mid-fifties Tide football was approaching its lowest ebb. Under J. B. Whitworth, an outstanding assistant coach and former Alabama star, the team managed only four victories in three years. This alarming famine set the stage for the dramatic and triumphant return of Paul ("Bear") Bryant.

The Bear

Heralded as "the Great Rehabilitator" after winning as a head coach at Maryland, Kentucky, and Texas A & M, Bryant accepted in 1958 the challenge of restoring the football prestige at his alma mater. "We have secured, to our way of thinking, the best football coach in the country for the position of head football coach at the University of Alabama," said Ernest Williams, chairman of the Alabama selection committee.

Bryant first became a legend in the Southern Conference by producing four bowl teams in eight seasons at Kentucky, previously a graveyard for coaches. He developed many outstanding players in the bluegrass, including quarterback Babe Parilli, tackle Bob Gain, and end Howard Schnellenberger, who in 1973 became the head coach of the Baltimore Colts. Several other of his alumni are now coaching, including the highly successful Charlie McClendon of Louisiana State, Bill Battle of Tennessee, and Steve Sloan of Vanderbilt.

"Winning isn't everything," says Bryant, "but it beats anything that comes in second." Totally dedicated to the game even after 29 seasons, he still arrives at his office at 7 A.M. He demands that his assistants and players give 120 percent, and no modern coach has had greater success in getting it. Before 1973, Bryant teams had a combined record of 220-69-16, the fourth best winning percentages of any coach in the history of college football and the best among active coaches at major colleges. His Tidesmen have played in 15 straight bowl games, won three national titles and seven SEC crowns, and finished in the top ten of the football polls in 12 of 16 seasons. From 1961-67, Bryant achieved a record of 68-6-2, the best in football.

Bryant is the only active coach whose players reside in a football dorm named after him. Paul W. Bryant Hall is equipped with assorted recreational facilities, plush carpets, piped-in music, and modern furniture. A former Alabama star, complimented on the luxurious living quarters that were his at Tuscaloosa said, "It is very nice, but you pay the full price, and the rent comes very high."

Clockwise from top: *Florida's Spurrier challenges Missouri; Florida State's Biletnikoff cuts upfield; Duke's Hart looks frantically for a receiver.*

Tackle Billy Neighbors in 1958 was the first of 20 All-Americans developed by Bryant at Alabama. The Tide's lengthy honor roll features such stars as Joe Namath, Lee Roy Jordan, Pat Trammel, Steve Sloan, Ken ("Snake") Stabler, Terry Davis, Dennis Homan, Ray Perkins, Johnny Musso, and John Hannah. Namath, later the New York Jets' superstar, was suspended by Bryant as a junior, but he returned and became the most publicized of all the Bryant pupils.

Namath's first game, in which he directed Alabama to a 31-3 victory over Johnny Griffith's Georgia Bulldogs, caused quite a furor in Dixie. The now defunct *Saturday Evening Post* charged that Bryant and Wallace Butts, then Georgia's athletic director, had conspired to fix the game—that Butts had given Georgia plays and data to Bryant in telephone conversations overheard in an insurance office by one George Burnett. Bryant, who already had filed a suit against the *Post* for charging in a story that he engaged in football brutality, eventually won $390,000 tax free. Butts collected $460,000, but most of it was taxable. Namath, the star of the controversial game, settled for $400,000 when he signed his contract with the Jets.

Football's Winningest General

General Robert Reese Neyland taught Bryant and countless other coaches priceless lessons in the art of defensive football. What McGugin did for Vanderbilt, Bob Neyland did for Tennessee. It is unlikely that any state has had two greater football coaches than Dan McGugin and Neyland. When sportswriters voted in an Associated Press poll to pick a coach of the all-time college team, Neyland finished behind only Knute Rockne, Pop Warner, and Amos Alonzo Stagg.

Tennessee followers are indebted to the United States War Department for assigning Lieutenant Neyland to Tennessee in 1925 as an instructor in military science and tactics. An all-around athlete at West Point, Neyland agreed to help coach the football team at Tennessee for a bonus of $500 annually. When Neyland arrived on campus, the football stadium seated 3,000. In 1973, Neyland Stadium seated 64,429.

The lieutenant fresh from West Point launched his Tennessee career by winning 66 of 68 games. Five of his first seven teams were undefeated.

George Mira of Miami waits for an opening downfield. Mira had sporadic success in the pros, where he played for three teams, ending up back in Miami.

Before being ordered to Panama by the War Department in 1935, Neyland completed nine seasons, in which he won 76 of 88 games. Overall, he had an imposing record of 173-40-12, though his career was interrupted twice more by military service. (He was a brigadier general in World War II). In 1939, Neyland's Vols did not yield a point in the regular season—the last team to achieve that feat.

Acclaimed as the greatest of the defensive coaches, Neyland was years ahead of his colleagues in football philosophy. He was a stern disciplinarian who did not tolerate sloppiness, but he did not subject his troops to the daily scrimmages that were routine elsewhere in his early coaching days. While rivals knocked themselves out on the practice field, Neyland devoted many hours to lectures and mental preparation for his team. He stressed sound fundamentals, the kicking game, and defense. Tennessee teams felt they had an advantage by being better prepared than their opponents, and they usually were. Therefore, the General did not feel it necessary to inspire his team with the flaming oratory that was fashionable at the time. Nor was Neyland expansive with the fans and the media. He declined all radio and later all TV interviews, refused to lecture at clinics, rarely spoke to a touchdown club, and never wrote a book or a magazine article on football.

Of the 225 games Neyland coached, he considered the 1932 duel with Alabama and coach Frank Thomas the most memorable. In driving rain in Birmingham, Beattie Feathers of Tennessee and Johnny Cain of Alabama staged perhaps the greatest punting duel in college annals. Each kicked 20 times, Feathers averaging 48 yards and Cain 45. Tennessee won 7-3 when Feathers scored the game's only touchdown.

Neyland had far greater difficulty pinpointing his best team. The best he could do was select *eight* of the teams he guided in his distinguished career; 1928-32, '38, '40, and '50.

In 1953, after picking Harvey Robinson to succeed him as coach, Neyland moved to the athletic director's job at Tennessee. However, Robinson was unsuccessful, so in 1955, Neyland lured Bowden Wyatt away from Arkansas. An All-American end and captain of the General's 1938 powerhouse, Wyatt reminded observers of his former coach. It was no secret that Wyatt idolized Neyland and emulated him in many ways.

Wyatt began successfully at his alma mater with an undefeated regular season in 1956. The team featured tailback John Majors, who later became a fine coach at Iowa State and Pittsburgh. But unfortunately for Tennessee and Wyatt, there was only one Neyland. By 1962, ill health among other factors forced Wyatt to leave his alma mater. Doug Dickey then put Tennessee back on the winning track before shifting to Florida. Bill Battle, who played for Bryant at Alabama, now has the Vols basking in the victory spotlight to which they were accustomed when the General ruled on the hill in Knoxville.

The Ramblin' Wrecks

One of Neyland's most famous players, Bobby Dodd, became his greatest coaching alumnus. At Georgia Tech football is as prominent as the slide rule. Tech is the only college that has had three coaches who have won more than 100 games each: John Heisman (102-29-6), William Alexander (134-95-15), and Dodd (165-64-8).

Alexander succeeded Heisman in 1920 and became more prominent in Dixie than even his famed predecessor. The first of Alexander's 25 teams at Georgia Tech lost only to Pittsburgh and was acclaimed national champion. Tackle Bill Fincher, quarterback Buck Flowers, and halfbacks Red Baron and Judy Harlan eased pressure on Alexander in Tech's first post-Heisman season.

Alexander had many respected teams, but his most famous edition of the Ramblin' Wrecks was the 1928 Rose Bowl team. Three All-Americans— halfback Warner Mizell, center Peter Pund, and tackle Frank Speer—led Tech to a national title capped by an 8-7 victory over California in an unforgettable Rose Bowl game.

The 1928 game is best remembered for one of the most bizarre plays in football history: "the wrong way run" of California's Roy Riegels. "The score was nothing-nothing," recalls Tech end Frank Waddy, "and we had the ball on our twenty-three. We had a play which faked toward the sideline and came back. Stumpy Thomason was carrying the ball and fumbled. Riegels grabbed it while it was still in the air. It was my business to block halfback

74

Benny Lom, but when Riegels got the ball, it became Lom's job to block me.

"Riegels took two steps in the right direction, but as I was bearing down on him, he headed for his own goal. Lom was caught short, and we both set out after the ball carrier.

"We ran like members of the same team, with me one stride behind Lom, who finally caught Riegels at the one. Lom grabbed Riegels by the right shoulder with his left hand and spun him around. Then I hit him high and spilled him into the end zone, where he lost the ball and we recovered. I've never been able to understand why we didn't get a touchdown, but they gave the ball to Cal on the one.

"The ball was so close to the sideline that [on the next play, a punt Vance Maree, our left

tackle, moved outside right tackle. No one stopped him as he went in with arms crossed to knock the punt clear out of the end zone for [a safety and] two points."

Waddy hasn't yet forgotten the reaction of Alexander to the Riegels caper. Says Waddy, "When Riegels started his run, coach Alex shouted, 'Sit down, all of you. . . .Let him go as far as he can.' "

Alexander earned virtually every honor his profession bestows and then retired in 1945 to the athletic director's chair. His successor, Dodd, became Tech's winningest coach.

In 22 seasons under Dodd, Georgia Tech teams won 165, lost 64, tied 8, and became perennial visitors to the various bowls. As an All-American quarterback under General Neyland, Dodd was

became successful coaches. When Dodd, now the
athletic director, greeted the 1973 season, it
marked his forty-second year at Georgia Tech.

Between the Hedges

The University of Georgia in Athens already had
a proud football heritage, thanks to such coaches
as Dr. Charles Herty, Pop Warner, Alex
Cunningham, and Harry Mehre, but Georgia
football reached its peak during the 22-year
regime of Wallace Butts. Butts's teams were
noted for wide-open offensive football and hard-
nosed defensive tactics. Frank Leahy, the former
Notre Dame headmaster, called Butts "an
offensive genius." The Bulldogs were running
pro-type patterns before the pros used most of
them.

Butts rates his 1942 team his best. With
Heisman Trophy winner Frank Sinkwich and
Charlie Trippi in the same backfield, the Bulldogs
capped a 10-1 season with a victory over UCLA in
the Rose Bowl. Trippi returned to Georgia after
army service in World War II and sparked the
undefeated 1946 Sugar Bowl champs, who
outdueled North Carolina and Charlie "Choo
Choo" Justice in a classic contest in New
Orleans. John Rauch, who later coached
Oakland to the Super Bowl, quarterbacked four
straight bowl teams for Butts.

Trippi, Sinkwich, Rauch, Fran Tarkenton, Zeke
Bratkowski, Joe Tereshinski, Johnny Carson, and
Jimmy Orr are some of Butts's Bulldogs who
enjoyed distinguished careers in the pro ranks.

Vince Dooley, a former Auburn star, has
continued the winning tradition at Georgia. In
his first nine seasons, Dooley coached six bowl
teams and was named SEC Coach of the Year on
three occasions.

Winning and Living Legends

When Harry Mehre's "lifetime" contract expired
at Georgia, he moved to the University of
Mississippi, where he preceded John Vaught. "I
was lucky to get out of there [Ole Miss] alive,"
says Mehre, a noted humorist, "but Vaught
became a living legend. Vaught should have
won with all that material he had. I had to play
such people as Charley Conerly and all those
Pooles and Kinards."

In 1947, his first season at Oxford, Vaught also
had Charley Conerly, who later became a great
pro quarterback with the New York Giants, and

an unorthodox, daring player, and he employed
the same philosophy as a coach. Other coaches
scrimmaged players for untold hours; Dodd
permitted his players to play volleyball and take
it easy during the week.

"I would like to play a team coached by some
coach other than Dodd who prepared for games like
he did," Bear Bryant often said. "But it works for
Dodd. His teams don't give you anything."

Dodd was the only coach to win six straight
bowl games. He coached 22 All-American
players, including such greats as centers Larry
Morris, George Morris, and Maxie Baughan,
quarterback Billy Lothridge, and halfbacks Leon
Harderman and Paul Rotenberry.

Frank Broyles of Arkansas and Pepper Rodgers
of UCLA are former Dodd quarterbacks who

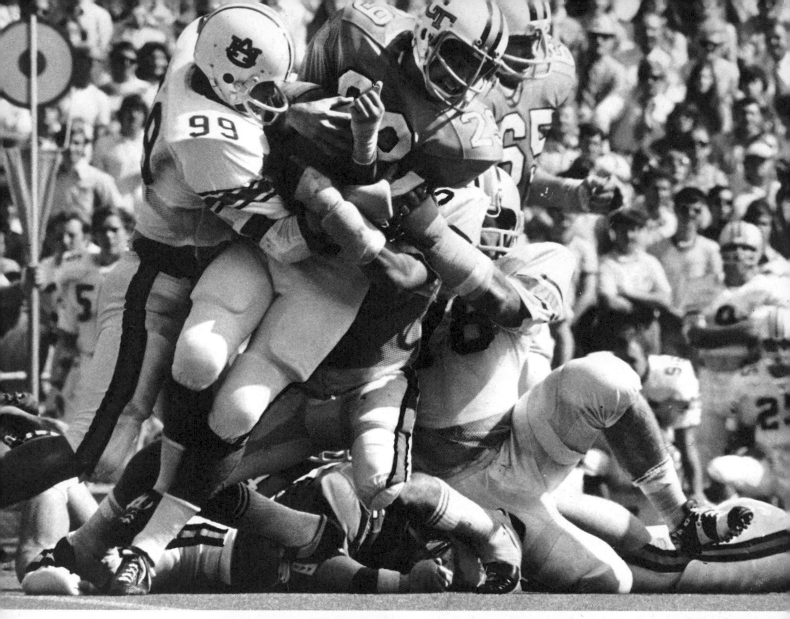

Clockwise from above: Georgia's Dooley; Tech's
McNamara is handled by Auburn's Welch;
Tennessee collides with Kentucky; NC's Vidnovic.

Barney Poole. The battery of Conerly and Poole enabled Vaught to become the first rookie coach in the SEC to win a title. Winning became a habit with the old TCU star; his Rebels won six championships and went bowling 17 times.

There are men in Mississippi who as youngsters never spent the holiday season at home, having played for Ole Miss in the era when Vaught produced a bowl team each year. Forced into temporary retirement because of a heart condition in 1970, Vaught qualified for the College Football Hall of Fame with a record of 185-58-12. He coached 20 All-Americans, from Charley Conerly to Archie Manning.

No coach in the history of Southern football is more respected than Ralph ("Shug") Jordan of Auburn. When Jordan started the 1973 season, it marked the beginning of his twenty-fourth year as head coach of his alma mater.

Jordan returned to Auburn as head coach in 1951 to a team that had won only three games in three seasons. Six years later Auburn was the undefeated and untied national champion and the next year celebrated its second consecutive campaign without defeat. Through 1972, Jordan had a coaching record of 156-69-5 and has had ten bowl teams.

When Jordan and Bryant shake hands after the annual Auburn-Alabama game, it is a meeting of the winningest coaches in football. They had 376 victories between them through the '72 season. Jordan has coached many All-Americans, including Heisman Trophy winner Pat Sullivan, flanker Terry Beasley, fullback Tucker Frederickson, guard Zeke Smith, and center Jackie Burkett.

The Tigers of Baton Rouge

No college students cheer their football teams with more enthusiasm than the War Eagles of Auburn and the Bengal Tigers of LSU. You have not fully experienced college football until you have seen a football game in Baton Rouge on Saturday night. Tiger Stadium seats 67,510 and is sold out for seven or eight games annually. From the moment the football Tigers follow the live Tiger mascot under the goal posts, the customers begin their night-long roaring of "Go Tigers! Go Tigers!" Countless coaches vow that there is no place precisely like it.

Huey Long, the late kingfish of Louisiana politics, was as interested in the Tigers winning as he was in becoming president of the United States. During the thirties, when Bernie Moore, later commissioner of the SEC, was head coach at LSU, the Bengals were Huey's pride and joy.

He induced railroads to run special trains to transport the student body to out-of-town games at vastly reduced rates. When railroad officials complained of losing money on the project, Huey reminded them that unless the ticket rates remained low, their taxes would soar.

Long did not welcome competition on weekends when his Tigers were playing. On one occasion, when the Ringling Brothers' circus was scheduled in Baton Rouge for the same Saturday on which LSU had a game slated, Huey strongly recommended that the circus change its date. Circus officials unwisely ignored Huey's advice, prompting him to invoke an ancient Louisiana tick law. No animals—including lions and tigers, of course—were permitted to enter the state unless they had been dipped in an antiseptic tank. The circus promptly rescheduled its performance for a date on which Long's football Tigers were idle.

In later years the Tigers would not need such help from Huey. After athletic director Jim Corbett imported an unknown coach, Paul Dietzel, LSU won a national championship in 1958. When Billy Cannon, Jimmy Taylor, and their playmates frolicked in Baton Rouge, tickets were always at a premium.

Though he later lost something of his touch at Army and South Carolina, Dietzel captivated Dixie fans with his three-team plan: the white team, the go team, and the Chinese Bandits.

When Dietzel, who had said a few days earlier that he hoped to spend his life at LSU, departed for West Point, Corbett wisely selected Charlie McClendon, an assistant and former Kentucky star under Bear Bryant, as the Bengals' new coach. In his first decade at LSU, McClendon's record was second only to Bob Devaney's at Nebraska. Entering his twelfth season in 1973, McClendon appeared a cinch to join the growing number of Dixie members of the 100-victory club.

No Southern college has a longer honor roll of stars than LSU. Y. A. Tittle, Steve Van Buren, Jimmy Taylor, Billy Cannon, Johnny Robinson, Fred Miller, Wendell Harris, and Tommy Casanova are a few of the players who have made Saturday nights so exciting in Baton Rouge.

Proving Grounds

Though Florida has never won a Southeastern Conference crown, the Gators have enjoyed considerable success under Bob Woodruff, Ray Graves, and Doug Dickey. They have had many stars, from Heisman Trophy winner Steve Spurrier to halfback Nat Moore, the junior college basketball player who in 1972 became the Cinderella back of major college football.

In recent years football fortune has been at low ebb at Mississippi State, but in the late thirties Major Ralph Sasse's Bulldogs were a power. State then hit its peak during the Allyn McKeen era, from 1939-48, when its mark was 65-19-4. Darrell Royal began as a head coach in Starkville in 1954 and moved on to a great career at Texas.

A major winner among the independents was Southern Mississippi's Pie Vann, who won some 200 games. And no honor roll of Southern football would be complete without A. C. ("Scrappy") Moore, who won 169 games and logged 35 colorful years at what is now the University of Chattanooga at Tennessee.

Two other coaches who won distinction in the Deep South are Andy Gustafson of Miami of Florida and Bill Peterson of Florida State. Peterson later moved to Rice and then became the head coach of the Houston Oilers.

The ACC and the Baron of Barlow Bend

Like the Southeastern Conference, the Atlantic Coast Conference is an offspring of the old Southern Intercollegiate Athletic Association, which became the Southern Conference and fathered the seven-college ACC in 1953.

Frank Howard, self-styled Baron of Barlow Bend, Alabama, is the winningest and most colorful of the ACC coaches. Howard frequently noted that he had coached more years in the ACC and had won more games than all his rivals combined. This boast would provoke his old sidekick, Peahead Walker of Wake Forest, to point out that Howard had also lost more games than all of his then current rivals. In the Southern and ACC, Howard logged a 165-118-12 mark.

In 30 seasons as head coach, Howard brought football fame to Clemson College. He named the school's stadium "Death Valley," and during the fifties, made his football team appropriately menacing. Clemson appeared twice in the Orange Bowl and once in each of the Sugar, Cotton, Gator, and Bluebonnet bowls.

A strong proponent of the single wing,

Above: *LSU's Warren Capone halts 'Bama's Wilbur Jackson. Opposite: Bill Luka of Auburn collars Oklahoma's Pruitt in 1972 Sugar Bowl game.*

Above and Right: *Football fanaticism surrounds Alabama games. Opposite: Morgan State's quarterback Bernard Jenkins starts a running play by handing off to scampering back Bobby Hammond.*

Above: *Garry Huff, Florida State's great passer, retreats to the pocket. Opposite top: Mississippi's opening charge. Opposite bottom: Upbeat Alabama.*

Howard had tailbacks such as Banks McFadden, Bobby Gage, and Jackie Calvert. Guard Harry Olszewski, end Joe Blalock, center Dave Thompson, and tackle Wayne Mass were other standouts.

Though much of its success was in the old Southern Conference, before the ACC was formed, Duke has more football tradition than its neighbors. The great Wallace Wade launched Duke's golden era in 1931 after a fabulous coaching career at Alabama. He had two Rose Bowl teams and a record of 110-36-7 at Duke. Wade's most famous team was the "the Iron Dukes" of 1938—undefeated, untied, and unscored on in nine games. Then, in the final seconds of the Rose Bowl game, third-string tailback Doyle Nave passed to Al Krueger, gaining for Southern Cal a 7-3 victory and administering Wade's most bitter defeat.

In 1941, Duke became the only college to host the Rose Bowl when World War II travel restrictions forced officials to play the game in Durham. The undefeated Dukes lost to Oregon State 20-16.

Bill Murray, who has had a distinguished career as a coach, spent 15 seasons as head coach at Duke. One of football's most respected men, Murray had a 93-51-9 mark in Durham. From Wade to Murray to Mike McGee, Duke has had many superstars: tackle Fred Crawford, Ace Parker, Dan Hill, George McAfee, Al DeRogatis, McGee, Eric Tipton, and Sonny Jurgenson.

The Atlantic Coast Conference is noted more for basketball than football; Duke and Clemson are the lone members that have more wins than losses on the gridiron. Though the league has had many fine teams, it won the national championship only once, under the late Sunny Jim Tatum at Maryland. Maryland was not thriving although H. C. Byrd had won 117 games there. When Tatum arrived in 1947, he quickly transformed the Terps into a national power, establishing a record of 73-15-4. He took Maryland to the Orange Bowl twice and to the Sugar and Gator bowls once each. He developed many outstanding players during his dynasty: Ed and Dick Modzelewski, Ray Krause, Bob Ward, Jack Scarbath, Bernie Faloney, Chet Hanulak, and Mike Sandusky.

Tatum had started his coaching career at North Carolina, his alma mater, in 1942, and he returned to Chapel Hill in 1956. His rebuilding campaign there, helped by his masterful recruiting, was gaining momentum when he died in 1958. Bill Dooley, brother of Georgia's Vince, later steered Carolina back to the prominence it knew in the Southern Conference under Carl Snavely.

In the late forties the Tar Heels attracted national attention with a Sugar Bowl team that featured Charlie ("Choo-Choo") Justice, who is generally acclaimed as the greatest of the Tar Heels. Art Weiner, George Barclay, later head coach at his alma mater, Don Jackson, Andy Bershak, Paul Seferin, and Don McCauley are other legendary figures at Chapel Hill.

In the days of Howard, Tatum, and Peahead Walker of Wake Forest, no conference had a more entertaining squad of banquet speakers. Peahead, who later served as an assistant under Herman Hickman at Yale and then became head coach of the Montreal Alouettes, firmly believed that football players should be supermen. Once, during one of his lengthy scrimmages, a player was injured and a doctor was summoned to the field. The alarmed physican shouted, "Coach Walker, this player is not breathing."

Continuing to observe practice manuevers at the other end of the field, Peahead drawled, "Well, you're a doctor, ain't you? You make him breathe!"

Deviously skilled at luring players to the small Baptist college, Peahead admitted that he showed linebacker Bill George the Duke campus and passed it off as Wake Forest's when he first attempted to recruit him. After George signed, Peahead informed him that the campus he had seen was for seniors—that he would spend three years on the other campus at Wake before moving there. In later years the ill-fated Brian Piccolo, who made All-American in 1964, helped to keep Wake Forest in the spotlight.

Though Virginia has had minimal success in the ACC, the Cavaliers were winners under Frank Murray and Art Guepe in the Southern. They also had one of the greatest players in tailback Bill Dudley, an All-American in 1941.

Tennessee's Conredge Holloway runs to daylight.

More recently, fullback Jim Bakhtiar, end Tom Scott, guard Joe Palumno, and halfback John Papit have starred at Virginia.

It is the consensus in the ACC that no coach got more out of his material than Earle Edwards, who won 77 games, many of them upsets at North Carolina State in 17 seasons. Dick Christ, Roman Gabriel, and Ron Carpenter are among the standouts who played for Edwards at State. However, the Wolfpack's boosters claim that now is their shining hour. Under coach Lou Holtz, the Pack has developed into one of the nation's most explosive offensive teams. In Raleigh they say that State has a football team the basketball team can be proud of.

Over the Rainbow

In 1972, when the Grambling Tigers performed in stadiums from New York to Honolulu before some 400,000 fans in the stands and before millions more on a 103-station TV network, it was a fitting salute to coach Eddie Robinson. Black colleges in the South have played football since 1892, but they did not attract national attention until Robinson launched his dynasty at Grambling. Dr. Ralph Waldo Emerson Jones, the highly respected sports-minded president of Grambling, hired Robinson in 1941. Major college football was unaware of the small Louisiana college, and when Robinson failed to win a game in his first season, skeptics at Grambling wondered whether Dr. Jones had selected the proper coach. He had. Robinson was to become one of the winningest coaches of all time. When Robinson started his thirty-second season as head coach of Grambling in 1973, only Alabama's Bear Bryant among active coaches boasted more victories. In establishing a fantastic 216-75-11 record, Robinson put Grambling and black college football in general in the national spotlight.

During his career, Robinson coached 50 All-Americans and sent more than 100 players to the pro ranks, including such titans as Tank Younger, Ernie Ladd, Willie Davis, Buck Buchanan, and Roosevelt Taylor.

Due to television, Robinson is the most widely acclaimed black coach in the nation at large, but in the Deep South, no black coach is held in

higher esteem than Jake Gaither, who had 25 straight winning seasons and bowl teams at Florida A & M in Tallahassee, Florida.

A brilliant leader, strategist, and orator, Gaither became head coach at Florida A & M in 1945. Only once in the next 25 years did his Rattlers lose more than three games or fail to win at least seven. His undefeated powerhouse in 1961 scored 506 points and allowed a mere 33 while winning ten in a row. All of Gaither's teams appeared in the Orange Blossom classic, the black equivalent of the Orange Bowl, played in the Miami arena in later years.

Gaither coached more future pros than any black coach except Robinson. Bob Hayes, of the Dallas Cowboys, and "the world's fastest

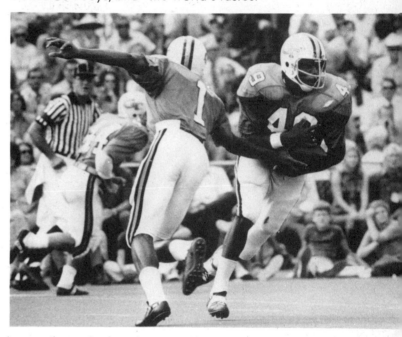

human," was the best known of his many stars.

Recently retired as athletic director at Florida A & M, Gaither is in constant demand on the banquet circuit, where he is among the most entertaining and inspirational of football speakers. Jake says a football player has to be "mobile, agile, and hostile" to be a winner.

He told Bob Gutkowski in an interview, "Whether he likes it or not, each man has got to cut it for himself. He can't blame the referee or the coach or the opposing player. He finds out about himself very quickly on that field. Where else do they become men quicker than on the football field? Somewhere along the line he's going to face the ultimate test, and he'll

Left: *Pat Sullivan, Heisman winner, cocks for a bomb.* Above: *Tech's Eddie McAshan (1) starts a running play. McAshan was later suspended.*

know right away if he has succeeded or not."

With similar old-fashioned simplicity, Gaither approached his coaching duties. "I had basic running plays and a couple of passing plays that everyone had to learn. We didn't get involved with a lot of fancy formations. I always stressed fundamentals . . . . That's the way I saw football." His record of 206-35-4 stands as a testimonial to his ability as a coach. He is the man with the highest victory percentage of any black coach at a major college.

His successors are likely to have a more difficult time than he had, because the white schools are no longer "thumbing their noses" at the black athletes. Gaither badly wanted Eddie McAshan who he feels will develop into the pros' first great black quarterback, but McAshan chose Georgia Tech over FAMU. That lost recruiting battle represented quite a turnabout from the old days when FAMU won by default. Hayes, Hewritt Dixon, and Willie Galimore among others, were all turned down by white schools before coming to FAMU. "I remember we used to meet these Southern schools at track meets and run them out of the park," says Gaither. "Now these same schools' recruiters come in like a locust invasion."

John Merritt of Tennessee State ranks just behind Robinson and Gaither. A master recruiter

and tactician, Merritt had a 143-47-7 record through the 1972 season, including a 23-game victory skein.

In his 21 years of coaching (10 at Jackson State, 11 at Tennessee State), Merritt has won five national championships and has seen 108 of his players drafted into the pro ranks. In fact Tennessee State has more graduates playing professional football today than any other school in the nation except two—Southern California and Notre Dame.

Merritt doesn't worry about losing blue-chip prospects to larger, whiter schools because he knows he will. His entire recruiting budget is only $4,000 to begin with, and facilities at State are less than ideal. Practice is cancelled when it rains because the grassless field becomes too muddy, there are never enough helmets until final cuts are made, and the living quarters for the team are functional at best. Why, then, do such exceptional football players show up at Tennessee State? As Merritt explains, "I've never heard a boy say he came here because of black pride or because it's a black school. He comes here because he knows he'll be a winner. We guarantee it. And he knows he'll be scouted by the pros."

Merritt's system seems to work. Tennessee State is the nation's number-one ranked small college football team.

Henry Kean, who had a combined record of 171-35-5 at Kentucky State and Tennessee State, was another extraordinarily successful pioneer of black college football in the South. Old-timers vow that Kean, who studied the game under Knute Rockne, introduced more offensive football in the area than all other coaches combined. "What you need for a passing game," Kean often said, "is a cross-eyed passer and catchers."

Ed Hurt of Morgan State once had a victory streak of 55 in a row and has a lifetime coaching record of 175-52-18.

There are many others who were unjustly ignored during great careers. Among them are Cleve Abbott of Tuskegee College, 224-74-20; Arnette Mumford of Southern at Baton Rouge, 230-84-24; William Nix of Morris Brown, 183-56-17; Vernon ("Ox") Clemons also of Morris Brown, 156-58-3; and Earl Banks of Michigan State, 92-22-2.

nts: the Midwest
by Maury White

Amos Alonzo Stagg was only seven years old in 1869, when collegians started quarreling over an inflated bladder, but he more than any other man shaped the game of football. Among other staples of today's game, Stagg introduced tackling dummies, diagrammed playbooks, huddles, direct passes from center, backfield shifts, men in motion, reverses, uniform numbers, and the awarding of letters. "All modern football stems from Stagg," flatly stated Knute Rockne.

From 1892 to 1932, Stagg coached the University of Chicago. His teams won only six titles in those 40 years, but it is not for his won-lost record that the game remembers him. He was the sport's premier legislator and jurist, a longtime member of the rules committee who wrote football law and interpreted it for the generations to come. His style was the strictest constructionism.

He once asked an official to nullify his team's touchdown because one of his players had committed an infraction. On a later occasion, he refused to send in a substitute with a play after his team had failed to score on the first three downs from the 1-yard line. "The rules committee deprecates the use of a substitute to convey information," Stagg explained loftily, unmoved as his team failed again on fourth down and then lost the game.

"He was a great leader on the rules committee," says H. O. ("Fritz") Crisler, formerly a coaching giant in his own right. "One time a coach came up with a formation in which the center stood with his back to the line of scrimmage. Stagg listened to all the arguments, then said simply, 'Football is a fighting game, and a fighter always faces his opponent.'" Following Stagg's simple edict (as well as the practical consideration that it's easier to block men you can see), the center today crouches over the ball, facing the enemy.

The first to be elected to college football's Hall of Fame and one of two men ever named a life

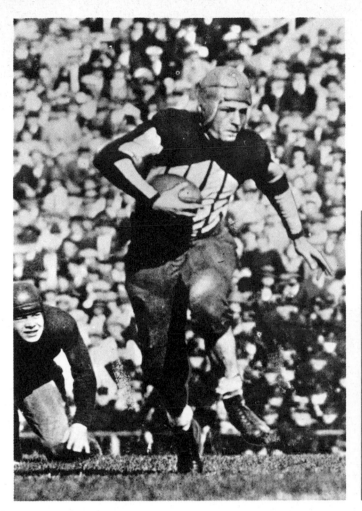

Preceding pages: Ohio State stops Iowa. Clockwise 97
from left: Bronko Nagurski; Red Grange;
Willie Heston; helmetless Duke Slater blocking.

member of the rules committee, (Crisler was the other), Stagg had such a formidable reputation that only incorrigible cynics dared question it. Feisty Bob Zuppke of Illinois, a Dutchman who concocted more trick plays and formations than anyone this side of touch football, sounded off publicly one day in 1930 after playing a round of golf with Stagg.

"Perfect my eye!" exploded Zuppke. "He doesn't smoke or drink. He doesn't chase skirts or swear. But Stagg has a vice worse than all those —he concedes himself all putts under six feet."

Ironically, the greatest football player that Chicago University produced blossomed after Stagg had left and only a few years before the school dropped the sport. John Jacob Berwanger, son of a blacksmith in Dubuque, Iowa, grew to 6 feet and 195 pounds, finished fourth in the decathlon at the Kansas Relays the first time he tried the event, and made 15 straight tackles in a Big Ten game. The 1934 Maroons voted their ace ball carrier the team's best blocker as well. The next year he won the first Heisman Trophy.

Playing with a specially designed face mask to protect a broken nose, Berwanger gained widespread acclaim while upgrading a mediocre team. In 1935, Ohio State arrived in Chicago as 40-point favorites but left breathing hard, happy to claim a 20-13 come-from-behind victory. On an 85-yard touchdown run in that game, Berwanger is credited with eluding eight tackles.

"Ohio State's right end jumped offside as the play started, and a horn blew. The Buckeyes relaxed and let me through for eighty-five yards. If that horn hadn't blown, I probably wouldn't be here," said Berwanger in New York in 1969, while being honored with the modern all-time All-American team.

Berwanger was the first man selected in pro football's first draft. Philadelphia claimed him, then sold their rights to the Bears, but Berwanger and George Halas couldn't agree on a contract. Berwanger wanted $25,000 per season at a time when Bronko Nagurski was making only about $7,000, so instead of becoming a pro football star, Jay opted for a businessman's career in Chicago.

While Stagg in Chicago towered over Midwest football, a host of nearly equal luminaries brought football tradition to the other schools in

98

Clockwise from left: *Jim Thorpe, 1912 All-American; Tom Harmon carries against Penn; Ed Widseth, Minnesota All-American; Ohio State's Chic Harley*

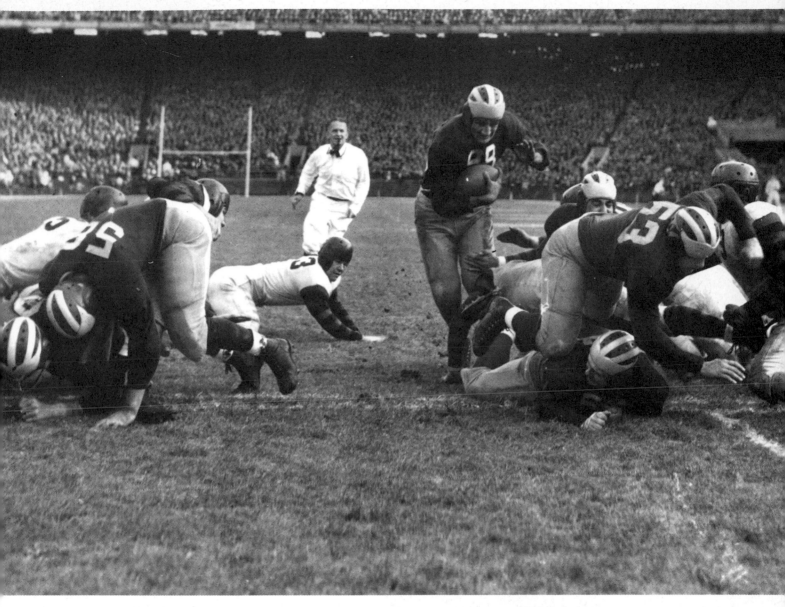

the Big Ten region. Near the turn of the century Dr. Henry Williams signed up at Minnesota, Howard Jones at Iowa, and Fielding H. ("Hurry Up") Yost at Michigan. Zuppke reigned at Illinois, and Norwegian-born Rockne, whose face resembled a battered oil can and whose high-pitched staccato voice inflamed football passions, ruled Notre Dame.

The honor roll of men who continued and embellished the tradition that these demigods spawned is a long one: Bo McMillin at Indiana; Clark Shaughnessy at Chicago; Ray Eliot at Illinois; Frank Leahy and Ara Parseghian at Notre Dame; Forest Evashevski at Iowa; Crisler, Bennie Oosterbaan, and Bo Schembechler at Michigan; Bernie Bierman and Murray Warmath at Minnesota; Charlie Bachman, Biggie Munn, and Duffy Daugherty at Michigan State; Dick Hanley and Pappy Waldorf at Northwestern; Ivy Williamson and Milt Bruhn at Wisconsin; Noble Kizer, Stu Holcomb, and Jack Mollenkopf at Purdue; and Francis Schmidt, Paul Brown, and Woody Hayes at Ohio State.

The Fighting Irish of Notre Dame

Knute Rockne was a young fellow who grew up in Chicago around the turn of the century and got to know and admire Stagg. He showed up at Notre Dame four years after completing high school, and the college has never been quite the same since. "The Rock" was assigned to a room with Gus Dorais. Three summers later the pair worked together at a Lake Erie resort, took along a football, and perfected the forward pass. It had been legal for a half-dozen years, but only when Notre Dame crashed into the big time with a stunning 35-13 upset of Army on the strength of Dorais's throwing and Rockne's receiving did people begin to concede that the forward pass was more a weapon than a toy or a gimmick. Upon graduating, Rock and Gus cooperated in one more important toss. They flipped a coin to see who would take the coaching job at what is now Loras College in Dubuque, Iowa. Dorais "won," and Rockne, a brilliant student, stayed at Notre Dame to teach chemistry and to assist Jess Harper in football. Taking over as head coach in 1918, Rock was 3-1-2 after one season. After thirteen, it was an amazing 105-12-5, including five undefeated seasons. When he died, the Irish had won 19 games in a row.

George Gipp, a breezy, talented young man full of habits that Stagg would never have tolerated, was Rockne's first and greatest All-American. The Rock was a firm disciplinarian, but he recognized a fellow genius in Gipp and generally allowed the young man's blithe spirit to blow where it would. "A reputation as a martinet is invaluable to a coach, providing he doesn't work at it too hard," Rockne admitted.

In 1921, well before the age of wonder drugs, Gipp lay dying from pneumonia. "I've got to go, Rock. It's all right. I'm not afraid," he told the coach from his deathbed. "Sometime, Rock, when things are wrong and the breaks are beating the boys, tell them to go in there with all they've got and win one just for the Gipper. I don't know where I'll be then, Rock, but I'll know about it. And I'll be happy."

Seven years later, in 1928, Rockne made his famous "Win one for the Gipper" speech. The Notre Dame squad returned inspired from the half-time pep talk, and the Irish beat Army 12-6. Pat O'Brien then made a mini-career of repeating Rockne's words in the movie with the inspiration of a man running for high public office. Perhaps the fervor rubbed off on Ronald Reagan, who played the Gipper in the film and who later became governor of California.

Gipp was only the start of Rockne's marvelous coaching career. Soon there were the Four Horsemen and the Seven Mules. Led by quarterback Frank Carideo, another brilliant backfield followed in 1929 and 1930. An oft-injured tackle those two seasons who needed a knee operation after the '30 season shared a room in the hospital with Rockne, in for repairs himself. They talked football hour after hour, day after day. In February, 1941, Frank Leahy, the former lineman, returned to the Fighting Irish as head coach and started to build the school's second greatest era: 97-11-9.

"Zygmont, if you do not care to rid yourself of excess avoirdupois, we will have to ask you to disassociate yourself from our little group," Leahy is alleged to have warned tackle Zygmont Czarobski. Leahy's speaking style was hardly informal, but he could teach and motivate his charges like no one but Rockne. His .888 victory percentage is the closest anyone has come to Rock's .898. The incumbent coach, Ara

Top: *Ernie Nevers with coach Pop Warner.* Above: *Angelo Bertelli shakes off a would-be Arizona tackler.* Opposite: *Elroy Hirsch scores for Michigan.*

Parseghian, is winning about 8 out of 10.

. Hunk Anderson (16-9-2) and Elmer Layden (47-13-3) coached with distinction between Rockne and Leahy, losing one less game between them in ten years than did Joe Kuharich in four (17-23 from 1959 to 1962), the only losing coach in the school's history. Layden was at the helm on November 2, 1935, at Ohio State when the Irish, trailing 13-0, scored three times in the last quarter, twice in the last three minutes, for an 18-13 victory that sportswriters voted "most thrilling football game of the first half of the century." Television was still in the future, but half the nation seemed to have its ear cocked to the radio for the game.

Andy Pilney passed to set up the first Irish touchdown and delivered the ball to Layden's brother, Mike, for the second. Buckeyes' coach Francis ("Show 'Em No Mercy") Schmidt then tried to calm his troops and run out the clock, but they fumbled, and Notre Dame recovered. Pilney promptly began his heroics again—he got off a dazzling run—but was hurt and left for the bench on a stretcher.

Bill Shakespeare, no relation to the dramatist, replaced Pilney and with little time left and his injured teammate watching from the stretcher found Wayne Millner in the end zone with the game-winning touchdown pass.

Gomer Jones, later Bud Wilkinson's top aide and then his successor at Oklahoma, was Ohio State's All-American center that year. At a squat 5 feet 9 inches, 210 pounds, he would vary his position in lining up for the snap. Following his instinct, he would sometimes play on the line

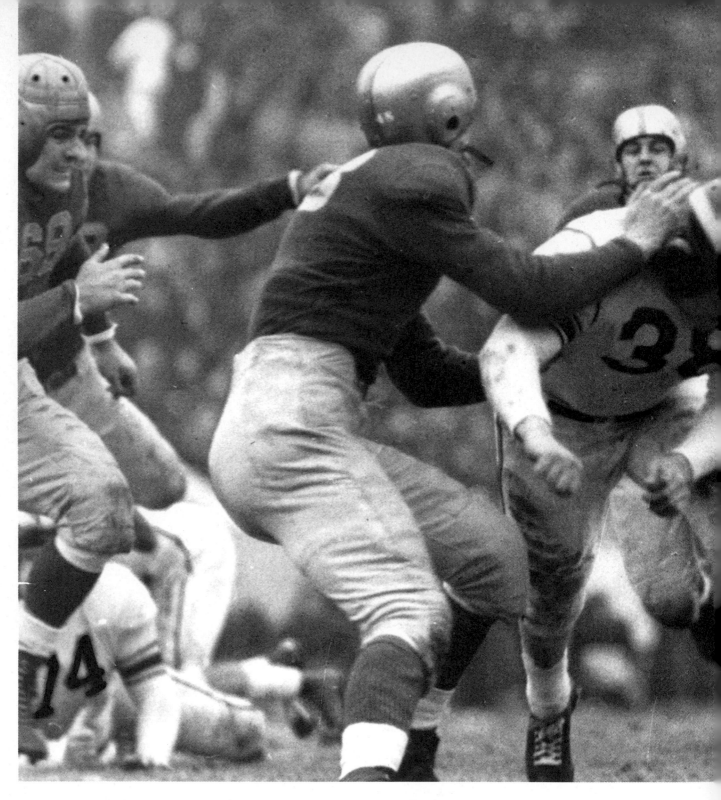

and sometimes behind it. It was the first time the Irish had faced this refinement. Years later Pilney and the Irish captain for the game, Wally Fromhart, in rehashing the game with Gomer, revealed that they'd created an audible on the spot to counter the mystifying tactics of the Buckeyes' center.

"Depending on where you were, we'd call 'Blubber in' or 'Blubber out,' " Fromhart revealed.

Jones winced and belatedly became serious about slimming down.

Of the many big games they have played, the Irish have been involved in two that may have been heralded with more ballyhoo than any of the others. Ironically, both wound up ties. Army's meat grinder had mauled the Irish 48-0 and 59-0 while Leahy and many of his Notre Dame players were in the service during the war. But when

Johnny Lujack led a resurrected postwar Irish team to five straight romps before the 1946 confrontation with Glenn Davis, Doc Blanchard, and company, football fiends were rapidly anticipating the rematch as the battle of the century. Unfortunately, both Notre Dame and Army played so conservatively that there were few exciting moments, and the game ended in a drab scoreless tie.

Two decades later, after almost a year's buildup, a national television audience snapped off their sets in disappointment when an Irish team featuring Terry Hanratty, Jim Seymour, and Kevin Hardy tied 10-10 with Michigan State, led by Clint Jones, Bubba Smith, and George Webster. Late in the game, instead of gambling for victory with last-ditch heroics, coach Ara Parseghian instructed Hanratty, a wondrous

Playing for Great Lakes, Minnesota's Heisman winner Bruce Smith scores against Notre Dame. Smith later made a movie, predictably—"Smith of Minnesota."

passer, to keep the ball safely on the ground. It was not a popular decision with the fans. Parseghian figured that a tie would preserve Notre Dame's number-one ranking in the wire service polls and a victory against Southern Cal the following week would clinch the national title. He was right. The Irish finished number one in both the AP and UPI polls, but there are those who have still not forgiven him for allowing the wire services to dictate his football strategy.

Such controversy is not foreign to South Bend. Old grads threatened mutiny when Leahy dictated that Notre Dame would use the T-formation instead of the hallowed "box" that Rockne employed. The critics quickly fell silent when quarterback Angelo Bertelli won the Heisman Trophy in 1943, but Leahy was never wholly free of the carping. There were rhubarbs over "the sucker shift" and alleged fake injuries.

When he retired in 1954, Leahy was a sick man, and the fans too were weary from the constant fussing.

From 1887 to 1958, the Fighting Irish finished under .500 in only five seasons. In the five years after 1958, they duplicated that figure, including a barely mediocre 2-7 effort in 1963. To rescue the beleaguered citadel of football, the trustees found an intense, hard-driving man. A French-Armenian Presbyterian, Ara Raoul Parseghian must be considered the architect of the third dynasty at the school that has come closer than any other to perpetual supremacy in college football. A stubby running back in college and pro ball, he studied under Woody Hayes and Paul Brown, coached with distinction at Miami of Ohio and at Northwestern, where he defeated Notre Dame four years in a row. The only private school in the Big Ten, Northwestern has more

106

Above: *Eye-greased Johnny Lujack attempts the extra point against Army.* Opposite: *Notre Dame stops Buddy Young of Illinois.*

Above: *Hall of Famer John Jay Berwanger.*
Opposite: *Ohio State fullback*
Vic Janowicz follows interference downfield.

money problems than its brethren, so there are fewer scholarships. Ara's teams at Northwestern frequently whipped through the first half of the season only to run out of bodies in the second half. People sometimes wondered how he would fare given better material. Now they know.

"It's going to be a lot of trouble to learn how to spell that name," former sports publicist Charles Callahan sighed after the Irish hired Parseghian.

"You mean Parseghian?" asked a friend.

"No. Presbyterian," said Callahan.

Actually, Rockne too had been a Protestant for most of his tenure, though he converted to Catholicism in his last years. Of more concern to the old grads than Parseghian's religion, however, was his football upbringing. For the first time in 46 years, the citadel of football would be commanded by a man who hadn't played at Notre Dame.

Even hallowed Notre Dame can benefit from a break with tradition. In one of the great turnabouts in college history, Notre Dame won its first nine games in 1964 under Parseghian before being upset by Southern Cal in the finale. Quarterback John Huarte won the Heisman, and end Jack Snow, linebacker Jim Carroll, and defensive tackle Kevin Hardy led the Irish charge back onto the All-American team. Since then, Notre Dame has missed finishing in the top 10 only once, topping the polls in 1966 and 1973. Halfback Nick Eddy, end Jim Seymour, defensive tackles Mike McCoy and Greg Marx, offensive linemen George Kunz and Larry DiNardo, defensive backs Tom Schoen and Clarence Ellis are all merely representative of the superior players Notre Dame has produced.

After the 1924 team won the Rose Bowl, school authorities banned postseason games until they finally relented after the 1969 season. The reason was familiar: money. The Irish lost to number-one rated Texas 21-17 in the Cotton Bowl but returned the next year after a 9-1 season for a heralded rematch. This time Notre Dame's huge line wrecked Texas's wishbone running attack, and Joe Theisman led a 24-11 victory that may have been the decisive factor in the Longhorns' failure to win the number-one crown again. Notre Dame missed a bowl after the 1971 season, then met Nebraska in the 1973 Orange

Bowl, but found themselves badly outclassed. The Huskers romped 40-6 as Johnny Rodgers ran for four touchdowns and passed for another. It was Parseghian's worst loss in nine years, and only with a late score did his team avert its first shutout in 73 games.

The outcome didn't please Irish fans, but if Gipp was still paying attention, he must have smiled two nights before the game when the television cameras at the Orange Bowl parade suddenly focused on a pair of young football players—Eric Penick and Art Best, Irish halfbacks who stepped out and joined the parade. Ara was amused, as Rockne would have been. "No, I'm not angry. The idea of coming to these games is for the players to have some fun," he said, unaware surely of what lay in store for his club against Nebraska.

The Golden Gophers of Minnesota

"When I'm traveling, I ask farm boys for directions. If they point with their finger, I move on. If they pick up the plow and point with it, I stop and sell them on the University of Minnesota," said Gil Dobie, who quarterbacked the Gophers to a tie with Iowa for the Big Ten title in 1900 and joined Dr. Williams's staff in 1904.

In 1926, one such pile of muscle, a 6-foot 2-inch, 225-pound behemoth raised in the wilds near International Falls, Minnesota, reported for football at Minnesota. Dr. Clarence Spears asked this thick-thighed youngster what position he had played as a prep.

"All of them," replied Bronko Nagurski. "When the other team had the ball, they put me wherever I could make the most tackles. When we had the ball, I carried it." There have been few better game plans in the history of football.

Nagurski is firmly enshrined in both the college and pro halls of fame. One of the legends of the Chicago Bears is that he once bulled head down into the end zone and churned into a mounted policeman, bowling over the horse. "I don't remember that," Bronko growled a few years ago in New York.

Having inspired many stories, Nagurski is understandably fuzzy in remembering, much less verifying all of them. Still, the legends persist. Gospel has it that the Minnesotan caused much blushing among proprietors of Manhattan's formal-wear rental stores when none of the outfitters could find a dress shirt with a 20-inch neck. Nagurski finally had to wear one of his own white shirts to the dinner.

In 1932, shortly after Nagurski had left for the pros, Bernie Bierman returned home to Minnesota to succeed Fritz Crisler. He brought with him a football program that produced a decade of excellence at Minnesota, unequaled anywhere until the 1950s, when one of Bierman's pupils, Charles ("Bud") Wilkinson, forged a similar dynasty at Oklahoma.

As a player, Bierman had learned much of his football under Dr. Williams, one of the tallest figures in the land of the giants before his retirement in 1921. As a member of the rules committee Williams was the first to advocate legalizing the forward pass. Under him the Golden Gophers won at least a share in eight titles early in the century, the last in 1915, Bierman's last as a player.

Returning as coach to the school at which he had been a star halfback, Bierman was a steely eyed, raspy voiced martinet dedicated to drilling his squad into near-perfect physical shape. He believed in the impeccable execution of a small number of plays and in blocks that could be heard as well as seen. Before long, his players shared the faith. In his second year, only four ties marred the Gophers' unbeaten season. Then came 1934, a vintage year: 8-0, a Big Ten title, and three All-Americans—halfback Pug Lund, who may have been Bernie's all-time favorite, end Butch Larson, and guard Bill Bevan, the last Big Ten player to play regularly without a helmet. At a time when the All-American team consisted of only eleven players, it was a formidable accomplishment for three of one school's players to win selection. Phil Bengtson, later to coach in the NFL, was a tackle on that team, and Wilkinson a guard.

"I have not seen a team anywhere—in person, on film, on television—that is better than my 1934 team. It was my best team—my favorite team—and it could do anything you'd want a football team to do," Bierman said in 1970. The 1934 squad couldn't have been an easy choice for Bierman because in that glorious 10-year period the Gophers went undefeated in five years, Big Ten champs in six, and national champs in four (1934, '36, '40, and '41). They sported such stars as tackles Ed Widseth and Urban Odson, end Ray King, and halfbacks Bruce Smith, the Heisman winner in 1941, and George Franck.

After three years in the service, Bierman resumed at Minnesota in 1945 but could never quite recapture his magic, although he had such stars as Leo Nomellini, Bud Grant, and Clayton Tonnemaker. As the T-formation took the nation by storm, the precision single wing that Bernie favored and its buck-lateral series that he originated fell out of fashion with the Gophers' fans. So, perhaps mistakenly, Bierman tried to use both the T and the single wing. In addition his strict discipline hampered him; young men just out of the service had had their fill of orders that couldn't be questioned. Finally, Minnesota failed to keep pace with its rivals in the latest craze—recruiting. Instead of receiving unsolicited visits from prep stars, schools now had to seek them out and lure them their way.

After 23 losses in the six campaigns after the war, Bernie resigned after the 1950 season with a still impressive 93-35-6 record. Since Bierman, the Gophers have claimed only one national title, when they moved from last in the Big Ten in 1959 to number one in the nation, as well as in the conference, in '60. Coach Murray Warmath, quarterback Sandy Stephens, and linemen Tom Brown and Bobby Bell led the squad.

Warmath was a dour, rumpled fundamentalist who served 18 seasons as the Gophers' coach, sometime picking up garbage tossed his way, sometimes almost blushing with acclaim. His teams were noted for tough defense; tackle Carl Eller and ends Aaron Brown, Bob Stein, and Doug Kingsriter were All-Americans. When Warmath was unable to satisfy the customers with his choice of quarterbacks, new athletic director Paul Giel, one of the school's greatest athletes, replaced him with Cal Stoll from Wake Forest. He started with a 4-7 year in 1972.

The Wolverines of Michigan

Michigan's strangleholds on the Big Ten Conference have made up in quantity what they lacked in duration. Fielding Yost, a fiery, incessantly talkative man, took the helm at Michigan in 1901 and five seasons later had compiled a 55-1-1 record. Wisely, Yost had sent to California for phenom Willie Heston, who scored over 100 touchdowns for the "point a minute" teams led by Heston, Dan McGugin, Neil Snow, and the great Adolph ("Germany")

Clockwise from bottom: J. C. Caroline gets 10 yards; Alan Ameche slams through Northwestern; Sandy Stephens hurdles Oregon.

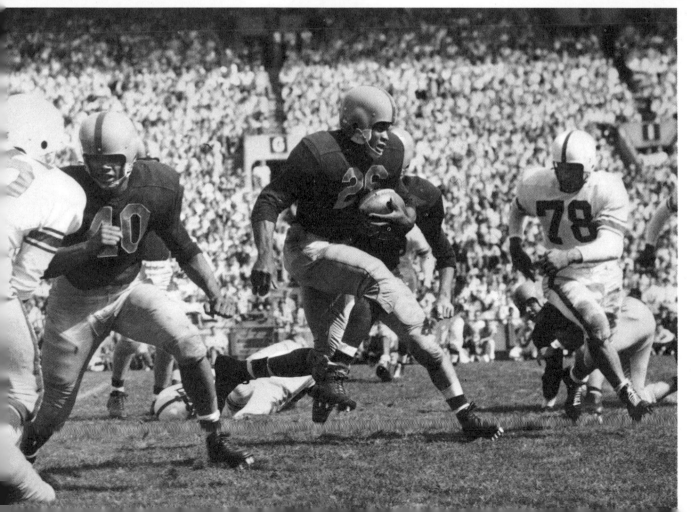

Schulz, a center who pioneered dropping behind the line on defense after the snap. "Use your searchlights, and jump the dead ones," was Heston's formula for success, not much different from Vince Lombardi's run for daylight. One statistic sufficiently demonstrates the breadth of Yost's dynasty: 2,821 to 42—the total points for and against Michigan in Yost's era. The lone setback was to Stagg's Chicago team, 2-0, after 56 straight without defeat.

Harry Kipke, a brilliant halfback, sparked a resurgence that brought undefeated seasons to Michigan again in 1922 and '23. Then Yost quit for one year but returned with the superlative aerial combination of passer Benny Friedman and the multi-talented Bennie Oosterbaan. Yost bowed out permanently as coach with titles in 1926 and '27 but remained as athletic director for many years.

A few years after graduating, Kipke came back to Michigan as coach and constructed the second Wolverines' dynasty, winning a share of the conference title in four straight years, starting in 1930. One of his greatest stars was Ivy Williamson, later the miracle man who overhauled Wisconsin football in the 1950s.

Fritz Crisler, an icy taskmaster, took over in 1938 and led the Wolverines to the head of their pack with tackle Ed Frutig, blocking back Forest Evashevski,and the remarkable Tom Harmon. In 1939, these men and their teammates prevented Dr. Eddie Anderson's glamorous "Iowa Ironmen" from capturing Iowa's first league title since 1922. (Iowa would have to wait until 1956, when ironically, Evashevski would be at the controls.) In his career at Michigan, Harmon scored 33 touchdowns and made "98" the most famous football number since Grange's "77". He even inspired a movie, "Harmon of Michigan," in which he starred.

After guiding Michigan to a flawless 10-0 mark in 1947, Crisler retired to the athletic directorship and left the reins to Oosterbaan, a tall, quiet man, whom everyone knew was a winner. He'd been an All-American in basketball, the Big Ten's leading hitter in baseball, and an all-time All-American in football. Predictably, his teams won the next three league titles.

Like Oosterbaan, Bump Elliott, who succeeded

112

Clockwise from above: Notre Dame's Paul Hornung scores first Irish touchdown of 1955 season; Wisconsin's Graff to pass; Northwestern's Murphy

him, did respectably, but the crowds in the 100,000-seat bowl declined sharply. After an 8-2 effort in 1968, Bump resigned as coach. Michigan followed a well-proven formula in finding his successor at Miami of Ohio, the largest little football brain factory in the Midwest and possibly anywhere. Paul Brown, Red Blaik, Ara Parseghian, Woody Hayes, John Pont, Weeb Ewbank, Stu Holcomb, Sid Gillman, and Paul Dietzel among others have all either played or coached there. In 1968, the resident genius was Glenn ("Bo") Schembechler, a tough, driving, explicitly profane perfectionist. "I don't consider it a building job. I want to win right now. But they'll have to do it my way," said Bo.

Four years later Schembechler had no one left to convince. He had fashioned a record of 38-6 —a higher winning percentage than Yost or Crisler—and had won at least a share of three titles in four years. In two of his four years, Michigan went bowling at Pasadena. They only just missed in 1972; they tied Ohio State for the conference crown with a 7-1 mark, but the Buckeyes beat them 14-11 at Columbus and thereby earned the Rose Bowl bid.

The Wolverines entered that pivotal game undefeated, having yielded only 43 points in 10 games, but Ohio State broke through when Harold Henson pounded over from the 1-yard line and hometown freshman Archie Griffin bolted 30 yards for the deciding score. Under the direction of their versatile junior quarterback, Dennis Franklin, the Wolverines amassed a large yardage advantage and gave themselves numerous scoring opportunities, but the Buckeyes prevailed.

With 13 seconds left in the game and Michigan on Ohio State's 41, some overzealous State fans who either had forgotten that there was time remaining or, more likely, knew it all too well, tore down the goal posts. Schembechler shrugged it off later and said he hadn't planned a field goal anyway. Earlier, he had twice ignored easy field-goal opportunities in favor of trying to ram through the Buckeyes' middle, but George Hasenrohl, Randy Gradishar, and the like claimed the ball both times after goal-line stands that have become part of Ohio State football lore.

It may have been best for Schembechler that

Ohio State won the trip to the Rose Bowl in 1973. He had suffered a heart attack just before the 1970 New Year's Day game, a 10-3 Michigan loss to Southern Cal, and he might not have born up well had swift, strong Southern California mistreated his Wolverines as it did the Buckeyes, 42-17.

The Buckeyes of Ohio State

It is not unusual for the Big Ten title to be at stake when Ohio State meets Michigan in their annual finale. Both teams are habitual winners. The last losing coach at Ohio State was Jack Ryder, who left in 1898 with a 22-24-1 mark. Five of the last eight coaches (Dr. J. W. Wilce, Francis Schmidt, Paul Brown, Carroll Widdoes, and W. W. Hayes) have won or shared a conference title.

The first of the trees in Ohio State's All-American Grove, where more than 50 have been planted in honor of Buckeyes' heroes, is for Charles ("Chic") Harley, an All-American in 1916, 1917, and 1919. Harley's nickname is spelled without a "k" at the end because with two simple strokes to fill out each "c" you make the word "Ohio." "Chic Harley is Ohio," they say in Columbus. Harley was a fleet, 162-pound running back who led the Buckeyes to a 21-1-1 record in his three seasons. He is credited as much as any man with raising football to Olympian status in the area.

The man who has done the most to keep it that way is Hayes, now 60, a controversial, paunchy extrovert who grimly roams the sideline, a baseball cap anchored on his head. Staunchly loyal to the robust T or any other power formation that facilitates the off-tackle smash, Hayes is one football fundamentalist who off the field can surmount his team's sometimes dreary on-the-field proficiency. One year he ordered then Big Ten Commissioner Tug Wilson and a 30-man party of sportswriters to leave a preseason practice. "I wanted to say something bad to a boy, and I won't let outsiders hear a boy being disciplined," said Woody. The next year he met the same writers at the hotel with a pep band and ordered chaises longues for practice.

Ohio State won the Big Ten in 1961 but couldn't accept the Rose Bowl bid because Woody lost a feud with a faction of the faculty.

Bob Ferguson, one of a long line of powerful Ohio State running backs, scores against Michigan, the last touchdown of his career.

The Hayes's Christmas cards that year read, "Merry Christmas, anyway." In 1968, when the Buckeyes were invited to Pasadena again and this time accepted, Anne and Woody made their Yuletide message "Ho ho ho! This year we get to go!"

A history major at Denison University, Hayes taught the subject briefly in high school and has read it consistently while coaching football at Denison, Miami, and Ohio State. Sometimes it's not clear what kind of scrimmage Woody is talking about.

"Xerxes told the Greeks at Thermopylae that his army would launch so many spears against them that they'd blot out the sun, and the Greeks replied, 'Fine and dandy. We'll fight in the shade,' " Hayes told a group of writers once, leaving it not entirely clear how this inventive defense applied to football.

Wary of the forward pass, Hayes has been castigated for an unispired "three yards and a cloud of dust" offense. But Hayes, like all good coaches, can be convinced by good talent to be more liberal. His precocious sophomore group of 1968 included brash rookie quarterback Rex Kern, who sometimes ignored plays that Hayes sent in from the bench. With Kern, Rufus Mayes, Dave Foley, Larry Zelina, Jim Otis, Jim Stillwagon, and a remarkable defensive back, Jim Tatum, the 1968 Ohio State team won mention as the National Collegiate Sports Service's Team of the 1960s.

After the Buckeyes beat Southern Cal in the 1969 Rose Bowl 27-16, Woody began at 9 A.M. to fight a letdown in his sophomore group. "Actually it was a few minutes later than that," he admits. "The meeting was at nine, but President-elect Nixon had me on the phone then. He mentioned that he got good grades his first year in law school, then slacked off the second."

The Buckeyes haven't relaxed, returning to the Rose Bowl after the '70, '72, and '73 seasons, nor has Hayes, unbearable as ever with sideline officials, photographers, and quarterbacks who throw interceptions.

Over the years the symbol of Ohio State football has been a big, crashing fullback. While other positions were slighted (Paul Warfield spent most of his senior season as a decoy), Ohio State has concentrated on developing power

backs. It is sometimes difficult to recall the difference between them: Will Sanders, Bob White, Hubert Bob, Bob Ferguson, Matt Snell, Otis, and John Brockington. They all seemed to ram equally hard. The incumbent is 6-foot 4-inch, 221-pound junior Harold ("Champ") Henson, who led the Big Ten in scoring with 20 touchdowns in 1972 and gained 772 yards. Oddly, freshman tailback Archie Griffin also gained 772 yards, including a school record 239 against North Carolina. Things haven't changed much at Ohio State; as Harley was, Griffin is a Columbus boy.

The Spartans of Michigan State

Like his successor at Michigan State, Duffy Daugherty, Biggie Munn belongs to the land of giants. Unfortunately, two of Munn's undefeated seasons at Michigan State, including one national title, came before the school joined the conference. Munn was an All-American guard under Crisler at Minnesota, served as an assistant to Bierman, Ossie Solem, and Crisler there, and took over at Michigan State in 1947, following Charles Bachman's long, respectable administration. The stocky Munn refined the multiple offense and soon developed a great back in Lynn Chandnois and an equally fine end in Dorne Dibble. Stars such as tackle Don Coleman, guard Frank Kush, and quarterbacks Al Dorow and Tom Yewcic led the Spartans through a 28-game winning streak, including undefeated seasons in 1951 and '52. After a Rose Bowl victory in 1954, Biggie retired with a 54-9-2 record. He is in the College Hall of Fame as both player and coach. When he quit coaching to become athletic director, he promptly hired assistant Daugherty, a former guard at Syracuse whom Biggie had coached there.

There has never been a more refreshing, wittier coach in the Big Ten than Daugherty. Perpetually optimistic before any season, he issued glowing appraisals of his teams, conditioning the fans to expect a national title for the varsity, and no worse than top-ten ranking for the second team. Duffy's teams did win two Big Ten titles, finished second four times, won the national championship once (in 1965), and finished second twice (in '55 and '66). Also, Daugherty was named Coach of the Year twice, yet some remained convinced that a comic couldn't coach. Assistant Dennis Stolz replaced him after the 1972 season.

For a kid from the Pennsylvania coal mines who survived a broken neck as a player, Daugherty found coaching fun while it lasted.

"Who are you happiest to see coming back this season?" he was asked once.

"Me," he retorted.

Of Duffy's many stars, quarterback Earl Morrall was the earliest, and in the hearts of the fans at least, linebacker George Webster was the greatest. In a 1969 poll of the Spartans' fans, the tall, lean, bone-jarring rover edged Morrall, end Gene Washington, and guard Don Coleman as State's best ever.

The Boilermakers of Purdue

Among Purdue's enticing attributes are its "Golden Girl" (a coed whose title is transferred when she graduates); its self-proclaimed "World's Largest Bass Drum;" and its nickname, the Boilermakers, which is sometimes amended to Spoilermakers because the team seems better at ruining the title hopes of others than at winning the crown itself. Stu Holcombe coached a Purdue team to a tie for the title in 1952, and Jack Mollenkopf repeated in 1967, but Purdue has a legacy of "almosts." For instance, a Boilermaker has never won the Heisman, although Bob Griese, now quarterbacking the 1974 Super Bowl champion Miami Dolphins, finished second in 1966, flanker LeRoy Keyes was third in '67 and second in '68, and quarterback Mike Phipps was second in 1969.

More than anything else, Purdue has had a run of great quarterbacks, starting with Bob DeMoss in 1945, who was eligible as a frosh and had four bright years. Since then Len Dawson, Dale Samuels, Ron DiGravio, Griese, and Phipps have earned high marks, most of them under Mollenkopf. When the earthy Mollenkopf ("Where's that * * * writer who wrote that I was profane?") retired after 1969, the Dallas Cowboys hired him to scout quarterbacks and nothing else. DeMoss took over and lasted three years before yielding to Alex Agase after the 1972 season. After a slow start, DeMoss's last team finished third (6-2) in the Big Ten, led by brilliant running back Otis Armstrong, who closed his career with 276 yards and three touchdowns against Indiana. That performance

Ohio State's Bob Vogel applies compress to a wounded mouth. Vogel later starred with the Baltimore Colts for 10 years.

made Armstrong the first in the league since 1945 to win its total offense crown (he had 1,176 yards) without throwing a pass.

Agase, a sophomore All-American guard at 5 feet 9 inches, 170 pounds for Illinois in 1942, made All-American the next year on Purdue's unbeaten team, playing as a Marine enlistee in the V-12 program. Since then, Purdue has traditionally stocked king-sized linemen, such as

Gene Washington reaches to catch
a bomb against Notre Dame. Washington finished third
in a poll to determine State's best player ever.

118

1972 All-American tackle Dave Butz (6 feet 7 inches, 264 pounds), who contributed more than his share to the average height and weight of Purdue's front four: 6 feet, 6 1/2 inches, and 249 pounds. (Butz's shoe size is 12 1/2 7E.)

Lured by the chance to dispense more scholarships, Alex came to Purdue after having rejected at least five other head jobs. Purdue's athletic director, George King, wisely looked beyond bare statistics in hiring Agase—his record was 29-52-1 in nine seasons—and grabbed the stocky, determined, cigar-chewing Assyrian.

In the winter of 1968, Alex decided that after 18 years of marriage, he owed it to his wife to learn to dance. "I was raised in a tough neighborhood where you weren't supposed to associate with girls," he recalls. "Sure I wanted to learn to dance, but I was bullheaded and wouldn't admit it."

Agase decided to refine his image in secret and then reveal his new talents at a party. He surreptitiously sought out a Fred Astaire studio, but the instructor there said he'd learn faster by practicing at home, so after two lessons, he broke the secret to his wife. She was very happy.

"That dance instructor made me a better football coach," Agase insists. "Being a student again—trying hard to do something I wasn't good at—made me realize the true importance of patience and understanding.

"I was vividly reminded of how much more can be accomplished by good teaching than by a kick in the pants. I think every coach would gain by being a student from time to time."

The Wildcats of Northwestern

With Agase's move from Northwestern to Purdue, Indiana's John Pont moved to Northwestern. Dissatisfied with contract dealings and no longer the hero he was when he brought the Hoosiers from last in 1966 to the Rose Bowl in '67, he left one tough job for another.

Northwestern will challenge Pont even more than Indiana did. The teams that Parseghian and then Agase produced weren't buried as deeply in the standings as were the Hoosiers before Pont, but Northwestern is no stranger to futility; it has not taken a title since 1936, when it won under Pappy Waldorf. To find a period

when the Wildcats dominated their conference for more than a year one needs to go even further back, to coach Dick Hanley and his 1930 and '31 championship teams, led by halfback Pug Rentner and tackles Dal Marvil and Jack Riley. Otherwise Northwestern managed only a few near misses, as in 1943 when the incomparable Otto Graham quarterbacked the team to a third-place finish.

The Hoosiers of Indiana

Indiana has had a few remarkably good players over the years—halfbacks Bill Hillenbrand and George Taliaferro, and end Pete Pihos in the 1940s; defensive end Earl Faison, and backs Marv Woodson and Tom Nowatzke in the early 1960s. Yet for the most part, the Hoosiers are losers. They have managed only two titles. The first came in 1945 when white-haired charmer Alvin ("Bo") McMillin arrived from Kansas State and brought with him the victory rains that alleviated a 14-year drought of losing seasons. He remained as adept at miracle working as he had been in 1921, when he ran 32 yards for the only score as the Praying Colonels of Centre shocked mighty Harvard 6-0. Dispensing solid fundamentals with Southern charm at Indiana, Bo quickly gained three first-division finishes, and his "Pore Li'l Boys" won the 1945 title, bringing him the league's first 10-year coaching contract, which he rejected for the Detroit Lions' job.

The situation that Pont inherited in 1965, after he had had big winning years at Miami of Ohio and Yale, was no better and possibly worse than the one in 1945 that McMillin rectified. When Pont took over, Indiana had mustered only one winning season in its last seventeen. Unfazed, Pont worked his miracle even faster than McMillin had his. Indiana recovered from 2-8 and 1-8-1 pre-Pont seasons when three jaunty sophomores—quarterback Harry Gonso, tailback John Isenbarger, and wide receiver Jade Butcher—led a blend of rookies and veterans to a tie for the 1968 title, winning fame as "the Cardiac Kids" and "the Happy Hooligans." Because Isenbarger had a habit of running when he was supposed to be punting, "Punt, John, punt!" became a happy war cry. Soon however, after three successive second-division finishes, Pont departed, and volatile, exuberant Lee

Corso came from Louisville as his replacement.

Corso, 37, may succeed Daugherty as the life of the party in the Big Ten. Among his credentials are an elephant ride in a parade a few years ago, a pregame trip to midfield with a turkey in hand (Corso was game captain that day), and a drive past a cemetery to remind himself that "Things could be worse." His optimism may be strained at Indiana.

The Hawkeyes of Iowa

A team doesn't need a dynasty to spawn memorable players. In 1970, a poll of veteran football experts picked an all-time Big Ten team of 21 men, on which Iowa placed four. No one could argue over the selection of tackle Fred ("Duke") Slater, star of the Hawkeyes' unbeaten 1921 outfit and the first black ever named an All-American. Nor was there any dispute when the experts chose Nile Kinnick, the scholar who won the Heisman and Maxwell trophies in leading the 1939 Ironmen to second in the league and first in the heart of the nation that exciting season. Kinnick's likeness appears on one side of the special coin that is used for every pregame flip in the Big Ten. The experts also remembered guard Calvin Jones, winner of the Outland Trophy as the nation's outstanding interior lineman in 1955, and tackle Alex Karras, also an Outland winner, in 1957, and later a perennial all-pro tackle with Detroit.

Howard Jones guided the Iowa Hawkeyes from 1916 to 1923 with 42-17 success before moving on to greater fame and glory at Southern California. The former Yale star, who also coached the Elis briefly, was a steely eyed, emotionless man who parlayed talented backs such as Aubrey Devine, Craven Shuttleworth, and Gordon Locke with linemen Slater, Les Belding, and Paul Minick into undefeated league champions in 1921 and '22. Then came a bleak period, brightened only by such stars as Ozzie Simmons, Dick Crayne, Kinnick, and Mike Enich. Not until the arrival of Forest Evashevski in the 1950s did Iowa recover. With the football mastery of Crisler, under whom he trained, and the derring-do psychology of a riverboat gambler, Evashevski treated the Hawkeye state to a decade of excitement and excellence. The cornbelt rocked and rolled as the high-flying Hawkeyes took a title in 1956 (the first since

Jones) and tied for the crown in 1958 and '60. Iowa featured the wing T, the decade's glamour formation, which Evashevski and an old Michigan teammate, Davey Nelson, had developed. With the wing T came two Rose Bowl victories and a half-dozen All-Americans: quarterbacks Ken Ploen and Randy Duncan, and ends Jim Gibbons and Curt Merz, as well as Jones and Karras.

Evashevski quit coaching after the 1960 season and started a controversial term as athletic director. After the football program deteriorated under Jerry Burns and Ray Nagel, Frank Lauterbur, a huge winner at Toledo, was summoned in 1971. Aided by the use of freshmen in 1972, the rebuilding seemed to be progressing.

The Badgers of Wisconsin

Before the turn of the century, Wisconsin fielded one of football's titans in Pat O'Dea, an Australian-born kicker who performed such feats as drop-kicking a 62-yard field goal and punting 110 yards—pretty good even for a man born on St. Patrick's day. O'Dea's fame lived on in Madison, partly because the Badgers did nothing to rival, much less equal it. They went without Big Ten titles from 1921 to 1952. Then stern, tough Ivy Williamson, who had succeeded Harry Stuhldreher in 1949, started a decade of prosperity.

End Dave Schreiner and backs Pat Harder and Jug Girard had been bright stars for Wisconsin in the period around World War II, but the brightest of all arrived in 1951. He ran erect, lifting his knees exceptionally high, flailing the arm that wasn't clutching the ball. Alan Ameche, "the Horse," had an exuberant style that pleased almost everyone in Madison except his parents, who came from Italy and thought little of fun and games like football. Because they refused to sign a permission card for Alan to play in junior high, it fell to brother Lynn to begin the football tradition in the Ameche family, for which Wisconsin should have awarded *him* a letter.

The 6-foot, 215-pound Heisman Trophy winner led his team to the Big Ten title in 1952. Four years later Williamson quit, and Uncle Miltie Bruhn carried on with back-to-back titles in 1958 and '59. He added another in 1962 before the dry spell that lingers today set in. Bruhn's

Clockwise from right: Ohio State diehards; gargantuan
Boilermaker Dave Butz; quarterback Clements
directs Irish offense against hated rival USC.

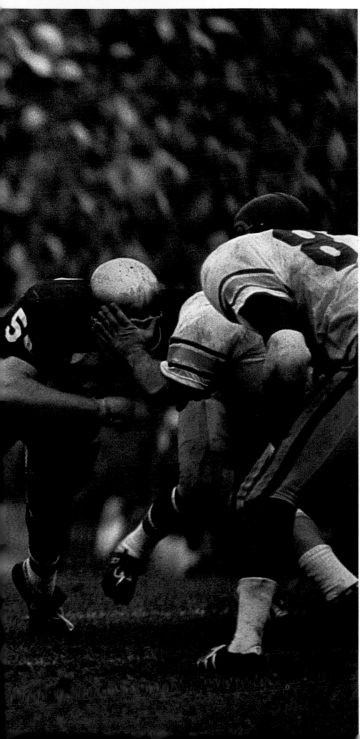

123

Opposite: Quarterback Harry Gonso of Indiana eyes his receiver. Right: Notre Dame's famed receiver Jim Seymour makes grab against Purdue.

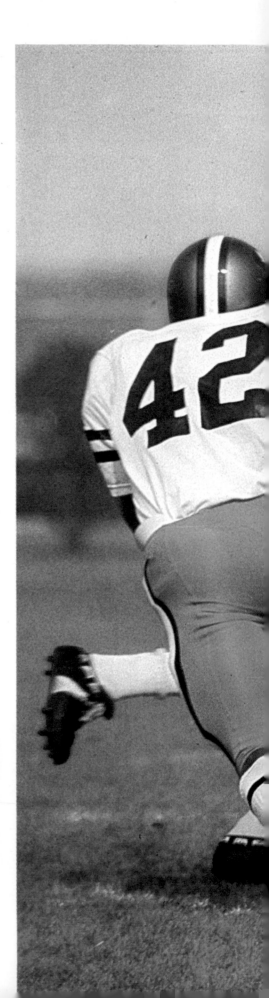

Clockwise from above: *The moods of coaches:
Hayes, Ohio State; Mollenkopf, Purdue; Pont
Indiana.* Right: *Kent State rebuffs Bowling Green.*

quarterbacks, Ron Miller and Ron VanderKelen, threw the ball, often to an end named Pat Richter. Jerry Stalcup and Dan Lanphear were the line stars of the period.

As of 1973, John Jardine had spent three futile years trying to rebuild.

The Fighting Illini

On the same October day that Notre Dame visited the Polo Grounds in New York and unleashed its four horsemen for a 13-7 victory over powerful Army, a swift 170-pounder from Wheaton, Illinois, was presiding over a dazzling christening ceremony for the new University of Illinois Memorial Stadium. While the maize and blue Michigan Spartans pursued him fruitlessly, Red Grange bolted 95 yards with the opening kickoff, scored thrice more before the game was 12 minutes old (on runs of 67, 56, and 44 yards), scored again in the second half, and threw for a sixth touchdown to conclude the one-man show. In the 39-14 romp, Grange rolled up 402 yards.

When asked what he remembers most about that memorable day, Grange emphatically replied "Stockings! The thing I'll never forget is that coach Bob Zuppke had us take off our long game stockings.

"It was a warm day, and we were sitting in the dressing room ready to go when Zup came in and told us to take them off. 'It'll make you faster,' he told us. So we took 'em off, feeling rather silly about it as no one played barelegged in those days. When we got out on the field, the Michigan players were amazed—thought we'd greased our legs—and stood and stared at us during our warm-up. I believe that old fox had a lot to do psychologically with winning that game."

As a prep coach in a Chicago suburb in 1906, Zup is credited with being the first to teach centers to spiral the ball instead of floating it back. He was a volatile, intensely proud man. The late Leo Johnson, longtime track coach and football aide at Illinois, was his chief scout for many years.

"Considering the intense scouting now, my reports were laughable," Johnson once recalled. "I'd stop by Zup's place for a half-hour when I got back on Sunday and give my impressions on the other team and the players. I was allowed to draw the formations they'd use but never a

play. When I tried to do that he'd snap, 'I know what plays can be run from that formation.' "

In 1910, Illinois staged college football's first homecoming game, and in 1925 the school became the first to retire a jersey number: Grange's "77," of course. Grange had come from Wheaton, Illinois, intending to play baseball and run sprints but his fraternity assigned him to football because it would bring the house better exposure. Johnny Hawks, a husky senior, used a paddle to persuade Red to work for Zup.

"Damn you! If it wasn't for you I'd never have gone out for football," Grange used to pretend to growl at Hawks, who never regretted his forceful influence.

Said Zuppke, "He was a natural. The number 'seven' is a natural in shooting dice, so I gave him two."

The number has been worn only once since at Illinois. Shortly after World War II, the equipment man loaned a jersey to a store for a display, and the store sewed on "77." When it returned, the jersey was inadvertently issued to a freshman tackle, who found himself virtually flung to the ground by his teammates before he could remove the hallowed jersey. There hadn't been as much commotion at an Illini practice since the previous fall, when coach Ray Eliot invited Jack Dempsey to give a midweek pep talk. The famed heavyweight boxer concluded his inspirational message with "Keep punching," and Eliot leaped to his feet and screamed, "No! No! Don't punch at all. It costs fifteen yards."

Illinois claimed titles under Eliot in 1946, '51, and '53. Its stars included Agase, tiny Buddy Young, who could run the hundred in 9.4, halfbacks John Karras and J. C. Caroline, and guard Bill Burrell. Pete Elliott put together a title team in 1963, featuring fullback Jim Grabowski and the brilliant middle linebacker, Dick Butkus. Sad times arrived shortly thereafter, and Bob Blackman, a big winner at Dartmouth, was hired as troubleshooter in 1971. He will do better if his teams can rid themselves of the habit of coming to life only after dropping their first half-dozen or so games each season.

Small College Powers

Until the early 1960s, the Big Ten was the only conference in the Midwest that offered big-time college football, but the Mid American

Conference, formed in 1946, came of age in dramatic fashion. Bowling Green (9-0) was named College Division national champion in 1959, and Ohio University, the only remaining charter member of the conference, won the honor the next year with a 10-0 mark. A few years later the league could claim to have graduated to the big time.

Its current members are Ohio, Bowling Green, Central Michigan, Eastern Michigan, Kent State, Miami, Toledo, Western Michigan, and Northern Illinois. The latter, which joined the league in March, 1973, was the small college king in 1963 when George Bork was throwing footballs for the school. Miami has won the most titles—eight—the last in 1966.

Coach Bill Hess's 1968 club at Ohio University, led by quarterback Cleve Bryant and split end Todd Snyder, finished 10-0 and became the first league team to finish in the national major college ratings—number 18 in the UPI poll, number 20 according to AP.

Stressing defense, Frank Lauterbur ignited his Toledo Rockets through 35 consecutive wins, the second greatest victory skein in modern major college history (Oklahoma had 47 from 1953 to 1957). Quarterback Chuck Ealey, who had never been beaten or tied in three years of high school ball in Portsmouth, Ohio, remained unbeaten in three years at Toledo, guiding the Rockets before heading north to Canadian football.

After undefeated seasons in 1969 and '70, Lauterbur left for Iowa, but his departure didn't diminish Toledo's success. In 1971, under Jack Murphy, Toledo was once again undefeated and became the first team ever to win three straight major college total defense titles (1969-71). In the 1972 opener, Tampa finally dumped Toledo, 21-0, ending the glorious string.

The 1972 campaign saw Kent State, 0-5 in the previous campaign, snap to attention with little prior notice and take the title and the Tangerine Bowl invitation. (They lost to Tampa 21-18.)

Few teams in the Midwest, with the prominent exception of Notre Dame, have fared well as independents. Detroit and Marquette, once respectable among the majors, have long since dropped out. Currently, Cincinnati, Xavier, and Dayton are playing as independents, having dropped their league affiliations.

Opposite: Ohio State's Stillwagon bursts through Minnesota's line. Above: Notre Dame's Ara Parseghian grimaces as he watches his team.

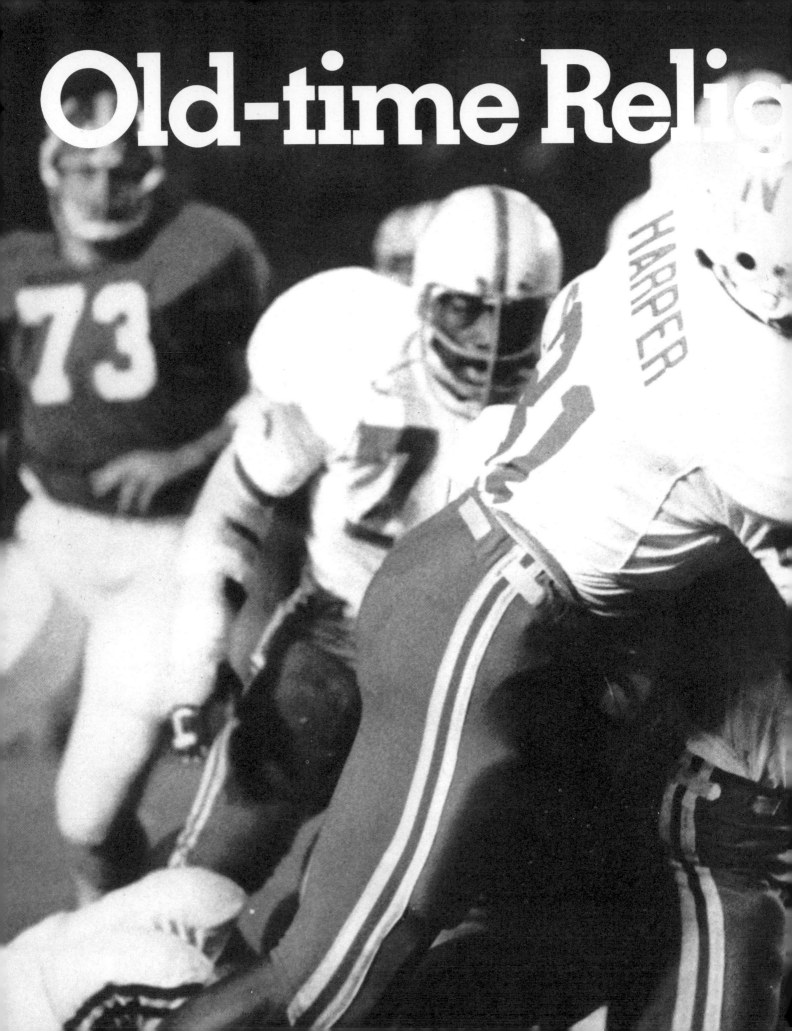

Old-time Relig

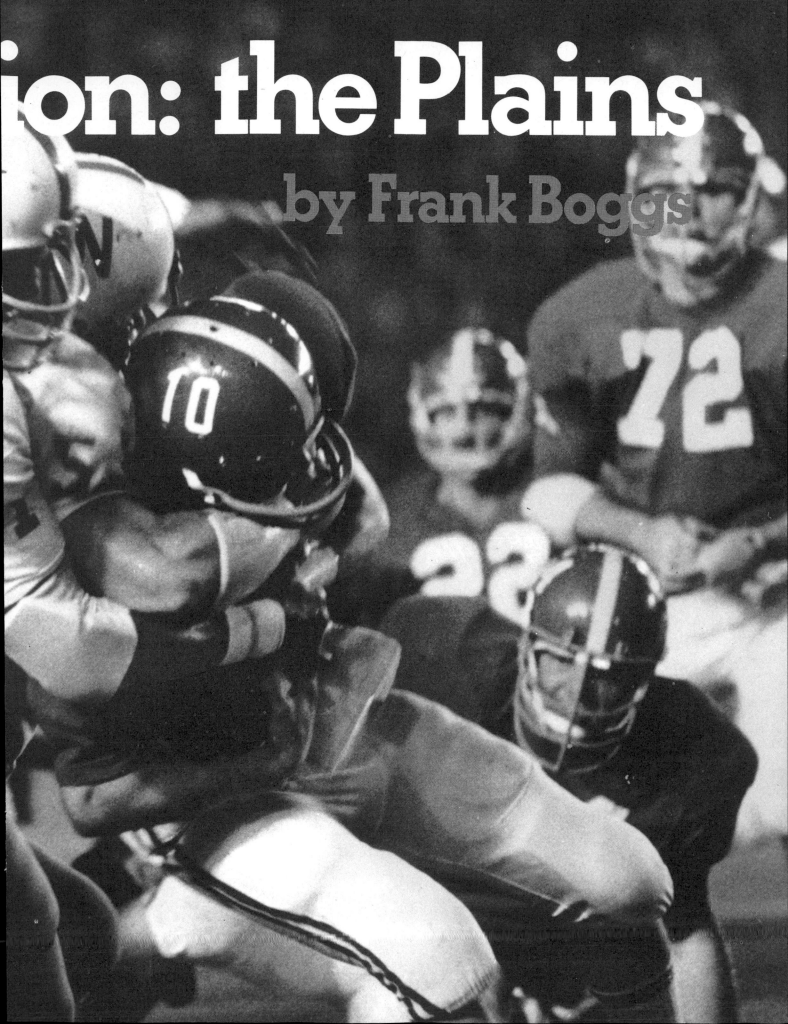

ion: the Plains
by Frank Boggs

In a divorce proceeding in Lincoln, Nebraska, Mrs. Fanatic has been awarded alimony, the house and its furnishings, the car, and the three kids, all of which Mr. Fanatic, knowing how courts go about this business, was ready to concede. Now, however, he begins to fidget in his chair. Sweat shows on his forehead, and muscles twitch in the face of his lawyer. The court is about to reach its big decision: who gets the season tickets to the University of Nebraska football games?

To the south, in Manhattan, Kansas, television viewers have a terrible time adjusting their color sets when Kansas State coach Vince Gibson does his weekly show. Soon after Gibson moved to Kansas from Tennessee, he discovered that the school colors are purple and white, so he introduced "Purple Pride." When he appears on the screen, everything but his skin is purple, and under the studio's bright lights, even that tends to catch a reflection. He wears purple suits, shirts, ties, and cowboy boots. He plays golf in purple golf shoes. When he began this fad among the school's loyalists, Gibson was often asked what goes with purple. He gave the obvious answer: "Purple goes with purple."

Still farther south is Big Red country and its center, the University of Oklahoma. Sometimes the school's football team experiences wonderful seasons, winning 11 games, losing none. Sometimes it suffers through hard times, winning 10, losing 1.

This area has steadily produced bowl teams, as in 1971, for example, when Nebraska, Oklahoma, and Colorado finished in precisely the same order in the national polls as they did in the Big Eight standings: one, two, three. Nebraska was unbeaten; Oklahoma lost only to Nebraska; and Colorado lost only to Nebraska and Oklahoma. Crowded car bumpers, already plastered with football-related stickers, had to accommodate one more proclamation: "1-2-3 = Big Eight."

In Oklahoma the new sticker covered the faded suggestion, "Chuck Chuck," or "Send Fairbanks Back to Alaska," coach Chuck Fairbanks having committed an unpardonable sin in 1970. His Sooners had won only seven

134

Preceding pages: *Nebraska swarms over Alabama.*
Right: *George Sauer of Nebraska skirts right end to score in East-West Shrine Game.*

Above: Bob Steuber gains 10 yards for Missouri in
1941 victory over Oklahoma that clinched Big Six
championship. Opposite top: Byron (``Whizzer'') White
listens to mentor, Colorado coach Bunnie
Oakes. Opposite bottom: Oklahoma's Tommy McDonald.

games and had accomplished nothing more noteworthy than tying Bear Bryant's Alabamans in the Astro-Bluebonnet Bowl.

The Big Eight Conference stretches from the corn fields of Iowa and the rich farm lands of Missouri through the waving wheat fields of Kansas and Nebraska and the red dirt of Oklahoma, to the foot of the Rockies in Colorado. In this Bible Belt, football is a religion. For years thousands have scrupulously attended service each Saturday afternoon.

Nothing New Under the Sun

In 1921, Bennie Owen, the first of Oklahoma's great coaches, led his team against Fred T. Dawson's Nebraska Cornhuskers on a field of mud that would have stuck a hog. After Nebraska won 44-0, a newspaper account explained why. "The Owen men bogged up to their ankles in the mire, for their football shoes did not have the mud cleats that Dawson had provided for his eleven. The Huskers had specially designed conical mud spikes, three inches in length on their shoes, which prevented them from sinking in and gave them a fairly firm hold in the mud. . . . Rubber soles kept the mud from sticking to the shoes."

In 1972, playing on a wet, slippery artificial turf at Boulder, Colorado, Oklahoma lost to Colorado. Several times Sooners' players tried to cut only to find themselves lurching ahead without changing direction. Compared to the Oklahomans, the Colorado players ran with the sure-footed ease of the mountain goats that may have been watching from the hills to the west. How, wondered many Oklahoma fans, could a well-paid football coach not know enough to have his players wear the proper type of shoes?

These two episodes, nearly a half century apart, are only one indication that very little has really changed in the Big Eight. Now as then, for example, the fans can be cruelly fickle to a particular player or team, but to their school's football tradition, they remain respectfully loyal. They are knowledgeable and intense about the game; they can crucify a 19-year-old who signals for a fair catch and then fumbles. Yet at the same game, they can relax and enjoy the carnival around them.

Coaches still depart for higher paying jobs,

Spears, the Dartmouth coach. The salary that lured Spears wasn't given out, but persons who attended the meeting say that Spears is to receive $7,500."

(Concessionaires of the day plied their trade with equal vigor and at similarly deflated prices. The Oklahoma vendors moved through the stands yelling, "Ice cold soda pop, chewing gum, candy, and peanuts. Hey you birds! Put your hands in your pockets and get your nickels out!")

Even sportsmanship, which appears to have waned since the old times, may not really have been forsaken by today's players, even if they consider it unfashionable to talk about. When Nebraska clinched the national championship in 1971 with its 35-31 victory over Oklahoma, the officials assessed only two 5-yard penalties, one against each team. Sportsmanlike sanity had prevailed despite the fact that one of the more frenzied buildups in the history of college football had preceded the game.

More than 50 years before, C. E. McBride, one of the more respected sports columnists in America, wrote on the subject of sportsmanship for the Kansas City Star. He had been impressed with the conduct of the Missouri team, coached by Johnny Miller. Wrote McBride, "Incidentally, it may be timely here to say a few words regarding the manner of football the Tigers have played under Johnny Miller—a clean, manly, sportsmanlike style of play that has made Missouri friends throughout the Valley."

Of course, as college football in the Plains grew from an adventurous cult to a well-heeled religion, there have been important modifications, some of the most important of which have been for the parishioners' benefit. Half-time shows have become spectacles. For no extra charge during intermission, you can witness Al Hirt playing a trumpet solo, or the Mormon Tabernacle Choir singing "Battle Hymn of the Republic," or perhaps Raquel Welch presenting a dramatic reading, followed by the homecoming queen parachuting onto the field while 57 area high school bands mass for the alma mater.

But if the showmanship is more grandiose, it is no more spirited than before. That time in 1921 when Nebraska wore the right kind of football shoes and whipped Oklahoma, "the Jazz

rarely admitting that the money lured them. They are more likely to talk of the "challenge" that the new opportunity presents. After the 1972 season, Chuck Fairbanks, for example, left Oklahoma for the New England Patriots of the NFL. He reportedly signed for $1 million over the next five years, and fringe benefits—healthy incentives for a man interested in challenges.

For considerably more modest offers, coaches 50 years ago switched camps with equal facility. In 1920, the Kansas City Star interviewed Bennie Owen to find out why Clarence W. Spears would leave Dartmouth for the football job at West Virginia. "The demand for good football coaches is country-wide," Owen told the Kansas City newspaper after returning from the annual intercollegiate meeting held in Chicago. "It was astonishing to note the number of schools that had men there looking for football coaches."

"At the meeting," reported the newspaper, "the announcement was made that West Virginia University had signed Clarence W.

138

Above: Paul Christman, who starred for Missouri from 1938-40. Opposite: Nebraska fans express their feelings for rival Oklahoma.

Hounds" were there—a noisy booster group whose purpose, said Oklahoma's student newspaper, was "to put spizzerinctum into the pep." The Jazz Hounds wore white trousers and red coats (but unfortunately, like the Sooners' football team, the wrong kind of shoes, so the white trousers never regained their virgin freshness). Before the game, this precursor of today's marching band paraded around the edge of the field, pulling a cow over whose back and sides was draped a sign that read, "This ain't no bull; we'll beat Nebraska."

At half time the Jazz Hounds squished to the middle of the field. Each carried an impeccably attired homing pigeon. Each bird sported a white streamer fastened to one foot and a red streamer attached to the other. On signal the Oklahoma pigeons were released. They flew to the top of the stadium, looked around a bit to get their bearings, and flew off toward their roosts in Norman, Oklahoma, arriving home before the Jazz Hounds, who had to contend with a slow train on their return trip.

Perhaps football lacks one thing it previously possessed—the nickname. If a young player today is named Robert, then Robert he remains. James plays halfback, Francis is at left guard, Michael is at safety.

Whatever happened to Cactus Face? Gilford ("Cactus Face") Dugan was a tremendous player in the late 1930s at Oklahoma. Lynn ("Pappy") Waldorf coached Kansas State to its last conference championship in 1934. Scrubby Laslett was a wonderful guard for Kansas in 1919. Iowa State had its great center, Polly Wallace, in the early twenties. Oklahoma had Roy ("Soupy") Smoot, Walter ("Waddy") Young, and Frank ("Pop") Ivy. W. C. ("King") Cole used to coach at Nebraska. Early in the century, Kansas had a 260-pound guard, Tubby Reed, who when the feeling moved him would spit tobacco juice in the eyes of the guy across the line.

Oklahoma had a great passer in the early years, Forest Geyer, nicknamed "Spot," because he always threw to the right one. Cussin' Smith kicked extra points for Kansas when Bennie Owen was a player there, his holder, in fact. One time Owen juggled the snap from center and had a terrible time placing it for Smith's big foot.

He finally managed to control the football, and Cussin' kicked the point, but he was angry. "Sit on it the next time, you little son-of-a-bitch, and I'll kick it anyhow," he remarked.

Nicknames used to be more common than given names. Long before baseball displayed its Dusty Rhodes, roads were in such poor condition that being dusty was the least thing wrong with them. That is why Nebraska had a famous back in 1924 named Choppy Rhodes.

An Anthropological Approach

Before retiring a few years ago, Harold Keith spent nearly his entire career as publicity director at the University of Oklahoma. He was one of the first sports publicity directors in the country and has given considerable thought to the origins and development of football in the Plains. "The Indians were the first ones here. When the Creeks and Choctaws had a game of Indian stickball (a species of shinny with its accompanying contusions, abrasions, and mayhem), they attracted spectators by the thousands. It was the only Indian sport I ever heard of that pulled tremendous crowds, although their horse races were fairly well attended.

"Then the ranchmen came and, after that, the Oklahoma land runs. The country was thinly settled by friendly, gutsy, impoverished white folks. At first the people were terribly lonely. You might not even have a neighbor, let alone see one more often than once a week. Back in the states they had run from, they were used to seeing people often. So they were starved for recreation and companionship. The first events they attended were the old-time square dances, to which they would ride fifteen, twenty, twenty-five miles on horseback or in a buggy and dance until sunup. The early rodeos, called steer-ropings then, also attracted a lot of fans. They were almost as rough as football, and Americans have always liked sports containing an element of roughness and danger and demanding considerable courage.

"That was followed by county-seat horse races, by town baseball, by collegiate football, and—hold your breath—by town football. Oklahoma University's first football game [in 1895] was against a town team from Oklahoma City and, from 1895 through 1906, Oklahoma

141 *Colorado's Davis is stopped by Nebraska's Mason (25) and Morelli (40). Colorado, even with good teams, has had trouble beating Nebraska.*

played town teams from Arkansas City, [Kansas]; Lawton, Pauls Valley, Fort Reno, and Pawhuska [Oklahoma]; and Dallas.

"This was in the days of the isolated small town. There was no radio or TV, and the newspapers arrived a whole day late. Roads were poor, and so were the people who walked and rode them. People were desperate for a place to go and something to do. People always have needed something to be proud of, to talk about, to brag about, to argue about. Sports provided a wonderful outlet."

A Numbers Game

On January 12, 1907, Kansas, Missouri, and Nebraska joined Iowa and St. Louis's Washington University to form the Missouri Valley Intercollegiate Athletic Association. A year later Iowa State, then known as Ames College, and Drake were admitted. Iowa dropped out in 1911 to join what is now the Big Ten Conference. Kansas State, not yet turned purple, became a member in 1913, Grinnell in 1919, and Oklahoma in 1920. Oklahoma State, then Oklahoma A & M College, left the Southwest Conference in 1925 to join.

On May 19, 1928, Kansas, Missouri, Nebraska, Kansas State, Iowa State, and Oklahoma decided to secede and form their own conference. They called themselves the Big Six, later to become the Big Seven, with the admission of Colorado for the 1948 season and finally the Big Eight, when Oklahoma State followed in 1958. (Renaming the conference has never posed much of a problem.)

Whatever its name, Nebraska and Oklahoma have dominated the conference from the beginning. Through 1972, Nebraska had won or shared twenty-nine conference championships,

Opposite: Colorado's Anderson scrambles before firing. 143
Above: Oklahoma's Pruitt. Tagged ``too
small'' by pro scouts, he made it in the pros anyway.

Oklahoma twenty-one. Missouri is a distant third, having won or shared twelve titles. Kansas follows with five, Iowa State has had two, and Colorado and Kansas State have taken one each. Oklahoma State has not won a title, although it fielded some excellent teams before entering the conference.

Oklahoma has produced three national championship teams, according to both the Associated Press and the United Press International polls—in 1950, 1955, and 1956. Nebraska topped the AP poll in 1970 and both the AP and the UPI polls in 1971.

The Sooners' greatest accomplishment and perhaps the college football record that will endure longest, was their 47-game victory streak. It began in the third game of 1953, a 19-14 decision over Texas, and ended in 1957 at Norman before 63,170 (the school's largest home crowd ever), who witnessed Notre Dame's stunning 7-0 upset of the Sooners. The coach of that Notre Dame team, Terry Brennan, was assisted by an energetic little defensive coach named Hank Stram, later to become one of professional football's recognized geniuses as coach of the Kansas City Chiefs.

Obviously, Oklahoma's record streak came at the height of the Sooners' domination of their conference. In its 10 years (1948-57), the Big Seven Conference had only one champion—Bud Wilkinson's Sooners. In 1946 under coach Jim Tatum, then in 1947, when Wilkinson took over, the Sooners shared the Big Six title with Kansas. And when the conference expanded to eight members, Oklahoma won the championship in 1958 and '59. So in 14 years, Oklahoma first shared the conference championship twice and then won it for 12 consecutive seasons. Not even the musical *Oklahoma!* could match that run.

All-Stars: Past and Present

This midlands conference has produced three Heisman Trophy winners: Oklahoma's Billy Vessels in 1952, the Sooners' Steve Owens in 1969, and Nebraska's Johnny Rodgers in 1972.

Ten of its products have been enshrined in the College Football Hall of Fame: Claude Reeds of Oklahoma, Bob Fenimore of Oklahoma State, Ed Weir of Nebraska, Jim Bausch of Kansas, George Sauer of Nebraska, Byron ("Whizzer") White of Colorado, Guy Chamberlin of Nebraska, Paul Christman of Missouri, Ray Evans of Kansas, and Ed Bock of Iowa State. All were backfield greats except Weir, a tackle, and Bock, a guard.

From the conference have come Hall of Fame coaches D. X. Bible of Nebraska, Bennie Owen of Oklahoma, Bill Roper of Missouri, Pop Warner of Iowa State, Fielding Yost of Nebraska and Kansas, Biff Jones of Nebraska and Oklahoma, E. N. Robinson of Nebraska, Don Faurot of Missouri, Lynn ("Pappy") Waldorf of Kansas State, and Bud Wilkinson of Oklahoma. Surely Bob Devaney's name will be added to that elite list. His Nebraska powers won 102 games, lost only 20, and played two ties during his 11-season reign, which ended after the 1972 campaign when he gave up coaching but remained as the Huskers' athletic director.

Dan Devine of Missouri was the first Big Eight coach to leave for the professionals, going to the Green Bay Packers. Chuck Fairbanks, after a six-year stay at Oklahoma during which his teams fared far better than some bumper stickers indicated, left for the New England Patriots.

Including those players later inducted into the Hall of Fame, more than 150 conference players have gained All-American honors—men such as Forest Geyer, Granny Norris, tackle Cash Gentry, Pop Ivy, and lineman Buddy Burris, all of Oklahoma; Polly Wallace of Iowa State; three tremendous late-twenties linemen, Dan McMullen, Ray Richards, and Hugh Rhea, fullback Sam Francis, and great runner, Bobby Reynolds, all of Nebraska; Bob Stueber of Missouri; and also from Oklahoma, quarterbacks Darrell Royal, now the head coach at Texas, and Eddie Crowder, now the head coach at Colorado.

Compared to the media-saturated fans of today, the public that acclaimed those stars hardly knew them, having had to rely on radio and, before that, impersonal newspaper accounts. Today, with television, folks can scrutinize their heroes, and therefore, perhaps the modern All-Americans seem greater than the old-timers, whose feats are recorded in yellowing pages of dusty books rather than in full color instant replays.

In 1972, Nebraska had a marvelous middle guard, Rich Glover, and a premier defensive end, Willie Harper. Oklahoma boasted scatback Greg Pruitt and center Tom Brahaney. The year before

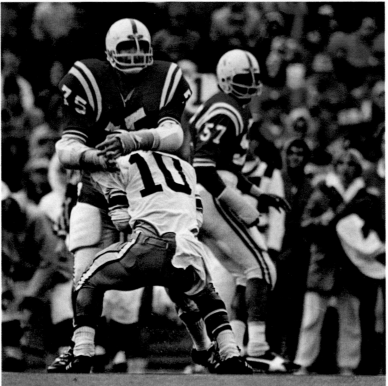

Clockwise from above:
Johnny Rodgers cuts
through Oklahoma;
Cornhuskers' Larry
Jacobson pulls down
Colorado's Joe
Duenas; Sooners'
defense is anchored
by Lucious Selmon
and Berland Moore.

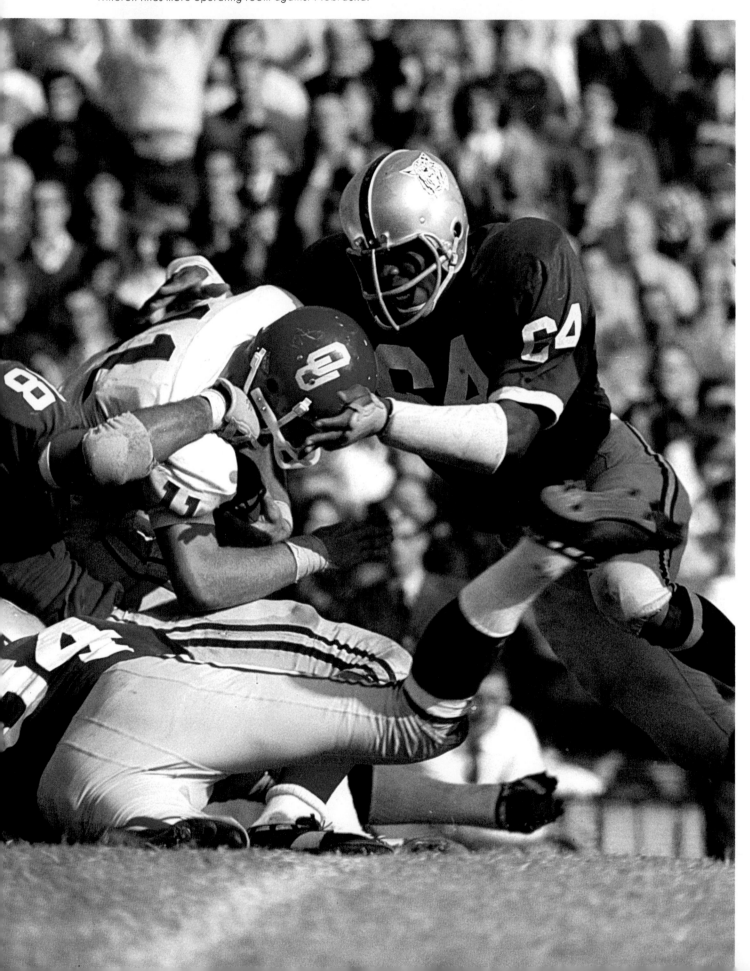

Following pages: Greg Pruitt (left) and Steve Davis.

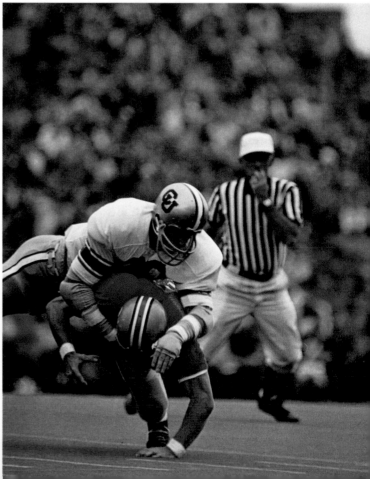

the Sooners' quarterback Jack Mildren matched wits and talent with his opposite number on Nebraska, Jerry Tagge. A sampling of other big names from the fairly recent past: Dwight Nichols and George Amundson of Iowa State; Joe Romig, Dick and Bob Anderson, and Herb Orvis of Colorado; John Hadl, Gale Sayers, and Bobby Douglass of Kansas; Ralph Neely and Granville Liggins of Oklahoma; Wayne Meylan and Jeff Kinney of Nebraska; Roger Wehrli of Missouri; John Ward of Oklahoma State; and Clarence Scott of Kansas State.

Big Eight schools, however, are not the only ones that supply the football talent from the flat lands. The University of Tulsa fielded some excellent teams under Henry Frnka and produced as well a one-armed All-American guard, Ellis Jones, in 1944. Other Tulsa All-Americans have included tailback Glenn Dobbs in 1942, later the Hurricanes' head coach; center Felto Prewitt in 1945; tackle Marv Matuszak in 1952; quarterback Jerry Rhome in 1964; and little Howard Twilley, who graduated in 1965 after catching passes worth 3,343 yards in 30 games.

Early in the century, Haskell Institute at Lawrence, Kansas, turned out a series of tremendously powerful football teams. The Haskell Indians were at their best when a back named John Levi ran wild. When a mid-century Associated Press poll named Jim Thorpe this country's greatest athlete, Thorpe himself denied it. He called Levi "the best athlete I ever saw."

Air Force Academy, a baby compared to most surrounding schools, has grown up under coach Ben Martin and produced one of the area's most exciting passing quarterbacks, Rich Mayo.

Among small colleges, Northeastern State of Tahlequah, Oklahoma, won the National Association of Intercollegiate Athletics (NAIA) championship in 1959. Central State of Edmond, Oklahoma, took that title in 1963.

Byron White and Claude Reeds

In 1934, Chester Nelson was a young sportswriter on the *Rocky Mountain News*. He is still there and still writes a daily column. "Of the men who have shown a world of promise," he wrote then, "Byron White, the shifty triple threat freshman star of 1934, appears the most likely candidate [to succeed] among the backs."

Sportswriters aren't always wrong. Mr.

Nelson, for one, knew talent when it ran past him. Byron White became well known at Colorado as Whizzer White, finished college impressively, and then gained the stature of one who can no longer be called by a college nickname. Today he is Byron White, associate justice on the United States Supreme Court.

In those formative years, there weren't many sportswriters to herald the coming stars. A boy came off the farm unrecruited and unscouted. He arrived at the university with no glossy high school reputation having preceded him. Most often he would serve his three years in oblivion, with few media representatives to be impressed and no publicity department to court them. Only occasionally could a player shine on his own.

Claude Reeds needed no sportswriters' ballyhoo. He was the tall, rugged, somewhat shy Oklahoma fullback for four seasons, starting in 1910. Reeds lettered four times in football and basketball, three times in baseball, and twice in track. Ed Meacham, later an Oklahoma assistant and scout, played with Reeds at Oklahoma. In an interview many years ago, Meacham spared no words in his praise of this Hall of Famer.

"Claude Reeds was the university's great punter; the most accurate passer, equaled in long passes only by Spot Geyer; the most terrific line-plunger and off-tackle driver; the greatest end runner from kick formation; and the hardest man to tackle Oklahoma has ever had. He was the strongest in running interference, seldom sent the kickoff short of the goal line, never sacrificed team play for individual play, anticipated opponents' attacks and moved quickly to points of attacks, was a sure tackler, and seldom if ever failed to break up a pass directed to his field of play. He was strong, fast, clean, determined, and was never injured."

One of Reeds's finer moments came in 1911, with the championship of the Southwest Conference at stake (Oklahoma was a member of the SWC until 1920). Bennie Owen's Sooners journeyed to Austin for their game with Texas. With them they carefully transported a large banner that read "Beat Texas," a war cry that is still heard today throughout the state of Oklahoma every October, when the Sooners and Longhorns collide at the state fair in Dallas in one of the land's great traditional matches.

153

Clockwise from left: Colorado takes on Ohio State; Oklahoma and Kansas State meet in Big Eight contest; Super coaches Bud Wilkinson and Nebraska's Bob Devaney.

"Alone and almost single-handed Claude Reeds kept the championship in Oklahoma that year," reported a campus magazine of the time. "In the wake of his long catapulting runs across almost the entire field were left a row of prostrate players who had been unfortunate enough to get in his way. His smashing interference and sensational long and well-placed punts were also a potent factor in Oklahoma's victory that day." (However, the Sooners did not, as this enthusiastic account implies, overwhelm Texas that afternoon. Their modest 6-3 victory indicates that even Reeds may have been more inspirational to the writer than he was potent on the field that day.)

Reeds later went into coaching, serving for a time as one of Owen's assistants. As a coach, he achieved his most notable success at Central (Oklahoma) State during the 1930s. His Central teams won eight conference titles in 10 years and from 1935-39 won 25 consecutive conference games.

The University of Oklahoma magazine writer who had waxed hyperbolic over Reeds as a player, later interviewed him when Reeds was a coach. "Once the cloak of reserve is penetrated," he wrote, "Reeds is found to be jovial and good-natured and talks freely of sports, something that few coaches will do for reporters. He is considerate of the players who are under his direction and talks of nothing but football while on the practice field. His psychology in developing winning teams is to make them play 'over their heads,' or, in other words, to get the team's morale to such a high pitch that the team will play with more than its actual ability."

To that spiritual approach to building winning teams, coaches would add a more materialistic one—a crude forerunner of recruiting. During Reeds's coaching days at Central State, scholarships were unheard of, but townspeople who liked football did have job offers that a coach could use to entice particularly fine prospects. In 1935, longtime Omaha sportswriter Fred Ware took a compassionate look at moonlighting college ballplayers when he wrote, "Next time you think one of them bobbles a play and you're all set to do a round of freestyle crabbing, just recall that the kid probably knocked off studying around 2 A.M. after spending the earlier hours of the night swabbing the marble floor of a bank lobby or dealing 'em off the arm at a lunch counter."

Reeds had a slightly more jaundiced view. "Some worked, and some of the boys didn't work so well," he recalls, chuckling as he remembers his recruits.

In 1941, Reeds purchased a farm near Newcastle, a small town southwest of Oklahoma City not far from the university in Norman where he starred as a player. He still lives on the farm and occasionally comes into Oklahoma City to eat at a cafeteria on the south side of town.

In the fall of 1972, Reeds was inducted into Oklahoma's athletes' hall of fame. He tries to avoid the arguments about which era produced the greatest athletes but occasionally offers an opinion. He begins by recognizing the talents of the modern players but then questions whether they have the stamina they would need if the game were played as it was in his prime. "Not many like to play like we did," he says. "We played the whole game. Now they play awhile and rest awhile."

An Oklahoma Idol

Were Claude Reeds and Steve Owens to be matched in a popularity poll today, it is very possible that Owens would win in a shutout. Steve Owens appears in the sports news quite regularly; Reeds is mentioned only when historical footnotes are required. Owens played for the Sooners from 1967-69. He scored 56 touchdowns, rushed for 3,867 yards, and by wholly dominating the football field made it a waste of money to buy a program to see who the other players were. It was sufficient to know that "36" carried the football. He rushed 358 times as a senior and 905 times in his three years, both school records.

Oklahomans idolize Owens for more than his football feats. He is the type of guy who salutes the flag, who never sassed his mom, who always did his homework before going out to play, who went to Sunday School every week, whose first words were "sir" and "ma'am." That is the Steve Owens that Oklahoma has placed on a pedestal, and there is none loftier than the one for a model football player.

Owens is from Miami, Oklahoma, a pleasant

place in the northeastern corner of the state. He never really thought about doing anything but playing football, which he began on an organized level in the fifth grade. "It seems like I've been playing football all my life," he says quite accurately.

When he was in the seventh and eighth grades he obtained a part-time job as a shoe salesman on Miami's main street. "I was walking down the street one day, and this friend of mine was standing there in front of the store. He told me they needed a boy to work on Saturdays in the shoe department. He took me in to meet the owner. I was wearing blue jeans and tennis shoes—I hadn't gone to town to apply for work—and the owner said, 'He's sure not dressed very nice.' But this friend of mine told him I didn't always look like that. I'd been out playing football." So Owens landed the job and worked at something other than football for one of the few times in his life.

"On Saturday afternoons we'd get the radio out and listen to OU football games. The whole store would gather around and listen to football. That was the first time I really got interested in Oklahoma football. Nobody got waited on from one to four P.M. in that shoe department."

Owens is an old-fashioned hard worker who claims, perhaps unfairly, that he never had great talent. But he cannot deny his dedication. "In high school you have heroes," he says. "I just always had a dream of playing at Oklahoma. Jim [Mackenzie, the Sooners' head coach who died of a heart attack after coaching Oklahoma in 1966, when Steve was a freshman,] sold me on Oklahoma," says Owens. "And it was everything I ever thought it could be while I was playing there."

During his great career he became the most tireless and most effective runner in the school's history. In his final game as a Sooner, he carried the football a record 55 times for 261 yards. Oklahoma needed every bit of his efforts to secure its 28-27 triumph over Oklahoma State.

Earlier in the week, Owens had won the Heisman Trophy. To escape the ringing telephone, he moved into the home of Barry Switzer, OU's assistant coach in charge of offense who replaced Chuck Fairbanks as boss in 1973. "There was so much pressure. There was a

Nebraska's Kenny (top) and Tagge starred on offense in national championship game with Oklahoma.

155

question in some people's minds if I was deserving of the Heisman Trophy."

Any dissenters were convinced by his work in that last game against Oklahoma State. "That's the only game at OU in which I ever got tired," Owens says.

Despite his performance, the pros still doubted whether Owens could star in the NFL. When he left college, the skeptics predicted he would join the legion of former heroes who wind up sitting on their Heismans. "I know that talk had to have an effect on me," he said. "I always knew I could play professional football. But you keep reading some of those things in the papers, and I was beginning to wonder if I *could* play. Is it true? Then I just said, 'To heck with it. . .' It made me try that much harder. I got so tired of hearing it. I always felt it was unjust criticism."

Owens went to Detroit, fought off a series of injuries, and then rushed for 1,035 yards as a sophomore with the Lions, becoming the first 1,000-yard rusher in the history of that club.

When he isn't playing football, he spends his free time with his wife, Barbara, a small son, Blake, and a pair of feisty poodles. He loves the life. "It flatters me for people to come up and ask for my autograph. It's amazing to me that I can pull into a service station at someplace like Welch, Oklahoma, and have a guy walk up and say, 'Well, how's it going with Detroit?' Oklahoma must have about two-and-a-half million people, and they're all football fans."

Owens spends many evenings in the off-season speaking to youth groups. He tells all of them basically the same thing, his credo: "Decide what you want in life. Then go out and get it."

Rivalries

Except in 1918, when World War I forced the cancellation of their match, Kansas and Missouri have played against each other every year since 1891. Their series is the oldest one west of the Mississippi and one of the best. After their meeting in 1921 (a 20-20 tie), the umpire, Dr. Isadore Anderson, offered a simple assessment of the match. "It was the most wonderful game I have ever seen," he said.

Like other great rivals, they are often more intent on beating each other than on accomplishing anything else in the football

season. Such devoted attention to one game, possibly at the expense of others, may seem irrational to a detached outsider, but the partisans' self-assurance overwhelms the timid skeptic, particularly when he realizes that the enthusiasm with which these two teams clash is hardly unique. With equal zeal every year, Army plays Navy, Southern California plays UCLA, Texas plays Oklahoma, Yale plays Harvard, and the Washburn Ichabods play the St. Benedict's Ravens, which, should you be an Ichabod and/or a Raven is more important than any other.

Before the 1959 Missouri-Iowa State game, coaches from both sides performed their normal ritual of testing the field telephones. Something was wrong. An Iowa State coach found himself talking to a coach from Missouri. By game time the problem had been solved but not forgotten. The Northwestern Bell Telephone Co. of Ames, Iowa, decided to commemorate the occasion. It had a trophy made and awarded it each year to the winning team. It seemed a fitting gesture, especially since later in the same season a similar problem plagued a game in Missouri.

While Kansas-Missouri and Texas-Oklahoma reduce the locals to a frenzy, the Nebraska-Oklahoma series has had a similarly unsettling effect on college football fans across the nation as well as the region. Until recently, the Nebraska-Oklahoma series has been one of streaks. From 1931-42, for example, Nebraska defeated the Sooners 10 times, Oklahoma won only once, and one game ended in a scoreless tie. Beginning in 1943, the Sooners whipped Nebraska for 16 consecutive years. Since then, however, the series has been the standoff that can be expected from two teams that have become superpowers of the football world. In the 1959-72 period, each team won seven times and neither won more than three in a row.

In 1971, Bob Devaney's Cornhuskers were ranked number one nationally, Chuck Fairbanks's Sooners number two. Their meeting had been arranged for national television on Thanksgiving afternoon at Norman. Because of the Thursday date, neither team played on the previous Saturday—a layoff that left their followers with more time to wrack themselves in the suspense and left the sportswriters with more pregame space to fill. By game time some

Steve Owens barreling to the Heisman. After graduating to the pros, Owens said, "I always knew I could play professional football, but then you start reading some of those things. . . ."

OU NO. 1 1971

30	SMU	0
55	PITTSBURG	29
33	USC	20
48	TEXAS	27
45	COLORADO	17
75	KAN. ST.	28
43	IOWA ST.	12
20	MO.	3
56	KANSAS	10
48	NEBRASKA	21
	OKLA. ST.	

TEXAS
OU 48 🐂 27
EAT STEER ALL YEAR

writers had probed the game's intricacies with everyone from the head coaches to the chain gangs. "This is what college football is all about," Fairbanks intoned as game day neared.

Writers for whom Norman had previously been Dr. Peale's first name encountered a mild case of culture shock in having to go there. Some of them gained admittance to the stadium press box only to find that there were not enough seats. Jostling for space at the additional counter tops that had been installed in the large, plush press box, they scribbled their notes, looking like slightly tipsy patrons at an overcrowded bar. An estimated 500 people stuffed a press box that can normally accommodate only half as many.

The epidemic of hyperbole that had swept through the football populace in the country before this game afflicted the writers especially. The most cautious scribe called the game a classic. The rest dubbed it "the game of the

century." By game day some of the less self-assured began to chide themselves for having given the game too big a buildup.

No one will ever know how much some of the more desperate 62,884 fans paid for the privilege of witnessing the game in person. Television moguls said the game was viewed by 55 million. The audience included President Nixon, who later telephoned both head coaches.

Oklahoma gained 467 yards in total offense. Nebraska gained 362. Both teams scored in every quarter. Oklahoma led twice, each time by three precarious points. There were 66 points scored that day, yet the game featured some stellar defense. With 7:10 to play, Jack Mildren moved the Sooners into a 31-28 lead when he sizzled a 16-yard touchdown pass to Jon Harrison, at 150 sweaty pounds, the smallest figure on the field. Sensing the Sooners' fourth national championship, the jubilant spectators allowed

Above: *Typically reserved Oklahoma football fan.* Opposite: *Coaches Devaney (left) and Wilkinson. Wilkinson's records at Oklahoma remain unbroken.*

themselves to forget for the moment that time enough remained for Nebraska to score.

It took the Huskers 11 plays. The key was a third-down pass from quarterback Jerry Tagge to Johnny Rodgers, who had electrified everyone earlier in the afternoon by returning a punt 72 yards for the game's first touchdown. Rodgers's reception kept the Huskers crunching onward. Finally, with the ball at the 2-yard line and only a couple of minutes remaining, Jeff Kinney, who already had rushed for 169 yards, crashed through an all but undetectable hole and scored the decisive points in Nebraska's 35-31 win.

Don Bryant, Nebraska's sports publicist, wrote, "Football fans will continue to savor their 1971 Turkey Day gridiron feast for years to come, not because of the score, not because one team won or another lost, but because they were fortunate enough to have witnessed two unbelievably great groups of young men meet in friendly competition before millions of their fellow citizens with both acquitting themselves with unparalleled valor. Nebraska was magnificent; Oklahoma was magnificent. Both rose to the challenge; both refused to buckle before the most pressure ever applied to two football teams. Both teams—and especially the Big Eight Conference—won on Thanksgiving Day, and it may even be said that these two magnificent football teams insured an even bigger victory, establishing a fact that sometimes may be overlooked but should never be forgotten: no sport can equal or approach the color, drama, excitement and excellence of America's college football. . . ."

Fairbanks later described his telephone conversation with the President. "President Nixon talked to me about some of the other big games, but he said this one fulfilled all the build-up, all the anticipation. His statement was one of

congratulations for both teams. I appreciated this, and it was a pretty good analysis of what happened."

A Political Issue

In early 1973, Oklahoma's football program found itself caught in the middle of a recruiting scandal. Two players had been declared ineligible, including a young man whom everyone had labeled the starting quarterback for the coming season. The assistant coach who had recruited him was fired. The scandal and the reaction to it are telling indications of the seriousness with which the region's fans follow their football. The scandal was sports page news, certainly, but it was also page one news and the lead story on the local television newscasts. Sports are mere games for only so long. Often they are too important to be segregated in the sports section at the back of a newspaper.

The following is part of an editorial in the *Oklahoma City Times* after the news broke.

"Grieving Sooner football fans found Wednesday that all the world's minor crises had been shunted to a siding by a tragedy of epic proportions. The great victories of last fall were suddenly ashes. Perhaps Elizabeth Barrett Browning anticipated such a sorrow when she wrote:

> . . . I overturn
> The ashes at thy feet. Behold and see
> What a great heap of grief lay hid in me
> And how the red wild sparkles dimly burn
> Through the ashen grayness. If thy foot in
>   scorn
> Could tread them out to darkness utterly
> It might be well perhaps.

"Due to infractions of recruiting rules (one of them involved a spectacularly successful freshman quarterback who had played in nine of last season's games), the Big Red is suddenly no longer No. 2 in the nation. In fact, it seems for a time to have been relegated to about ninth place in the Big Eight.

"Bureaucratologist James Boren advises, 'When in doubt, mumble!' There must have been a lot of doubts in Sooner land, to judge by the amount of mumbling going on. 'Honesty is always the best policy, and college kids have to know that their university sets the example,' said one loyal rooter, 'but this is ridiculous!'

"But in the tradition of the playing fields, OU and its team will survive. If we could only be as sure about the fans. . . ."

A Psychological Phenomenon

Perhaps this football craze should be viewed by a psychiatrist as well as mere sports enthusiasts and editorial writers. Dr. Joseph B. Ruffin moved to Oklahoma 10 years ago, having lived in such places as Chicago, California, and Japan. The "rambunctiousness" of the citizenry immediately impressed him. This world consists of two types of people, he says: those who sit still and those who get up and go. "The United States was populated by those who got up and went," he claims, "action-oriented people. . . ."

Oklahoma was one of the last available spots for the get-up-and-goers. In their rush to settle there, some of them claimed land early, earning the nickname "Sooners," which the University of Oklahoma later adopted. Oklahoma City was settled in one day in "the Run of '89," on April 22.

The descendents of these impetuous frontiersmen have a favorite pastime on Saturday evenings in the fall, after they return from the big stadium. They like to get together, have some drinks, and discuss the game. Dr. Ruffin has managed to be invited to such parties, never revealing beforehand that he is not the typical Midwestern football fan. He takes great interest in these gatherings.

"There will be eighteen TV sets on around the house," he says, "and it's lots of fun. But I have noticed [that] those of us who are not all that hopped-up about football soon find ourselves on the outside of the conversation. . . . They think maybe I'm queer, I guess. [For a man here] to be appropriately 'studly.' he ought to be excited about football."

As a psychiatrist, the doctor has been involved many times in group therapy with homosexuals from this area. Nearly always football enters the discussion, because, he says, so many homosexuals have had to struggle with their lack of interest in the sport. Football, it seems, has at least as dramatic an impact on some of those who don't follow it as on those who do.

The doctor extends his analysis to the strategy of the game. It is no coincidence, he believes, that in this section of the country such a premium is placed on running. (Teams from the Big Eight

and its predecessors have won the NCAA rushing championship nine different years, yet none has ever won an NCAA passing title.) He firmly believes that athletics are an important mode for discharging whatever it is that man needs to discharge in order to remain on an even keel. In football, running is one of the better ways, he implies. "Who the hell wants to throw a pass?" he asks. "You're not going to get out any aggression that way."

Perhaps the Southwesterners' propensity for rough-and-tumble also explains why their schools have long produced such powerful wrestling teams. Oklahoma State has been the dominant wrestling power for years, and Iowa State has moved steadily nearer the top in recent years.

A Final Anecdote

In 1903, when every Oklahoma town wanted its own town football team, Lawton, Oklahoma, boasted a squad so strong that it challenged the University of Oklahoma to a postseason game. It was no idle talk. The town offered the university $300 to participate in what was surely one of the country's earliest bowl games. Before the

Sooners could meet to decide whether to accept, the Lawton backers became impatient and wired that they'd be willing to pay $400. That clinched it. After an ambitious 11-game schedule that had taken the Sooners as far afield as neighboring Arkansas, they needed to strengthen their frail financial condition.

Before the big game with Lawton (which OU won 27-5), an Oklahoma end, one Alex Clement, came down with a severe cold. His parents forbade him to make the trip and his brother offered him the staggering sum of $40 not to play, fearing that if he did, the cold might develop into pneumonia. But Alex Clement was not persuaded. He played, claiming that if he had to die, there was no finer way to go than playing football.

Perhaps it was such unwavering dedication and the slightly mad justification of it that coach Bennie Owen sought to instill in his OU squads in later years when he told them, "Think fight, talk fight, always fight. And use your noodles—that is what they are for." Judging by the spirit with which they continue to play, football players of the Plains seem to have followed his advice.

Big Shoot-out:

the Southwest
by Dave Campbell

For a few tantalizing seconds, the ball spiraled through the freezing mist. On the Texas 40-yard line, the Longhorns' quarterback, James Street, watched his pass in dismay, for he thought he had never thrown a poorer one. Downfield, frantically pursued by Arkansas defensive back Jerry Moore, Texas tight end Randy Peschel raced toward the ball he was sure had been overthrown. As the two players swept inside the Arkansas 20-yard line, the ball descended and both of them lunged for it. It cleared the hands of Moore by inches, and Peschel had it, sprawling at the Arkansas 13-yard line. On fourth and 3 with time running short in the fourth quarter, desperate Texas had been reprieved.

Two plays later, the Longhorns, less desperate now, scored, and for the first time that long and anxious afternoon, they took the lead. For the moment they could revel in their startling turnabout; no matter that their margin was a single point. From fourth and 3 on their 43, trailing by six points with less than five minutes to play, the Longhorns had struck on the implausible 44-yard fourth-down pass. They had then quickly added Ted Koy's twisting 11-yard run and sophomore Jim Bertelsen's 2-yard plunge for the touchdown that had tied the game at 14-14. Kicker Happy Feller had promptly added the go-ahead extra point. With three minutes and 58 seconds remaining in the biggest game of their young lives, the Longhorns were jubilant.

Although stunned, Frank Broyles's Razorbacks were not ready to surrender a game that had for most of the afternoon been theirs. Most of the spectators at the game vividly remembered that four years earlier in that same emotion-swept stadium another number-one-ranked Texas team had failed to check the rallying Razorbacks in the final moments of a game. On that occasion Arkansas passed its way 80 yards downfield to the winning score with 92 seconds left. Having scored that delicious 27-24 victory over their arch-rivals, the Razorbacks had completed a perfect season and garnered a second consecutive

164

Texas sophomore backfield sensation Jack Crain swings around right end for a first down in Longhorns' 1939 defeat of Rice at Austin.

Southwest Conference championship.

But in 1965, the two teams had clashed at their usual time, in mid-October, when victory, however uplifting, had not been decisive. The television cameras had beamed the game across the country, but most other college teams had played too that day, so the memorable 1965 Texas-Arkansas game commanded only one prominent stage among many.

In the cold, gray late afternoon of December 6, 1969, the stakes were incomparably greater. For one thing, this game was the climax of college football's centennial.

Since the 1869 contest between Princeton and Rutgers, football had come a long way, both in the development of the game itself and in the autumnal hurrah it inspired. In an all-out effort to demonstrate how far the game had progressed, the National Collegiate Athletic Association (NCAA) took a number of steps before the season to give it a special flavor. Among other things, the NCAA approved a television network's suggestion that one game be switched from its usual place on the schedule to a special December date. It would be the only game played that day. It would, it was hoped be the final, climactic game of the regular season, and with the aid of national television, the entire college football world would focus on it. The centennial celebration planners admitted that they would have to be outrageously lucky to select the season's best game for December, but in early spring they chose anyway: Texas versus Arkansas. They hit a bullseye.

"It [the selection] makes them look wiser than a tree full of owls," cracked Texas coach Darrell Royal as he prepared to send his undefeated, untied, number-one-ranked Longhorns against Broyles's number-two-ranked but equally unmarred Razorbacks. With the 1969 crown of major college football at stake, half a continent clamored for tickets to what Royal deftly tagged "the Big Shoot-out."

Only 44,000 of the swarm of ticket seekers gained admittance to the game, packing Razorback Stadium beyond its capacity and doing their best to ignore the raw and often wet weather. The audience included evangelist Billy Graham, United States Senator William Fulbright, an assortment of congressmen,

governors, show biz people, and sports figures, and on the 50-yard line, the President of the United States himself, Richard Nixon. He was there, the White House had announced, to award a special presidential plaque to the winners, proclaiming them national college football champions. The jubilant centennial celebration planners, basking in their prediction-come-true, only feared that the game itself could not live up to its billing. But it did.

With less than four minutes to play and favored Texas finally in front by a point, the game already qualified as a classic. A poll by ABC-TV Sports would later certify it as "the best game of the sixties." Arkansas had jumped in front early with a short scoring drive following a fumble recovery. Then in the third quarter, after losing a touchdown because of a penalty, the Razorbacks had moved ahead by two touchdowns. Passer Bill Montgomery and prime

receiver Chuck Dicus pierced the Texas secondary, and the quick, well-schooled, fired-up Razorbacks' defense consistently thwarted Texas's famed wishbone T. Texas finally scored early in the fourth quarter when James Street, who had not tasted defeat in his 18 games as the Longhorns' starting varsity quarterback, broke loose on a 42-yard touchdown run. As he slashed across the goal line again, on a 2-point conversion play, he left the Longhorns only a touchdown behind at 14-8.

Midway through the fourth quarter, after driving almost the length of the field on passes, Arkansas found itself on the Texas 7-yard line, ready to kick the field goal that would have clinched victory. But on third down Montgomery aimed a touchdown pass toward Dicus in the end zone, and Texas's Danny Lester intercepted. It was the first interception Montgomery had thrown since midseason.

Now, with Arkansas trailing by a point after the stunning Street-Peschel bomb and Texas's subsequent touchdown, Montgomery had to start throwing again. Quickly the Razorbacks moved upfield from their 20 to the Texas 39. As 1:38 flashed on the scoreboard clock, he needed only one more first down to maneuver Arkansas within range for expert long-range kicker Bill McClard. Montgomery looked toward Dicus but then shifted targets and threw toward end John Rees, who was open for a fleeting moment on a sideline pattern. As the pass arrived, so did Texas defensive halfback Tom Campbell, the son of the Longhorns' defensive coach. Campbell stepped in front of Rees, intercepted the throw, and tumbled out of bounds. Texas, at last, truly was number one.

"This was one of the greatest games of all time," President Nixon told the Longhorns in their dressing room. "The wire services will

name Texas the number-one team [which they did], and this is a great honor in the one hundredth year of college football. The fact that you won a tough game and the fact that you didn't lose your cool and didn't quit makes you deserving of number one."

Valiant Arkansas, conceded Royal, certainly wasn't far behind. "Arkansas is as good as we are, and I thought that most of the time today they may have been better," the Texas coach said.

Four years later, Frank Broyles still found it "the biggest game I've ever been involved in, without question. I think everyone in Texas and Arkansas still feels that way. The game and the circumstances were unique. The excitement around the game was unequaled by any game I've ever been around. It was one of those games where the fans never sat down. In my travels around the country, people still come up to me and want to discuss that game."

An Extraordinary Conference

In college football's hundredth season, the Southwest Conference enjoyed its finest hour, and its finest hour featured many of the qualities that over the years have distinguished the league. An excellent brand of football, nationally famous coaches, flaming rivalries, home-grown teams, a "one-big-family" relationship, and go-for-broke tactics—all those are typical of Southwest Conference football.

Since its birth in 1915, the conference has produced seven teams that finished first in one or more of the major polls, and sixteen others that finished in the top six. It has produced 121 All-Americans and 26 members of the National College Football Hall of Fame. The league helped to pioneer the forward pass in the twenties and thirties and spawned the earth-scorching wishbone attack in the sixties. It is the only league that has a major bowl of its own, the Cotton Bowl, where the Southwest Conference champ is required by league statute to play on New Year's Day. It has boasted some of the most heated rivalries, producing some of the nation's most memorable games.

What makes the SWC most special, however, is its home-grown flavor. Most major conferences sprawl over five or six states. The Southwest Conference, apart from charter member

Opposite top: *Don Hutson beats his man by yards.*
Opposite: *John Kimbrough besieged.*
Above: *Texas A&M stops Fordham's Eshmont.*

*Behind fine blocking, Bobby Layne, heads for a
score against Oklahoma. Joe Mitchell,
at left, plays with only one hand.*

Arkansas, is strictly Texan: Texas, Texas A & M, Texas Tech, Rice, Baylor, Southern Methodist (SMU), Texas Christian (TCU), and member-elect Houston. The rosters of teams in other conferences are crowded with out-of-state players. Southwest Conference teams have traditionally used native sons: Sammy Baugh, Davey O'Brien, Doak Walker, Bobby Layne, John Kimbrough, Jack Pardee, Don Meredith, Donny Anderson, Lawrence Elkins, Clyde Scott, Billy Moore, and the league's first black All-American, Jerry Levias.

After Texas end Hook McCullough, a Missouri native, made the all-SWC team in 1920, the league did not have another all-conference player who was not a Texas or Arkansas product until Kansas-reared Billy Dewell, also an end, made all conference at SMU in 1938. After Dewell, no import made the league's all-star team until still another end, Tennesseean J. D. Ison, starred at Baylor in 1949. Of the conference's many All-Americans, all were home grown until Arkansas's Lance Alworth, who was recruited from the neighboring state of Mississippi, made the All-American team in 1961.

The foremost heroes of that '69 Texas-Arkansas classic—Street, Peschel, Lester, Campbell, and Koy for Texas; Montgomery, Dicus, Rees, linebacker Cliff Powell, and tailback Bill Burnett for Arkansas—were all products of the Texas and Arkansas high school football programs. Indeed, except for Bertelsen, a Wisconsin native, most of the key figures that day came from the sprawling Texas school athletic system, which has long been recognized as one of the nation's largest and best. When the 1973-74 school year began, the Texas interscholastic league system included 999 teams that competed in 11-man football and vied for the state championships in five classifications (Class B through Class AAAA). The teams begin their seasons as early as September and finish as late as December. Texas schoolboys often begin formal football competition before they are teen-agers, and more of their heroes wear cleats and pads than chaps and spurs. Basketball coaches in Texas bemoan a situation in which "there are only two sports in Texas—football and spring football practice."

The products of these extensive programs are high school football players prized from border to border. Understandably, they become the object of a great manhunt. A 1973 NCAA survey showed that Texas had produced more consensus All-Americans in the last 25 years than any state—46 compared to runner-up California's 36, Ohio's 35, and Pennsylvania's 31.

Those Texans have come from throughout the state, from such hamlets as Magnolia (population 800), home of Rice All-American Buddy Dial, and Iraan (population 996), home of Texas All-American Bud McFadin, to the metropolitan centers, which produced such talents as Doak Walker, Bobby Layne, Tommy Nobis, and Bill Glass. Each year college football recruiters besiege Texas high schools. They come from the Southwest Conference, from the non-SWC schools in Texas, and from major schools in the Big Eight, the Southeastern Conference, the Western Athletic Conference, and even the Big Ten and Pacific Eight Conferences.

Some of the schoolboy prizes get away each year, especially to Oklahoma. Since World War II, Oklahoma has produced one powerhouse after another, many if not most of them with football talent originally trained in Texas. Other prize players choose non-SWC schools in Texas. For instance, one of college football's all-time greats, Clyde ("Bulldog") Turner, was a West Texas schoolboy who made headlines at Hardin-Simmons. Such schools as Texas Western (now Texas at El Paso), West Texas State, Texas A & I, and North Texas State have produced a number of truly formidable talents—North Texas State's Mean Joe Greene, Abner Haynes, and Ray Renfro, for example.

But most Texas schoolboys graduate to the Southwest Conference and play against other former Texas schoolboy stars whom they have been reading and hearing about for several years. Such a closed system makes for great competition both on the field and in the living rooms where the prize schoolboy prospects are wooed and won.

"We have a most unusual conference," sums up Broyles. "It's unusual in that we're all so close together both in geography and in the players we try to recruit; we're all thrown together all the time. It's a unique situation—when one

school goes up, several others go down. It works like balance scales. When one school—let's say Baylor—signs an outstanding boy, it detracts from the other seven members of the conference who were all after the same boy. So you can go from first to last in the Southwest Conference in a hurry. Now that's not the usual situation elsewhere. In the Big Eight, for instance, Oklahoma and Nebraska aren't necessarily going after the same boys. Oklahoma can have a great year recruiting, and it won't necessarily affect what Colorado or Missouri or Nebraska do. They can have great years at the same time. But when someone in the Southwest Conference has a great year, it's often at the expense of the other members.

"Another thing: with the conference so localized, our alumni are thrown together all the time. And you always want to beat your friends more than strangers because you have to live with your friends. You have to listen to them kid you and needle you after their school has beaten yours. So all that adds to the rivalry and competition. It just makes the Southwest Conference a unique situation."

The Evolution of the SWC

On May 6, 1914, representatives of seven institutions met in Dallas for the purpose of founding an organization that would "enlarge and more closely relate the athletic activities of the larger institutions of the states represented." A second meeting was held in December of that year, and from that meeting came the organization that would become known as the Southwest Athletic Conference. There were eight charter members: Texas, Arkansas, Baylor, Texas A & M, Oklahoma, Oklahoma A & M (later State) Southwestern of Texas, and Rice. Southwestern withdrew after two seasons, Oklahoma after five, Oklahoma A & M after eleven. Rice competed the first year, withdrew for two years, and then returned. Phillips entered in 1921, then withdrew shortly thereafter, but SMU entered in 1918 and became a permanent member. TCU became a member in 1923.

After Oklahoma State withdrew in 1925, the conference became a seven-member league and remained so for 30 years, starting a highly satisfactory round-robin schedule in 1934. Texas. Tech finally won admission in the mid-fifties after a long and bitter struggle in which droves of legislators, lobbyists, and wealthy West Texans began boycotting Dallas department stores. They concentrated on Dallas because it harbored both the headquarters of the league and SMU, the school that had long opposed SWC expansion. When Dallas merchants got the message, so did SMU. In 1956, Tech joined the conference and began formal football competition in 1960. Houston, a mushrooming school that plays its home games in the glamorous Astrodome, campaigned for admission almost as long as Tech but less heatedly, and the Cougars finally gained acceptance in May, 1971 (to begin conference gridiron play five years later) after Texas decided to sponsor their bid.

Adding Houston to the football lineup in 1976 will make the SWC a nine-member league for the first time in its history and will mark the beginning of what many predict will be a new era. Already a highly successful independent with a tradition of top-heavy scores (example: the 1968 Cougars 100, Tulsa 6) and some outstanding players (Elmo Wright, Warren McVea, Robert Newhouse, Riley Odoms), Houston appears likely to compete strongly for the championship from the start, much as Michigan State did when finally admitted to Big Ten competition in the early fifties.

The first SWC era ran from 1915 to the late twenties or early thirties and featured some fine teams, some torrid title fights, and some outstanding players, but for the nation at large, most of the decade and a half unfolded in relative obscurity. It wasn't until 1929 that Southwest Conference players (Arkansas end Wear Schoonover and SMU tackle Marion Hammon) won All-American recognition. Not until 1930 did one of the league's representatives, Baylor's Barton ("Botchey") Koch win consensus All-American honors. And not before 1934 did the league gain a broad measure of national prestige—most of it, oddly enough, from a single afternoon's work. On October 6, 1934, Rice traveled to Lafayette, Indiana, and upset Purdue 14-0. On the same Saturday in South Bend, Texas upset Notre Dame 7-6. Three weeks later, SMU, which in 1928 had played a powerful Army team to a

virtual draw before losing 14-13, visited New York and beat Fordham 25-14 in the Polo Grounds.

For the first time, the opinion-makers' eyes turned toward Southwest football. They saw wide-open, razzle-dazzle, unpredictable football and were impressed. The Southwest Conference had come of age nationally, and a new era had begun.

It was a 20-year golden era. It featured the league's first national champions (SMU in 1935, TCU in 1938, and Texas A & M in 1939) and its first great nationally publicized showdowns, starting with a battle of the unbeatens, SMU and TCU in 1935 with the Rose Bowl invitation at stake. The era included the league's first Heisman Trophy winner, Davey O'Brien of TCU in 1938; such thunderous runners as the legendary fullback, John Kimbrough; such pinpoint passers as Baugh, O'Brien, Layne, Billy Patterson, and Dwight Sloan; and finally the Golden Boy himself, the fabulous three-time All-American, Doak Walker. The flock of folk heroes of the era was tutored by coaches who would themselves become household words among football fans—such Hall of Fame coaches as Dana Bible, Ray Morrison, Matty Bell, Dutch Meyer, Homer Norton, Francis Schmidt, Jess Neely, and Morley Jennings.

Actually, Bible, Morrison, and Schmidt had already established their reputations by the time the league blossomed into a national power. Morrison won three titles at SMU, witnessed the mid-thirties bloom, and then moved to Vanderbilt. Schmidt laid the foundation at Arkansas and moved to TCU, where he won that school's first conference title in 1929 and then won another in '32 before leaving for Ohio State. Bible arrived before the golden thirties and lasted far beyond them, although he did interrupt his Southwest Conference career for eight years at Nebraska. He won big at Texas A & M in the league's early era, returned to revive Texas in the thirties, and stayed with the Longhorns as a pivotal figure, either as head coach or athletic director, through the mid-fifties, when the league's latest era began. That was the age of the Young Turks, led by Darrell Royal and Frank Broyles.

Starting in 1959, two years after Bible helped

172

select Royal for Texas and a year after Broyles began at Arkansas, one or the other finished at the SWC summit every season but two. SMU's Hayden Fry captured the crown after a dizzy series of improbable comebacks in 1966, and Texas A & M's Gene Stallings won the following year after another run of miracle finishes. The Royal-Broyles domination was new for the league. It once had prided itself on the fact that its champions simply didn't repeat. From the SWC's first conference champion, Oklahoma in 1915, to TCU's national champions of 1938, not a single winner managed to repeat the following season. Texas A & M broke the pattern by winning in 1939, sharing the title in '40, and then taking another undisputed crown in '41. Texas captured back-to-back titles during the war years of 1942 and '43. And SMU repeated as champion with the legendary Walker in 1947-48. But for the most part, the first four decades of Southwest Conference football were marked by different champions every year. Through the thirties and forties, every member of the seven-team league except enigmatic Baylor won at least one title.

Early Champs: the Aggies and the Longhorns

Baylor won a share of the title in 1915, the very first year of championship competition in the newly formed league, but had to forfeit its victories because it had used an ineligible player. No official SWC champion was recognized in 1916. Thus, when Texas A & M won in 1917 and again in 1919, it became the league's first uncontested champion, followed by Texas in 1920. It was appropriate that these two ancient enemies were the first champs, for it had been largely because of them that the league had been formed in the first place. When they had met on neutral ground in Houston in 1911, violence had erupted between their partisans while Texas was scoring a 6-0 upset victory. Officials of the two state schools promptly severed athletic relations, a ban that would last for three years. The two arch-rivals resumed their football warfare on November 19, 1915, in a game that rates special mention for several reasons: It was the first time the two teams met on A & M's field; the Aggies defeated the heavily favored Longhorns, although they made only three first downs; A & M's Rip Collins

173

exhibited some of the greatest punting in the 58-year history of the conference, averaging 44.6 yards on 23 punts; and the final score—A & M 13, Texas 0—led directly to the naming of the Texas mascot.

That christening occurred a year and a half later. By then some of the Texas grads had purchased a uniquely colored longhorn steer (the legend persists that he was orange and white, the official Texas colors) and made him the school's mascot. The next March, following Texas's revenge victory over the Aggies in Austin—a 21-7 conquest on Thanksgiving Day—Texas enthusiasts planned a big gathering at which to brand the longhorn with the "21-7" score. When some A & M students heard of those plans, they went to Austin, slipped into the animal's barn, and branded him with the "13-0" reminder of A & M's victory in 1915. When the longhorn's chagrined chaperones discovered what had happened, they converted the "13" into a "B", made an "E" out of the dash, and inserted a "V" before the zero. That's how Bevo got his name.

Of greater, if not more lasting significance were A & M's accomplishments in 1917. The Aggies hired a new coach, Dana X. Bible, who promptly produced a championship team that won eight games, lost none, scored 270 points, and allowed not a single point to be scored against it. When Bible and most of that 1917 Aggies team returned from World War I (in which Bible served as a pursuit pilot), they improved their record in the 1919 season. The 1919 team was 10-0, scored 275 points, and again allowed none.

Led by three-time all-conference fullback Jack Mahan, the 1920 Aggies were about to achieve still another perfect season when misfortune struck in the same form it would strike so many Aggies teams over the years. Undefeated and unscored on in 27 games since 1917, A & M fell victim to a fired-up underdog Texas team at Austin. Texas won 7-3, scoring the only points that the Aggies surrendered in three years.

Bible avenged the defeat two years later in Austin, but by then the tradition had been established that any A & M team is ill-fated on Texas's home turf. After Bible's 1922 team won in Austin 14-7, the Aggies were not to triumph

there again until 1956, during Paul ("Bear") Bryant's brief but colorful reign at College Station. Nor have the Aggies won at Texas's field since '56.

The Longhorns victory over the previously unblemished Aggies in 1920 was the league's first big showdown. It attracted 20,000 fans, the largest crowd that had ever seen a college game in Texas.

Texas won with a pass on fourth and 7 at A & M's 11-yard line with time growing short and the Aggies leading 3-0. Coach Barry Whitaker ordered a razzle-dazzle reverse on which the ball found its way into the hands of little-known sophomore Bill Barry. Barry ran a few steps, stopped, turned around, and threw to star tackle Tom Dennis, who had become an eligible pass receiver on the play. Dennis made a lunging catch at the 4-yard line, and the Longhorns scored one play later for their first conference title.

That pass was the first of many improbable last-minute feats that would characterize SWC games. The Southwest Conference didn't invent the forward pass, but it played a pioneer role in proving that the forward pass could be one of football's most devastating weapons. Starting in 1923 when Ray Morrison first launched his Flying Circus at SMU, the SWC wrote a record of aerial proficiency unsurpassed in college football history.

Before Morrison's first bombs began falling, Bible led Texas A & M to another conference crown in 1921, and then on the second day of 1922, his team won what might be termed the first bowl game ever played in the Southwest. As they won, the Aggies established a proud tradition that remains undiminished today, the tradition of the Aggies' "twelfth man."

Played in Dallas and billed as the Dixie Classic, the game matched the champion Aggies, distinct underdogs that day, against heralded Centre College of Kentucky, one of college football's powers, especially after its defeat of mighty Harvard. From the start the Aggies, led by Puny Wilson, carried the battle to the Bo McMillin-led Centre team and won a shocking 22-14 upset. Late in the game, as injuries began to take their toll, Bible found himself alone on the bench; all his able-bodied players were in the game. He recalled that King Gill, a sophomore whom he had released from the team several days earlier to start basketball practice, was working as a spotter in the press box. Bible rushed word to Gill to suit up and hurry to the bench. Gill did, and although he wasn't needed that day, the Aggies never forgot. Since that game a half century ago, the entire Texas A & M corps has stood throughout each football game, ready if needed.

Baylor's Early (and Only) Titles

Baylor won championships twice in the early years, in 1922 and again in '24 under the direction of the inimitable Frank Bridges, one of the most original and inventive football coaches who ever lived. Mixing such outstanding talents as high-scoring Wesley Bradshaw (119 points in 1922, fourth-highest total in league history) and three-time all-SWC tackle Sam Coates with hidden-ball tricks, eight-man offensive lines, tackle-arounds, and sideline kickoffs, the Harvard-trained Bridges drove his SWC contemporaries and the rules makers wild.

Bridges left Baylor after the 1925 season following a dispute with the president of the school, and though no one realized it at the time, the Bears had begun a championship famine that would last at least through 1972. They have had fine coaches since 1925, including Morley Jennings, George Sauer, Bob Woodruff, and John Bridgers. Nine of their players have been chosen All-Americans, starting with the unforgettable Barton Koch and extending through Larry Isbell, Bill Glass, Don Trull, Jim Ray Smith, and their one-man gang on defense in 1972, Roger Goree. Sixty-seven of their players have made the consensus all-league team. The Bears have won great victories, enjoyed lofty national rankings, and scored astonishing upsets, such as their victory over number two-ranked Tennessee in the 1957 Sugar Bowl game. At one time Baylor had more graduates in pro football than any other SWC school. Seven times they have finished second in the conference race, and seven times they have won bowl invitations. But after 48 years, they are still trying to win another conference championship.

The Flying Circus

After Baylor's first championship in 1922, SMU's Morrison introduced the league to quarterback Logan Stollenwerck and then to Gerald Mann.

Before those two gunners had ceased firing, to such receivers as Jimmy Stewart and Gene Bedford, they had transformed Morrison's clownish aerial circus into deadly serious legitimate theater. Starting in 1923, Morrison won two titles (1923 and 1926) in the next five years, finished second twice, and lost a total of two conference games.

"Ray Morrison is deserving of credit for giving the Southwest Conference its reputation as a passing league, although even before World War I, Pete Edmond and Clyde Littlefield had been a fine passing combination at Texas," says one of Morrison's protégés, TCU's famed Dutch Meyer. "Morrison was an innovator. The first time I ever saw a trap play, one of his teams used it."

Matty Bell, who succeeded Morrison at SMU in 1935 after coaching stints at TCU and Texas A & M, remembers the problems he had when he sent his Frogs or Aggies against Morrison's passing Mustangs. "I don't know that it ever got to the point when I told my defensive secondary to play the pass first and then the run," says Bell, "but you were always conscious of what SMU could do. . . . At SMU in 1934 and 1935, it was a way of life to throw the ball."

A High School Sub

While SMU in the mid-twenties was perfecting its passing attack, D. X. Bible was beginning his second era at A & M. "In my own mind, I always divide the A & M period of my coaching career into the 1917-21 period and then from 1925-27, when Joel Hunt came into prominence," says Bible.

Hunt had been a substitute at Waco High under the legendary Paul Tyson, the most famous high school coach in the state in his day. Tyson won four state titles during one 6-year span at Waco High. His 1927 team was 14-0, averaged 56 points per game, surrendered an average of 2.4 points, overwhelmed a Houston opponent 124-0 in the state play-offs, and climaxed its season by crushing Latin Cathedral of Cleveland 44-12 for the unofficial national schoolboy title. A confidant of such immortals as Pop Warner and Knute Rockne, Tyson once worked under Rockne at Notre Dame. Tyson and such high school coaching wizards as Blair Cherry, who won three straight state titles at Amarillo in the thirties, helped to make Texas

schoolboy football an ever-expanding assembly line of great college prospects. Although only a substitute for Tyson, Joel Hunt was one such prospect.

Hunt came to A & M on his own, unwanted and unrecruited. Recruiting, notes Bible, was much different in those days. "When you started fall practice, you literally met your football squad. Many of them were boys you had never seen before. One thing we had at A & M that other schools did not have was a truly strong program of intramural football. Athletics and the military were the two great things at A & M in that period, and we picked up some good football players off the company teams there. And the military influence made it quite easy to have discipline as far as varsity and freshman football were concerned. One reason recruiting was on such a low key then, of course, was that a head coach had little help. He had a line coach and a freshmen coach. That was about it."

One of Bible's mainstay linemen on the A & M 1923-25 teams was Barlow ("Bones") Irvin, who later became a fine high school coach and then athletic director of A & M. "I think Mr. Bible undoubtedly is right in his recollection that A & M did almost no recruiting while he was there," says Irvin. "In my case, and probably in the case of a number of others who came in during the fall of 1922, A & M's victory over Centre was a glamour factor that made a lot of boys decide to go there. At one time we had fifteen or sixteen players who had captained their high school teams. I think Joel Hunt may have been somewhat typical of the type player we had. He had been an understudy to the famous Boody Johnson when both played for Paul Tyson at Waco High, and he really didn't do much at A & M until about midseason of his sophomore year. Then A & M's starting tailback got hurt, early in the Baylor game at Waco as I recall, and Hunt came off the bench and scored two touchdowns. He was an outstanding player from then on. He wasn't especially fast, but he had an uncanny ability to follow his blockers. You could hear him talking to them sometimes when he was running down the field. And he had the knack of being able to change directions at full speed."

Hunt was 5 feet 10 inches, 158 pounds, and all-conference as a sophomore in 1925, 160

176

Clockwise from top: *Dana X. Bible; Lawrence Elkins; Doak Walker; Bobby Layne; James ("Froggie") Williams. Opposite: Walker in action against Texas Tech.*

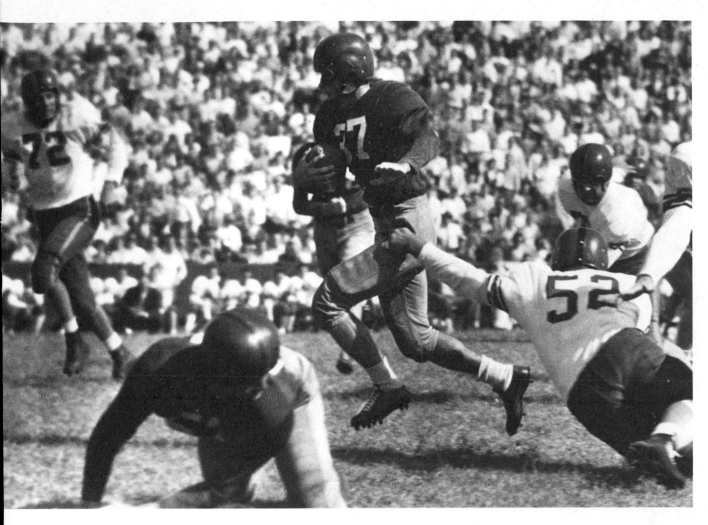

pounds and all-conference as a junior in 1926, and 162 pounds and all-conference for a third straight year in 1927. Gerald Mann at SMU was all-conference both in '26 and '27, and for three years the SMU-A & M, Mann-Hunt duels overshadowed all other league showdowns. Hunt, Bible, and the Aggies won in 1925, 7-0, as Hunt threw for the game's only touchdown. Mann, Morrison, and SMU got revenge in 1926, 9-7, as the Mustangs' ace threw for one touchdown and kicked the game-winning field goal. In the 1927 rubber game between the rivals, Joel Hunt staged an extravaganza. He scored three touchdowns, threw for a fourth, intercepted no less than four of Mann's passes, and averaged over 40 yards on his punts. The Aggies won 39-13.

"A & M stopped Mann almost cold and went on to an unbeaten season," recalls Irvin. "I think that game showed how sound Mr. Bible's football philosophy was. He was as devoted

a student of the game as anyone I've ever known."

Joel Hunt's performance in that big showdown was the stuff of which All-American honors are won. And his nationwide scoring record that year—128 points, which still stands as the all-time SWC record—also was classically All-American. But the nation did not recognize the Texan's talents until postseason play in the East-West Shrine game in San Francisco, when Hunt and Mann teamed in the same backfield for the West. Hunt and Mann played superbly in that game, each scoring a touchdown in the West's 16-6 victory. Later, the experts hailed them as two "lost All-Americans."

Two Receivers

Another star of that Shrine game was TCU's fabulous end, Raymond ("Rags") Matthews. A quarter of a century later Jack McDonald wrote in the *San Francisco Call Bulletin*, "Matthews played the most devastating game we've ever

Above: *Rice's Tobin Rote breaks up TCU pass play.*
Opposite top: *John Kimbrough, A&M fullback.*
Opposite bottom: *Weldon Humble, Rice Hall of Famer.*

witnessed . . . never before or since has a wingman so dominated the play. If we were choosing sides and I had first choice of any athlete who ever appeared in the series, Matthews would be my first choice."

The immortal Rags was only 6 feet and 176 pounds, but to Dutch Meyer, a freshman coach at TCU at the time, "Rags Matthews was, bar none, the greatest competitor I ever saw. . . ."

As Matthews finished his career at TCU, another remarkable end began his at Arkansas. His name was Wear Schoonover, 6 feet 3 inches, 190 pounds. By 1929, the conference had won enough of a national reputation so that there was no overlooking him, although to be sure, it would have been difficult to overlook him in any era. In 1929, he played every minute of every game. Against Baylor he caught thirteen passes; against A & M he intercepted five. He caught seven touchdown passes that season and kicked several game-winning extra points. His performance convinced the famed Grantland Rice to name him to his first All-American team.

Horned Frogs and Stampeding Longhorns

If Texas A & M of 1927 was the conference's strongest team of the twenties, TCU's first championship team, in 1929, was probably runner-up. By then the colorful Francis Schmidt had shifted his coaching operations from Arkansas to Fort Worth, succeeding Matty Bell, who in turn succeeded D. X. Bible at A & M. Bible had gone north to the midlands to rebuild Nebraska's fortunes. Schmidt produced a winner for the Horned Frogs his very first year, thanks to a rawhide-tough line led by Mike Brumbelow and Noble Adkins, a blazing speedster named Cy Leland, and another Texas passing wizard, Howard Grubbs. Grubbs was only 5 feet 11 inches, 165 pounds, but he could magically execute the big play. He became athletic director at TCU in the mid-thirties and in 1950 became executive secretary of the Southwest Conference. When he retired in 1973 after serving 23 years in that capacity and establishing himself in the first rank of conference commissioners in all college athletics, the league honored him as "Mr. Southwest Conference."

After upsetting A & M's previously unscored-on Aggies in 1920 for their first conference title, the

Texas Longhorns failed to reach the winner's circle until 1928, when sophomore Dexter Shelley starred in their backfield. Clyde Littlefield, an earlier football and track hero at Texas, had moved in as head coach by then. Two years later he hit the jackpot for the Longhorns again, this time with Shelley as a senior and two marvelous sophomore backs named Harrison Stafford and Ernie Koy. All three made the all-conference team in 1930. In 1932, following SMU's championship season in 1931, when Ray Morrison produced still another star passer in Weldon Mason, the Longhorns rose again, but they didn't win.

Instead, Schmidt's TCU team triumphed, proving that it is better to have a great line than a great backfield. TCU had no less than six linemen who won all-SWC honors: end Madison Pruitt, tackles Foster Howell and Ben Boswell, guards Lon Evans and Johnny Vaught, and center J. W. Townsend. Vaught also made the All-American team and years later became the winningest coach in Ole Miss history.

"TCU had a great football team in 1932, and that was one of the great lines in conference history—big, strong, and agile," notes Dutch Meyer. "That team was 10-0-1, and it never got as much as a nibble from the Rose Bowl."

At Fort Worth, in the celebrated Texas-TCU showdown, Texas tried to exploit the talents of its three all-conference backs—Stafford, Koy, and flashy John Hilliard—against that rugged TCU line. The Frogs prevailed 14-0 despite a block so crushing that it has become as famous as the game's final result. Stafford, 6 feet 1 inch, 185 pounds, caught Vaught, 6 feet, 185 pounds, with an open-field block that knocked Stafford dizzy and Vaught cold. Forty years later, when SWC old-timers speak of "that block," no one asks which one they mean.

Stafford still ranks as one of the league's all-time greats. One of the conference's pioneers, Joe Utay of A & M, calls him "the fiercest football player I ever saw." Says Littlefield, "There's no doubt in my mind that I've never seen a player with the all-around ability that Stafford had. There's never been a man who could block, run, catch passes, and play defense like Harrison Stafford." Says Weldon Hart, a student of Texas football for 40 years, "Today's athletes are so superior that there was only one prewar [World War II] star at Texas who could be a star today. That's Harrison Stafford. In fact, Stafford could play defensive back or tight end or running back and be greater today than he was then."

Intersectional Triumphs: the New Era

The big breakthrough came in 1934, the same year that four new head coaches entered the league. Dutch Meyer succeeded Schmidt at TCU, Jimmy Kitts replaced Jack Meagher at Rice, Jack Chevigny supplanted Littlefield at Texas, and Homer Norton succeeded Matty Bell at A & M. Rice was to win the title that '34 season—its first conference crown in SWC history—with two of the finest backs ever to play in the same conference backfield: John McCauley and Bill Wallace. Led by those two, the Owls also staged the conference's greatest coup.

In early October, Rice traveled to Purdue and upset the Boilermakers 14-0. Purdue had lost only four games in four seasons and had scored in 49 straight games. Rice scored when McCauley went 43 yards with a pass from Wallace, and later when Red Bale, who is now the Rice athletic director, jarred the Purdue passer loose from the ball in the end zone and Owls end Frank Steen recovered.

Texas's 7-6 victory that afternoon in South Bend over Notre Dame was even more dramatic. A famous Notre Dame product himself, Texas coach Jack Chevigny was for the first time opposing his alma mater, which was directed that day by one of the famous Four Horsemen, Elmer Layden. Not having lost an opener in 40 years, Notre Dame was not expected to lose this one.

Chevigny's pregame dressing room speech would have done credit to Rockne. "We thought at the time that was the greatest speech we had ever heard. We were a bunch of demons when we went out to play Notre Dame," recalls J. Neils Thompson, a reserve end that afternoon who today is one of the more prominent voices in NCAA affairs. Texas struck quickly. End Jack Gray recovered Notre Dame's fumble on the opening kickoff on the Irish 18. John Hilliard scored four plays later from the 8-yard line and then kicked the extra point, the point that made the difference at the finish. Across the nation the headlines belonged to the Southwest Conference that day. SMU completed the SWC's triumph a couple of weeks later by trouncing a fine Fordham team 26-14.

Texas and Rice had their own showdown for the title in late October. The Owls won 20-9 when Harry Fouke, today the University of Houston's athletic director, intercepted a pass late in the game and returned it for the decisive touchdown. "Much has been written of Rice's win over Purdue and Texas's win over Notre Dame the same day and of the prestige it gave the Southwest Conference," Fouke notes. "As players, we were very conscious of the impact. But we were also aware, after hearing of Texas's win, of what a tremendous game was in prospect when we played Texas. And it was. It was also the game in which the first radio play-by-play of a Southwest Conference game was made. The strange thing about it was that the team didn't even know about it. Otherwise it might have had the same impact on us that playing on national television has now for players.

"Jimmy Kitts was a great innovator. Other practices in other years had run from three to three-and-a-half hours, but he rarely kept us on the field for more than two hours. He stressed the mental rather than the physical approach, and our workouts had a lot of zest to them. Things were different in another respect, too. There wasn't anything of what they call bowl fever now. The Rose Bowl was about the only bowl we knew anything about then, and I don't recall any of our players even thinking about it during the 1934 season. The big reason was probably because Rice had never won a conference football championship and that was the only thing we thought about."

SMU versus TCU

Wallace, McCauley, and two-year all-conference end Leche Sylvester, were back at Rice in 1935, but TCU and SMU were the biggest powers in the conference that year. SMU boasted broken-field wizard Bobby Wilson, a 5-foot 10-inch, 150-pound explosive. The Mustangs also had all-league fullback Harry Shuford, a pair of all-conference tackles, Truman Spain and Maurice Orr, and a new head coach, the well-traveled Matty Bell, who had already coached two other conference teams. Bell had moved to SMU as Ray Morrison's assistant after being fired at A & M in 1934. When Morrison moved to Vanderbilt, Bell won promotion at SMU.

"Our team had improved tremendously in 1934 over what it had been in '33," recalls Matty. "Morrison had always wanted to coach at Vanderbilt, and when he got the chance, he left. He never said a word that I can recall about the 1935 team's potential. I knew we had a good ball club coming up, but I never expected it to do as well as it did."

SMU started by blanking four of its first five opponents, including defending champion Rice 10-0. Then it shut out Texas, UCLA, and Baylor, and beat Arkansas 17-6. In late November the Mustangs were undefeated and untied. They had scored 244 points, had permitted only three touchdowns, and were generously contributing to the wildest football hysteria the state had ever known as they challenged TCU for the conference crown.

That was Dutch Meyer's second TCU team, with end Walter Roach, guard Tracy Kellow, center Darrell Lester, and halfback Jimmy Lawrence. Best of all it had 6-foot 2-inch, 175-pound passing-punting genius Samuel Adrian Baugh. Thirty-nine years later, in the centennial year of college football, the Football Writers of America would select Sammy Baugh as college football's greatest quarterback.

He had grown up in the little football-minded Texas towns of Temple and Sweetwater, but when he graduated from high school, he thought he'd rather play baseball than football. He planned to go to Texas on a baseball scholarship, in the company of a Sweetwater teammate, Red Sheridan, who was a widely coveted running back. Legend has it that Baugh enrolled at Texas, stayed a few days, and then got a longing to combine his baseball with football. His thoughts turned toward TCU.

"I was baseball coach at TCU then [in the summer of 1933], and we went to Abilene to play an exhibition game," says Dutch Meyer. "Baugh was playing for the Abilene team and was outstanding. We had no baseball scholarships then, but someone told me Baugh was a good football player. When I got back to Fort Worth, I asked Schmidt to give him a football

scholarship. He mumbled something about, 'I'll think about it.' The next day I went back and then the next and the next. Finally, to get rid of me I think, he told me to write Baugh and tell him he had a scholarship.

"When Baugh reported to my freshman football practice in the fall of 1933, I really had no idea where I would use him. He had been, of all things, a blocking back in high school at Sweetwater. Once I saw Baugh throw the football, though, there was no doubt in my mind where he belonged. He was as good as any human I ever saw throw the ball. From the time he played his first freshman football game, he absolutely stood them on their ears.

"He was a man who could take mediocre personnel further than anybody I ever knew. He was a great kicker—I think his punting actually was as good as his passing. In 1935, against Santa Clara, one of the best teams on the Pacific Coast, he kicked six balls out of bounds inside their ten-yard line. Against SMU, he had to punt three straight times on one down because of penalties. He kicked all three punts out of bounds inside their ten. In one of the great plays in our Sugar Bowl game against LSU, played in heavy rain on a sloppy field and with a heavy ball, Sam one time kicked fifty-five yards out of bounds from the end zone."

Later Slingin' Sam would set an NFL season punting record that still stands. But his passing was most magnificent. J.T. King, today the athletic director at Texas Tech, played against Baugh as a 160-pound guard for Texas. He remembers how quickly Baugh could release the ball.

"They were just passing us to death," King recalls about one Texas game against TCU. "We were running up and down the field, and then they'd get it and go about sixty yards in three plays. I was playing defensive guard, and one time I jumped over and shot a gap, and nobody touched me. I really clobbered ol' Sam. I put my shoulder into him and drove him to the ground. I heard the crowd cheering, and I thought, 'They're really cheering ol' Jake for putting this guy on the ground this time.'

"About that time, Sam patted me on the back and said, 'Jake, we're fixin' to run down there now and kick the extra point.' He had had the

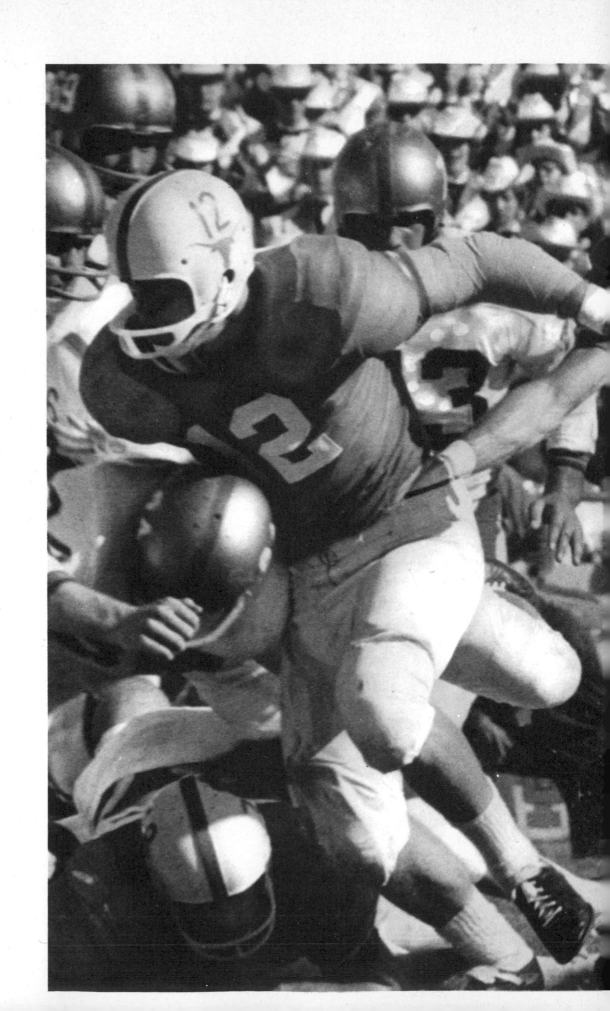

ball when I hit him, and he had thrown it on his way to the ground. It went about sixty yards in the air for a touchdown."

With Baugh passing as no one before him ever had, the '35 Frogs dispatched their opponents as decisively as their SMU contemporaries were trouncing theirs. Boasting perfect records, the Frogs and Mustangs met on November 30 to decide a conference crown, a national title, and a coveted Rose Bowl bid. It would be the first invitation to the Rose Bowl for a team west of the Mississippi.

Plans were quickly made to broadcast the game on nationwide radio. The showdown at TCU's stadium commanded the presence of the nation's sportswriting elite, including Grantland Rice, and such famous coaches as Bernie Bierman of Minnesota, Pappy Waldorf of Northwestern, and D. X. Bible of Nebraska. "There was nothing like it in our league until the '69 Texas-Arkansas game," says Wilbur Evans, now a veteran Southwest Conference and Cotton Bowl executive who was then a rising young sportswriter in Texas.

Grantland Rice described the struggle as "one of the greatest games ever played in the 60-year history of the nation's finest college sport. In the most desperate game this season has known from coast to coast, Southern Methodist beat Texas Christian [20-14] and thereby carved a clear-cut highway right into the middle of the Rose Bowl. . . ." According to Rice, the game was "a swirl of action that no other section of the country could approach . . . the climax game of 1935."

Two aspects of that showdown are remembered better than any others: all the passes that TCU's receivers dropped and one fourth-quarter pass that SMU's Bobby Wilson caught. Dutch Meyer still blames himself for the dropped passes. Just before he sent his team out for the opening kickoff, he gave them a raging fight talk. "It was the most grievous mistake I ever made in coaching," he says today. "I can't remember exactly what I said, but I told them this was the most important game of their lives. It was the greatest loss of my career to this day. I shouldn't have made a speech."

Sam Baugh agrees. "You don't need anybody to get you up for a game like that," says Sam,

James Saxton (10) of Texas follows Mike Cotton (12) into the line.

who today is a Texas rancher at Rotan. "Dutch's talk got everybody tight as ticks, and we dropped some passes."

The Frogs dropped nine. They were "so nervous they couldn't get their hands relaxed, and this was the greatest bunch of receivers I ever had—Walter Roach, Will Walls, Jimmy Lawrence, my nephew Little Dutch. He was the only one who caught 'em," says Meyer.

While the Frogs fretted and dropped passes, the Mustangs performed coolly. "When I was at A & M, we played Tulane's 1933 Rose Bowl team," explains Matty, "and I never forgot the ice-water poise they had, the unexcited way they went about their business. I told myself then that if I ever had a great team I'd keep them in the same frame of mind." So Matty discarded ringing pregame speeches and instructed his team to *walk* onto the field.

Mainly because SMU was without its all-league fullback, signal-calling Harry Shuford, it had been rated a slight underdog. To take Shuford's place, Bell turned to junior Bob Finley, who like Wilson was a product of the bustling little central Texas town of Corsicana. All week after practice, Finley recalls, "Matty kept drilling me on the idea that it was easier for us to score from the forty than it was from the ten."

For a while it appeared that the Mustangs could score from anywhere. They quickly jumped to a 14-0 lead on 73-yard and 74-yard scoring drives. But Baugh revived the Frogs in the second quarter with a 50-yard punt that went out of bounds on SMU's 4-yard line. TCU regained possession following the Mustangs' short punt and quickly scored. At half time, with the score 14-7, Bell decided the time had come to say a few words after all. "My high school coach had a favorite pregame statement," says Matty, "and I always remembered it. That was the only thing I said to the squad before the second half: 'Men, you've got thirty minutes to play and a lifetime to think about.' "

With about 10 minutes left in the game, the score tied 14-14, and the Frogs no longer dropping Baugh's passes, the Mustangs were stalled at the TCU 37, on fourth and 4. Substitute J. R. ("Jackrabbit") Smith, who also had been trained as a signal-caller, ordered a bit of fakery: "Ends down and out, fake punt, and pass to Wilson." Finley was the passer as well as the punter. He swung his leg in the fake punt, then dropped back 8 more yards and threw.

"When they lined up to kick," remembers Matty, "I thought to myself, 'I hope old Bob kicks it out on the one.' His pass was thrown so high and long it looked like a dying dove hanging up there. Wilson fielded it like an outfielder."

"The pass was thrown to the wrong side of Wilson," notes Dutch Meyer. "He had to twist in midair to catch it over his right shoulder. It took a great athlete to make that play, but of course Wilson was a great athlete. He just fell into the end zone for the touchdown."

The Frogs never recovered. "Lots of people have changed things around, so they think the touchdown pass was thrown with three or four minutes left in the game," says Finley. "But it came three or four minutes deep in the fourth quarter, and TCU still had plenty of chances to tie or win it. As a matter of fact, coach Bell substituted Shelley Burt for me in the last few minutes, and Baugh threw a long pass almost to the end zone that Burt barely knocked down at the last second. I never had a touchdown pass thrown over me in my college career, but I'm not sure, as tired as I was, that I could have broken up that one if I had still been in there.

"A lot of things have been said and written about that pass to Wilson. I never saw the catch because they buried me, but I was told Wilson jumped up between two men about the one-yard line and caught the ball. I could throw a ball around fifty yards, and I wound up and threw it as high and as far as I could, so I don't imagine it was what you'd call a picture pass. Matty says he almost passed out when he saw it. One of the ends said he was wide open about ten yards downfield, and he probably wouldn't have spoken to me again if Bobby hadn't caught the ball."

After the game, Sam Baugh approached Finley, put his arm around his shoulder, and said, "By George, Bob, you put it on us. You're real champions."

Inevitably perhaps, the sequel to the big game was anticlimactic. SMU went to the Rose Bowl and lost to Stanford 7-0, and TCU went to the Sugar Bowl and beat LSU 3-2. "If anyone is to be blamed for our Rose Bowl defeat it would be

John Crow of Texas A & M can't shed Buddy Dial of Rice. Both men had fine pro careers, Crow with St. Louis and Dial with Pittsburgh.

Clockwise from top: Super linebacker Tommy Nobis
(60) leads charge against SMU; Donny Anderson
makes one-handed grab; Jerry Rhome grimly fires away.

me," says Bell. "We went to the Coast to have fun, and we didn't really push the players hard. Stanford had a senior team that had lost the 1934 and 1935 Rose Bowl games and was determined to go out with a win. Still, we had our chances, fumbling on the four-yard line on a first-down play. I still take pride in the fact that we had Stanford superbly defensed. I had had a man scouting them from midseason on."

The Cotton Bowl

Baugh graduated after the 1936 season, the year Arkansas won its first official title. (The Razorbacks had forfeited one in '33 for having used an ineligible player.) Jack Robbins and Dwight Sloan, two splendid passers, led the Razorbacks to the title, with considerable assistance from a superlative end, Jim Benton. Although TCU had a poorer record against conference opponents than did the Razorbacks, and therefore finished second, the Frogs had tied Arkansas 7-7 and had a better overall season record. So when an East Texas oil man, J. Curtis Sanford, and some of his friends decided that the time had come to stage a postseason game in the Southwest, they invited TCU and Slingin' Sam to come over to Dallas on January 1 and be the host team in what Sanford called the "Cotton Bowl." They invited Marquette, with a 7-1 season record and a fine passer of its own, Buzz Buivid, to be the guest team. TCU won that first Cotton Bowl game 16-6.

In October, 1940, the Bowl became the first major bowl to come under the direct and exclusive control of an athletic conference, the SWC. In May, 1942, the league's governing committee decreed that its champion could not play in any other postseason game if it declined the host role in the Cotton Bowl. Since then the Dallas New Year's Day football game has grown into an extravaganza. The 1971 Cotton Bowl game, which featured a rematch between Notre Dame and number-one-ranked, defending national champion Texas drew the largest television audience in the history of college football. (Notre Dame won 24-11, snapping Texas's 30-game winning streak.) The first game between the two teams, the 1970 Cotton Bowl game, won by Texas 21-17, drew the second largest television audience ever to see a college game. From 1970-73, the Cotton Bowl's television rating stood number one among all the bowls.

A Second Sammy Baugh

Baylor had one of its near misses in 1937. Led by their great aerial battery, Billy Patterson and Sam Boyd, the Bears were undefeated and ranked fourth in the nation after six games. Rose Bowl talk abounded in Waco. Then in its first year under the new coach it had just lured from Nebraska, the widely respected D. X. Bible, Texas shocked the Bears 9-6. Baylor promptly went to pieces, and Rice put all its pieces together for a second title for Jimmy Kitts. In the Cotton Bowl, Rice beat a Colorado team that boasted a legend of its own, Byron ("Whizzer") White.

Then all eyes in the Southwest Conference turned toward Dutch Meyer, little Davey O'Brien, and those fast-firing Frogs of '38. "That [1935] SMU game," says Dutch Meyer, "made me a Presbyterian. I thought right then that it was repayment to Matty for the humiliation he suffered in 1933 when Texas A & M let him go while there were still two games on the schedule. Also, the mistake I made before the game helped me in 1938 when we went to play A & M. I kept the boys calm and we won with ease."

With the exception of the 21-14 victory over Arkansas in their second game of the season, the '38 Frogs beat everyone easily until they encountered Carnegie Tech in the Sugar Bowl. That 1938 TCU team stands as the masterpiece of Meyer's 18-year career as a head coach. Undefeated, untied, and never behind in a game until they met Carnegie Tech, the Frogs were armed with a great line, anchored by two All-Americans: tackle I. B. Hale and center Ki Aldrich. The Frogs' offense was led by the fabulous mighty mite, Davey O'Brien, who stood 5 feet 7 inches, weighed 150 pounds, and could pass like—well, almost like Sam Baugh. "A man who gets two kids like that in a row is lucky as heck," says Meyer.

Responding to the new frenzy of enthusiasm that was gripping college football from coast to coast, the Associated Press in 1936 had inaugurated its weekly poll of the best college teams. After ranking the top ten through the season, it then climaxed the polling of sportswriters across the land by naming a national champion. Minnesota won in 1936, Pittsburgh in 1937. Then it was time for TCU.

"Baugh might have been a better all-around player than Davey O'Brien and a better passer," Meyer says, "but as a field general, O'Brien has never been equaled. He was the finest play selector I have ever seen. And as for Ki Aldrich, he was the best man I've ever seen at sizing up plays. He was out of this world, a football bird dog who played a ferocious game."

With O'Brien and Aldrich in command, the Frogs ripped off 10 straight wins, came from behind to beat Carnegie Tech in the Sugar Bowl 15-7, and won Associated Press recognition as 1938's national champion. O'Brien, who between the '37 and '38 seasons had mastered the long pass, threw 19 touchdown passes and became the first player in SWC history to win the Heisman Trophy. After Davey produced 377 yards in total offense against Carnegie Tech's highly rated team, the losers said, "We don't feel a bit disgraced, losing to a great little guy like that."

"Jarrin' Jawn"

What O'Brien and the Frogs achieved through the air in 1938, Homer Norton's Texas A & M team and its powerful fullback, John Kimbrough, accomplished on the ground in '39. For the second straight season, the Southwest Conference produced college football's national champion, and for the second straight season, that champion took its perfect record to the Sugar Bowl, where it disposed of a strong challenger (fifth-ranked Tulane this time, 14-13). With Hale, Aldrich, and O'Brien, the '38 Frogs had had three All-Americans. The '39 Aggies settled for two: Kimbrough and tackle Joe Boyd. Both were as rugged on defense as on offense. That Aggies' team permitted only 18 points while scoring 198, and even today SWC old-timers debate the question as to which was best: SMU in '35, TCU in '38, or A & M in '39. "I don't think it would be fair to make comparisons involving those three, although A & M probably was the strongest physically," offers Matty Bell.

The strongest Aggie of them all surely was the immortal Kimbrough. He was 6 feet 3 inches, 220 pounds, and could run the hundred in 10 flat. "He could run the ends as well as he could crash through the line," the late Norton used to marvel. "He had more straight ahead power than anyone I ever saw."

Norton had failed to recruit Kimbrough when Jarrin' Jawn was a schoolboy in the little West Texas town of Haskell. Kimbrough said he wanted to go to Tulane and become a doctor, like his brothers. He did go to Tulane but stayed on campus only two weeks before writing Norton, "Dear Coach: You were right. I'm unhappy here, and I plan to change schools. Would you still have me at Texas A & M?" Norton's reply was brief: "Dear John," he wrote, "Enclosed please find one (1) railroad ticket...."

Midway in 1938, his sophomore season, Kimbrough came off the bench and sparked the Aggies to a 6-6 tie with favored Baylor. By the next week he was already the league's irresistible force. Against Arkansas that day, A & M guard Bill Minnock first expressed the sentiment that was to be applied at one time or another to every great fullback since Kimbrough. Lining up opposite a Razorbacks defender, Minnock told him, "Big Jawn's fixin' to come through here, and I don't know what you're going to do, but I'm gettin' the hell out of the way."

The Austin Jinx

An All-American in 1939 and about to become one again in 1940 as the Aggies fielded what they considered an even better team than their '39 version, Kimbrough planned to finish his college career in the Rose Bowl. Texas A & M had won 19 games in a row and was again ranked number one nationally. The Aggies needed only one more victory, over D. X. Bible's Texas team in Austin, for an invitation to Pasadena. Of course, that assignment should have given them pause because no A & M team since 1922 had defeated the Longhorns in Austin. Even in 1938, when the Longhorns won only once and A & M was on the verge of beginning its 19-game winning streak, Texas took a 7-6 decision from the Aggies. Also, by 1940, Bible's program at Texas was beginning to produce results. The Longhorns had won only twice in D. X.'s first year back in the SWC, 1937, only once in '38, and they had finished in the cellar four straight years, but by midseason of '39, some of their splendid sophomores—end Malcolm Kutner, guard Chal Daniel, wingback

Noble Doss, fullback Pete Layden, and tailback Jack Crain—had begun to mature. They first erupted in the final 30 seconds against Arkansas when the nimble Crain ran 67 yards for a touchdown. Bible later labeled that game the turning point.

"That play and that victory changed our outlook—mine, the players', the student body's, and the alumni's," he said. "Things had been going pretty badly up until that game. The way back was still long, but we had the fruits of victory, and we were on our way."

Texas had won seven games and lost two when Thanksgiving Day, 1940, and the number-one ranked, favored Aggies arrived. Bible knew his team had a chance. To mentally invigorate his players, he passed out copies of Edgar Guest's poem, "It Can Be Done," just before game time and then read the lines aloud:

Somebody said that it couldn't be done
but he with a chuckle replied
That maybe it couldn't but he would be one
Who wouldn't say so till he'd tried.

Then Bible's Longhorns did to the Aggies what the 1920 Texas team had done to Bible's unbeaten, untied, unscored-on Aggies, and with the same weapon—a forward pass.

On the first play, Layden threw a 32-yard pass to Crain. Two plays later Doss made a remarkable over-the-head catch at the Aggies' 1-yard line. Layden squirmed the remaining yard, Crain kicked the extra point, and the 'Horns spent the rest of the afternoon holding off Kimbrough and his surprised teammates.

"We had one foot in the Rose Bowl and the other one in Memorial Stadium, and Texas cut one of them off," Norton lamented after the Aggies and their coach had drowned their grief with tears in the dressing room. Texas used only 13 men in scoring the upset. Those are still known in the Longhorns' ranks as "the immortal 13."

Instead of going to Pasadena and the Rose Bowl, Kimbrough and the Aggies went to Dallas and the Cotton Bowl, and there they beat Jim Crowley's Fordham team 13-12. The Texas defeat cost the Aggies a clear-cut claim on the SWC title, forcing them to share first place with SMU. (In the final AP national ranking they finished sixth.) It was the first time since the

Texas's Ernie Koy keeps his balance for a few extra yards. Koy followed his father and preceded his brother in playing for Texas.

birth of the conference in 1915 that a team had managed even a share of the title after winning it the previous year. Norton's Aggies then won the crown outright in 1941 and went to the Cotton Bowl for a second straight year (where they lost to Alabama 29-21). But as it had the previous year, Texas once again overshadowed the Aggies' run to the title.

A Dream Season Destroyed

Although it was a while before many people noticed, Bible's arrival at Texas had signaled a big change in one aspect of SWC football recruiting. "When coach Bible returned in 1937 to coach at Texas, it went on a highly specialized basis, with the areas of the state being divided up so the talent could be assessed and contacted," remembers Bones Irvin. "Mr. Bible put organization into recruiting, and it wasn't long before the other schools went into it with the same intensity as Texas."

Adds J. T. King, "Mr. Bible just put a lot more emphasis on recruiting than the other schools had been putting on it. And from a practice standpoint, the big change he brought to Texas was a stress on team play, particularly on offensive and defensive timing."

189

Texas steadily increased its manpower, and once trained, the young Longhorns showed their power when they upset the 1940 Aggies. That delicious Thanksgiving Day victory served as a springboard for '41. For six straight games, the Longhorns, featuring the lethal broken-field runs of Jack Crain, were undefeated, untied, and unchallenged (their closest games were 34-0 victories over LSU and SMU). Texas ranked number one nationally. On the cover of its November 17 edition, *Life* magazine ran the pictures of 14 of Bible's finest. Inside was an eight-page spread on Texas football, showing the Longhorns in various scenes on and off the field. Surely, the natives agreed, this was the Southwest Conference's greatest team yet.

Then Texas encountered Baylor, a team that had lost two weeks earlier to A & M 48-0 and now met the stampeding Longhorns without its finest player, halfback Jack Wilson. To be sure, Texas too suffered from injuries that day, but the Bears still seemed outclassed. The Bears trailed 7-0 and faced fourth and 4 (it's remarkable how often that particular situation has figured in historic SWC moments) from the Texas 18-yard line with 18 seconds left to play. Baylor's Kit Kittrell threw a touchdown pass to sophomore Bill Coleman, and the wounded Wilson hobbled onto the field to kick the point that tied the game and stunned the world of college football. Even the Longhorns' tough end coach, Blair Cherry, broke down after the game and sobbed.

Later that tie game would be voted the greatest upset in the first 40 years of SWC football. Ironically, shortly before sending his underdogs out for the opening kickoff, coach Frank Kimbrough (John's brother) had read to them the very lines that Bible had used to inspire his Longhorns before they upset the Aggies the season before—the lines from Edgar Guest's "It Can Be Done."

The tie dropped the Longhorns from number one to number two in the AP poll. Then, the next Saturday in Austin, Dutch Meyer's underdog Frogs completed the destruction of Texas's dream season. They beat the Longhorns 14-7 with a 19-yard touchdown pass—sophomore Emory Nix to halfback Van Hall—with eight seconds left to play. As Weldon Hart, the sports editor of the *Austin American-*

Statesman, wrote that day, "When the spry young blades of Texas U., current vintage, are old and gray and come back to the Forty Acres as honored guests, they will still be trying to explain the inexplicable Longhorns of 1941."

Texas regrouped after losing to TCU and defeated A & M at College Station for the first time since 1923, but the Longhorns season had been wrecked. The Aggies by then had clinched the championship. Having missed both the title and the bowl bids, the frustrated Longhorns erupted in fury against an Oregon team that had just lost to Rose Bowl bound Oregon State 12-7. On that December afternoon in Austin, the Longhorns decimated Oregon 71-7, but it was inadequate compensation for not having been invited to Pasadena.

The victory celebration was further muted less than 24 hours later when the Japanese forces attacked Pearl Harbor. Most of the Longhorns as well as other SWC gridders were soon serving in the military.

The War Years

Texas would present Bible his first championship as a Longhorns coach in '42, the 'Horns would win again in '43 and in '45, and the Frogs would win one for Dutch Meyer in '44, but in those war years, SWC football was in disarray. One team, the Baylor Bears, elected to drop the game for the duration of the war. There were, however, some fine players during that era, including an end at Texas, Hubert Bechtol, who became the SWC's first player to win All-American recognition three straight years.

Texas's championship in 1945 was D. X. Bible's third at Texas, his eighth as a Southwest Conference head coach, and the last he would ever win. His Longhorns, strongly favored the next season, ranked number one in the AP's first poll of 1946 after blitzing Missouri 42-0, Colorado 76-0, and All-American Bob Fenimore's Oklahoma A & M team 54-6. But they fell victim to Rice and then TCU and consequently finished third in the SWC race. On January 1, 1947, adhering to the plans he had announced a year earlier, Bible yielded the Texas reins to his longtime assistant, Blair Cherry. Bible's teams at Texas A & M had posted a 72-19-2 record; his Longhorns were 63-31-3, and 53-13-1 for his last seven seasons.

After favored Texas stumbled in 1946, Jess Neely's Rice squad, with guard Weldon Humble, and John Barnhill's Arkansas Razorbacks tied for the crown. Arkansas won the Cotton Bowl invitation, having beaten Rice in their showdown. That was Neely's first taste of the championship after taking over the Owls in 1940. He was to win three more before finishing 27 remarkable years as Rice's head coach in 1966.

Golden Boys

On November 3, 1945, in Dallas, Texas's Bobby Layne and SMU's Doak Walker, the players who would become the brightest stars of the league's exciting first postwar years, met in their first showdown. They had been high school teammates at Highland Park in Dallas. Layne, the older, had enrolled at Texas in 1944 and had promptly made the all-SWC team as a freshman while Walker was finishing at Highland Park, making all-state after sparking his team to the state finals. For the 1945 season, however, both were in the merchant marine until late October when, with the season half gone and World War II over at last, both received their military discharges in New Orleans.

Layne hurried back to Austin to resume his football career at Texas. Walker planned to take a short vacation in Dallas and then begin his college career, also at Texas. But it happened that SMU was playing Tulane that weekend in New Orleans, where Walker met his former high school coach, H. N. ("Rusty") Russell. By then Russell had joined Matty Bell's SMU staff. He persuaded the Doaker to ride back to Dallas on a train with the SMU team, and somewhere along the way, Walker changed his mind about going to Texas. When Layne next saw him, the next weekend, Walker was wearing the red and blue of SMU as the Mustangs warmed up before the game against the Longhorns.

"If Rusty Russell hadn't gone to SMU as an assistant coach that year, I'm convinced we'd have had Walker and Layne as teammates," Bible said later, wistfully contemplating what those two extraordinary performers might have accomplished in the same backfield. As it was, Layne and Walker achieved All-American and Hall of Fame acclaim playing on opposite sides. Before leaving the SWC and becoming teammates once more, with the Detroit Lions,

they produced two unforgettable shoot-outs. Layne and Texas won the 1945 thriller 12-7. Walker and SMU triumphed 14-13 in 1947. (Walker missed the 1946 season because of more military service.)

In the 1945 game, Walker had run 30 yards for a touchdown and kicked the extra point for SMU before Layne's 33-yard touchdown pass to Peppy Blount with three minutes remaining decided the issue. Blond Bobby was even more impressive in the Cotton Bowl game that followed the '45 season. Texas defeated Missouri and its new-fangled split-T formation 40-27 that January afternoon. Layne scored four touchdowns, kicked four extra points, and completed 11 of 12 passes for 158 yards and two more touchdowns. "I never saw a better job by anybody," said Missouri coach Chauncey Simpson as he walked to the Texas team bus after the game to shake Layne's hand.

When Walker and Layne met in their second and final duel in 1947, both SMU and Texas were undefeated. Texas, ranked number three nationally, was slightly favored over the eighth-ranked Mustangs, who had the home advantage that day. SMU scored first after Walker passed on fourth down for a key first down at the Texas 4-yard line early in the game. Texas tied it with an 11-yard plunge by fullback Tom Landry, the man who now guides the Dallas Cowboys of the NFL. Shortly before the half, Walker caught a 54-yard pass from SMU passing ace Gil Johnson that carried to the 1-yard line, and the Mustangs scored on the next play. Walker again kicked the extra point, for a 14-7 lead. In the fourth quarter, Layne threw a touchdown pass to Byron Gillory, but the extra point went wide, and that miss made the difference. SMU won the first of two consecutive conference titles, finishing the season with a 9-0-1 record and a number three ranking nationally. Texas won the remainder of its games and was ranked fifth. The Mustangs went to the Cotton Bowl and tied Penn State 13-13 while Layne ended his splendid career by hurling Texas to a 27-7 victory over Harry Gilmer and Alabama in the Sugar Bowl.

Layne had gone to Texas intending to play baseball, as Sammy Baugh had intended a decade earlier. But also like Baugh, Layne had been an outstanding high school football player,

191

and by the time the Longhorns held their first scrimmage in 1944, Layne was in pads and cleats, firing bullets to All-American Hub Bechtol. He was to make all-conference four straight years. (Only two other players in league history have ever done so—the remarkable Walker at SMU and Layne's teammate at Texas, lineman Dick Harris.) Layne also made the All-American team in 1947. "His passing form wasn't classic, and he wasn't a clever runner," Blair Cherry later admitted, "but Bobby was a winner."

Doak Walker may have said it best: "Bobby never really lost a football game. Time just ran out on him."

As for the Doaker himself, "He was the greatest player I ever coached or hope to coach," Matty Bell declares to this day. "He could have been All-America on his blocking alone. Nobody ever played football like Doak Walker." He made the All-American team in 1947, 1948, and 1949, and he won the Heisman Trophy as a junior in 1948. His boyish good looks graced the covers of a dozen magazines, including *Life*, *Look*, and *Collier's*. He was only 5 feet 11 inches, 165 pounds, and he was not especially fast, "but his presence lifted a team like no individual I have ever seen," says Frank Broyles.

Walker led a backfield of Dick McKissack, Paul Page, and a rugged sophomore named Kyle Rote. Combined with Gil Johnson's magical passing, the razzle-dazzle Ponies swept to the title again in 1948, although TCU managed to hold them to a 7-7 tie in their final game of the season. SMU beat Texas handily 21-6 as Walker triggered two touchdowns, bested A & M 20-14 as Walker ran 13 yards for the decisive points, and finally overcame Arkansas and All-American Clyde Scott 14-12 by scoring all their points in the last four minutes and their last seven after time had run out. With five seconds to play and the ball on the Arkansas 16, Gil Johnson dropped back, evaded a heavy Razorbacks rush, and fired to Paul Page as the final gun sounded. Page caught the ball at the Arkansas 2-yard line and stumbled into the end zone for the winning score, to which he added his second extra point of the game.

An Inspiring Finish

By 1949, the pattern for settling the league race appeared well established: The battle for the

championship would always include a bit of everything, but finally it would be decided by one fateful pass. Rice's All-American end, James ("Froggie") Williams, changed the pattern in 1949 when he kicked a field goal with eight seconds remaining to nudge Rice past Texas in a 17-15 thriller. Jess Neely took that '49 championship team to the Cotton Bowl and soundly defeated North Carolina and Charley ("Choo Choo") Justice 27-13.

Favored to claim their third conference crown in a row, Walker, Rote, and associates had bounced Oregon and Norm Van Brocklin 21-13 in the first game of the 1949 season. But beset by injuries, SMU dropped to a fifth-place finish in Doak Walker's farewell season. The Mustangs lost 35-26 to Baylor and the Bears' outstanding passer, Adrian Burk, although Walker caught a touchdown pass while lying on his back in the end zone.

The Mustangs of the Walker era had the stage to themselves for their final game of the '49 season, a December nonconference game against Frank Leahy's undefeated, untied, number-one-ranked Notre Dame team. Walker was too injured to play, and the Fighting Irish were a 27 1/2-point favorite, having won 37 games in a row. Just before the Mustangs went out to play, the injured Walker stood up to say a few words. "I looked forward all my life to playing against Notre Dame," he said. "I wanted to end my career in this game. I can't be on the field with you today, but you know I'll be with you. . . ." He was too choked-up to finish. Led by Kyle Rote, the inspired Mustangs rushed out and played the Irish to a near standstill. They gained a 20-20 tie on Rote's third touchdown of the game in the fourth quarter before finally bowing 27-20. SWC football writers later voted the game the Southwest's greatest in the 1945-65 span.

Matty Bell walked off the field as the Mustangs' grid boss for the last time that afternoon. "Only once in a lifetime does a coach have a boy like Walker and one like Rote. I had them both the same year, and I figured that was a good time to end it," explained Matty. "Of all the guff I ever took for losing games, it's funny that I got more praise from that Notre Dame game than for any game I ever won."

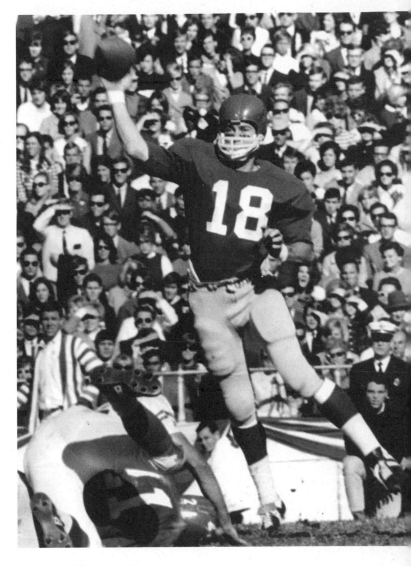

Opposite: *Wooster of Texas springs forward.* Above: *Livingston of SMU avoids sprawling tackler. After success in 1966, SMU has had problems.*

Relinquishing the National Spotlight

Edged by SMU teams for the championship in '47 and '48, Blair Cherry fielded a powerhouse at Texas in 1950. The Longhorns won the conference title and only barely missed a perfect season and a national title when they fumbled a snap on a fourth-down punting situation against Oklahoma. That miscue late in the game enabled the Sooners to beat the Longhorns 14-13 and best them for the national title (their first). Texas finished number two in the new UPI poll and number three in the AP balloting. Rote was the league's most publicized player that season, but two others also won considerable fame. Bud McFadin, 6-foot 3-inch, 240 pound Texas tackle, established himself as one of the Longhorns' all-time best and won consensus All-American honors. At A & M fullback Bob Smith, playing with a broken jaw, posted records that still stand: 1,302 net yards rushing in 10 games and a single-game total of 297 yards rushing against SMU.

Both the TCU team that won in 1951, overcoming favored Baylor, and new coach Ed Price's Texas champs in 1952 were teams that suffered solid thumpings before securing their crowns. Not until 1953, when Jess Neely produced another cochampion at Rice, did the conference have another highly rated team. The Owls won a sixth-place ranking in the final AP poll, after they had conquered the cochampion Longhorns 18-13 in October on a 31-yard touchdown pass—Leroy Fenstemaker to Dan

Opposite: *Texas coach Darrell Royal. Content at Texas,* 197
Royal turned down a million-dollar pro
offer. Above: *The Astrodome, home of the Houston Cougars.*

Hart— with 55 seconds remaining.

The Owls needed no such rescue against Alabama in the Cotton Bowl. A relatively unknown halfback, Dick Moegle, gained 265 yards, averaged 24 yards per carry, and scored on runs of 34 and 79 yards. He was loose on a 95-yarder when an Alabama player, Tommy Lewis, leaped from the bench and tackled him as he passed the 'Bama reserves. The officials promptly awarded Moegle and Rice a touchdown, and the football world was given a prime conversation topic that still has appeal.

Having tied for the title with sophomores in 1953, Texas was heavily favored in 1954. Instead, "the Little Piggies" of Arkansas's Bowden Wyatt upset the field, after which Wyatt received and accepted an invitation to return to Tennessee to coach his alma mater. He drove off in a new Cadillac that Arkansas fans had just given him, leaving them considerably upset.

The Bear Conquers Texas

While Arkansas, sparked by fullback Henry Moore and All-American guard Bud Brooks, won the title in '54, Texas A & M failed to win a single conference game. That was the first Aggies' team coached by that celebrated rebuilder of lost causes, Paul ("Bear") Bryant, who had been brought from Kentucky in early '54 to get the Aggies back on top, where they had not been since 1941. Bryant took the '54 squad to a remote little town, Junction, Texas, housed his players in old military barracks, and there, in merciless West Texas heat and dust, forged the core of a team that two years later would carry the maroon and white to an undefeated season and a number-five national ranking.

The Aggies began their renaissance in 1955 with a crunching junior, Jack Pardee, and a hard-running halfback, John David Crow. Although A & M defeated TCU that season, the Frogs and their remarkable runner, Jim Swink, prevailed as champs of the conference. Slick Jim, a native of the little East Texas town of Rusk, accumulated a record 20 touchdowns in 1955, scored 26 points and rushed for 265 yards against Texas alone, made the All-American team, and sparked TCU to the first of three titles under coach Abe Martin.

The Aggies won it all in '56, however. They disposed of TCU in a blinding rainstorm 7-6 when halfback Don Watson threw a touchdown pass to Crow late in the fourth quarter and Loyd Taylor kicked the extra point that settled the issue. Asked whether the game had gone according to plan, Bryant rumbled, "No, it went according to prayer." The next week the Aggies rallied late and beat Baylor 19-13 in what Crow later called "the meanest, bloodiest, toughest game I ever played, college or pro." Then they closed their season by doing what no A & M team had done in more than four decades: they beat the hated Longhorns in Austin. With that Thanksgiving Day victory, 34-21, A & M almost compensated for missing the Cotton Bowl trip. The Aggies were forbidden to go because they were on probation for recruiting violations—the first such punishment in league history. Instead of A & M, runner-up TCU went to Dallas and outlasted Jim Brown and Syracuse 28-27.

The Rise of the Young Turks

Bryant was holding court at A & M following an Aggies' victory one Saturday night when a sportswriter asked him to name some good young coaches in the country. Already it was obvious that some coaching changes would be forthcoming in the league either the next year or in 1958. "There are three great young ones right now," Bryant replied, and he named them. Two of them would rule the SWC within the next few years—Darrell Royal and Frank Broyles.

Following a disastrous 1-9 season in 1956, all the more bitter for that loss to the Aggies, the Longhorns turned to Royal, a former Oklahoma All-American who was then coaching at the University of Washington. Arkansas changed coaches two years later, luring Georgia Tech trained Broyles from the University of Mississippi. By then Bryant had departed from the conference, having moved to Alabama after A & M's near miss in '57. The nation's top-ranked team in mid-November of that year, the Aggies boasted a Heisman Trophy winner, the extravagantly talented Crow. But they lost by a point to Rice's Cotton Bowl bound Owls, then lost by two points to Texas and Darrell Royal in another upset, and finally lost by three points to Tennessee in the Gator Bowl. Rice's championship, engineered by quarterback King Hill, was Jess Neely's fourth and last.

TCU won the title outright in 1958 and gained a share in '59 on the muscle of Abe Martin's strong fullback, Jack Spikes, and two mighty tackles, All-Americans Don Floyd and Bob Lilly. In a preview of their coming success, Texas and Arkansas shared the title with TCU in '59, besting SMU and its talented youngster, Don Meredith.

Although no one realized it at the time, Broyles at Arkansas and Royal at Texas had arrived at the summit to stay. The dynasties they began in 1959 would stretch into the seventies, yielding outright titles to Texas in 1962, '63, '69, '70, '71, and '72, outright titles to Arkansas in '60, '64, and '65, and cochampionships to each in '61 and '68. Texas under Royal in league play alone was 80-16-1 from 1959-72; Arkansas under Broyles was 74-21-2. No other SWC school was, as Bear Bryant once put it, "even in the same orchard." Texas finished number one in the UPI (coaches') poll in '63, '69, and '70; number four in '59, '61, and '62; and number five in '64, '68, and '72. Arkansas finished number two in both '64 and '65, made the top ten in '59, '60, '61, '62, '68, and '69, and won the Grantland Rice Trophy in '64 as the top team in the opinion of the Football Writers of America. While the Longhorns and Razorbacks dominated the league over that 14-year period, only one other SWC team, SMU, with its championship in 1966, managed a final rating in the top ten. The '66 Mustangs finished number nine.

A Royal-coached Longhorns' team went to the Cotton Bowl for the first time in 1959. (Cochampions Arkansas and TCU traveled to the Gator Bowl and Bluebonnet Bowl respectively.) Texas had lost only once in 10 games, to Abe Martin's last great TCU team in an upset on a snow-laced gridiron in Austin. Then the '59 Longhorns met defeat in the Cotton Bowl at the hands of what chief defensive assistant Mike Campbell still insists was the finest one-platoon college team he ever saw—Ben Schwartzwalder's number-two-ranked Syracuse Orangemen, led by the great Ernie Davis.

The '59 upset was not the last time that Martin's Frogs would plague Royal. A four-touchdown underdog in '61, they beat the Longhorns again and cost them both uncontested possession of the SWC title and the national title.

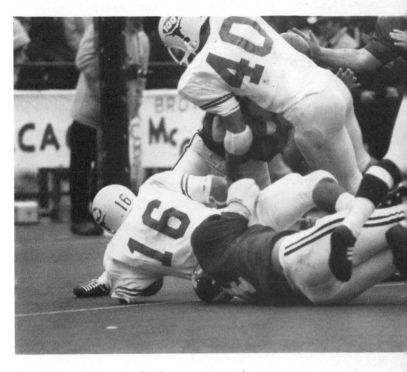

James Street (16) carries for Texas against Arkansas. The "100" on Texas's helmets signifies the hundredth anniversary of college football.

That '61 squad was probably Royal's finest of the one-platoon era, his '63 national champions notwithstanding. Texas hit the league in 1961 with a new offense, "the flip-flop," which featured the constant breakaway runs of jittery James Saxton, who averaged 7.9 yards per carry that season and won All-American honors.

The Longhorns were rolling along unchallenged (their closest game had been their 28-3 opening game victory over California) with a solid number-one position in both polls when TCU's four-times beaten Frogs came to town. With Saxton injured the Frogs repeatedly thwarted the Longhorns' scoring threats and finally triumphed 6-0. They scored with an aerial thunderbolt—some backfield trickery followed by a 50-yard touchdown pass from tall Sonny Gibbs to end Buddy Iles. A summer later, well after Texas had defeated favored Mississippi in the Cotton Bowl 12-7, Royal still grieved over that loss to TCU. When he saw a magazine picture of the fatal Gibbs-to-Iles play, he blurted out, "There's that damn pass."

Texas had deprived Arkansas of an outright title in 1959 with a 13-12 victory in Little Rock.

Arkansas responded by upsetting the 'Horns 24-23 in Austin in 1960 while winning for Frank Broyles his first championship. In 1962, the two teams had another memorable meeting in Austin. Arkansas led until the final 36 seconds, when Texas completed a 20-play, 85-yard drive and won the game 7-3.

The next year Texas won its first national title with a team that survived a number of close calls. Outland Award winner Scott Appleton, a big tackle, and All-American tailback Tommy Ford were the leading men for Royal's cast in '63, but it was quarterback Duke Carlisle who made the season's single biggest play. In early November Baylor came to Austin unbeaten in league play, largely thanks to a scorching aerial battery—All-Americans Don Trull and Lawrence Elkins. Texas finally won the showdown 7-0 after Carlisle trotted onto the field as a special pass defender and one play later picked off what looked like a sure Trull-to-Elkins touchdown pass with 29 seconds remaining in the game. After that shaky triumph, the Longhorns used their own aerial fireworks to fuel a dramatic fourth-quarter comeback and nipped upset-minded Texas A & M 15-13 at College Station. On New Year's Day Texas blitzed Roger Staubach and number two-ranked Navy 28-6 in the Cotton Bowl. The Longhorns' knockout plays against Navy: 58- and 63-yard touchdown passes from Carlisle to wingback Phil Harris. "When you pass, three things can happen, and two of them are bad," Royal had said, but he proved he would pass as quickly as the next coach, given the need and opportunity.

Preludes

The '64 Longhorns had bounded to the top in the national polls with a 15-game winning streak when the Razorbacks appeared in Austin in mid-October to avenge their last-minute defeat of two years before. With one of the league's all-time greats, redheaded linebacker Tommy Nobis, who logged 24 tackles against Army and 25 the next week against Oklahoma, the Texas defense appeared to be even better than the year before. But the underdog Razorbacks, undefeated and rebounding strongly after their down year in 1963, stunned Texas when Kenny Hatfield returned a punt 81 yards for a touchdown. After Texas had tied the score at 7-7,

Arkansas surged ahead again in the fourth quarter when quarterback Fred Marshall threw a 34-yard touchdown pass to end Bobby Crockett. Trailing by seven points, the Longhorns launched a final, fateful fourth-quarter drive from their 30-yard line, resurrecting memories of the 1962 game as they ground out the yardage.

With 87 seconds remaining, big halfback Ernie Koy (an older brother of Ted Koy, one of the Texas heroes of the '69 classic) supplied the 2-yard scoring plunge that made it 14-13. Royal quickly decided to shoot the works on the conversion, but quarterback Marv Kristynik, "Marvelous Marv" rushed his flare pass to halfback Hix Green, and it never had a chance. Thus the Texas winning streak died and the Longhorns fell from their perch atop the ratings.

The most prominent chronicler of the Razorbacks, Orville Henry, sports editor of the *Arkansas Gazette* in Little Rock, told of a peculiar postscript to the big game. "After I finished my story that night, I went back to my motel room, and my wife and a few of our friends were sitting around still talking about the game. In their hands all of them were clutching tufts of grass. They had gone down to the field after the game, gotten down on their knees, and plucked a handful of grass down near the goal line, at the same spots where Danny Brabham had fumbled and Tommy Ford had scored [the key plays in Texas's 1962 victory] and where the ball had fallen behind Hix Green [on the unsuccessful conversion attempt in '64]." The Arkansas-Texas rivalry reduces reasonable people to bizarre cultists.

The Razorbacks used their momentum to sweep through the remainder of their schedule. Then they overcame Nebraska in the Cotton Bowl 10-7. Texas righted itself after the numbing setback, won the remainder of its games, and went to the Orange Bowl, where the Nobis-led defense thwarted Joe Namath and top-ranked Alabama 21-17. When Texas knocked off Alabama on New Year's Day, Arkansas became number one, at least in the minds of the football writers who awarded the Grantland Rice Trophy.

When the Razorbacks and Longhorns tangled in 1965, Texas was again rated number one nationally, and Arkansas, victorious in its last 16

Left: *Terry Champagne mans the line for TCU against Ohio State.* Above: *Baylor's All-American defensive end, Roger Goree, ready to charge.*

Above: Aggies fullback Alvin Bowers on the run
with SMU's Ed Johnson (66) in close pursuit.
Opposite: Quarterback Allan Lowrey of 1971 Longhorns.

Left: *Longhorn Randy Braband (63) forces Alvin Maxson of SMU to fumble.* **Above:** *Music, Texas-style. Drum was used in halftime show at 1974 Superbowl.*

Doug McCutchen carries for Texas Tech.

games, ranked number three. They staged what might be called a prelude to 1969's big shoot-out, but in '65, the Razorbacks completed the key pass—Jon Brittenum to Bobby Crockett for 14 yards to the Texas 1-yard line with less than two minutes to play—and won the game 27-24. "I would have to think it was the greatest game in the history of football. There'll never be another one like it," bubbled Frank Broyles afterward, unable to imagine what the future held in store four years hence.

While Arkansas completed another undefeated season, after its memorable midseason conquest of Texas, two non-Razorbacks made headlines by signing with the pros for huge bonuses. Texas's Nobis, for two years an All-American, and winner of both the Outland and Maxwell awards, signed the second richest pro bonus contract in the history of the NFL: unofficially, $700,000. And another two-time All-American, Texas Tech's Donny Anderson, the Red Raiders' most brilliant star since their entrance into the SWC in 1960, signed with Vince Lombardi and Green Bay for $711,000. Seven and eleven—the figure had a nice ring to it, Donny thought.

Last-Minute Heroics

Still armed with mighty tackle Loyd Phillips, who also would win the Outland Trophy, Arkansas seemed likely to repeat in '66. Instead, Baylor and Texas Tech upset the Razorbacks, and SMU, propelled by a genuine miracle-maker named Jerry Levias, capitalized on Arkansas's misfortune. Hayden Fry's Mustangs conquered Rice with 9 seconds remaining, overcame Texas with 15 seconds left, and edged Baylor with 18 seconds to go. "Our team just wouldn't give up," explained Fry. Only a sophomore, Levias gained an average of 17 yards for every time he touched the football. "I can't really say anything about Jerry that isn't unbelievable—because that's what he is," Fry said of the SWC's first black football star.

If SMU's string of success in '66 was improbable, A & M's run to the Cotton Bowl the following year was even more remarkable. The Aggies lost their first four games, including their opener to SMU when Levias caught a touchdown pass with four seconds remaining. ("Levias is the greatest big play man that's been in the

conference for years and years, maybe since Doak Walker," suggested Tech's J. T. King at the time.) Coach Gene Stallings's Aggies trailed Texas Tech in Lubbock as time ran out. But the final play, which officially began with three seconds remaining, did not end until quarterback Ed Hargett had scrambled 15 yards for the touchdown that lifted the Aggies to a 28-24 victory and started them on the road to the Cotton Bowl. To get there they also overcame Texas, for the first time since Royal had become the Longhorns' coach. They did it with a fourth-quarter pass, from Hargett to Bob Long for 80 yards. In the Cotton Bowl on January 1, 1968, A & M defeated Alabama 20-16, a victory for coach Stallings over his old mentor, Bear Bryant, after which Bryant hoisted Stallings to his shoulders and carried him off the field.

New Formation; Familiar Finishes

In 1968, the wishbone was born. Royal's explosive new offense, geared to allow the quarterback a triple option, brought the Longhorns roaring back to the top after their four-year absence. Guided by Street, Eddie Phillips, Donnie Wigginton, and Alan Lowry, in that order, and swept along by such blistering runners as Chris Gilbert (3,231 yards in three seasons), Steve Worster, Jim Bertelsen, and their 1972 sophomore sensation, Roosevelt Leaks, the Longhorns grabbed five consecutive conference titles, an unprecedented feat but not necessarily their most amazing. For instance, they fell behind Notre Dame by 10 points in the 1970 Cotton Bowl game, with their national championship on the line, and then rallied in the fourth quarter to win 21-17. The key play: Street's barely complete pass on fourth and 2 to Cotton Speyrer at the Notre Dame 2-yard line with 2:26 left to play.

Another unforgettable moment: Texas, unbeaten in 22 straight, trailed UCLA 17-13 with 20 seconds remaining. The Longhorns faced a third-and-19 situation from the UCLA 45-yard line. Coolly Eddie Phillips threw to swift Cotton Speyrer cutting across the middle. As two UCLA defenders lunged for the ball and missed, Speyrer caught it and flashed across the goal line, saving the victory string and the number-one rating with all of 12 seconds to spare. Such are the economies of football shoot-out style.

More Than Fittir

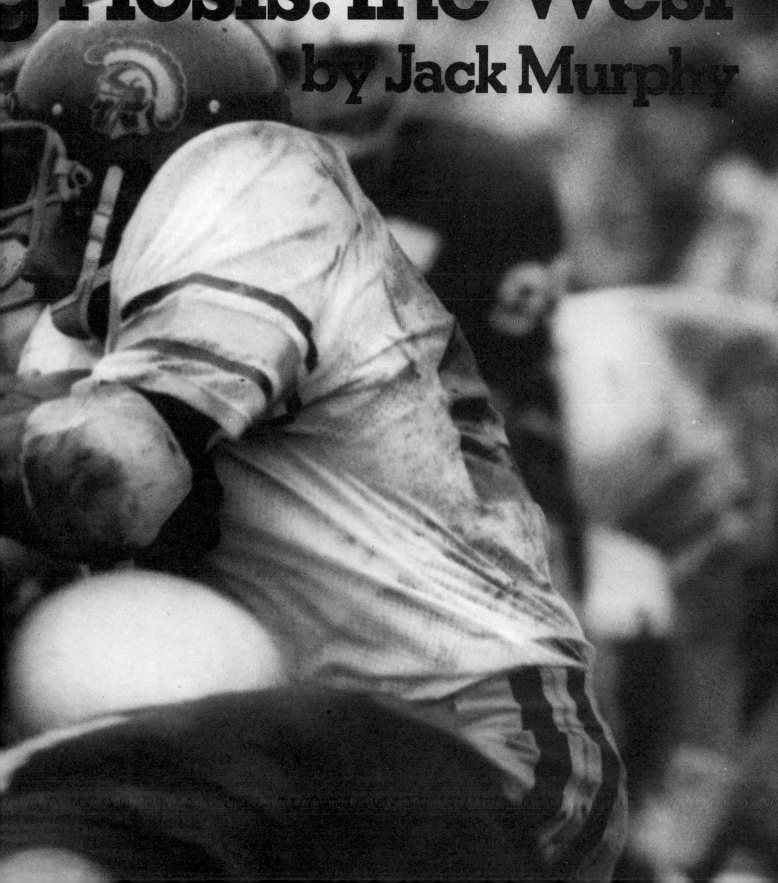

Hosts: the West
by Jack Murphy

**N**ot long after he had
established himself as
head football coach at
UCLA, the late Henry
R. Sanders decided he
had misjudged the
life-style of lotusland.
"When I came to
Southern California,"
reflected Sanders, "I expected to find the
Hollywood types sitting around a swimming pool
with a dry martini in one hand and a wet blonde
in the other." Sanders chuckled at the memory.
"Actually, that's an exaggeration. I discovered
some of these fellows don't even like martinis."

There is an exotic quality to Western living
that has been reflected in the region's collegiate
football for the past 60 years, most of all in the
high drama of the Rose Bowl. The football buff
will easily recall Roy Riegels of California
running in the wrong direction against Georgia
Tech in 1929; the theatrics of Alabama's Dixie
Howell and Don Hutson in 1935; Doyle Nave
scrambling off the bench in the waning seconds
to hurl four consecutive passes to Al Krueger as

USC defeated Duke 9-3 in 1939; more recently,
the passing skills of Stanford quarterbacks Jim
Plunkett and Don Bunce; and the acrobatic
running of such USC backs as O. J. Simpson and
Anthony Davis.

This showcase of Western football wasn't even
known as the Rose Bowl or established at its
current site in Pasadena when it began, after the
1901 season. That first game was called "the
East-West Game" and was played in
Tournament Park in Pasadena between
Michigan and Stanford. Michigan zapped
Stanford 49-0. Then the game was discontinued
until 1916.

During this fallow period, Gilmour Dobie
established a record at the University of
Washington that would prove to be as durable
as the soaring Douglas firs of the Pacific
Northwest. In his nine years in Seattle, ending in
1916, Dobie never tasted defeat. His teams won
58 games and were tied three times. Some
football historians jeer that Dobie's talent as a
schedule maker surpassed his ability as a coach;
his opponents often were high school teams and
service clubs. Yet it was no minor feat to avoid
defeat for nine years, regardless of the
opposition. His teams scored a total of 1,927
points over the nine-year span and only once
yielded as many as two touchdowns in a game.

Dobie is remembered as a perfectionist who
would compel his athletes to devote an entire
afternoon to polishing a single play. The Spartan
discipline paid off when the East-West Game
resumed in 1916, Dobie's last season at
Washington. His Huskies defeated Brown 14-0.

The Wonder Teams

The reinstated forerunner of the Rose Bowl later
featured a game that has been described as the
most important football game ever played in the
Far West. That was the East-West Game of 1921,
in which the Wonder Teams of the University of
California carved their niche in the history of
college football. In the game that created
national interest in Western football, the first of
Andy Smith's unbeaten teams blitzed Ohio State
28-0. An exceptional athlete, Harold ("Brick")
Muller accounted for the key play. After lining up
in the backfield instead of at end, his usual
position, and then taking a deep lateral from his
teammate, Pesky Sprott, Muller zipped a line

212

drive pass 53 yards to Brodie Stephens on the Ohio State goal line. The long pass deceived the Ohio State safety, Pete Stinchomb, who later ruefully admitted, "I simply didn't believe anybody could throw the ball that far."

Actually, the line of scrimmage was the Ohio State 37-yard line, so under modern rules the scoring pass would have been measured as only 37 yards. But it was a prodigious achievement in that day, and Ohio State spent a long time recovering from it. The Buckeyes didn't return to the Rose Bowl for 26 years.

Muller also made a vivid impression on Gus Henderson, then head football coach at USC. Henderson termed Muller "the best man I ever saw in a football suit."

Muller was one of the four San Diego athletes who had accompanied their high school coach, Nibs Price, to the University of California, where they formed the nucleus of the Wonder Teams. When Andy Smith hired Price as an assistant, he also netted Sprott, Stanley Barnes, and Cort Majors, as well as Muller. During the five-year era of the Wonder Teams, 1920-24, California won 44 games and was tied four times. They never knew defeat.

Old-timers say the 1920 team was the best of the five. It was composed of ends Muller and Stephens, tackles Stan Barnes and Dan McMillan, guards Cort Majors and Lee Cranner, center Fat Clark, quarterback Charlie Erb, halfbacks Crip Toomey and Pesky Sprott, and fullbacks Duke Morrison and Archie Nesbit.

The quality of the Wonder Teams was suggested by the reaction of their head coach in 1920, when he was asked to pick an all-Pacific Coast team. Andy Smith ignored the rest of the league and chose his entire varsity, a team that had scored an average of 60 points per game, a point a minute.

Games Coaches Play

In 1923, the Rose Bowl assumed its modern identity with the construction of a horseshoe facility with 57,000 seats. The structure was eventually enlarged to seat 104,594, but sometimes not even that is large enough. A record mob of 106,869 witnessed the 1973 contest between USC and Ohio State.

The fifty-ninth Rose Bowl game, in 1973, was not unlike the first game played in the arroyo

seco (dry wash) structure, in 1923. Both events were enlivened by controversy. In 1973, Ohio State coach Woody Hayes, an admirer of the late General George S. Patton, was formally charged in court with striking a *Los Angeles Times'* photographer. A half century earlier, a fistfight was barely averted between the rival coaches, Gus Henderson of USC and Hugo Bezdek of Penn State. Henderson was angry because the Penn State athletes arrived late at the stadium, 15 minutes after the scheduled 2:15 P.M. kickoff. The USC coach believed the delay was a calculated psychological ploy by Bezdek. The Penn State coach protested that his team had been a captive of traffic in the streets of Pasadena.

Joe Hendrickson, sports editor of the *Pasadena Star-News* since 1961, has extensively researched the 1923 Rose Bowl game and tells of the confrontation between Bezdek and Henderson when they met outside the Penn State dressing room.

"Where have you been?" demanded Henderson.

"We got caught in the traffic jam trying to get here," said Bezdek.

"You're a lot of bunk," said Henderson.

"Remove your glasses," challenged Bezdek.

Fortunately, bystanders intervened before he could.

Later, Henderson would tell Rube Samuelson, "I wasn't about to fight anybody, especially

Left: California's Sottari scores against UCLA. Above: Amos Alonzo Stagg, voted the best coach in the first 100 years of college football.

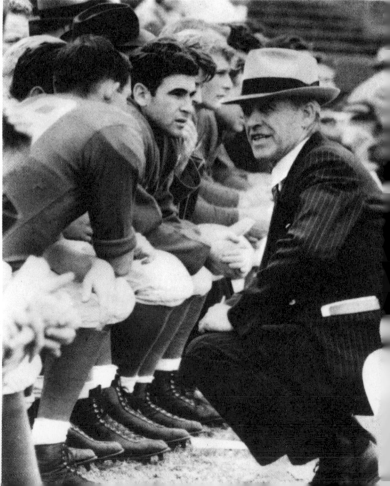

Preceding pages: *UCLA's Jackie Robinson. Clockwise from above: Buckeye Ray Hamilton reaches for a pass in 1950 Rose Bowl; coach Clark Shaughnessy; scampering Frankie Albert; Huskie Hugh McElhenny.*

Bezdek. I knew he had earned his way through the University of Chicago fighting as a pro under an assumed name."

The game finally commenced at 3:05 P.M. and concluded, according to press box poets, by "the light of the moon." USC had scored 14 points to Penn State's 3. The bitterness of the occasion was reflected by the postgame comments of the coaches. "The best team won," jeered Henderson. "Good coaching, like the effect of cigarettes, always tells in the long run. We should have won by four more touchdowns. Hugo Bezdek is no gentleman."

"The best team lost," countered Bezdek. "The best team and the best coaching in the world couldn't have won against the luck USC had today. At its best my team could beat USC by forty points."

Henderson was a bad humored Rose Bowl winner partly because California had declined an invitation to represent the West at Pasadena. The last of the Wonder Teams refused to play in the Rose Bowl a third straight season because it objected to sharing the game's proceeds with other conference schools and because many California athletes preferred to go home for the Christmas holidays.

The Wrong Way Run

Cal's next appearance, in 1929, would be remembered as long as Americans play and speak of football. That was the occasion on which Roy Riegels ran the wrong way, much to the astonishment and delight of the Georgia Tech football team.

The play began at the Georgia Tech 20-yard line early in the second period. Tech back Stumpy Thomason fumbled when he was hit by Cal's Benny Lom on a sweep. Riegels caught the ball at midfield, started for the Tech goal, then unaccountably reversed directions and streaked toward the California goal, 65 yards away. Lom set out in pursuit of his confused teammate, shouting at Riegels but unable to make himself heard above the tumult. Finally, Lom caught Riegels near the California goal line and brought him down at the 1-yard line.

On the ensuing play Lom's punt was blocked by Tech tackle Vance Maree, and the ball squirted through the end zone for a safety. That made the difference as Georgia Tech prevailed 8-7.

Howard Jones's Thundering Herd

The teams of Howard Harding Jones of USC dominated the region in the thirties. Jones took five USC football teams to the Rose Bowl and came away with a 5-0 record against such coaching notables as Jock Sutherland, Bernie Bierman, Wallace Wade, and General Bob Neyland. Jones's teams were known as "the Thundering Herd," the coach himself as "the Man." He got his sobriquet from Al Wesson, then the USC athletic publicity director and later chief publicist at the Hollywood Park race track.

"Jones was in complete command always," remembers Wesson. "He would try to delegate responsibility to his assistants, but it wasn't in him. On the practice field, he'd see something that displeased him, so he'd take charge and begin demonstrating how it should be done. He didn't care much for advice. Of the people on his staff, only Bill Hunter had his ear. Hunter was assistant football coach as well as athletic director, and he was always at Jones's side during the games."

Athletes of superior ability found their way to Jones. Through the years he was blessed by 19 All-Americans, including Ernie Pinckert, Johnny Baker, Aaron Rosenberg, Jess Hibbs, Tay Brown, Ernie Smith, Francis Tappaan, Morley Drury, Cotton Warburton, Granny Lansdell, Orville Mohler, and Russell Saunders (known as "Racehorse Russ").

Jones is remembered for his successes in the Rose Bowl and his spirited rivalry with Pop Warner of Stanford. His most celebrated victory came against Notre Dame in 1931. Notre Dame led 14-0 until early in the fourth quarter and was preparing to celebrate its twenty-seventh triumph without defeat and a national championship. Then, astonishingly, USC rallied for 16 points in the time remaining, culminated by a dramatic 23-yard field goal by guard Johnny Baker. Thus, Baker became a hero instead of a villain. Earlier, he had missed the conversion after the Trojans' first touchdown, and he was heavy with guilt until his late field goal provided redemption.

The drama touched off a celebration that lasted for days. A film of the game was rushed to Los Angeles, where it was a highly successful full length feature at Loew's State Theater. When

Jones and his athletes returned by train to Los Angeles, they were received with great pomp and ceremony and were paraded up Spring Street, through downtown Los Angeles.

"It was wild," recalls Al Wesson. "Thousands turned out to cheer along the parade route. We all wore derbies provided by Bill Hunter. The town was mad about the Trojans. The only other time I experienced such excitement was at the end of World War II."

Little Irving Warburton, known as "Cotton," held a special enchantment for fans in the early thirties. He never grew heavier than 147 pounds, but he often appeared to be the biggest man on the field. His fame began in 1931 in a storied game between USC and California. California was leading 3-0 in the fourth quarter when Warburton took the football and sprinted 59 yards down the sideline for the deciding score in USC's 6-3 triumph.

"A couple of guys thought they had him," says Wesson, "but, boom! he was gone. He was a real speed demon."

Warburton also scored two touchdowns as USC demolished Pittsburgh 35-0 in the 1933 Rose Bowl, a shattering experience for Pitt coach Jock Sutherland. Sutherland had come to Pasadena intent on revenge, for three years earlier USC had ravaged Pittsburgh 47-14. But the '33 Rose Bowl was not the occasion to redress old wrongs. The Trojans that crushed Pitt had not only won 10 consecutive games but had yielded only 13 points in the full season while scoring 201.

With the best team in its history, Colgate had hoped to be invited to the '33 Rose Bowl. Instead, Bill Hunter phoned Sutherland at Pittsburgh, and Colgate coach Andy Kerr waited for a call that never came. That inspired Kerr's classic description of his Colgate football team: "unbeaten, untied, unscored upon, and uninvited."

Jones experienced a four-year slump in the mid-thirties, then reasserted himself by leading his 1938 and 1939 teams to the Rose Bowl. In the Trojans' 7-3 triumph over Duke in the 1939 Rose Bowl contest Doyle Nave, a fourth-string tailback in Jones's single-wing formation, became an instant celebrity. The game had entered the final two minutes with Duke leading 3-0 when Nave transformed the dreary game into an event of surpassing excitement. Nave completed four consecutive passes to Al Krueger, the last for a touchdown that triggered a monumental celebration.

As Al Wesson reconstructs this episode, putting in Nave was the inspiration of Jones's aide and confidant, Bill Hunter. Seated beside Jones, Hunter said to the head coach, "Why don't you give Nave a chance? You've tried all those other guys, and we're getting nowhere."

There is another, less heroic version of how Nave came to prominence against Duke. The late Maxwell Stiles, a Los Angeles sportswriter of excellent reputation, credited the appearance of Nave to the whim of a USC assistant coach, Joe Wilensky. According to Stiles, Wilensky pretended he had received instructions from Trojans' coaches who were observing the game from the press box.

"They said to rush in Nave and Krueger," Wilensky told Jones. Before the head coach could react, Nave and Krueger were joining the Trojan huddle. Actually, Wilensky had been holding a dead phone. The coaches in the press box had left their station and were trying to reach the field.

It's a charming story either way, part of the Jones legend. Later, in the tumult of the dressing room, Wesson was approached by Nave. "Do you think I'll get a letter?" he asked.

Nave wasn't being modest. "He had played about fifteen minutes all season," recalls Wesson. "But he earned his letter with four passes. It had been a very dull game until the finish. Then it became one of the most memorable Rose Bowl games ever played."

Wesson was curious about the single-minded way in which Nave destroyed Duke. "Why did you throw to Krueger on every play?" he asked.

The answer was obvious to Nave: "When you've got the best pass catcher on the field, why bother looking elsewhere?"

Nave had an opportunity to become USC's starting tailback the following season but soon lost the job to Amby Schindler. It was Schindler, a powerful, high-stepping runner, who paced USC through another season without defeat. Then came a 14-0 conquest of Tennessee in the Rose Bowl, the last of Jones's five victories at Pasadena. The Man left his mark on the Rose

Bowl: In 1930 USC 47, Pittsburgh 14; 1932, USC 21, Tulane 12; 1933, USC 35, Pittsburgh 0; 1939, USC 7, Duke 3; 1940, USC 14, Tennessee 0.

Jones's last team, in 1940, went flat with a 3-4-2 record. The Howard Jones era of USC football began in 1925 and continued until he suddenly died of a heart attack after the 1940 season.

Pop Warner

Jones's major rival in the Far West was innovative Pop Warner of Stanford. Warner originated the double-wing formation and defeated Jones's first two USC teams in 1925 and 1926, 13-9 and 13-12. The third meeting of the masters ended in a 13-13 tie, before Jones won five straight from Warner. Jones was a colossus of Western football, but many believe Pop Warner made a more meaningful contribution to the game. Warner brought imagination and invention to his work. He devised the wingback formations and is credited with creating the reverse. He also was one of the pioneers of the forward pass. Grantland Rice has written that it would be difficult to say whether Warner or Knute Rockne had the more profound influence on college football.

Red Smith described Glenn Scobey Warner as a "gruff old gent, kind and forthright and obstinate and honest. He was one of the few truly original minds in football coaching, and that made him a big man in his world."

Warner came to Stanford in 1924 through a novel agreement that demonstrated his integrity. When approached by a Stanford emissary, Warner accepted the job at Stanford with the stipulation that he would first honor the last two years of his contract with Pittsburgh. He sent two assistants, Andy Kerr and Tiny Thornhill, to install the "Warner system" during the 1923 and 1924 seasons.

Stanford had good reason to wait for Warner. He had been a successful coach at Cornell and Carlisle (where Jim Thorpe became famous), as well as at Pittsburgh, where he had four consecutive undefeated seasons from 1915-18. At the conclusion of his career, Warner would look back on 451 collegiate football games in 44 years and an overall record of 313-106-32.

In one sense Warner was extraordinarily lucky. He coached not only Thorpe at Carlisle but Ernie Nevers at Stanford. Nevers blossomed into an all-time, All-American fullback and even now is regarded as the Stanford football player without equal. Warner termed Nevers the greatest player he ever coached, granting him an edge over Thorpe because of his industry. Thorpe, said Warner, had a tendency to coast at times. Nevers gave his greatest effort at all times. "If their skill is about the same," reasoned Pop, "I'll take the all-outer over the in-and-outer every time."

The Vow Boys . . .

Warner left Stanford after the 1932 season at age 61 to begin still another career, this time at Temple, where he was less fortunate. Indeed, his timing was wretched. Warner had become discouraged at Stanford after losing five consecutive games to USC and feared he would not have personnel to compete in the near future. Moving to Temple, however, was a bitter miscalculation. He walked away from the teams that would become known as "the Vow Boys," the athletes who vowed as freshmen they never would lose to USC, and never did. They kept their pledge without Warner, who was replaced by Tiny Thornhill.

Warner would say later that defecting to Temple was the worst mistake of his life. He should have known better than to part company with Bobby Grayson, Monk Moscrip, and Bob Reynolds, "the Horse," who would play 180 minutes in the Rose Bowl and become an All-American and all-time Stanford and Pacific Coast tackle.

In *The Color of Life Is Red*, a history of Stanford athletics, Don Liebendorfer recalls introducing Reynolds to Warner in his workshop at home. When Reynolds came into the room, says Liebendorfer, "the old man nearly fell out of his chair at the sight of that magnificent hunk of man. Never did I see Warner move any faster than when he brushed past me . . . in his haste to shake hands with Bob. He actually offered Horse his chair, which I had never seen before and never saw again."

Thornhill would become Reynolds's coach and experience the sweetness of three triumphs over USC and three Rose Bowl appearances, though Stanford lost to Columbia 7-0 in 1934 and to Alabama 29-13 in 1935 before conquering Southern Methodist 7-0 in 1936.

In three seasons, 1933-35, the Vow Boys won

twenty-five games, lost four and tied two. They played defense so well that the opposition scored only 99 points in that span of 31 games while they scored 476. They were remarkably durable; it was rare for more than 20 of the Stanfords to enter a game. During the 1934 season halfback Bones Hamilton logged 544 minutes of playing time. Bobby Grayson had five 60-minute games.

... And the Wow Boys

After the Vow Boys, came Clark Daniel Shaughnessy and the Stanford "Wow Boys" in 1940-41. With Thornhill out of favor with the alumni after a lean period, athletic director Al Masters turned to Shaughnessy. Shaughnessy gathered an exceptional staff of assistants: Marchie Schwartz, Phil Bengtson, Bernie Masterson, Jim Lawson, and Husky Hunt. He introduced the T formation to Stanford as well as a left-handed quarterback, Frankie Albert. In time Shaughnessy would be acclaimed as the inventor of the T formation, an honor he quickly disclaimed. "I appreciate the compliment," he said, "but I must admit I played the T under Doc Williams at Minnesota in 1911. I've just added a few little extras."

Shaughnessy perfected the T with such men as fullback Norm Standlee, halfback Hugh Gallarneau, tackle Bruno Banducci, and a young man from Cut Bank, Montana, Vic Lindskog, who would be remembered as one of Stanford's finest centers.

In the view of some football historians, Shaughnessy and his Wow Boys changed the course of the sport. Rube Samuelson, in his definitive history of the Rose Bowl through 1951, regards the Stanford team of 1940 as a milestone. "The 1941 Rose Bowl game revolutionized football," contends Samuelson in his book, *The Rose Bowl Game.*

As Samuelson notes, the 1941 Stanford-Nebraska Rose Bowl game created national interest in the T formation. Shaughnessy didn't create the T, but he made it fashionable. This, Samuelson believes, was football's most significant development since Knute Rockne and Gus Dorais displayed the forward pass as Notre Dame shocked Army 33-13 in 1913. As Stanford defeated Nebraska 21-13, the public was fascinated by an offense in which both the

players and the fans had difficulty locating the ball.

Before the contest, Nebraska rejoiced over the opportunity to compete at Pasadena. The Rose Bowl invitation was termed "the greatest thing that has happened to Nebraska since William Jennings Bryan ran for the presidency." The announcement touched off a 24-hour celebration, during which, it is said, Nebraska coeds were locked in their dormitories. But they quickly escaped through the windows with the help of stepladders graciously provided by their boyfriends. Ten thousand football freaks came to Pasadena with the Cornhuskers, full of hope and bottled spirits.

The Nebraska head coach, Major Biff Jones, sought to acquaint his athletes with the T formation in various ways. He seized on an opportunity to expose his squad to the T as practiced by the Chicago Bears. Jones took his athletes to a game between the Bears and the Los Angeles All-Stars that resulted in an easy victory for the Chicago professionals.

The event that followed was one of the Rose Bowl's more distinguished games. Stanford led 14-13 at half time. Then came the play that resolved the issue. Stanford's Pete Kmetovic fielded a punt at the Nebraska 39 and threaded a path to the end zone behind a wave of efficient blocking. The scoring play, wrote Rube Samuelson, was "one of the greatest in all football history."

Of Kmetovic's decisive run, Shaughnessy would say, "It was the most savage blocking I've ever seen on any gridiron, college or professional."

An Unfair Reputation

During Stanford's 20 glorious years, California sent only one team to the Rose Bowl. (The Golden Bears defeated Alabama 13-0 in the 1938 game.) Then a large, jovial man named Pappy Waldorf brought another era of prosperity to Cal. In three seasons, Waldorf's teams won 29 games and tied once, each year winning the championship of the Pacific Coast Conference and going to the Rose Bowl.

It was Waldorf's ill luck that California came away empty from Pasadena, losing to Northwestern 20-14 in 1949, to Ohio State 17-14

Clockwise from left: 1973 Rose Bowl; Oregon's
Alan Pitcaithley *fumbles*; Sonny Sixkiller.
Following pages: Trojan band; floats and displays.

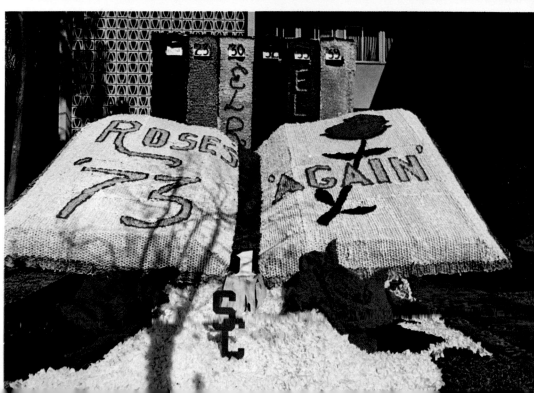

in 1950, and to Michigan 14-6 in 1951. Those defeats nourished the theory that Western college football was somehow inferior to the game played by those fellows in the Big Ten.

The idea first sprouted in 1947 when Illinois, an object of scorn to the Los Angeles press, abused UCLA 45-14 in the first Rose Bowl game after the Big Ten and the Pacific Coast Conference had formally mandated the champs of the two conferences to face each other at Pasadena each New Year's Day. The previous year, Alabama had blitzed USC 34-14 in the Rose Bowl, and the West lost too in the Sugar Bowl. Squirmin' Herman Wedemeyer ran St. Mary's into the New Orleans game, only to be overmatched against Oklahoma A & M (now Oklahoma State). St. Mary's absorbed a 33-14 drubbing. Then Michigan deflated USC 49-0 in the 1948 Rose Bowl and California lost three straight.

That losing streak was a distinction Waldorf didn't covet because, among other reasons, it left him subject to the barbs of the press. He was the first coach to lose three consecutive Rose Bowl games, and the writers freely assigned him the blame. When in '51 California submitted to a Michigan team that had been beaten by Michigan State, Army, and Illinois during the season, the critics showed their teeth. Wrote Braven Dyer in the Los Angeles Times, "Credit victory to [Charles] Ortmann [the Michigan quarterback who completed six of eight passes for 64 of the 80 yards on Michigan's winning drive]. Charge defeat to Waldorf."

Yet Waldorf had been responsible for a football renaissance at Berkeley. When he arrived from Northwestern, the Berkeley campus had a reputation as a graveyard for coaches. Pappy couldn't be buried. He developed such gifted players as Jackie Jensen, Les Richter, Johnny Olszewski, and Pete Schabarum. Richter, a linebacker, was a prodigious talent who later came to the Los Angeles Rams at the cost of 11 players; he was worth an entire team. Jensen was a superb running back, regarded by many as without peer in the history of California football. He subsequently enjoyed a fine career as an outfielder with the Boston Red Sox. The Golden Bears of California had emerged from the doldrums of World War II.

The Master and the Magician
The story of Western football is essentially the development of the sport at the major schools of the Pacific Coast Conference, now the Pacific Eight Conference. But there were periods when the independents (notably St. Mary's, Santa Clara, College of Pacific, and the University of San Francisco) competed favorably for attention.

During the 1946 season two noteworthy events occurred at College of Pacific. First, Amos Alonzo Stagg retired from active coaching. Second, Eddie LeBaron appeared, like an elf from beneath a mushroom, and with similar trickery earned a reputation as a masterful quarterback.

Stagg had been 71 when he joined College of Pacific after 41 seasons at the University of Chicago. He was 84 when College of Pacific asked him to become a consultant. Instead, he chose to remain on the field and joined his son, Amos Alonzo Stagg, Jr., at Susquehanna College in Selinsgrove, Pennsylvania. He quit, finally, in his ninetieth year. In sum Stagg was a head football coach for 57 years, including 14 at College of Pacific. His 14-year record at Pacific: 60-75-7, despite the fact that he was often overmatched in personnel by the bullies of the West.

Eddie LeBaron was only 17 in 1946 when he established himself as the Pacific quarterback. Soon he was being acclaimed as the finest T-formation quarterback in the Far West. His ball-handling finesse gave him the aura of a magician. His admirers swore he could hide an elephant in a phone booth. Pacific opponents, bewildered in their efforts to find the ball, just swore.

The South Comes West
As the Waldorf era at California ended with the 1951 Rose Bowl game, other schools became more assertive. The Chuck Taylor period (1951-57) was beginning at Stanford, and the wit and guile of Red Sanders at UCLA became better appreciated. Sanders had come to UCLA from Vanderbilt for the 1949 season. To some his credentials were suspect. Westerners doubted that a man from the Old South could be free of racial bias. Seemingly an old-fashioned sort with his single-wing offense, he impressed observers as a horse-and-buggy football man. "Maybe it's a horse-and-buggy offense," countered the

Preceding pages: *Trojan Anthony Davin a-ꞓ--ᴉᴇ·. und·
·I-ᴜᴍᴜᴉᴇ Charles Anthony stalks in USC Rose Bowl victory over Ohio State. Left: UCLA's Gary Beban.*

Left: *USC's Mike Battle makes his initial move.*
Opposite: *Southern Cal's Sam ("the Bam")*
Cunningham hurdles Ohio State's line.

new UCLA coach, "but there's a TV set in the dashboard."

Sanders proved his point when his second UCLA team shattered USC 35-0. Until Sanders arrived, college football in Los Angeles had been USC's domain. Suddenly, L.A. was a two-school city. Sanders's Bruins upheld their newly found respectability by defeating the Trojans three straight seasons, 1953-55. A popularity poll conducted by the *Los Angeles Mirror* established Sanders as the most admired man in Los Angeles. Not even Bob Hope or Walt Disney could match him.

UCLA students were so enthralled that they presented Sanders a certificate saluting him as "the finest, most beloved and respected coach in the nation." When the undergraduates appeared at Sanders's home demanding a speech from their hero, Sanders was pleased but skeptical. "Which one's got the rope?" he whispered to his wife, Anne.

During a four-year period, 1952-55, his teams lost only 3 games while winning 34. They were twice defeated in the Rose Bowl (1954 and 1956) and were ineligible to play at Pasadena after the 1955 season despite a 9-0 record.

Sanders was a relaxed, witty man who nevertheless enforced strict discipline among his athletes. No UCLA football player dared to unfasten his chin strap much less remove his helmet on the practice field or during a game.

The Bruins prospered with Paul Cameron, Donn Moomaw, Jack Ellena, Bob Davenport, Hardiman Cureton, and Ronnie Knox. They became as adored as such former Bruins' celebrities as Kenny Washington and Bob Waterfield.

Sanders termed his unbeaten team of 1954 the best he ever coached, despite its 17-14 loss to Michigan State in the 1956 Rose Bowl game, doubtless his most bitter football experience. This was the famous contest in which the Spartans' Dave Kaiser kicked a 41-yard field goal with only seven seconds to play. It was the first field goal of Kaiser's career.

The officiating may have unduly influenced the outcome. UCLA was severely punished by five penalties in the closing moments, three for coaching from the sideline, one for interfering with a punt receiver, and one for

having an ineligible pass receiver downfield.

During the same period that Sanders reigned at UCLA, Chuck Taylor was providing a lively football atmosphere at Stanford. He had Bob Mathias and Bill McColl in the 1952 Rose Bowl game, and thereafter he brought high excitement with such passers as Bobby Garrett and John Brodie. But Taylor's teams were more entertaining than successful. He resigned to become assistant athletic director after the 1957 season, providing an opportunity for Jack Curtice.

That Reputation Repudiated

There is an ebb and flow to football similar to the tide of other events. In the first 13 years of Rose Bowl jousting between Western teams and the Big Ten, the milkshake set managed only one victory, USC's 7-0 decision over Wisconsin in 1953. From 1947 through 1959 Jess Hill of USC was the only Western coach who established a respectable Rose Bowl record.

Then, in 1960, the downtrodden arose. Jim Owens and his robust charges from the University of Washington stomped Wisconsin

Top: *Jim Plunkett looks for a man.* Bottom: *UCLA coach Tommy Prothro. Prothro left his job for the pros.* Opposite: *Gary Beban of UCLA.*

44-8, then returned to Pasadena the next year to defeat Minnesota 17-7. Suddenly Western football was more fashionable. Those who believed that the game could be played only by steelworkers and coal miners began to reconsider. And today there is no longer any ground for such prejudice. In the last six Rose Bowl games through 1973, the Big Ten has had but one winner.

An Heir to Howard Jones

Western football in the sixties and early seventies focused on the skills and varying fortunes of four coaches: Jim Owens of Washington, John McKay of USC, Tommy Prothro of UCLA, and John Ralston of Stanford. Owens was the toast of the Coast when, astonishingly, Washington won the 1960 and 1961 Rose Bowl games. Prothro returned to UCLA from Oregon State (he had previously been a UCLA assistant under Red Sanders) and found success in his first season with the Bruins. Sophomore quarterback Gary Beban led them to the Rose Bowl, where they surprised Michigan State 14-12. After six splendid seasons, Prothro resigned to become head coach of the Los Angeles Rams and was succeeded by Pepper Rodgers.

Ralston attracted attention quite suddenly with the flowering of Stanford quarterbacks Jim Plunkett and Don Bunce. First in the 1971 Rose Bowl Game, Plunkett foiled Ohio State, the nation's number-one-ranked college team 27-17. Then in the '72 Rose Bowl Bunce, similarly deflated Michigan, also number one, 13-12. After that rousing encore, Ralston quit to become head coach of the Denver Broncos of the National Football League.

Of the four prominent Western coaches in the last two decades, John McKay is preeminent, the spiritual heir of Howard Jones. Beginning at USC in 1960, McKay guided three national champions (in 1962, 1967, and 1972) and led the Trojans to the Rose Bowl six times. Moreover, he became the only coach ever to field a team in four consecutive Rose Bowls, 1967-70. Fittingly, his one hundredth victory as a head coach came in the 1973 Rose Bowl game, a 42-17 rout of Ohio State, coached by Woody Hayes, who, as a student of military history, perhaps appreciated the furious precision of the Trojans' blitzkrieg.

McKay is a calm, humorous man, perhaps because he hasn't often had to cope with defeat. As a halfback at Oregon in 1948, he teamed with Norm Van Brocklin on a squad that produced a 9-1 season and a trip to the Cotton Bowl. As a coach he has continued to win with such sterling running backs as Mike Garrett and O. J. Simpson, both Heisman Trophy winners, and Anthony Davis, who in one prodigious afternoon against Notre Dame in 1972 scored six touchdowns. With the exception of Don Coryell at San Diego State, an ambitious football school with a less ambitious schedule, no coach in the West approaches the success of McKay. And not even Coryell will surpass him; he defected to the St. Louis Cardinals of the NFL.

As the years have passed, McKay has become the white-haired coach, as well as father, of J. K. McKay, a talented wide receiver. John McKay, head coach, was never concerned about losing J. K. to another school. "I had one big advantage in recruiting the boy," he says. "I've been good friends with his mother for twenty years."

McKay claims he has noticed a subtle change in the comments of fans since J. K. joined the Trojans' varsity. According to John, the fans used to yell, "McKay, you idiot!" Now, he says, they yell, "There's that idiot McKay playing his idiot son."

More Than Fitting Hosts

The current popularity of Western football is mirrored by the growth of the annual pageant of flowers and football, the Tournament of Roses parade. The idea of Dr. Charles Frederick Holder, an author who lived in Pasadena, sprouted in 1890 as a village celebration during which members of the Valley Hunt Club festooned their buggies and surreys with flowers from local gardens. As the years passed, the festivities expanded into today's famous parade on the first day of each year. The 1973 parade involved 59 floats, 22 bands, 200 equestrians, 2,500 marchers, and, via television, millions of spectators.

Western college football has expanded and improved as spectacularly as the Rose Bowl parade. After years of losing to the Big Ten, the Westerners have gloriously risen and become more than fitting hosts for their great tournament.

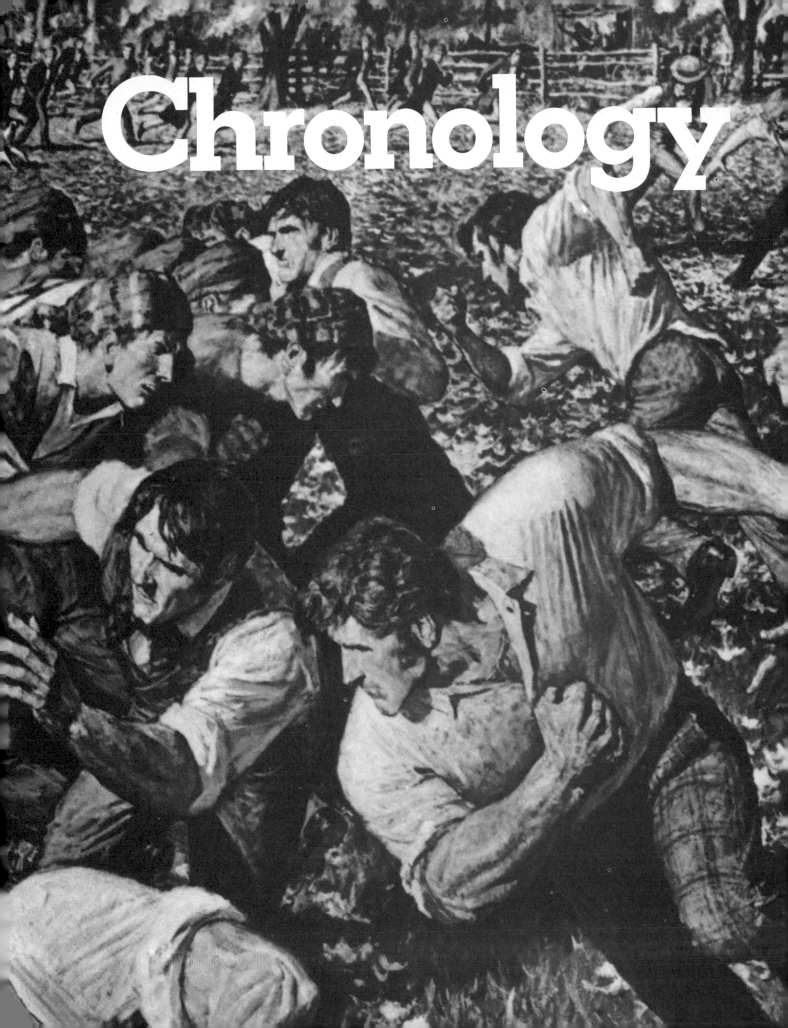

Chronology

1869 The beginning of college football as well as the beginning of the home-field advantage. Rutgers defeats Princeton at Rutgers 6-4, then Princeton defeats Rutgers at Princeton 8-0. These first games, played by teams of 25 men, were played soccer-style.

1871 The first set of rules appears, including the decision to make all fields 500 feet by 300 feet.

1872 Stevens Tech and Yale take up the sport, each playing one game. Harvard puts out rules combining association football and rugby.

1873 In the North teams are reduced to 20 men, while in the South a game is played with 50 men per team. In the latter game Washington and Lee defeats Virginia Military.

1876 With the "Father of American Football," Walter Camp (then aged 17) at halfback, Yale defeats Harvard 1-0.

1877 Appearance of first full uniform, created by L. P. Smock, a Princeton player. The uniform includes a jersey with an orange "P," a tight canvas jacket, black knee pants, and stockings.

1878 Hoboken, New Jersey, is site of football's first great crowd, 4,000 people who see Princeton play Yale. The $300 paid to rent the field is felt to be extravagant.

1880 New rules are set forth by Yale graduate Camp. They lower the size of teams to 11 men and create a scrimmage system for putting the ball into play. To begin each play, the ball is passed back to a quarterback. This new set of rules allows a team to keep the ball unless it is kicked or lost through a fumble.

1882 Camp revises his rules. Unless five yards are gained in three downs, a team loses possession of the ball. This new rule leads to institution of planned strategy, signals, and chalk lines drawn parallel to the goal line. Thus the field comes to resemble a gridiron.

Right: Princeton-Yale, 1889—a romanticized representation. Opposite: Dartmouth-Harvard, 1903. Note referee with horn at left.

1883 The rugby system of scoring is replaced by a system of point values: safety scores one point, touchdown two, goal from try four, and goal from field five.

1884 The first use of "the V trick" or wedge formation, which hides the ball carrier. Also, the first use of interference, or "guarding," whereby players run on either side of the ball carrier.

1885 Use of first true referees hired to assess first penalty: five yards for delay of game.

1888 The end of rugby-style play. The height at which a legal tackle may be made is lowered from waist to knees and players in the rush line are prohibited from joining hands and forming a line across the field. With these changes come mass formations and plays. Football's first "perfect" record is established when Yale blanks all 13 opponents, scoring 694 points.

1889 Caspar Whitney, with the aid of Camp, creates the first All-America team. It is limited to players from the Big Three (Harvard, Yale, and Princeton) and has as end Amos Alonzo Stagg of Yale. At Madison Square Garden in first indoor game, Rutgers defeats Pennsylvania 10-0.

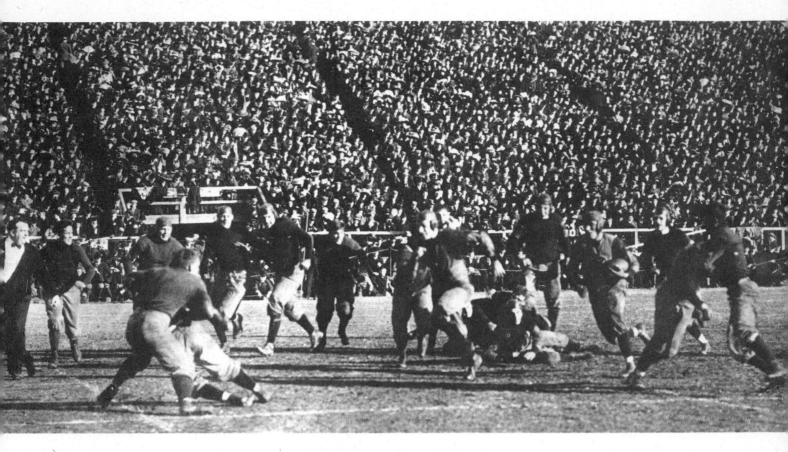

1892 "The Flying Wedge," invention of chess expert Lorin Deland, is used by Harvard. First West Coast intercollegiate game is played between Stanford and California. (Stanford is managed by Herbert Hoover.)

1894 The Flying Wedge and the V trick are prohibited by a new rule that allows no more than three offensive players to group more than five yards behind the line of scrimmage to launch momentum play.

1895 Groundwork is laid for Intercollegiate Conference (formed in 1896 and later known as the Big Ten) by presidents of seven Midwestern universities meeting in Chicago.

1898 A touchdown is given the value of five points, and the goal achieved thereafter is reduced in value to one point.

1900 In Des Moines, Drake defeats Grinnel 6-0 in the first outdoor night game. However, because of poor illumination of the field, not all the spectators see the game.

1903 Two hundred sixty-seven years after its founding, Harvard dedicates nation's first modern football stadium. Quarterbacks are allowed to run five yards forward with the ball from where it is put into play.

1905 President Teddy Roosevelt warns that he'll ban the game if the brutality is not ended. In response to this threat, a 62-college conference is held on December 28. The meeting is the beginning of the National Collegiate Athletic Association (so named in 1910).

1906 In first regular season game against Carroll College, St. Louis University becomes first team to score on newly legalized forward pass.

1909 Field goal drops in value from four to three points.

1910 New rules end the use of mass play: seven players must line up on the line of scrimmage; pushing and pulling the ball carrier are outlawed; and interlocked interference, crawling, and flying tackles are also prohibited. Illinois University hosts college football's first homecoming game, against Chicago.

1912 Army sophomore halfback Dwight Eisenhower gains 29 yards in nine carries against Carlisle one week before a knee injury ends his football career. Carlisle's Thorpe, acclaimed world's greatest athlete after winning Olympic decathlon and pentathlon, totals 340 yards in one game, and finishes with 1,869 rushing yards in 10 games. This, his last season, ends with three rules changes: touchdown becomes six points, fourth down added, and length of the field reduced from 110 to 100 yards.

1916 Georgia Tech makes history on October 7 by defeating Cumberland (of Tennessee) 222-0. The Rambling Wrecks gain possession 32 times, score 32 times, and, not surprisingly, agree to end the game 15 minutes early.

1920 After leading Notre Dame in two perfect seasons and amassing unparalleled career records of 2,341 rushing yards and 4,833 yards in all, Notre Dame's George Gipp, gives football one of its great rallying cries. Dying of pneumonia, he says to coach Knute Rockne, "Tell them to go in there and win just one for the Gipper."

1924 "The Four Horsemen" of Notre Dame (Harry Stuhldreher, Don Miller, Jimmy Crowley, and Elmer Layden) defeat Army 13-7 in New York's Polo Grounds. On the same day, October 18, "the Galloping Ghost" of Illinois, Red Grange, returns the first kickoff 95 yards for a touchdown and scores three more times (from 67, 56, and 44 yards) all in the first 12 minutes.

1926 When 111,000 people flood Chicago's Soldier Field to see the Army-Navy game, it marks the first time more than 100,000 fans see a football game.

1927 Goal posts are moved back 10 yards from the goal line in an effort by the rules committee to protect against a scrimmage

Top: *Harry Stuhldreher plunges through Stanford line in 1925 Rose Bowl.* Bottom: *Army's famous duo: Doc Blanchard, left, and Glenn Davis.*

near the unpadded posts. For the first time in 41 years, no team has a perfect record.

1928 Before a crowd of 66,404, Roy Riegels of California, playing against undefeated, untied Georgia Tech in 1929 Rose Bowl game, runs the wrong way. Rule is created outlawing opponents from advancing fumble that hits the ground.

1931 Knute Rockne is killed in a plane crash near Bazaar, Kansas.

1932 Colgate, under coach Andy Kerr, is undefeated, untied, unscored on, and uninvited to the Rose Bowl.

1934 Ball is reduced one inch in circumference. Sammy Baugh of Texas Christian throws 11 touchdown passes.

1936 For the last time in the century, there are no teams with perfect records. In a Thanksgiving Day game against NYU, Fordham's "Seven Blocks of Granite" permit only one touchdown (on a 1-yard run), but that score gives NYU a 7-6 victory and keeps Fordham out of the Rose Bowl.

1939 First televised football game—Fordham over Waynesburg 34-7. Tennessee shuts out all 10 regular season opponents.

1941 To compensate for the loss of manpower to World War II, the rules committee legalizes substitution.

1944 "Mr. Outside and Mr. Inside," Glenn Davis and Doc Blanchard, lead Army to nine victories and a 48-year high of 56.0 points per game.

1952 The rules committee outlaws two-platooning. The Ivy League college presidents ban spring practice and postseason games for their schools. The Southern Conference becomes the Atlantic Coast Conference. After three years of waiting and 24 wins in a row under Coach of the Year Biggie Munn, Michigan State enters the Big Ten.

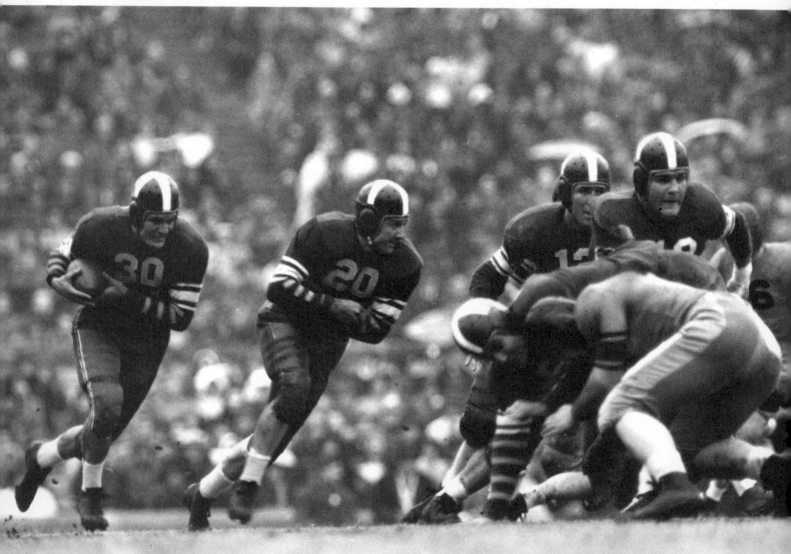

1957 With a 7-0 decision, Notre Dame ends two Oklahoma streaks: 47 victories in a row, the longest winning streak in the first century of college football, and 123 games in a row without being shut out. Dick Lynch leads Notre Dame.

1958 The first change in scoring rules since 1912 gives the team that scores a touchdown the option of trying for a two-point conversion by run or pass from 3-yard line. Major colleges try for two 51.4 percent of the time. "The Lonely End"-formation with Bill Carpenter and Heisman Trophy winner Pete Dawkins helps keep Army undefeated.

1959 Goal posts are widened (for the first time in 83 years) from 18 feet 6 inches to 23 feet 4 inches. Field goals increase 93 percent.

1961 Paul ("Bear") Bryant leads his alma mater, Alabama, to a 10-0 season. Previously, Bryant had resuscitated three other teams: Maryland, Kentucky, and Texas A & M.

1965 In college football's ninety-sixth year, Amos Alonzo Stagg dies at 102.

1966 After trailing 10-0, top-ranked Notre Dame ties Michigan State 10-10 in the waning minutes of "the Battle of the Decade." One of the great football debates: should the Irish have tried to score again, from their 30-yard line with 84 seconds left, or should they have run out the clock, as they did?

1968 The end of college football's first century, at 10:51 P.M. January 1.

1969 A consensus of 100 surveyed coaches, athletic directors, and sportswriters names Knute Rockne the greatest coach in the first 100 years of football.

1970 Yale becomes the only leading major college to win over 600 games.

1971 Florida quarterback John Reaves sets national career record by passing for 7,549 yards.

1972 NCAA adopts 24 rules changes including one that makes an untouched kickoff entering the end zone a dead ball. NCAA also gives permission for major colleges to use freshmen on their varsity teams.

1973 In an eerie parallel to the 1966 Game of the Decade, number-one-ranked Ohio State meets number-four-ranked Michigan at Ann Arbor. Strangely, the game ends in a 10-10 tie, but this time as a result, another team, Alabama, gains the number-one ranking. Of greater concern to the participants is the Rose Bowl bid, left unsettled by the tie. A poll of the athletic directors of the Big Ten decides in favor of Ohio State, to the bitter disappointment of Michigan.

Clockwise from above: *Frank Leahy dwarfed by his Notre Dame players at Pitt game, 1953; Duke's Tom Davis (30) and Winston Siegfried running in near symmetry against Oregon in 1942 Rose Bowl; Oklahoma's mastermind, Bud Wilkinson, 1958; TCU's Davey O'Brien shedding Arkansas defenders.*

A consensus of each decade's best
college football players, compiled by the editors
and authors of THE COLLEGE GAME.

All-Decade
All-America

illustrated by
George Smith

1890-1899

a.a. Stagg

Interior Line Play

The Flying Wedge

End—Frank Hinkey, Yale
End—Charles Gelbert, Pennsylvania
Tackle—Marshall Newell, Harvard
Tackle—Langdon Lea, Princeton
Guard—Pudge Heffelfinger, Yale
Guard—Truxtun Hare, Pennsylvania
Center—Andrew Wyant, Bucknell and Chicago
Back—Charles Daly, Harvard and Army
Back—Lee McClung, Yale
Back—Charles Brewer, Harvard
Back—Pat O'Dea, Wisconsin

Pudge Heffelfinger

John Heisman and the Trophy

1900-1909

Tournament of Roses

Willie Heston

End—Thomas Shevlin, Yale
End—Mark Catlin, Chicago
Tackle—Hamilton Fish, Harvard
Tackle—James Hogan, Yale
Guard—Albert Benbrook, Michigan
Guard—Nathan Dougherty, Tennessee
Center—Germany Schulz, Michigan
Back—Walter Eckersall, Chicago
Back—Willie Heston, Michigan
Back—Harold Weekes, Columbia
Back—Ted Coy, Yale

1910~1919

GEORGIA TECH 222
CUMBERLAND 0

Jim Thorpe

"Ban the Brutality"

Pop Warner

End—Tack Hardwick, Harvard; Bert Baston, Minnesota
End—Guy Chamberlin, Nebraska; Bill Fincher, Georgia Tech
Tackle—Wilbur Henry, Washington & Jefferson; Belford West, Colgate
Tackle—Josh Cody, Vanderbilt; Dan McMillan, California and Southern Cal
Guard—Clarence Spears, Dartmouth; Stanley Pennock, Harvard
Guard—Robert Fisher, Harvard; Joe Alexander, Syracuse
Center—Robert Peck, Pittsburgh; Paul Des Jardien, Chicago
Back—Bo McMillin, Centre; Ray Morrison, Vanderbilt
Back—Jim Thorpe, Carlisle; Elmer Oliphant, Purdue and Army
Back—George Gipp, Notre Dame; Joe Guyon, Carlisle and Georgia Tech
Back—Chic Harley, Ohio State; Edward Mahan, Harvard

George Gipp

Bronko Nagurski

Knute Rockne

The Four Horsemen

1920~1929

End—Bennie Oosterbaan, Michigan; Wes Fesler, Ohio State
End—Brick Muller, California; Wear Schoonover, Arkansas
Tackle—Bronko Nagurski, Minnesota; Duke Slater, Iowa
Tackle—Ed Weir, Nebraska; Bud Sprague, Texas and Army
Guard—Iolas Huffman, Ohio State; Frank Schwab, Lafayette
Guard—Ed Garbisch, Washington & Jefferson and Army;
    Jack Cannon, Notre Dame
Center—Mel Hein, Washington State; Adam Walsh, Notre Dame
Back—Benny Friedman, Michigan; Joel Hunt, Texas A&M
Back—Red Grange, Illinois; Sleepy Jim Crowley, Notre Dame
Back—Red Cagle, Southwest Louisiana and Army;
    Morley Drury, Southern Cal
Back—Ernie Nevers, Stanford; Ken Strong, New York U.

Sammy Baugh

Forward Pass

1930-1939

The Seven Blocks of Granite

End—Don Hutson, Alabama; Jerry Dalrymple, Tulane
End—Larry Kelley, Yale; Gaynell Tinsley, Louisiana State
Tackle—Ed Widseth, Minnesota; Fred Crawford, Duke
Tackle—Bruiser Kinard, Mississippi; Bob Reynolds, Stanford
Guard—Bob Suffridge, Tennessee; Bill Corbus, Stanford
Guard—Aaron Rosenberg, Southern Cal; Nick Drahos, Cornell
Center—Alex Wojciechowicz, Fordham; Ki Aldrich, Texas Christian
Back—Sammy Baugh, Texas Christian; Bobby Wilson, Southern Methodist
Back—Jay Berwanger, Chicago; Nile Kinnick, Iowa
Back—Tom Harmon, Michigan; Whizzer White, Colorado
Back—Bobby Grayson, Stanford; Marshall Goldberg, Pittsburgh

Forward Pass

1940-1949

Charlie Justice

Doak Walker

Blanchard and Davis

End—Leon Hart, Notre Dame; Dave Schreiner, Wisconsin
End—Froggie Williams, Rice; Art Weiner, North Carolina
Tackle—Dick Wildung,
Minnesota; Don Whitmire, Alabama and Navy
Tackle—George Connor,
Holy Cross and Notre Dame; Alvin Wistert, Michigan
Guard—Buddy Burris, Oklahoma;
Weldon Humble, Rice
Guard—Bill Fischer, Notre Dame; Rod Franz, California
Center—Chuck Bednarik,
Pennsylvania; Clayton Tonnemaker, Minnesota
Back—John Lujack,
Notre Dame; Frank Albert, Stanford
Back—Doak Walker,
Southern Methodist; Frank Sinkwich, Georgia
Back—Charlie Justice,
North Carolina; Glenn Davis, Army
Back—John Kimbrough,
Texas A&M; Doc Blanchard, Army

Jim Brown

Bud Wilkinson

The Lonely End

1950~1959

End—Willie Davis, Grambling; Ron Beagle, Navy
End—Ron Kramer, Michigan; Bill McColl, Stanford
Tackle—Jim Weatherall, Oklahoma; Dick Modzelewski, Maryland
Tackle—Alex Karras, Iowa; Bob Gain, Kentucky
Guard—Jim Parker, Ohio State; Les Richter, California
Guard—Bud McFadin, Texas; Calvin Jones, Iowa
Center—Jerry Tubbs, Oklahoma; Bob Pellegrini, Maryland
Back—Paul Hornung, Notre Dame; Dick Kazmaier, Princeton
Back—Howard Cassady, Ohio State; Billy Cannon, Louisiana State
Back—Willie Galimore, Florida A&M; Tommy McDonald, Oklahoma
Back—Jim Brown, Syracuse; Alan Ameche, Wisconsin

Hopalong Cassady

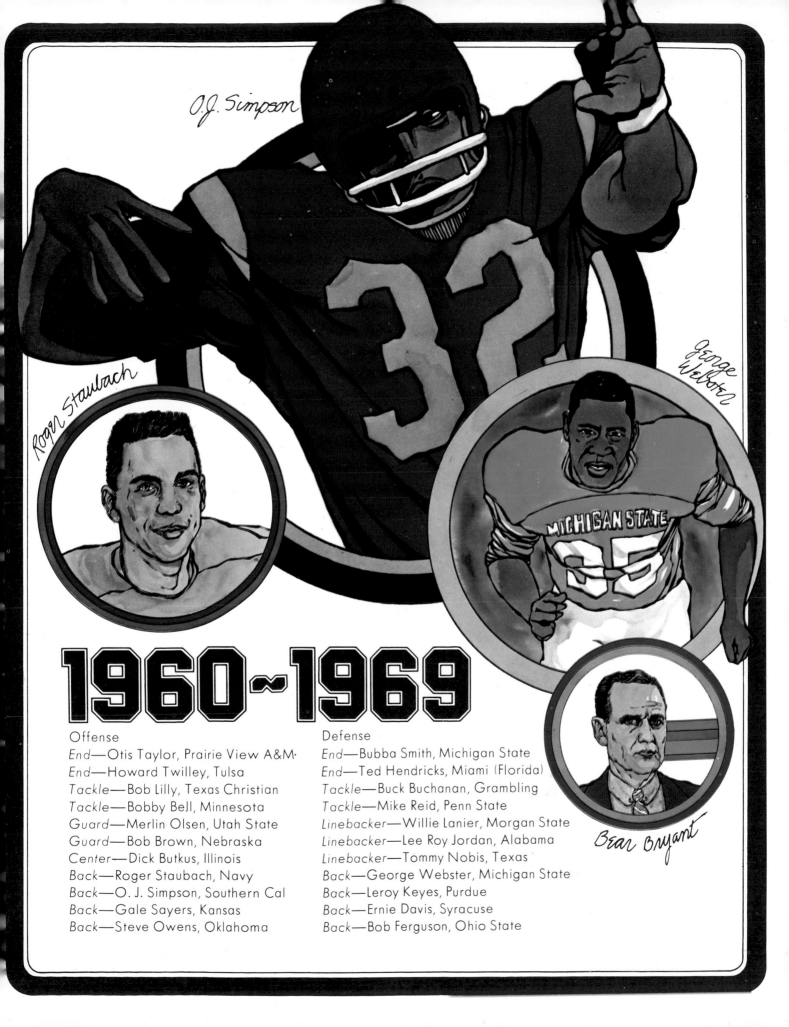

O.J. Simpson

Roger Staubach

George Webster

Bear Bryant

1960~1969

Offense
End—Otis Taylor, Prairie View A&M·
End—Howard Twilley, Tulsa
Tackle—Bob Lilly, Texas Christian
Tackle—Bobby Bell, Minnesota
Guard—Merlin Olsen, Utah State
Guard—Bob Brown, Nebraska
Center—Dick Butkus, Illinois
Back—Roger Staubach, Navy
Back—O. J. Simpson, Southern Cal
Back—Gale Sayers, Kansas
Back—Steve Owens, Oklahoma

Defense
End—Bubba Smith, Michigan State
End—Ted Hendricks, Miami (Florida)
Tackle—Buck Buchanan, Grambling
Tackle—Mike Reid, Penn State
Linebacker—Willie Lanier, Morgan State
Linebacker—Lee Roy Jordan, Alabama
Linebacker—Tommy Nobis, Texas·
Back—George Webster, Michigan State
Back—Leroy Keyes, Purdue
Back—Ernie Davis, Syracuse
Back—Bob Ferguson, Ohio State

PHOTO CREDITS

Acme Photo 107,109,168 bottom, 219
Baylor University 176 center right
Dave Campbell 203,204,206-207,208
Chicago Tribune 108
Columbia University 20 top,25 bottom
Cornell University 20 bottom
Melchior DiGiacomo 82,84,87 bottom
Malcolm Emmons 1,2-3,4-5,8,33,38,39
  top,41,51,52,56,58-59,71 left,72-73,
  75,76-77,78,79,81,83,86,87 top,88,
  90,91,93,94-95,112,113,114-115,117,
  118,121,122-123 bottom,123 right,
  124,125,126,130,131,132-133,139,
  140-141,142,143,145,146,147,148,
  149,150,151,152,155,156,158,159,
  160,161,162-163,192-193,194,195,
  199,201,202,205,207,210-211,225,
  226 top, 227,230-231,232,234,235,
  236,237
James Flores 229
Florida A&M 92
Georgia Tech 60
Fred Kaplan 226 bottom,228
Jerry Klein 240,241
Ross Lewis 6-7,46-47,48 top,54,55
North Carolina State University 64-65
  bottom
Northwestern University 100-101
  bottom
Ohio State University 99 left
Press Gazette 168 top
Richard Raphael 42-43,45 top, 48
  bottom
Ken Regan 16-17,44,45 bottom,50,85
Rice University 176 center left,179
  bottom
Rutgers University 19
Southern Methodist University 176
  bottom right
Stanford University 102 top
Texas A&M 179 top
Tony Tomsic 122-123 top, 126-127,128
United Press International 22,23,25 top,
  27,28-29,30,31,33,35,36,61,63 top,
  64-65 top,66-67,68,71 right,71 top,
  98,99 top,100-101, 100 left,102
  bottom,103,104-105,106,111,112,
  134-135,136,164-165,166-167,169,
  171,173,176 top,177,178,182-183,
  184,186 left, right,213,214,215,216-
  217,218,220,221,222-223,242-243,
  244,245
University of Colorado 137 top
University of Delaware 39 bottom
University of Georgia 63 center
University of Houston 196-197
University of Illinois 97 top
University of Iowa 97 bottom
University of Michigan 97 right
University of Minnesota 96,99 right
University of Mississippi 64 right
University of Missouri 138
University of Oklahoma 137 bottom
University of Oregon 220
University of Pittsburgh 18,53
University of Tennessee 63 bottom,64
  left
University of Texas 176 bottom left,
  186 top, 196
Victor's Photography 238-239
West Point 25 top right
Yale University 21,212

Printed in Italy by Arnoldo Mondadori Editore, Verona

EAST EUROPEAN
COOKBOOK

EAST EUROPEAN
COOKBOOK

Discover the traditional tastes of Russia,
Romania, Hungary, Scandinavia, and Poland

EDITED BY CAROLINE BALL

CHARTWELL
BOOKS, INC.

A QUINTET BOOK

Published by Chartwell Books
A Division of Book Sales, Inc.
114 Northfield Avenue
Edison, New Jersey 08837

This edition produced for sale in the U.S.A., its
territories and dependencies only.

ISBN 0-7858-0558-3

This book was designed and produced by
Quintet Publishing Limited
6 Blundell Street
London N7 9BH

Creative Director: Richard Dewing
Designer: Michael Head
Editor: Caroline Ball

Typeset in Great Britain by
Central Southern Typesetters, Eastbourne
Manufactured in China by Regent Publishing Services Ltd
Printed in China by Leefung-Asco Printers Ltd

Material in this book previously appeared in *New Jewish
Cooking*, by Elizabeth Wolf Cohen, *Recipes from a Polish
Kitchen*, by Bridget Jones, *Russian Regional Recipes*, by Susan
Ward, and *Scandinavian Cooking*, by Sonia Maxwell.

CONTENTS

INTRODUCTION

Stretching from the Arctic Circle to the shores of the Mediterranean, the chain of countries loosely referred to as "Eastern Europe" is home to a wide variety of peoples of very differing traditions. There is no common origin: Magyars and Slavs, Vikings and Mongols have all conquered and settled here, bringing with them their own cultures and languages. There is no common religion: Catholic Poland and Lithuania share borders with Orthodox Russia and Lutheran Latvia; many thousands of Jews worldwide come from old Polish and Russian families, and Islam is well represented. The region has suffered a seemingly endless history of political upheaval and redefined boundaries – and yet, there is a culinary tradition which has survived and unites these very different neighbors. Again and again the same ingredients and combinations are favored, albeit with different labels and variations imposed by climate and custom. The little pastries known as *piroshki* in Russia resurface as *pierogi* in Poland; those staple vegetables, cabbage and beet, are served up in countless ways from Karelia to Kiev; dumplings, sour cream and sweet and sour are recurring themes.

FOOD FIT FOR TSARS . . . AND EMPERORS
Visitors who ventured behind the old Iron Curtain almost inevitably found uninspiring and often downright unpalatable fare. But this was not always so. The court of the Austro-Hungarian emperors was one of glittering sophistication, with menus and chefs to rival any in Europe. Similarly, the great families of

Above: Steak Tartare

Poland were well traveled and sociable. They visited other European countries and allowed foreigners to live among them, encouraging a cosmopolitan social style and a varied repertoire at table.

Many dishes which later became internationally famous were culinarily translated from the Russian colloquial by gifted French chefs. The great Anton Carême, who cooked for Tsar Alexander I, is probably the most famous, but many others followed in his wake, working not only for the royal family but also for the lesser nobility. Ethnic influences from the Russian heartland, from the rich estates in Ukraine and Belorussia and from the lands of the south, were refined by these culinary artists. Dishes such as beef Stroganoff, steak tartare, and rum baba spread from Russian to Parisian society, and onto the *nouveau riche* tables of Delmonicos in New York.

It is not only to the French, however, that the classics of the high table owe thanks. In the early 18th century, Peter the Great also employed Dutch, German, and Swedish chefs, and an initially bemused, then enthusiastic court was introduced to sausages, hard cheese, fruit sauces, and compôtes. It was, perhaps, the Swedes, more than any, who influenced the style of entertaining, by introducing to the Russians their beloved smörgåsbord. Christened *zakuski* (small bites), the Russian adaptation of this initial medley of tidbits – smoked fish, caviar, cold ham, preserved vegetables, and savory pastries – had evolved by the last years of the 19th century into an intricate marriage of the culinary and visual arts so lavish that foreigners understandably mistook it for the whole meal. Even in today's straitened circumstances, nowhere is the generosity and imagination of the native Slav character made more apparent than in this traditional first act of a meal. The smörgåsbord is said to go back over 200 years, when it was the traditional meal of rural Swedes. Conversely, in Russia, the zakuska table filtered down the social scale – and throughout the empire – until it is now a fixture everywhere within the old Soviet sphere of influence, from the Baltic to Caucasia and Central Asia.

THE CRADLE OF RUSSIAN CIVILIZATION
Although a separate republic with a people fiercely proud of their different language, literature, culture, and cuisine, Ukraine is, in fact, the cradle of Russian civilization. Kiev, its capital, was originally the premier town and capital of Russ, the first unified "Russian-Slavic" state, founded in the 9th century. At its height, the kingdom stretched from the Baltic to

Above: Sweet Caraway Biscuits

the Volga and Danube, its rulers crushed invaders from the south and east and assimilated its previous Scandinavian lords. However, by the 12th and 13th centuries disputes over successions, devastating attacks by the Tartars and the expansion of the Polish-Lithuanian alliance had pushed the center of power east – to Novgorod and eventually to Moscow.

Ukraine was known as the breadbasket of the old Soviet Union, and with good reason: its extensive fields of grain and traditional creativity in baking have resulted in a fabled 70 types of loaves, rolls, and buns, ranging from white to black and flavored with sour cream, honey, or molasses.

The Ukranian influence extends beyond its wheatfields: the ubiquitous beet was an introduction from Ukraine, as was borscht itself. Peter the Great's present to his people, the potato, was exploited to the fullest in the fields and kitchens of Ukraine and Belorussia and then again in Russia.

Within the old Soviet Union, the Ukrainians have always carried a reputation as chefs, using a greater variety both of ingredients and cooking methods than the Russians. Because Ukraine stretches into the Crimea, historical home to immigrant Tartars and Turks as well as Slavs, eastern influences permeated northwards. From these regions came the Eastern and Middle Eastern custom of grilling cubes of meat on skewers and a taste for honey, nuts, and dried fruits in both sweet and savory dishes.

PEASANT TRADITION

At the heart of eastern European cookery, however, is the stockpot and grain store of the peasant. Bread was the staple, served up in black, brown, or white doorsteps, used in stuffings, soups and, together with barley or rye flour, as the basis for *kvas* (near beer), an invention of the early Slavs. "If we have bread and *kvas*, what more do we need?" says the anonymous peasant of Russian folklore. This was likely to have been a stoical acceptance of the poor man's lot rather than an out-of-hand rejection of improvement, since the chances of much else in medieval to 19th-century Russia were limited.

With the Great Reforms of the 1860s, serfs were freed, the lot of the small landowner improved, and village communes were set up. By the late 19th century, Russia and Ukraine were exporting wheat to a needy Europe. The physical limitations imposed by the size of the country, the corruption of officialdom, and the intransigence of the class system would eventually combine with other political factors to bring about revolution, but for the first time in many homes there was meat in the pot, if only poorer cuts which could be ground or stewed while the better ones went to market. For this reason, the Russian tradition of peasant cookery is particularly rich in recipes for leafy vegetables, dumplings, and pastries

Above: Steamed Lamb Dumplings

stuffed with meat, as well as meatballs, patties, and rissoles.

The countryman's larder was reliant on the grains and vegetables which would survive the long winters in earth cellars or on the shelf: salted or pickled cabbage, yellow turnips, buckwheat groats, barley, millet, onions, beet, and potatoes. Perhaps the greatest contribution of the homely Russian cook is the range of wonderful comfort soups originally made to sustain laborers and farmers during the long cold winters, and of light chilled soups devised to bring refreshment in the hottest of humid summers. Many exhibit an idiosyncratic sour tang provided by adding pickles, capers, lemon juice, vinegar, *kvas*, sour cream, sorrel, or sauerkraut, while a strongly flavored meat and vegetable stock acts as a foil. Typically, ingredients, too, have body – barley or hunks of bread, chunks of potato, beet, cabbage, and cheaper cuts of meat thicken the broth of winter soups, while finely chopped or puréed vegetables, wild mushrooms, fresh or dried, greens, and sometimes fruits form the basis of summer specialties.

The wholesome, if basic, Russian peasant cuisine, if treated with respect, could have developed like the cooking traditions of nearby Germany, Poland, and Hungary, enriched even from within the republic's borders: from the Cossack, Tartar, and Turkic people of the lower Volga-Don and northern Transcaucasian regions; from the Karelians in the north and from the eclectic mixture of indigenous and exiled races in Siberia. But circumstances of history and economics conspired to make that scenario impossible. But almost three quarters of a century of neglect is finally being countered by a rising interest in traditional cuisine from within the new Russia and from abroad.

SCANDINAVIAN INFLUENCE

As we have seen, Swedish chefs helped shape the cuisine of the Russian court of the 19th century, but links were forged much earlier than that. In the 9th and 10th centuries Viking trade routes ran the length of the Slav homeland, from the Baltic to the Black Sea. To survive the long winters, these northerners had to store supplies and, as a result, every possible method of preservation was used to produce a selection of dried, smoked, and cured meat and fish unmatched anywhere else. The Vikings took these preserves with them on their long voyages for sustenance and as a means of bargaining, and their methods were adopted wherever they traded.

When affordable, salt was always a favorite condiment, and it would be used with such zeal in

Above: Blinis

the preservation of food that violent thirsts were commonplace. Although salt is no longer used so liberally, Scandinavians still have a taste for salty foods. Many of their recipes use fresh meat that has been boiled for some time in brine and then left to soak for several days to impart flavor and tenderize it.

When salt was too expensive or in short supply other means of preserving had to be found. Meat would be stored in butter or whey, and smoking houses provided a wide range of smoked meats and fish for the table. Herring and cod were hung up and left to dry and because they were so readily available and so easily preserved, they have become two of Scandinavia's principal sources of food, and major exports. Fish was sometimes buried in a crude attempt at refrigeration – the fish often fermented, and this was considered a delicacy. Swedish *surstromming*, a Baltic herring preparation based on this practice, is one dish that still survives today.

The brief hot summers have ingrained in the north a love of the outdoor life and a passion for food from the wild. Fall brings fruits such as blackberries, blueberries, and cranberries, and an exotic variety of mushrooms, still an obsession throughout the region today. In season, hunting is popular, adding elk, venison, hare, and all types of game to the menu.

VARIATIONS ON A THEME

Stuffed cabbage rolls and meat patties are to be found in various guises from Norway to Bulgaria, and soured creams and cultured milk – whether Romanian yogurt, Polish smetana or Swedish buttermilk – are characteristic of eastern European cooking as a whole. The cuisines of the region are far from homogeneous, however. A country's cooking is based on its local produce and its cultural influences through history. Sweden and Russia fought over Finland for centuries and, after more than 600 years of Swedish rule and 100 under the Tzars of Russian, it is inevitable that Finland should bear traces of their two cultures. The Finns produce their own version of smörgåsbord, but their cuisine also includes borscht soup and meat kebabs. The countries bordering the Baltic – Estonia, Latvia, and Lithuania – similarly reflect their strong cultural ties with Scandinavia at least as much as with the Russia which subjugated them.

The borders of Belorussia have moved east and west between Russia and Poland for centuries, a dichotomy reflected in the food. Pigs have overtaken cattle in agricultural and culinary importance, while eastern Polish specialties like pork crackling in dripping, a wide variety of ham sausages, beef rolled and stuffed with sour pickles, the preference for sauerkraut rather than fresh cabbage and a weakness for poppyseed pastries have become Belorussian fixtures.

Across the north, caraway and poppy seed flavor Scandinavian aquavits and add crunch to Russian biscuits, and the ubiquitous dill is inseparable from pickles and gravad lax. Further south, these sharp, aniseed tastes give way to the fiery warmth of paprika and chili which characterizes the dishes of Hungary and Romania. In Romania and its neighbor Moldova, stews and sausages can be surprisingly spicy, while red and haricot beans, sweetcorn, fresh bell peppers, grilled meats and fish, smoked and aged ewe's cheeses speak more of the Balkans and the Levant than of northern steppes. Here, grapes replace hops and barley in the fields, and so wine replaces beer at the table.

The long northern coastline means that fish (fresh, smoked or pickled) plays an important part in the diet in Scandinavia, with herring, presented in innumerable ways, a specialty. Shellfish is popular in the south, while whalemeat is considered a delicacy in the north of Norway. Crystal clear rivers provide a wealth of freshwater fish, including the noble salmon.

Across the Baltic, Estonia, Latvia, and Lithuania share a fishing tradition, but one shaped by politics. Latvia's fishing industry, one of the world's richest during the years of independence between the two world wars, was afterwards commandeered by the Soviets to feed the Russian heartland. This meant that its wealth of sea and freshwater fish was largely unavailable to the local people and much of its fine heritage of recipes for fresh and smoked fish has long been unappreciated. Here, both the potato and the apple are treated with special respect: mashed, grated, in dumplings and pastries, the former appears in everything from suppers to desserts, while the latter features in sweet biscuits, fritters, tarts, cakes, sauces, and candy as well as combining with potatoes in a savory pudding. Lithuanian sausages – particularly a pork and beef version called *sviezia desra* – are reputed to be the most flavorful in eastern Europe.

Above: Potato Pancakes

In Russia and landlocked Hungary, fish from the rivers and, more especially, the huge lakes, are especially sought after. Sturgeon from the Caspian, with its precious caviar eggs, is probably the most widely known, but the unique trout from Lake Sevan and Hungary's Lake Balaton carp are prized locally.

Although Poland has access to the sea, its primary source of food is through agriculture, with hearty root vegetables and cabbages surviving the harsh climate. Traditionally, Poland is a nation of great meat eaters; it is known for its game, venison and wild boar in particular. A 16th-century queen of Poland, the Milanese Bona Sforza, was horrified at the quantities of meat and lack of vegetables that were consumed in her adoptive country. So she began the process of introducing variety to the diet in the way of fresh vegetables and other foods such as pasta. Many of the dumplings, noodles, and the use of garlic owe a certain amount to the Italian influence.

The Jewish population of Poland also contributed their ideas to the cooking and these are particularly noticeable in the preparation of cold platters of fish in aspic, in baking and dumplings.

KOSHER CUISINE

As the Jews migrated throughout the world, their cooking was borrowed from the local cuisine, using native ingredients. While keeping their kosher requirements and observing their holiday customs, each group of Jews developed dishes suited to the country in which they had settled. Eastern European Jews salted herrings for use during the long winters and rendered goose or chicken fat for cooking hearty stews and potato kugels.

Broadly speaking, Jews fall into two groups: the Sephardic Jews came from Spain, Portugal and the Middle East, and the Ashkenazic Jews came from central and eastern Europe, including Austria, Germany, Hungary, Poland, and the former Soviet Union. However, as the Soviet Union was so large, some of the Jews near the Turkish and Iranian borders more closely resemble their Sephardic neighbors in their cooking traditions.

Ashkenazic cooking tends to be subtle and delicate, with many well-flavored, long-cooked dishes of beef and sometimes lamb, with onions, paprika and sparingly used garlic. Parsley and dill are the most

Above: Cholent

frequently used herbs. Horseradish is the spicy accompaniment used for meat and fish dishes and always accompanies gefilte fish; pickles and pickled cucumbers are favorite condiments. The sweet and sour combination of vinegar or lemon juice with sugar or honey is used to create dishes such as sweet and sour cabbage.

Much of the cooking of central Europe was based on rendered goose or chicken fat, and smoked or salted fish, as these ingredients were inexpensive and widely available. Once potatoes were introduced from the New World, they became as popular as egg noodles, a specialty of Ashkenazic cuisine and the base of many traditional dishes, such as kreplach and kugels. Barley, lentils, and buckwheat are also popular ingredients.

Austrian, Hungarian and German Jews are renowned for their baking. During the great migration of Europeans to the United States at the end of the 19th century, German Jews set up bakeries in their adopted homeland. The strudels, yeast-cakes, bagels and other breads they popularized are now accepted as Jewish-American foods.

COFFEE AND CAKES

Although Austria's coffee houses are the most celebrated internationally, Latvia and Estonia share with Poland and Hungary an almost Viennese appreciation of coffee, and of the pastries to go with it. Budapest's coffee houses were the lively meeting places of the literary world, and Warsaw was renowned for its wonderful gateaux and pastries. Taking coffee and cake is still very much a social event, an occasion to share with friends or an opportunity for entertaining.

Above: Beet & Watercress Salad

SOUPS

SOUR MILK AND BARLEY SOUP

PEA SOUP

BEER SOUP

MOLDOVAN POTATO CHEESE SOUP

"ALMOST NOTHING" SOUP

BORSCHT

RASSOLNIK

KRUPNIK

MEAT AND KVAS SOUP

NETTLE SOUP

RASPBERRY SOUP

CHERRY SOUP

SOUR MILK AND BARLEY SOUP

This is a very old Latvian recipe, handed down through generations and still popular today. It is a cold summer soup, for that surprisingly warm season. The coastal strip of Latvia is lapped by the northeasterly waves of the Gulf Stream, making the climate slightly milder than that of its Scandinavian neighbors.

SERVES 6

1 lb field or brown mushrooms, finely sliced then chopped
¼ cup vegetable oil
1 large onion, finely chopped
1½ tbsp tomato paste
2 tbsp fresh lemon juice
8 cups chicken stock
½ lb pearl barley
salt and freshly ground black pepper
1 cup buttermilk
1 cup sour cream
3 tbsp finely chopped fresh dill
2 hard-boiled eggs, chopped
1 Polish-style sweet-sour pickle, finely chopped

In a large saucepan, sauté the mushrooms in the oil over medium high heat. Stir until the mushroom juices have evaporated, about 15 minutes. Add the onion and stir until softened, about 8 minutes. Stir in the tomato paste, lemon juice, and chicken stock and bring to the boil over high heat.

Slowly stir in the barley and seasoning to taste. Bring back to the boil, cover, and lower the heat. Simmer until the barley is tender, about 30–40 minutes.

Take the soup off the heat and leave to cool. When it is at room temperature, stir in the buttermilk, sour cream, and dill. Taste and adjust the seasoning. Chill for at least 1 hour (or overnight, covered) before serving.

Ladle the soup into individual serving bowls and garnish each with the chopped egg and pickle.

PEA SOUP

Sliced kabanos are tasty in this delicious soup, added after sieving or blending.

SERVES 4

1 onion, roughly chopped
1 clove garlic, crushed
1 bay leaf
a little fat or butter
1 lb frozen peas or shelled fresh peas
3¾ cups stock such as ham, beef, veal, or chicken
1 small potato, cubed
salt and freshly ground black pepper
⅔ cup sour cream

Cook the onion, garlic and bay leaf in a little fat in a saucepan over low heat until soft but not browned – about 10 minutes. Add the peas, pour in the stock and stir in the potato. Sprinkle in a little seasoning. Bring to the boil, reduce the heat, cover and simmer for 30 minutes.

Sieve or blend the soup until smooth. Return it to the pan and heat through. Taste for seasoning, stir in the sour cream and serve at once.

Right: Pea Soup

BEER SOUP

This very popular Danish soup, rarely tasted by foreigners, should be as thick as porridge. A sweet, dark, non-alcoholic malt beer is traditionally used.

SERVES 4–6

8 slices pumpernickel
2½ cups dark malt beer
or brown ale
1 cup water
grated rind and juice of 1 lemon
sugar, to taste
⅔ cup whipped cream

Cut the bread into small pieces, and place in a deep dish. Pour the beer and water over the bread, and leave to soak for a minimum of 3 hours.

Transfer the mixture to a saucepan, and simmer over a low heat until it thickens to the desired consistency. Purée in a food processor at medium speed. Add the lemon rind and juice, and sweeten with sugar to taste. Return to the heat and bring to the boil. Serve hot with whipped cream.

MOLDOVAN POTATO CHEESE SOUP

This is a soup for potato-lovers, traditionally made with aged *brynza*, a hard ewe's cheese. It is lip-smacking good made with the Basque variety. You can use any other hard cheese, but the results will not be as authentic.

SERVES 6

¼ cup unsalted butter
2 large onions, finely chopped
3 large carrots, chopped
2 large potatoes, peeled and chopped
¼ tsp sweet paprika
large pinch of cayenne pepper
1 tbsp finely chopped parsley
4 cups chicken stock
½ lb ewe's cheese (Basque Ektori or similar) or other hard cheese
salt and freshly ground black pepper
finely chopped chives

Melt the butter in a large saucepan over medium heat. Add the onions and carrots and sauté gently for about 20–25 minutes, until they are tender and lightly colored.

Stir in the potatoes, spices, and parsley, then add the chicken stock and bring to the boil. Reduce the heat, cover, and simmer for 30 minutes, or until the potatoes are soft.

Strain the soup into a bowl and purée the vegetables in a blender or food processor with a little of the stock until smooth. Return the purée to the saucepan and add as much stock as necessary (about 3½–4 cups) to obtain a good consistency. Set the soup over low heat and stir in the cheese. Continue stirring until it has dissolved into the soup, but do not allow to boil. Adjust the seasoning to taste and serve immediately in individual bowls, topped with the chives.

"ALMOST NOTHING" SOUP

This Russian soup, made from scraps, has a surprising flavor, smoky and nut-like. Add a little cream to make it more sophisticated.

SERVES 4-6

3 lb beef, chicken, veal, or mixed bones
1 onion, unpeeled
salt and freshly ground black pepper
7 cups water
2 lb potatoes, scrubbed and dried
1 onion, finely chopped
¼ lb bacon fat or melted butter
½ cup light cream (optional)
2 tbsp chopped fresh chives

Place the bones, the unpeeled onion, and seasoning to taste in a large pot. Cover with the water and put over high heat. Bring to a boil, then cover and simmer for 1 hour. Uncover and continue to simmer until the stock has reduced to almost half. Strain the stock and return to the saucepan.

Meanwhile peel the potatoes. Reserve the potatoes themselves for another use. Melt the bacon fat or butter in a frying pan and sauté the onion until soft, about 6 minutes. Add the potato skins and continue to cook until they too are tender.

Transfer the potato skins and onion to the saucepan containing the stock. Bring to the boil, then reduce the heat and simmer for 10 minutes. Purée the soup in batches; return to the saucepan and reheat. Thin, if necessary, with a little water or the light cream. Ladle into individual bowls and serve sprinkled with the chopped chives.

15

BORSCHT

There are many versions of borscht; the only ingredient which does not vary is the beet. This soup is made all over eastern Europe and served hot or cold. It can be made with beef or without, with vegetables or without, and served chunky or smooth.

This elegant ruby-red soup is most delicious served with a swirl of sour cream, chives and dill, and for an extra treat, serve with a tiny piroshki or two (*see* pages 38–9).

SERVES 6

1½ lb small beets with tops
1 onion, chopped
3¼ cups beef, chicken or vegetable stock, or water
1 tsp salt
freshly ground black pepper
3 tbsp fresh lemon juice or cider vinegar
2 tbsp light brown sugar, or to taste
sour cream for serving
chopped fresh chives and dill for garnish

Cut tops from beet, leaving 2–3 in of stalk attached. Scrub beet thoroughly under cold running water, being sure to remove all grit and sand. If tops are young and tender they may be added, well washed.

In a large saucepan, over medium heat, place beet and chopped onion and cover with stock or water. Bring to a boil, then simmer, partially covered, until beet is tender, 20–30 minutes. Carefully strain liquid through a sieve into a large heatproof bowl; rinse saucepan.

Remove beet and peel off skin. Quarter beet and add to a food processor fitted with metal blade. Add onions (and tops if using) from sieve to the beet, process until finely puréed.

Return beet and onion purée to washed saucepan and add reserved cooking liquid, being careful not to add any sand or grit which may have settled on bottom.

Over medium heat, bring soup to a boil. Season with salt, pepper, lemon juice or vinegar, and brown sugar. Simmer 5 minutes and serve hot with a swirl of sour cream. Sprinkle with fresh chives and dill. Alternatively, cool and chill to serve cold.

If serving cold, reseason before serving and thin with a little water if necessary.

RASSOLNIK

A soup which crept from lowly origins in Russia to the highest tables in the land. This is a St Petersburg favorite, served chilled as often as hot.

SERVES 8

⅓ cup butter
¼ cup vegetable or sunflower oil
1 medium onion, finely chopped
1 stalk celery, finely chopped
1 medium carrot, finely chopped
1 large potato, peeled and cubed
1 lb lamb's kidneys, trimmed and cut into ½ in pieces
⅓ cup all purpose flour
6 sprigs parsley, chopped
2 lb fresh sorrel leaves or 1 lb each sorrel and young
spinach leaves, stripped from their stems and
finely chopped
salt and freshly ground black pepper
6 cups beef stock
1 bay leaf
2 sour pickled cucumbers, finely chopped, with ⅓ cup
pickling juices
1 egg yolk
sour cream

Melt ¼ cup butter and 2 tbsp oil in a large saucepan and gently sauté the onion, celery, and carrot until they are softened and lightly colored, about 10 minutes. Add the chopped potato and continue cooking, stirring for a further 5 minutes. Transfer the vegetables to a bowl and set aside.

Heat the remaining butter and oil in the pan. Dip the kidney pieces into the flour and gently fry them until they are slightly browned, about 3 minutes. Remove with a slotted spoon and set aside. Stir the parsley and sorrel (or sorrel and spinach) into the pan and add the cooked vegetables. Toss everything gently until the leaves are wilted. Season to taste with salt and pepper and add the beef stock and bay leaf. Bring to a boil, then cover, lower the heat and simmer for about 25 minutes.

Remove the bay leaf and mash the vegetables to thicken the soup. Stir in the pickled cucumbers and their juice, together with the cooked kidneys. Simmer for a further 5 minutes.

Remove a cupful of the soup and beat with the egg yolk in a small bowl. Stir the egg mixture back into the soup and heat it briefly. Do not boil or the egg will curdle.

If serving hot, transfer the soup to a large tureen and pass the sour cream separately. If serving cold, cool to room temperature, then chill for 2–3 hours before dividing between individual bowls, each topped with a spoonful of sour cream.

KRUPNIK

This Polish soup is made of grain – barley usually, or buckwheat may be used – and has the same name as a potent drink made from caramel, honey, spices, and Polish spirit.

SERVES 6

1 onion, chopped
2 carrots, cubed
1 leek, sliced
2 tbsp fat
5 cups beef stock
½ cup pearl barley
salt and freshly ground black pepper
1 bay leaf
½ small celeriac (celery root), cubed

Cook the onion, carrots, and leek in the fat in a large saucepan, until slightly softened but not browned. Pour in the stock, then add the barley with a sprinkling of seasoning and the bay leaf. Bring to a boil, reduce the heat and cover the pan. Simmer for 30 minutes.

  Add the celeriac (celery root) to the soup, give it a good stir and re-cover the pan. Simmer the soup for a further 30 minutes by which time the barley should be plump and tender. Taste for seasoning before serving. This soup should be served freshly cooked otherwise the barley swells and absorbs all the liquid.

MEAT AND KVAS SOUP

The *kvas* (*see below*) can be replaced by flat beer or semi-sweet cider, though the slightly sour flavor of rye will be missing. This dish may be served hot or cold.

SERVES 6 – 8

2 hard-boiled eggs, separated
2 tsp dry mustard powder
⅔ cup sour cream
salt and freshly ground black pepper
5 cups kvas, flat beer or cider
1 medium cucumber, peeled, seeded and finely cubed
2 scallions, including trimmed green top, finely chopped
2 medium potatoes, cooked, peeled and finely cubed
½ lb cold cooked roast beef or pork, finely cubed
large pinch of cayenne pepper
⅓ cup dill or chives, finely chopped

KVAS (MAKES 5 PINTS)

1 lb slightly stale black or dark rye bread
11 cups boiling water
5 tsp dry yeast
⅔ cup sugar
3 tbsp lukewarm water
1 large sprig of mint
raisins

Finely chop the whites of the eggs and set aside. In a bowl, mash the yolks with the dry mustard powder and a teaspoonful of the sour cream until you have a paste. Then slowly whip in the rest of the sour cream until smooth. Season with 1½–2 tsp salt and pepper to taste. To make the Kvas, preheat the oven to 225°F. Place the bread in the oven for about 1–1½ hours, or until it is very dry. *Do not let it burn.* Crumble the bread into a bowl and pour the boiling water over it. Cover with a dish towel and leave for at least 8 hours.

Line a fine sieve with cheesecloth and strain the bread liquid through it into a large bowl, pressing the bread with a spoon to extract as much liquid as possible. Discard the bread.

Sprinkle the yeast and a large pinch of sugar over the 3 tbsp lukewarm water and stir to dissolve completely. Set aside in a warm spot for about 10 minutes, or until the mixture is foamy and almost double in volume. Stir the yeast mixture, the rest of the sugar and the mint sprigs into the bread water. Cover with a dish towel and set aside for another 8–12 hours.

Strain the liquid again through a cheesecloth-lined sieve placed over a large bowl. Sterilize 5 × 1 pt bottles. Pour the liquid into each bottle until it is about two-thirds full, then drop 4–5 raisins in. Cover the tops with plastic wrap secured with a rubber band.

Place the bottles in a cool dark place for about 3 days, until the raisins have risen to the top and the sediment sunk to the bottom. Carefully pour off the clear liquid into a bowl, leaving the sediment behind. Thoroughly clean the bottles, remove the raisins from the *kvas*, and funnel it back into the bottles (there will be slightly less). Cork the bottles or cover with plastic wrap and refrigerate until ready to use. This will keep for several weeks well covered in the fridge.

Whisk in the *kvas*, little by little, until the liquid is thoroughly combined with the sour cream mixture. Stir in the egg whites, cucumber, onions, potatoes, meat, and cayenne pepper. Chill for 15 minutes, then ladle into bowls and garnish with dill or chives.

19

NETTLE SOUP

All that is needed for this Scandinavian spring treat is a plastic bag and a pair of gloves for picking those young, tender shoots while out on a spring walk. For color, add hard-boiled eggs, shrimp, and croûtons.

SERVES 4 – 6

½ lb fresh young nettles
salt and pepper
5 tbsp chopped fresh chives
2 tbsp butter
3 tbsp flour
5–6 cups beef stock

Rinse the nettles thoroughly in cold water. Boil them for about 15 minutes until tender in lightly salted water. Drain and finely chop the nettles with the chives.

Melt the butter, add the flour, and cook for 2–3 minutes, stirring continuously. When golden brown, add the beef stock and boil for 10 minutes. Add the nettles and chives to the soup. Season with salt and pepper. If liked, serve with a poached egg or half a hard-boiled egg per person.

RASPBERRY SOUP

This is a favorite summer soup of Estonia, and indeed of other Baltic and Eastern European states. It is considered a specialty by the restaurants of Tallinn, Estonia's capital. In season, whortleberries – wild blueberries – can be substituted.

SERVES 6

1½ lb raspberries or blueberries
6 oz redcurrants
1¼ cups water
1 tbsp cornstarch
juice and rind of ½ lemon
⅔ cup light brown sugar
½ tsp cinnamon
1¼ cups whipping cream
⅔ cup sour cream

Reserve a large handful of berries for garnish. Place the remainder in a liquidizer or processor fitted with the metal blade and process until the berries are liquefied.

Place a fine sieve over an enamelled or stainless steel saucepan. Press the puréed fruit to extract the seeds, stirring through the sieve in batches until all the liquid has passed through.

Add the water to the strained fruit. Place over high heat and bring to the boil; lower the heat and simmer for 15 minutes. In a small bowl, mix the cornstarch with a little water. Whisk into the soup, turn up the heat, and continue whisking as the soup begins to boil and the soup thickens. Lower the heat and whisk in the lemon juice and rind, sugar, and cinnamon. Take off the heat, allow to cool, then chill for several hours or overnight.

Before serving, whisk in the whipping and sour creams. Ladle into individual soup bowls and garnish each with some of the reserved berries.

CHERRY SOUP

Fruit soups are a feature of many eastern European countries, plum and cherry being particularly popular. This delicate and refreshing recipe is a Polish version.

S E R V E S   4

1½ lb cherries, stalks removed
1 cinnamon stick
2½ cups water plus 2 tbsp
½ cup sugar
2 tbsp arrowroot
⅔ cup sour cream

Put 1 lb of the cherries in a saucepan with the cinnamon stick and all but the 2 tbsp water. Bring to a boil, reduce the heat and cover. Simmer the fruit for 30 minutes, then cool slightly. Pit the reserved cherries.

Discard the cinnamon stick and press the cherries through a sieve, with all the cooking liquid. Pour the sieved fruit back into the rinsed pan. Add the sugar and reserved cherries. Heat, stirring, until the sugar has dissolved. Blend the arrowroot to a smooth paste with the remaining water. Add a little of the hot soup, then pour the mixture into the pan of soup and bring to a boil, stirring. As soon as the soup is boiling, remove the pan from the heat and cool slightly. Whisk in the sour cream and cover the surface of the soup with plastic wrap or waxed paper. Cool and chill.

Stir the soup well before serving, ladled into delicate soup dishes or glass dishes.

APPETIZERS

HERRINGS IN
SOUR CREAM

FISH SALAD

EWE'S CHEESE
WITH PAPRIKA

MUSHROOM
CAVIAR

HARE PATE

CABBAGE AND
MUSHROOM
ROLLS

GLASSBLOWERS'
HERRING

ZAKUSKI

PASHTET

MARINATED
MUSHROOMS

EGGS A LA
RUSSE

CHEESE
KNISHES

HERRINGS IN SOUR CREAM

Herrings became a staple of the Jewish diet in Poland, Hungary, Czechoslovakia, and other eastern European countries because they were economical. If using salt herrings, soak them in cold water for at least 4 hours.

SERVES 6 – 8

1 lb jar pickled herrings or herrings in wine sauce, drained

1 red onion, thinly sliced

4 crisp apples, halved and cored but not peeled

½ tbsp lemon juice or cider vinegar

½ tsp ground cinnamon

2 tsp sugar

1 cup sour cream or yogurt

freshly ground black pepper

radicchio and fresh dill sprigs for garnish

black bread for serving

Pat herrings dry with paper towels. Discard onions and liquid from the jar. Lay each herring flat on cutting board and, holding sharp knife at an angle, cut each into 5–6 diagonal slices. Remove to mixing bowl and add thinly sliced red onion.

Lay each apple half cut-side down on cutting board and cut into thin slices. Add to herrings and onions.

In a small bowl, combine lemon juice or vinegar, cinnamon, sugar, and sour cream or yogurt. Season with black pepper.

Pour dressing over herrings, onions, and apples. Toss to blend well, cover with plastic wrap and refrigerate 2 hours or overnight.

To serve, arrange a leaf or two of radicchio on individual serving plates, spoon on equal amounts of herring mixture and garnish with sprigs of fresh dill. Serve with black bread.

FISH SALAD

A delicate salad that may be served as a light main course as well as for the first course of the meal.

SERVES 4

½ lb cod fillet
1¼ cups fish stock
1 medium potato, cooked and cooled
1 pickled cucumber, sliced
¼ cucumber, peeled and cubed (about ¼ lb)
2 tbsp chopped chives
⅔ cup sour cream
1 tbsp horseradish sauce
salt and freshly ground black pepper
24 cucumber slices to garnish

Place the fish in a shallow pan. Pour in the stock and heat until simmering. Poach gently for 3–5 minutes, until the fish is firm and just cooked. Set the fish aside to cool in the stock.

Dice the potato and mix it with the pickled and fresh cucumber. Drain the fish and flake the flesh off the skin, removing all the bones. Stir the chives, sour cream, and horseradish into the vegetables, adding seasoning to taste. Add the fish and mix very lightly to avoid breaking the flakes. Divide the salad between four small plates and garnish with cucumber.

EWE'S CHEESE WITH PAPRIKA

This spread is good with rye bread or it may be used on canapés. Try healthfood stores for ewe's cheese or use a good feta cheese instead.

SERVES 4

¼ lb ewe's cheese
6 tbsp sour cream
½ tsp paprika
1 tbsp chopped chives

Mash the cheese with a fork, then gradually work in the sour cream to make a smooth paste. Stir in the paprika and chives. Chill lightly before serving with rye bread.

MUSHROOM CAVIAR

Eastern Europeans, particularly Russians and Poles, are mushroom fanatics. Dawn expeditions into the wooded countryside in search of fungi are a common sight in the fall.

SERVES 8-10

¼ lb fresh mushrooms (the more varieties, the better – field, shiitake, oyster, girolle, etc), finely chopped
1 medium onion, finely chopped
½ cup butter
1 tbsp dry sherry
½ cup curd cheese
½ cup full-fat cream cheese
2 oz fresh parsley, finely chopped
1 oz fresh tarragon, finely chopped
1 oz fresh marjoram, finely chopped

In a large skillet, sauté the mushrooms and onion in the butter over medium heat, stirring often. When the mushrooms are browned and softened, add the sherry. Remove from the heat.

In a bowl, beat together the two cheeses and herbs. Stir in the mushrooms, onion, and their juices. Beat the mixture with a wooden spoon until it is well combined. Spoon the pâté into a small pot, smooth, swirl the top and cover. Chill overnight or up to 3 days before serving with small rye rounds.

HARE PATE

Traditionally, game such as venison and hare makes an important contribution to meat eaten in eastern Europe. This fine pâté would probably be cooked by steaming on the hob rather than in the oven.

SERVES 12

1 lb fresh pork sides, skin removed
2 lb hare joints
2 medium onions, halved
2 bay leaves
parsley sprig
salt and freshly ground black pepper
1 tsp ground allspice
½ tsp ground ginger
freshly grated nutmeg
2 cups fresh bread crumbs
1 egg, beaten
8 slices rindless streaky bacon
a little butter

Brown the pork in a heavy skillet, then transfer it to a large saucepan. Brown the hare joints all over in the fat from the pork. Add the joints to the pork and pour some water into the skillet. Bring to a boil, stirring, to save all the cooking residue and pour it over the meat. Add the onions, bay leaves, and parsley with some pepper and just a little salt.

Pour in enough water to just cover the meat. Bring to a boil, reduce the heat and cover the pan. Simmer for 1 hour. Leave until the meat is cool.

Scoop the onions out of the pan and grind them or process until smooth in a food processor. Cut all the meat off the hare joints and grind it twice or process until smooth. Cut the pork into chunks and grind it in the same way. Bring the cooking liquid to a boil and boil hard, in the open pan, until reduced to 1¼ cups – this will take 30 minutes, if not longer.

Mix the meats with the onions, spices, bread crumbs, and egg. Strain the reduced liquid through a fine sieve into the pâté and mix well. Add plenty of seasoning – taste a little of the mixture to check for saltiness. Set the oven at 350°F.

Stretch the bacon with the back of a knife, then use it to line a 10 × 4 in loaf pan, overlapping the slices slightly. Press the pâté mixture into the pan. Fold the ends of the bacon over the top. Butter a piece of waxed paper and press it on the pâté, then cover with foil. Place in a roasting pan and pour boiling water around the loaf pan. Bake for 1 hour. Weight the pâté until cool (*see* page 106/7), then chill overnight. Unmold and serve in slices.

CABBAGE AND MUSHROOM ROLLS

These are delicious as a snack or as an accompaniment to soup.

MAKES 24

1 tsp dried yeast or ½ oz fresh yeast
(½ cake compressed yeast)
2 tbsp lukewarm milk
1 tsp sugar
2 cups hard wheat flour
⅓ cup butter
pinch of salt
1 egg yolk
2 tbsp sour cream
beaten egg to glaze

FILLING

¼ lb green cabbage, trimmed of tough stalk
3 dried mushrooms
1 small onion, finely chopped
2 tbsp butter
½ tsp sugar
½ tsp vinegar
salt and freshly ground black pepper

Sprinkle the dried yeast over the milk and sugar or blend the fresh yeast with the milk and sugar. Leave in a warm place until frothy. Sift the flour into a bowl and blend in the butter. Stir in the salt, then make a well in the mixture and add the egg yolk and sour cream. Stir the yeast liquid into the egg and cream, gradually incorporating the dry ingredients. Mix to a soft dough.

Turn out the dough onto a lightly floured surface and knead for about 10 minutes, until it becomes smooth and elastic. Place in a clean bowl, cover with plastic wrap and leave in a warm place until doubled in size. This will take 1½–2 hours.

For the filling, cook the cabbage in boiling water for 10 minutes. Place the mushrooms in a small pan and add just enough water to cover. Heat until simmering and cook for 10–15 minutes, until tender. Drain the cabbage well, then squeeze out all the water and chop finely. (A food processor is useful for this.) Drain and chop the mushrooms, saving the liquid to flavor a sauce or soup.

Cook the onion in the butter until soft but not browned – about 10 minutes. Mix the cabbage and mushrooms with the onion, adding the sugar, vinegar, and seasoning to taste.

Set the oven at 425°F. Lightly knead the risen dough and divide it in half. Break one portion into 12 equal pieces. Roll a small piece of dough into an oblong measuring about 3 × 4 in. Use your fingertips to press out the corners of the dough. Mound a teaspoonful of the filling in the middle of the dough, then fold one end over it. Brush the opposite end with a little beaten egg, then fold it over to make a neat roll. Place on a greased baking sheet with the join down. Continuing rolling and filling the dough. Leave the rolls to rise in a warm place, loosely covered with plastic wrap, for about 30 minutes. Brush the rolls with beaten egg.

Bake for 10–15 minutes, until golden. Transfer to a wire rack to cool slightly. The rolls are at their best while still hot or warm but they are also perfectly good when cold.

GLASSBLOWERS' HERRING

These tasty, spicy herrings are at their best when they have been marinated for a few days.

SERVES 4 – 6

4 medium herrings
3 medium red onions, sliced
2 carrots, sliced

MARINADE

1¼ cups pickling vinegar
1¼ cups sugar
2½ cups water
20 whole allspice
20 white peppercorns
4 bay leaves

Gut and clean the herrings, then soak in cold water overnight. Drain and dry the herrings. Cut across in slices 1½–2 in thick.

For the marinade, mix the vinegar, sugar, water, allspice, white peppercorns, and bay leaves. Bring to the boil, then allow to cool at room temperature.

Put the herrings and vegetables in layers in a glass jar. Pour in enough marinade to cover completely. Refrigerate for at least 24 hours before serving. Serve with boiled new potatoes and brown bread.

ZAKUSKI

Traditionally, a colorful array of canapés is served with vodka to welcome guests. Known in Russia as the zakuska table (the little snacks are *zakuski*), the custom was adopted from the Swedish smörgåsbord and variations on the theme are to be found throughout the region. Many of the dishes in the book, especially from this chapter and the next, could contribute to a zakuska table – the suggestions here are a few simple ideas with a bread base. If possible use thinly sliced rye bread; if using white bread, toast it first. Remove the crusts and cut into neat squares or use a cookie cutter to stamp out small rounds.

SMOKED SALMON

Place a piece of smoked salmon on buttered bread. On top of that, diagonally across the bread, spoon a strip of cold scrambled egg. Garnish with finely chopped dill.

For a different presentation, top rounds of buttered bread with tiny smoked salmon rolls. Add a little sour cream to each and garnish with quartered lemon slices and dill sprigs.

THE HANS ANDERSEN SANDWICH

A Danish creation. Butter a piece of bread, and put two rows of crisp bacon on top. Spread liver pâté across one row of bacon, and place tomato slices across the other. Top the tomato with horseradish and a strip of jellied consommé.

COLD ROAST PORK

Spread thin slices of roast pork on buttered bread. Garnish with crisp pieces of crackling, slices of jellied consommé, pickled cucumber, and beet or red cabbage.

ITALIAN SALAD

Mix together cooked chopped carrots, finely cut asparagus, peas, and mayonnaise. Place a lettuce leaf on buttered bread, and arrange a thick layer of the Italian salad on top. Garnish with tomato slices and cress. If you are using homemade mayonnaise, add a few drops of tarragon vinegar to the vegetables.

TOMATO WITH RAW ONION

Place several slices of tomato on buttered bread. Put a pile of finely chopped raw onion in the center.

CHEESE AND TOMATO

Spread small rounds of buttered bread with cottage cheese and garnish with quartered tomato slices. Sprinkle with chopped chives.

EWE'S CHEESE WITH CUCUMBER

Top small triangles of buttered bread with thinly sliced cucumber and small dollops of ewe's cheese with paprika (see page 25).

HERRING SPREAD AND EGG

Mash herring fillets and spread on buttered bread. Add halved hard-boiled egg slices and sprigs of dill for garnish.

HERRING AND PICKLED CUCUMBER

Top rounds of buttered bread with a slice of pickled cucumber. Cut rollmops into thin slices and place a slice on each canapé. Top with a tiny dollop of sour cream and a sprig of dill or parsley.

PATE AND PICKLED MUSHROOMS

Spread small squares of buttered bread with thin slices of hare pâté (see page 27). Slice pickled mushrooms (available from delicatessen) and place a slice on each canapé. Add a sprig of parsley to each.

ROAST BEEF AND FRIED EGG

Place tender slices of cold roast beef on buttered bread. Fry onions until golden and crisp and spread on the slices of beef. Top with a fried egg, and serve before the egg cools. Note: eggs should be sunny side up!

PASHTET

This pâté can be made with veal and liver, pork and liver, or just liver; it can be served plain, set in aspic or baked in pastry. This is a fairly simple recipe enlivened with dried mushrooms, a favorite Ukrainian ingredient.

SERVES 8

½ lb calves' liver, chopped
1 cup milk
¼ cup butter
½ lb fatty bacon, sliced
1 small onion, chopped
1 stalk celery, chopped
1 small carrot, chopped
1 bay leaf
4 peppercorns
½ lb lean veal, chopped
1 cup chicken stock
1 oz dried boletus or porcini mushrooms
2 slices stale white bread, crusts removed
2 small eggs
pinch of allspice
salt and freshly ground black pepper

In a bowl, soak the calves' liver in the milk for 1 hour. Drain thoroughly and discard the milk.

In a frying pan with a lid, melt the butter over medium heat and coarsely chop and fry 6 oz of the bacon for 3–4 minutes. Add the onion, celery, carrot, bay leaf, peppercorns and veal; toss to coat in the bacon fat and butter for a few minutes. Then pour over the chicken stock and add the dried mushrooms. Cover and simmer gently for 1 hour. Add the liver and cook for a further 30 minutes.

Remove from the heat. Strain the stock into a bowl and soak the bread in it for 5 minutes. Squeeze out as much moisture from the bread as possible and process in batches with the meat and vegetables in a blender or a processor fitted with a metal blade. As the mixture is ground up, transfer to a large bowl. With the hands, work in the eggs, allspice, and salt and more pepper to taste.

Preheat the oven to 350°F. Line a 9 x 5 x 3 in loaf pan with the remaining bacon. Pack in the meat mixture, smooth the top, and cover the pan with foil. Bake for 45–60 minutes, until the pâté is browned and a wooden cocktail stick inserted in it comes away clean. Cool, remove from the pan, then chill. Serve in thick slices with black bread and butter and pickled cucumbers.

MARINATED MUSHROOMS

In Russia, Ukraine and the Baltic states, some of the enthusiasm for wild mushrooms is now tempered with fear, since fungi – particularly the thick-stalked *cep* or *boletus* known colloquially as the "Penny Bun" – have been shown to be severely contaminated by the fallout from Chernobyl. Fortunately our own wild mushrooms, and those available from an increasing number of suppliers, are unaffected.

SERVES 4 – 6

1 lb fresh whole button mushrooms, or a mixture of button and oyster mushrooms
2 cloves garlic
2 cloves
1 bay leaf
sunflower or vegetable oil
1 tbsp sugar
2 tsp salt
1 cup red wine vinegar
⅔ cup water
3 peppercorns

Trim the stalks of the mushrooms so that they are flat with the caps and remove any discolored parts from the oyster mushrooms. Place the garlic, cloves, bay leaf, peppercorns, sugar, and salt in an enamelled or stainless steel saucepan and cover with vinegar and water. Bring the liquid to a boil, add the mushrooms and reduce the heat. Simmer uncovered for about 20 minutes, until the mushrooms sink to the bottom. Remove from the heat, take out the garlic, and let the mixture cool.

Pour the mushrooms and their liquid into 1 pt jars and pour over just enough oil to create a film on top. Cover with plastic wrap secured with rubber bands and refrigerate for at least 10 days before using. (They should keep for several months if refrigerated.)

Right: Marinated Mushrooms

EGGS A LA RUSSE

While the origins of this dish lie within the borders of the Austro-Hungarian rather than the Russian Empire – it was a favorite of turn-of-the-century Viennese chefs – the marriage of ingredients justifies the name they gave it.

SERVES 6

6 hard-boiled eggs, halved
2 tbsp mayonnaise
½ tsp dry mustard powder
1 tbsp Dijon mustard
3 tbsp finely chopped sour-sweet pickled cucumbers
2 tsp finely chopped scallions
salt and freshly ground black pepper
capers and paprika to garnish

Remove the yolks from the halved eggs, reserving the whites, and place them in a small bowl. Mash them thoroughly, then blend the mayonnaise, the two mustards, the chopped cucumbers, and scallions, and seasoning to taste. Spoon the mixture into the egg-white halves and garnish decoratively with the capers and paprika.

CHEESE KNISHES

Knishes, tiny filled pastries, are multipurpose, traditional Jewish fare. Sometimes served with soup or on their own as an appetizer they are traditionally eaten at Shavuot with a moist cheese filling. Other fillings include potato, chicken, and *kasha* (buckwheat). Many different kinds of pastry can be used but this sour cream pastry made in the food processor makes the whole job quick and easy.

MAKES ABOUT 2 DOZEN

PASTRY

1 cup all purpose flour
1 tsp baking powder
½ tsp salt
1 tsp confectioners' sugar
½ cup unsalted butter or hard margarine, cut into small pieces
⅓ cup sour cream
1 egg, beaten, to glaze

CHEESE FILLING

1 cup cottage cheese
2 tbsp sour cream
2 tbsp fine matzo meal
1 tbsp sugar
1 tbsp melted butter
2 eggs, beaten
¼ cup golden raisins, or 1 tbsp chopped fresh parsley

Into a large bowl, sift flour, baking powder, salt, and sugar. Transfer to a food processor fitted with metal blade. Add butter and process until mixture resembles fine crumbs. Remove cover and spoon the sour cream evenly over flour-butter mixture. Using pulse action, process until mixture begins to hold together. Do not allow dough to form into a ball or pastry will be tough. If dough appears too dry, add a little cold water, 1 tablespoon at a time.

Turn out dough onto lightly floured work surface and knead lightly. Form dough into a ball and flatten; wrap well and refrigerate 2 hours or overnight. Leave dough to soften 15 minutes at room temperature before rolling out.

In a large bowl, combine all filling ingredients until well blended.

Grease 2 large baking sheets. Cut dough in half and work with one half at a time. Roll out dough to an 8 × 12 in rectangle about ⅛ in thick. Cut dough into 4 in squares. Place filling in center of each square.

Brush edges of each square with a little egg glaze and fold lower-left corner up to upper-right corner to form a triangle. Using a fork, press edges together to seal well. Place on baking sheet. Continue with remaining dough and filling. You will need to bake in batches.

Preheat oven to 400°F. Brush each triangle with a little egg glaze and score top of pastry to let steam escape. Bake until a rich golden brown, 17–20 minutes. Cool 15 minutes before serving.

NOODLES, GRAINS, DUMPLINGS, AND PANCAKES

PIROSHKI

HOMEMADE
NOODLES

ŁASANKI
WITH
CABBAGE

POTATO
DUMPLINGS
WITH PRUNE
AND NUT
FILLING

SAVORY
NOODLE
KUGEL

MAMALIGA

EGG
NOODLES
AND
BUCKWHEAT
GROATS

KREPLACH

PLUM
KNEDLE

PANCAKES

SAVORY
FILLED
PANCAKES

PANNKOOGID

CHEESE
BLINTZES
WITH
STRAWBERRIES

APPLE
PANCAKES

BLINIS

PIROSHKI

Piroshki are tiny pastries, originally from Russia, usually eaten with a clear meat or chicken broth, but also delicious on their own. They make a delightful canapé or hors d'oeuvre. Traditionally made with a yeast-based dough, a good flaky pastry or commercial puff pastry can be used. The filling can vary from meat to fish, to mushrooms, to cheese and spinach, or any combination you like.

MAKES ABOUT 25–30

FOR THE DOUGH

¼ cup lukewarm water
1 tbsp fine granulated sugar
2½ tsp dry yeast
3½ cups all-purpose flour
1½ tsp salt
⅔ cup warm milk
⅓ cup unsalted butter, melted
3 large eggs
oil

Place the water in a small bowl and sprinkle 1 tsp sugar and the yeast over it. Leave to stand for 15 minutes or until foamy. In a larger bowl, combine three-quarters of the flour with the salt. Make a well in the center and pour in the yeast mixture, the milk, the melted butter, 2 of the eggs, and the rest of the sugar. Using your hands, turn the dry ingredients into the wet and combine thoroughly until you have a soft dough. Remove to a floured board and knead, adding more flour if necessary, to keep it pliable and not sticky. Continue kneading until the dough begins to blister.

Form the dough into a ball with your hands and place it in an oiled bowl, turning to cover with oil. Cover with plastic wrap and let the dough rise in a warm place until it has doubled. Punch it back, cover and chill overnight. Prepare the filling (*see* opposite). This can be done several hours ahead and chilled until needed.

The piroshki will probably need to be baked in two batches. Divide the ball of dough in half. Return one half to the fridge and roll out the other into a thin rectangle. Cut out 3 in rounds with a cookie cutter or lid. Reserve the scraps.

Preheat the oven to 400°F. Make an egg wash by beating the remaining egg with a pinch of salt. Place a heaped teaspoon of the filling on each round, brush the edges with some of the wash, and fold over to make a crescent, pinching the edges together. Use the scraps to make further piroshki. Place them on a lightly greased baking sheet, cover with a towel, and allow to rise for 15–20 minutes. Brush the tops with the wash and bake in the oven for 20–25 minutes or until lightly golden.

Roll out the remaining dough and bake in a similar fashion.

The piroshki can be baked ahead and frozen. Defrost and reheat at 350°F for 10–15 minutes.

POACHED PIROSHKI

Piroshki may also be made without yeast and cooked briefly in boiling water, which makes them similar to ravioli. They can be sweet or savory.

2 cups all purpose flour
salt and freshly ground black pepper
1 egg
⅛ cup water
beaten egg, to seal
½ lb bacon fat or rindless streaky bacon slices, cubed (optional)
a little fat or butter (optional)

Sift the flour into a bowl with ½ tsp salt. Make a well in the middle, then add the egg and water. Mix the flour in to make a firm dough. Use your hands to knead the dough together in the bowl. Turn out the dough onto a surface and knead well until smooth. Divide the dough into quarters and wrap in plastic wrap while you prepare the chosen filling.

On a lightly floured surface, roll out a quarter of the dough quite thinly. Cut out, fill and seal the piroshki as above.

Cook the piroshki in a large saucepan of steadily boiling salted water or stock for about 4 minutes. If making savory piroshki, while the piroshki are cooking, brown the bacon in the fat. Drain the piroshki, transfer them to a warmed serving dish and top with the bacon and fat. If the piroshki are cooked in stock, then ladle just a little stock over them.

38

FILLINGS

PORK

1 small onion, very finely chopped
2 tbsp fat or butter
1¼ cups ground cooked pork
2 tbsp stock

Cook the onion in the fat or butter until soft – about 10 minutes. Add the remaining ingredients and season to taste.

BEEF OR VEAL AND HERBS

1 tbsp vegetable oil
1 medium onion, finely chopped
1 cup ground beef or veal
1 tsp salt
freshly ground black pepper
¼ tsp dried thyme
¼ tsp grated nutmeg
1 egg, lightly beaten

Fry onion in the oil over a medium heat for about 5 minutes until soft and beginning to color. Add meat and cook, stirring occasionally, until the meat has lost its pink color and any liquid has evaporated. Season with salt, pepper, thyme, and nutmeg and remove from heat to cool slightly. Mix in the beaten egg.

CHEESE

1½ cups cottage cheese
2 cups fresh bread crumbs
2 egg yolks

Strain the cottage cheese to remove as much liquid as possible. Mix with the remaining ingredients and season to taste.

SALMON AND CABBAGE

2–3 dried boletus or other wild mushrooms
1 lb cabbage, cored and trimmed of old leaves
3 tbsp unsalted butter
salt and freshly ground black pepper
4 oz salmon fillet
2 tbsp sour cream
1 tbsp caraway seeds
1 tbsp dill seeds
1 egg

Soak the mushrooms in hot water for 30 minutes. Drain and chop them finely. Shred the cabbage in a food processor, then chop into shorter lengths. Place in a large saucepan of boiling water and boil for 3 minutes. Drain, refresh under cold water and drain again, squeezing out the excess water.

In a large skillet, sauté the cabbage in the butter for about 15 minutes. Season to taste and stir in the salmon and the mushrooms. Stir in the sour cream, then the caraway and dill seeds. Chill until needed.

HOMEMADE NOODLES

Pasta in some form or other is surprisingly widely used throughout eastern Europe. Lokshen, Yiddish for noodles, are used by eastern European Jews as an accompaniment to meats, stews, in soups, or in puddings called kugels – egg-enriched dishes of baked noodles with sweet or savory additions. This homemade pasta can be cut into soup noodles or any other shape you like. The food processor makes this easy work.

SERVES 4-6

2 cups all-purpose flour
2 eggs
½ tsp salt

In a food processor fitted with metal blade, process flour, egg, and salt until blended. With machine running, add 1–2 tablespoons water until dough forms a ball in the machine. (If dough is too sticky, add a little more flour.) Process 30 seconds.

Turn out dough on to a lightly floured surface and knead lightly until dough is smooth and elastic. Cover dough on surface with inverted bowl and leave to rest 30 minutes.

Flour 2 large baking sheets. Cut dough in half and work with one half at a time. On lightly floured surface, roll dough as thin as possible into a 14 in square. Place dough square on floured baking sheet and sprinkle with flour; leave to dry 25 to 30 minutes. Repeat with second half of dough.

When dough is slightly dry, roll each square sheet of pasta into a loose, flat jelly-roll shape. Slice crosswise into noodles ⅛ to ½ in wide.

Unroll noodles and shake to separate, letting them stand 1 minute longer. (For later use, hang noodles over the back of a chair or wooden rack to dry.)

Bring a large saucepan of water to a boil. Add noodles and cook about 5 minutes for wide noodles and 2 to 3 minutes for thin noodles. Drain and add to boiling chicken soup or toss with butter and cheese and serve immediately.

VARIATIONS

NOODLE SQUARES
Prepare dough as above, but do not cut into noodles. Cut the dough squares into ½ in strips, then cut strips into ½ in pieces, to form squares.

BOW TIES
Roll out dough as directed but do not leave to dry. Cut dough into 1 in strips, then cut strips into 1 in pieces to form squares. Pinch squares in center to form bow ties.

THIMBLE NOODLES
Prepare dough as above, but dry only 15 minutes. Fold dough sheet in half lengthwise and, with a floured thimble or tiny round cutter, cut through the double layer of pasta. Fry pasta circles in oil heated to 375°F until golden brown and slightly puffed. Drain on paper towels, then serve in soup.

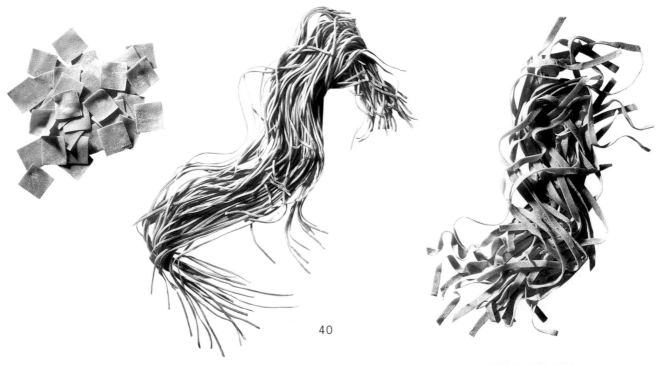

ŁASANKI WITH CABBAGE

**Łasanki is the Polish name for tiny squares of
pasta, boiled and served as an accompaniment to
a main dish, tossed with some sour cream or
mixed with vegetables as here.**

SERVES 4

3 cups all purpose flour
salt and freshly ground black pepper
2 eggs
⅔ cup water
*1½ lb green cabbage, trimmed of tough stalk
and shredded*
1 large onion, thinly sliced
¼ cup butter or fat
1 tsp caraway seeds
1 clove garlic, crushed (optional)

Sift the flour into a bowl with ½ tsp salt. Make a well
in the middle, then add the eggs and water. Gradually
stir the flour into the liquid. Use your hand to
gather the dough together, then knead until
it is smooth. Cut the dough in half and
wrap one piece in plastic wrap.

Roll out the remaining dough on a lightly floured
surface into a 14 in square. Dust with a little flour,
fold in half and cut into thin strips. Dust with a little
flour, fold in half and cut into thin strips. These should
be ¼–½in wide. Cut across them to make tiny squares.
Dust these łasanki with a little flour and sprinkle on a
large plate. Repeat with the remaining dough.

Cook the cabbage in boiling salted water for 3–4
minutes, then drain. Cook the onion in the butter with
the caraway and garlic, if used, until soft – about 15
minutes.

Cook the łasanki in a saucepan of boiling salted
water for 4 minutes, then drain. Stir the cabbage into
the onion and heat for 1 minute. Mix in the łasanki
and transfer the mixture to a warmed serving dish.
Serve at once.

POTATO DUMPLINGS WITH PRUNE AND NUT FILLING

Potatoes have a revered place in the east European kitchen, and are exploited fully These dumplings are a specialty of the lower Ukraine and Moldova.

MAKES ABOUT 30-36

1¼ lb floury potatoes, cooked, peeled, mashed, and cooled
2 cups all purpose flour
⅓ cup fat
1 egg yolk
salt
¼ tsp cinnamon
1¼ cups fresh bread crumbs, toasted
⅔ cup sugar

FOR THE FILLING

15 ready-to-eat prunes
½ tsp grated lemon rind
1 tbsp lemon juice
¼ cup walnuts, finely chopped
⅓ cup sugar

Make the filling first. In a saucepan, just submerge the prunes in water. Bring to the boil, then lower the heat and simmer for 20 minutes. Cool the prunes in the liquid then drain them, reserving 2 tbsp of the liquid. Pit and chop the prunes, place in a bowl and mix together with the lemon rind and juice, walnuts, and sugar.

In a large bowl, beat the potatoes with most of the flour, the fat, egg yolk, and salt to taste. Use your hands to work the mixture into a dough. Transfer to a floured surface and knead, adding a little more flour if necessary to get a smooth, glossy dough. Roll out until it is a large rectangle ⅛ in thick, then cut into squares of about 3½ in.

Place a heaped teaspoon of the filling in the center of each square. Pull up the corners to enclose the filling and form the dough around it to make a ball.

Bring a large saucepan of salted water to a boil, drop in the dumplings and poach for about 25 minutes, or until they are glossy and float to the surface.

Drain the dumplings thoroughly. Mix together the cinnamon, bread crumbs, and sugar and roll the warm dumplings in the mixture. Serve immediately with sour cream.

MAMALIGA

Moldovan food exhibits a legacy of the days between the wars when it was a part of Romania, and of the generations before that when it had many unofficial links with that country. This polenta-like hard cake has a Balkan flavor; it is often served with borscht or cabbage dishes.

SERVES 6

1 cup stone-ground yellow cornmeal
4 cups water
1–1½ tsp salt
¼ cup butter
pinch of dried marjoram
large pinch of cayenne pepper
10 oz hard ewe's or goat's cheese
salt and freshly ground black pepper

Stir the cornmeal in a large frying pan over medium heat for 4 minutes, or until it loses its bright yellow color and becomes light beige.

Pour the water into a saucepan. Put the hot cornmeal into the water, it should hiss; then stir in the salt to taste. Cook over moderate heat for 5 minutes, stirring, until the liquid begins to boil. Cover, lower the heat and simmer for 20 minutes, stirring frequently.

Preheat the oven to 375°F. Uncover the saucepan and continue to stir until the mixture is very thick and the spoon is drawing it away from the bottom and sides of the pan. Remove from the heat, add the butter, marjoram, and pepper, and stir until the butter is melted. Stir in three-quarters of the cheese, then turn the mixture into a shallow buttered baking dish.

Bake for 40 minutes on the top shelf of the oven, until the cake has a skin over it. Remove from the oven and allow to cool and set for at least 1 hour. (The cake can be kept refrigerated for up to 3 days.)

To serve, heat the broiler to hot. Slice the cake into squares or wedges and sprinkle over the remaining cheese. Broil until the cheesy crust is golden-brown and the mamaliga is hot. Serve immediately.

EGG NOODLES AND BUCKWHEAT GROATS

Noodles and dumplings of all types are popular in Ukraine and Belorussia. They range from little misshapen egg pasta droplets to potato and rice dumplings. They are served on their own with butter, accompanied by meat sauces, or baked with other ingredients, as here.

SERVES 6–8

½ cup unsalted butter
2 onions, sliced
½ lb field or brown mushrooms, sliced
6 oz whole buckwheat groats (kasha)
1 large egg, beaten
1¼ cups boiling water
1 tsp salt
½ lb fresh egg noodles, cut into quarters
freshly ground black pepper
½ cup fine dry bread crumbs
sour cream

Melt a quarter of the butter in a large skillet and sauté the onions until they are soft and lightly colored, about 8 minutes. Add the mushrooms and cook, stirring, until the mushrooms are soft. Transfer the vegetables to a casserole.

Wash and dry the skillet. Place over moderate heat and add the buckwheat, stirring, and the beaten egg. Continue to stir until the groats are separate and egg-coated. Pour in the boiling water and add 1 tablespoon butter and salt. Cover and simmer until all the liquid is absorbed and the buckwheat just tender, about 25 minutes. Transfer the buckwheat to the casserole.

Preheat the oven to 350°F. In a large saucepan, cook the noodles in boiling water until just tender, about 4 minutes. Drain thoroughly and stir the noodles into the casserole with the buckwheat, onions, and mushrooms, adding 3 tablespoons of butter and seasoning to taste. Melt the remaining butter and combine with the bread crumbs. Scatter over the top of the casserole and bake in the oven until warmed through and the bread crumbs are toasted, about 20 minutes. Serve with sour cream to spoon over.

SAVORY NOODLE KUGEL

A kugel is a baked pudding popular with eastern European Jews. Traditionally, a kugel was simmered in a separate dish, inside or alongside a stew and then served as an accompaniment or afterwards with pickles. Cheese-based kugels can be served as an accompaniment dish or a main dish. Noodle kugels can also be made with sugar and fresh or dried fruits.

SERVES 4–6

½ cup unsalted butter or margarine, at room temperature
1 cup cream cheese, at room temperature
1 cup cottage cheese
5 eggs, beaten
1¼ cups milk
grated rind and juice of 1 lemon
2 scallions, finely chopped
1½ oz raisins (optional)
salt
freshly ground black pepper
¼ tsp grated nutmeg
½ lb egg noodles, cooked and drained

Preheat oven to 350°F. Lightly grease a deep baking dish. In a large bowl, blend butter and cream cheese together until smooth. Beat in cottage cheese and eggs, then slowly beat in the milk.

Stir in lemon rind and juice, scallions, raisins, if using, salt and pepper to taste, and nutmeg. Add noodles and toss to mix well.

Turn into baking dish and cook until mixture is set and top is puffy and golden brown, 1 hour. Serve hot or cold from dish.

Right: Savory Noodle Kugel

KREPLACH

Yiddish for "little crêpe," kreplach were originally from Russia and Poland. These are small filled dumplings, sometimes referred to as Jewish ravioli or Jewish wontons. They can be made in various shapes and filled with meat, chicken, or cheese. The meat filling is usually made from the shin of beef which has been used to make stock, but ground beef can be used instead.

MAKES ABOUT 75

1 cup cooked beef, ground, or ground beef, browned
1 small onion, chopped
½ tsp salt
freshly ground black pepper
1 tbsp chopped fresh dill (optional)
1 egg
1 recipe Homemade noodle dough (see page 40)

Into a food processor fitted with metal blade, process beef and onion until finely chopped but not pasty. Add salt and pepper to taste, dill, if using, and the egg and, with pulse action, process until meat mixture is moist and holds together. Scrape into a bowl and refrigerate until ready to use.

Prepare noodle dough and roll out as directed but do not leave to dry. Cut into 2 in squares. Put 1 teaspoon filling in the center of each square and brush corners with a little water. Fold lower-left corner over upper-right corner to form a triangle, pressing the edges firmly together to seal.

Transfer to a lightly floured baking sheet and continue until all dough is used. (Kreplach can be made up to this point ahead and refrigerated until ready to cook.)

Bring a large saucepan of water to a boil. Add some of the kreplach but do not overcrowd. Simmer gently 12–15 minutes. With a slotted spoon, remove and drain in a colander. Bring water back to a boil and continue until all kreplach are tender. (Cooked kreplach can be refrigerated or frozen for future use.)

To serve, simmer kreplach in chicken or meat soup until heated through, 10–12 minutes.

Kreplach can be served other ways. Cook in boiling water as directed and serve tossed with butter or oil and grated cheese or a tomato sauce. For a main meal, fry kreplach in butter or oil and a little chopped onion and sprinkle with cheese.

Kreplach can also be made with a cheese filling. Combine 2 cups cottage cheese, 2 tbsp sour cream, 3 tbsp fine bread crumbs or matzo meal, salt and pepper to taste, 1 tbsp chopped fresh parsley, 1 tbsp chopped fresh chives and 1 egg. Mix well and use to fill kreplach as above.

PLUM KNEDLE

A family meal in Poland does not necessarily consist of a main course followed by pudding; sweet dishes, such as this one, may be served as a light meal on their own. Other fruit may be used instead of the plums: try lightly poached chunks of cooking apple, hulled strawberries or stoned cherries. The knedle may also be filled with preserves or marmalade.

MAKES 12

1 lb potato dumpling mixture (see page 42)
12 ripe plums
¼ cup unsalted butter, melted
confectioners' sugar to dust

Prepare the knedle dough as described in the recipe. Divide it into 12 pieces. Remove the stalks from the plums but leave the fruit whole.

Lightly flour your hands and flatten a portion of dough into a neat patty on your palm. Place a plum in the middle, then ease the dough around it to enclose completely.

Cook the plum knedle in a saucepan of steadily boiling water for about 3 minutes, until the dumplings are cooked. Drain and serve at once, with the butter poured over and dusted with confectioners' sugar. Warmed honey is also good with the plums instead of confectioners' sugar.

PANCAKES

Here is the basic recipe for pancakes. They may be filled with a savory stuffing or served with fruit bottled in syrup or liqueur, with jelly or with plum spread.

MAKES 8

1 cup all purpose flour
1 egg
½ cup water
½ cup milk
oil or butter to cook

Sift the flour into a bowl and make a well in the middle. Add the egg and about a third of the water. Beat the egg and water, gradually working in the flour and adding more water with the milk to make a smooth batter. Leave to stand for 30 minutes. You may have to thin the batter with a little extra water if it thickens a great deal on standing.

Heat a large skillet and grease it lightly. Ladle some of the batter on to it, rolling the pan to ensure the base is evenly coated. Cook the pancake over a medium heat until golden underneath and fairly dry. Use a spatula to loosen the edges, then turn the pancake over and cook the second side. Repeat with the remaining batter. Place paper towels between the pancakes as you stack them to prevent them sticking together.

The pancakes freeze well when cool. Pack them interleaved with freezer film so that a few may be lifted off without having to thaw the whole batch. Heat them individually in a greased pan or use for stuffed pancakes.

SAVORY FILLED PANCAKES

Select either of these fillings to stuff eight pancakes.

SERVES 4

8 pancakes (see previous recipe)
oil or butter to cook

COATING

1 egg, beaten
1 cup white bread crumbs

Prepare the pancakes before making the chosen filling.
Divide the filling into eight portions. Lay a pancake on a board and place a portion of filling in the middle. Fold one end of the pancake over the filling, then brush the pancake with beaten egg. Fold the sides over and lastly fold the end over to enclose the filling in a neat parcel. Brush all over with egg and coat with bread crumbs. Repeat with the remaining pancakes and filling.
Heat a little oil or butter in a large skillet and cook the pancakes, turning once until the coating is golden. Serve at once.

CABBAGE FILLING

¾ lb green cabbage, trimmed of tough stalk
salt and freshly ground black pepper
6 slices rindless smoked streaky bacon, cubed
½ tsp caraway seeds
4 tbsp drained sauerkraut
2 tbsp sour cream

Cook the cabbage until soft. Drain, cool and chop finely.
Cook the bacon until browned. Mix the cabbage, bacon, caraway, sauerkraut, and sour cream with seasoning to taste.

MEAT FILLING

1 onion, finely chopped
2 tbsp butter
½ tsp dried marjoram
2 tbsp chopped fresh parsley
1½ cups ground cooked meat
4 tbsp sour cream

For the meat filling, cook the onion in the butter for 10 minutes. Add the marjoram, parsley, and meat. Stir in the sour cream and season to taste.

PANNKOOGID

These Estonian pancakes are huge – the size of plates – and have a fluffy consistency quite unlike the familiar pancake. In their native land they would often be served with lingonberries, but raspberries or blueberries are just as scrumptious.

SERVES 6

1 cup all purpose flour
¼ cup sugar
pinch of salt
2 eggs, separated
⅞ cup milk
½ tsp vanilla essence

FOR THE FILLING

½ lb fresh raspberries or blueberries
2 tbsp water
⅔ cup sugar
1 tbsp cornstarch

Sift the flour, sugar, and salt into a large bowl. Make a well in the center. Drop the egg yolks, the milk and vanilla into the well, then beat to combine thoroughly with the flour. The batter will be thin. Cover it with a cloth and leave in a cool – not cold – place overnight to mature.

To make the filling, rinse and drain the berries and place in an enamelled or stainless steel saucepan, together with the water and the sugar. Cook over medium heat, stirring, until the berries are dissolving into a sauce, with some remaining whole. Bring to a boil, stir in the cornstarch and reduce the heat. Cook for 5–10 minutes, stirring until the filling mixture has thickened. Remove from the heat, pour into an attractive bowl and allow to cool.

Before using the batter, beat the egg whites in a large bowl until they form stiff peaks. With a rubber or plastic spatula, carefully fold them into the batter.

Lightly coat a large non-stick crêpe pan or skillet with butter and heat until medium hot. Remove from the heat and pour in ½ cup of the batter. Tilt the pan to spread it evenly, then replace on the heat and fry the pancake for about 3 minutes a side, until golden. Slide the pancake on to a dish and keep warm while you make the rest of the pancakes.

Serve each pancake flat on a plate, accompanied by the bowl of fruit sauce.

CHEESE BLINTZES WITH STRAWBERRIES

Blintzes are a symbol of Jewish cooking around the world, with the name coming from the Yiddish for pancake. It is a simple crêpe or pancake filled with cheese or fruits or savory fillings such as potato and mushroom, chicken livers, cabbage, or meat.

SERVES 6 – 8

3 large eggs
½ tsp salt
½ tsp sugar
2 tbsp butter or margarine, melted
1½ cups milk or water
¾ cup all purpose flour
butter or margarine for baking or frying, melted

FILLING

2 cups cottage cheese
⅔ cup cream cheese, softened
⅓ cup sugar
1 tsp vanilla extract
1 lb strawberries, thawed if frozen
sugar
juice and grated rind of 1 lemon

In a large bowl, beat eggs, salt, sugar, melted butter or margarine, and milk or water until well blended.

Into a medium bowl, sift flour; make a well in center. Using a wire whisk, gradually stir beaten egg mixture into flour, drawing in flour from edges of well until all egg mixture is added. Whisk until smooth. Strain into a measuring jug. Cover and refrigerate about 1 hour. (Batter may thicken; add milk or water to thin if necessary.)

Over medium heat, heat a 7 in crêpe pan or skillet. Brush with a little melted butter. Pour 3 to 4 tablespoons (about ¼ cup) batter into pan, tipping pan to coat bottom with batter. Cook until top looks set and bottom is lightly browned, about 2 minutes. Using a spatula, loosen edges and flip blintze, then cook 10 seconds. Slip cooked blintze onto a piece of waxed paper. Repeat until all batter is used, stacking blintzes between sheets of waxed paper. Blintzes can be used immediately or stored in the refrigerator or frozen.

Preheat oven to 350°F. Brush a 15 × 10 in jelly roll tin with butter or margarine.

Make filling. In a medium bowl, with a mixer at medium speed, beat cottage cheese, cream cheese, sugar, and vanilla until smooth.

On a clean work surface, spread 1 heaped tablespoon of cheese mixture down center of each blintze. Fold sides towards center, so each side covers about half the filling. Beginning at bottom edge, roll up blintze. Arrange seam-side down on buttered pan. Brush each folded blintze with a little butter. Bake until heated through, about 10 minutes.

Reserve 6 to 8 strawberries: slice each in half lengthwise and set aside. Hull remainder. Into a food processor, fitted with metal blade, place half of the strawberries. Add sugar to taste and lemon juice and grated rind. Process until smooth and pour into small bowl. Chop remaining strawberries and add to purée. Add more sugar if necessary.

To serve, place 2 blintzes on a plate, spoon over a little strawberry sauce and garnish with 2 strawberry halves.

APPLE PANCAKES

These are so moreish that once tried they are not easily forgotten! The great surprise is that they are really quick and easy to make, too.

MAKES 10

½ cup all purpose flour
2 tbsp superfine sugar
1 egg, separated
4 tbsp sour cream
½ lb cooking apples, peeled, cored, and finely sliced
butter to cook
confectioners' sugar to dust
sour cream to serve (optional)

Sift the flour into a bowl. Stir in the sugar, egg yolk and sour cream to make a thick batter. Add the apples, stirring for a while without breaking the slices. Whisk the egg white until standing in stiff peaks. Fold it into the apple mixture, making sure it is well combined with the other ingredients.

Heat a little butter in a large skillet or griddle. Drop spoonfuls of the apple mixture onto the hot surface. Use the spoon to arrange the mixture in fairly thin, neat rounds measuring about 2½–3 in across. Cook fairly slowly until golden underneath and almost set on top. Turn the pancakes over and cook the second side until golden. Serve at once, dusted with sugar, with some sour cream, if liked.

BLINIS

Leaving the batter for the blinis to stand overnight allows it to acquire its distinctive sour flavor. Blinis freeze well, and are delicious paired with smoked salmon or smoked meats such as ham and turkey and with cottage cheese accompanied by dried or fresh soft fruits.

SERVES 8-10

⅓ cup lukewarm water
2½ tsp active dry yeast
2 tbsp sugar
1¼ cups milk
1 cup unsalted butter, melted
½ cup buckwheat flour
½ cup all purpose flour
1 tsp salt
2 large eggs, separated, at room temperature
⅔ cup sour cream

TO SERVE

½ lb black caviar or lumpfish roe
½ lb golden or red salmon roe
sour cream
hard-boiled egg, finely chopped
1 lemon, sliced
dill

Pour the lukewarm water into a small bowl. Sprinkle the yeast and ½ tablespoon sugar over it and leave for 3 minutes. Stir to dissolve completely, then set in a warm spot for another five minutes, until it is foamy and doubled in volume.

Heat half the milk to lukewarm and stir into the yeast mixture together with the remaining sugar and 1 tablespoon of the butter. Beat in the buckwheat flour for about 1½ minutes, then cover tightly with plastic wrap and chill it overnight.

Next day, let the batter come to room temperature. Heat the remaining milk to lukewarm and stir into the batter together with the all purpose flour, salt, egg yolks, and sour cream. Beat the mixture for about 1 minute, then cover and leave to rise for 1 hour or until foamy and double in size. In a metal bowl, beat the egg whites to stiff peaks. Fold them gently into the batter.

Place a griddle or a shallow skillet over medium heat and, when it is hot, brush lightly with butter. Drop about 2 tbsp butter on to the griddle so that it spreads into a 3–4 in circle. Repeat twice and fry the blinis for 2 minutes, or until the undersides are golden. Brush the tops lightly with melted butter and turn them over to cook for 1 more minute. Repeat until all the batter is used up, meanwhile keeping the blinis warm, covered with foil, in an oven set at 250°F. (The blinis may be made up to 2 days before and kept covered and chilled. Reheat in a 350°F oven for 15 minutes.)

Serve the warm blinis wrapped in a napkin on a heated platter, accompanied by pots of the caviar and roe in ice and an attractive arrangement of sour cream, finely chopped hard-boiled egg, sliced lemon and finely chopped dill.

FISH

HERRING AND
BEAN SALAD

HERRING
WITH LEEK
AND LEMON

MARINATED
FISH

ONION AND
MUSTARD
HERRINGS

MATJES
HERRING
WITH
TOMATOES
AND OLIVES

FISH IN
HORSERADISH
SAUCE

FISHBALLS

GEFILTE FISH

GRAVAD LAX

PATAKUKKO

OVEN-
ROASTED
PIKE

LAKE FISH
IN MUSTARD
SAUCE

SMOKED EEL
SALAD

SWEET AND
SOUR FISH

SHRIMP IN
DILL CREAM

HERRING AND BEAN SALAD

Dried beans are used in a variety of ways, to make soups, in stews or cold in salads as here.

SERVES 4

1 cup dried fava or lima beans, soaked overnight in cold water to cover
salt and freshly ground black pepper
4 salted herring fillets
2 tbsp olive oil
1 medium potato, cooked and cubed
1 pickled cucumber, sliced
½ cup shelled peas, cooked
4 tbsp sour cream
4 tbsp mayonnaise
2 tbsp chopped fresh dill or parsley
2 tbsp finely chopped onion
1 tsp grated lemon rind
lemon wedges to garnish

Drain the soaked beans. Cook them in plenty of fresh, boiling water for 1 hour, until tender. Add salt to the water halfway through cooking. Drain well and cool.

Cut the herring fillets into strips and mix with the cooled beans and olive oil. Add the potato, pickled cucumber, and peas, mixing lightly to avoid breaking up the ingredients. Transfer to individual bowls or a large dish.

Mix the sour cream, mayonnaise, dill, onion, lemon rind, and seasoning to taste. Spoon this dressing over the salad and add lemon wedges to garnish. The dressing should be tossed into the ingredients just before the salad is eaten. Lemon juice may be squeezed over to sharpen the salad.

HERRING WITH LEEK AND LEMON

The leek and lemon juice add a tangy flavor to the herring – one of the many ways of serving this bountiful fish from the northern waters.

SERVES 4 – 6

2 salt herrings (4 fillets)
1 leek, cleaned and sliced
1 small bunch of dill, coarsely chopped

MARINADE

juice of 2 lemons
2 tbsp pickling vinegar
1 cup water
¾ cup sugar
½ tsp whole allspice
½ tsp white peppercorns
1 bay leaf

Fillet the salt herrings, and soak them in water overnight. Mix all the ingredients for the marinade in a saucepan and bring to a boil. Leave to cool.

Slice the herrings into 1-inch strips. Layer in a glass jar with the sliced leek and dill. When the marinade is cold, pour over enough liquid to cover the herrings. Leave in the refrigerator for 24 hours before serving. Serve with boiled new potatoes.

MARINATED FISH

Use the freshest possible fish. If you are using mackerel look for small, young specimens that tend to be fine-flaked and not over rich. The fish rolls may be served with boiled potatoes and beet salad, or accompanied by rye bread.

SERVES 4

2½ cups water
1 bay leaf
1 onion, thinly sliced
salt and freshly ground black pepper
2 tbsp vinegar
4 mackerel or herrings, cleaned with heads off
1 small carrot
1 pickled cucumber
1 pickled cucumber, sliced, and dill sprigs to garnish

Simmer the water, bay leaf, onion, and seasoning for 10 minutes with a close-fitting lid on the pan. Add the vinegar and cool.

Bone the fish. Lay each one flesh side down on a board and press firmly down the middle of the bone. Turn the fish over and the main bone should lift off easily, bringing with it most of the small bones at the side. Pick off all remaining bones. Cut each fish in half lengthways to give eight fillets.

Cut eight thin sticks from the carrot and blanch them in boiling water for 1 minute. Drain and rinse under cold water. Cut eight thin sticks lengthways from the pickled cucumber. Place a stick of carrot and pickled cucumber at the wide end of each fish fillet and roll up to the tail, then secure with wooden toothpicks. Place in the prepared, cooled liquid. Heat very gently until the liquid is steaming but not simmering. Cover and leave at this heat for 10 minutes. Remove from the heat and leave the fish to cool completely in the liquid. The rolls should be cooked through by the time they have cooled.

Lift the fish rolls from the cooking liquid when cool. Serve garnished with pickled cucumber and dill, whole or chopped.

ONION AND MUSTARD HERRINGS

Onions and mustard appear in combination with herring in several Baltic recipes. Sometimes the fish is in a mustard sauce but in this Latvian version, the overnight marinade enhances the finished dish.

SERVES 4

1½ lb fresh small herring, gutted, head, backbone, and bones removed, washed and patted dry
8 tbsp rye flour
¼ cup unsalted butter
1 medium red onion, peeled, sliced, and separated into rings
2 tbsp finely chopped parsley
lemon quarters

FOR THE COATING

4 tbsp German-style mustard
1 tbsp French-style mustard
3 small egg yolks
⅓ cup heavy cream
salt and freshly ground black pepper

To make the coating mixture, mix together the two mustards in a small bowl. Whisk in the egg yolks, one by one, then the cream. Season to taste and whisk lightly again.

Spread out one herring on a flat plate. Spoon a little of the coating over the inside of the fish, fold together, and brush the skin on both sides with the mixture. Push to one side of the plate and continue with each of the remaining fish. Use any remaining mixture to recoat the fish. Cover with foil and leave overnight in the refrigerator.

Spread the rye flour on a plate and dip each of the fish into it. Melt the butter in a large skillet over medium heat. Fry the fish in batches, turning to cook both sides, until they are golden brown, about 6 minutes. Keep warm until all the fish are cooked.

Arrange the fish attractively on a serving dish, with the onion rings and parsley scattered over them. Serve garnished with lemon quarters.

MATJES HERRING WITH TOMATOES AND OLIVES

A traditional recipe for herrings in brine with the flavors imparted by the marinade. The matjes are a perfect contrast to plain new potatoes.

SERVES 4

2 matjes herring fillets, canned in brine
4–6 shallots or small pickling onions
12–14 olives with pimento

MARINADE

¼ cup tomato catsup
1 tbsp pickling vinegar
2 tbsp sugar
pinch of salt
1 tsp crushed white pepper
3 tbsp oil

Slice the herring into 2-in strips. Slice the shallots into fine rings. Layer the herring, shallots, and olives in a glass jar.

For the marinade, mix the catsup, pickling vinegar, sugar, salt, and pepper together. Stir and add the oil slowly. Pour the marinade over the herring to cover, and leave in the refrigerator for a few hours before serving. Served with new potatoes and brown bread.

Right: Matjes Herring with Tomatoes and Olives

FISH IN HORSERADISH SAUCE

This simple dish of cod in a creamy horseradish sauce is quite delicious.

SERVES 4

1 lb cod fillet, skinned and cut into four portions
2 bay leaves
salt and freshly ground black pepper
1 cup water
2 tbsp butter
¼ cup all purpose flour
3 tbsp grated horseradish
1¼ cups sour cream
dill or parsley sprigs and lemon slices to garnish

Place the fish in a shallow pan and add the bay leaves. Sprinkle with seasoning, pour in the water and heat gently until simmering.

Cook gently for 3–5 minutes, until the fish is just cooked. Use a spatula to transfer the pieces of fish to an ovenproof dish. Strain the fish cooking liquor and reserve.

Set the oven at 425°F. Melt the butter in a small saucepan and stir in the flour. Gradually pour the reserved fish cooking liquor onto the flour mixture, stirring all the time. Add the horseradish and bring to a boil to make a very thick sauce. Stir in a little seasoning and the sour cream. Spoon the sauce over the fish.

Bake for about 10 minutes, until the sauce is just beginning to brown. Garnish with dill and lemon, then serve at once.

FISHBALLS

These fishballs may be served as part of a salad, as below, or they may be served hot, coated with horseradish sauce made in the same way as in the previous recipe (Fish in horseradish sauce).

S E R V E S   4

1 small onion, finely chopped
2 tbsp butter
⅔ cup fresh white bread crumbs
¼ lb cod fillet, skinned
1 egg white
2 tbsp chopped fresh dill
salt and freshly ground white pepper
3¾ cups fish stock
white part of 1 leek, thinly sliced
1 lettuce heart, shredded
¼ cucumber, thinly sliced (about ¼ lb)
8 radishes, sliced
6 tbsp mayonnaise
dill sprigs to garnish

Cook the onion in the butter for about 10 minutes, until soft but not browned. Mix with the bread crumbs in a bowl. Grind the fish or purée it in a food processor and add it to the crumb mixture. Stir in the egg white, dill, and plenty of seasoning.

Using clean hands, wet them and roll small portions of the fish mixture into walnut-sized balls. The mixture should make 16 balls. Heat the fish stock in a saucepan until simmering. Add the fishballs and simmer for 10 minutes. Drain and cool.

Blanch the leek in boiling water for 30–60 seconds, drain immediately and rinse under cold water. Drain and pat dry on paper towels.

Arrange the lettuce, leek, and cucumber on individual plates or on one platter. Group the fishballs on the salad, adding the radish slices for color.

Mix the mayonnaise and sour cream with a little seasoning to taste. Spoon this dressing over the fishballs. Garnish with dill and serve.

61

GEFILTE FISH

The name "gefilte" comes from the German for "filled." Originally, skinned and boned fish was stuffed with a minced fish mixture and slowly simmered. After chilling, the rich stock became jellied and was served as part of the dish or separately. Nowadays, however, the mixture is generally formed into balls and simmered in stock. It is also very attractive when packed into a ring mold and baked in the oven, or even microwaved! Of course, cooked in this way there is no jelly as an accompaniment.

Although freshwater carp and pike were traditional for making gefilte fish, most cooks prefer a mixture of saltwater white fish. But whatever fish you use, gefilte fish is always served with carrot slices and beet-flavored horseradish sauce.

SERVES 6

FISH STOCK

3–4 lb fish bones and heads (white fish only), well rinsed
2 onions, sliced
1 carrot, sliced
1 stalk celery, sliced
1 leek, split lengthwise, sliced and well rinsed
4 sprigs fresh parsley
1 tsp salt
1 tsp black peppercorns
2 sprigs fresh thyme (optional)

FISH MIXTURE

3 lb white fish fillets, such as cod, whiting, snapper (a little carp or pike can be mixed in)
2 onions, quartered
salt
3 eggs, lightly beaten
½ tsp fresh ground white pepper
¼ tsp grated nutmeg (optional)
¼ cup medium matzo meal
1 carrot, thinly sliced

TO SERVE

fresh parsley sprigs and lemon slices
Horseradish-beet sauce (see right)

Prepare stock. Into a large stockpot, place all ingredients for fish stock. Cover with cold water and, over high heat, bring to a boil. Skim off any foam that comes to the surface. Reduce heat and simmer for 20 minutes. Strain stock into a large saucepan or casserole. Set aside.

Prepare fish mixture. Into a food processor fitted with metal blade, place fish and onions and process to a fine purée. (You may need to work in batches.) Add 1½ teaspoons salt, or to taste, eggs, pepper, and nutmeg and process to mix.

Stir in matzo meal; add ¼ cup water, a little at a time. The mixture should be light and slightly sticky, but hold its shape. Cover and refrigerate for 30 minutes.

Using 2 tablespoons, form mixture into ovals, placing each on a baking sheet sprinkled with water. Continue until all mixture is shaped.

Bring stock to a boil. Add carrot slices and carefully drop fish ovals into stock. Reduce heat and simmer gently for 1 hour. (Do not leave water to boil.)

Leave fish to cool in stock. Using a slotted spoon, remove fish ovals to a large shallow baking dish or serving platter. Strain stock over the fish ovals and place a carrot slice on top of each oval; scatter remaining slices around the dish. Refrigerate 4 hours or overnight. Garnish with parsley sprigs and lemon slices and serve with Horseradish-beet sauce.

HORSERADISH-BEET SAUCE

MAKES ABOUT 1 ¼ pt

1 medium fresh horseradish root
3–4 beet, cooked, peeled, cut to fit food processor tube
1 tbsp light brown sugar or honey
freshly ground black pepper
¼ cup distilled white wine or cider vinegar

Wearing rubber gloves, use a swivel-vegetable peeler, peel horseradish root. Trim ends. In a food processor fitted with grating disc, grate horseradish.

Without removing processor cover, grate cooked beet onto horseradish.

Remove cover and scrape into a bowl, mixing well with brown sugar or honey, pepper to taste, and vinegar. If mixture is too dry, add a little more vinegar. Store refrigerated in a covered jar.

GRAVAD LAX

Prepare your own gravad lax with salmon, trout, or mackerel. You will be surprised how easy it is, and how delicious. The dill and mustard sauce is a perfect accompaniment.

SERVES 4 – 6

2–3 lb fresh salmon (middle cut)
¼ cup salt
⅓ cup sugar
plenty of fresh dill
1½ tbsp crushed whole white peppercorns

Ask for the salmon to be cut into fillets, and have the central bone removed. Remove any remaining small bones. Mix the salt and sugar together.

Take a shallow, non-metallic dish and sprinkle with half of the dill. Place one of the salmon fillets on the dill, skin wide down. Rub half the mixture of salt and sugar into the salmon. Sprinkle with crushed white peppercorns and half the remaining dill. Repeat the process on the other side of salmon and sandwich together, skin side up. Cover with foil.

Refrigerate for 3 days, turning the salmon every 24 hours. To serve, scrape off the seasoning and cut in slices, discarding the skin. Serve with dill and mustard sauce.

DILL AND MUSTARD SAUCE

As well as accompanying gravad lax, this sauce can also be served with other types of fish.

SERVES 4 – 6

1 tbsp sugar
2 tbsp malt vinegar
2 tbsp mild mustard
finely chopped fresh dill
7 tbsp oil
salt and white pepper

Mix the sugar, vinegar, mustard, and dill together. Pour the oil slowly into the mixture, stirring thoroughly. Season with salt and white pepper.

PATAKUKKO

This fish pie is a typical dish from Karelia, in eastern Finland, and can easily be carried around. As it is so portable, try it in the children's lunch box or on picnics.

SERVES 4 – 6

2 lb small perch or vendace
10 oz fatty pork, cut into strips
1½–2 tbsp salt

DOUGH

1¼ cups rye flour
⅓ cup water
⅓ cup white flour
1 tsp salt

Clean the fish, and sprinkle with salt. Leave the fish to stand in the refrigerator for a few hours or overnight to allow the salt to soak in.

Line a baking dish with strips of the pork. Place the fish in the baking dish and add a drop of water.

Preheat the oven to 325°F. Mix together the rye flour, water, white flour, and salt to make the dough. Knead it well on a floured board. Roll out the dough and use to cover the fish in the baking dish. Bake for 2–3 hours until golden.

OVEN-ROASTED PIKE

Though a somewhat undervalued fish elsewhere, pike is popular in the Baltic States and Scandinavia. It has a delicious, unusual flavor, that is well worth exploring.

SERVES 4 – 6

2 lb pike
2 tsp salt
1 egg, beaten
bread crumbs for coating
1 tsp ground white pepper
4–6 anchovy fillets
½ cup butter, melted
3 cups grated hard cheese

Preheat the oven to 400°F. Scale the fish, leave the head on for flavor, but cut off the fins. Rinse and dry. Sprinkle with a little salt and leave for 5 minutes. Turn the fish in the beaten egg, then coat in bread crumbs mixed with a little white pepper. Arrange the anchovy filets on top of the fish.

Wrap in foil and bake for 20–30 minutes. Baste with melted butter a few times. Sprinkle with the grated cheese 5 minutes before the end of the cooking time. Serve with steamed vegetables of your choice and boiled potatoes.

LAKE FISH IN MUSTARD SAUCE

Omul is a delicious relative of the salmon, found only in Siberia's Lake Baikal, one of the most beautiful lakes and on record as the deepest (1 mile) in the world. This recipe would use local wildflower honey and the fish would be baked over an open brushwood fire; here we must be content with ordinary honey, best Scottish salmon and a barbecue or grill.

SERVES 6

2 tbsp sunflower oil
3 lb salmon fillet, washed and dried
2½ tbsp German-style mustard
1½ tbsp honey
grated rind and juice of ½ small lemon
1 tbsp finely chopped fresh dill
salt and freshly ground black pepper
dill sprigs

If you are broiling the fish, brush a sheet of foil with a little sunflower oil before placing the salmon skin-side down on it. Whether broiling or barbecuing, place the fish (and foil, if used) on a baking tray. Mix together the remaining oil, mustard, honey, lemon rind and juice, and chopped dill. Brush the fish liberally with the mixture.

Pre-heat a broiler to hot. (If you are using a barbecue, the coals should be greying. Place the fish in a fish holder and turn it flesh-side down towards the coals.)

Broil or barbecue the fish about 5 in from the heat for about 10 minutes, or until slightly translucent. Transfer to a serving platter and garnish with dill sprigs before serving.

SMOKED EEL SALAD

Smoked eel makes a tasty salad which may be served with vegetables – try cucumber salad (*see* page 118) and boiled new potatoes – or with thinly sliced rye bread.

SERVES 4

½ lb smoked eel fillet
4 small tomatoes, thinly sliced
2 tbsp finely chopped onion
1 tbsp vinegar
1 tsp sugar
2 tsp water
1 small lettuce heart, shredded
salt and freshly ground black pepper
4 tbsp sour cream
a little paprika

Cut each piece of eel in half lengthways and pick out all the bones. Arrange the strips of eel on individual plates with the tomato slices. Sprinkle the onion over the tomato.

Stir in the vinegar, sugar, and water together until the sugar has dissolved. Toss this dressing with the lettuce and seasoning to taste.

Arrange the lettuce on the plates. Top the fillets of eel with a little sour cream and sprinkle with paprika.

SWEET AND SOUR FISH

In eastern Europe, sweet and sour fish was generally prepared with carp. In France it is known as *carpe à la Juive* (Jewish-style carp) and it was traditional to serve the head of the fish to the head of the house on the Jewish New Year, Rosh Hashana. This recipe uses fish steaks rather than a whole fish.

S E R V E S 6

6 fish steaks, such as carp, pike, salmon, or trout,
1 in thick (3 lb total weight)
salt
freshly ground black pepper
1 onion, thinly sliced
1 carrot, thinly sliced
1 bay leaf
4–6 whole cloves
1 lemon, sliced and pips removed
2–4 slices fresh ginger root
1 tbsp black peppercorns
½ cup red wine vinegar
⅔ cup light brown sugar
¼ cup raisins
4 ginger cookies, crushed to crumbs (optional)
3–4 tbsp chopped fresh parsley
lemon twists, for garnish

Rinse fish steaks under cold running water and pat dry with paper towels. Sprinkle lightly with salt and pepper to taste and set aside.

In a large, non-aluminum deep skillet combine onion, carrot, bay leaf, cloves, lemon slices, ginger root, and peppercorns with 3¾ cups cold water. Over high heat, bring to a boil, then simmer, covered, for 15 minutes.

Add fish steaks and cook over medium low heat, covered, until fish pulls away from center bone and turns opaque, 10–12 minutes. Using a spatula, carefully remove fish steaks to a large deep glass or ceramic baking dish.

Bring cooking liquid to a boil again and cook until liquid is reduced by half, 7–10 minutes. Strain into a smaller saucepan and add the vinegar, brown sugar, and raisins. Simmer 2–3 minutes longer, stir in the ginger cookie crumbs, if using, and chopped parsley. Cool slightly, then pour over fish. Cool completely, then refrigerate overnight. Serve chilled, garnished with lemon twists.

SHRIMP IN DILL CREAM

It is always an advantage when food can be prepared in advance for a dinner party. This dish can be served as a starter or for lunch.

S E R V E S 4

1 lb peeled shrimp
1½ cups finely chopped dill
1¼ cups whipping cream
gelatine
2 tbsp sherry
salt and white pepper
finely chopped fresh dill
1 large cucumber, sliced
1 lettuce
4 oz jar lumpfish roe

Place the shrimp in a bowl, and add the finely chopped dill. Pour in the cream, and place in the refrigerator for a couple of hours.

Dissolve the gelatine in warm water. Drain the shrimp from the cream, and whisk the cream into the gelatine. Add the sherry and seasoning to taste. Add the shrimp to the cream. Pour the mixture into a chilled ring mold and keep in the refrigerator for 5–6 hours, until set.

Turn out the molded shrimp ring onto a serving plate. Sprinkle finely chopped dill on top. Garnish with cucumber slices, lettuce leaves, and lumpfish roe.

Right: Shrimp in Dill Cream

MEAT

BEEF STROGANOFF

BOILED BEEF WITH HORSERADISH SAUCE

KARELIAN STEW

BEEF ROLLS

GOULASH

KJOTTKAKER

SPICED OXTAILS WITH BUCKWHEAT

RAW SPICED FILLET OF BEEF WITH SPICY SAUCE

VEAL STEW

ROAST VENISON WITH JUNIPER

STEWED LAMB WITH MUSHROOMS AND BARLEY

SHASHLIK

BIGOS

PORK WITH BEANS

PORK LOIN WITH APPLE PRESERVE

ROAST PORK

PIGS' FEET

HAM IN RYE PASTRY

PORK WITH APPLES

CHICKEN KIEV

ROAST TURKEY

SALAT OLIVIER

EASTER CHICKEN CASSEROLE

DUCK WITH RED CABBAGE

PICKLED AND COOKED GOOSE

ROAST GOOSE

BEEF STROGANOFF

The Stroganovs became one of the wealthiest members of the Russian merchant aristocracy through their exploitation of Siberia's fur resources. The French chef of a late 19th-century Count Stroganov created this now internationally popular dish. It should *not* be served over rice – a heresy introduced by the West – but a tuft of straw potatoes on top is classically acceptable.

SERVES 6 - 8

1 tbsp dry mustard powder
1 tbsp sugar
6 tbsp sunflower oil
3 large onions, sliced
1 lb fresh mushrooms, sliced
2½ lb tenderloin of beef cut into ½ in wide strips
salt and freshly ground black pepper
2¼ cups sour cream
6 fresh parsley sprigs, stems removed, chopped
deep-fried straw potatoes (optional)

Combine the mustard and sugar in a bowl with water to make a paste. Let the flavors mingle while completing the recipe.

Heat half the sunflower oil in a large, heavy-bottomed shallow casserole. When just crackling, add the sliced onions, reduce the heat to low, and stir. Gently soften the onions, covered, for about 25 minutes, stirring occasionally. During the last 10 minutes, uncover and add the mushrooms. Remove from the heat, drain the mixture, and set aside in a bowl.

Heat the remaining oil in the casserole. Drop in half the meat, stirring with a wooden spoon and turning the strips over to brown evenly. Transfer with a slotted spoon to the bowl with the vegetables; sauté the remaining meat. When all is browned, return the meat and vegetables to the casserole, together with the mustard mixture. Season to taste and add the sour cream, a little at a time, stirring continuously. Cover the casserole, heat through gently for about 5 minutes, and serve. Top each serving with a light scattering of parsley, and the straw potatoes, if desired.

BOILED BEEF WITH HORSERADISH SAUCE

The stock from the beef makes wonderful soup. Any leftovers from the joint may be ground for making patties or for filling piroshki. Authentically, the horseradish sauce should be very hot, laden with plenty of fresh horseradish. However, if you are unsure of your liking for horseradish it is a good idea to taste the sauce before adding the full amount. Serve boiled potatoes, carrots, green beans, or other fresh seasonal vegetables with the meat. Sauerkraut with mushrooms (page 113), carrot and potato hotpot (page 105) or cucumber salad (page 118) are alternative accompaniments.

SERVES 8

2¼ lb joint of rolled (fresh) brisket
a little fat
1 carrot, sliced
1 large onion, sliced
1 dried mushroom or the stock from simmering dried mushrooms
1 leek, sliced
large piece of celeriac (celery root) (about 1/4 lb)
1 clove garlic, crushed
1 bay leaf
2 large parsley sprigs
3 tsp salt
freshly ground black pepper
1 tsp allspice berries

HORSERADISH SAUCE

2 tbsp butter
¼ cup all purpose flour
4 tbsp grated horseradish
1¼ cups sour cream

In a large, heavy-based skillet, brown the joint of meat all over in a little fat – beef dripping is ideal. Add all the vegetables, garlic, herbs, and salt, then pour in enough water to just cover the meat. Bring to a boil and skim any scum off the surface. Reduce the heat, cover and simmer for 3 hours, until the meat is very tender.

For the sauce, melt the butter in a pan and stir in the flour. Stir in 1¼ cups of the beef cooking liquid and the horseradish. Bring to a boil to make a thick sauce, stirring all the time. Simmer for 3 minutes, then stir in the sour cream and season to taste. Heat through until just simmering.

Serve the beef carved into slices, with some of the horseradish sauce poured over. Offer the remaining sauce separately.

KARELIAN STEW

Karelia is eastern Finland, and this Karelian stew is an easy start to get acquainted with the eastern flavors. As with all slowly cooked stews, this dish is best cooked a day ahead. Refrigerate and skim off the fat. Reheat in the oven at a medium heat for about 30 minutes, until piping hot.

SERVES 4-6

1 lb pork
1 lb mutton
1 lb beef
1½ tbsp salt
15–20 whole allspice
2 onions, sliced
5 cups beef stock

Preheat the oven to 300°F. Cut the meat into 1-in cubes and place in a casserole dish. Add the salt, allspice, and onions to the casserole. Add sufficient beef stock to cover the meat. Cook until tender, 30–40 minutes, stirring occasionally. Cover the dish with a lid toward the end of the cooking time. Serve with mashed potatoes.

BEEF ROLLS

Small fingers of bacon fat should be used instead of the bacon in these rolls if possible. If you have a good continental delicatessen near you, buy *speck* – cured pork fat coated in paprika.

SERVES 4

1 lb frying steak
1 pickled cucumber, quartered lengthways
4 fingers of bacon fat or 2 slices rindless bacon, halved
4 tbsp all purpose flour
salt and freshly ground black pepper
a little fat
1 small onion, finely chopped
2½ cups water
1 bay leaf
1 dried mushroom or 6 open mushrooms, sliced
⅔ cup sour cream
2 tbsp chopped fresh parsley

Cut the steak into four equal pieces. Place each piece in turn between sheets of waxed paper and beat out until very thin. Use a meat pounder or rolling pin for this. Place a piece of pickled cucumber and a finger of fat or half bacon slice on each slice of steak. Roll up and secure with two wooden cocktail sticks. Coat the rolls with flour and plenty of seasoning.

Heat a little fat in a flameproof casserole – beef dripping is best, butter or oil will do. Add the beef rolls and brown them all over. Add the onion and reduce the heat, then continue to cook for about 5 minutes, stirring the onion as best you can until it is slightly softened. Pour in the water, add the bay leaf and mushroom.

Heat until the liquid is simmering, then cook, uncovered, at a steady simmer for 40 minutes. Turn the rolls over halfway through cooking and baste them often with the liquid. By the time the beef rolls are cooked through the sauce should be reduced by half. Transfer the rolls to warmed serving dish, remove the cocktail sticks and keep hot.

If there is a lot of liquid in the pan, boil it hard for a few minutes to reduce it to about 1¼ cups. Achieving the exact quantity is not important but the sauce should be slightly thickened and full flavored. Remove from the heat and stir in the sour cream. Taste and adjust the seasoning, then warm through without boiling. Stir in the parsley and pour the sauce over the rolls. Serve at once, with boiled potatoes and other vegetables.

GOULASH

There are many variations and different additions in goulash recipes around the world – this is the authentic basic recipe, great in itself, and you can add to it as you wish.

6 tbsp oil for cooking
4 oz smoked bacon, finely chopped
3 lb beef fillet, cut into 1 in chunks
salt and pepper to taste
3 red bell peppers, chopped
3 onions, finely chopped
paprika, to taste

Place the oil, then a layer of bacon into a large casserole dish with a lid. Add a layer of beef to that, with salt and pepper to taste, then a layer of red bell peppers and then a layer of onions.

Continue the layering until everything is used up, then add enough water to cover all the ingredients.

Cook over a medium heat for approximately 1 hour, or until the meat is tender.

Add salt and pepper to taste and add the paprika powder to taste before serving.

KJOTTKAKER

Ginger and nutmeg give these Norwegian meat cakes their distinctive flavor.

SERVES 4

1 lb ground beef
¼ tbsp salt
¼ lb suet, finely chopped
2 tbsp potato flour or cornstarch
1¼–2¼ cups cold water or milk
pinch of pepper, ginger, and grated nutmeg
2 tbsp wholewheat flour
¼ cup butter for frying
2¼ cups boiling water
1 onion

Mix the meat with the salt, suet, and potato flour. Stir well in one direction only. Gradually add the cold water or milk until the mix becomes firm in texture. Add all the spices. Divide into four and shape into round patties.

Dab each meat cake in flour and fry until brown. Place in a saucepan as they are ready. Add the boiling water and simmer for about 15 minutes. Blanch the onion and cut into slices. Brown, then simmer in the cooking liquid. A sauce may be made by browning butter and flour, gradually adding the cooking water or stock.

Right: Kjottkaker

SPICED OXTAILS WITH BUCKWHEAT

In the Russian and Polish countryside you can still see oxen pulling ploughs. A tough, gelatinous meat, oxtail needs slow cooking but the resulting tender flesh, falling off the bone, and the rich, thick sauce are worth the wait. This recipe is an adaptation from the Lower Volga region, nearing the Caspian Sea.

SERVES 6–8

5 lb oxtail pieces, trimmed
⅓ cup sunflower oil
3 medium onions, sliced
4 cloves garlic, crushed
1½ tbsp tomato paste
14 oz can chopped chili tomatoes
3¼ cups beef stock
3 cinnamon sticks
1 tsp ground cumin
1 tsp ground ginger
1 tsp mustard seeds
¼ tsp turmeric
4 tbsp finely chopped parsley
4 tbsp finely chopped cilantro
1½ cups buckwheat groats
2¼ cups boiling water
salt and freshly ground black pepper
2 tbsp butter
3 carrots, halved and thinly sliced
¼ lb turnips, halved and thinly sliced
1 small celeriac (celery root), quartered and thinly sliced
2 medium zucchini, halved and thinly sliced
½ lb baby leeks, trimmed and left whole
parsley and/or cilantro sprigs, to garnish

In a large enamelled or stainless steel casserole, brown the oxtails in the oil. Remove with a slotted spoon to a plate and set aside. Add the onion to the pot and fry gently over medium heat until lightly colored and soft. Stir in the garlic and cook for 1 minute, then stir in the tomato paste, the tomatoes and their juice, and the beef stock. Drop in the cinnamon sticks, and stir in the cumin, ginger, mustard seeds, turmeric, parsley, and cilantro. Bring to a boil, then cover and lower the heat. Simmer for 4 hours over a low heat, until the meat from the larger pieces is falling off the bone. If necessary, add water to keep the stock covering the meat.

Take the casserole off the heat and allow to cool. Refrigerate for 12 hours or overnight.

Preheat the oven to 350°F. Dry roast the buckwheat in a skillet over medium high heat, stirring constantly, until it begins to pop. Add the boiling water and salt to taste. Dot the butter over the surface and bake in the oven for 45 minutes, or until the grains are soft. Keep warm.

Meanwhile, lift off the solidified fat from the top of the casserole. With a slotted spoon, take out the oxtails, place them in a large baking dish and pour over enough boiling water to cover the bottom of the dish to about ½ in. Cover the dish with foil and reheat in the oven for the last 30 minutes while the buckwheat is cooking.

Strain the stock from the casserole into a bowl and discard the solids. Return the stock to the casserole and add the carrots, turnips, and celeriac. Bring to the boil, then cover and simmer the vegetables for 15 minutes, or until they are tender-crisp. Stir in the zucchini slices and the baby leeks and cook for a further 5–10 minutes until they are also soft.

Drain the sauce through a strainer into a saucepan. Set the vegetables aside. Strain the reheated oxtails, allowing the cooking liquid to flow into the same saucepan. Quickly bring the sauce to a boil.

Pile the cooked buckwheat onto a large serving dish. Spoon the strained vegetables on top of the buckwheat and surround it with the oxtails. Drizzle some of the sauce over the vegetables and buckwheat and serve the remainder separately in a sauceboat. Garnish the dish with the sprigs of parsley and/or cilantro.

RAW SPICED FILLET OF BEEF WITH SPICY SAUCE

Often simply served with an undressed green salad and bread. Delicious with small bread croûtons scatter on top.

SERVES 4

1 lb piece tenderloin of beef
cress, chopped

MARINADE

¼ cup Madeira
2 tbsp red wine
1 tbsp olive oil
2 tbsp each of crushed white peppercorns and allspice
(or black pepper)
1–2 tsp grated horseradish
plenty of chopped chives or leeks
chopped fresh parsley

SPICY SAUCE

3 tbsp unsweetened mustard
½ tsp sugar
½ tsp salt
1 egg yolk
generous ½ cup oil

Mix the marinade ingredients together. Place the meat in a shallow bowl, and pour the marinade on top. Turn the meat, and be sure to dab the marinade all over it. Sprinkle chopped cress over the entire surface. Cover with plastic wrap and refrigerate for 48 hours.

Scrape off the spices and cress. Place the meat in a plastic bag and refrigerate for another 48 hours.

For the sauce, mix all the ingredients together, stirring thoroughly and adding the oil slowly. If required, dilute the sauce with a couple of spoonfuls of water or a little lemon juice.

Slice the beef thinly with a very sharp knife. Serve together with the spicy sauce.

VEAL STEW

SERVES 4 – 6

2 lb stewing veal, cubed
2 tbsp fat
1 clove garlic
1 large onion, sliced
½ tsp dried marjoram
½ tsp ground allspice
½ tsp paprika
salt and freshly ground black pepper
2 tbsp all purpose flour
2½ cups veal or chicken stock or half and half stock
and red wine
1 bay leaf
2 parsley sprigs
1½ lb potatoes, cubed
⅔ cup sour cream

Lightly brown the veal in the fat in a heavy-based flameproof casserole. Beef or pork dripping or butter may be used; if you prefer, substitute a little oil. Stir in the garlic and onion and continue to cook until the onion is slightly softened. Stir in the spices, seasoning, and flour. Cook for 1 minute, then stir in the stock. Add the bay leaf and parsley (tie them together if you like). Bring to a boil, then reduce the heat so that the stew simmers. Cover and cook for 1 hour, stirring occasionally.

Add the potatoes, stir and cook for a further 20–30 minutes, or until the potatoes are very tender. Lastly stir in the sour cream and heat through for a few minutes. Check the seasoning before serving.

ROAST VENISON WITH JUNIPER

This is a simple method of cooking a roasting joint, based on an old-fashioned Polish method from days when venison was freely available. Offer boiled potatoes and Polish-style cauliflower (page 112) with the venison. Beet in sour cream sauce (page 120) may also be served as an accompaniment.

SERVES 8

3 lb rolled haunch of venison
2½ cups water
1 onion, sliced
3 bay leaves
3 tbsp vinegar
¼ lb bacon fat
1 parsnip, cubed
1 carrot, cubed
1 leek, sliced
¼ lb celeriac (celery root), cubed
4 juniper berries
4 allspice berries
salt and freshly ground black pepper
¼ cup rendered bacon or pork fat or butter
1¼ cups red wine
1¼ cups sour cream

Make sure that the venison is trimmed of all fat and membranes, as venison fat has an unpleasant taste. Put the joint of venison in a bowl. Heat the water, onion, and 2 bay leaves slowly until boiling. Reduce the heat, cover, and simmer for 5 minutes. Allow to cool completely, then add the vinegar and pour the mixture over the venison. Cover and chill for 24 hours, turning the joint at least twice.

Cut the bacon fat into strips. Drain the venison and pat it dry on paper towels. Use a meat skewer to pierce holes through the joint. Use a larding needle to thread the bacon fat through the holes. If you do not have a larding needle, then use the meat skewer to push the fat into the joint as far as possible. This is known as "larding," a process of introducing fat to very lean meat to keep it moist during cooking.

Set the oven at 375°F. Place all the vegetables in a roasting tin with the remaining bay leaf. Crush the juniper and allspice and mix with seasoning, then rub the mixture all over the venison. Stand the joint on the vegetables and smear it generously with fat or butter. Roast the venison for 1 hour, basting often with fat, adding extra fat if necessary, to keep the meat moist. The venison should be cooked until still slightly pink in the middle.

Transfer the joint to a serving platter and keep hot. Pour the wine over the vegetables in the pan and heat slowly, stirring all the time until boiling. Simmer for 5 minutes, stirring and scraping the pan all the time. Sieve the sauce, stir in the sour cream and taste for seasoning. Heat gently, then serve the sauce with the venison, carved into thick slices.

STEWED LAMB WITH MUSHROOMS AND BARLEY

This is a Moldovan dish, from the foothills of the Carpathian mountains. It is unsophisticated and hardly pretty-pretty, but it is nutritious, inexpensive, and full-flavored, a true rustic feast.

SERVES 6

2½ lb shanks or neck of lamb, cut into pieces
⅓ cup vegetable oil
1 medium onion, chopped
2 long red medium-hot chili peppers, seeded and chopped
6 oz fresh mushrooms, wiped and sliced
1 tbsp German-style mustard
2¼ cups chicken stock
⅓ cup white wine vinegar
1¼ cups pearl barley
1 tsp cumin seeds
2 whole cloves
2 tsp dried dill
salt and freshly ground black pepper
1 cup sour cream or yogurt
2 oz flat-leaved parsley, finely chopped

In a heavy casserole, brown the lamb shank or neck pieces in half the oil until they are colored. Remove with a slotted spoon and set aside. Add the onion to the casserole, and cook until it is soft and lightly colored, about 6–8 minutes. Remove with the slotted spoon and set aside. Add the rest of the oil and sauté the peppers and mushrooms for about 5 minutes, or until the mushrooms are softened. Remove to a bowl and set aside.

Preheat the oven to 325°F. Stir the onions and lamb back into the casserole, together with the mustard. Add the chicken stock and the wine vinegar, bring to a boil, and transfer the casserole to the oven. Bake for 1½ hours, until the lamb is very tender and falling off the bones.

Remove the lamb from the casserole. Using your hands and a fork, pull the meat from the bones and chop it. Return to the casserole and stir into the stock with the barley, cumin seeds, cloves, dill, and seasoning to taste. Bring to a boil, cover, and lower the heat. Simmer for about 1 hour, until the barley is tender and most of the stock has been absorbed.

Stir the pepper and mushrooms into the stew, together with the sour cream or yogurt. Heat through for about 10–12 minutes, take off the heat, stir in the chopped parsley, and serve.

SHASHLIK

Shashlik, shish kabob and kebab are terms which mean lamb or beef grilled on a skewer. Skewered meat cooked over an open fire was probably one of the original ways of cooking meat. Traditional in the Russian republics, the Balkans and the Middle East, its popularity has spread, and many Russian-Jewish immigrants now sell shashlik beside the traditional hot dog men in New York City!

SERVES 6

4 lb boneless lamb shoulder, trimmed of all visible fat and cut into 2 in cubes
4 small onions, root ends attached, cut into eighths
1 lb cherry tomatoes
2 yellow or red bell peppers, cored, seeded, and cut into 1 in squares
fresh rosemary sprigs for garnish

MARINADE

⅔ cup olive oil
½ cup lemon juice
½ cup dry red wine or dry sherry
2–3 tbsp chopped fresh rosemary, or 1 tbsp dried
½ small onion, finely chopped or grated
4–6 cloves garlic, peeled and finely chopped
1 tsp salt
freshly ground black pepper
½ tsp red pepper flakes (optional)

In a large, shallow non-metallic baking dish, combine marinade ingredients, stirring until well blended and creamy. Add lamb cubes and stir around until well coated. Cover and refrigerate 6 hours or overnight, stirring occasionally.

Position barbecue rack about 5 in above preheated coals.

Thread lamb cubes onto metal skewers, leaving a small space between cubes so meat cooks evenly. Thread onion pieces, cherry tomatoes and pepper squares onto separate skewers; brush with some remaining marinade.

Arrange lamb skewers over center of coals and cook, turning and basting with marinade occasionally, 17–20 minutes. Halfway through cooking time, add vegetable skewers to barbecue and cook, turning and basting with marinade, 8–10 minutes.

Arrange skewers on long serving platter and surround with fresh sprigs of rosemary. Serve with rice, salads or other accompaniments.

BIGOS

Among the best known of Polish dishes, Bigos is a meat stew with sausage, sauerkraut, and cabbage. Since it is traditionally a hunter's recipe, the meat used in the stew may be anything, from wild boar to hare, rabbit, venison, or game birds. Indeed, a combination of different meats, including leftover roasts, may be added. Polish sausage contributes a wonderful smoked, garlic flavor to the stew. Serve with potatoes or chunks of rye bread – delicious!

SERVES 6

1 lb pork, cubed
12 slices smoked rindless streaky bacon, chopped
2 onions, sliced
2 bay leaves
2 cloves garlic, crushed
1 lb sauerkraut, drained
1 lb wiejska sausage, cut into chunks
1 cup red wine or stock
2 dried mushrooms or 1 cup mushrooms, sliced
salt and freshly ground black pepper
1 lb green or white cabbage, trimmed and shredded
2 tbsp all purpose flour
2 tbsp water

Cook the pork and bacon together in a large, heavy-based flameproof casserole until the fat runs and the cubes of pork are lightly browned. Stir frequently at first to prevent the meat sticking. Add the onions, bay leaves, and garlic and cook, stirring, for 5 minutes until the onions are slightly softened.

Squeeze all the liquid from the sauerkraut, then cut across the pat of vegetable to shred it finely. Add to the meat with the sausage and wine or stock. If using dried mushrooms, simmer them in just enough water to cover for 5 minutes. Strain the liquor into the stew and chop the mushrooms. Add the mushrooms and seasoning, then heat until simmering. Cover and simmer for 1 hour, stirring occasionally, until the meat is tender.

Cook the cabbage in boiling salted water for 2 minutes, then drain well. Blend the flour with the water, stir the paste into the stew and bring to a boil, stirring. Cook, uncovered, to evaporate any excess liquid, for about 5 minutes. Stir in the cabbage, heat for 1–2 minutes and serve.

Bigos should be juicy but not too wet. Its flavor improves with keeping, so it is ideal for making a day in advance. Make sure the stew is thoroughly heated through before serving. If liked, cook and add the cabbage at the last minute instead of leaving it overnight.

PORK WITH BEANS

An easy and hearty winter meal, guaranteed to bring a glow to the face after a walk in even the worst of winter weather.

SERVES 4

2 slices rindless smoked bacon, chopped
1 clove garlic, crushed
1 leek, sliced
1 onion, thinly sliced
2 carrots, sliced
1 bay leaf
1 lb lean, boneless pork, cubed
1 cup dried fava or lima beans, soaked overnight
salt and freshly ground black pepper
5 cups water
salt and freshly ground black pepper
1 lb celeriac (celery root), cubed
2 tbsp all purpose flour
4 tbsp sour cream
3 tbsp chopped fresh dill or 1 tsp dried dill

Cook the bacon and garlic in a large, heavy-based flameproof casserole until the fat runs. Add the leek, onion, carrots, and bay leaf and cook for about 5 minutes, until the onion begins to soften. Stir in the pork and drained beans. Pour in the water and bring to a boil. Make sure that the beans are well covered with water, adding extra if necessary. Reduce the heat, cover and simmer for 30 minutes. Check to make sure that the beans do not dry up on the surface during cooking.

Add plenty of seasoning at this stage and stir in the celeriac. Continue to cook the stew, half uncovered so that excess liquid evaporates, for a further 30 minutes, or until the beans are cooked.

Stir the flour and sour cream into a smooth paste and add a little cooking liquid from the pot. Stir the paste into the stew and bring to the boil. Simmer for 3 minutes, add the dill and serve.

PORK LOIN WITH APPLE PRESERVE

The accompanying preserve for this dish must be made at least 3 days ahead of time; the meat should be marinated for 24 hours. Leftover cooked meat, topped with the apple chutney, makes a good cold sandwich on rye bread.

S E R V E S   4

2 lb rolled pork loin
½ cup light beer

F O R   T H E   P R E S E R V E

¼ cup dry cider
1 cup light brown sugar
3 eating apples, peeled, cored, and chopped
1 small onion, finely chopped
juice and rind of ½ lemon
½ red bell pepper, cored, seeded, and chopped
1 clove garlic, crushed or finely chopped
2 tbsp finely chopped fresh peeled ginger
large pinch cayenne pepper
¼ tsp salt

F O R   T H E   M A R I N A D E

1 tbsp honey
1 tbsp finely chopped fresh marjoram or oregano
1 tsp juniper berries, crushed
1 clove garlic, crushed
¼ tsp dried black peppercorns

Make the preserve first. Bring the cider and brown sugar to a boil in a large saucepan; stir until the sugar dissolves. Add the remaining ingredients and bring to a boil again. Reduce the heat and simmer, stirring occasionally, until the mixture reduces to 1½–2 cups. Cool, then chill for at least 3 days before using.

Place the marinade ingredients in a large plastic bag. Add the pork loin and roll it around in the bag to coat it. Tie the bag shut and place on a dish in a cool place. Turn it occasionally in the next 24 hours.

Preheat the oven to 375°F. Remove the pork from the marinade and discard the marinade. Place the pork on a rack over a baking pan and roast until the meat is done, about 50–55 minutes.

Skim the fat from the drippings in the pan and discard. Pour the beer into the pan and bring to a boil over high heat, stirring the dripping into the beer. Reduce the liquid until thickened. Pour into a sauceboat and serve with the pork and preserve.

ROAST PORK

Caraway seeds and garlic make this an aromatic roast.

S E R V E S   8

3 lb rolled fresh ham
1 large clove garlic
salt and freshly ground black pepper
2 tsp caraway seeds
8 medium cooking apples, peeled, cored, and halved
5 cups water
2 tbsp honey

Set the oven at 375°F. Make sure the pork skin is well scored, then rub the joint all over with the cut clove of garlic. Place the garlic in a roasting pan. Rub salt all over the skin, then sprinkle the joint with pepper and place it on top of the garlic in the pan.

Roast the joint of 30 minutes. Baste it with the cooking fat and place the apples in the pan around the joint, basting them well. Roast for a further 15 minutes, then transfer the apples to an ovenproof dish, basting them with just a little fat. Set aside. Pour about a third of the water around the pork and continue to roast for about 1½ hours, adding more water from time to time to prevent the base of the pan from drying out.

Trickle the honey over the apples and put them back in the oven for about 10 minutes before serving the joint. Transfer the meat to a warmed serving platter. Boil the cooking liquid (add the extra water if necessary), scraping all the residue from the sides of the roasting pan. When the liquid is reduced to a full-flavored thin gravy, carve the pork into slices, moisten with a little gravy and serve with the apples.

Right: Pork Loin with Apple Preserve

PIGS' FEET

Lent is traditionally a time for outdoor get-togethers in Scandinavia, where lanterns and candles are placed in trees. It requires food that can be prepared beforehand.

SERVES 4 – 6

4–5 lb pigs' feet, preferably forelegs
1 gallon water
4 tsp salt
20 whole white peppercorns
2–3 bay leaves

Rinse the pigs' feet well in cold water. Place in a saucepan, cover with the cold water and bring to a boil. Skim off any foam, and season with the salt, peppercorns, and bay leaves. Simmer over low heat for 2–3 hours, until tender. Leave to cool in the pan. Remove and serve cold. This dish is easiest eaten with your fingers.

HAM IN RYE PASTRY

This is a popular Russian Easter dish which can be served either hot or cold, as here. It would be well partnered by cabbage cooked with sour cream, boiled potatoes with dill, and a pot of German-style mustard. The rather hard, dry pastry can be discarded before serving, if desired; it is really there to seal in the flavor of the spiced ham.

SERVES 10 – 12

½ cup dark brown sugar
1 tsp dry mustard powder
¼ tsp ground cloves
large pinch of ground cinnamon
5 lb canned Polish ham
milk

FOR THE PASTRY

2½ tsp dry yeast
3 tbsp lukewarm water
⅓ cup caraway seeds
⅔ cup cold water
2 tbsp molasses
3 cups rye flour

Make the pastry first. Dissolve the yeast in lukewarm water in a small bowl. Add the caraway seeds and set aside in a warm place for 10 minutes to become foamy and double in volume.

Stir in the cold water, the molasses and half the flour, a little at a time. Take the resultant dough out of the bowl and place on a floured surface. Knead in the remaining flour, little by little. The dough should be stiff. Cover with plastic wrap and set aside for 30 minutes. Meanwhile, remove the aspic from the ham and pat the ham dry with paper towels.

Roll out the dough to form a 26 × 10 in rectangle. Mix together the sugar, mustard, cloves, and cinnamon in a small bowl. Sprinkle a heaped tablespoon of the mixture in the center of the dough. Place the ham on top and pat the remaining mixture over the ham.

Preheat the oven to 350°F. Fold the dough neatly over the ham, tucking the corners in and sealing it with a little water where the edges meet. Set the ham on a foil-lined baking sheet, brush with milk, and bake for 1¾–2 hours. Remove from the oven and allow to rest for 15 minutes before slicing the ham (and removing the pastry surround, if desired).

PORK WITH APPLES

Denmark's favorite meat is pork. The pig in one way or another is the Danes' key export. They have numerous ways of preparing pork, but it would be hard to find a more delicious version than this particular dish.

SERVES 4

1 lb bacon slices
2 lb eating apples
¼ cup sugar

Fry the bacon gently and pour off any excess into a dish during frying. This will make the bacon nice and crispy. Remove the bacon and keep warm.

Wash, core, and slice the apples, but do not peel them. Fry the apple slices in a little of the bacon fat until soft. Sprinkle a little sugar over the apples. Place the fried apples and warm bacon slices in a serving dish. Serve with fried onions or leftovers. This recipe can also be used as a topping for open sandwiches.

CHICKEN KIEV

Chicken Kiev has become a familiar dish, stacked frozen and ready-to-heat in markets. But the real thing bears little resemblance, in appearance or taste, to such orange monstrosities. The recipe has been simplified to take advantage of prepared chicken breasts.

SERVES 6

⅔ cup unsalted butter, softened
grated rind and juice of 1 large lemon
3 tbsp freshly chopped tarragon
6 large skinless boned chicken breasts
salt and freshly ground black pepper
2 small eggs
4 cups fresh fine bread crumbs
oil for deep-frying

Combine the butter, lemon rind, and tarragon in a bowl. With a fork, work the mixture until it is thoroughly mixed. Shape into a block, wrap in foil, and chill until hard.

Lay the chicken breasts on a sheet of waxed paper. Trim away any bits attached by membrane. Cover the breasts with another sheet of greaseproof paper and pound with a meat pounder until they are flattened. Season the breasts as desired.

Cut the butter block into 6 pieces and place one piece in the center of each breast. Fold the top and edges over, then roll neatly. Tie the roll with thread.

Beat the eggs lightly in a shallow bowl. Spread the bread crumbs on a large plate. Dip the breast rolls in the egg then coat them in the bread crumbs, pressing into the crumbs to make sure they adhere. To obtain a thick "skin" brush the coated rolls with a little more egg if necessary and press into the crumbs again. Place the rolls on a plate and chill for 2–3 hours.

In a deep fryer or heavy saucepan, heat enough oil to cover the breasts completely. When it spits at water droplets (or reaches 375°F), lower in 3 breasts with a slotted spoon. Fry until golden-brown, about 5–6 minutes. (The oil must not get too hot or the coating will brown before the chicken is cooked.) Drain on absorbent kitchen paper and repeat with the remaining 3 breasts. Serve immediately. Potatoes and cabbage or peas would make a typical accompaniment.

ROAST TURKEY

Roast turkey is uncomplicated and familiar; the stuffing in this Polish version is pleasingly different. Turkey used to be very popular and prized for its quality in centuries past. It would have been eaten on Christmas Day, although most households would also eat up the remains of puddings and sweet delights from the Christmas Eve meal.

SERVES 8-10

8 lb turkey with giblets
1 small onion, quartered
1 bay leaf
1 large onion, finely chopped
¼ cup butter
salt and freshly ground black pepper
½ tsp ground ginger
½ tsp grated nutmeg
½ tsp ground allspice
good pinch of ground cloves
⅔ cup raisins
3 tbsp chopped fresh parsley
5⅓ cups fresh bread crumbs
2 eggs, separated
3 tbsp all purpose flour

Trim the wing ends off the turkey. Cut away any lumps of fat and singe off any small feathers with a long match – let the match burn for just a few seconds before doing this to avoid making the turkey smoky. Rinse the bird inside and out under cold running water, then dry it thoroughly with paper towels.

Chop the turkey liver and set aside. Put the other giblets in a pan with the wing ends, quartered onion, and bay leaf. Pour on water to cover, bring to a boil, cover, and simmer for 1 hour. Strain this stock for making gravy.

Cook the onion in half the butter for about 15 minutes, or until softened but not browned. Stir in the chopped turkey liver and cook until firm. Add seasoning, all the spices, and the raisins. Continue to cook, stirring all the time, for 2–3 minutes, until the raisins are slightly plump. Add the parsley, then pour the cooked mixture over the bread crumbs and mix well. Mix in the egg yolks until they are evenly distributed. Whisk the egg whites until they stand in soft peaks and stir them into the stuffing.

Set the oven at 350°F. Spoon some of the stuffing into the neck end of the bird and put the rest into the body cavity. Truss the turkey neatly with string, tying the wings together, then bringing the string up to the legs and tie it off. Smear the remaining butter over the turkey breast. Roast, covered with foil, for 2½ hours. Baste the bird frequently with the cooking juices.

Pour off most of the fat from the roasting pan and add some of the giblet stock, stirring the roasting residue off the sides of the pan around the turkey. Roast the bird, covered, for a further 15 minutes. Uncover and continue to cook for 30–45 minutes, until the turkey is browned and cooked through. Pierce the bird at the thickest part of the thigh to see if the meat is cooked: if there is any sign of pink meat or blood then continue to roast the turkey.

Keep topping up the stock in the roasting pan to make a rich gravy. When the turkey is cooked, strain the cooking juices. Thicken them with the flour blended with a little water. Bring to a boil and simmer for 3 minutes.

SALAT OLIVIER

A near relative of the "Russian salad" so dear to the hearts of caterers and delicatessen owners, this real Russian salad is a traditional favorite, again refined and Frenchified by an imported chef. It would make a delicious main course for a summer luncheon or picnic.

SERVES 6

1½ lb cooked, boned, and skinned chicken
5 hard-boiled eggs
½ lb new or small red potatoes, boiled in their skins and thinly sliced
¼ lb cooked fresh or frozen peas, drained
¼ lb black olives, halved
2 large sour pickled cucumbers, finely chopped
⅔ cup mayonnaise
½ cup sour cream
2 tsp Worcestershire sauce
salt and freshly ground black pepper
1 tbsp chopped fresh dill
2 tbsp capers

Slice the chicken into ½ in wide strips. Finely chop two of the eggs. Place the chicken and chopped eggs in a large bowl, together with the potatoes, peas, and pickled cucumbers. In a smaller bowl, beat together the mayonnaise and the sour cream. Fold the Worcestershire sauce and half the dressing into the chicken mixture, seasoning to taste.

To serve in the Russian manner, mound the chicken salad in the center of a large serving dish. Slice the remaining eggs and arrange the slices around the salad. Top each slice with a halved olive. Spoon the remaining dressing over the salad and scatter the chopped dill and capers over the top. Chill for 30 minutes before serving.

EASTER CHICKEN CASSEROLE

This dish is traditionally served in Denmark on Easter Monday with decorated eggs, new potatoes, carrots, and peas, followed by a cheese board and a dessert.

SERVES 4 – 6

¼ cup butter
3 lb chicken joints
3 medium onions, chopped
2½ cups chicken stock
½ lb mushrooms
2 tbsp chopped fresh parsley
salt and pepper
2 cups peas
2 eggs
2 tbsp milk
butter for cooking
2 tbsp cornstarch

Melt the butter and fry the chicken joints and onions until golden brown. Add the chicken stock, mushrooms, and 1 tablespoon of the chopped parsley, and season with salt and pepper. Cover and simmer for 35 minutes, adding the peas for the last 5–8 minutes.

Beat the eggs and milk together and season. Fry the egg mixture in a little butter in an omelet pan until firm. Put the chicken and vegetables on a heated serving dish and keep warm. Thicken the cooking liquid with the cornstarch blended with water to make the gravy. Pour the gravy over the chicken and vegetables. Cut the fried egg into thin strips, and use to garnish the chicken, along with the remaining chopped parsley.

Right: Easter Chicken Casserole

DUCK WITH RED CABBAGE

Succulent duck portions braised on a bed of red cabbage and apple are a typically eastern European combination.

SERVES 4

4–4½ lb duck
1 small whole onion
a little fat
1 onion, thinly sliced
1 bay leaf
½ tsp caraway seeds
salt and freshly ground black pepper
1 lb red cabbage, shredded
1 lb cooking apples, peeled, cored, and sliced
2 tbsp sugar
1 tbsp all purpose flour
⅔ cup sour cream (optional)

Trim any large pieces of fat from the duck and trim off the large flap of skin from the neck end. Cut off the ends of the joints and put them in a saucepan. Turn the duck breast down on a board and use a heavy knife to split it along the back. Open out the duck and cut it in half through the inside of the breast. Cut each half into two portions. Trim off the small and broken bones from the breast portion. Add all the trimmings, except lumps of fat, to the joint ends. Wash and dry the duck joints.

Cut the whole onion in half without peeling and add it to the duck trimmings in the saucepan. Pour on water to cover, bring to a boil and simmer, covered, for 40 minutes. Drain the liquid off, return it to the pan and boil it until reduced to 1½ cups.

Meanwhile, brown the duck joints all over in the minimum of fat in a heavy-based flameproof casserole. Drain off excess fat. Add the sliced onion, bay leaf,

94

and caraway seeds with plenty of seasoning. Pour in the reduced stock and bring to a boil. Cover and simmer for 30 minutes. Lift the duck joints from the stock. Add the cabbage, apple, and sugar, stir well to mix thoroughly, then replace the duck on top. Cover and simmer duck, fruit and vegetable for a further 30 minutes.

Taste and adjust the seasoning. Blend the flour to a smooth paste with the minimum of water, then stir it into the cabbage mixture. Bring to a boil, all the while stirring as best you can. Simmer for 3 minutes and serve. Sour cream may be served with the casserole, if liked.

PICKLED AND COOKED GOOSE

The cooking of eastern Scandinavia has had a pronounced influence on the cuisine of Estonia. This recipe is a variation of an old Swedish dish; like ham, the cured bird could be kept until needed, a boon when refrigerators were unknown. The berry condiment is a typical Estonian touch.

SERVES 8

juice of ½ lemon
1 cup salt
1½ tsp sugar
10 lb goose, cleaned, washed, and dried
½ lb canned lingonberries or cranberries, crushed

FOR THE BRINE AND AND POACHING BROTH

⅓ cup salt and 1 tbsp sugar to each 2¼ cups water
1 medium onion, unpeeled
1 carrot, scraped
1 clove garlic, unpeeled
6 whole black peppercorns
2 bay leaves

Combine the lemon juice, salt, sugar, and saltpeter in a bowl. Rub the goose all over inside and out with the mixture, being sure to reach all parts. Place in a shallow non-metal baking dish or pan and set aside in a cool place for 24 hours, turning it several times.

Place the goose in a large saucepan or pot. Add enough water to cover it with about 1½ in to spare. Remove the goose and transfer the water with a measuring cup to a large bowl. Pour the water back into the pot and add salt and sugar in the proportions given in the ingredients above. Bring the brine to a rolling boil over high heat, then remove from the heat and leave to cool to room temperature.

When the brine is cool, put the goose into it. Weight the goose down to make sure it is totally submerged (a small weight inside the goose or a plate on top will do). Leave the bird in a cool place for 3 days, turning occasionally.

Lift out the goose and drain it thoroughly. Sew or skewer the openings shut and truss it. Place in a large saucepan or pot and add just enough water to cover. Drop in the vegetables, garlic, peppercorns, and bay leaves and bring to a boil. Cover, lower the heat and simmer gently for about 1¾ hours or until the bird is fork-tender.

Drain the goose thoroughly and remove the trussing string and skewers. Serve warm or cold, with a sauceboat of the crushed lingonberries or cranberries on the side.

ROAST GOOSE

The main dish at the Christmas table in Denmark is roast goose. Tradition demands the goose be stuffed with peeled and sliced apples and prunes. It is served with cooked apples stuffed with prunes.

SERVES 8-10

1½ cups prunes, pitted
9–10 lb goose
juice of 1 lemon
2 medium apples, cored and peeled
1 tbsp salt
2½ cups chicken stock or water
1 tbsp sugar
pepper

Soak the prunes in water for 12 hours. Preheat the oven to 350°F. Rinse the goose thoroughly under cold running water. Dry with paper towels. Brush the goose both inside and out with the juice from the lemon, and then rub the inside of the goose with the sugar, pepper, and onion. Cut the prunes and apples into small pieces, sprinkle with salt, and place inside the goose. Secure with skewers, or sew the skin together. Sprinkle with salt. Place the goose in a baking pan and put it on the bottom oven shelf. Roast for about 20 minutes to brown.

Drain off the fat and pour the boiling stock or water, sugar, and pepper into the pan. Turn the goose over so the back is facing up, and roast for 1 hour. Turn it breast up and roast for a farther 1½–2 hours. Leave for 15 minutes in the switched off oven with the door open. Remove the stuffing and discard it – it is too fatty to eat.

Serve the goose with apples stuffed with prunes, red cabbage (page 114), and boiled potatoes.

APPLES STUFFED WITH PRUNES

MAKES 8

1 cup sugar
port to taste
16 prunes
8 large apples, cored and peeled
4 cups cold water

Put 2 teaspoons of the sugar, the port, and prunes in an ovenproof dish. Leave to macerate for 6–8 hours. Preheat the oven to 325°F. Cook for 20–30 minutes, until soft.

Cut the apples in half. Mix the remaining sugar and water in a pan then boil for 2–3 minutes. Add the apples, and leave to simmer for 10 minutes, uncovered, over a low heat. Remove the apples with a slotted spoon, and place in a serving dish. Put one prune on each apple half.

SUPPER DISHES

SWEET
POTATO AND
PARSNIP
KUGEL

ROSSOLYE

BORNHOLM
OMELET

SWEET AND
SOUR
STUFFED
CABBAGE

CABBAGE
ROLL PIE

CARROT AND
POTATO
HOTPOT

BITKI

CARROT
TZIMMES
LOAF

HAM
SAUSAGE
WITH RED
CABBAGE

POTATO AND
APPLE
PUDDING

SWEET POTATO AND PARSNIP KUGEL

The kugel must be one of the greatest contributions of Jewish cooking to the world. It is a baked pudding which can be savory or sweet, and, depending on the ingredients, eaten as a vegetable or dessert.

Sweet potatoes, carrots, and parsnips are all naturally sweet vegetables. They combine to make a baked vegetable pudding which is particularly delicious as a supper dish on its own or with roast turkey or duck.

SERVES 6-8

2 sweet potatoes, peeled
2 carrots, peeled
2 parsnips, peeled
1 apple, peeled, cored, and quartered
1 onion, quartered
¼ cup butter or margarine
salt
freshly ground black pepper
1 tsp ground cinnamon
½ tsp grated nutmeg
⅓ cup light brown sugar
4 tbsp light molasses or corn syrup
2 eggs, beaten
1 oz fine matzo meal (cake meal)
¼ cup vegetable oil

In a food processor fitted with grater attachment, grate potatoes, carrots, parsnips, and apple. Scrape into large bowl and set aside. Wipe processor clean. Grate onion.

Preheat oven to 375°F. In a large deep skillet, over medium-high heat, melt butter or margarine. Add onion and cook until beginning to soften, 2–3 minutes. Stir in grated vegetables and apple and cook just until vegetables begin to soften 4–5 minutes. Scrape into large bowl.

Add salt and pepper to taste, cinnamon, nutmeg, brown sugar, molasses or corn syrup and water. Stir well and leave to cool slightly. Add beaten eggs and matzo meal.

In a medium roasting pan or 9 × 13 in cake pan, heat vegetable oil. When a small amount of vegetable mixture sizzles when added to the oil, turn vegetable mixture into the baking tin, smoothing the top evenly. Bake, covered with foil, 30 minutes. Uncover and bake until vegetables feel soft when pierced with a knife and top is brown, 15–20 minutes longer.

ROSSOLYE

Rossolye is a signature dish of Estonian cuisine, rather like borscht is of Russian. It is no surprise that both are based on beet. Rossolye is a common component of the Estonian version of the zakuska table and makes a delicious luncheon dish on a warm summer's day.

SERVES 8

3 tsp dry mustard powder
½ tsp sugar
1¼ cups whipping cream
5 large boiled beet, peeled and cubed
2 tart apples, cored, peeled, and cubed
6 large potatoes, boiled, peeled, and cubed
2 sweet-sour Polish-style cucumbers, cubed
2 fillets of pickled herring, drained and cubed
1 lb leftover lean cooked beef or pork, trimmed and cubed
salt and freshly ground black pepper
2–3 tbsp dry white wine
2 hard-boiled eggs, chopped
lettuce leaves

To make the dressing, combine the mustard, sugar, and whipping cream in a large bowl. By hand or with an electric mixer, whip the mustard cream until it holds soft peaks. Set aside.

In another large bowl, combine the beet, apples, potatoes, cucumbers, herrings, meat, seasoning to taste, and the wine. Toss to combine. Then gently fold in the hard-boiled eggs and three-quarters of the dressing. Chill for 30 minutes, then transfer the salad to a lettuce-lined plate or glass bowl and top with the remaining whipped cream.

BORNHOLM OMELET

Bornholm is the little paradise island in the Baltic Sea, famous for its unique cliffs, sandy beaches, woods, picturesque little towns, and fresh or smoked herring. This unusual omelet has an excellent combination of flavors.

SERVES 4–6

6 eggs
¼ cup milk or light cream
1 tsp salt
¼ cup butter
3 small smoked herrings, boned
15–20 radishes
1 head of lettuce
2 tbsp chopped fresh chives

Beat the eggs, milk, and salt together. Melt the butter in a skillet and add the egg mixture. Cook to the desired consistency.

Slice the herrings, radishes, lettuce, and chives, Sprinkle on top of the omelet.

SWEET AND SOUR STUFFED CABBAGE

There are many versions of this dish to be found throughout eastern Europe. In Russia the rolls are called *goluptsy*, meaning "pigeons", and are made with a sweet and sour tomato-based sauce. In other countries, such as Ukraine, they are often stuffed with mushrooms rather than meat, while the Hungarians use a paprika-flavored sauce.

SERVES 6-8

1 large cabbage
⅔ cup dried seasoned bread crumbs
½ cup milk
1 tbsp vegetable oil
1 onion, finely chopped
2 garlic cloves, peeled and finely chopped
2 lb ground beef
¾ tsp salt
freshly ground black pepper
4 tbsp tomato catsup
2 eggs, beaten
2-3 tbsp chopped fresh dill
½ cup long-grain rice
chopped fresh dill for garnish

SAUCE

2 x 14 oz cans tomatoes
1¼ cups tomato sauce
8 tbsp tomato catsup
salt
freshly ground pepper
2 onions, thinly sliced
grated rind and juice of 1 lemon
⅓ cup light brown sugar
⅔ cup golden raisins

Core center out of cabbage and gently remove as many leaves as possible; smaller leaves can be overlapped to form a large leaf. Bring a large saucepan of water to a boil. Plunge in leaves (it may be necessary to do this in batches) and simmer until the leaves are softened, but not tender, 3–5 minutes. Drain and rise under cold running water; set aside.

In a small bowl, combine bread crumbs and milk and leave to stand until milk is absorbed.

In a small skillet heat oil over medium heat. Add onion and cook until onion is softened and beginning to color, 3–5 minutes. Add garlic and cook 1 minute longer, stirring occasionally. Remove from heat and set aside.

In a large bowl, with a fork, mix beef, salt and peppers to taste, catsup, eggs, chopped dill, and rice. Stir in milk-soaked bread crumbs and cooked onions; mix until very well blended.

In a shallow roasting pan with tight-fitting lid, combine all sauce ingredients. Over medium heat, bring to a boil, then reduce heat and simmer, stirring occasionally 15–20 minutes.

Preheat oven to 325°F. Arrange a cabbage leaf on a flat work surface, remove any heavy core from leaf if necessary. Place 1–2 tablespoons meat mixture (exact amount will depend in the size of the leaf) in center of each cabbage leaf. Fold sides over stuffing, then roll cabbage leaf jelly-roll fashion to completely enclose the stuffing. Place on a baking sheet or tray and continue until all meat mixture is used. (Any leftover cabbage can be thinly shredded and added to the sauce.)

Arrange all cabbage packages, seam sides down, in the sauce-filled roasting pan and spoon some sauce over cabbage packages. Add a little water if necessary; cabbages should be just covered with liquid. Cover and cook about 1½ hours.

Remove lid and baste cabbage packages with sauce. With a slotted spoon, remove packages to a deep serving plate and keep warm. If liquid is very thin, reduce over medium heat until slightly thickened. If it is too thick, add a little water; pour over cabbage and sprinkle with the chopped dill.

CABBAGE ROLL PIE

This recipe gives stuffed cabbage rolls, that favorite east European dish, a distinct Estonian-Finnish twist, by burying the rolls under a layer of puffy yeast dough.

SERVES 6 – 8

⅔ cup pearl barley
3 lb head white Dutch cabbage
2 tbsp vegetable oil
1 onion, finely chopped
1 small red bell pepper, cored, seeded, and chopped
1 cup ground lean pork
1 cup ground veal
2 sweet-sour pickled dill cucumbers, chopped
1¼ cups chicken or beef stock
salt and freshly ground black pepper
1 tbsp butter
4 tsp flour
1 tbsp tomato paste
⅔ cup sour cream
½ recipe sour cream rye dough (see page 156)
or 1 lb wholewheat bread dough
1 large egg

Fill a large saucepan with water. Bring to the boil, add the barley and lower the heat. Simmer, covered, until the barley is tender, about 30 minutes. Drain the barley thoroughly and reserve.

Meanwhile, soften and remove the cabbage leaves as described on page 103. Repeat the process until you have about 18 leaves. Cut out the toughest part of the central stem in each leaf. Set aside.

Heat the oil in a skillet and stir in the onion. Sauté until limp, about 6 minutes. Add the pepper and cook for another 5 minutes, until that too is limp. Take the mixture off the heat. Transfer to a bowl and add the meat, chopped cucumbers, 2 tablespoons stock and salt and pepper to taste. Use your hands to combine well and divide into as many portions as there are leaves. Put a portion at the stalk end of each leaf, tuck in the ends, and roll to make a neat packet. Place the cabbage rolls in a baking dish just large enough to hold them in one layer. Set aside.

Melt the butter in a saucepan. Stir in the flour and cook for 3 minutes, or until the mixture is smooth. Whisk in the remaining stock and tomato paste, continue until the sauce boils and thickens. Take the sauce off the heat and stir in the sour cream. Pour the hot sauce evenly over the cabbage rolls.

Roll the dough out to a rectangle just larger than the baking dish. Lay over the top of the cabbage rolls and tuck the edges in. Use a fork to pull the dough gently towards the rim of the dish, crimping it. Cover the pastry with a dampened dish toweL and leave to rise in a warm place for 20 minutes, or until risen and puffed up.

Preheat the oven to 350°F. Make an egg wash by lightly beating the egg with a little water. Brush the wash over the pastry and bake until golden brown, about 45 minutes.

CARROT AND POTATO HOTPOT

A simple, warming vegetable dish.

S E R V E S   4

1 large onion, thinly sliced
6 tbsp butter
¼ lb carrots, thickly sliced
1½ lb potatoes, peeled and cut in large chunks
salt and freshly ground black pepper
1 bay leaf
2½ cups water
⅔ cup fresh bread crumbs
6 tbsp all purpose flour
⅔ cup sour cream
2 tbsp chopped fresh dill

Cook the onion in one third of the butter for 10 minutes. Stir in the carrots and potatoes, then sprinkle in some seasoning. Add the bay leaf and pour in the water. Bring to a boil, then simmer, uncovered, for about 15 minutes, until the vegetables are tender.

Meanwhile, cook the bread crumbs in half the remaining butter until golden. Set aside.

Drain the vegetables, reserving the liquid, and put them in a warmed serving dish. Melt the remaining butter in a saucepan and stir in the flour. Gradually add the cooking liquid and bring to a boil, stirring. Simmer for 3 minutes, add the sour cream and dill, and taste for seasoning. Pour this sauce over the vegetables and top with the crumbs. Serve at once.

BITKI

These tasty little patties can be made with either beef or pork – the latter is probably more common in western Russia and the Ukraine. While the recipe offers the option of cranberry jelly as an accompaniment, in its home regions bitki would more usually be paired with lingonberries.

SERVES 4 – 5

¼ cup butter
1 medium onion, finely chopped
1½ lb lean ground pork or beef
1 cup ground veal
¼ cup ground fresh pork fat
2 cups dry bread crumbs
1 large egg, beaten
salt and freshly ground black pepper
⅓ cup chicken fat or dripping
⅔ cup sour cream (optional)
½ cup cranberry jelly (optional)

Heat the butter over medium heat and add the onions. Cook, stirring occasionally, until lightly colored and softened, about 8 minutes. Transfer to a large bowl and add the ground meats, fat, bread crumbs, egg, and seasoning to taste. Work with your hands until all the ingredients are well combined.

Form the bitki into 8–10 thick patties. Turn each of the patties over in the remaining bread crumbs to coat them. Melt half the fat in a skillet over high heat. Fry the patties until they are golden brown, about 5 minutes a side. Transfer to a serving dish and keep warm. Repeat with the remaining fat and patties.

Serve the bitki in either of two ways: sour cream can be stirred into the skillet after the patties are finished, warmed through, and then poured over the bitki. Alternatively, serve the bitki plain, accompanied by a sauceboat of cranberry jelly.

CARROT TZIMMES LOAF

In Yiddish, a tzimmes means a mess or a fuss; to make a tzimmes over someone or something means to make a great fuss – usually the grandmothers' province. This recipe is particularly fussy, but is well worth the effort and can be prepared ahead. Using traditional ingredients, this version is based on an appetizer at the Quai d'Orsay restaurant in Paris, Chef Antoine Bouterin's individual carrot "pâtés" made with carrots and blanched artichokes and served with a butter sauce.

SERVES 8 – 10

2 leeks, cut in half lengthwise and well rinsed
2 large carrots, cooked and mashed
1 large sweet potato, cooked and mashed
2 tbsp melted margarine, or vegetable oil
2 tbsp honey
1 tbsp lemon juice
salt
freshly ground black pepper
1¼ tsp cayenne pepper, or to taste
¼ tsp grated nutmeg
4 scallions, finely chopped
4 eggs
2 egg yolks
2 large potatoes, cooked and mashed
14 oz pitted prunes, soaked in hot water 10–15 minutes
fresh parsley sprigs and lemon twists for garnish

Fill a large saucepan with water and, over high heat, bring to a boil. Add leeks and cook until slightly softened and the color brightens, 1–2 minutes. Drain and rinse under cold running water to stop the cooking and keep color. Separate and remove to a clean dish towel and drain and dry well. Set aside.

In a large bowl, combine mashed carrots and sweet potato with melted margarine or oil, honey, lemon juice, salt and pepper to taste, cayenne pepper, nutmeg, and half the chopped scallions. Set aside.

In a small bowl, beat 2 of the eggs and 1 yolk. Stir into carrot-sweet potato mixture. Set aside.

In another bowl, place mashed potatoes. Season with salt and pepper and add the remaining scallions. In another small bowl, beat remaining 2 eggs and 1 yolk. Add to potato-scallion mixture, beating well until well blended.

Preheat oven to 375°F. Lightly grease a 9 × 5 × 3 in loaf pan or long terrine dish. Lay leeks across pan or dish, overlapping each slice and alternating tops and bottoms, so dish is lined with white and green parts. Leave leeks to hang over sides.

Drain prunes and pat dry with paper towels. Carefully spoon in half of the carrot-sweet potato mixture, smoothing to make an even bottom layer.

Place one-third of the prunes onto carrot layer, leaving space between prunes. Cover with half the potato-scallion mixture, smoothing top to make an even layer. Sprinkle in another third of the prunes. Repeat layers with the remaining carrot-sweet potato mixture, prunes and potato-scallion mixture.

Fold over ends of leeks to cover top of tin or dish and cover tightly with foil.

Place dish in a shallow roasting pan or baking dish. Fill the roasting pan with boiling water to about 1½ in up side of loaf pan or terrine. Bake 1¼ hours, until knife inserted in center comes out clean, adding water to water bath if necessary. Cool tzimmes loaf completely in water bath.

Remove loaf pan or dish from water bath and dry bottom of tin. Place on a dish and weight the top overnight. To weight loaf, cut a thin piece of cardboard the size of top of loaf. Wrap with foil and press against surface of the loaf. Place 2 heavy cans on top of board; refrigerate overnight.

To serve, run a sharp knife around edges of tin, shake gently to unmold onto plate. To slice loaf, use a sharp knife. Run under hot water and wipe dry before cutting each slice. Serve chilled, garnished with parsley sprigs and lemon twists.

HAM SAUSAGE WITH RED CABBAGE

Kolbasa is a smoked ham sausage common throughout the eastern European states. Like many processed pork products, it is largely produced for sale in Poland and nearby Ukraine and Belorussia. It can be eaten hot or cold.

SERVES 4 – 6

1 large head red cabbage, shredded
1 oz butter
⅓ cup lemon juice
½ cup beef stock
¼ cup red wine
salt and pepper
2 tsp brown sugar
1 tbsp cornstarch
1 lb kolbasa or other smoked ham sausage,
thinly sliced

Place the shredded cabbage in a colander and pour boiling water over it. Drain thoroughly.

Melt the butter in a heavy flameproof casserole over medium heat. Stir in the cabbage and sauté for 5 minutes. Add the lemon juice and continue stirring for another 5 minutes: the cabbage will be bright pink. Pour over the stock and wine, cover, and lower the heat. Simmer for 45 minutes.

Mix together the sugar and cornstarch in a small bowl; stir in a little of the cooking liquid. Stir the mixture into the cabbage and raise the heat to high. Stir as the sauce thickens, then add the sausage. Cover and simmer for 30 minutes. Serve with thick slabs of rye bread.

POTATO AND APPLE PUDDING

In addition to potatoes, apples are a passion in Lithuania; they appear in everything from desserts to first courses with herring. This pudding also has variations in Denmark and Germany, where there is a predilection for sweet-savory combinations. It goes particularly well with pork, goose, and duck.

SERVES 4 – 6

1 lb floury potatoes, unpeeled
1 lb tart apples, peeled
½ cup butter
2 tsp sugar
¼ tsp nutmeg
⅔ cup milk
¼ cup heavy cream
⅔ cup bread crumbs

In a large saucepan cover the potatoes with water and bring to the boil. Lower the heat and simmer until the potatoes are tender. Meanwhile, in another large saucepan, sauté the apples in three-quarters of the butter until softened. Toss the hot apples with the sugar and nutmeg and set aside.

Drain the potatoes and peel while still hot. Mash them with the milk until as smooth as possible. Add the apples in their butter, and the cream. Mash and beat vigorously to combine.

Preheat the oven to 400°F. Transfer the mixture to a baking dish. Scatter the bread crumbs over and dot with the remaining butter. Bake for 25 minutes, until the top is golden.

VEGETABLES AND SALADS

POLISH-STYLE
CAULIFLOWER

SAUERKRAUT
WITH
MUSHROOMS

KALE IN
CREAM SAUCE

SWEET AND
SOUR RED
CABBAGE

LATKES

CUCUMBER
SALAD

RUTABAGA
CASSEROLE

RUSSIAN
POTATO
SALAD

BEET IN
SOUR CREAM
SAUCE

STUFFED
ONIONS

ODESSA-
STYLE
MUSHROOMS
IN SOUR
CREAM

BRAISED
CUCUMBER
WITH DILL

JANSSON'S
TEMPTATION

WEST COAST
SALAD

POLISH-STYLE CAULIFLOWER

**When the topping of bread crumbs, browned in
butter, is used the dish may take the title "à la
Polonaise."**

SERVES 4

1 cauliflower, cut into flowerets
salt and freshly ground black pepper
¼ cup butter
1 cup fresh bread crumbs
a little chopped fresh dill (optional)

Cook the cauliflower in boiling salted water for about
5 minutes, or until tender. Drain thoroughly and
transfer to a warmed serving dish.

Melt the butter and add the bread crumbs. Cook,
stirring, until golden. Add a little seasoning and some
dill, if liked. Sprinkle this topping over the cauliflower
and serve.

SAUERKRAUT WITH MUSHROOMS

Dried mushrooms enrich sauerkraut but the vegetable may be cooked with a sauce made from meat stock instead. Offer as a side dish to broiled or roast pork, boiled beef, or other meats, including roast game.

SERVES 2 – 4

2 large dried mushrooms
1¼ cups water
1 onion, thinly sliced
2 tbsp butter
1 tbsp all purpose flour
1 lb sauerkraut, drained
⅔ cup sour cream
salt and freshly ground black pepper

Simmer the mushrooms in the water for 5 minutes. Drain, reserving the liquor, and chop the mushrooms. Cook the onion in the butter for 10 minutes, until softened but not browned. Stir in the flour, then gradually add the mushroom liquor and bring to a boil. Add the mushrooms to the sauce.

Squeeze the sauerkraut to extract all the liquid (save some to add at the end of cooking if you like fairly sour vegetables), then slice the pat of vegetable with a sharp knife to shred it. Add to the sauce, stirring well. Cover and simmer for 20 minutes.

Stir in the sour cream, heat gently and taste for seasoning before serving.

KALE IN CREAM SAUCE

Vegetables that keep well through the winter play a large part in eastern European cooking. Kale served this Danish way makes an excellent side dish to accompany cured loin of pork, a favorite traditional dish.

SERVES 4-6

1 lb kale
2 tsp salt
¼ cup butter
4 tbsp flour
1 cup milk
1 cup whipping or heavy cream
½ tsp freshly ground pepper

Pick the tender kale leaves from their stalks, and wash thoroughly under cold running water. Shake off the water, and tear the leaves into large pieces. Cook the kale in boiling salted water for about 10–15 minutes. Drain thoroughly, then finely chop the kale.

For the sauce, melt the butter in a pan. Remove from the heat and stir in the flour. Pour in the milk and cream at the same time, whisking vigorously. Return the pan to a low heat, whisking continuously, until smooth. Season to taste. Add the finely chopped kale, and heat for a few minutes.

SWEET AND SOUR RED CABBAGE

Cabbage is an important ingredient in the Russian and central European kitchen, where unfortunately it is mostly overcooked. This braised cabbage dish is especially delicious with rich meats, such as goose, duck, and pot roasts. The recipe can also be made with green cabbage, a variation which goes well with turkey.

SERVES 6-8

2 tbsp vegetable oil
1 onion, cut in half and thinly sliced
2 eating apples, peeled, cored, and thinly sliced
1 red cabbage, about 1½ lb, quartered, cored, and shredded
¼ cup red wine vinegar
2–3 tbsp light brown sugar
⅓ cup golden raisins (optional)
½ cup vegetable stock or water
salt
freshly ground black pepper

In a large, heavy-bottomed, non-aluminum pan, over medium heat, heat oil. Add onion and cook until soft and golden, 5–7 minutes. Add sliced apples and cook until beginning to brown, 2–3 minutes.

Add cabbage and remaining ingredients. If you want to make the green cabbage version, use white wine vinegar or lemon juice and white sugar. Simmer, covered, stirring occasionally and adding water if necessary, until cabbage is tender, 30–40 minutes. Uncover and cook until liquid is absorbed. Spoon into serving bowl. Sweet and sour cabbage is also delicious served cold.

Right: Sweet and Sour Red Cabbage

LATKES

Latkes are a well-known and well-loved Jewish contribution to the culinary repertoire. They are delicious with rich roast poultry, such as duck and goose, but can also be eaten as a brunch dish or on their own sprinkled with sugar or topped with apple sauce or sour cream.

SERVES 6 – 8

6 medium potatoes, peeled
1 onion
2 eggs, lightly beaten
¼ cup fine matzo meal, or all purpose flour
1 tsp salt
pinch ground white pepper
vegetable oil for frying
apple sauce or sour cream for serving

In a food processor fitted with grater attachment, grate potatoes and onion. Drain in a colander, pressing to squeeze out as much liquid as possible. Place in a large bowl and beat in remaining ingredients except oil and accompaniments. (Work as quickly as possible so potatoes do not turn brown.)

In a large, heavy skillet over medium heat, heat about 1 in vegetable oil or just enough to cover pancakes. Drop batter by tablespoonsful into hot oil and cook until underside is browned, 2 minutes. Turn and cook until second side is browned, 1–2 minutes longer.

Remove to a serving platter and keep warm in a 300°F oven. Continue until all batter is used, adding a little more oil if necessary. Serve immediately with apple sauce or sour cream.

CUCUMBER SALAD

This cold variation of the previous recipe may be offered as an accompaniment to boiled meats.

SERVES 4

½ cucumber, peeled (about ½ lb)
salt and freshly ground black pepper
⅔ cup sour cream
1 tbsp chopped fresh dill

Thinly slice the cucumber and place the slices in a colander, sprinkling the layers with a little salt. Stand the colander over a bowl and leave to drain for 15 minutes.

Shake all the liquid off the cucumber and pat the slices dry on absorbent kitchen paper. Mix with the sour cream, adding pepper to taste. Sprinkle with dill and serve.

RUTABAGA CASSEROLE

This Finnish casserole is delicious, but, in fact, any vegetables can be used.

SERVES 4-6

2 lb yellow turnips (rutabagas), peeled
1½ tsp salt
4 tsp bread crumbs
¼ cup heavy cream
½ tsp grated nutmeg
2 eggs, lightly beaten
2 tbsp butter

Cut the turnips into ¼-inch cubes, and put into a saucepan. Cover with cold water, add ½ teaspoon of the salt, and bring to a boil. Lower the heat, and simmer for about 20 minutes until soft. Drain, and purée in a blender.

Preheat the oven to 325°F. Soak the bread crumbs in the cream for a few minutes. Stir in the nutmeg, remaining salt, beaten eggs, and puréed turnip.

Grease a large casserole dish, and pour in the mixture. Cut the butter into tiny pieces, and dot over the turnips. Bake, uncovered, for about 1 hour, until golden brown. Serve with meat or fish, or on its own.

RUSSIAN POTATO SALAD

This delicious salad incorporates the dressing which has now become internationally known as "Russian dressing."

SERVES 6-8

2 lb new potatoes
2 tbsp finely chopped scallions
3 tbsp finely chopped fresh dill
6 tbsp finely chopped sweet-sour pickled cucumber
6 radishes, thinly sliced
fresh dill sprigs to garnish

FOR THE DRESSING

⅔ cup mayonnaise
½ tsp Worcestershire sauce
1½ tbsp catsup
2 tbsp dry white wine
1 tsp horseradish sauce

Put the potatoes in a large saucepan of water and bring to a boil. Cover, lower the heat and simmer for about 20–25 minutes, or until the potatoes are done. Drain and when cool, cut into ¼ in slices.

In a small bowl, whisk together the ingredients for the dressing. In a large bowl, assemble the potatoes, onion, dill, cucumbers, and radishes. Pour the dressing over and toss gently to combine. Garnish and serve.

BEET IN SOUR CREAM SAUCE

Sugar and vinegar are added to give the beet a sweet and sour flavor. The vegetable is served with cooked meat, fish, game, or poultry.

SERVES 4

1 large onion, finely chopped
2 tbsp butter
1 tbsp all purpose flour
1 tbsp sugar
2 tsp cider vinegar
1 tbsp beet juice
⅔ cup sour cream
1 lb freshly cooked beet, peeled and coarsely grated
salt and freshly ground black pepper

Cook the onion in the butter for 15 minutes, until very soft but not browned. Stir in the flour, then add the sugar, vinegar, beet juice, and sour cream.

Bring to a boil, then stir in the beet with a little seasoning. Cook, stirring occasionally, for 5 minutes. Check the seasoning and balance of sweet to sour before serving.

STUFFED ONIONS

These old-fashioned stuffed onions are a Swedish delicacy, well worth a revival in their popularity. It is difficult to understand why this fine dish has been forgotten.

SERVES 4–6

3–4 large yellow onions
1 tbsp bread crumbs
½ cup light cream
5 oz ground veal, or 1 cup cooked rice
1 small can of mushrooms
1 egg yolk
salt and white pepper
celery salt
2 tbsp butter

Peel the onions, and make a deep cut through half of each onion. Boil the onions in lightly salted water until semi-soft. Drain, reserving the cooking liquid, then rinse them under cold water. Separate the layers carefully and leave to drain. Take the cores of the onions and chop finely.

Stir the bread crumbs into the cream, and leave to swell. Mix with the veal or rice, mushrooms, chopped onion cores, and egg yolk. Season well with salt, pepper, and celery salt.

Place 1 tablespoon of the mixture on every large onion layer and fold. Melt the butter in a skillet, and brown the stuffed onion layers all over. Add ⅔ cup of the onion water and simmer, covered, until soft. Add more onion water, if needed.

Stuffed onions can also be baked in a greased ovenproof dish. First brush with melted butter or margarine, then bake in the oven at 425°F for 30 minutes.

ODESSA-STYLE MUSHROOMS IN SOUR CREAM

The combination of mushrooms and sour cream is a popular one all over Ukraine, Belorussia, and Moldova and understandably, as it is mouthwateringly delicious. However, the version that originates from the holiday port of Odessa, on the Black Sea, has a widespread reputation among cognoscenti. At home it would be made with *brynza* or *seerh*, but any hard, crumbly cheese with a good flavor will be suitable.

SERVES 6

⅓ cup unsalted butter, at room temperature
4 scallions, finely chopped
1 lb field or brown mushrooms, wiped and patted dry
1 tbsp flour
salt and freshly ground black pepper
½ cup sour cream
⅓ cup heavy cream
½ cup grated cheese (see above)

Melt half the butter in a skillet over medium heat. Add the scallions and sauté briefly, then stir in the mushrooms and continue to cook for about 5–6 minutes, until the mushrooms are browned and just going soft.

In a small bowl, combine 1 tablespoon of the butter with the flour, working it to make a *beurre manié*. Stir the *beurre manié* into the mushrooms and cook for 3 minutes, or until thickened. Season to taste, and stir in the sour cream and heavy cream.

Preheat the oven to 350°F. Pour the mushroom mixture into an attractive baking dish. Sprinkle the top with the cheese, and dot with the remaining butter. Bake for 20–25 minutes, until the mushrooms are bubbling and the top just coloring.

Left: Odessa-style Mushrooms in Sour Cream

BRAISED CUCUMBER WITH DILL

This deliciously delicate dish from Poland is good with chicken or fish.

SERVES 4

1 cucumber, peeled and halved lengthways (about 1 lb)
1 small onion, halved and thinly sliced
2 tbsp butter
salt and freshly ground black pepper
⅔ cup water
1 tbsp sugar
1 tbsp cider vinegar
2 tbsp sour cream
2 tbsp chopped fresh dill

Use a teaspoon to scoop all the seeds out of the cucumber. Cut each half into 2 in lengths. Cook the onion in the butter for 10 minutes. Add the cucumber and stir for 2 minutes to coat the pieces. Sprinkle in seasoning, then pour in the water and heat until simmering. Cover and cook for 5 minutes. Remove the lid and cook for a further 5 minutes, so that some of the water evaporates. The cucumber should be tender but not soft.

Stir in the sugar, vinegar, and sour cream. Taste the sauce and adjust the seasoning before serving. Sprinkle with dill.

JANSSON'S TEMPTATION

No wonder Jansson was tempted! The saltiness of the anchovies is tempered by the potatoes. Onions add a contrasting flavor and the cream makes this Swedish specialty irresistible.

SERVES 4 – 6

6 medium potatoes
10 anchovies in brine
2 medium onions, thinly sliced
2–4 tbsp butter
generous 1 cup heavy cream

Preheat the oven to 325°F. Peel the potatoes and cut into thin strips. Soak them in cold water to get rid of the starch – it will make the potatoes crispier. Meanwhile, cut the anchovy fillets in half, if preferred. Reserve the brine. Fry the onions gently in half the butter until golden brown.

Grease an ovenproof dish. Dry the potatoes with paper towels. Put the potatoes, anchovies, and onions in layers, beginning and finishing with potato. Pour over half of the cream. Dot with the remaining butter and pour over 4 tablespoons anchovy brine. Bake for about 25 minutes. Pour over the rest of the cream and anchovy brine, then bake for another 20 minutes. Serve with cold beer.

WEST COAST SALAD

This delicious salad comes from Sweden and makes use of the harvest from the country's long coastline. Serve it for lunch or supper, or as a starter. The salad can be prepared in advance and kept in the refrigerator, but add the dressing just before serving.

SERVES 4 – 6

½ lb cooked fresh shrimp
1 cooked fresh lobster or crab, or 6 oz canned
2 tomatoes
¼ lb mushrooms, sliced
1 lettuce, shredded
1 small can asparagus and/or 1 small packet frozen peas
4½ oz packet frozen corn
3 pickled cucumbers
hard-boiled egg wedges, to garnish

DRESSING

2 tbsp red wine vinegar
salt and white pepper
6 tbsp oil

Peel the shrimp. Pick the meat from the lobster or crab, and cut it into small pieces. Cut the tomatoes into thin wedges. Mix and gently stir together the seafood, mushrooms, lettuce, and tomatoes. Blend with the asparagus and/or peas, corn, and cucumbers. Chill before serving. Shake the dressing ingredients together and pour over the salad.

Right: West Coast Salad

DESSERTS

APPLE
STRUDEL

KISEL

BAKED
BUCKWHEAT
PUDDING

PASHA

SWEET
APPLE
BREAD
PUDDING

CHARLOTTE
RUSSE

RASPBERRY
TART

CRANBERRY
PARFAIT

DRIED FRUIT
COMPOTE

TROLL'S
DESSERT

NOODLES
WITH POPPY
SEEDS

BLUEBERRY
PIE

FRUIT-
FILLED
LOKSHEN
PUDDING

APPLE STRUDEL

Strudel is popular all over eastern Europe, and in Poland it may well be served as one of the sweet dishes for the Christmas Eve meal. Filo pastry is an easy but effective substitute for making your own strudel pastry.

SERVES 8

2 lb cooking apples, peeled, cored, and roughly chopped
¼ cup superfine sugar
1 tsp ground cinnamon
pinch of ground allspice
½ cup raisins
6 sheets filo pastry
¼ cup butter, melted
1⅓ cups fresh bread crumbs
confectioners' sugar to dust

Set the oven at 375°F. Grease a large roasting pan. Lay a clean cloth on a work surface. Mix the apples, sugar, spices, and raisins.

Lay two sheets of filo pastry on the cloth, overlapping them by about 2 in along the long side. Brush very lightly with a little butter, then top with two more sheets, butter and top with the remaining filo. Sprinkle the bread crumbs over the pastry, leaving a 1–1½ in border. Spread the apple mixture all over the bread crumbs. Fold the border of pastry over the edge of the apples, then roll up the pastry and its filling from the long side. Use the cloth to help roll the strudel. Lift the strudel in the cloth (this is its real purpose in this recipe) and roll it onto the pan, so that the pastry join is underneath. Gently pat the strudel into shape and brush it all over with the remaining butter.

Bake for 30–40 minutes, taking care that it does not become too brown. Serve the strudel hot, dusted with confectioners' sugar. You will need two large spatulas and a serving platter or board if you intend to serve the strudel whole.

NOTE: Always keep filo pastry covered with plastic wrap while you work, as it dries rapidly and crumbles into bits if allowed to lay uncovered in the air. Also, make sure the surface is absolutely dry as spots of water will cause the pastry to become sticky and break. If you do not have a large pan, then curve the strudel on a baking sheet.

KISEL

Kisel is a traditional summer dessert, changing its character as the different fruits come into season. It can also be thinned to become a sweet drink, a summer treat in the days before fizzy drinks became the norm, even in Russia.

SERVES 4 – 6

1 lb raspberries, strawberries, blueberries, cherries, peeled apricots, or peaches
2¼ cups water
⅔ cup sugar
2–2½ tbsp arrowroot
⅔ cup white or red wine (optional)

Place the washed and cleaned fruit into a saucepan with the water. Bring to a boil, then simmer for 15–20 minutes. The fruit should be very pulpy. Strain the liquid from the fruit into a bowl. Be careful not to press on the fruit too hard; it will make the juice cloudy.

Discard the solids and return the juice to the saucepan, together with the sugar. Bring to a boil, then lower the heat and simmer. In a small bowl, whisk the arrowroot with 4 tablespoons of the juice (use 2 tablespoons arrowroot if not including the wine; otherwise, add 2½ tablespoons). Stir the thickening into the juice and the wine, if using. Continue to simmer, whisking, for a few minutes. Remove from the heat, cool slightly, pour into individual glasses and chill for at least 4 hours before serving.

BAKED BUCKWHEAT PUDDING

The addition of dried fruits and lemon rind lifts an old-fashioned and inexpensive pudding. Serve with vanilla custard or offer a warmed fruit syrup or honey instead.

SERVES 6

4 eggs, separated
½ cup superfine sugar
1 tsp natural vanilla essence
scant 1 cup sour cream
grated rind of 1 lemon
½ cup raisins
⅔ cup candied peel
1¼ cups buckwheat flour
confectioners' sugar to dust

Set the oven at 350°F. Base-line and grease a 7–8 in charlotte mold or deep round cake pan.

Blend the egg yolks, sugar, and vanilla in a bowl until pale and thick. Beat in the sour cream, lemon rind, and fruit, then stir in the buckwheat flour. Whisk the egg whites until stiff and fold them into the mixture using a metal spoon. Take care to keep the mixture light. Turn the pudding into the prepared mold or pan.

Bake for 1¼ hours, until risen and browned. Check the pudding about 8 minutes before the end of cooking and cover loosely with a piece of foil if it is likely to become too dark. Turn out the pudding onto a clean dish towel, remove the lining paper, and invert the pudding onto a warmed serving dish. Dust with confectioners' sugar and serve.

PASHA

For centuries Karelia in eastern Finland was the point of entry for many dishes out of the east, and many Scandinavian dishes bear the unmistakable stamp of Russia. This traditional Easter cheesecake originated in Russia, but has been much more widely adopted.

SERVES 4–6

2½ lb curd cheese
1 cup butter
1 egg
3 egg yolks
⅔ cup sugar
1 cup whipping cream
1 split vanilla pod
scant ½ cup candied orange peel
scant ½ cup candied lemon peel
½ cup chopped almonds
½ cup raisins
½ tbsp ground cloves
½ tbsp ground cinnamon
2 tbsp lemon juice
20 whole ground almonds
candied cherries

Put the cheese into a piece of cheesecloth, and squeeze out the liquid. Melt the butter and mix with the cheese. Cream the whole egg and egg yolks with the sugar. Gradually whisk in the cream, and add the vanilla pod. Put the bowl over a pan of simmering water over a low heat. Stir the mixture until it becomes thick and creamy. Remove from the heat, and continue stirring until cooled. Remove the vanilla pod, then fold in the curd cheese. Stir in the candied peels, chopped almonds, sultanas, cloves, cinnamon, and lemon juice.

Line a 5-cup earthenware mold with a large, dampened piece of cheesecloth, and spoon in the mixture. Fold the cloth loosely over the top, and place a weight on top. Leave to stand for 1–2 days. Turn out the pasha onto a serving dish. Decorate with almonds and candied cherries.

Right: Pasha

SWEET APPLE BREAD PUDDING WITH LEMON SAUCE

The valued apple makes another appearance in this Luthianian dessert, the sugar addict's answer to the savory potato and apple pudding on page 109. Vanilla ice cream makes a yummy cold partner for this warm pudding, as do mashed and sugared cranberries.

SERVES 6–8

½ cup unsalted butter
1⅔ cups milk
⅔ cup light brown sugar
6 slices stale white bread, crusts removed, cubed
2 eating apples, peeled, cored, and sliced
2 eggs
¼ cup Greek- or Bulgarian-style yogurt
½ tsp vanilla essence
dash of almond essence
¼ tsp ground allspice
¼ tsp salt
3 oz dates, stoned, and finely chopped
5 tsp wheatgerm

FOR THE SAUCE

⅞ cup sugar
2 tbsp cornstarch
1¼ cup water
3 tbsp butter
3 tbsp fresh lemon juice

Heat the butter, milk, and sugar together in a saucepan over low heat until the butter has melted and the sugar has dissolved. Set aside.

Combine the bread cubes and apple slices in a baking pan that will take them in one layer. In a bowl, whisk together the eggs, yogurt, vanilla and almond essences, the allspice, and salt. Stir in the milk mixture and the dates.

Pour the liquid over the apples and bread and leave to soak for 10–15 minutes. Meanwhile, preheat the oven to 350°F. Sprinkle the top of the pudding with the wheatgerm and bake for 40 minutes, or until puffy and golden brown.

Meanwhile, make the sauce. In a saucepan, stir the sugar and cornstarch in the water over high heat until boiling. Add the butter and lemon juice, stirring, and when the butter is dissolved, remove from the heat.

Serve the apple bread pudding warm, accompanied by the warm lemon sauce.

CHARLOTTE RUSSE

This famous dessert was the creation of Anton Carême, chef to Tsar Alexander I in the first quarter of the 19th century. The great French cook exploited the Russian love of fruit purées – charlottkas usually have apple or soft fruit fillings or accompanying sauces. This popular version makes use of apricot custard.

SERVES 8–9

1–2 tbsp apricot jelly
16–18 sponge fingers
⅔ cup whipping or heavy cream
½ cup canned baby mandarin segments, drained

FOR THE CUSTARD FILLING

1 lb can apricot halves in syrup, drained and syrup reserved
5 tsp gelatine
8 egg yolks
⅔ cup sugar
1¼ cup milk
⅔ cup heavy cream
½ cup sour cream
6 tbsp Cointreau, Grand Marnier or other orange liqueur

Spread the jelly thinly around the inside edge of a 8–9 in, deep springform cake pan. Measure the sponge fingers against the sides of the pan and cut off one end so that they will stand up. Line them up side-to-side, around the inside of the pan, pressing them into the jelly.

apricots in a blender or a food processor fitted with the metal blade. Add ½ cup of the apricot syrup and purée the apricots. Place 3 tablespoons apricot syrup in a small bowl and sprinkle the gelatine into it. Put the bowl into a pan of hot water and stir the syrup and gelatine until the latter has dissolved.

Beat the egg yolks with the sugar in a bowl placed over a pan of hot water until the mixture is creamy and lemon yellow. Bring the milk to simmering point and slowly stir it into the egg mixture, stirring all the time. Continue to stir over the hot water until the mixture has become a spoon-coating custard. Stir the gelatine into the custard, take off the heat and allow to cool to room temperature.

Whisk the apricot purée into the custard, then cover and chill in the refrigerator until the mixture is satiny and just beginning to set. In a bowl, combine the heavy cream and sour cream and whip until they reach stiff peak stage. Fold into the apricot mixture, together with the orange liqueur.

Pour the mixture into the sponge finger-lined pan. Chill for 4 hours or overnight.

To unmold, run a knife around between the pan and the sponge. Spring open the pan and slip the charlotte out. Whip the whipping or heavy cream, fill a piping bag and circle the top of the charlotte with piped rosettes. Place a mandarin segment on top of each rosette. Keep chilled until served.

RASPBERRY TART

A delicious fresh tart consisting of a thin, rich pastry shell filled with a fine lemon cream and raspberries, topped with lemon jelly. Suitable both for tea and as a dessert.

SERVES 6

PASTRY

2 cups flour
pinch of salt
½ cup soft butter
2 tbsp sugar
1 egg yolk

LEMON CREAM

2 egg yolks
2 tbsp sugar
¼ tbsp cornstarch
generous 1 cup light cream
2 tbsp softened butter
grated rind of ¼–½ lemon

DECORATION

gelatine
1 cup water
2 tbsp sugar
juice of ½ lemon
about 2 cups fresh raspberries, or ½ lb frozen raspberries

Preheat the oven to 350°F. Place the flour and salt in a bowl, then blend in the butter until the mixture resembles bread crumbs. Stir in the sugar. Add the egg yolk, and stir until it forms a dough. Add water as necessary. Knead lightly. Use to line a shallow, straight-sided flan dish, 9 in in diameter. Bake blind for about 10 minutes, until golden. Cool slightly, then release carefully from the pan.

For the lemon cream, whisk together the egg yolks, cream, cornstarch, and sugar in a saucepan. Simmer the mixture, whisking, until the cream is thick and fluffy. Remove from the heat, add the butter, and whisk occasionally while it cools. Flavor the cold cream with the lemon rind.

Dissolve the gelatine in the water for the jelly. Add the sugar and lemon juice.

Fill the pastry shell with the lemon cream, and cover with raspberries. Pour the jelly over the top when it starts to set. Leave the tart in a cold place until serving.

CRANBERRY PARFAIT

A parfait is a stylish and always successful dessert. Any berries can be used.

SERVES 4–6

2 egg yolks
⅔ cup sugar
⅔ cup cranberry purée
1¼ cups heavy cream

Whisk the egg yolks and sugar until fluffy. Stir in the cranberry purée. Whip the cream, and fold gently into the cranberry mixture. Taste to see if more sugar is needed.

Rinse a 3–5-cup mold with cold water. Pour in the mixture and freeze. To remove the parfait before serving, dip the mold into hot water for a few seconds. Serve with fresh berries and whipped cream.

DRIED FRUIT COMPOTE

The compôte, a favorite for Christmas Eve, may include any dried fruits that are available. The fruits are steeped in a thick, sweet syrup.

SERVES 8

1½ lb dried fruit, such as prunes, apricots, pears, peaches, apples, raisins
¾ cup sugar
pared rind and juice of 2 lemons
pared rind and juice of 1 orange
about ½ cup blanched almonds, cut into slivers and toasted

Place the fruit in a bowl and pour in enough water to cover the fruit well. Cover and leave to soak overnight.

Next day, drain the liquid from the fruit into a saucepan and add the sugar, fruit rind, and juices. Bring to a boil, then add the soaked fruit and simmer for 3–5 minutes, until the fruit is tender. Drain, reserving the liquid, and place the fruit in a bowl. Return the fruit rind and liquid to the pan and bring to a boil. Boil the syrup until reduced and thickened slightly. Strain the syrup over the fruit. Leave until cold before serving topped with the almonds.

TROLL'S DESSERT

Whip up this light, creamy Norwegian dessert flavored with fruit sauce or sliced strawberries and you will have a delightful end-of-meal treat in no time.

SERVES 4

2 egg whites
1 cup lightly sweetened apple sauce or ½ lb (about 1½ cups) fresh or frozen strawberries, sliced

Whisk the egg whites until stiff. Add the apple sauce or strawberries. Continue whisking until the mixture is stiff and fruit and egg whites are well blended. Use an electric whisk for quick results. Serve with cream.

Right: Dried Fruit Compote

NOODLES WITH POPPY SEEDS

This was part of the traditional Polish Christmas Eve meal, although other desserts have replaced it in some households.

SERVES 6

2 cups all purpose flour
½ tsp salt
1 egg
3 tbsp water
2 tbsp butter, melted
3 tbsp clear honey
⅓ cup poppy seeds, ground

Sift the flour and salt into a bowl and make a well in the middle. Add the egg and water, beating the two together. Mix in the flour to make a very stiff dough. Gradually knead the dough into a ball. Turn out onto a surface and knead until smooth. Cut the dough in half and wrap one piece in plastic wrap.

Roll out the second piece into an oblong measuring 12 × 7 in, dust with flour and fold in half. Cut across the fold into thin noodles, measuring ¼ –½ in wide. Dust the noodles with a little flour and shake them on to a plate. Repeat with the remaining dough.

Cook the noodles in plenty of boiling water for about 4 minutes, until tender but not soft. Drain and toss with the melted butter, honey, and poppy seeds. Serve hot.

BLUEBERRY PIE

Berries are loved by the Finns, and there are plenty for picking in the forests.

SERVES 4 – 6

CRUST

¼ cup butter
⅓ cup sugar (optional)
1 egg
⅓ cup whipping cream
2¼ cups flour

FILLING

2 pints blueberries
sugar to taste (optional)
1 tsp bread crumbs or potato flour

Soften the butter and add the sugar, if using. Mix in the egg thoroughly, then add the cream and flour. Mix well, but do not beat the dough. Leave the dough to stand in a cool place for 15 minutes.

Preheat the oven to 400°F. Roll out the dough into a thin sheet and transfer to a greased baking sheet, shaping a raised edge all the way around. Mix the blueberries with the sugar, if using, and the bread crumbs or potato flour. Spread the filling on the dough. Bake until the crust is golden brown.

FRUIT-FILLED LOKSHEN PUDDING

A sweet kugel is an old-fashioned Ashkenazic dessert – rich and heavy. This creamy version with dried fruits makes a delicious change. Use vermicelli or angel hair pasta for a very creamy pudding.

SERVES 4

1¼ cups milk
¼ lb vermicelli, angel hair pasta or thin spaghetti
2 eggs
¼ tsp salt
grated rind of 1 lemon
grated rind of 1 orange
½ tsp ground cinnamon
¼ tsp grated nutmeg
⅓ cup sugar
2 tbsp butter or margarine, melted
¼ cup no-soak dried apricots, chopped
⅓ cup pitted dates chopped
⅓ cup sultanas
2 tbsp slivered almonds

In a medium saucepan, over medium heat, bring milk to a boil. Add noodles and cook over low heat until noodles are just tender and have absorbed most of the milk, 15 minutes. Cool slightly.

Preheat oven to 350°F. Lightly grease a 4-cup baking dish or soufflé dish. In a large bowl, beat eggs, salt, lemon and orange zests, cinnamon, nutmeg, and sugar until well blended. Add melted butter or margarine and dried fruits.

Add cooked pasta to the egg mixture; toss together to distribute the dried fruit evenly. Turn into the baking dish and sprinkle with almonds. Bake until a knife inserted in to the center comes out clean, 40–50 minutes.

For a softer, creamier pudding, bake pudding in a water bath. Prepare as above but place baking dish or soufflé dish into a larger roasting pan. Fill pan with boiling water to come about half way up side of baking dish. Cover for first 25 minutes, then uncover to brown top and almonds.

BAKED GOODS

PIERNIK

"JEWISH"
APPLE CAKE

EIVOR'S
ORANGE
CAKE

LEKACH

KERMAKKU

BABA

SERNIK

VATRUSHKI

POPPY SEED
PARCELS

APPLE
PASTRIES

FAWORKI

BUCHTY

BALABUSKY

PLAITED
BREAD

NORWEGIAN
WHOLEWHEAT
BREAD

LITHUANIAN
COTTAGE
CHEESE
BACON BREAD

PIERNIK

¼ cup clear honey
1 tsp ground cinnamon
4 cloves
½ tsp grated nutmeg
3 cups all purpose flour
2 tsp baking soda
¼ cup butter
¼ cup sugar
⅓ cup candied orange peel, finely chopped
⅓ cup raisins
⅓ cup golden raisins (optional)
about ½ cup filberts
1 egg, beaten

Heat the honey and spices in a small pan until boiling. Reduce the heat so the honey is just boiling for 3–4 minutes, until darkened. Put the pan into cold water and stir 1 teaspoon cold water to the honey. Leave to cool. Remove the cloves. Base-line and grease an 8 in square cake pan. Set the oven at 350°F.

Sift the flour and baking soda into a bowl. Rub in the butter, then stir in all the dry ingredients. Mix in the honey and egg. Turn the mixture onto a floured surface and knead well – the dough is soft but keep it moving to prevent it from sticking. Turn the dough into the tin, pressing down evenly. Bake for 50–60 minutes. The piernik is cooked when a skewer inserted into the middle comes out free of any sticky mixture. Cool the piernik on a wire rack, then wrap in plastic wrap and a plastic bag to mature.

This is a honey cake, although it is often described as gingerbread because of its color and the combined flavor of other spices and honey rather than the ingredients. It should be stored for at least a week before it is eaten, preferably a few weeks so that it has time to soften. It is traditionally kept for several months. The uncooked dough may be left for several days, even weeks, before it is baked.

"JEWISH" APPLE CAKE

These layers of tangy apples baked in a moist, sweet, lemon-scented mixture make a teatime favorite.

SERVES 16-20

APPLE FILLING

2 lb cooking apples, peeled, cored, and thinly sliced
4 tbsp sugar
1 tsp ground cinnamon
grated rind and juice of 1 lemon

CAKE

4 eggs
1 cup superfine sugar
scant cup vegetable oil
1 cup self-raising flour, or cake flour plus 2 tsp baking powder
1 tsp vanilla extract
sugar for sprinkling

Preheat oven to 350°F. Grease a 9 × 13 in cake pan. In a large bowl, toss apple slices with sugar, cinnamon, lemon rind, and juice.

In a large bowl, with electric mixer at medium speed, beat eggs with sugar until thick and lemon colored and mixture forms a "ribbon" when beaters are lifted from bowl, 3–5 minutes. Beat in oil until well blended. Stir in flour and vanilla just until well mixed and smooth.

Pour half the mixture into prepared pan. Spoon half the apple slices over mixture. Cover apple slices with remaining mixture; top with remaining apple mixture. Sprinkle with about 2 tablespoons sugar.

Bake until apples are tender and cake is golden brown and puffed and top springs back when gently pressed with a finger, 1¼–1½ hours. Cover with foil during baking if top colors too quickly. Remove to wire rack to cool. Cut cake into squares and serve at room temperature.

EIVOR'S ORANGE CAKE

This orange cake is light and airy, with a pleasant, fresh flavor. Try it served with coffee or tea as the Swedes do, or as a dessert accompanied by fruit salad.

SERVES 4–6

⅔ cup butter
½ cup sugar
3 eggs
grated rind of 2 lemons
¼ cup fresh orange juice
2 cups flour, sifted with 2 tsp baking powder
butter for greasing
bread crumbs for coating pan

GLAZE

½ cup confectioners' sugar
2 tbsp fresh orange juice
a few drops of oil and yellow food coloring
candied orange peel

Whisk the butter and sugar until smooth and pale. Add the eggs, one at a time, stirring vigorously. Mix in the lemon rind and orange juice, together with the flour. Grease a 9-in round cake pan with the butter, and sprinkle in the bread crumbs. Pour the batter into the pan. Place in a cold oven. Heat the oven to 325°–350°F and bake for 1 hour. Turn out and leave to cool under the upturned pan.

Mix the confectioners' sugar and orange juice to a smooth glaze. Add a couple of drops of oil, and color the glaze light yellow with food coloring. Spread over the cake and scatter the orange peel on top.

LEKACH

This honey cake is the traditional Jewish New Year's cake. Sweet honey as we know it did not really become available until Roman times and even then was prized for its medicinal uses and saved for joyful holidays and special occasions. Lekach, Yiddish for honey cake, or *pain d'épices* (spice bread) as it is called in France, is heavily flavored with ginger and other spices and resembles the German-style gingerbread, although that cake uses molasses instead of honey.

SERVES 12

generous cup all purpose flour
1 cup wholewheat flour
⅔ cup dark brown sugar
1 tbsp baking powder
1 tsp baking soda
2 tsp ground ginger
1 tsp ground cinnamon
½ tsp ground allspice
⅓ cup walnuts or almonds, chopped and toasted (optional)
¼ cup golden raisins (optional)
1½ cups honey
scant cup strong black coffee
3 tbsp bourbon whiskey, brandy or water
4 eggs
¼ cup vegetable oil
8 tbsp ginger preserve or chopped stem ginger in syrup
confectioners' sugar for dusting or honey for glazing

Preheat oven to 350F. Grease a 9 × 13 in cake pan; line with waxed paper; grease and flour paper.

In a large bowl, combine flours, sugar, baking powder, baking soda, ginger, cinnamon, and allspice. Stir in chopped walnuts or almonds and raisins if using. Set aside.

In a small saucepan, over medium heat, heat honey with coffee until warm and remove from heat. Stir in whiskey, brandy, or water.

In a large bowl, beat eggs with vegetable oil until well blended. Beat in ginger preserve or stem ginger. Alternately, in 3 or 4 batches, stir warm honey mixture and flour mixture into the beaten egg mixture until well blended.

Pour mixture into prepared pan. Bake until skewer inserted in center comes out with just a few crumbs attached and top springs back when gently pressed with a finger, 1 hour. Remove pan to wire rack and cool completely.

Turn out cake onto a rack and then back onto serving plate, so cake is right side up. Dust with confectioners' sugar or, if you do not mind a sticky cake, brush with slightly heated honey, and cut into squares to serve.

KERMAKKU

This feather-light Finnish sponge is made with sour cream and delicately spiced with cinnamon and cardamom or ginger.

SERVES 6 – 8

⅔ cup softened butter
1 cup sugar
3 eggs
4 cups flour
1 tsp baking soda
1 tsp ground cinnamon
1 tsp ground cardamom or ginger
1 cup sour cream
1 tsp vanilla sugar
butter for greasing
bread crumbs for coating pan

Preheat the oven to 325°F. Mix the butter and sugar until light and creamy. Add one egg at a time, stirring constantly. Mix all the dry ingredients together, except the vanilla sugar (sugar that has been left with a vanilla pod to absorb the flavor) and bread crumbs. Beat half of the flour mixture into the creamed mixture. Whisk in the sour cream, the rest of the flour mixture, and the vanilla sugar.

Grease a 9-in round cake pan with butter, and sprinkle in the bread crumbs. Spoon in the mixture. Bake for 50 minutes. When ready, turn out onto a wire rack and leave to cool.

BABA

When made for Easter the traditional decoration for baba is a small lamb molded from sugar paste placed in the middle of the baba, with tiny Easter eggs all round and sprigs of fresh green foliage added.

MAKES A 9IN BABA

3 tsp dried yeast or 1 oz fresh yeast (1 cake compressed yeast)
½ cup warm milk
scant 1 cup confectioners' sugar
4 cups hard wheat flour
⅔ cup raisins
⅓ cup chopped candied peel
1 cup blanched almonds, chopped
2 eggs, beaten
4 egg yolks
½ cup butter, melted
confectioners' sugar to dust or boiled frosting

Sprinkle the dried yeast over the milk and 1 teaspoon of the confectioners' sugar or blend the fresh yeast with the milk and 1 teaspoon of the sugar. Leave in a warm place until frothy. Sift the flour into a bowl and mix in the fruit and nuts with the remaining confectioners' sugar. Make a well in the middle, add the eggs, yolks, melted butter, and yeast liquid. Mix the dry ingredients into the liquid to make a very soft dough. Beat this with your hand until very elastic and smooth. Cover and leave to rise in a warm place until doubled in size – about 2 hours.

Thoroughly grease a 9½ cup kugelhopf mold or bread pan 10½ × 5½ in (top measurement). Punch down the dough with your hand, then put it in the pan pressing it down well. Cover loosely with plastic wrap and leave in a warm place until the dough has risen to the top of the pan. Meanwhile, set the oven at 350°F.

Bake the baba for about 40 minutes, until risen and well browned. Leave in the pan for a few minutes, then turn out to cool on a wire rack. Dust with confectioners' sugar or coat the baba with frosting while still warm. Leave to cool before serving. Cut at a slant into slices.

Right: Baba

SERNIK

This Polish cheesecake has a firm texture and deep golden-colored baked crust. Sernik is made for Easter, whether it be this version, one with a double crust (*see* method) or a cheesecake baked on a sponge base.

SERVES ABOUT 10

BASE

1½ cups all purpose flour
1 tsp baking powder
½ cup unsalted butter
4 tbsp superfine sugar
2 egg yolks

TOPPING

2 cups curd cheese
½ cup sugar
¼ cup all purpose flour
⅓ cup candied orange peel, chopped
⅔ cup raisins
grated rind of 1 lemon
4 eggs, separated
confectioners' sugar to dust

For the base, sift the flour and baking powder in a bowl. Blend in the butter, then stir in the sugar. Mix in the yolks to make a soft dough. Grease a 10 in springform pan or loose-based cake pan and press the dough into it. Chill for 15 minutes. Set the oven at 375°F. Bake the base for 10 minutes, then set aside to cool. Reduce the oven temperature to 325°F.

For the topping, place the cheese in a double thick piece of scalded cheesecloth and squeeze as much liquid as possible from it (avoid squeezing the cheese through the cloth). Scrape all the cheese into a bowl, then beat in the sugar, flour, fruit, lemon rind, and egg yolks. Whisk the whites until stiff, fold them into the mixture. Turn the mixture on top of the prepared base. Spread the cheese mixture evenly.

Bake for 1¼–1½ hours, until well browned, risen and fairly firm to the touch. Leave the cheesecake to cool in the pan. Dust with confectioners' sugar before serving.

To make a double-crust cheesecake, double the quantity of the base ingredients and save half until the cheesecake topping is in place. Roll out the reserved dough and trim it to fit the top of the pan. Lift it carefully on top of the cheesecake and bake as above.

VATRUSHKI

Vatrushki are served as a savory zakuska, as a sweet to go with tea or as a large dessert tart.

MAKES ABOUT 16 TARTLETS

1½ cups all purpose flour
½ tsp baking powder
⅓ cup sugar
pinch of salt
1 large egg
⅓ cup sour cream
5 tbsp unsalted butter

FOR THE FILLING

¼ cup rum
2 tbsp water
¼ cup raisins
2 cups cottage cheese
4 eggs
⅞ cup sugar
2 tsp grated lemon rind
½ cup clarified butter, melted
¼ tsp salt
½ cup flour

Make the filling first. Heat the rum and 2 tbsp water in a saucepan over high heat until almost boiling. Remove from the heat and stir in the raisins. Set aside.

Line a colander with cheesecloth and pour in the cottage cheese. Leave to drain for 3 hours.

In a large bowl, beat the cottage cheese using an electric mixer. Beat in the eggs, one at a time, and the sugar, until the mixture is pale in color. Stir in the lemon rind, melted butter, salt, and flour, 1 tablespoon at a time. Drain the raisins, discard the liquid and fold the raisins into the cottage cheese.

To make the dough, sift the flour, baking powder, sugar, and salt into a large bowl. Beat the egg, sour cream, and butter in a small bowl. Make a well in the center of the flour and pour the egg mixture into it. With your hands, slowly work the flour into the liquid, then beat until the mixture forms a ball. Wrap in plastic wrap and chill for 1 hour.

Preheat the oven to 400°F. On a well-floured surface, roll the dough out into a rectangle as thinly as possible. Cut out 16 or so 4 in rounds from the dough. Make a rim around each circle by folding over and pinching up the dough, so that you end up with shallow tartlet cases.

Place the cases on a greased baking tray and spoon some of the filling into each case. Bake for 15–20 minutes, or until the vatrushki are golden. Remove and cool on a wire rack.

POPPY SEED PARCELS

These little Polish sweetmeats taste terrific!

MAKES 16

2 cups all purpose flour
6 tbsp unsalted butter
2 tbsp superfine sugar
1 egg, separated
3 tbsp sour cream
½ cup poppy seeds, ground
2 tbsp butter
4 tbsp raisins, chopped
2 tbsp clear honey
½ tsp grated nutmeg
superfine sugar to sprinkle

Sift the flour into a bowl. Blend in the butter, then stir in the sugar. Mix in the egg yolk with the sour cream to make a fairly stiff dough. Knead the dough, then wrap in plastic wrap. Chill for 30 minutes.

Meanwhile, make sure the poppy seeds are ground. Mix them with the butter in a small pan. Cook for a few minutes, stirring all the time. Add the raisins, honey, and nutmeg and set aside to cool. Set the oven at 375°F.

On a lightly floured surface, roll out the dough into a 14 in square. Cut this into sixteen 3½ in squares. Divide the poppy seed mixture between the squares, piling it in the middle of each with a teaspoon. Lightly whisk the egg white and brush it on the edges of the pastry. Fold the corners of each pastry square up to meet over the middle of the poppy filling. Pinch all the pastry edges together to seal them thoroughly. Use the blunt edge of a knife to knock the pastry edges down, holding them with two fingers, to ensure they are sealed and neat.

Place the parcels on greased baking sheets and brush them with a little egg white. Bake for 20–25 minutes, until golden. Sprinkle with superfine sugar as soon as they are cooked. Cool on a wire rack.

APPLE PASTRIES

These are slightly fiddly to make but they are worth the effort.

MAKES ABOUT 30

1½ cups all purpose flour
6 tbsp unsalted butter
3 tbsp superfine sugar
½ cup cottage cheese
2 tbsp sour cream
3 full-flavored eating apples, peeled, cored, and quartered
1 egg, beaten
confectioners' sugar to dust

Sift the flour into a bowl. Blend in the butter and stir in the sugar. Drain any liquid from the cheese, then press it through a sieve. Mix the cheese and sour cream into the flour mixture to form a soft dough. Knead gently into a ball and cut in half.

Set the oven at 400°F. Roll out one piece of dough quite thinly and cut out 2½ in rounds. Cut each apple quarter into two or three pieces. Place a piece of apple on a round of pastry. Brush the edge of the pastry with egg, then fold it in half to enclose the apple. Pinch the edges together to seal them well. Place the parcel on a greased baking sheet. Fill and seal all the rounds, re-rolling the trimmings. Repeat with the second piece of dough. Brush the pastries with beaten egg.

Bake for about 20 minutes, until golden and cooked. Cool on a wire rack and dust with confectioners' sugar while warm. Serve warm or cold.

FAWORKI

The dough from which these cookies are made is called *chrust*; sometimes the cookies are also given this name. If you are inexperienced at making these little cookies, make sure you have enough time to get the knotting just right! They are sometimes made larger than here.

MAKES 24

1 cup all purpose flour
2 tbsp butter
2 egg yolks
1 tbsp water
oil to deep fry

Sift the flour into a bowl and blend in the butter. Mix in the egg yolks and water to make a smooth dough. On a lightly floured surface, roll out the dough into an oblong measuring 18 x 6 in and cut in half lengthways. Cut each half into twelve 1½ in wide strips.

Take a strip of dough and cut a slit down the middle of it. Push one end of the dough through the slit, then flatten it out to make a neat little knot. Keep the dough covered with plastic wrap while you knot and cook the strips, otherwise it dries out and breaks as you try to knot it.

Heat the oil for deep frying to 340°F. Fry the pastry knots in batches until crisp and golden. Drain them on double thick paper towels. Dust with confectioners' sugar while hot. Cool on a wire rack.

BUCHTY

These versatile rolls are of German origin but they are a popular Polish bread. They may be served in a number of ways: as a rich bread for breakfast, hot with fruit syrup or bottled fruit as a sweet dish, or the rolls may be filled with some fruit conserve or marmalade as they are shaped. The cooled rolls may be sliced and toasted or baked until golden to make crisp rusks for serving with smoked meats. They are certainly worth the hard work involved in the hand-beating of the dough. You will need a strong arm for this recipe!

MAKES 16

3 tsp dried yeast or 1 oz fresh yeast
(1 cake compressed yeast)
½ cup warm milk
6 tbsp sugar
4 cups hard wheat flour
1 tsp salt
10 tbsp butter
3 eggs
confectioners' sugar to dust
preserved fruit or fruit syrup to serve

Sprinkle the dried yeast over the milk and 1 teaspoon of the sugar or blend the fresh yeast with the milk and 1 teaspoon of the sugar. Leave in a warm place until frothy. Place the flour and salt in a bowl and make a well in the middle. Melt 6 tablespoons of the butter and pour it into the flour with the eggs. Add the yeast liquid and beat the liquids together. Gradually work in the flour to form a very soft dough. The mixture is a cross between a batter and a dough: too stiff to beat with a spoon, too wet to knead.

Wash your hands in hot water and dry them, and beat the mixture with the palm of one hand. Once you get the hang of it the process is not too bad. As the mixture develops it becomes elastic and tends not to stick to your hand. Carry on beating the mixture for about 15 minutes, by which time it should be coming cleanly away from the bowl as you work it. It should not be too sticky. Cover with plastic wrap and leave to rise in a warm place until doubled in size – about 2 hours.

Thoroughly grease and base-line a 7-in square deep cake pan. Melt the remaining butter. When the mixture has risen, beat it back slightly with a spoon. Moisten your hand with butter and take a portion of the dough about the size of a small tomato. (The dough should be divided into 16 portions but this is not always easy so you may have to use a certain amount of judgment.) Gently mold the dough portion into a small, round roll, then place it in the prepared pan. Keep your hand buttered while shaping the remaining dough into 15 more small rolls. Place them in the pan, slightly apart, in neat rows. Cover with plastic wrap and leave to rise in a warm place until they just cover the base of the tin and no gaps are visible. Meanwhile, set the oven at 350°F.

Pour the remaining melted butter all over the rolls. Bake for 30–35 minutes, until risen and browned. Turn out and break off rolls to serve hot with fruit syrup or bottled fruit. Leave any leftover rolls to cool on a wire rack.

BALABUSKY

Ukraine is renowned for the variety of its breads. These sour cream rye rolls are one of the types most commonly encountered. They make delicious sandwiches when filled with smoked ham, kolbasa or salt beef, spread with plenty of mustard.

MAKES 10-12 ROLLS

⅔ cup lukewarm water
2½ tsp (¼ oz) dry yeast
1 tbsp sugar
½ cup sour cream
1 cup rye flour
1–1¼ cups all purpose flour
1½–2 tsp salt
1½ tbsp caraway seeds

Place the water in a large bowl and sprinkle the yeast and sugar into it. Leave for 5–8 minutes, or until the mixture is foamy. Stir in the sour cream, then slowly work in the rye flour and most of the all purpose flour. Add salt to taste and 1 tablespoon of the caraway seeds. Work the dough with your hands until it forms a ball and turn out onto a floured surface. Knead in as much of the remaining flour as will make the dough smooth and still slightly sticky; this will take about 8–10 minutes.

Transfer the dough to a buttered bowl, turning it to coat with butter, then cover the bowl with plastic wrap and leave to rise in a warm place for 1 hour or until doubled in volume. Turn the dough out onto a floured surface and pull into 10–12 equal pieces. Shape each into a flat-bottomed oval, scatter the remaining caraway seeds over the tops and press in lightly.

Place the ovals on a lightly oiled baking sheet and leave to rise, covered with a damp dish towel, for 45–60 minutes, or until doubled in size.

Preheat the oven to 400°F. Bake the rolls for 18–20 minutes, or until they are golden brown.

The rolls may be frozen. Reheat wrapped in foil for 30 minutes at 375°F.

PLAITED BREAD

A rich bread that is popular for breakfast.

MAKES 1 LOAF

2 tsp dried yeast or ¼ oz fresh yeast (¾ cake
compressed yeast)
½ cup warm milk
1 tsp sugar
3 cups hard wheat flour
1 tsp salt
¼ cup butter
1 egg
beaten egg to glaze

Sprinkle the dried yeast over the milk and sugar or
blend the fresh yeast with the milk and sugar. Leave in
a warm place until frothy. Place the flour and salt in a
bowl. Blend in the butter and make a well in the
middle. Add the egg and yeast liquid and beat
together. Mix in the flour to make a firm dough.

Knead the dough into a ball, then turn out onto a
surface. Knead well for about 10 minutes, until
smooth and elastic. Put the dough back into the bowl
and cover with plastic wrap. Leave to rise in a warm
place until doubled in size – about 1½–2 hours.

Turn out the dough and knead it lightly. Divide into
three equal portions. Roll each portion into a long
sausage measuring about 16 in. Grease a large baking
sheet and lift the strips onto it, pinching their ends
together. Plait the strips into a neat loaf. The plait
must not be too tight nor too loose. Cover loosely
with plastic wrap and leave to rise in a warm place
until doubled in size. Meanwhile, set the oven at
425°F.

Brush the loaf with beaten egg. Bake for about 30
minutes, until glossy, brown, and cooked through.
Check that the loaf is browned underneath and that it
sounds hollow when tapped on the base. Cool on a
wire rack and store in an airtight container.

NORWEGIAN WHOLEWHEAT BREAD

Anybody who has traveled in Norway must have envied the Norwegians their fine bread. Here is one example.

MAKES 1 LOAF AND 10 ROLLS OR 2 LOAVES

1¼ lb wholewheat kernels
2¼ cups skim milk
4 tbsp fresh yeast
2 tbsp salt
1 tbsp oil
½ cup cottage cheese
8½ cups wholewheat flour
1½ cups white flour
crushed wheat for coating

Soak the wholewheat kernels for about 1 hour in lukewarm water. Heat the milk to body temperature, and stir the yeast into the liquid.

Add the salt, oil, cottage cheese, wholewheat flour, well-drained wheat kernels and, finally, the white flour. Knead the dough until smooth. Leave to rise for 30 minutes.

Shape into one loaf and 10 rolls, or 2 loaves. Roll everything in crushed wheat. Place the loaf in a greased 2 lb loaf pan and the rolls on a greased baking sheet, and leave to rise until doubled in size. Preheat the oven to 400°F. Bake the loaf for about 40–45 minutes. Bake the rolls at 425°F for about 20 minutes.

LITHUANIAN COTTAGE CHEESE BACON BREAD

Varske – cottage cheese – and honey are commonly used as a baking ingredient in Lithuania. This recipe mixes wholewheat and white flour to give a hint of the sturdier type of bread you will find in the Baltic States.

MAKES 1 LOAF

¼ cup vegetable oil
6 oz lean bacon, finely chopped
2 heaped tbsp finely chopped scallions
¼ cup honey
⅔ cup milk
1 egg
6 oz cottage cheese
1¼ cups wholewheat flour
1¼ cups white flour
2 tsp baking powder
½ tsp baking soda
scant tsp salt

In a small saucepan, heat the vegetable oil over medium heat. Add the bacon and fry for a few minutes, until the bacon is cooked. Turn down the heat and stir in the scallion, allowing it to wilt slightly. Then add the honey, heat through, and remove from the heat. Beat in the milk, egg, and then the cottage cheese. Blend thoroughly and set aside.

In a large bowl, sift together the two flours, baking powder and soda and the salt. Make a well and pour in the cottage cheese mixture, beating gently – do not overbeat.

Preheat the oven to 375°F. Scrape the bread dough into a buttered and floured 9 × 5 × 3 in loaf pan. Flatten the top of the loaf with a spatula and drop the loaf sharply twice on a hard surface to eliminate air pockets. Bake for 45–50 minutes, or until the top is golden brown.

Place the pan on a wire rack to cool for 15 minutes before turning out. Cool completely before serving.

Right: Lithuanian Cottage Cheese Bacon Bread

INDEX

160

A Tribute to

Trucking

Northeast Edition

Doug Condra, Consulting Editor
Foreword by Gene Williams

"Partners in Progress" by
Gene Williams and Mark H. Dorfman

Windsor Publications, Inc.
Chatsworth, California

A Tribute to Trucking

Northeast Edition
by Jack Thiessen

Windsor Publications, Inc.—
    History Book Division

Managing Editor: Karen Story
Design Director: Alexander D'Anca

Staff for *A Tribute to Trucking*:
Associate Editor: Jeffrey Reeves
Photo Editor: William A. Matthews
Senior Editor, Corporate Biographies:
    Judith L. Hunter
Production Editor, Corporate Biographies: Una
    FitzSimons
Editorial Assistants: Kim Kievman, Michael
    Nugwynne, Kathy B. Peyser,
    Theresa J. Solis
Publisher's Representatives, Corporate
    Biographies: Bill Koons, Diane Murphy
Layout Artist, Corporate Biographies:
    Mari Catherine Preimesberger
Designer: Tom McTighe

Library of Congress Cataloging-in-
    Publication Data
Thiessen, Jack.
    A tribute to trucking / Jack Thiessen. — 1st ed.
    p. cm.
    Bibliography: p.
    Includes index.
    ISBN: 0-89781-295-6
    1. Trucking — Northeastern States. 2. Truck-
ing — Middle West. 3. Trucking — United States.
I. Title
HE5632.A115T48 1989
388.3' 24' 0973 — dc20   89-33173
                                          CIP

Windsor Publications, Inc.
Elliot Martin, Chairman of the Board
James L. Fish III, Chief Operating Officer
Michele Sylvestro, Vice-President/Sales-Marketing

*Frontispiece: To drive the long haul is
to travel over open roads and under a
big sky, a lifestyle many truckers have
found irresistible. Photo by Kent
Knudson/ The Photo File*

*Right: A 1920s 'Diamond T'. Courtesy,
American Truck Historical Society*

Contents

Facing page: Some trucks have evolved past the point of cargo transportation to show pieces, often spending more time on display than on the road. Photo by Sam Sargent/ The Photo File

Page 9: The Chevrolet 80 series, introduced in 1962, came equipped with Detroit Diesel Series 53 diesel engines. The truck had a 25,000-pound gross vehicle weight. Courtesy, PR Counselors

*S*incere thanks to Senior Editor Pat McCullough, Washington Editor Bill Smith, and Managing Editor Debbie Whistler, of **Heavy Duty Trucking Magazine,** *and to Editor Tom Berg, of* **American Trucker Magazine,** *for their considerable help and encouragement.*

Jack Thiessen

Whether sunup or sundown, trucks are rolling to destinations all across the country. Photo by David Pollack

Picture this:

Thousands of truck drivers, their rigs laden with highly sought consumer and industrial goods from their home bases in the frigid Northeast and Upper Midwest, beam as thoughts of the warm and beckoning climes of Florida and the West Coast dance in their heads. They think of the time in the not-too-distant future when they will be able to doff their foul-weather gear, roll up their sleeves, flip down sun visors, maybe even turn on the air conditioning in their tractors.

Is this the annual exodus from the icy, snowy grip of their home turf to more pleasant surroundings for the winter? Hardly. It's just

another over-the-road trek in a year-long routine that sees truckers from the Northeast and Upper Midwest travel America's highways and byways with the cargo that keeps Americans going. Of course, few would say that the change in scenery isn't welcome.

On the other hand, during the summer, it's just as likely that

these same drivers from the northern climes are just as happy to leave the hot and humid territories of the South and the searing heat of the Western deserts to gather their cool closer to home.

Regardless of all that, it's the reasons rather than the seasons that put truckers on the roads to their destinations. Chief among those reasons is the transporting of the goods so essential to conducting the everyday life of all Americans—those at both ends of the trucking line. For every load of cargo originating in the Industrial Crescent that is the Northeast and Upper Midwest and destined for a section of the country so much in need of those products, another load originating at the other end is ready to make its way to a destination just as much in need of that cargo.

For example, the prime seafood of the New England coast is relished in places south and west of there. And, in the same way, the flowers, plants, and fresh produce of the South and West are welcomed with open arms and mouths in the homes of the shorter growing seasons of the Northeast. Raw materials come from one direction, finished products go in another. Food, clothing, automobiles and other vehicles, electronic gadgetry, pharmaceuticals and other health aids, cosmetics, wood products, stone, and countless other bits and pieces that fit into the fabric of everyday life find themselves some time in their existence on a roll with trucking.

This goes on day in and day out in this broad segment of America that stretches from the rocky coasts of Maine on the north to the nation's capital of Washington, D.C., on the south, and in a westward band to the Great Lakes states of Illinois, Indiana, Michigan, and Ohio. This whole clutch of industrialized and metropolitanized territory, which also includes New Hampshire, Vermont,

By 1910 White had converted from steam to gasoline powered engines. This 1910 White was owned by W.J. Sloane, decorators and furnishers. Courtesy, Volvo GM Heavy Truck Corporation

Massachusetts, Connecticut, Rhode Island, New York, New Jersey, Delaware, Maryland, and Pennsylvania, teems with approximately 92 million people, more than one-third of the nation's 1985 population figure of 239 million. Within the crescent lie 13 urban centers each jammed with more than one million inhabitants.

Most of the names of those urban areas conjure visions of huge, bustling centers of production and distribution, the backbone of American industry, the heart of the financial and business world, the use and/or abuse of natural resources and, finally, legendary figures on the face of America. They are Boston, the cradle of revolution; New York, the booming metropolis that exemplifies all that is good and bad in huge cities; Philadelphia, the birthplace of independence; Pittsburgh, Cleveland, and Detroit, giants of industry; Washington, D.C., that political swirl that serves as the capital of the Western world; Baltimore, which has one of the busiest ports in the country and the second largest (behind New York, of course) container facility on the East Coast; and Chicago, a city of such fascination that it led the poet Carl Sandburg to sing of it: "Hog butcher for the world, tool maker, stacker of wheat, player with railroads and the nation's freight handler; stormy, husky, brawling, city of the big shoulders."

In these cities alone, the numbers of mouths to feed and bodies to clothe, the homes to furnish, the business buildings to service, the automobiles to move across cramped and often crazed highway systems all are staggering. And that's only a beginning. That crescent also contains all those other things that speak so loudly of America: farming and dairy products from Vermont, upstate New York, Maryland, and Pennsylvania; truck farming in New Jersey; poultry production in Maryland and Delaware; rugged terrain in New England tamed by equally rugged individuals; fishing fleets in the area's coastal waters; a huge and still growing educational center in the Boston area; and an emerging emphasis at various points in the region, but particularly in the Boston area, on high technology and its applications to most every facet of the everyday lives of individuals, industry, and business.

And what part does trucking play in all of this? Statistics show that more than 76 per-

cent of the total freight revenues generated in the United States go to the nation's mammoth truck fleet, a figure that has risen in the 1980s from 72.9 percent at the start of the decade. In recent years, trucking's intercity revenues have been about 5 times higher than rail revenues, 7 times those of water transport, and about 18 times those of air freight. In tonnage, trucking claims $1\frac{1}{2}$ times that of rail carriers, about $2\frac{1}{2}$ times that of water-borne

The White 3000 series became the best-selling cabover in the United States in the 1950s. This 3022 PLT was produced in 1953. Courtesy, Volvo GM Heavy Truck Corporation

Virtually any trucking operation must deal with one or more of the seemingly countless government agencies known by such acronyms as ICC, FHWA, EPA, and others. Photo by Sam Sargent/The Photo File

cargo, and 364 times that of air freight. All of this, of course, creates a massive infusion of money, through a variety of taxes, into state treasuries that winds up going toward preserving a high level of highway maintenance as well as undergirding the development of any number of other programs designed to improve the public's well-being.

Much of the overall totals in both revenues and tonnage, naturally,

would come from the Northeast and Upper Midwest, criss-crossed by thousands of miles of highway and featuring large populations and concurrently large daily needs. Taking care of New York City alone each day produces, according to statistics compiled by the National Geographic Society, these hard-to-comprehend figures: 10,000 long-haul trucks arrive at city warehouses; feeding the populace requires at least seven million pounds

of meat, fish, and fresh vegetables and fruit that must be brought in and distributed; keeping the city clean requires hauling away twice that poundage in household refuse.

And all of that in a city that is a maze of approximately 6,000 miles of streets criss-crossing its five boroughs, which are linked to each other and surrounding communities by 62 bridges, four tunnels, and a ferry. Certainly, if a trucker can make his way in, out, and around New York, New York, he can make it anywhere.

Mastering New York serves truckers well throughout that area known geographically as the Middle Atlantic states (including New York, New Jersey, Pennsylvania, Delaware, and Maryland) because it is the most urbanized region of North America, where about a fifth of the U.S. population lives on one-twentieth of the nation's land. What seems to be an

From bringing in the food to hauling away the trash, the populous Northeastern United States is especially dependent upon trucking for everyday needs. Everyday in New York City 10,000 long-haul trucks arrive at city warehouses. Photo by Bette Garber

unbroken string of communities reaches all the way from New York City to Washington, D.C., making it the most populous portion of a massive urban megalopolis that stretches to Boston on the north. A growing part of this Eastern cityscape are myriad suburbs that no longer serve only as bedroom communities but have become active seekers of white collar businesses and light, "clean" industry, thus adding them to the nation's transportation map.

However, away from the Middle Atlantic urban and suburban mass lie fertile farming areas that produce tons of foodstuffs for the thriving region, poultry farms that could put at least one chicken in every pot of the Northeast, and dairies that pour billions of gallons of milk annually into city markets. How do they get to market? The trucking industry provides the answer, naturally. Legions of trucks traverse the region's thousands of miles of highways and byways daily, not to recreate any of the convoys or roadblock-running from the trucking songs or motion pictures of the 1970s, but to do what's all in a day's—or week's—work: taking care of the needs of their neighbors and the huge numbers of other fellow Americans in

their corner of the nation.

The northern reaches of the megalopolis is capped by Boston, the commercial, cultural, and industrial drive shaft of all of New England. Though it boasts one of the world's great harbors and shipping is a major industry, Boston serves also as a citadel for high finance and high technology. The latter is represented by scores of companies involved in the production of computers, software, electrical machinery, and systems for defense and space exploration. Serving as the backbone of these industries, which if not born during the second half of this century certainly have been nurtured to maturity during the past 40 years, has been a talent pool of design and management skills fed by a steady flow of graduates from 65 institutions of higher education— with MIT and Harvard at the head of the class. This gives the Boston area a reputation as one of the nation's leaders in research and education and make the business of learning a major industry in the area.

Beyond Boston lies the bulk of New England, featuring a coastline that is whipped with capes and inlets along its serpentine stretch of 6,130 miles and characterized for the most part by the rough, rocky land of the interior that's unsuited for the mechanized farming of the latter part of the 20th century. Those independent, flinty Yankee farmers of the 1800s have all but left the land in many places in New England, although some localized farming does persist, most notably in the Connecticut River Valley. The hardy and versatile potato still sustains Maine's Aroostook County, a longtime haven for the palatable tuber. Vermont stands out as a dairying state, Massachusetts and New Hampshire crate and ship apples, and New Hampshire and Vermont offer the nation's waffle and pancake lovers the sweet taste of maple syrup.

Famed Barre granite is still carved from the walls of quarries in Vermont, but the days of the thriving textile mills, shoe factories, clock and small-arms production are things of New England's rich and famous past. But ever the survivors, New Englanders, whose land was shaped by cataclysmic crustal collisions and glacial grinding, have fought back against the problems of competing imports, aging equipment, and the beckoning of the rising-again South. Instead of bowing to this pressure, this territory where the Pilgrims observed the first Thanksgiving and where a tea party signaled the patriots' dream of a land free from British rule has adjusted its industrial output to the age of technology, producing computers and their components, high tech software that seems bound to fit any personal, business, or industrial need, machine tools, aircraft engines, and precision instruments.

Swinging to the west into America's industrial heartland, the trucking industry rolls through territory

with far more open spaces than it encounters in the urbanized and industrialized East, but finds the same deep dependence on 18-wheelers and their kin. It also finds itself in somewhat of a stiffer competitive situation with railroads and water transport because of the huge rail impact on Chicago and the heavily used waterways of the Great Lakes and the busy Ohio and Mississippi rivers. Even so, trucking plays an immense role in this area too, particularly in the realm of transporting the goods that result

from heavy manufacturing.

This region between the four western Great Lakes and the winding, vibrant Ohio River is America's anvil, embracing the greatest concentration of heavy industry in the nation and accounting for the value of one-fourth of the country's manufactured goods. That manufacturing muscle hammers out a quarter of the nation's steel production in the area around Chicago. A third of the nation's automobiles roll off assembly lines in Detroit and its environs, and the mills, factories, and refineries of Cleveland span 65 miles near the shores of Lake Erie.

Though the Upper Midwest is home to the brawny cities of Pittsburgh, Cleveland, Detroit, and Chicago— and their burly industries—the region isn't overpowered by massive urban sprawl as the Northeast is. While the northernmost tier of the region is part of the huge industrial complex that stretches from the East Coast to Chicago, the region's four states—Ohio, Michigan, Indiana, and Illinois—also show a pastoral, agricultural side that puts much of the territory in the forefront of crop production for the United States. In many areas the ribbon of concrete and asphalt that is the interstate highway system is bordered by vast croplands that often seem to reach to the far, blue horizons.

Ohio, for example, balances the steel, heavy machinery, and automotive parts of its north with the corn, soybeans, tomatoes, and livestock that dominate the economy of much of the rest of the state.

In similar fashion, Indiana's industrialized northern stretch that

Some of the nation's largest and busiest ports are located on the East Coast, with much of the freight shipped out on trucks. Photo by Bette Garber

includes the rugged, steel-making cities of Gary and Hammond hard against Chicago's big eastern shoulder turns much gentler throughout its broad expanses of rolling farmlands and woodlands. Even the stone quarries of central Indiana from which much of the limestone used in the nation's buildings is cut have something of a pastoral feel, located as they are near farming areas and not too far from the state's seat of higher learning, Bloomington, home of Indiana University. Farming provides huge cash crops of corn, soybeans, hogs, and cattle, and the woodlands of the southern part of the state provide the raw materials for furniture and other wood-products plants there.

Indianapolis, the state's capital and home to the famed 500-mile auto speedway race, has long looked on itself as "the crossroads of America." The nation's interstate highway system puts an exclamation mark to that as several major roads in the system converge on this transportation hub.

To the north of the Hoosier state, Michigan struggles with its heavy industry, turning to robots, computers, and the like to modernize working conditions reeling under the pressure of foreign competition. The state's Lower Peninsula continues along its industrial way, but also boasts outstanding fruit and vegetable farms that help to balance the state's economy. Dairy products, livestock, and corn are major products. The state's

Upper Peninsula, on the other hand, sings a vacationer's siren song of remote and challenging trout streams and lovely beaches all along a lakeshore that also is a playground for those hardy souls enamored with such water sports as water skiing, sailing, and speedboating.

In a game of word association in the state of Illinois, quintessence probably would be far down the list. Lincoln probably. Corn most likely. Chicago and wind certainly. And yet Illinois, with its big, boisterous, and Bearish Chicago set against a backdrop of a more stable and staid agricultural economy serves as the quintessential Midwestern state, the nearest thing to an ideal example. The fierce independence of the farmer and the fierce competitiveness of the big-city worker and business executive make for a mix that gives Illinois a vast reservoir of energy and muscle, truly the heartbeat of the heartland.

The state is first in the nation in agricultural exports, with fertile farms that cover four-fifths of the state producing primarily high-yield corn and soybeans and supporting a massive hog industry. Illinois' corn crop, in value, produces approximately one-fifth of the nation's total, and the soybean harvest accounts for a sixth. Naturally then, it would follow that the manufacture of farm equipment—mostly in the central and southern reaches of the state—is a major contributor to the state's economy.

Illinois ranks third in the nation among manufacturers, with Chicago, which counts nearly three-fourths of the state's population, leading the way as the nation's number one manufacturing city. It also is the nation's leading mail-order center. Chicago, too, is a center without peer in North America for transportation, acting as a major, if not the most major, hub for the nation's highway, railroad, and air systems. In addition, Chicago is a major Great Lakes port, moving products by barge down the Illinois Waterway to the Mississippi River, by ship to other lake ports and overseas through the St. Lawrence Seaway. And, of course, that kind of trade works both ways, with the Windy City also receiving goods the same way.

Above: An unbroken string of cities stretching from New York City to Washington, D.C., is tied together with an interstate system that supports a growing population dependent on trucking. Photo by David Pollack

Inset: The tons of agricultural and dairy products generated by the fertile farming areas of the Northeast, Middle Atlantic, and farther inland are transported by truck in the surrounding cities daily. Photo Bette Garber

But there's another sense of Midwestern essence in this region, one that belongs to the people of the vast farmlands that stretch away from the industrialized urban areas. It was on farms such as these during those formative years for this nation that the true Midwestern spirit was born and which persists even today. It's a spirit that emanated from people of the land—conservative but friendly, skeptical but optimistic, hard-working, church-going, and civic-minded. There are those who insist that this robust, no-nonsense state—birthplace of the vacuum cleaner, the Cracker Jack, the Ferris wheel, and the steel skyscraper—not only lies in the heartland, but is the true heart of this nation, the most distinctly American of any of its regional counterparts.

The Northeastern Trucking Industry

While much attention has been given to the somewhat glamorized—in song and on film—long-haul version of trucking, it's not all over-the-road for carriers in the Northeast and Upper Midwest. Many, maybe even a majority, spend most of their time taking care of business closer to home as regional carriers. This is particularly common in New England, where one trucking-industry official made it eminently clear how important trucking is in that part of the country: "Without trucks up here we would not have any transportation. We don't have a rail system per se—primarily everything in the Northeast is transported by truck."

With that scenario in mind, it doesn't take much imagination to conclude that the people of the Northeast would be hard-pressed to survive without this industry that has experienced such dramatic change since the advent of deregulation. There have been large companies that have failed, others that have bought up smaller companies and grown larger. There have been smaller companies that, through prudent and patient handling, have risen to positions of prominence. And there are those—giving deregulation a black eye—that jumped in and out of business in the time it took to make one run. There are union and non-union carriers; there are general-freight

Below: The industrial output of the New England region ranges from gravel to computer components. Photo by David Pollack

Inset: The Upper Midwest, between the four western Great Lakes and the Ohio River, accounts for one-fourth of the country's manufactured goods. Photo by Bette Garber

Above: While the Upper Midwest is home to steel and coal industries, the area is known even more for its agriculture. Photo by Bette Garber

Below: Illinois is the country's leading state for agricultural exports. Photo by George Olson/The Photo File

handlers, specialty carriers, and manufacturers that find a special kind of profit center in having their own fleets.

While many carriers continue to flex their muscles nationally, those who have chosen to stay in their own corner of the nation are emphasizing their ability to deliver regional excellence. This seems to have special importance in the Northeast in general and to New England in particular. In many cases, New England carriers put emphasis on six-state or three-state service, but with major runs to the New York-New Jersey area for its customers for both delivery and pickup. Much of that traffic is tied to the huge container lines that ply the harbors of the New York metropolitan area, the inbound traffic bringing regional products in for shipping out on freighters and tankers, while the backhaul traffic brings raw materials, components, and consumer goods back to home base for distribution in the region.

Actually, that's the way it is through all corners of the Northeast and Upper Midwest. Both ends of the line are equally important and each truckload in either direction serves its own special purpose and that—ultimately—is to serve people some where along the line, whether it be

through an immediate consumer product for everyday subsistence or the raw materials or parts that go into an eventual product for the consumer or the materials that bring light, power, and heat to the home, factory, and office.

Among the New England states, Rhode Island and Maine offer interesting examples of how trucking serves the people of a region. The old song, "Poor Little Rhode Island," doesn't really fit these days, though it still is "the smallest of the 48." Thanks to its fine deep-water port at Providence, the state stands as a major distribution center for coming-and-going carriers. Huge amounts of petroleum flows out of the harbor aboard trucks on their way to service mainly Eastern Connecticut and parts of Massachusetts, but with other stops scheduled in other parts of New England. Providence also is a major clearinghouse for imported automobiles coming into the area, and has a huge chemical storage plant at the port and one of the few asphalt mix plants in the region.

For Maine, it has hitherto been considered the end of the line on the distribution and origination charts, with its trucking firms doing mostly a short-haul business, seldom carrying cargo beyond Boston. That has meant a lot of dead-heading in the past, and counting on non-domiciled carriers to haul products out of the state, particularly potatoes from the spud capital of Aroostook County in the northernmost reaches of the state. However, with the expected increase in the flow of trade to and from Canada, the future looks much brighter for Maine, which, if all goes well, could become a bridge state, much like Connecticut, along at least one United States-Canada trade route. That could mean a steady stream of goods flowing both north and south to Canada and back into New England, thus reducing dead-heading for Maine trade, encouraging establishment of trucking operations, and expanding service into a longer-haul mode.

The opening up of Canada is just one of the many changes coming to America's trucking industry since the advent of "let's make a deal" rate structures created by deregulation of the industry in the early '80s. The environment trucking found itself in during those years was full of uncertainty and turmoil, but that is beginning to change. Among other things, deregulation has given a number of new companies the flexibility to enter and exit the industry at their discretion, and that has led to fluctuating and competitive rates on truckload traffic in particular because these com-

panies will go anywhere they want to go and haul just about anything they're capable of.

There are two primary patterns of long-haul business: full truckload (TL) and less-than-truckload (LTL). Both have grown dramatically since the move to "just-in-time" delivery. Larger carriers handle most LTL shipments because they're more able to guarantee a receiver overnight or second-day delivery for loads that usually range from 1,000 pounds to 10,000 pounds. The LTL material is handled across a terminal, meaning that a company has to have a fixed-space facility that allows unloading of one vehicle and loading of another. Since its rates are higher, LTL is profitable for companies that can handle it.

"Just in time" inventory management, otherwise known in business circles as cost optimization, is being used by more and more manufacturers and distributors since they've found that carrier delivery times have become so reliable, assuring those customers of prompt delivery of supplies ordered just before inventories run out. Thus, in-transit inventories—rolling warehouses, if you will—are becoming steadily flowing streams in production and distribution channels in both TL and LTL shipments. Even if freight rates are high, this is consid-

Above: Drivers in Michigan and the surrounding area are as likely to be carrying computers as compost. Photo by David Pollack

Facing page: North America represents a huge market for truck sales. Manufacturers from abroad have become very active by investing in U.S. truck builders, and importing their own trucks. Photo by David Pollack

Facing page, inset: Many truckers in the Northeast spend their time hauling regionally rather than cross-country, especially in New England, where the dense population demands a lot of deliveries. Photo by Bette Garber

Left: Many New England truckers emphasize regional service, usually in three to six states. Photo by Bette Garber

ered a favorable trade-off when the action lowers inventory-holding costs by a greater amount.

For example, a Pennsylvania company dealing in industrial chemicals and lubricants which not only has its own leased fleet of trucks but also uses contract carriers for some of its transport is convinced it couldn't exist without trucking, particularly in this day of "just in time" delivery. The move to shorter inventory time has put greater demands on delivery systems, but trucking has come through even under extreme conditions and "sometimes ridiculous time schedules," as one sales executive put it. But customer satisfaction is paramount and when that customer says the material must be delivered in no more than 48 hours a company must be able to rely on on-time deliv-

ery. The trucking industry, in that executive's mind, has responded beautifully.

"Just in time" delivery isn't a positive only for the receiver. On the contrary, it speeds up the entire process, allowing the shipper to bill more quickly and get paid in 30 days, which, in turn, allows the contract hauler to see his pay sooner.

And a corporate leased fleet has a number of advantages, also, not the least of which is the potential for becoming a considerable profit center. It means that a company—in this instance, again, the Pennsylvania firm—can not only move customer materials when a common carrier isn't available, but also can move raw materials from one of its plants to another for production purposes. A customer's order could also go on one

of those trips for drop-off on a tight delivery schedule that perhaps could not be demanded of a common carrier. This means moving the company's own raw materials quickly and profitably and keeping the customer happy, also. In addition, a fleet truck can pick up empty hazardous-materials drums for return to a manufacturing plant, something Interstate Commerce Commission regulations won't let a common carrier do. That means fewer empty trips—and more profit.

Survival and competition have become trucking's bywords in the deregulated '80s. That environment has been characterized by a high entry rate, intense price and service competition, advancements in logistics systems, and associated improvements in productivity. A steady influx of carriers and departures of marginal ones, especially smaller, non-union truckload carriers, is expected to maintain

competitive pressure. All carriers will continue their efforts to offset high labor costs through improved productivity.

Industry performance ultimately is contingent on the state of the economy, the major determinant of overall national tonnage and the demand for transportation. These factors, in turn, have a direct impact on industry pricing practices and total industry revenues.

And, of course, the trucking industry in the Northeast and Upper Midwest isn't just trucks, drivers, business executives and maintenance and warehouse workers. Far from it. Putting trucks on the road and keeping them there is a monumental task requiring dedication and expertise in numerous allied businesses. They include those that produce original equipment; replacement parts; and such primary components as engines,

Above: Transportation has become more than a means of employment for some truckers, as two wheels can replace 18 for an after-work interest. Photo by Bette Garber

Facing page: The raw materials produced on the East Coast, like this potash, are trucked to area processing centers. Photo by David Pollack

brakes, and suspension systems and, certainly, a range of enough other important components to line a substantial stretch of interstate highway. In addition, there are those who produce electrical systems; trailers of all shapes and for innumerable uses; fuels, lubricants, and special aids for extreme weather conditions; seats; sleepers; graphics that give trucks distinctive looks and spread a company's name across the land; and, of course, insurance.

The outlook for trucking over the long haul appears favorable. The var-

ied performance of the general economy throughout the '80s has given the industry more experience with its new environment, which appears to be on the road toward further refinement and adjustment. That experience certainly should prepare the trucking industry for something of a smoother ride into the 20th century.

Gene Williams
Louisville, Kentucky

Above: Truck racing on dirt tracks and pavement ovals is becoming increasingly popular. Photo by Bette Garber

Left: The people of the Northeast would be hard pressed to survive without the trucking industry, which spans from one-truck family operations to huge fleets. Photo by Bette Garber

Facing page: There have been a few twists in the road to financial stability in the trucking business. For one, pay increases for drivers have lagged behind those in other professions. Photo by Robin Riggs/After Image

PART

One

Moving Through the Years

The outlook for long-haul trucking is favorable, as the industry has experienced a changing business climate in the 1980s and has proven adaptable to change. Photo by Christopher Springman/The Photo File

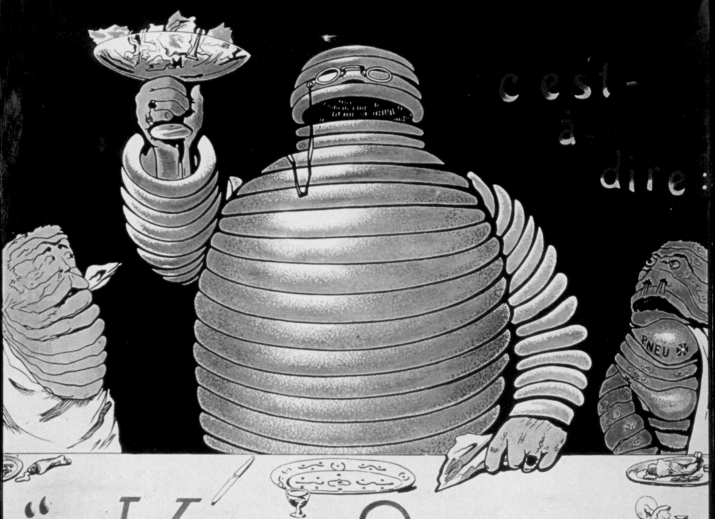

An Industry Sputters to Life

American trucking didn't begin in America. It began in France, or in Czechoslovakia, or in Germany. And the year was 1769, 1817, or 1896, depending on what one considers a truck.

Artillery Captain Nicholas-Joseph Cugnot, a native of Lorraine, is generally credited with creating the first steam-powered wagon. Designed for pulling heavy cannon, the vehicle was tested in 1769 in front of a number of French military dignitaries. The machine was incredibly clumsy. A heavy, pear-shaped copper boiler was suspended ahead of the single front wheel, which was flanked by a pair of cylinders. These functioned like a small child's legs and feet on the pedals of a tricycle: as steam was admitted alternately into the cylinders, a rocking beam pulled one piston rod up while the other was being pushed down, moving the wheel forward.

A witness to the demonstration later wrote, "I have verified it would have covered 1,800 to 2,000 toises [about 2.3 miles] in an hour had it not experienced setbacks." One problem was that the limited boiler capacity could only propel the machine for 12 or 15 minutes before it ran out of steam. The vehicle's steering stability was also so poor that during the demonstration it crashed into a stone wall, resulting in the first truck accident statistic and setting back truck development for almost four decades. In 1815 a Czechoslovakian engineer named Josef Bozek built a little one-half horsepower steam engine and installed it in a small carriage. Initial trials were so suc-

Facing page: Michelin, a French company, has had a great impact on the trucking industry as a leading developer of improved tires. This ad from the 1920s marked the first appearance of Michelin's symbol, Mr. Bib. Courtesy, Michelin Tire Co.

Above: According to this advertisement, Oshkosh "4-Wheel-Drive" trucks could travel anywhere where "wheels can touch the ground." Courtesy, American Truck Historical Society

As part of a promotional campaign, the Saurer Motor Company sent this truck on the first transcontinental trip. The truck was driven from Denver to San Francisco, then, after being shipped back to Colorado by train, it was driven to New York. In 1911 roads were so poor that the truck often had to ford streams and even make its own road. Here the truck climbs Telegraph Hill in San Francisco. Courtesy, Motor Vehicle Manufacturing Association

cessful that he built a larger version, which he publicly demonstrated in 1817 to a large crowd gathered in Prague's Stromvoka Woods.

Cheered on by the spectators, Bozek was prompted to pass the hat among the crowd to pay off debts he had incurred while building the vehicle. Nobody knows how much he collected because in the confusion of a sudden thunderstorm that sent everyone scurrying for cover, someone stole the gate money. Bozek was convinced it was a sign that God did not intend for man to ride on mechanical contrivances. So he took an axe to the carriage and to the two steamboats he also had built, destroying them completely.

The first steam vehicle propelled on land in this country actually preceded Bozek's by almost a dozen years. The vehicle—if indeed it could be called that—was a 20-ton dredging scow built by Oliver Evans for the city of Philadelphia in 1804. When it came time to move the cumbersome boat the mile and a half from his shop to the Schuylkill River, Evans fitted it with wheels and chugged over the cobblestones to the water's edge and into the stream. Later he wrote that

though it was equal in weight to two hundred barrels of flour, and the wheels fixed with wooden axle trees for this temporary purpose in a very rough manner, and with great friction, of course, yet I transported my great burden to the Schuylkill with ease; and when it was launched in the water, I fixed a paddle wheel at the stern and drove it down the Schuylkill . . . leaving all the vessels going up behind me, at least, half way, the wind being ahead.

The question remains whether Evans' contraption was truck, boat, or the world's first amphibian.

Richard Dudgeon's vehicle, built in New York City in 1855, never pretended to be a truck even though it looked like one. He called it a steam carriage, but when it huffed and puffed down East Broadway for the first time at a breakneck 20 miles per hour, the newspapers quickly labeled it the "Red Devil Steamer" and condemned it for its noise and the ruts it cut in the street.

Nor did the city fathers take any kindlier to the new contraption. In fact, they quickly passed an ordinance restricting operation of the vehicle to

selected streets—and only if Dudgeon hired someone to run ahead waving a red flag to warn travelers of the hulking menace that followed.

Thus rebuffed, Dudgeon moved out to Long Island where he operated the vehicle for almost ten years, logging hundreds of miles. His longest trip was from Locust Valley, Long Island, to Bridgeport, Connecticut, and his fastest time was a mile covered in one minute and 52 seconds—about 33 miles per hour.

Dudgeon, though, was almost a generation ahead of his time. Although steam engines had long been used by fire departments to power the pumps that were pulled by horses, steam power did not move from rail to road until the latter part of the nineteenth century. But around 1872 the LaFrance brothers in Elmira, New York, discovered that coal burners could actually propel a vehicle much faster than oat burners could. Similarly, farm machinery manufacturers began harnessing steam instead of horses to new harvesting and threshing equipment.

The steam-powered trucks introduced in ever-increasing numbers in the early 1890s bore a great resemblance to the railroad locomotives of the day, complete with smokestack, protruding boiler, and iron wheels. They had tremendous power, but their equally tremendous consumption of fuel and water was self-defeating; the bigger they got, the less room, proportionally, was available for cargo.

Emerging almost simultaneously in the late 1800s was the electric truck, energized by storage batteries. These battery-powered trucks had many advantages over steam. They started instantly, were simple to operate, and the electric motors were easy to maintain. They also had fewer moving parts than steam engines and more cargo space, and they didn't have to be stoked up, fed, or bedded down.

From about 1900 onward, large cumbersome electric trucks crept slowly and silently over city streets, carrying everything from beer to newsprint to building materials. They were workhorses—not racehorses— capable of carrying up to 10 tons but seldom able to move faster than 8 miles per hour. Yet they were so reliable and so nearly indestructible that one Philadelphia publishing company continued to use them into the mid-1950s, hard rubber tires and all.

The Sampson truck train of 1900 ran on a stream. While it is hardly comparable to modern triples, it does demonstrate an early use of the semitrailer concept. Courtesy, Motor Vehicle Manufacturing Association

Above: The Commercial Truck Company was based in Philadelphia and its market was confined to that area. This 1915 Commercial truck was electrically powered and carried explosives. Courtesy, American Truck Historical Society

Below: Although the American Automobile Association and the trucking industry have not always seen eye to eye, the AAA did promote a Packard truck as part of their tour. Courtesy, Motor Vehicle Manufacturing Association

Electric trucks did have limitations. A single electric motor was not large enough to provide the necessary power, so a motor was often installed in each rear wheel and sometimes in all four wheels. This modification not only provided four-wheel drive but also four-wheel braking, unknown in other trucks of this era.

Another disadvantage was the truck's batteries, which were exceptionally heavy and severely restricted in range. Under the most ideal conditions, they could barely eke out 100 miles before running out of juice and requiring an overnight recharge.

For almost ten years, steam-and electric-powered trucks vied for supremacy until a young upstart drove onto the scene—a truck powered by an internal combustion engine. Historians credit Germany's Gottlieb Daimler with building and successfully operating the world's first truck with a gasoline engine. It looked like a wagon in search of a horse, yet when its engine sputtered to life in early 1896, it signaled the beginning of a worldwide revolution in commercial transportation.

Although the gas-powered truck was not initially as powerful as the steamer or as durable as the electric, its speed, carrying capacity, and longer range quickly boosted its fame and popularity.

The great-great-granddaddy of American-built gasoline trucks is conceded to have been the small delivery wagon built in 1896 by the Winton Company of Cleveland, Ohio, just a few months after Daimler cranked up his first truck.

But the Winton was not alone for long. Barely 15 years later the ranks of American truck builders mushroomed to an amazing 461 whistle-blowing, horn-tooting manufacturers. By 1912 they produced 100,000 commercial vehicles—putting the trucking industry on the road for good. But the manufacturing bubble burst soon after. Many smaller manufacturers, unable to stand the competitive pressure and the strain on their meager financial resources, were merged into healthier companies. Others, with imaginative names like Me serve, Package-car, Gasmobile, and Famous, ingloriously went out of business unnoticed and unmourned. Today only seven nameplates of that era have survived to celebrate diamond anniversaries: Autocar, Ford, FWD, GMC, International, Mack, and White. And two of those now are merged into the single nameplate, WHITEGMC.

In terms of continuous truck manufacturing, White ranks as the oldest survivor. The company's first truck was a steam-powered, light delivery wagon built in 1900 and put into service a year later by the Denver Dry Goods Company. It was probably the fastest commercial vehicle on the road, thanks to the innovative flash boiler perfected by brothers Windsor, Walter, and Rollin White in a back room of their father's Cleveland sewing machine factory.

Because their steamers were ready to roll only moments after the boilers were fired, the Whites' vehicles quickly became the hottest things on wheels—literally and figuratively. In 1905 their "Whistling Billy" racer averaged more than 74 miles per hour to set a world's record for a mile in 48.3 seconds.

White trucks and cars were also well suited for long-distance touring, as demonstrated in 1910 by an American who drove one through France and across the Alps to Italy, returning via Austria and Germany. That same year the White brothers quit the sewing machine company, organized a separate company to handle the automotive line, and introduced their first gasoline-powered model.

In 1903 another brother act stepped onto the bus and truck scene. The five Mack brothers, who operated a wagon and carriage manufacturing plant in Brooklyn, New York, built a gasoline-powered sight-seeing bus, the *Manhattan*, for a local tour agency. The *Manhattan* was such a hit with rubberneckers that the Macks suddenly found themselves out of the wagon business and in the bus business.

Within the year the company moved its factory to Allentown, Pennsylvania, to accommodate a growing demand for sight-seeing and hotel buses and a combination express and passenger vehicle, all built to the same basic specifications.

The Macks also contemplated construction of a pure motor truck in 1904, but it was 1905 before they actually found the time to put together a prototype using the one-and-one-half to two-ton bus chassis. Later that same year they built a 5-ton version with the driver's seat located over the engine instead of behind it.

The bigger unit won immediate acceptance and was Mack's mainstay for the next five years. Nationwide, however, the biggest growth market was in smaller-size trucks. Consequently, in 1910 the brothers introduced the Mack Junior, a speedy delivery truck with a 32 horsepower engine which became a favorite of American merchants.

The Ford Motor Company, incorporated in 1903 to build automobiles, introduced its first commercial vehicle two years later. It was little more than a car with the rear third chopped off and fitted with a short pickup box. Packed to capacity, it could hold two bushels of apples with space left over for a half-pound of pears.

Henry Ford, the company's founder, wasn't really interested in pure truck manufacturing. Most of his time was devoted to the development of mass production. Still, Ford was persuaded in 1914 to extend the truck bed a bit further—just long enough for fellow Detroiter August Fruehauf to attach one of his funny-looking two-wheel trailers, creating the world's first semi.

As its name implies, Autocar began life as a passenger vehicle—but with an engine no bigger than found in today's smallest gas-powered mowers. Autocar was the 1892 brainchild of Louis S. Clark, a Pittsburgh pharmacist whose neighbors claimed he must have inhaled a whiff too much of the gasoline he sold along with his pills, potions, and poultices. Indeed, drug stores were the primary "filling stations" of the 1890s.

Apparently Clark was a better inventor than he was a pharmacist. He is credited with inventing the porcelain spark plug, the engine oil circulating system, the double-reduction rear axle, and the drive shaft which eventually replaced oversize bicycle chains and sprockets to power truck wheels.

The first Autocar truck, produced in 1899, was little more than an experimental model. Serious truck production began in 1907 with the introduction of a one-and-one-half to two-ton model with the engine under the seat. Then in 1910, after the company moved production to Ardmore,

Above: John M. Mack, an inventive genius and a man of determination, is credited with the founding in 1893 of the truck manufacturing enterprise which eventually became Mack Trucks, Inc. Courtesy, Mack Trucks, Inc.

Below: A 1918 Old Reliable dump truck was utilitarian, but had no safety features. Courtesy, American Truck Historical Society

The first White truck was a light steamer built in 1900 and delivered to the Denver Dry Goods Co. in 1901. Courtesy, Volvo GM Heavy Truck Corporation

Pennsylvania, near Philadelphia, it stopped making automobiles altogether. The company kept the Autocar nameplate while producing more than 3,000 trucks a year, making it the dominant truckmaker of the young century.

International Harvester's first truck was produced in 1907. Like Daimler's original creation, it looked like a farm wagon in search of a horse. With its high wagon wheels it was ideal for dirt roads and appealed to farmers— a natural market for McCormick and Deering, two farm implement manufacturers. Aptly named Auto Wagon, it sold well in the farm market, although some detractors claimed farmers bought the vehicle merely to park outside the barn as a reminder to the horses that they could be replaced.

The GMC nameplate made its first

highway appearance in 1912, the result of a consolidation four years earlier of two truck manufacturing companies that had enjoyed considerable success as independents. One half of the joint venture was the Rapid Motor Company, founded in 1902 by Max Grabowsky, who built his manufacturing plant two years later in Pontiac, Michigan. The other partner was the Reliance Motor Company of Owosso, Michigan.

Early on in the race for truck customers, both companies staged successful cross-country demonstrations of their trucks, adding to the internal combustion engine's growing reputation for reliability.

In 1907 a Reliance three-ton truck was driven from Detroit to Chicago with a two-ton load and four passen-

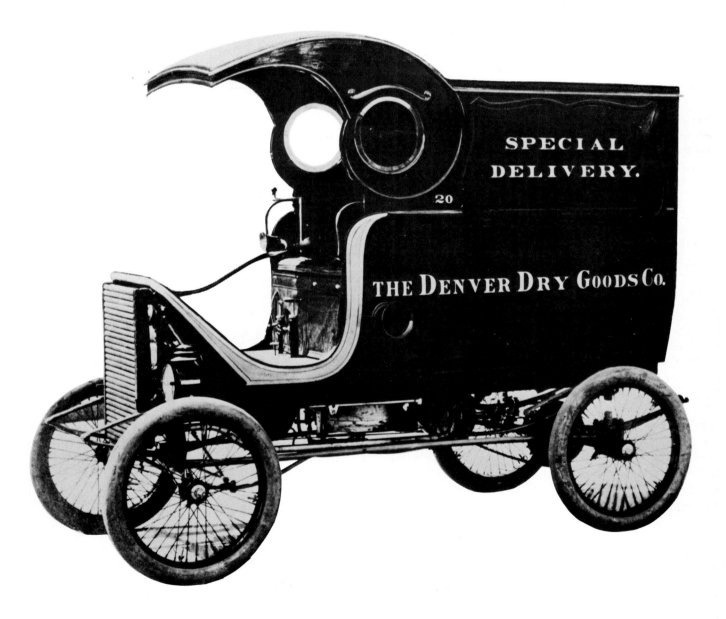

gers, in a demonstration coinciding with the Chicago Auto Show. The trip over 304 miles of frozen roads took 33 hours and 49 minutes of actual driving time. The truck arrived in good condition—which is more than could be said for the four frostbitten passengers.

Three years later it was the Rapid Motor Company's turn to show off. And not to be outdone, the company sent Reliance its truck on a 3,000-mile jaunt, starting and finishing in Detroit—but this time during the summer months.

The Four Wheel Drive Auto Company was formed in 1912 by Otto Zachow, a blacksmith and car dealer who earlier had built a passenger car with front- and rear-wheel drive. The car performed so well on Wisconsin's muddy roads that Zachow persuaded his well-to-do brother-in-law to back him in the design and manufacture of a three-ton all-wheel drive truck powered by a four-cylinder engine developing 56 horsepower.

This truck quickly caught the eye of the U.S. Army. Based on its own tests the army ordered 38 of the rugged vehicles for General Pershing's Mexican campaign against Pancho Villa,

which permanently established FWD as a builder of tough, special purpose vehicles.

Pressured by so much competition, the pace of truck design and manufacturing in those early years was too frantic to permit methodical pre-production testing. New ideas had to be literally tested on the road.

As one publication of the era observed, "The man behind the wheel is more often somewhere else around the truck. In front, cranking the truck. Behind, pushing the truck. Beside, repairing the chain. Or under, keeping out of the rain."

Truck driving in the first decade of this century required nerves of steel and blood that could run hot or cold, depending on the season. With only a partial roof over their heads and no windshield, drivers had little protection from the elements. They were frostbitten in the winter, drenched in the spring, sunburned in the summer, and blown to pieces in the fall.

The ride was equally uncomfortable. The stiff leaf suspension used on most makes was designed to cushion the load, not to keep the driver from bouncing like a rubber ball. And the unyielding wooden plank that served

Above, left: The 1909 International Auto Wagon was aimed at the rural market. It had a 20-horsepower "Big Twin" engine and large wheels to handle rough country roads. Courtesy, Motor Vehicle Manufacturing Association

Top: The Pittsburgh Motor Vehicle Company, which produced its first truck in 1899, subsequently changed its name to the Autocar Company. Autocar is the oldest continuing truck nameplate and the second oldest motor vehicle nameplate. Only the Oldsmobile nameplate precedes it. This 1909 Autocar was used as an ambulance. Courtesy, Volvo GM Heavy Truck Corporation

Above: A 1910 Autocar built to haul liquids is pictured outside Autocar headquarters. Courtesy, Volvo GM Heavy Truck Corporation

Above: The 1917 "International Harvester" model H had acetylene headlights and a kerosene taillight. The four-cylinder gas engine could generate almost 20 horsepower. Courtesy, American Truck Historical Society

Above: In 1908 General Motors was organized and acquired the Rapid Motor Company. The following year Glidden Tours used the durable and strong gasoline-powered Rapid to climb Pike's Peak at an elevation of 15,000 feet. Courtesy, Motor Vehicle Manufacturing Association

Below: In 1910 the Four Wheel Drive Auto Company (FWD) produced its first truck and tested it thoroughly on the muddiest roads. Courtesy, Motor Vehicle Manufacturing Association

as seating was hard as stone. It is no wonder that some drivers spent many of their off-duty hours perched on padded stools at the local tavern.

In their bids for new business, truckmakers increasingly turned to public demonstrations of their vehicles' rugged reliability. Whereas the automakers met their competition on the racetrack as a means for generating publicity, truckmakers competed to establish new cross-country records. And with few good roads outside city limits, most of the trips were truly cross-country.

One of the most ambitious demonstrations was staged by the Saurer Motor Company, which had begun exporting trucks from Switzerland in 1905. As part of a sales campaign launched shortly after opening an American manufacturing plant in 1911, Saurer sent a truck on the first-ever transcontinental trip.

The first leg was westward from

Denver to San Francisco with a cargo of timber—not for delivery but to bridge gullies and provide solid footing when rainstorms turned dirt roads into quagmires. It took three months just to get the *Pioneer Freighter* over the mountains and through the desert. The journey across New Mexico took almost another month. And when the road disappeared—a frequent occurrence—the driving team was forced to take a teeth-rattling ride on the railroad right-of-way.

The truck was shipped back to Colorado and then driven east to Chicago and on to New York, where it arrived after logging more than 5,000 miles, including diversions and demonstrations. The total elapsed time for both journeys was slightly more than a year. Following Saurer's lead, GMC set out in 1916 to cross the continent in both directions in a one-and-one-half ton truck loaded with a ton of canned Carnation evaporated milk. Setting out from Seattle, destined for New York, William Warwick and his wife were under solemn oath to make their own repairs and to keep the truck rolling unassisted by any external power. The couple kept their word, turning down friendly offers of a helping hand when they became stuck.

In Colorado the truck was washed down the side of a canyon in a cloudburst. In Illinois it broke through the bottom of a ferryboat in midstream. It was mired up to the axles at least once

in practically every other state on the route. But amazingly, the Warwicks completed the trek in 68 days elapsed time, 31 days of actual road travel, without a single mechanical breakdown.

The real test of trucks and trucking, however, awaited the outbreak of World War I. Even before America's entry, nearly every major manufacturer converted production to a broad array of motorized vehicles, from cargo carriers and tankers to munitions movers and ambulances.

Although thousands of trucks were exported overseas, none was more endeared than the Mack AC model, by far the ugliest of breeds. It was the first truck built with a steel cab and optional roof. The pugnacious styling

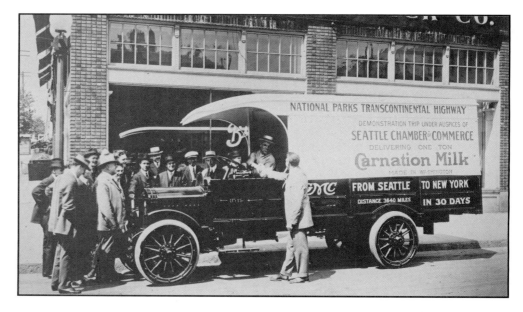

Above: The American trucking industry boomed in World War I as the Allies purchased mass quantities of American trucks to supply the trenches. When the United States entered the war, thousands more were shipped to Europe. These trucks served as ambulances to ferry the wounded from the battlefields. Courtesy, Motor Vehicle Manufacturing Association

Right: Workers at the Port of Newark, New Jersey, load Mack "Bulldogs" for shipment to Europe. Courtesy, American Truck Historical Society

of its steel hood prompted British troops to christen it the Bulldog—a name that has endured as the company's logo ever since. In toughness and tenacity, it lived up to its name. It was a boom era for American truck manufacturers whose combined output reached 19,000 units a month, many of them marked for use on the home front as well as for the war front. It was this phenomenal growth in trucking that spawned the beginnings of intercity travel.

In New York City the Beam Fletcher Company began running 22 trucks a day on round-trips to Philadelphia. The Liberty Highway Company started daily motor service between Detroit and Toledo, using a five-ton truck to pull three five-ton trailers—requiring a mere eight hours to make the 63-mile run. And in Alabama, the Birmingham Civic Association prevented a severe coal shortage by contracting with Jenkins Motor Company to haul in 200 tons a day directly from outlying mines.

A serious transportation crisis in 1917 opened the door to additional growth for trucking. The railroads,

Above: Dodge Brothers of Detroit introduced their first truck in 1917. Courtesy, Motor Vehicle Manufacturing Association

Top: Since early trucks were basically motorized wagons, few came with enclosed cabs. This 1918 model TT Ford came equipped with attachable side curtains to keep out some of the winter's blast. Courtesy, Ford Motor Corporation

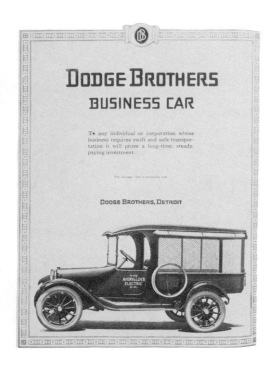

after years of neglect and with many of their underpaid employees fleeing to join war industries, nearly came to a standstill under the strain of the nation's wartime transportation requirements. Poor carloading and antiquated business practices resulted in incredible congestion and tieups at rail terminals. It was not unusual for trucks to wait up to four days to pick up a few boxes of freight. The railroads' only solution to the problem was to embargo certain freight, refusing to haul many shipments, including foods over short distances. And in so doing the railroads opened the door for trucking. One city broke the embargo on package freight by trucking small shipments to 14 outlying points within a 20-mile radius. A New York drug firm began weekly truck deliveries to Boston. Several Cleveland factories bought their own trucks

and began hauling in raw materials from as far as 30 miles away.

Not surprisingly, the federal government finally stepped in toward the end of the war and took over the rails and instituted the first large-scale break-bulk system. Cities were divided into zones and the unloaded freight was delivered by truck directly to customers within each zone. Most bottlenecks were broken within a matter of weeks.

The conclusion of the war was as much a victory for American trucks as it was for American troops. Both had proved their mettle under fire. And when the soldiers came marching home victorious, gas-powered trucks, too, had proved their supremacy over steam and electricity.

Suddenly, trucks were in demand. No longer limited to delivery chores, trucks were recruited for a variety of

Facing page, top: The Dodge Business Car, introduced in 1918, was the Dodge Brothers' most famous truck. It was popular with many small urban businesses. Courtesy, Motor Vehicles Manufacturing Association

Facing page, bottom: The Four Wheel Drive Auto Company built this truck in 1916. The truck can be viewed at the British Columbia Provincial Museum. Courtesy, American Truck Historical Society

Above: A 1912 Peerless stake truck was used by the firm of Morgan and Bolton. Courtesy, American Truck Historical Society

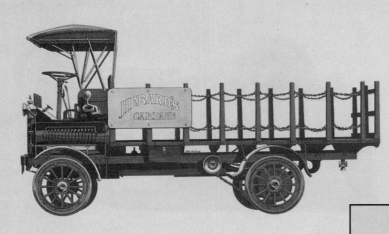

Above: With a partial roof and no windshield, the driver of this 1912 Pope Hartford truck was fully exposed to the elements. Courtesy, American Truck Historical Society

Above: This 1914 Selden "JL" truck carried fruit and vegetables for T. Kupfer and Sons. Courtesy, American Truck Historical Society

Above: A 1918 Saurer stake truck took to the streets just as World War I was ending. Courtesy, American Truck Historical Society

Below: This 1918 Ford served as a police wagon. Although Ford did produce some commercial vehicles of its own during this era, many of its "trucks" were actually cars converted to trucks by other companies. Courtesy, Ford Motor Corporation

Bottom: On the home front during World War I, trucks were used to help provide the materials needed for the war effort. Here a GMC hauls logs from a Washington forest in 1917. Courtesy, Motor Vehicle Manufacturing Association

jobs—repairing overhead power lines, hauling logs out of the forest, delivering mail, and moving mountains of dirt at construction sites. Yet despite the truck's versatility, the lack of adequate roads connecting the cities and towns of the nation largely confined its work to the limits of a given city.

The idea of a single transcontinental highway linking the Atlantic and the Pacific coasts was first conceived in 1912 by Carl G. Fisher, founder of

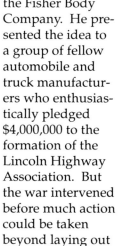

the Fisher Body Company. He presented the idea to a group of fellow automobile and truck manufacturers who enthusiastically pledged $4,000,000 to the formation of the Lincoln Highway Association. But the war intervened before much action could be taken beyond laying out

the route and publicizing the need for such a highway. In 1919 Captain Dwight D. Eisenhower led a convoy of army trucks over the proposed Lincoln Highway route and was convinced of the importance of good roads to the strengthening of American commerce and its military defenses.

As early as 1916, Congress passed the Federal Aid Road Act which offered up to $10,000 per mile in government funds for construction of adequate rural routes while leaving the actual construction in the hands of the individual states. But World War I put an end to the program before it was barely begun.

The war almost put an end to American roads as well. Built mostly of macadam, the roads' thin shells were ground to dust under the weight of millions of tons of war materials. To make matters worse, some believed that road building, including road repair, was non-essential work and should be suspended until after the war.

Yet it was clear that the nation needed a national network of roads that would encourage interstate commerce as well as provide a growing mass of motorists easy access to the seashore and the mountains, as well as to the homes of friends and relatives in distant parts of the country.

Although the first concrete pavement had been laid in 1909—a one mile stretch on the outskirts of Detroit that cost a total of $13,000—it remained virtually the only example of highway paving until after the war.

The American road of the 1920s was a dust bowl in the summer, a sea of mud in spring and fall, and a series of bone-jarring, frozen ruts in the winter. Motorists and truckers alike seldom needed a signpost to mark a state or county line: the sudden change in road conditions—for better or worse—told the story.

It was road building as much as the bathtub gin that put the roar in the Roaring Twenties. The federal government again passed a bill appropriating $200 million for road construction. To help implement the program most four-wheel-drive trucks that had served army duty overseas were brought back by the government and consigned to road-building contractors.

Actual design and construction of the Lincoln Highway remained unfinished until the 1920s when the Federal government took over the project. Specifications—generous for that decade—called for a 40-foot wide concrete pavement, capable of carrying four lanes of traffic, flanked on each side by pedestrian side paths included within the 110-foot wide right-of-way. Not so generous were the proposed speed limits, 35 miles per hour for cars and 10 miles per hour for trucks— a rate that would take a truck from New York to San Francisco in a mere 32 days.

Other federal highways quickly took shape as road building reached a fevered pitch in the mid-1920s. Bridges were built, mountains were excavated, swamps were crossed, a uniform system for route signs was created, and the general quality of the nation's roads improved immensely in just a few short years.

The truck, too, was improved. Some cabs were fitted with doors, windows, and windshields. Transmissions were improved and work continued on improving the reliability of pneumatic tires. Some manufacturers even began to offer such options as padded seats, electric lights, speedometers, bulb horns, and rearview mirrors.

Interstate truck driving was still a challenge, however, fraught with many uncertainties. Brakes caught fire as heavily loaded trucks descended long slopes in the West. On the upgrade they often came to a steaming, sizzling stop, forcing the drivers to leap out and quickly block the wheels. And although the cab was enclosed, no provison was made for cold weather except in a few models that diverted heat directly from the manifold. Truckers had to choose between freezing or suffocating from the fumes.

But as trucking continued to grow at a phenomenal pace, interstate travel was limited to the more densely populated states in the Northeast. Gradually, toward the end of the decade, a few semis and doubles began operating regularly between cities no farther than a single day's drive, forging the beginning links in a chain of interstate operations. Shipping coast to coast by truck also was possible although the consignment might be transferred to seven or more different carriers before reaching its destination. The railroads, however, still ruled interstate commerce with an iron fist. But as trucking entered its fourth decade, the road signs already pointed away from the tracks. Trucks were becoming America's prime mover.

Below: For a time, southeastern Pennsylvania was a leading motor transport center. In this view of the "Alco" car and truck plant in Philadelphia, completed trucks can be seen at rear, center, and touring cars at right, rear. Courtesy, American Truck Historical Society

Bottom: Production was at maximum in this GMC plant in 1917 as America's truck manufacturers rushed to supply trucks for the Allies in Europe. Courtesy, Motor Vehicle Manufacturing Association

From Regulation to Deregulation 2

O n a spring morning in 1934, in an elegant leather and stainless steel men's washroom aboard a Pullman railroad car heading west from Pittsburgh, the foundation for an orderly, prosperous trucking industry was established.

In the years following World War I, trucking service became chaotic, unreliable, and fiercely competitive. Any entrepreneur with a few bucks and a bit of fire could enter the motor carrier business, his financial fitness or reliability never questioned.

Owners often competed for the most profitable routes and ignored the needs of shippers along less lucrative routes, mostly smaller rural communities. Operators set their own rates, often shaving them slightly above the break-even point to stave off cutthroat competition. Trucking gypsies preyed on the customers of responsible operators. Although failing at an alarming rate, gypsies undercut the more realistic rates of established firms and raised havoc with the economics of the industry.

Capitalizing on the trucking industry's unstable pricing, the railroads waged an all-out war on their strident young competitor, using the political influence in statehouses and the federal government that they had built up over decades. It became increasingly evident that truck operators would have to join hands if they were going to fight back and develop a reliable industry. There was also an obvious need for some sort of regulation—either voluntary or government-imposed.

During the early 1920s many state and local trucking associations

Above: Drivers have been lining up for positions with less-than-truckload carriers, but deregulation and the resulting expansion have proved troublesome for truckload operators trying to fill vacancies. Photo by Kent Knudson/The Photo File

Facing page: Certain truck fleets, and often independent owner-operators, continually strive to make their trucks stand out from the rest. Photo by Mark E. Gibson

Above: American Trucking Association's first Washington office was rather spartan in appearance, fitting well with the Depression-era economy that gave birth to the organization. Courtesy, American Trucking Association

Below: This picture of the first ATA executive committee was taken in 1936. Seated, left to right, are Lewis J. Benton, H.D. Horton, Ted V. Rodgers, Griswold B. Holman, and Fisher G. Dorsey. Standing, left to right, are Glenn R. Ward, James B. Godfrey, Jr., Hugh E. Sheridan, Frank Flanagan, Walter F. Carey, M.B. Emerson, Al Meyers, John L. Wilkinson, W.H. Brearly, John F. Winchester, Chester G. Moore, and John V. Lawrence. Courtesy, American Trucking Association

had been formed to counter railroad-backed legislation that restricted the use of heavier trucks to haul bigger loads. Although many of these state and local groups became a viable force in their own areas, they lacked any significant influence at the national level.

It soon became apparent that a national organization was needed to bring the widely fragmented industry together. Responding to this need, Ted Rodgers of Scranton, Pennsylvania, John W. Blood of Kansas, and Jack Keeshin of Chicago organized a group of carriers called the American Highway Freight Association, with Rodgers at the helm.

At the same time A.J. Brousseau of Mack Motor Truck and Frank Schmidt of the National Automobile Chamber of Commerce formed the Federated Truck Association of America, composed of state affiliates. They brought in Edward F. Loomis from the auto group to head the federation.

Both organizations quickly merged in 1933 when newly elected president Franklin D. Roosevelt created the National Recovery Administration (NRA) to administer the National Industrial Recovery Act, a depression-born measure that called for all businesses to develop "a code of competition." The act called for a code of fair practice for

businesses and industries, setting minimum wages and maximum work hours and promising higher prices for all industries, including trucking.

In the spring of 1933 leaders of the two national trucking organizations met in Chicago to write the required code for the trucking industry. As might have been expected, nothing was resolved. Despite meeting after meeting the two disparate groups ended up submitting 90 different versions of the proposed trucking code.

Impatient with these internal differences, the NRA demanded one code—and fast. General Hugh Johnson, head of the NRA, told the industry that if it did not draw up a single code, "the government will write one for you."

By the summer of 1933 the two trucking groups had merged, forming the American Trucking Associations (ATA)—still the industry's most vocal group—and work was under way on the final NRA code. One of the driving forces behind the industry's organization was Rodgers, the dynamo from Scranton. He was elected president of ATA, a post he held until 1946. He was also the key participant in that historic moment on the Pullman car.

By the spring of 1934 the newly formed ATA had hammered out a code

for the industry, but the participants were impatient for federal approval. It was no secret that the fledgling organization wanted fast approval because it needed the income the government would provide to ATA to keep the depression-strapped organization going.

However, a hitch developed—good old government paperwork—delaying approval and signing of the ATA's code-papers by the NRA administrator. Learning of the delay, Rodgers tried to reach the administrator, who was enroute to the Pacific Coast—which would mean another delay of three to four weeks.

Rodgers hurriedly obtained an official copy of the papers, hopped a plane and followed the route of the federal official's train west to Pittsburgh, where he boarded it late at night. The following morning, he found the NRA official in the Pullman washroom and there the papers were signed.

The code required every for-hire trucking company to register with the government. All trucking companies had to observe maximum hours of service and minimum rates of pay for all employees. In addition, each carrier had to file a schedule of minimum rates and tariffs. Although the code did not pro-

duce the benefits many operators hoped for, it did create unity in the industry and an awareness among many that regulation was indeed viable.

In May of 1935, however, the Supreme Court declared the National Industrial Recovery Act unconstitutional. But by this time the industry was ready to go along with permanent federal intervention in its affairs.

A few months after the Supreme Court ruling, Joseph B. Eastman, federal coordinator of transportation and a friend of the industry, drafted a regulatory bill that provided for safety regulation of interstate carriers and economic regulation of for-hire operations. The bill, drafted under the supervision of the Interstate Commerce Commission, was rushed through Congress and signed into law by President Roosevelt on August 9, 1935.

President Roosevelt characterized the Motor Carrier Act of 1935 as "terribly long and frightfully confusing," yet its effect on the growth of the trucking industry was immense. The complex bill described in detail how the various provisions of the law would be carried out and what motor carriers had to do to conform.

ATA's newspaper, *Transport Topics*, warned the industry:

Above: The **A.T.A. Registration Bulletin** *was the voice of the American Trucking Association and continues today as* **Transport Topics**. *This early issue annouced the beginning of the first trucking code, including the national license plate that was issued to registered carriers. Courtesy, American Trucking Association*

Because most truck drivers are unfamiliar with the intricacies of the new law, they readily may fall victims to the various individuals who will set themselves up as experts on the law—for a fat fee. The law may be steeped in mystery, at least that is the impression these experts will impart to their prospective customers. If the bill is as mysterious as they will picture it, it would require a squad of Philadelphia lawyers, two accountants and several politicians to unravel it.

Despite the bill's complexities, it gave rise to a new, unified trucking industry. Economic regulation was finally in place, but nagging complaints persisted about the condition of trucks and their safety on the highways. Many trucks operated without windshields, with failing brakes, stripped gears, few or inadequate lights, and other hazardous conditions.

Above: Most truck manufacturers in the 1920s and 1930s also made buses, as cities expanded and mass transit became a necessity. This private coach was made for Franklin D. Roosevelt for his 1932 presidential campaign. Courtesy, Volvo GM Heavy Truck Corporation

Right: Labatt Brewing Company of Canada contracted Count Alexis de Sakhnoffsky to design a rolling promotion. The Labatt's Streamliners were a familiar sight from 1932 until 1955. This reconstruction of an old frame, which took seven years to complete, is powered by a 1948 White. Courtesy, American Truck Historical Society

Sensing growing public concern over truck safety, the industry joined forces with the federal government in drafting what became the 1937 law that placed truck safety under federal regulation for the first time—a precedent that continues to this day.

The Depression ironically was a boon to many fledgling interstate carriers. For years slow, unpredictable rail service had forced merchants, manufacturers, and warehousers to stock sizable inventories of raw materials or finished goods. But in the iron grip of hard times, they no longer could afford the luxury of buying by the carload.

Truckers took advantage of this opportunity, creating new, flexible routing to meet merchant's needs. Merchants were able to order smaller quantities, which were delivered right to their doors in a much shorter time than by rail. The new arrangement benefited both trucker and merchant. For exam-

Above: In 1934 Dodge Brothers introduced this one-ton panel truck. Courtesy, American Truck Historical Society

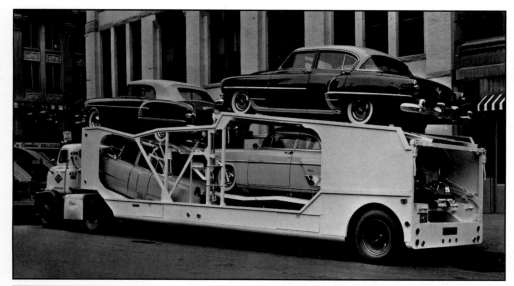

Above: When car carriers came into use, cars were larger than today. Although this Dodge tractor could have pulled more, there was no way to do so practically, and legally. Courtesy, American Truck Historical Society

Top: In the 1950s Fruehauf was working to redesign the car carrier to make it more economical. One thing going for the designers was that cars couldn't stay 20 feet long for ever. Courtesy, American Truck Historical Society

As with the auto industry, the booming oil business also meant more business for trucks. Trucks were driving through back roads, mud, and in bad weather to get pipe and machinery to drilling sites. Much the same conditions prevailed for truckers specializing in hauling farm goods. Tales were common of such feats as driving a load of eggs through a blinding snowstorm with one arm out the window to brush off the snow just so the delivery would get to the market on time.

As the industry grew the truck itself underwent many improvements. Some design standardization had been forced on the manufacturers during World War I. And now truckmakers began to standardize even further, turning to outside suppliers for design and manufacture of major components such as axles, transmissions, and engines.

Since the introduction of the Winton in 1896, gasoline had fueled the internal combustion engines in all American trucks. Yet as early as 1923 the German firm of Benz had successfully demonstrated a truck diesel engine, which was not marketed in the United States. But nearly a decade passed before Clessie L. Cummins introduced and marketed an American-made version of the diesel engine.

The engine was not an easy sell. In fact, Cummins tried to get auto manufacturers interested in his engine for more than five years, using a mixture of engineering know-how and Barnum & Bailey showmanship. Cummins' diesels raced at Indianapolis, set speed and endurance records, and toured the United States and Europe, often with Cummins behind the wheel.

Cummins' finest hour came in the fall of 1931 when his diesel-powered truck set a non-stop endurance record—a 14,600-mile run around the Indianapolis Speedway oval without ever shutting off the engine. "After that," Cummins remarked later, "truckers were lined up at the door every morning for two weeks waiting to buy an engine." The first Cummins diesel installed in a truck was put in a Kenworth in 1932. Mack introduced its own 131 horsepower diesel six years later, as did Caterpillar.

While Cummins dramatized the durability of his engine, movies began to glamorize the role of trucking. *California Straight Ahead*, for example, featured

ple, after a year of truck deliveries, the Otis Elevator Company discovered it had saved $100,000 in the cost of packaging as well as a savings in paperwork. And whereas rail shipment required anywhere from six days to six weeks, trucks could make a delivery in 24 hours—and with considerably less damage to the freight.

As a result common carriage of less-than-trailerload (LTL) shipments grew rapidly. New carriers were born, and some blossomed quickly into giant transportation companies—among them Consolidated Freightways, Yellow Transit, and Roadway Express.

Trucking also benefited from the growing automobile industry. As more Americans purchased cars, car dealers needed a better way to deliver new cars from the factories. As a result, auto haulers began springing up rapidly with rigs that could haul four or five vehicles at a time.

John Wayne as a school bus driver who got fired and ended up owning a fleet of trucks. Other films depicting the struggles of truckers featured actors such as Humphrey Bogart and Ida Lupino. But despite the publicity trucking's growth did not come easily.

The railroads continued to resist the growing trucking industry, although it was acknowledged that trucks would continue to be a formidable competitor. The National Transportation Committee, a group created by insurance companies and railroad interests, concluded: "One thing is certain, automotive transportation is in advance of the march of progress. It is here to stay. We cannot invent restrictions for the benefits of the railroads. We can only apply such regulations and assess such taxes as would be necessary if there were no railroads and let the effect be what it may." Taxes remain a battleground between railraods and trucks to this day.

In many parts of the country public attitude still ran heavily against trucks—especially in those areas where coal influenced the economy. Railroads were heavy users of coal for their steam locomotives and were also the primary means of transporting coal to market. In 1938 the 1,500 citizens of Whitwell, Tennessee, a coal-mining town, voted an embargo on trucks for two months.

With the mines hit hard by layoffs, the town adopted the slogan, "We don't dig no gasoline, we dig coal." Local merchants were told citizens would refuse to purchase their goods unless they were hauled by rail and not trucks. With rail cars sitting idle, the town resented truck deliveries. Trucks, however, were allowed to deliver "perishable goods, fresh fruits, vegetables, etc., not including potatoes; packing house products, meats, lard, cheese, etc., but not including soap; bakery products, coffee, tea, spices, mayonnaise and other relishes, candy and tobacco, bottled drinks and petroleum products."

Embargos such as this one died out quickly and trucks began to haul more essential consumer goods. However, politicians continued to play on the public's fear about large trucks—a political tactic still used today.

One of the biggest flareups over trucking occurred in 1939 within President Roosevelt's cabinet. The President's flamboyant, controversial

Secretary of the Interior, Harold Ickes, speaking to the American Automobile Association in 1939 advocated all trucks be banned from the highways on weekends and holidays and that automobile transporters and diesel-powered vehicles be banned altogether.

Ickes also promised that someday he would enjoy the "pleasure of driving down a truck-infested road in the biggest armored truck I can find and bumping these pests from the road, regardless of where they may light." Ickes' speech touched off a furor—mostly by anti-Ickes forces—all across the country. But the controversy soon died down as the trucking industry continued to play a prominent role in the U.S. economy during the last year of the Depression.

By the outbreak of World War II, trucks were recognized as an essential part of the U.S. freight transportation

Below: Clessie Cummins climbs into his test bus equipped with his diesel. Courtesy, Motor Vehicle Manufacturing Association

Bottom: This restored 1932 "Kenworth" is a model 88. The first Cummins diesel installed in a truck was put in a Kenworth in 1932. Courtesy, American Truck Historical Society

system—a role that was accelerated greatly by the war. As the war effort heated up in 1942, there was a growing fear that a truck shortage would develop if older trucks were not kept running. President Roosevelt wrote special letters to "owners and drivers" reminding them that the nation's five million trucks were a vital asset to the war effort. "It has become the patriotic duty of every truck operator in America to help in every possible way to make his truck and tires last longer," Roosevelt stated. During a recruiting drive in October of the same year, the U.S. Army Quartermaster Corps recruited about 5,000 truck dispatchers, mechanics, and drivers for foreign service.

Among the many famous truck units serving the war effort, none was more famous than the Red Ball Express, a 400-mile truck service built at the height of the war, following the historic D-Day invasion of France on June 6, 1944. It ran from the beaches of Normandy to Germany and back again on parallel highways open only to trucks bearing the red ball symbol on their windshields. At times more than 400 trucks an hour stretched out along the route, delivering supplies to front-line troops.

During the first 26 days of its operation, Red Ball trucks delivered more than 200,000 tons of supplies to the Western Front. In the most critical stages of General George S. Patton's race halfway across Europe, trucks delivered 7,000 tons daily, prompting Patton to proclaim, "The truck is our most important weapon."

At the war's close General Eisenhower, in a report to President Truman, wrote: "When one looks back on those amazing days, it seems . . . incredible that at no period up until the time we stood on the threshold of Germany was the momentum of the drive retarded through lack of essential supplies. The spectacular nature of the advance was due in as great measure to the men who drove the Red Ball trucks as to those who drove the tanks."

The memory of the Red Ball Express and the 1919 convoy he had led across America remained with Eisenhower many years later when he signed the largest highway construction bill in the nation's history.

The close of the war brought with it dramatic changes for the trucking indus-

try. Larger, more efficient equipment was introduced, and U.S. economic growth opened new and larger markets. A vast new system of roads made access to shippers more efficient. The trucking industry was growing and prospering at a speed that old-timers could only have dreamed about.

However, there were clouds on the horizon. Lawyers in the Justice Department were becoming concerned over rate bureaus, the regional organizations of trucking companies that set rates on various types of freight. Many of these organizations had been operating freely for as many 50 years with the support of the industry, which considered them a sensible way to bring order out of pricing chaos.

Yet this traditional collective ratemaking process was under fire. Justice Department lawyers filed a number of lawsuits against the rate bureaus. And President Harry S. Truman argued that the bureaus violated antitrust laws. To counter these heated arguments bills were introduced in Congress by Senator Clyde Reed, a Kansas Republican, and Congressman Alfred L. Bulwinkle, a North Carolina Democrat, to preserve the collective ratemaking process. The bills received almost unanimous support from shippers, carriers, and unions.

As the acrimonious debate continued in Congress, Senator Alben Barkley, the Democrat from Kentucky, later to be Truman's vice president, called the measure "a vicious piece of legislation." And Senator Reed, one of the bill's sponsors, called the Justice Department "a

bunch of screwballs."

When the dust settled the famous Reed-Bulwinkle Act of 1948 had passed—despite Truman's veto—and collective ratemaking was preserved for another 30 years.

Following World War II the trucking industry experienced a revolution in truck design and manufacturing. The diesel engine came of age. Although it had been introduced at the outbreak of the war, it was not until the late 1940s and early 1950s that it became the workhorse of the trucking industry.

Truck design was changing rapidly. Although the first tilt cab was introduced in 1935, it was not until after the war that a highly tooled forward tilt model came on the market. Not long after, the forward tilt became standard equipment. Post-war trailers were also being made with lighter materials, to some extent the result of aircraft research for warplanes.

In Portland, Oregon, Consolidated Freightways applied aircraft engineering techniques and materials to create an all-aluminum tilt cab, christened the Freightliner and marketed through the White Truck organization.

As truck equipment became larger, more powerful, and more efficient, there was an increasing need for bigger, better-designed highways. In 1956 President Eisenhower, Congress, and the trucking industry joined forces to secure funding for the largest public works project in U.S. history—building the interstate highway system.

The effort that led to signing the bill into law was not easy—and neither was

Above: The loss of available new trucks during the war was coupled with the loss of drivers. Erwin Schwandt, a livestock transporter, put his daughters to work to replace drivers who had joined the Army. Courtesy, PR Counselors

Facing page, top: After the bombing of Pearl Harbor, maintenance became the byword of the nation's fleets, since new trucks were no longer available. Here several Whites are checked in late 1942 so they will keep rolling "for the duration." Courtesy, Motor Vehicle Manufacturing Association.

Facing page, middle: In 1943 Franklin D. Roosevelt reviewed the troops in a White Scout Car. Courtesy, Volvo GM Heavy Truck Corporation

Facing page, bottom: With the onset of war, America's truck manufacturers quickly converted their factories to build military vehicles. Here, White 666 armored transports are assembled before shipment to Europe in 1942. Courtesy, Volvo GM Heavy Truck Corporation

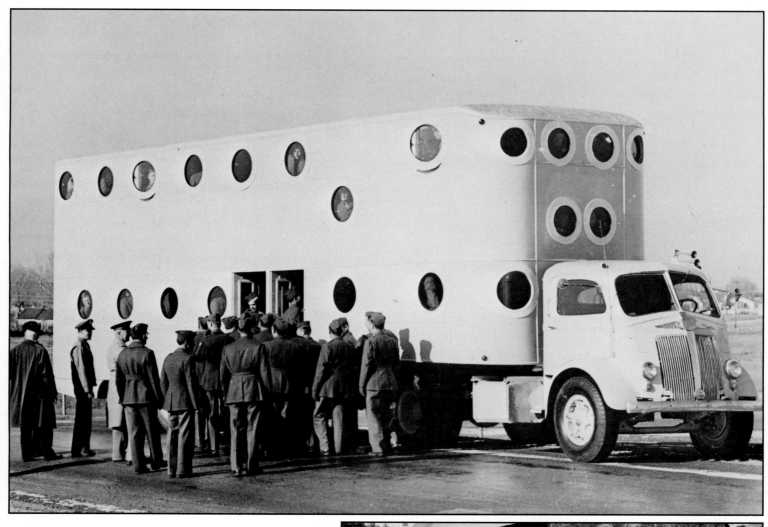

Above: Trailer manufacturers contributed to the war by making troop transports. This Gillespie Double-Decker is pulled by a White 800-series tractor in 1943. Courtesy, Volvo GM Heavy Truck Corporation

Right, top: A White Half-Track cruises through a Normandy town in June 1944. Courtesy, Volvo GM Heavy Truck Corporation

Right, bottom: Motorized transportation quickly replaced animals in the war effort, but horses and machines served together briefly. Here White Scout Cars accompany the 107th Cavalry in early 1942. Courtesy, Volvo GM Heavy Truck Corporation

implementing it afterward. A bitter fight in Congress over apportionment of the funds among the states resulted in a compromise formula, and the bill was passed just before adjournment. Yet even before the bill reached the White House, the Internal Revenue Service began issuing regulations implementing the new taxes on trucks and equipment that were part of the funding package.

The project was plagued by other problems as well. Shortages were predicted for concrete, steel, and asphalt when construction began. The Bureau of Public Roads—in charge of the huge project—was also 900 engineers short. To make up for the shortage, engineers were asked to make greater use of aerial surveys and "electronic devices" in making their calculations.

Despite these problems, the massive 42,000-mile, $50 billion project—first estimates escalated rapidly—was under way. Its biggest supporter was President Eisenhower. He had been impressed with the German Autobahn he saw while serving in World War II and saw America's need for a similar

Above: Freightliner Corporation was originally established to provide trucks for its parent corporation, Consolidated Freightways. This Freightliner, nicknamed "Bubblenose," was the first Freightliner sold commercially in 1950. It was re-purchased by Freightliner in the late 1970s and fully restored. Courtesy, Freightliner Corporation

Below: These Mack dump trucks haul gravel for cement during construction of Interstate 78 in New York. Trucks played a vital part in the building of the interstate highway system. The interstates of the 1960s came much closer to matching the plans of the 1920s than those actually built in that era. Courtesy, PR Counselors

Above: This 1952 "Freightliner" was the first truck that company sold commercially. Courtesy, American Truck Historical Society

Left: American trucks appeared on European roads more frequently after World War II leveled domestic manufacturers' factories. The "Indiana" pictured here hauled for the Nederland Expresse in Holland, around the early 1950s. Courtesy, American Truck Historical Society

Facing page: The 1965 COF 4000 International cabover pictured here stood in the middle of a gradual evolution in the looks of International cabovers as they progressed from the late 1950s to the early 1970s. Courtesy, Navistar International

national highway system, for national defense as well as economic reasons.

As anticipated by the president and other proponents of the project, the interstate system provided an important network of highways among cities, increasing commerce and travel to all parts of the United States. The contribution of the interstate system and other highways to the burgeoning growth of the trucking industry in the 1960s and 1970s is difficult to determine; however, most transportation experts agree it was

substantial. Without modern roads today's larger, more efficient tractor-trailers could not operate.

Although the trucking industry benefited economically from a new, efficient system of roads, more economic troubles were on the horizon as deregulation became a major issue. Cries to deregulate grew more strident as the Carter administration took office in 1977. Banks, airlines, and railroads—among others—were all cut loose from the government's regulatory apron strings.

By the 1950s containerized cars began to catch on. The longshoremen's unions didn't like it, but it was a natural way to keep costs down and transport companies solvent. Courtesy, American Truck Historical Society

With the passage of the Motor Carrier Act of 1980, the trucking industry was also deregulated. The act was the most comprehensive overhaul of motor carrier regulation since the passage of the Motor Carrier Act of 1935, which originally placed the industry under federal surveillance.

The original act had set up entry standards to ensure carrier dependability. The 1980 reform legislation, however, relaxed those standards. Deregulation also lifted the 1935 restrictions on where a carrier could operate and restored much of the pricing freedom that had been taken away in 1935. Single-line ratemaking—a major feature of the 1948 Reed-Bulwinkle bill—was phased out.

Experts are still debating the long-term effects of the act. But the short-term effect has meant rate wars, entry and exit of hordes of newcomers, and the demise of many old-line firms unprepared for the new, unrestricted competition.

The ink was barely dry on the unsettling 1980 act when the industry was hit again with more legislation—the Surface Transportation Assistance Act of 1982. The "Assistance" act was a mixed blessing for the industry. Under this act truckers were able to take advantage of larger, more productive equipment coming on the market. It allowed use of twin combinations of 28 feet for each unit, 48-foot single trailers and a trailer

width of 102 inches (an increase of six inches). In return, however, the diesel fuel tax was increased by five cents per gallon, and the heavy-vehicle use tax also took a substantial jump.

One of the most important, unresolved problems remaining from the passage of the 1982 act is exactly where the longer, wider vehicles can operate. By law, these larger trucks are still able to travel over interstate highways. However, the states were given the right to designate what interstate access roads these bigger rigs could use. By the end of 1987 many states—most mired down in politics—had not made all their final road choices.

As the 1990s approach, transportation experts are watching with interest the developing relationship between trucking companies and the railroads—especially at the regional level. Railroads have bought some motor carriers to improve regional service. And some regional trucking carriers have reached agreements for handling the railroads' pickup and delivery of freight. This arrangement is known in the industry as "intermodalism," a buzzword meaning a combination of several forms of transportation—land, sea, and air—into one giant interlocking system, worldwide as well as nationwide. Trucking, of course, will continue to play a leading role in this intermodalism, keeping the wheels of commerce turning.

There are some things, such as blizzards, that advances in trucking technology can do little about. Courtesy, American Truck Historical Society

Spanning the Spectrum of Services 3

*I*n Tonopah, Nevada, the owner of a small grocery store rubs the last vestiges of sleep from his eyes as the truck arrives with fresh vegetables and fruit from California.

In Pontiac, Michigan, a tractor-trailer pulls up to a loading dock with parts for the morning's auto production. In High Point, North Carolina, trucks loaded with the newest line of sofas and bedroom suites head for furniture stores across the country.

In San Antonio a fleet of garbage trucks are well into their morning rounds, while in Atlanta a truck pulls onto a construction site with steel beams for the city's newest office tower.

In rural Colorado farmers load open-top trailers with alfalfa destined for a feed lot 100 miles away. In Boston street vendors are setting out cut flowers trucked in overnight from Florida.

In Oregon a logging truck rumbles down a mountainside with logs for a paper mill. In Indiana a driver maneuvers his twin trailers into a terminal where cartons of everything from blackboards to Band-Aids will be unloaded, sorted, and transferred to other trucks for delivery to their final destinations.

Trucking has become so important to American commerce and industry that few people realize the role it plays in our daily lives. Without trucks we could not heat our houses on a blustery cold night. And seldom does anyone consider how a potato can make the trip from a farm

Above: Few people see the voyage freshly-cut trees make before they are turned into paper or lumber. Photo by Dave Bartruff/ The Photo File

Facing page: From the harbor docks to the local grocery store, trucking plays a vital role in daily commerce and shipping in America. Photo by Mike Mitchell/After Image

Bottom: In the 1940s, with the advent of more powerful planes, shipping freight by air became a widespread practice. Perishable goods could be sent to distant markets faster than on trucks or trains. Courtesy, American Truck Historical Society

Below: This 1955 "Diamond T" pulled what must have been the most peculiar of many promotional road shows— "Elsie the Borden's Cow in person and her Famous Barn Boudoir." Courtesy, American Truck Historical Society

in Idaho to a supermarket in New Jersey and still be sold for something less than tax on a bus ticket. But the wheels keep turning, despite more roadblocks and economic pitfalls than most travelers would endure.

The Motor Carrier Act of 1980 is commonly referred to as "deregulation," implying that the trucking industry was left to proceed unfettered by bureaucratic red tape. This is hardly the case. In order to legally haul commercial freight between any or all states, a company or individual still must be licensed by the Interstate Commerce Commission. There are several different kinds of authority but all applicants must show that they are fit, willing, and able to provide beneficial and safe service according to public needs.

Only a few truckers who haul commodities categorized as "exempt" do not need a federal license. Exempt commodities are generally defined as livestock or agricultural and horticultural products in an unprocessed or sometimes semi-processed state. A glance at the exempt list shows the legislative successes and failures of various interest groups. For example, pasteurized and powdered milk is exempt, but sterilized milk in hermetically sealed cans is not. Manure in its natural, dried, or dehydrated state is exempt, but fertilizer is not.

Drivers must also adhere to strict safety regulations. Any truck that operates on public highways—no matter what it is hauling—must comply with federal safety standards administered by the Department of Transportation.

In roadside inspections mandated by the 1984 Motor Carrier Safety Act, trucks are scrutinized for required equipment and accessories. Trained inspectors also check the operating condition of brakes, coupling devices, exhaust systems, fuel systems, lighting, load securement,

steering mechanisms, suspensions, frames, wheels and rims, windshield glazing, and windshield wipers. A truck can be taken out of service for excessive steering wheel play, ineffective wipers, broken or missing leaf springs, and brakes or tires which show too much wear.

Drivers, too, can be taken out of service if they have been on the road too long. Like many workers, truck drivers must punch a time clock, so to speak. Truckers cannot legally get behind the wheel of a truck if they've been on duty (though not necessarily driving) for 15 hours. After 8 hours off duty they can drive for 10 more hours. However, they must be off duty for another 8 consecutive hours before they are allowed back on the road.

Drivers must also keep written records or logbooks noting every hour of every day, including days off. The driver and the driver's employer can be prosecuted for inaccuracies, falsifications, or failure to keep logs as required.

In order to be eligible for an interstate truck driving job, a person must be at least 21 years old, must pass a Department of Transportation (DOT) prescribed physical every 24 months, must also pass a DOT road test, and must take a written exam to demonstrate knowledge of highway rules and regulations.

Off the road, trucking companies are governed by an alphabet soup of federal agencies. The Federal Environmental Protection Agency (EPA) has rules regarding the disposal of used oil, rags, and other materials used in the shop, plus increasingly strict rules regarding fuel storage.

The Occupational Safety and Health Administration (OSHA) has assorted rules covering employee safety. And, of course, there is the Internal Revenue Service. In addition to income tax and social security, the IRS collects a federal use tax levied annually on each heavy truck.

But the tax requirements do not end with the federal government. Interstate as well as intrastate truckers must register with the proper authorities in any

Specialized cabs and trailers are often found in off-road applications. This half-cab model was produced by Fabco, which only produces off-road vehicles. Courtesy, PR Counselors

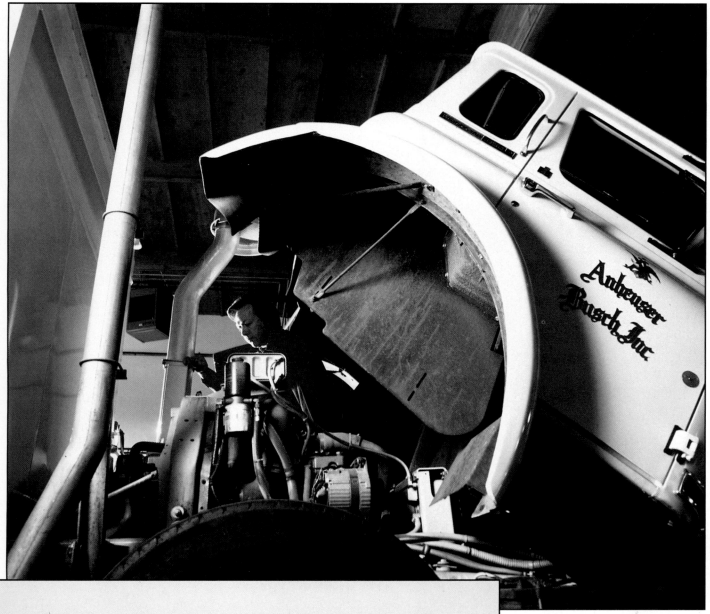

state that they operate in or pass through. They must also pay their "fair share" of fuel taxes, which are used to maintain state roads.

Truckers are also required to keep records of mileage to establish the amount of fuel consumed within each state's borders. Tax rates and reporting requirements vary, but generally truck operators must submit a quarterly report to each state indicating miles traveled, fuel taxes paid, and taxes or credits due.

A few states also charge a weight-distance tax, multiplying the mileage driven within their borders by a tax rate determined by the weight category of the truck.

Individual states may also impose safety regulations, although most state regulations mirror the federal rules.

Left: Interstate truckers are required to take a written exam to demonstrate knowledge of highway rules and regulations. Photo by Kent Knudson/The Photo File

Above: Trailer length limits differ from state to state, which sometimes makes interstate hauling difficult for truckers. Photo by L. Linkhart/The Photo File

Facing page, top: Truck maintenance shops are required to meet Environmental Protection Agency (EPA) guidelines regarding disposal of used motor oil and other materials. Photo by Tom Tracy/The Photo File

Facing page, bottom: Exempt cargo, such as unprocessed agricultural products or livestock, does not require the trucker to possess authority from the Interstate Commerce Commission. Photo by R. Hamilton Smith/After Image

State regulations usually specify limits on size and weight of big trucks, which often creates an expensive barrier for interstate commerce. For example, a trucking company using the popular 53-foot semitrailers can travel on interstates and other roads in Kentucky—as long as the overall length of the combined tractor-trailer is no more than 57 feet, 9 inches. (The Surface Transportation Assistance Act of 1982 set a length limit of 48 feet for semitrailers, with no overall tractor-trailer length limits on interstate and designated highways.)

The trucking company can deliver that same load to Alabama with no problem, since the overall length limit in Alabama is a comfortable 60 feet. But the shortest route from Kentucky to Alabama is through Tennessee. And by state law, 53-foot trailers are prohibited from traveling any highways in Tennessee—interstate or otherwise.

So the trucking company hauling between Kentucky and Alabama has to make one of two choices: it can use a smaller trailer, with less revenue-producing payload, or it can make a wide swing through Missouri, Arkansas, and Mississippi, which will be a costly detour.

While deregulation did not create a free-for-all within the industry, it did open a floodgate of new competition at a

Trucks can be adapted to carry anything, but highway and bridge restrictions limit what and where they can haul. In 1953 Leonard Brothers of Miami, Florida, moved this giant tank with a "push-me pull-you" arrangement. Courtesy, American Truck Historical Society

time when the economy wouldn't allow a leisurely transition. Between 1980 and 1985 the Interstate Commerce Commission (ICC) granted operating authority to 27,000 first-time applicants. Another 59,000 received authority to expand their operations. By the end of 1985 there were more than 33,000 ICC-regulated motor carriers—twice as many as there were in 1979. Most of the new entries were relatively small fleets.

An additional estimated 100,000 owner-operators were also on the road in the mid-'80s, hauling exempt commodities or operating under the authority of other companies. And some 40,000 to 50,000 private fleets carried freight exclusively for parent companies such as a local appliance store, a national supermarket chain, or big oil and chemical companies. This competition alone might have been enough to choke all but the most stalwart participants, but there were other, equally heavy pressures.

The country was shifting from a manufacturing to a service-based economy. And service businesses have little freight to haul. Moreover, imports were on the rise, which meant truckers in Europe and the Far East were moving raw material and parts to production plants while U.S. truckers waited for finished

goods to arrive at a shipping port.

By the mid-1980s the amount of freight moved annually by all modes of transportation had dropped approximately 400 million tons below the amount of freight moved in the late 1970s. The trucking industry had managed to hold its own against its biggest competitor, the railroads. Yet twice as many motor carriers were slugging it out for the same-sized piece of a shrunken pie.

The insurance industry also dealt a damaging blow. During the late 1970s and early 1980s, interest rates were high and insurance rates were low. But when interest rates dropped reinsurance became expensive and truckers' losses started to climb.

In 1984 the loss ratio for commercial auto liability insurance was 112 percent, which meant that insurance companies were paying $1.12 in claims for every $1 collected. Such deficit spending prompted some insurance companies to retreat, leaving uninsured trucking companies in their wake. Other insurers made some overnight adjustments, increasing rates by as much as 500 percent. The effects of deregulation and a changing economic base were felt throughout the entire industry, even

by the most established trucking companies.

With gross revenues of more than $500 million, McLean Trucking Company would have been the eighth largest carrier in the country. Yet in January of 1986, when the standings were still being tallied, McLean announced it was bankrupt. In one fell swoop 3,800 tractors and 9,600 trailers were parked. Some 9,800 workers in 45 states were looking for work.

McLean was hardly alone. Between 1980 and 1986 an estimated 3,500 regulated carriers went out of business. In 1987 alone more than 1,500 carriers—roughly 2 out of 10—closed their doors. Most were small companies, but some familiar names disappeared, such as Spector Red Ball, Branch Motor Express, Gordons Transport, and Mason & Dixon.

Other companies acquired new parentage. Coastal Tank Lines, the twelfth-largest for-hire bulk carrier, was acquired by Chemical Leaman Tank Lines, the number two for-hire tankline. And Associated Truck Lines, Graves Truck Line, and Garrett Freightlines combined to become ANR Freight System. Roadway Services, parent of the giant less-than-truckload (LTL) carrier

Roadway Express, acquired Spartan Express, Roberts Express, and Nationwide Carriers.

Not all buyers were trucking companies, however. Since 1983 the big services conglomerate, IU International, has unsuccessfully attempted a merger between two old-line trucking companies, Pacific Intermountain Express (P-I-E) and Ryder Truck Lines. (Although originally founded by the same man, Ryder Truck Lines is a separate company from Ryder System.) In 1986 the floundering P-I-E Nationwide was acquired by a Chicago investment group headed by a former department store executive.

Railroads also got into the act. North American Van Lines, one of the country's biggest household moving and storage companies, was acquired by Norfolk Southern Railroad. And Overnite Transportation, another motor carrier company long envied for its operating efficiency and profitability, was snapped up by Union Pacific Railroad—at a premium price.

Amid the chaos, an industry once described as "staid" emerged as a big, powerful business with a knack for change. The 1.2 million medium- and heavy-duty trucks operating today hard-

Right: With importation on the rise, U.S. truckers are carrying increasingly more freight unloaded at ports on both coasts, coming in direct competition— or working directly with—the railroads. Photo by John Lund/The Photo File

Below: More than half of the freight-carrying trucks on the road are operated by private carriers to haul their own goods. Since deregulation, such carriers may also haul freight for others. Photo by Tom Tracy/After Image

ly compare with the 176 million total vehicles on the road. Yet the workhorses on wheels haul more than two billion tons of freight each year, or roughly 12 times the combined weight of every car, bus, pickup, and truck in the United States.

The American trucking industry employs an estimated 7.1 million people. Including spouses and children, that means some 31 million people depend on the industry's $150 billion annual payroll.

Of course, this figure does not include workers who rely on trucking for their non-trucking businesses. The stockboy at the supermarket, for example, could not stock the shelves if trucks did not deliver the goods. The sales manager in Connecticut would not *absolutely, positively* get his package to Boise, Idaho, the next morning if companies such as Federal Express did not have a well-orchestrated distribution network of airplanes and trucks. Like other industries, trucking has taken the high-

Above: Private carriers, hauling solely for their own companies, tend to worry more about operating costs than competition from other trucking companies. Photo by Tom Tracy/The Photo File

Left: Some large truck lines, like North American Van Lines, have been bought up by the railroads. Photo by L. Linlkhart/The Photo File

The Gemini space capsule got a different kind of boost in 1965 from this 1960 Chevy tractor on its way to Cape Canaveral. Courtesy, PR Counselors

tech road, using computers for customer service, truck maintenance, and even in the cab as the trucker's companion. Today many trucks are equipped with computerized trip recorders that measure speed, shift patterns, stops, idle time, and braking, which increase driver efficiency and safety.

In maintenance shops, computers are rapidly becoming part of the landscape. Mechanics are learning to operate keyboards with the same ease they turn wrenches. By tapping a few numbers they instantly know what work was done on a specific truck, the last time it was in the shop, and what work should be done this time through the service bay. The objective

is preventive maintenance.

In most trucking company offices, computers handle the time-consuming customer service tasks. If shippers want to know how much it will cost to transport 600 pounds of bicycle chains from Mississippi to West Virginia, the clerk simply dials a special number offered by companies like Carolina Freight. A computer called "Sally" will answer. Carolina Freight's mainframe computer can also help a customer who wants information about freight movements or any number of special reports. And if the company wants to know where any shipment is and when it will be delivered, Carolina's computers can tell customers what terminal a carton last

passed through and when. All has been dutifully recorded with bar-coded labels and laser scanners.

But if technology is rampant, ingenuity still prevails among truckers who have always had a knack for fine-tuning. Shortly after the Surface Transportation Assistance Act of 1982 mandated 48-foot minimums for semi-trailers, Dart Transit Company began designing 53-footers. Obviously a bigger trailer could carry more freight, but loading was another issue.

Door frames had to be beefed up to support walls and ceiling, but the big door frames got in the way. So Dart narrowed the frame on one side and made it wider on the other. Now there is only one cumbersome corner to maneuver around, but structural integrity is maintained.

Watching lift truck operators load tall stacks of cereal boxes, Dart executives noticed that the lightweight cargo tended to sway at the top. If a stack being loaded hit one already in place, progress stopped until another dock worker came to the rescue.

Dart solved the problem by raising the center of its trailer floors a fraction of an inch. So now when the cereal boxes lean, they lean toward the smooth trailer wall. And one big boy, no doubt fueled with cornflakes, can load one very big trailer all by himself.

Many miles of red tape had to be cut in order to transport this 107-ton electro-magnet from Illinois to California for Stanford University's linear accelerator. The 1979 trip marked the heaviest load ever carried on U.S. highways up to that time, and a Kenworth conventional did the work. Courtesy, PAC-CAR, Inc.

The Business of Trucking

4

S omewhere in the dusty corners of a marketing executive's library is a neatly drawn pie chart labeled "The Trucking Industry." Undoubtedly, the pie has been divided into four slices: for-hire, private, owner-operator, and leasing— four tidy segments into which were fitted some 1.2 million medium- and heavy-duty trucks.

The chart is not entirely obsolete. The categories still exist. But in the tumultuous decade following deregulation in the early 1980s, the pie was subdivided and reworked to create a patchwork industry of some 180,000 participants with businesses as diverse as the sizes of their repair shops.

When most people think of the business of trucking, they think of for-hire trucking—companies that move freight for a living. And anyone who has ever counted logos on the highway most certainly thinks of giants like Yellow Freight Systems, Consolidated Freightways (CF), and Roadway Express.

Through years of hauling less-than-truckload (LTL) shipments over networks that span the United States and Canada, these three giants have earned their stripes as trucking's "big three." Collectively, they own more than 30,000 tractors and 80,000 trailers. They also account for

Above: Yellow Freight Systems is a prominent sight on the nation's highways, as it is one of the largest for-hire trucking companies in operation. Photo by Sam Sargent/The Photo File

Facing page: Trucking has evolved into a giant industry, with independent truckers, small fleets, and giant fleets combining to fill virtually any shipping need. Photo by Tom Tracy/The Photo File

Facing page: United Parcel Service has earned a reputation for being one of the best-operated motor carriers in the world. Photo by David Pollock

Below: Driving for less-than-truckload carriers offers the alternative to operating independently. Photo by George Olson/The Photo File

about one-fifth of the revenues earned annually by the nation's 50 biggest for-hire carriers.

But the big three hardly stand alone. In terms of revenues United Parcel Service (UPS) has long been the biggest motor carrier of all, outranking Yellow, CF, and Roadway combined. Known best for its little brown vans that comb cities and even rural areas in their daily small-package rounds, UPS feeds those little vans a steady stream of cargo shuttled from terminal to terminal by some

6,000 big rigs and a fleet of aircraft.

UPS also has a well-earned reputation for being one of the best-operated fleets in the world. Its drivers are still neatly uniformed—a throwback to the 1950s when most fleet drivers were provided with uniforms. The company promotes almost entirely from within, making it possible for today's dockworker to become tomorrow's UPS president. It spends nearly $3 million annually on washing its trucks. Every truck, every night.

On the other side of the big three are other LTL carriers such as Overnite

Transportation, Carolina Freight, Preston Trucking, Holland Motor Express, and A-P-A Transport. Their revenues place them among the 50 largest trucking companies in the country. Their fleets, ranging in size from several hundred to several thousand trucks, rate top honors in just about anybody's book. Although their operations are similar, each company is a unique business.

Overnite Transportation, for instance, built a thriving business by keeping operating costs well below most of its competitors—performing so well that when Union Pacific decided to expand its business using trucks, it bought the trucking company at a premium price.

Carolina Freight took the high-tech bull by the horns early in the 1980s, becoming one of the first trucking companies to use computers in its operation. Computers made it possible for Carolina Freight to trace almost instantly a customer shipment, tracking its present location and where it will be in five hours. And Preston Trucking has a penchant for both productivity and a family-type management style with minimal supervision and lots of participation among its 5,000 employees.

As many LTL companies moved up the big carrier roster in the 1980s, some relatively unknown companies emerged victorious in another for-hire segment—truckload carriage.

In the late 1970s few people in the trucking industry had heard of Johnnie Bryan Hunt or his fleet of five trucks. By the mid-1980s J.B. Hunt Transport's annual revenues had quadrupled, its income multiplied roughly ten times, and its fleet increased to more than 6,000 tractors and trailers. Soon everyone knew of J.B. Hunt and knew there were a lot more like him.

Hunt slipped unheralded into the trucking industry fast track along with companies like Builders Transport, M.S. Carriers, CRST, Dart Transit, and Schneider National Transport—all building businesses on their ability to get a shipper's trailerload of freight anywhere in the country at a highly competitive price.

These truckload super-carriers also shared some common characteristics: they employed non-union drivers and closely supervised them in order to control costs. Typically, in the late 1980s they paid their drivers 18 to 22 cents per mile, compared to the 37 cents per mile paid union drivers. They also were very selective about where they offered low rates to shippers; they were careful not to compete, for example, where a rail corridor existed and double-stack freight rates were low.

At the same time, other fledgling carriers were carving out niches in the industry. PST Incorporated began operation well after deregulation, at a time when farmers and their farm equipment suppliers were feeling an equally rocky economic pinch. Still, PST saw a need for heavy equipment haulers that could offer manufacturers trailers and services tailored specifically to their needs. In three years the new company's earnings quadrupled and its fleet of 500 tractors was turning a tidy profit.

Perhaps more typical of little companies growing up in the 1980s was the one started by Pam and Will Maas, who in the late 1970s quit their corporate jobs to go trucking. With a small down payment on a truck and offices anywhere they could find a telephone booth, the couple began hauling meat from Chicago to Texas. By 1987 they had over 40 trucks, a thriving business hauling meat and deli items, and a bona fide headquarters with their name on the door.

But the telephone booth office is still occupied by many others. For despite early speculation that a deregulated industry's cutthroat competition would put the independent owner-operators on the endangered species list, thousands of these companies are still trucking. Many companies with interstate authority still run under their own company banner. Most, however, contract their services to other companies to haul everything from steel beams to aluminum cans, apples to applesauce, or museum pieces to household goods.

Whatever the cargo, it takes a special breed of man or woman to be an owner-operator. They are, in many ways, the industry's true entrepreneurs—one per-

Above: Truckload carriers control costs carefully and select target areas they will service. Photo by John Lund/The Photo File

Right: Owner-operators are free to choose with what and how they outfit their rigs, sometimes bringing the driver special recognition. Photo by Susan Davison

son, one truck businesses, where the president is also the Corporate Executive Officer as well as the driver, mechanic, accountant, safety supervisor, and marketing manager. Owner-operators include people like Bill Means, a 25-year veteran who has driven more than a million miles without an accident. Or Robert Swisher, who, in nine years of independent trucking, has hauled everything from electronic equipment to boats. Or Charlene and Willard Davis, who travel and work side by side, hauling general freight and produce coast to coast. Or Brad Hille, a trucker who enjoys teaching teenage drivers how to share the roads with big trucks.

As owner-operators survived and thrived, so did the private fleet sector of the industry. The history of private carriage can be traced back to the early days of trucking. When the industry became regulated, private fleets were severely restricted as to what they could haul with their own trucks. If, for instance, a manufacturer transported its own goods from a plant in Mississippi to a warehouse in Indiana, it could either

Above: Deregulation has opened up virtually all types of freight hauling for the trucking companies. Photo by Tom Tracy/The Photo File

Left: Many companies have found that the only practical way to ship their cargo is through the operation of their own private truck fleet. Photo by Tom Tracy/The Photo File

Above all, deregulation has put tremendous cost pressures on the trucking industry. Many major fleets were forced out of business. Photo by Phillip Wallick/The Photo File

pick up a load of exempt commodities or go home empty.

Despite the inefficiencies many companies felt it was still better than the for-hire alternative. For one thing, rates were high in those days (or higher than shippers thought they should have been). More importantly, manufacturers and retailers did not want a trucking company's schedule to determine when their shipments would be picked up and delivered. They wanted to determine that themselves.

Over the years the private carrier industry has grown to staggering proportions. Names such as Safeway, Frito-Lay, and Burlington shared the highways with Roadway Express and Yellow Freight.

Companies such as Conoco, Texaco, and Union Carbide, whose needs were so specialized, had little choice but to operate their own fleets. They joined thousands of furniture stores, wholesale florists, food distributors, and other businesses operating small fleets of trucks to meet delivery needs of their local and regional customers.

Together, companies technically "not in the trucking business" came to control the majority of medium- and heavy-duty trucks in operation. And after deregulation they prospered as never before.

For-hire rates came down, service improved, and private fleets had several options to pursue. Many companies obtained limited or full interstate operating authority so they could fill empty backhauls with somebody else's paying freight. More new companies were added to the for-hire trucking industry roster as manufacturers formed trucking subsidiaries as profit centers, under such banners as Howard Industries, a manufacturer of electrical transformers; Ghent Manufacturing, a maker of blackboards and flipcharts; and Bendix and Borg-Warner, both manufacturers of automotive and truck components.

Other private carriers chose to concentrate on the most service-sensitive portions of their fleet operations, handing off the rest to for-hire carriers. Still others took a slightly different course—negotiating freight hauling contracts with for-hire carriers.

Before deregulation, there was a clear distinction between "common" and "contract" carriers. A common carrier was required to haul freight for any customer—at published rates. A contract carrier could only haul freight under contract for a limited number of companies. The Motor Carrier Act of 1980, however, gave shippers and carriers significantly more freedom to do business under contracts. A common carrier could also be a contract carrier serving unlimited customers under separate agreements. Those agreements could be negotiated with few regulatory limitations, and the terms were confidential.

That confidentiality was especially appealing in a highly competitive environment, where it was advantageous for shippers and carriers not to let competitors know costs of distribution and carrier prices. Shippers also benefited from handing over all fleet responsibilities—including trucks, drivers, maintenance, and a myriad of administrative tasks required to run a trucking company. Additionally, as part of the contract, shippers still had a tight control over schedules.

Other companies that needed their own fleets but did not want the headaches of maintaining trucks turned to leasing. In one package they could get a truck and all necessary maintenance. If, for some reason, that truck broke down, all they had to do was call for a replacement.

For years the growth in the truck leasing industry paralleled that of private carriage. And when deregulation threatened to shrink leasing's customer base, full-service truck leasing rose to the challenge.

Truck leasing created huge networks of transportation services. Their service menus expanded from vehicles and maintenance to include permits, licensing, fuel tax reporting, drivers, freight brokerage, and even contract carriage—thinly disguised under the term of "dedicated carriage." Essentially truck leasing began to look less like an alternative to traditional ownership and more like an alternative to running a fleet. It was a big, expensive order which, coupled with fiercely competitive leasing rates, created a situation not unlike the fluctuating state of key players in the rest of the industry. Some leasing companies closed their doors. Many more merged or were acquired by others. It was a rocky time for small companies and for big operations like Saunders, which sold its truck leasing division to Ryder System, and Leaseway, which off its truck leasing operations in an acquisition by Hertz Penske.

At the same time old names became more visible and new names appeared. Many years before the battle began, local and regional independent leasing companies had banded together to offer their customers nationwide service. In the 1980s NationaLease and Amtralease moved into position as full-service networks aiming to meet the big boys head on. It gave any small, local leasing company the ability to bid on the business of a national shipper, confident that if a truck should break down 3,000 miles away, a member of the fraternity of lessors would get it quickly back into service at a reasonable cost.

Attracted by the boom in leasing and worried by declining sales, truck dealers—the traditional truck retailers—threw their hats into the full-service leasing ring. Navistar International dealers formed their own Idealease truck rental and leasing network. Paccar set up PacLease, franchising Kenworth and Peterbilt dealers. Ford and Mack also launched truck leasing systems. Volvo GM started Integral Truck Leasing. All this activity put a lot of new kids on an already crowded block. Yet full-service leasing revenues grew at a compound rate of almost 15 percent, and the industry expects continued growth for the rest of the decade.

Conservative estimates set the number of trucks owned by full service leasing companies at more than 800,000. With trailers, the leasing fleet numbered well over a million. Approximately one out of every three trucks built was purchased by leasing companies.

With growth of the industry, there emerged a giant of massive proportions. From a solid footing as the country's biggest truck rental and leasing company, Ryder System marched resolutely into transportation—perhaps signaling the direction of the rest of the industry in the next decade.

Like many companies, Ryder pursued any available opportunity. Through acquisition and expansion it has become the country's largest transporter of new cars and trucks. Setting its sights on contract carriage, the company's dedicated services division uses sophisticated computer modeling techniques to map out logistical plans for everything from home delivery of furniture and appliances to warehousing and transportation of computers. In the truck leasing and rental segment of the industry, Ryder Truck Rental's fleet of approximately 120,000 trucks, tractors, and trailers put it far ahead of its competitors and far ahead of even the biggest for-hire fleets. Add operations in Canada and the United Kingdom and Ryder ranks as the largest full-service truck leasing and rental company in the world.

As pies go, nobody had a bigger slice.

Above: Truck leasing has created huge networks of transportation services, including vehicle maintenance and freight brokerage. Photo by Tom Tracy/The Photo File

Below: In the race for customers in the truck leasing business, most truck manufacturers have offered some type of leasing program. Photo by Sam Sargent/The Photo File

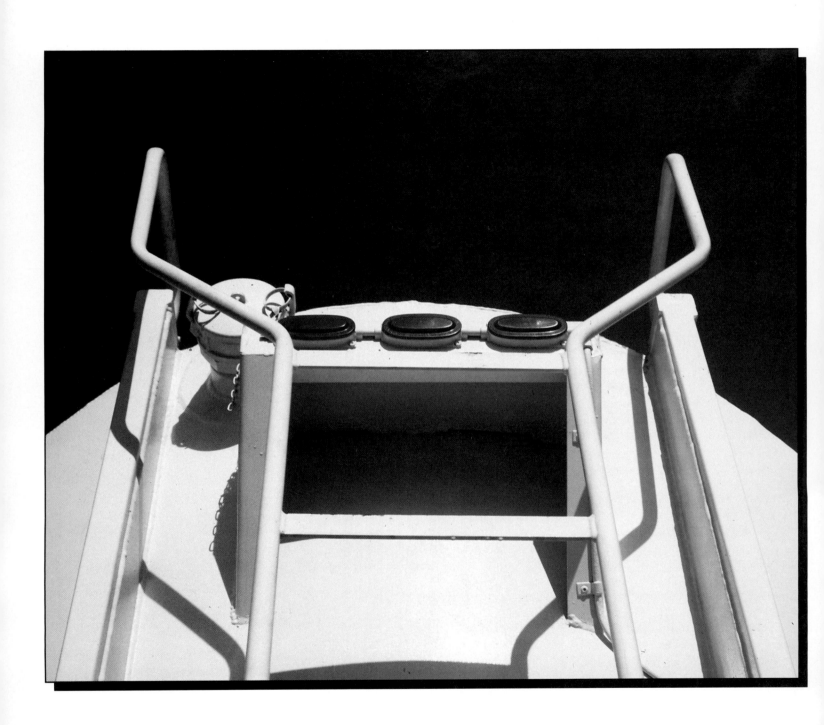

Driving for Safety

5

*P*robably in no other decade since trucking came of age was more emphasis placed on safety than in the 1980s. Big and small fleets alike adopted new safety programs or reemphasized existing safety efforts, making safety a buzzword of the industry.

Not that safety had never been important. The industry has always been concerned with safety on the highways. In fact, many of the most prosperous companies of the 1940s and 1950s were recognized for their safety programs, which rewarded individual driver achievement in the area of courtesy as well as safety. Both Yellow Freight Systems and Consolidated Freightways, for example, equipped their drivers with "courtesy cards" —prepaid postcards that could be mailed back to the safety supervisor by motorists who had been aided by a company driver during a roadside emergency.

The industry's safety campaign of the 1980s, however, was the result of several pressures: soaring insurance rates in which premiums more than quintupled—if coverage could be obtained at all; federal and state legislation and rulemaking aimed at tightening the reins on trucking; increased lobbying by several organizations critical of trucking, chiefly the American Automobile Association; and misleading media coverage of accidents which applied the term "truck" to virtually any vehicle that was not an automobile.

Media coverage, in particular, often reinforced an already growing attitude among motorists that trucks were dangerous and truckers were reckless. It was not unusual, for example, to see a front-page ban-

Above: Safety has become especially important in light of soaring insurance rates and federal and state legislation aimed at tightening the reins on trucking. Photo by Kent Knudson/The Photo File

Facing page: Safety on and off the highway has never been a matter of hindsight for the trucking industry, which boasts an exemplary record. Photo by Mark E. Gibson

Michigan inspector Clair McWhorter examined the rig of Charles Parkins in Edmore, Michigan, in 1948. The instrument shown is a fire extinguisher. Courtesy, American Truck Historical Society

light trucks, pickups, and even family vans. Consequently, there was no way, even on a national level, to determine accident rates involving heavy trucks. Authorities argued vigorously over the meaning of the data.

Unfortunately, little has changed since a 1968 Department of Transporation report found truck accident data so confusing and unreliable that it could not be used to determine whether the situation was improving or worsening from one year to the next. Statistics on accidents involving heavy trucks were based on reports submitted by carriers to the Office of Motor Carriers (OMC), formerly the Bureau of Motor Carrier Safety (BMCS), or on Fatal Accident Reporting Systems (FARS data compiled by the National Highway Traffic Safety Administration).

Officials admitted that both data bases had serious shortcomings. The BMCS' reports did not cover intrastate carriers and also suffered from underreporting by private interstate carriers. FARS data, although more accurate, was limited to fatal accidents and did not provide specific information on vehicle configuration, cargo, operating conditions, or other environmental factors.

Taken at face value the FARS figures were as disturbing as they were deceptive. They showed that heavy trucks, while comprising only one percent of the vehicle population, were involved in nearly 10 percent of fatal highway accidents. This alarming statistic was also misleading; it did not take into consideration that the average truck annually covers more than 10 times the mileage of the average car.

Exposure factors also were missing from the BMCS' "Accidents of Motor Carriers of Property" report—a compilation from thousands of accident reports filed annually. For many years the Interstate Commerce Commission (ICC) compiled overall mileage statistics on reporting carriers which were then

ner headline proclaim:
"Trucker Slams Bus: 24 Killed, Scores Injured" —only to discover the so-called trucker was a teenager driving a pickup. Unfortunately the casual reader often never got beyond the grim headline which suggested that the accident was caused by a professional big-rig driver.

Such wrong impressions are often compounded by the fact that when a big truck is involved in an accident—be it the fault of the truck operator or not—it is most likely to be a sensational accident. Even if everyone involved walks away unhurt, a jackknifed or overturned tractor-trailer can jam a freeway for hours, frustrating motorists and increasing anti-truck sentiments.

When trucking was deregulated in 1980, industry leaders became concerned about the law's effect on highway safety: Would heavy truck accidents increase at a dramatic pace? Were twin trailers as safe as tractor-trailer combinations? Were drivers the cause of most accidents, was faulty equipment the culprit, or was it a combination of both?

Truck-involved accident statistics did little to clarify the situation. Data compiled by individual states often combined tractor-trailer figures with those of

compared with accident data to obtain a "per million mile" accident rate. But this data likewise became unavailable when the ICC dumped its mileage figure reporting requirements.

Equally unreliable were government accident figures based on exposure, size of vehicle, type of carrier, and other factors, using information obtained during annual safety audits. Because the companies targeted for auditing were usually chosen because of their poor safety records, it was not surprising to find an unusually high accident rate among those groups.

Furthermore, accident figures were open to various interpretations which caused controversy within the industry as well. In 1987 the American Trucking Associations (ATA) pointed to an 18 percent rise in truck accidents between 1983 and 1984 to prove its point that deregulation had a negative impact on safety. The National Private Truck Council (NPTC), which favors further decontrol of the industry, used the same data to demonstrate an improvement in roadway safety.

Neither group was entirely incorrect. ATA's conclusion was based on the number of reported accidents of $2,000 or more damage, which increased from 31,628 in 1983 to 36,633 in 1987. PTCA, however, noted that more minor accidents had crossed the $2,000 threshold as result of inflation—and that both the number of trucks and miles traveled had increased during the same time period. NPTC insisted that accident frequency rates could not be shown to have increased but were actually on the decline. Moreover, argued PTCA, truck accidents only slightly exceeded the pre-deregulation figure of 35,541, and truck accident fatalities actually declined.

This post-deregulation highway safety controversy prompted Congress to move into an area previously deemed to be outside its national purview. Traditionally, the federal government left regulation and licensing of commercial drivers to state governments. But spurred by increased trucking industry pressure for more federal control in the safety arena—especially in the area of driver licensing—Congress passed the Commercial Vehicle Safety Act, which became effective on July 1, 1987. The law mandated extensive and far-reaching rules to regulate truck drivers on a nationwide scale.

The safety act had been passed in part to curb the practice of duplicate licensing, which could be easily done in several states. Drivers often obtained several licenses from different states so they could allocate current driving violations to the license with the fewest black marks. Duplicate licensing enabled drivers who had been suspended on one license to use another license from a different state and continue to legally drive.

Because licensing requirements varied from state to state, duplicate licensing was fairly easy and became a common practice among truckers. In addition, there was little standardization among states for licensing of big-rig drivers. Only 32 states required truck drivers to be road tested in a commercial vehicle. In some states a driver could

To promote public confidence in trucking in 1947, states and companies sponsored public safety inspections. The tractor pulling this car carrier is a 1941 model. Courtesy, American Truck Historical Society

Above: Government statistics regarding accidents based on truck size and other factors obtained in annual safety audits often proved misleading, due to the records of the individual companies surveyed. Photo by Mark E. Gibson

Top: Tracking driving records of individual drivers has been hampered by multiple licenses that some truckers obtained. Photo by Roger Tully/ After Image

qualify to drive an 18-wheeler simply by passing a road test in a car.

This lax commercial licensing proved a nightmare for carriers trying to track the safety records of individual drivers. With little communication or cooperation among state agencies, duplicate licenses were an effective way for drivers to get around deserved penalties.

The federal safety act, however, made

duplicate licensing punishable by fines up to $2,500 or jail terms. In certain cases a criminal violation might be involved, leading to fines up to $5,000 and a prison term up to 90 days. The same penalties applied to fleets that knowingly hired multi-licensed drivers. The legislation also included provisions for standardized licensing and testing procedures established by the Department of Transportation. All states are required to comply with this new amendment by 1992 (California rushed its program into effect on January 1, 1989).

Significantly, within the first six months of the law's enactment, more than 30,000 multiple licenses were voluntarily surrendered.

In addition to the single-license law, the safety act passed other rules which gave trucking management more control over drivers. One rule requires drivers to report all moving violations to employers within 30 days, including any infractions while driving a personal vehicle. Home-state authorities must be notified of any violations in other states and employers must be notified of license suspensions, revocations, cancel-

Left: Truck drivers had better stay on the wagon while driving, as the Commercial Vehicle Safety Act calls for permanent license suspension on second conviction of driving while intoxicated. Photo by George Olson/The Photo File

Below: Truck drivers, whether specialized, local haulers, or cross-country drivers, are prohibited from operating with multiple licenses from different states under the Commercial Vehicle Safety Act. Photo by Pete Saloutos/After Image

This fleet photo from the 1920s features in front, from left to right: 1918 White with two newer Whites, 1922 International Harvester, 1920 Mack. In the rear, from left: 1909 White, 1916 Buick, 1917 or 1918 Jumbo. Courtesy, American Truck Historical Society

lations or other disqualifications. In addition, drivers will be prohibited from driving a commercial truck if their personal license has been suspended or revoked because of violations committed while off duty. This commercial suspension lasts as long as the personal one.

The safety act also took a hard line on drivers convicted of operating while under the influence of alcohol or other drugs, leaving the scene of an accident, or being involved in two or more serious traffic violations within three years. If convicted a driver would be disqualified for one year for a first offense or permanently disqualified upon a second conviction. And if a driver is convicted of using a vehicle during the commission of a felony or possessing, manufacturing, or selling controlled or illegal substances, his license would be suspended for life.

The fact that most federal truck safety regulations focus on the driver is no fluke. During the 1980s a majority of the regulations enacted had been originally lobbied for by the major trucking organizations. Their aim was to save lives, gain better control of drivers, project a better image—especially among lawmakers—and reduce soaring insurance premiums.

Now the industry must contend with a new problem—a full blown driver

shortage that is expected to worsen in the coming years. By the turn of the century, according to Department of Labor statistics, the demand for drivers is expected to reach as high as 600,000. And some industry and government experts predict that as early as 1992 the number of available drivers could decrease by 30 percent.

Some 10 percent of that decrease is attributed to the stricter federal driver regulations, qualifications, and licensing, plus enforcement of those rules by means of stepped-up roadside safety checks and carrier safety auditing. Retirement will account for another 10 percent decrease in drivers. The loss of experienced, professional drivers is expected to hit the industry hard, especially since the number of qualified new drivers who would take their place is expected to decline dramatically.

One of the more novel solutions to the driver shortage is one suggested by the Interstate Carriers Conference. The conference has proposed an on the job driver training program for 18- to 20-year olds. The program, of course, would require approval by the Federal Highway Administration since it calls for lowering the federal minimum age of 21.

The idea of teens rumbling down the road in 40-ton rigs has raised more than a few eyebrows. But the program would include rigorous training and an extensive copilot apprenticeship. In addition, a driver-trainer would be in the cab with the trainee for at least the first 65,000 miles or one year, with the youngster operating the vehicle between 35 and 45 percent of the time.

In the meantime, a concerned trucking industry has united and begun to actively campaign for a set of training standards and certification for driver training schools. According to the National Transportation Safety Board many graduates of truck driver-training schools are still not prepared to handle a heavy-duty truck. In an effort to standardize instruction and evaluation of driver-training schools, industry leaders established the Professional Truck Driver Institute of America (PTDIA). Provided with both manpower and money from fleets, truck manufacturers, and other industry organizations, the institute established voluntary minimum driver-training standards and developed an inspection program that would result in accreditation of driver-training school curricula that met rigorous standards.

Truck leasing companies have already initiated programs focused on driver training. Many provide their private carrier customers with advice on compliance with new federal and state safety

According to the National Institute on Drug Abuse (NIDA), another 10 million people occasionally use cocaine and amphetamines. And thousands of Americans drink alcohol to excess.

To combat the substance abuse problem, many trucking companies have begun to implement pre-employment drug screening programs to identify habitual substance abuse. Motor carriers, in particular, have been in the forefront in intiating drug and alcohol screening programs. As early as 1984 the motor carriers reached an agreement with the Teamsters National Grievance Committee which would allow employers to make mandatory blood and urine screening a part of the

Long trailers make ideal billboards. The Transport Motor Express put its whole route map on a Fruehauf trailer, which was pulled by a 1949 22 series White. Even though the truck is equipped with extended mirrors on both sides, the mirrors are quite small. Courtesy, American Truck Historical Society

regulations. Nationwide networks of safety managers are made available to fleets providing driver testing and screening, safety meetings, and driver performance monitoring.

But improving driver safety and efficiency through better training programs is just one of the many steps the industry is taking to make America's highways safer. Like the rest of the country, the industry now faces an increasing problem of drug and alcohol abuse among its drivers.

It is estimated that about one in 10 Americans smoke marijuana on a regular basis—a total of more than 20 million people from all walks of life.

required biannual driver physicals.

The motor carrier screening programs initiated in the 1980s covered three basic categories: (1) screening of potential employees, (2) regular screening of employees as part of required physical exams, and (3) cause-related testing either after an accident or when a worker showed signs of substance abuse. Random screening, once confined to high-security industries, remained rare among trucking companies but is slowly gaining acceptance among trucking company officials, who seek to lower liability exposure and boost overall performance.

The American Trucking Associations (ATA), for example, recommends a pre-employment drug and alcohol screening program along with "reasonable" cause testing. The ATA also supports voluntary random tests and post-accident testing, limited to fatal accidents and accidents causing more than $50,000 in property damage.

The ATA, while endorsing most aspects of drug testing proposals, has stopped short of supporting mandatory random roadside testing. And independent trucker organizations and the Teamsters are opposed to random testing, citing the fallibility of such tests and their inability to truly address the nationwide drug problem.

No industry official, however, disputes the bottom line—that drug screening of some sort is certain to become routine in the trucking industry. And there is also no arguing the fact that drugs adversely affect driving ability.

Marijuana, for example, reduces reaction time almost to the same extent as alcohol. Cocaine and other stimulants often give users a feeling of power and mastery behind the wheel, encouraging the driver to speed up—along with his heart rate—and take unnecessary risks. Even over-the-counter or prescription medications can cause driver impairment when improperly used.

The Federal Highway Administration in 1988 put into effect a rule disqualifying both interstate and intrastate commercial vehicle drivers found to have an alcohol concentration of 0.04 percent, measured in either blood or breath. First-time violators are subject to a one-year disqualification. A second violation of the proposed 0.04 percent standard results in lifetime disqualification. Furthermore, a driver found to have *any* trace of alcohol in the bloodstream will be barred from driving for 24 hours.

"While the vast majority of America's commercial drivers avoid alcohol use when working, we cannot and will not tolerate those few operators who ignore common sense and endanger themselves and others on the highway by drinking and driving," said then-Secretary of Transportation James Burnley. Burnley admitted that the industry's new standard "is significantly below" the 0.10 percent alcohol level required in most states.

The 0.04 percent blood alcohol level means that a couple of beers could end a professional truck driver's career. Yet, said Burnley, "The stricter standard of

Mobile radio was an important post-war development in local deliveries. Turnaround time was cut, a traffic manager's efficiency was increased, and it was a vital safety-oriented tool. Courtesy, American Truck Historical Society

0.04 [percent] for truck and bus operators is proper considering the potential risk to life, limb and property posed by these larger vehicles should there be an accident."

But the industry's standard is not tough enough, according to the National Transportation Safety Board (NTSB), which is arguing for even stricter standards—zero tolerance. NTSB Chairman James Burnett said disqualification at 0.04 percent was much too lenient. Burnett believes that a truck or bus driver's permit should be yanked if any trace of alcohol is detected.

The industry's attempt to alleviate alcohol and drug abuse among its drivers is just another example of its dedication to making America's highways safer for everyone.

Safety has also been increased by the introduction of improved technology and equipment. Safer drivers are alert, efficient, and, of course, comfortable. Drivers now benefit from improved truck suspension systems, tilt steering wheels, and power steering which relieve arm and back strain. Better heating, defrosting, air conditioning, and thicker-insulated cabs make for a comfortable ride and a

contented driver. Truckers who run long hauls now have customized sleepers, cozy homes away from home.

The introduction of motorized or cable mirrors on the passenger side of cabs increased the driver's field of vision and dramatically reduced blind side and backing accidents. Brightly illuminated signals mounted midway down the lengths of semitrailers at eye level warn motorists of wide turns. Convex mirrors, some with built-in heating elements—further increase trucker visibility. The ultimate in advanced technology may be the closed-circuit TV mounted on the rig to scan blind spots; however, its high cost has precluded a buying stampede.

The installation of computerized trip recorders was initially viewed by a few drivers as the proverbial Big Brother. However, these black boxes have increased driver safety while improving fuel economy and lowering maintenance costs. Trip recorders enable drivers to handle their vehicles better, reduce idling time and speeding, as well as accidents. On-board computers also reduce illegal runs in which drivers may be forced to drive extensive distances in limited time frames.

Increasingly concerned about the safety of heavy-duty trucks on crowded freeways and highways, the industry has focused on making big rigs more conspicuous to motorists, day or night, to prevent fatal underride accidents. "We just want to make trailers so obvious they [motorists] must see them," said an insurance company representative. The use of highly reflective tape, applied like running stripes along the sides and backs of trailers, is another simple yet inventive way of creating safer co-existence between trucker and motorist.

The introduction of these safety measures was prompted by research showing that tractor-semitrailers traveling at night on rural non-interstate highways have the greatest statistical chance of being involved in fatal accidents. A University of Michigan survey of approximately 25,000 fatal truck accidents occurring between 1980 and 1984 showed that truck-trailers involved in accidents had an 8.6 fatality rate for rural non-interstate roads and only a 2.9 fatality rate for rural interstates, per 100

million miles traveled.

The chances of an accident occurring increase at night. Research also indicates that a high incidence of fatal truck accidents occur at dawn—so many, in fact, that it became known as the "dawn phenomenon."

Surprisingly, statistics show only 14.4 percent of the drivers involved in early morning accidents had been at the wheel for six or more hours, compared with 27.5 percent of accidents overall and 39.1 percent of accidents occurring at dusk. The discrepancy has prompted further study into the dawn phenomenon.

Not all safety measures were readily accepted, however. The passage of the front-brake law, effective February 26, 1987, created a great deal of controversy within the industry. The front brakes of as many as 200,000 trucks were either missing or inoperable because their owners were convinced that front brakes caused jackknifing in emergency stopping situations.

Experience proved otherwise. Tests and truck accident records kept in Cali-

In 1944 Kenworth became a division of the Pacific Car and Foundry Company. Manufactured on the West Coast, many of Kenworth's trucks were used in logging applications, as was this model 588 in 1948. Courtesy, PACCAR, Inc.

Splash and spray caused by big rigs has been a problem eluding solution. Flaps and skirts offer some help, but truck aerodynamics appear to be the best answer. Photo by L. Linkhart/ The Photo File

fornia, where front brakes had been required since 1982, showed that drivers handled their vehicles better with working front brakes. One test, for example, demonstrated that a fully loaded tractor-trailer traveling 60 miles per hour on dry concrete needs 250 to 300 feet to stop safely with all brakes working. Shutting off the air on front brakes increased the required stopping distance by as much as 139 feet.

Trucks without working front brakes after the deadline faced the prospect of being slapped with an "out of service" sticker until corrected. Faulty brakes were cited in an earlier study by the National Highway Traffic Safety Administration as the contributing factor in nearly one-third of all heavy-truck crashes.

With the industry's emphasis on safety, the Commercial Vehicle Safety Alliance (CVSA), a voluntary organization that coordinates member states' highway safety inspections, continued to

expand its influence. The group had grown to encompass 44 states, two Canadian provinces, and more than 100 associate members by 1988. Its aim is to establish more uniform, cost-effective, and less burdensome procedures for state vehicle safety inspections.

Working with the Department of Transportation, members of CVSA agreed on out-of-service criteria based on a Critical Item Inspection Procedure designed to decrease costs to truckers and delays in deliveries while increasing the number of inspections. In CVSA member states, each inspected truck receives a sticker that is good for three months. This frees roadside inspectors to examine more vehicles and reduces the chance of a truck already judged "clean" being stopped needlessly for inspection in other jurisdictions.

Highway funding and safety issues also received a boost in 1986 when Congress enacted a five year, $68.5 million highway authorization bill that

included funds to complete the interstate system, improve primary, secondary, and urban highways, and upgrade bridge replacement programs. Still, the specter of budget cuts continued to loom over the industry, and federal officials confirmed that they had not been spending all the funds available in the Highway Trust Fund.

"That policy must be reversed," said Congressman John Paul Hammerschmidt, ranking minority member of the House Public Works and Transportation Committee. The congressman and other industry watchdog groups continued to put pressure on Washington to get a fair share of road improvement funds to further assure highway safety.

From time to time, the marriage between federal authorities and commercial interests has been a rocky one. One of the major flaps involved mud flaps. After a decade of testing and bickering, the Department of Transportation backed down on an effort to require controversial anti-spray flaps on all big trucks. DOT researchers tested all types of devices in rain, mud, sleet, and snow, but eventually concluded that the flaps and skirts it proposed to mandate in 1985 did little to cut spray or improve motorist visibility.

As promoted by Senator Danforth, the flap proposal would have cost the trucking industry an estimated $620 million. (Coincidentally, Danforth's home state was also the home of a major manufacturer of anti-spray flaps.) But the National Highway Safety Administration (NHTSA) said there would be no new regulations unless they saw evidence that flaps or any other anti-spray device could significantly reduce water spray and thus could save more lives.

The federal government and motor carriers are not always on opposite sides of the fence, however. For years the government had permitted heavy trucks

Research indicates the chances of an accident involving a truck increase at night, with a high incidence of accidents occurring during the dawn hours. Photo by Frank Siteman/After Image

Today's trucks offer amenities to make drivers more comfortable and safe, such as improved suspensions and quieter cabs. Photo by Gerry French/The Photo File

operating in and around major cities to bypass federal regulations on driver qualification and equipment safety. The predictable result was several horrendous freeway accidents attributed to poor vehicle maintenance. In a petition filed with the Federal Highway Administration, the American Trucking Associations (ATA) dubbed the exemptions a "legal anachronism" that allowed metropolitan areas to become potential dumping grounds for "unqualified and unfit truck drivers with unsafe trucks." Consequently, the 50-year-old commercial safety zone exemption was repealed following yet another industry campaign to improve truck safety.

Skyrocketing insurance costs had a major impact on motor carriers in the mid-1980s, forcing hundreds of fleets and owner-operators out of business or to "run bare" because they could not afford—or even get—increasingly expensive coverage. Although availability was improved, the high cost of insurance is expected to remain a hot issue through the 1990s.

In an effort to bring the insurance

tempest under control, trucking companies have redoubled their efforts to increase driver safety. Statistics show, for example, that a $1,000 accident actually costs an additional $8,000 in uninsured costs such as production and distribution delays, time lost by workers, paperwork, and replacement of lost equipment. By reducing the number of accidents, companies hope to lower damage costs, injury rates and liability.

As the trucking industry enters the last decade of this century, federal officials and industry leaders will have to work together to improve safety on the road. Accurate and comprehensive accident statistics are essential in determining what safety measures must be taken. The driver shortage, too, will have to be tackled head-on with better training and consistent standards. Drivers and management will have to join forces in an effort to eradicate substance abuse.

Throughout the 1980s industry leaders have put safety first, providing better training, equipment, and support to drivers, making America's highways safer for everyone.

Sharing the Road with a Truck

Ask the average truck driver to name the cause of most car/truck accidents and he will likely point an accusing finger at the automobile operator. And not without justification.

Scores of highway accidents have been caused when a car cuts in front of a truck and immediately slows down, its driver oblivious to the fact that 40 tons of truck and cargo cannot possibly stop as quickly as a one-ton automobile. In such situations, the truck driver is often obliged to choose between two evils: hit the car or run his truck off the road.

Truck drivers also get very nervous about motorists who tailgate or "draft" big trucks, following only a few feet behind the trailer out of the trucker's view, "That's like asking to get your head taken off," observes one driver. "If I have to slam on the brakes, your car's going to go right under the trailer, which will peel back the roof like a sardine can."

Similarly, few motorists are aware of another blind spot—the area next to the right front fender of a conventional truck/tractor. Because of the height of the cab, a car in that position is invisible to the trucker; it cannot be seen in the truck's rearview mirror nor over the hood. A car in that position is in danger should the unknowing trucker move into that lane.

Another truck driver beef: motorists who use their high beams when passing a truck at night. The truck's big west coast mirrors can magnify the glare, blinding the driver and causing him to become disoriented and drift out of his lane.

Just as dangerous is the automobile driver who plays cat and mouse, speeding up to pass a truck, then slowing down so that the truck is forced to pass him. Then doing this again and again.

In the late 1980s a couple of attempts were made to educate the motorist on how to safely share the road with big trucks. Booklets published by the ATA described the importance of safe driving habits on the freeways of several U.S. cities, for example in Washington, D.C., Los Angeles, Chicago, and Boston.

The American Automobile Association (AAA) sponsored a 25-minute film, *Sharing the Road With Big Trucks*, which is one of the best films ever done on the subject. Copies are available at many AAA offices throughout the United States.

Some trucking experts have also proposed a car and truck safety program directed at the high school level. They point out that some 3,000,000 youths are annually enrolled in driver education programs that could easily include a section on how to share the road with trucks, but funding has been lacking.

Tests have shown that a fully loaded tractor-trailer with working front brakes can actually stop safely in a short distance. But some drivers still fear front brakes can cause jackknifing. Photo by Sam Sargent/The Photo File

The ABCs and XYZs of Trucking 6

*I*t's alphabet soup," decried one harried trucking executive as he raced from one government agency to another on his first business trip to Washington, D.C. He was describing the array of agencies and trade associations the trucking industry has to deal with, such as the DOT, ICC, OMC, IRS, NHTSA, DOD, DOL, FHWA, and OSHA.

Need a loan? Unless you are a very large firm, you visit the Small Business Administration (SBA).

Hauling agricultural commodities? The Department of Agriculture (DOA) is the first stop.

Want to haul furniture for military families (a very lucrative business)? Head for the Department of Defense (DOD).

Terminal and truckstop operators are facing new rules concerning their underground fuel storage tanks. The new federal laws will be handled by the Environmental Protection Agency (EPA).

Labor problem? The obvious agency is the Department of Labor (DOL). But if the possibility of discrimination of any sort is involved, the Equal Employment Opportunity Commission (EEOC) may be involved.

If you're involved in international trade, the Department of Com-

Above: A mid-1970s move to have heavy duty rigs equipped with electronic anti-lock brakes, a system that had not proven reliable, was eventually stymied by a federal lawsuit. Photo by Roger Tully/The Photo File

Facing page: Along with other organizations, many state trucking associations exist to facilitate industry growth. Photo by Erik Svensson/After Image

Bottom: The competition was fierce between the many post-Prohibition brewers, and trucks became mobile billboards for their owners. This 1930s Mack CJ heralds the taste of Goetz Country Club Beer. Courtesy, Motor Vehicle Manufacturing Association

Below: This 1936 Indiana Glass truck was built by White after White purchased Indiana in 1932. White continued to produce Indiana trucks as a less expensive line until 1939. Courtesy, Volvo GM Heavy Truck Corporation

merce, Federal Maritime Commission, or State Department all might be places to visit.

As the trucking industry has grown into a complex, intricate business, the number of federal agencies with fingers in the pie has also proliferated. A half-century ago when trucking first came into its own, most trucking affairs were administered by the Interstate Commerce Commission (ICC). Since its formation in 1887, the ICC has been primarily responsible for regulating routes and ratemaking practices, originally for the railroads and later for the trucking industry. However, in 1980 when Congress passed the Motor Carrier Act, many of the ICC's regulatory powers were taken away. Even now some in the industry are calling for sunsetting the commission altogether.

Today most of trucking's interests are handled by the Department of Transportation (DOT) and its myriad satellite agencies. A relatively new cabinet agency, the DOT was established in 1967 to pull together an assortment of transportation agencies, ranging from trucking and aviation to the Coast Guard.

DOT's Federal Highway Administration (FHWA) is the first port of call for most trucking executives who deal

with Washington. The FHWA oversees all federal highway safety regulations and safety programs. One of its main functions is to conduct roadside inspections of heavy trucks to ensure that drivers and rigs pass federal safety laws, authorized by the federal Motor Carrier Safety Assistance Program (MCSAP). FHWA also enforces the new statute restricting truck drivers to one commercial operator's license. And it published stiff rules aimed at permanently grounding truck drivers who are substance abusers.

The Office of Motor Carriers (OMC), a new group within the FHWA, has special responsibility for dealing directly with the trucking industry and its relations with the federal government. It was the moving force, for example, in the FHWA's adoption of the single driver's license rule.

Another DOT satellite agency with a close relationship to trucking is the National Highway Traffic Safety Administration (NHTSA), which plays a major role in the development of heavy truck design technology. For example, NHTSA and truck manufacturers tangled for more than a decade over attempts to develop a device that would significantly reduce splash and spray thrown up by trucks in a rainstorm. Manufacturers insisted there was no single viable, cost-effective device that would solve the problem, yet NHTSA continued to test scores of systems before finally throwing in the towel in 1988. In the meantime, aero-

dynamic truck designs substantially reduced splash and spray on newer models.

NHTSA was also embroiled in a major controversy over its mandate in the mid-1970s requiring heavy-duty rigs to be equipped with electronic anti-lock brakes. Truck manufacturers and anti-lock suppliers alike complained that NHTSA had not allowed enough time for such systems to be perfected and thoroughly tested. Predictably, anti-lock brakes' performance was erratic at best and disastrous at worst—and was ultimately scrapped as the result of a federal lawsuit filed by a major truck manufacturer. Unfortunately, that did not happen until more than $1 billion had been invested—and lost—by both suppliers and truckmakers. The case underscored the fact that dealing with the government's "alphabet soup" of bureaus can be both time consuming and expensive—but necessary.

Although the DOT today dominates relations between trucking and the federal government, the shadow of the Interstate Commerce Commission remains. Shorn of most of its power, the ICC still is the federal force that shapes government-industry relations. Anyone seeking entry into interstate trucking must still make application to the ICC for permission. However, few applications have been denied in recent years. The commission also set the stage for the remarkable growth of private interest groups within the industry—both within the states and

carriers specializing in various kinds of hauling.

Federal involvement in the trucking industry started in the early 1930s when dozens of new trucking companies were created, each fighting for a piece of the less-than-truckload business forfeited by the railroads because of the Depression. In 1935 Congress passed the Motor Carrier Act, which permanently put Uncle Sam in the passenger seat of interstate trucks—frequently functioning more as a meddlesome backseat driver than as a helpful navigator. And the ICC climbed aboard as a non-paying passenger.

Most of the responsible operators in the industry welcomed the 1935 Motor Carrier Act. In fact, the act prompted several trucking companies to form—that same year—the American Trucking Associations (ATA) with the single purpose of lobbying for better industry regulation.

As a sort of benevolent ogre, the ICC continued its strong regulatory control over the trucking industry for nearly 50 years. Many less-than-truckload carriers would have preferred to see its federal control continued because, in effect, the agency protected their ICC-approved routes from competitors. To obtain an ICC-approved common carriage route involved a

Bottom: White designed this special cab and trailer for Labatts Beer shortly after the repeal of Prohibition. Although the streamlined truck looked spectacular, it was not very practical when it came to hauling beer kegs. The truck was delivered in 1937. Courtesy, Volvo GM Heavy Truck Corporation

Below: The United States Government continues to be as big a customer for truck manufacturers as it was in the 1930s. This 1936 photo of Tennessee Valley Authority trucks shows a pair of 1931 Federals. Federal began building trucks in 1910. Courtesy, Motor Vehicle Manufacturing Association

Above: The Commercial Motor Vehicle Safety Act of 1986 included a provision that truck drivers pass a much tougher test than was previously required. Photo by Ron Hussey/The Photo File

Top: Nearly all aspects of trucking interests are handled in some way by the Department of Transportation (DOT), established in 1967. Photo by John Lund/The Photo File

The commission's quarterly reports of Class I and II carriers (the largest) are considered the basis for analyzing performance for the entire industry. The ICC's annual report includes an overwhelming amount of detail about every trucking company registered with it. The information ranges from total revenues, profits, and operating ratios to the number of tractors and trailers rented or owned, and the number of miles traveled in intercity or intrastate operations.

Although relatively few applicants have been turned down since 1980, the commission still retains the right to determine the physical and financial fitness of the applying company. And although it has relaxed its standards in recent years, the commission still has the power to revoke licensed authority. The agency also has investigatory power to assure that any truck operator has sufficient insurance as mandated by federal law.

At a time when many carriers are seeking to sell out, the ICC has the power to challenge any merger or acquisition it decides is not in the public interest. Also, interstate carriers are still required to file their rates with the commission, although they are seldom challenged.

In the heyday of the ICC—from 1935 to 1980—the American Trucking Associations served as the principal voice of trucking in Washington—a position it still maintains, although not with the preeminence it once had. At its peak of power the ATA was as potent a lobbying force as the National Rifle Association. ATA emissaries were once welcome walk-in regulars in the Capitol Hill offices of scores of senators and congressmen.

Significantly, the organization's name is plural. ATA comprises numerous truck-related associations, each with a specialized interest. Not the least of these are individual state trucking associations that have consistently played a major role in the growth and regulation of the industry. Many of these state associations predate ATA and the 1935 Motor Carrier Act by several years.

In the far West, for example, the Washington Trucking Association was founded in 1922 to "protect the rights of motor carriers" certified under

long and costly application and review procedure that could take months and even years—and which too often was eventually turned down because it was "not in the public interest." Even purchase of existing rights from another carrier involved tortoise-paced approval by the ICC. Consequently, a carrier's ICC authority to ship from point A to point B over specified highways became a valuable, negotiable commodity.

However, on July 1, 1980, President Jimmy Carter signed a new Motor Carrier Act which greatly diminished the regulatory power of the ICC. As a direct result many old-line common carriers, no longer protected from either route or rate competition, were forced to close their doors.

The ICC, however, still plays a fairly significant role. Corporate and financial officers within the industry— as well as outside financial analysts— rely heavily on the commission for details pertinent to the fiscal performance of the industry and individual companies.

state legislation passed in 1921, and to "establish and publish a set of rates and tariffs."

In 1925 a group of local cartage men in the Chicago area met in a local coffee shop to form the Central Motor Freight Association to deal with interstate problems truckers were then having with the neighboring states of Indiana, Michigan, and Wisconsin. Recalled one of the original members, "There were times when we held banquets or had a dinner meeting when we didn't have sufficient funds to cover the tab, so a number of us picked up the balance and shared alike. It was a struggle." Out of those gatherings grew the Illinois Trucking Association.

About the same time in Ohio, perhaps even a bit earlier, a number of carriers formed the Toledo Hi-Ways Transport Association. Two years later it banded together most of Ohio's major carriers and the name was changed to the Ohio Association of Commercial Haulers. Its aim: Move to Columbus and influence legislation involving trucking. Thus the Ohio Trucking Association was born.

As trucks began to overtake railroads in the hauling of goods, there was greater need for carriers in each state to band together and lobby state legislatures, which often viewed trucking as an easy target for additional taxation. By the time the American Trucking Association was formed and the ICC was given regulatory control over the industry, about half the states had active trucking associations.

Although publicity usually focuses on federal activities, state associations have been a vital force in protecting regional interests. During 1987, for example, state associations accomplished the following:

—In Florida two bills were killed that would have raised fuel taxes, another authorizing a 55-cent sales tax on freight services died, and a five cent per gallon diesel fuel tax was repealed.

—Efforts in Michigan to raise diesel taxes and truck registration fees were defeated.

—Minnesota was thwarted in its attempt to add a six percent sales tax on new truck and trailer purchases, and increased highway user fees were defeated.

—In Oklahoma trucking interests

persuaded the legislature to eliminate a 3.25 percent excise tax on sales of trucks in excess of 54,000 pounds, reduce the diesel fuel tax three cents per gallon and cut the trailer tag from $40 per year to $40 for the life of a trailer.

In addition to these more notable accomplishments, a spot check in late 1988 showed that about half the states were considering some kind of legislation involving trucks.

Lending strong backup support to both ATA and the state trucking associations are a complex of ATA-affiliated groups representing specialized carriers within the industry. Over the years the most powerful has been the Regular Common Carrier Conference (RCCC). It represents carriers of less-than-truckload general freight and includes the giant firms of the industry. Any time there is a fight over more deregulation of the trucking industry, the RCCC can be counted on to take a strong stand against such changes.

Bottom: The American Truck Dealers Association represents nearly 1,700 truck dealers, and is located in Washington, D.C. Photo by Tom Tracy/The Photo File

Below: Industry associations form a powerful lobbying body in government, and aim to protect truckers' rights and interests. Photo by Phillip Wallick/ The Photo File

In the fall of 1983 the Cavalcade of Trucking took to the road to celebrate the 50th anniversary of the American Trucking Associations. A 41-foot trailer was donated by Fruehauf and converted into a museum with pictures, displays, and artifacts from trucking history. The museum, pulled by a state-of-the-art 1984 White tractor, toured the nation. It stopped at malls, stste capitals, and even sat on the mall in our nation's capital. Courtesy, PR Counselors

The Interstate Truckload Carriers Conference (ITCC) represents carriers of truckload freight. They lease or hire many of the truck drivers who own their own rigs—commonly known as owner-operators. Most of their freight moves in truckload lots directly from shipper to customer.

The National Tank Truck Carriers (NTTC) represents firms that haul petroleum products, chemicals, and other liquid or dry bulk materials. Hardly a day goes by that this group is not involved in some issue regarding hazardous materials on the nation's highways.

Two rapidly emerging groups are regional trucking firms and couriers that run around urban areas with fast delivery and pickup, such as Federal Express, Purolator, Roadway Package Express, and Emery. The issues of the regional carriers are handled by the Regional and Distribution Carriers Conference (RDCC), while the needs of the couriers are handled by the Film, Air and Package Carriers Conference (FAPCC).

There are other ATA-affiliated groups representing household goods movers, auto haulers, munitions and oil field equipment transportation, and heavy machinery movers.

Another group with a major influence on trucking industry policies is made up of private truck carriers. These carriers are owned by firms whose primary businesses are other than trucking, such as petroleum companies, grocery chains, and automotive parts manufacturers, to name a few. As a group, they represent the largest single body in the trucking industry, and with economic regulation loosened, they are able to compete for freight with for-hire carriers.

As 1988 drew to a close, the two major organizations representing the private-carrier segment of the industry were merged, forming the National Private Truck Council, an organization second in size only to the ATA. The groups were the Private Truck Council of America (PTCA) and the National Private Trucking Association (NPTA). NPTA, formerly the Private Carrier Conference (PCC) of ATA, broke away from ATA in 1987 after a dispute over the deregulation issue. The ATA, primarily at the urging of its powerful RCCC membership, was pushing for federal reregulation of the industry, while the PCC strongly favored doing away completely with the few vestiges of regulation that still existed.

Also emerging was a powerful group of leasing firms—comprising most of the nation's leading truck leasing companies—organized as the Truck Renting and Leasing Association (TRALA). As capital costs continued to rise and competition in the industry intensified, more private trucking operations began leasing their equipment from firms that would assume truck ownership and operation responsibilities. These companies provide services ranging from purchasing and full-service maintenance to insurance, and, in some cases, even driver hiring and training.

In the 1980s the trend was toward "dedicated carriage," a service originated by lessors that relieves the customer company of virtually every responsibility but dispatching. Not counting the several thousand trucks in daily rental, TRALA members own and operate nearly a million Class 6, 7, and 8 trucks and trailers. It is small wonder that industry analysts consider leasing the fastest-growing segment of the industry and predict it will continue to exercise greater influence on government policy.

TRALA is also responsible for spawning the Alliance for Simple, Equitable & Rational Truck Taxation (ASERTT), formed originally to show Capitol Hill politicians the error of their ways in attempting to use the trucking industry as a tax cash cow. More recently, however, ASERTT has focused its attention on proposed legislation deemed detrimental at the state level. At times, ASERTT lends welcome support to state associations. Yet the organization is also unafraid to vigorously oppose a state trucking association when its cause would be harmful to private trucking.

Included among the plethora of agencies associated with the trucking industry are state associations and organizations representing special interests in the industry. The American Truck Dealers Association, for example, is a division of the National Automobile Dealers Association representing some 1,700 truck dealers in the United States from a lobbying base in Washington. Used truck dealers are part of a new group called the Used Truck Sales Network (UTSN), which represents organizations that acquire and dispose of used equipment—some of which has come on the market as result of trucking company bankruptcies.

The Commercial Vehicle Safety Alliance (CVSA) is made up of state highway safety officials. The alliance is concerned with highway safety, especially rules and regulations involving heavy trucks. Also concerned with the nation's highways is the Highway Users Federation (HUF), which is composed primarily of companies and government officials interested in the future of the nation's highways, both how they are constructed and used. The group often has been headed by a trucking industry executive, who is elected annually.

The Western Highway Institute (WHI) is composed of members who represent trucking companies, truck manufacturers, and other industry suppliers. This organization is noted for its research on safety-related industry issues such as splash and spray, the use of double and triple trailers, and brakes.

Members of the Motor Vehicle Manufacturers Association (MVMA) include major truck and auto manufacturers, representing this segment of the industry in Washington. The Association also produces economic reports on both trucks and autos. A parallel organization is the Heavy Duty Manufacturers Association (HDMA), which represents companies that supply the truck builder with component parts.

The National Association of Truckstop Operators (NATSO), based in Alexandria, Virginia, represents a majority of the nation's rapidly growing contingent of truckstop operators, now estimated to exceed 3,000 in number.

The American Association of Motor Vehicle Administrators (AAMVA) represents the state motor vehicle administrators. It is primarily interested in the licensing of drivers and vehicle safety.

The Truck Trailer Manufacturers Association (TTMA) serves the nation's truck trailer and truck body makers. It functions as both a watchdog in Washington and central administrator of financial and research information for its members.

The American Association of State Highway and Transportation Officials (AASHTO), as the name implies, is composed of state highway transportation officials who conduct research on the nation's future highway needs.

And representing American motorists is the American Automobile Association, the well known AAA. The AAA generally opposes trucking advocates and consistently pushes for state trucking laws that are restrictive at best, punitive at worst.

There are also organizations representing owner-operators. Among them: The Independent Truckers and Drivers Association (ITDA), based in Maryland and headed by Rita Bonz; the Independent Truck Owner-Operators Association (I-TOO), led by Marshall Siegel and based in Massachusetts; and the Owner-Operators Independent Drivers Association of America (OIDA), operating from headquarters in Missouri, headed by Jim Johnston.

The alphabet soup of state and government agencies is the penalty an industry pays when it gets as big and complex as the trucking industry has become. And the maze of agencies and special interest groups is not likely to get any less complicated.

John F. Kennedy welcomed the leaders of the ATA to the White House on October 13, 1961. They are (left to right) John J. Gill, ATA board chairman; Clarence A. Kelley, ATA president; Neil J. Curry, chairman of the ATA executive committee; John F. Kennedy; John M. Akers, ATA treasurer; Welby M. Frantz, retiring ATA board chairman; Harry L. Gormley, ATA secretary. Courtesy, American Truck Historical Society

The Driver

To some he still conjures up a rugged John Wayne image, crossing lonesome prairies and climbing steep-graded mountainsides, logging hundreds of miles before he heads home. But this image has given way to a new breed of truck driver, who could be a company man or woman, a husband and wife team, or an independent owner-operator.

Nearly three million strong, the driver is the linchpin that holds the industry together. The full weight of the industry rests squarely on his or her shoulders, relying on skill and ability to get the cargo to its destination safely and on time.

Some drivers own their equipment. Others are company drivers, working either for a common carrier or for a private manufacturing or marketing company that operates its own truck fleet. Either way, when one climbs behind the wheel of that big rig, he instantly becomes his own boss. No time card to punch. No foreman looking over his shoulder. No button-down collar or necktie.

If he wants to take an extra 10 minutes for a second cup of coffee at the truckstop, who's to say no? If he wants to turn up the stereo volume high enough to split the seams of the cab upholstery with Waylon Jennings wailin', who's to complain? He enjoys a freedom others sometimes envy, but the hours are long and the work is demanding.

In an industry as diverse as trucking, it is difficult to paint a picture of the typical driver. In over-the-road service, for example, the typi-

Above: To truck drivers' credit, statistics indicate that alcohol use was a factor in only 5 percent of all fatal accidents involving big rigs.
Photo by Greg Olson/The Photo File

Facing page: Owner-operators have the option of outfitting their rigs to their specifications, almost always more elaborately than fleet-owned trucks.
Photo by Susan Davison

cal driver may be a non-union employee of a company with a fleet that hauls general commodities by the van trailer-load to all 48 contiguous states. He may earn between $20,000 and $30,000 a year, work an 80-hour week, and may get home as infrequently as once a month.

Or perhaps the typical driver pulls a refrigerated trailer, hauling produce or frozen foods; or drives a moving van, packing, loading, and transporting precious family possessions across town or across the country; or hauls a tanker, delivering fuel, chemicals, or bulk foodstuffs a few hundred miles; or pulls a flatbed trailer hauling machinery, coiled steel, piping, or building materials.

Some drivers never leave the city limits. They wheel short semis or straight trucks in and out of nerve-wracking urban traffic on peddle runs to and from loading docks. These drivers are the vital door-to-door link between trucking company and customer and between manufacturer and consumer.

Some drivers are independent contractors who own their own rigs. In addition to hauling goods they also must maintain their trucks and tend to an incredible array of paperwork. One trucking magazine estimates there are between 330,000 and 350,000 such owner-operators in the United States; other estimates go as high as 500,000.

The wide spread in the estimate is indicative of the independents' elusiveness. Many of them come from rural backgrounds and still prefer the small town to big-city living. When they're home for a week or a weekend, they want to purge themselves of diesel fumes in the clean, fresh country air.

Dozens of attempts have been made—and will continue to be made—to bring them together into a cohesive bloc, capable of exerting tremendous clout among shippers and politicians alike. A handful of organizations have had moderate success in organizing them— among them the Independent Truck Owner-Operators Association in Massachusetts, the Owner Operators Independent Drivers Association of America in Missouri, and the Independent Truckers and Drivers Association in Maryland.

Most over-the-road drivers are family men. They have neither the time nor the money to fool with wine, women, and drugs. They dislike being away so long

from their families. As one says, "Every time I pass a man watering his lawn, I say to myself 'I wish I could do that instead of being confined behind this steering wheel.'"

But in the same breath, he brags about his distinctiveness: "I'd go nuts if I had to go to some dull office every day or do the same boring thing over and over again on a factory assembly line. Where I work, there's no time clock to punch. Every day the scenery is different. I watch the sun rise over a wheat field in Nebraska and set over a mountain in Colorado."

That's on good days. It's not so glamorous when a torrent of rain is beating on the windshield . . . or worse, when swirling snow cuts visibility to a few feet . . . or worse yet when an inch-thick layer of ice encrusts every square inch of tractor and trailer and turns the road surface into a skating rink.

Whatever they do and wherever they go, most believe their jobs are dangerous—and they are right. A federal government report in 1988 said truck drivers have a higher fatality rate from accidents than all worker occupations except mining and quarrying.

Traffic accidents are the leading cause of sudden deaths among drivers, yet as few as five percent of truck drivers use their seat belts. Most truckers, like some motorists, believe that a seat belt will trap them in the cab after an accident, barring their escape from a fire. They ignore statistics showing that fire seldom kills a driver, but that nearly 40 percent of all trucker fatalities result from their being thrown from the cab following impact.

Drivers also are prone to injury from slipping while getting into or out of the cab or while loading or unloading cargo. They face many health dangers, too, chiefly lung disorders from the bad air they breathe while in traffic and from cigarettes. In fact, 63 percent of drivers are smokers, more than double the national average, which now has slipped below 30 percent. The truck's relatively rough riding characteristics over long periods can cause back problems and internal injuries. And the stress of coping with traffic can result in high blood pressure, ulcers, and other nerve-related maladies.

Actually the occupational hazards of truck driving are more difficult to deal

Truckers have always been a tough breed, but perhaps more so in the past than today. Driving horrendous hours with little technology or laws to protect them, they gained a reputation in the 1930s and 1940s that approached legendary proportions. Courtesy, American Truck Historical Society

with than the actual driving of the truck. Contrary to general belief, wheeling a big rig is not all that difficult once it has been learned and practiced.

Managers spend thousands of hours and millions of dollars devising procedures and designing equipment to do the work of trucking in the most efficient manner possible. For example, advances in engines, drivetrains, and aerodynamics have improved vehicle fuel efficiency by more than 50 percent in the last 10 years.

But when all is said and done a truly good driver can add about 35 percent to a given truck's fuel economy performance by starting and stopping smoothly, by keeping engine revs low through proper use of transmission gears, and by shutting down the engine when it is not needed. Moreover, if he treats the equipment well, the driver can greatly reduce maintenance expenses and extend the truck's life.

A driver also can make or break the image of his company—and the industry. Most motorists expect courteous, professional behavior from the driver of a big rig, and they react angrily when a trucker tailgates or cuts them off. Worse yet is the prospect of an 80,000-pound truck being driven by someone who is drunk, drugged, or just dead tired.

However, as in virtually every other occupation, it is the few bad apples that give the whole barrel a rotten odor. The actual number of truckers on drugs or other mind-altering subtances probably hovers around five percent. Some of this minority pop stimulants to keep awake, while others—mirroring the problems of drugs in society as a whole—may use more diabolical concoctions. To the trucker's credit, government statistics show that alcohol was a factor in barely five percent of all fatal accidents involving big trucks. That compares with accident statistics showing more than 50 percent of car drivers to be alcohol impaired.

Despite these figures, in 1988 federal agencies and the Congress were being pressured to enact and enforce tougher regulations against driving a truck while under the influence of drugs or alcohol. A Senate bill called for random testing of truckers, similar to testing proposed for airline pilots and railroad engineers. Predictably, the International Brotherhood of Teamsters, which had already taken a

strong stance against alcohol and drug abuse, opposed such testing as unreliable and discriminatory.

Meanwhile, the Department of Transportation's Federal Highway Administration (FHWA) sought to standardize widely varying state rules and procedures for granting commercial driver's licenses and to enforce stricter testing of an applicants' mechanical knowledge and driving skill. In some states a truck driver was eligible to drive a big rig simply by passing an automobile driving test. In other states prospective truck drivers were merely obliged to take a written test—no road test was required to check their ability to operate an 18-wheeler.

However, by 1992 all commercial truck and bus drivers will be required to apply for a standardized truck license (some states' programs will go into effect earlier). The Federal act which outlawed duplicate licensing also set tougher criteria for application and testing in all states.

Old-timers lament the loss of the truckers' legendary image as a "knight of the road"—always courteous and ever ready to lend assistance to a stranded motorist. A generation ago, when that image was popular, trucking was a different game. Roads were narrower, speeds lower, and more direct contact was made between truckers and motorists. Truck drivers would flash their lights or signal with their hands to assist motorists in passing, and often they would stop to help someone in trouble.

But today's higher interstate speeds and greater pressure to deliver the goods

Harry Truman gave his famous double handshake to the trucking industry's driver of the year, John Castner, 34, and runner up George Neff, 32. Winners were chosen on the basis of good driving records, citizenship, and being good samaritans. Courtesy, American Truck Historical Society

road drivers stopped at the scene and saved 34 others by getting the bus' jammed rear emergency door open before fire consumed it.

For some truckers deregulation of the trucking industry, which began in 1980, has been more bane than blessing. Many lost their jobs when a host of old-line common carriers found they could not compete with the new kids on the block and simply went out of business. With new trucking companies springing up like dandelions, driving jobs became easy to find. But cutthroat rate wars reduced most driver's paychecks. Consequently, drivers' wages did not keep up with pay hikes granted in other industries; the average pay increase for truck drivers was only about 20 percent in 1979 compared to 50 percent in other occupations. And by the late 1980s, many owner-operators were actually earning less than they did in 1980 while their expenses for vehicles, fuel, and maintenance were somewhat higher. Because most drivers were non-union, and because independent truckers were still reluctant to band together, their ability to force up wages was greatly eroded.

Moreover, the once-powerful Teamsters Union became a thin shadow of its former self in the early '80s, representing fewer than one in five truck drivers. Instead, it derived more than 9 out of 10 of its members from non-trucking occupations, ranging from airline clerks and teachers to police officers.

Many Teamster drivers were forced into "give backs," taking cuts in wages and fringe benefits in an attempt to keep their jobs. Refusal by drivers to accept employers' reduced wage and benefits offers was followed by shutdowns of many of the old-line companies. Consequently, the Teamsters, wracked by both deregulation and a deep recession, grudgingly conceded that three-quarters of a loaf was better than no loaf at all.

Yet in terms of wages, non-union drivers were getting half a loaf. Some earned as little as $18,000 anually while pushing their rigs upward of 100,000 miles a year. Because deregulation spilled too many trucks onto the highways in pursuit of too little freight, something had to give, and it was usually the driver who had to sacrifice. Displaced by bankruptcies, many drivers were forced into lower-paying jobs.

By 1985 the economy rebounded and

on time make it tougher for a trucker to play Sir Galahad. Moreover, in the lawsuit-prone atmosphere of the 1980s, truckers are reluctant to come charging to the rescue of motorists in distress for fear of litigation if something should go wrong in the performance of the good deed. For the same reason, most fleets prohibit their drivers from signaling a motorist to pass.

But in the shadow of this fading legend, there is still a glimmer of the old hero. Truckers are repeatedly cited for heroism—pulling people from burning cars and icy lakes, and sometimes losing their own lives in the process. An annual Highway Heroes award, sponsored by the Goodyear Tire & Rubber Company, honors latter-day knights with cash and public acclaim.

Unfortunately, the news media—too often preoccupied with the sensational story—focuses on the big-rig wreck and freeway jam-up. Typical was the highway tragedy near Louisville, Kentucky, in 1988 when a pickup truck going the wrong way on an interstate highway smashed head-on into a church bus, killing 27 people, mostly children. The media consistently called the pickup operator a "truck driver," and barely mentioned the fact that two over-the-

Above: Husband-and-wife driving partnerships have been making the long haul together more often in recent years. Photo by R. Hamilton Smith/After Image

Top: Although truck drivers have a much better record than automobile motorists on alcohol or drug use while driving, measures have called for random testing. Photo by Roger Allyn Lee/The Photo File

freight tonnage gradually increased. However, trucking firms still struggled with rate-cutting and their profits remained dismal. Despite wage concessions Teamster drivers for less-than-truckload carriers still earned a decent living and there were plenty of applicants for any vacancies. This generally was also true of private fleets, which paid well and operated comfortable equipment.

It was a different story, however, in the truckload area which had expanded as a result of deregulation. By 1986 these carriers began having trouble filling driver vacancies because they paid low wages and often required drivers to spend weeks and sometimes months on the road. Driver turnover in many truckload fleets soared to as high as 200 percent. Drivers drifted from company to company, often quitting after only a few weeks or months to take jobs that paid another penny a mile, promised better dispatching procedures, or put them in the cab of a fancier truck. Some carriers enticed drivers with better pay, $20,000 or more to start, plus extra money for loading and unloading and bonuses for fuel efficiency or longevity. Other companies launched programs that focused on driver's needs, showing them how they fit into the entire operation.

Experts have cited a number of contributing factors to the persistence of the driver shortage: government and insurance regulations which effectively barred many potential young drivers from employment and sent them to work in other industries; tougher regulations requiring drug screening; and the lower birthrates of the 1960s and 1970s, which reduced the total number of young people entering the work force.

Barring another deep recession, the trucking industry will be short tens of thousands of drivers by the early 1990s. One estimate puts the shortage as high as 600,000. To alleviate this shortfall the industry is studying better pay and benefits for drivers to compete with other industries. Furthermore, the industry may be obliged to get its drivers from non-traditional sources. And some industry experts have suggested recruiting immigrants to fill truck driver vacancies.

Just fifteen years ago women truck drivers were about as scarce as ants at an exterminators' picnic. They were so rare,

in fact, that their male counterparts gave them wide berth—on the road as well as in truckstops. Women's restroom facilities were inadequate at best, non-existent at worst. And short of renting a motel room, it was impossible for a female driver to take a shower while she was on the road.

No one has made an accurate count, but it has been estimated that upward of 100,000 women now answer to the title of truck driver. And nobody makes jokes about their driving skills, either. Women drivers have proven themselves to be just as dextrous, efficient and sharp on the job as their male counterparts.

With the distressing shortage of well-trained drivers, one of the salvations of over-the-road trucking has been the husband-and-wife driving team. This partnership is not new; household goods carriers have long encouraged wives to join their husbands on the road. Today it is not unusual to see couples at loading docks and truckstops. If a husband and wife like the nomadic life, it seems a perfect arrangement. Drivers can enjoy the companionship of their spouses, who also drive and help with the paperwork and customer contacts. Together they can see the country while earning a decent living—two paychecks instead of one. The employers also benefit from a more content, stable, and productive driver team, and shippers and consignees get more reliable, prompt, and friendly service. As the driver shortage worsens, carriers may recruit more drivers' spouses as a way to get more productivity out of each vehicle.

A majority of the new recruits probably will learn their truck-driving skills at one of approximately 300 truck driving schools in the United States—a number that is expected to triple by the early 1990s to meet the shortage-inspired demand for training.

As a sign of the times, a couple of driver-hungry truckload carriers started apprenticeship programs, taking high school graduates and giving them further training. Some also backed a plan to allow closely supervised 18-year-olds to drive, con-

Bottom: Women today are finding their place in trucking—behind the wheel. This was hardly the case 15 years ago, however. Photo by Susan Davison

Below: Truckstop restaurants have come a long way since the time they were known for greasy hamburgers. The quality and variety is often on par with the best national restuarants. Photo by Susan Davison

Above: Just as train engineers posed with their engines in the 1800s, truckers posed proudly with their rigs. And, also like the old engineers, drivers maintained their vehicles and were solely responsible for anything that happened to truck or cargo. Courtesy, American Truck Historical Society

Top: Though it looks like a scene from a B movie, this is actually a pinochle game in the drivers' room of Anchor Motor Freight Corporation in Linden, New Jersey. The dealer in the April 1945 game is the drivers' boss, Barkley W. Fox (in white shirt). Courtesy, American Truck Historical Society

stituting a break with a long-standing federal regulation setting 21 as the minimum driving age for interstate truck drivers, despite insurance companies' demand for even higher minimum ages.

As tough as the shortage will be on management, it can only enhance the drivers' position. For a while, at least, the forces of supply and demand will push up pay, increase fringe benefits, and improve working conditions.

The owner-operator trucker who will probably benefit the most is as misunderstood as he is difficult to define. He has often been hailed as a folk hero and the "last American cowboy," independent and seemingly answerable to no one. Granted, owner-operators are free from over-the-shoulder supervision. But in truth, they face many deadlines. Loads must be delivered on time and in good condition. So the independent trucker is often dependent on several bosses—the broker who lines up the load, the dispatcher of the carrier he is leased to, and the shipper and consignee of the cargo.

One of the independent's greatest freedoms is his choice of the kind of truck he owns and how it is equipped and painted. It is almost axiomatic that it will always be more comfortable and more powerful than the average fleet vehicle. It will also sport more chrome, more lights and much more gadgetry—from heated remote control mirrors and automatic oil changers to color television sets and microwaves. A few even boast waterbeds.

In short, the truck expresses the owner-operator's individuality. But aside from a few major components, such as engine, transmission, and rear axle, the independent owner-driver tends to leave the rest of the component specifying to the dealer—unlike fleet equipment managers who practically specify down to the last nut, bolt, and cotter pin.

Truck purchase is no small item for the independent owner-operator. A "plain vanilla" tractor—austerely equipped and powered—will cost a minimum of $63,000. Add another $27,000 for a refrigerated van-type trailer and it

equals an outlay that will buy a three bedroom house with two baths, a family room, and a two-car attached garage on a half acre in Toledo. But there's one big difference: the bank will give the driver-owner 20 years to pay for the house—but perhaps only three years to pay off the truck.

Consequently, the independent operator is obliged to be less cowboy and more businessman. He must be able to make truck payments of up to $2,500 a month, handle truck maintenance, and file countless tax and operating reports with state and federal authorities. For example, if his annual travels take him into all 48 states, he must file a report and/or pay a tax on the fuel he purchased in each state.

Unlike most businessmen the owner-operator has little negotiating power. The price of his equipment and services are usually set—as well as the price he will receive for hauling a load from point A to point B. At worst, he goes broke. Many freight rates are well below the trucker's break-even point. In such cases he keeps few of the dollars that pass through his hands, and may earn little or nothing for his efforts.

There are many exceptions, of course. Independents who have good business sense and are able to control their costs earn comfortable livings. They know how to choose commodities that pay top dollar, where to get good loads, when to contract with a carrier, and are able to recognize and select honest companies to pull for.

Actually there are few genuinely independent truckers —owner-operators—who have their own operating authority and who line up their own loads. The majority of the independents contract their trucks and their services to large carriers and let them arrange loads. The carrier also handles much of the paperwork required by state and federal regulations. Sometimes the carrier may even require the trucker to paint his vehicle in company colors, stipulate where he must buy insurance, or even help him buy a truck. North American Van Lines, for example, recruits potential owner-operators, puts them through the company's own extensive training program, then finances the purchase of a new or used tractor already painted to company specifications.

But life on the road is no sightseer's holiday. The independent trucker puts in long days and spends weeks and sometimes months away from home and family. Economic pressures also force some drivers to over-extend themselves. Some shippers are repeatedly guilty of making unrealistic delivery demands. The truckers' choice is either take the load and push himself at an illegal and unsafe pace or refuse the load and lose the revenue. With truck payments to make and a family to feed, the trucker may have virtually no choice at all.

Some of the traditional loneliness of driving a truck while the rest of the nation sleeps has been alleviated by electronics—the CB radio, television, and the stereo radio/tape player. Abuse and foul language, however, have diminished the popularity of CB, although most drivers still keep their sets tuned to traffic and road condition reports from drivers who are traveling in the opposite direction. Occasionally, a driver who missed his calling as a comedian will entertain a score of travelers within wavelength for a hundred miles or more.

A good AM/FM radio lets the trucker tune in to all-night deejays who tailor their programming exclusively for truckers. Typical of the breed is Fred Sanders, who began his midnight-to-dawn stints 13 years ago over Chicago's powerful WMAQ. He now has organized a coast-to-coast network that feeds his program live via satellite to 18 affiliated stations. Most trucks are also equipped with good stereo systems with enough wattage to drown the drone of the diesel in a sea of sound—usually country and western music. And recorded books, according to one driver, "can make whole states disappear."

Truckstops are a trucker's oasis. Some of the fanciest offer saunas, exercise rooms, barbershops, and therapy clinics for taking the kinks out of ailing backs. Nearly all of them now are equipped with laundromats and private shower facilities. And whereas greasy hamburgers were once the mainstays of the menu, truckstop food now competes in taste and variety with the best of the national restaurant chains. One Georgia truckstop, in fact, operates a gourmet restaurant serving haute cuisine dinners amid crystal chandeliers and original paintings, all prepared by a gourmet chef whose specialties include Noisettes d'Agneau Perigeaux and Filets of Beef Richard III.

The trucks of the 1980s have also attained haute cuisine status. All are quieter and smoother riding than they were even a decade ago. Sleeper compartment accommodations are more refined, with more storage space for clothes and other personal items. Auxiliary power units are available to run heating and air conditioning systems, making it unnecessary to idle the truck's noisy engine. Posh custom sleeper boxes offer stove, refrigerator, sink, television with VCR, large bed, and even a shower and chemical toilet. The vast majority of drivers, however, are obliged to settle for something more mundane.

Although the pressures and stresses are the same from behind the wheel of a rolling palace as they are in a plain vanilla company truck, thousands of big-rig drivers have logged thousands of miles without so much as scratching a fender. And several thousand truckers have passed the million mile mark without a chargeable accident.

The million milers have one thing in commom: they know the importance of safety on the road. With powers of concentration equal to those of a professional athlete, these professional drivers are alert and quick. Never diverting their attention from that white line, they are aware of every intersection ahead and every vehicle that shares the road with them. They seldom watch the clock, understanding full well that traffic and road conditions will determine their arrival time. They play it safe on the road, avoid speeding, weaving in and out of traffic, or tailgating slow drivers to frighten them into moving over.

Fortunately for America and American trucking, such drivers represent the majority of the men and women who keep the wheels of industry and commerce turning by keeping the wheels of trucking turning.

Above: In the 1950s and 1960s truckers were known as the "Knights of the Road," often stopping to help "damsels in distress" such as this one. Many freight carriers encouraged their drivers to be courteous and helpful. Courtesy, PR Counselors

Top: Fruehauf sponsored a contest for truckers who could improve the image of truckers and Fruehauf trailers. Courtesy, American Truck Historical Society

Equipment Evolution

S The trucks America uses today to muscle its loads to market are as diverse as the trucking industry itself—a nearly limitless variety of power units, truck bodies, and trailers, often custom built for a specific hauling job. The eclectic parade of tractor-trailers coming down the highway reflect their owners' preferences, not only in paint and detail but in wheels, tires, engines, transmissions, axles, interior trim, trailer or body design, and operation. Except for some fleet trucks, hardly any two heavy-duty tractors are alike.

As trucking has grown during this century, the evolution of equipment has been marked by a number of major advancements. Some of these parallel modifications made in the automobile industry, but many are unique to trucks. Revolutionary changes tend to be a hard sell to most truckers, who are skeptical of such change and have reason to be. A truck down for repairs is not on the road earning money.

Originally built as motorized wagons perched on early auto chassis, trucks soon emerged as heavy-duty vehicles. By the time America entered Europe's Great War in 1916, trucks had shed their spindly appearance for a hefty body needed for serious cargo hauling. Mack's "Bulldog" AC model typified the crude-but-tough truck that helped muscle the Allies to victory. In yellowed photographs of trucks from that era, two mechanical features stand out: hard rubber tires with wooden spoked wheels and stout chains linking power-delivering sprockets to

Above: Trucking industry interests are frequently faced with measures from the American Automobile Association calling for more restrictive trucking laws. Photo by Tom Tracy/The Photo File

Facing page: Diesel engines gained favor over gasoline engines for their reliability and strength, features required on the grades found in the western United States. Photo by Sam Sargent/The Photo File

Above: The semi-trailer, introduced by August Fruehauf in 1915, began to gain popularity in the 1920s. This White two-ton tractor, pictured in the early 1920s, was owned by Runkel Brothers in New York. Courtesy, Volvo GM Heavy Truck Corporation

Top: The 1903 Gulf tank wagon shows how little trailers were to evolve past mere wagons until the late 1920s' at which time more powerful trucks and better "fifth wheels" were available. Courtesy, American Truck Historical Society

the rear wheels. In the 1920s hard rubber gave way to the pneumatic "balloon" tire, which increased carrying capacity, enhanced traction, and softened the ride for driver and cargo. Much publicity was generated for the pneumatic tire when the Goodyear Tire & Rubber Company sent a large truck, the "Wingfoot Express," on a coast-to-coast run over the primitive roads of the day.

By the end of the 1920s, heavier trucks had abandoned wooden spokes and were rolling on metal wheels. The convenient but clumsy chain drive was also replaced with a drive shaft which delivered more power via an axle differential directly to the axle. Semitrailers, which are supported by the chassis of the vehicle ahead, came into wider use. Trailers were especially useful because they greatly increased the amount of goods a truck could haul over long distances.

The first semis were the product of Detroit blacksmith August Fruehauf. Fruehauf noticed the horses he shoed were healthier if they pulled their loads rather than carried them on their backs. He reasoned that the same principle could be applied to trucks, so he began building trailers which could shoulder much of the burden. He established the Fruehauf Corporation, now the nation's largest manufacturer of truck trailers.

Trailers, indeed, are a story in themselves. They come in as many varieties as the power units that pull them and are built to carry specific types of commodities. The ubiquitous box-type van, for example, is able to carry a variety of dry cargo. But the van may also be insulated and heated to keep foodstuffs from freezing in winter or with the addition of plumbing and a heater-refrigeration unit, it becomes a "reefer."

Unlike truck manufacturing, which went through a great economic shakeout that reduced the field to a handful, truck body and trailer building has remained a booming business including scores of companies that serve mostly local and regional markets. To stay competitive these companies must keep abreast of advances in materials and construction, as well as manufacturing techniques. Up to the early 1950s, most perishables in transit were kept cool with ice, until engineers at Thermo King in Minneapolis pioneered the application of mechanical refrigerators driven by gasoline engines. By the 1980s diesel engines and sophisticated electronics had taken over the task of keeping food—and commodities like cosmetics—under high pressure. Flatbeds, drop decks, and low boys now tote construction materials, aircraft engines, or huge electrical transformers. Specially ventilated trailers with built-in ramps carry livestock to market and giant hopper trailers transport such dry bulk materials as flour and cement. Other trailers today have side curtains to facilitate side-loading of bulky objects, such as factory machinery. Auto carriers are ingeniously fabricated so their hydraulically operated ramps can be configured to haul as many as 10 new cars from factory to dealer.

As the loads got heavier and trucks got bigger, more gears were needed to get the vehicle moving and to keep the engine from bogging down. In the early 1920s a coal dealer in Green Bay, Wisconsin, had his mechanics bolt on a three-speed auxiliary gearbox behind a truck's original four-speed transmission. This multiplied the ratios through which the engine worked from 4 to 12 (each of the main transmission's gears was "split" by 3 auxiliary ratios), and the truck could then pull a trailer. Although they added to the difficulty of shifting gears, these two-stick transmissions enjoyed much popularity.

A few years later, single rear axles on trucks were doubled as another means to boost payload and pulling capacity. Even these tandems, however, were solidly mounted on the truck's frame. Only the tires provided cushion as the vehicle climbed over bumps, driveway aprons, and other vertical obstacles. Complex suspension systems for tandem rear axles thus came into being. Today, multiple sets of leaf springs, beams, or air bags equalize weight between axles by tying them together. Rods connect the axles securely to the frame, preventing them from being twisted off their springs by engine torque. Magnus Hendrickson, a Swedish immigrant who settled in Chicago, invented one of the first

"walking beam" tandem suspensions in the late 1920s, and sold the first units to International Harvester Company.

Air brakes, which greatly increased stopping power over hydraulic or mechanical brakes, came on the scene in the 1930s. Compressed air, pumped through hoses to brake mechanisms, proved an effective means of remotely controlling trailers not permanently coupled to power units.

When the Great Depression boosted trucking's fortunes, truckers faced increasing constraints from state lawmakers. Authorities, concerned about the safety of long trucks sharing the highways with increasing numbers of cars, imposed length restrictions which changed the shape of over-the-road trucks. In conventional truck designs the engines of most big trucks were housed in an auto-like hood ahead of the driver's cab. Faced with length limits, truckers were relunctant to give up cargo-carrying space behind the cab, so they got builders to place the engine under the cab and shorten the overall length by eliminating the hood.

These first cab-over-engine (COE) units had non-tilting cabs, making maintenance of engine components difficult. To replace an engine required either unbolting the cab from the chassis or pulling the engine out of the front of the vehicle. But the COEs did cut down on the tractor length and added to the cargo-carrying capacity of the trailer.

Weight, though, was another critical payload factor. Trucks were made mostly of heavy steel. But when Leland James, president of Consolidated Freightways, suggested to truck builders that they try using lightweight materials like aluminum, he was virtually greeted with boos, hisses, and catcalls. So James called together five of his best mechanics, cleared out a corner of a repair shop, and set them to work designing and building trucking's first lightweight tractor. Although development was interrupted by World War II, James' team eventually designed an aluminum cab tractor called the Freightliner—a nameplate that survives as a major U.S. manufacturer today. The company rose to prominence under the presidency of Kenneth W. Self, a self-styled country boy who was one of the original five mechanic-designer-builders.

Perhaps trucking's single greatest advancement was the diesel engine. Diesel engines began appearing on the road as early as the 1940s. Named after German engineer Rudolf Diesel, who patented his design in 1892, the automotive diesel was pioneered in this country

Above: With better refrigeration trailers available, food companies built long range fleets and expanded their markets. In 1940 Cuday packing used large "Diamond T's" to service the Midwest. Courtesy, American Truck Historical Society

Top: This 1926 Chevrolet utility truck was restored by Winross Restorations. Courtesy, American Truck Historical Society

Above: This 1929 Ford "A" tractor was restored in 1965. Courtesy, American Truck Historical Society

Top: Trailers have become specialized to accommodate many types of cargo, everything from frozen foods to livestock. Photo by Tom Tracy/The Photo File

by Clessie Cummins, a Hoosier inventor from Columbus, Indiana. Installed in heavy trucks, the diesel boasted high stamina and economy—as well as much noise and smoke. But with the availability of cheap gasoline throughout America, gas-fueled engines remained popular in trucks for another 25 years, especially in the relatively flat Great Plains states.

In the West, however, where long steep grades put tremendous strain on engines, the oil-burning diesel was accepted much more readily by those wise enough to recognize its virtues. Gas engines often broke down in the mountains, leaving driver and load stranded and the trucker broke. But as a trailer builder in Salt Lake City noted in the late 1930s, "The people who paid their bills were running diesels."

Early truck diesels rarely delivered more than 80 horsepower. After World War II, however, horsepower ratings climbed from 180 to 220, then 250 and up. Cummins, Mack, Caterpillar, and Detroit Diesel introduced larger engines,

allowing drivers to haul more freight. The rounded trailer noses of the 1930s were also squared off to make room for more cargo. Although the flat-faced trailers generated considerably more wind resistance, the higher horsepower diesels were more than equal to the task. Besides, with diesel fuel priced at 18 to 20 cents a gallon, who cared?

Most postwar diesels required the use of multiple gear ratios—10, 13, 15 or more speeds—to keep the trucks moving in a narrow engine operating range of only a few hundred revolutions per minute. Outside that range power dropped considerably. To solve this problem, Mack introduced its revolutionary Maxidyne with a wide power band that allowed for a five-speed transmission. At the lower end of the band, torque output increased to make up for declining horsepower. The result was that drivers did not have to shift as often, and fuel economy was better. It became a popular idea, and a few major fleets embraced the idea and benefitted from the high torque rise.

By the early 1970s both Consolidated Freightways and United Parcel Service were buying Detroit Diesel and Cum-

mins Engine diesels with less than traditional ratings, but which maintained
horsepower and torque over a wide
operating range. Six- and seven-speed
transmissions—instead of 10- or 13-
speed units—quickly became practical.

Although diesels were economical
and durable, many truckers, especially
independent owner-operators who drove
their own rigs, clamored for more raw
power. For example, in the mid-1960s,
an owner-operators' hot setup might
include a 318 horsepower Detroit V8 or
335 horsepower Cummins in-line 6.
These were later eclipsed in the 1970s by
450 horsepower Detroit V12s and huge K
series Cummins I-6s, and by 425 horsepower V8s from Caterpillar.

The horsepower war was on—at least
until the Middle East changed forever
America's approach to fuel use. Trucking, like the rest of industrialized and
motorized America, was profoundly
affected by the 1973 Arab Oil Embargo.
Almost overnight fuel supplies dried up,
while the trickle still available doubled in
price.

Truck designers, pressured by the
sudden scarcity of diesel fuel, began to
work feverishly on designs that would
decrease fuel consumption. Air deflectors sprouted from cab rooftops to bend
rushing air around and over the flat
noses of trailers. In less than 10 years the
deflectors evolved into full fairing packages with bulbous roofs, panels extending from the sides of cabs to close the
gap with the trailer, air-dam bumpers,
and even side skirts on tractors and trailers. Truck builders streamlined their
hoods and cabs to smooth the passage of
air over sheet metal and past turbulence-
creating gaps and holes. New aerodynamic designs became popular, saving
fuel and big money. A 5 or 10 percent
reduction in a truck's fuel bill added up
to hundreds, even thousands of dollars
for a rig running 100,000 miles a year,
especially with fuel soaring to $1 and as
much as $1.50 per gallon. And the horse-
power race was over, at least temporari-
ly.

In 1985 Kenworth Truck Company
introduced its T600A conventional, probably the decade's most influential vehicle. With a severely sloped nose, the KW
"anteater," as drivers quickly dubbed it,
was radical in appearance. But it saved
fuel. Its overwhelming acceptance even
caught the manufacturer by surprise;

within three years T600As accounted for
the majority of Kenworth's conventional
cab sales. Competitors designed and
built fast-selling aerodynamic models of
their own. Like it or not, America's
truckers were latching on to high-tech-
nology.

Engine makers, meanwhile, worked
equally feverishly to improve the efficiency of their power plants. Turbocharging was added to those diesels
that did not already have it, and
advanced aftercooling systems began
appearing by the late 1970s. New, smaller engines began doing the work of
large-displacement engines, lowering
buying and operating costs and saving
weight. Electronic controls, which precisely meter the supply of fuel to the

*Above: An Avery farm truck had steel
wheels consisting of wooden and metal
cleats. The metal cleats were bolted on
while the wooden ones were pounded
in. If not kept wet, the wooden cleats
would fall out. Courtesy, American
Truck Historical Society*

*Top: Truck manufacturers have
increased diesel fuel effecincy through
continuing design changes from the
frame up. Photo by Tom Tracy/The
Photo File*

UNPRECEDENTED in the history of civilization stands the vast communications service—the world-girdling telephone and telegraph. The fate of nations, the gearing of commerce, the saving of countless lives depend on endless careful planning, on workers' skill—yes, and likewise on the horde of good trucks—GMCs—servicing this communication web. The Makers of General Motors Trucks salute the service of a trillion wires and its controllers, providers of close ties for all human relations!

Time payments through our own Y. M. A. C. Plan at lowest available rates

GENERAL MOTORS TRUCKS AND TRAILERS

GENERAL MOTORS TRUCK & COACH
DIVISION OF
YELLOW TRUCK & COACH MANUFACTURING COMPANY
PONTIAC, MICHIGAN

GMC saluted the communications services and the GMC trucks that service the "communication web" in this advertisement. Courtesy, PR Counselors

engine and allow mechanics to quickly diagnose an engine's internal problem, were introduced in the mid-1980s. Accessories like fan clutches were added to save even more fuel.

Tires, too, underwent change. Radials, which had already caught on in the auto market, swept the heavy truck industry in the mid- to late 1970s. Truckers found out what motorists already knew: radials deliver much longer mileage and save fuel by reducing rolling resistance. New radial designs hit the market. Low-profile radials cut rolling resistance even more than standard-size radials, and further lowered operating costs. Even the "super single," one large tire that replaces the dual wheel-and-tire assembly on most axles, began catching on. Although big singles

roll easier than low-pros, they often stumble on roadblocks raised by highway engineers concerned about pavement "rutting" from the singles' greater footprint pressure. Retreading, although never popular with automobile drivers, gained acceptance among truckers because a well-cared-for radial casing can be given new life two or three times with the application of new tread. Retreading can stretch the total lifespan of the original tire to 600,000 or more miles.

Long life became a rallying cry among fleet managers who demanded more durable engines, driveline components, cabs—virtually every component housed between the headlights and taillights. But specifically, they wanted a tractor that could be operated for 500,000 miles before requiring a major engine overhaul. The builders delivered, improving engine life from 300,000 miles to the targeted 500,000 miles. Transmissions and axles were designed and built to pass the 600,000-mile mark before requiring serious attention. Cabs were made of more rust-resistant materials—like aluminum and galvanized steel—to keep them from deteriorating before the chassis and driveline components were ready for the scrap yard. Today the current target is a one million-mile tractor—an achievable goal already attained by a small number of exceptionally well-maintained trucks.

Perhaps the most controversial design was the introduction of anti-lock brakes, which were subsequently required in the mid-'70s on all trucks under a federal law. Reasoning that huge jumbo jets could stop safely on slick runways, federal regulators demanded the same life-saving performance from trucks. But the bureaucrats overlooked two factors: (1) Trucks must make many more stops and work in a much harsher daily environment than an airplane, and (2) technology, mostly in the form of microcomputer-controlled electronics, was not yet perfected for the harsh realities of the road. Horror stories abounded of air brakes suddenly coming on by themselves or not coming on at all when the driver wanted to stop. Brake maintenance costs soared. Challenged in a lawsuit by Paccar Incorporated (a parent company of Kenworth and Peterbilt), the anti-lock requirement ultimately was thrown out by a federal circuit court. But it was a bitter pill for manufacturers and

truckers alike who by this time had to swallow losses in excess of a billion dollars.

Electronic anti-lock braking, using more rugged and advanced components, reappeared on the market in the mid-1980s. These modified designs had been successfully tested and used in Europe and were considered more safe and efficient than earlier designs tried in the U.S. Federal authorities, too, proceeded more cautiously in formulating new anti-lock brake requirements.

By the mid-1970s, modern truck designs were well established. For local and short-haul service, there were low cabovers which were easy to climb into and out of, and short-nose conventionals which cost less but were almost as easy to maneuver in traffic and into tight loading areas. Over-the-road operations used high cabovers, whose entire cab structure tilted forward for easy access to engine and transmission. And if an operation did not require especially long trailers or worked in states that permitted generous overall lengths, the long-nose conventional was favored.

Many states imposed length limits on trailers. Out West a single tractor could pull two or three trailers legally, but doubles and triples were not allowed in most Midwest and Eastern states where the mere mention of "road trains" on generally narrow and crowded highways gave politicians palpitations. Exceptions were turnpikes in New York, Ohio, and Florida, which were built to superhighway standards and whose authorities gladly collected the higher tolls the longer trucks paid.

Even with the expansion of the interstate system, many state officials ignored the proven fact that long truck-trailer combinations could operate safely; they continued to ban them from their highways. Not until the U.S. Congress intervened in late 1982 were more productive doubles (each trailer could be up to 28 feet long) and longer semitrailers (up to 48 feet) allowed on the interstates throughout the country. Congress also decreed that loaded rigs could weigh a total of 80,000 pounds and, in a separate law, increased the maximum width limit from 96 to 102 inches—a width used for years by intercity and transit buses. But even the so-called "STAA" vehicles (the Surface Transportation Assistance Act that legalized them) still faced many

Above: Dodge offered an economical lightweight diesel engine in 1962 for use in short-haul trucks such as this one. The engine was a Dodge-Perkins six-cylinder, four-cycle model with direct injection, and was capable of 10-14 MPG in local service. Courtesy, Chrysler Motor Corporation

Below: Federal introduced its 2 model Style Liner series in 1951. The unique feature was a hinged fender that swung up for ease of maintenance. But although Federal survived the Depression, it could not survive postwar competition and ceased operation in 1959. Courtesy, PR Counselors

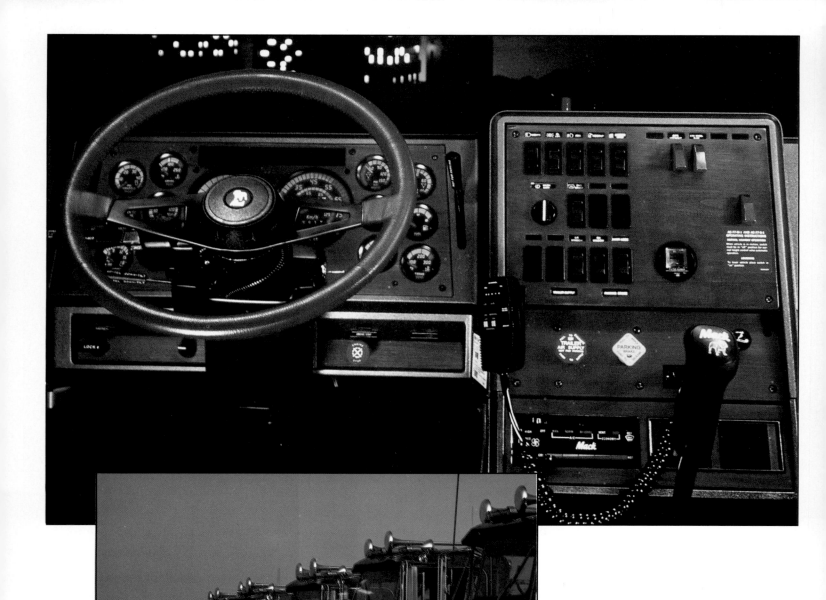

Top: Mack introduced its CH 600 conventional truck in the fall of 1988. Its sleek lines add to its aerodynamic values, yet it retains the pugnacious appearance that typifies Mack. Pictured is the CH-600 instrument panel designed for easy access. Courtesy, Mack Truck Corporation

Above: Truck manufacturers cater to fleet operators by outfitting trucks with special equipment specified by the purchasers. Photo by Mark E. Gibson

Right: Advances in engine technology have enabled manufacturers to create smaller, more efficient power plants that reduce weight and cost. Photo by Tom Tracy/The Photo File

restrictions laid down by lawmakers in individual states. Some, for example, allowed them to venture no farther than a quarter-mile from interstates. And the "access" issue was still being grappled with by federal and state authorities six years after passage of the STAA.

Nonetheless, the law had a major effect on truck configuration: it made the long-nose conventional the king of the road because no overall length limits existed for STAA vehicles. If a tractor pulled a pair of 28-foot trailers, or a single 48-footer, and no cargo was carried by the tractor itself, it theoretically could be 1,000 feet long and still be legal. But most truckers were practical and knew their rigs still had to maneuver through city streets to get to their loading and unloading points. This was their chance to change from the high cabover to the conventional. The long-nose tractor was preferred by most drivers because of its crash protection, more "macho" looks and, some thought, its better ride. Managers, too, preferred it because it generally cost less to buy and maintain. But high cabovers, with their good maneuverability and constantly improving ride, are still popular with many truckers.

Heavy trucks used in local operations were largely unaffected by the federal law. Primarily employed in construction and garbage hauling, these vehicles are built to meet varying state limitations. Generally, Eastern and Midwestern states favor shorter, more maneuverable trucks; western states have always encouraged long wheelbases that provided equal weight over greater distances and put less stress on bridge spans. Federal authorities, favoring the longer designs, began pressuring eastern states to enforce the federal "bridge formula" on interstate highways.

In the near future trucks will become even more aerodynamic, more efficient in componentry and more reliant on high technology for diagnosing problems. Electronics will become widely used on engines and chassis to achieve greater efficiency in maintenance and operations. Electronic data recorders, which capture vast amounts of trip information and virtually place the manager over the driver's shoulder, are already in use. They can save bundles of money by pinpointing wasteful driver habits and vehicle abuses, but they can also work to the driver's advantage by verifying his performance and saving him from unjustified speeding tickets. To comply with federal Environmental Protection Agency standards, diesel exhaust emissions will have to get cleaner. This will require more sophisticated electronic controls,

Above: Transmissions in modern trucks can be tailored to the user's goal: line-haul fuel economy, stop-and-go efficiency, or off-road guts and durability. Photo by Jack Williams/The Photo File

Top: Truck tire carcasses can last as long as 600,000 miles through repeated retreading. Retread use on the front wheels is subject to various state regulations. Photo by Sam Sargent/The Photo File

In the late 1960s most truck manufacturers experimented with gas turbine engines in an attempt to apply aircraft technology to trucking. But although the engines provided plenty of power, they were not economical. Pictured is the Chevy version, the Turbo Titan III, on the road in 1968. Courtesy, General Motors Corporation

perhaps low-sulphur fuel and/or alternate fuels like methanol, and/or unwieldy particulate traps to scrub diesel smoke of unsightly, unhealthy contaminants. As diesel fuel again climbs in price, more futuristic aerodynamic designs will provide a better friction coefficient than those in today's automobiles. Like technology in general, truck design will evolve at a pace far faster than it did in the first 70 years of this century.

Many advances in principle componentry of trucks before and after World War II were carried out by independent suppliers rather than the truck builders themselves. This aspect of North American truck equipment evolution came about for two primary reasons: the proliferation of small truck manufacturers with limited research and development resources in the early part of the century, and larger companies' preoccupation with products other than heavy trucks. Because their volume was limited, the smaller firms found it less expensive to buy engines, transmissions, clutches, axles, and other parts from established suppliers than to develop and manufacture these parts themselves.

Only those companies that survived the tumultuous ups and downs of the economy in the first three decades could

afford to design their own gasoline engines, for example, and many gas engines were still bought from suppliers like Hercules. When the diesel really began catching on after World War II, few truck builders had the money or expertise to bother with it. This gave Cummins, Detroit Diesel, and Caterpillar a ready-made market.

Giant corporations like General Motors and Ford Motor Company seemed to concentrate on higher volume: light- and medium-size trucks and, primarily, autos. International Harvester also built light- and medium-size trucks and, of course, farm equipment. White similarly branched out into farm machinery and large stationary engines. What little research and development capital was left for heavy trucks went into the cab and chassis.

In order to please a wide range of buyers and capture as many sales as possible, truck assemblers, as they were sometimes called, found themselves offering a growing list of component options. From this came the North American practice of customers specifying or "spec'ing" the components they want.

Fleet maintenance managers spec'd equipment in great detail. Radiators, batteries, windshield wiper motors—

nothing was too small to include on the order. Managers had found through experience what worked best (or what did not) in their operations. And the practice enabled them to keep the fleet parts standardized, reducing inventories in maintenance shops and maintaining vehicle familiarity for mechanics. If the truck builder changed the "standard" wheel seal sometime during the model run from Brand Y to Z, it did not matter—Acme Trucking's vehicles would come off the line with Brand X, because that is what the fleet ordered. So detailed did the art of spec'ing become that maintenance managers—who sometimes achieve vice presidential status in their corporations—would brag that "the truck is only an envelope for my components."

A downside to all this spec'ing was the truck builder's high cost of engineering and installing all these pieces into the chassis, and of carrying so many parts in inventory. By the early 1980s the manufacturers showed signs of rebellion. They began weeding out seldom ordered options and continued to offer only the most popular ones. They encouraged acceptance of a factory standardized set of components by pricing these considerably lower than the optional parts. And, in a move that made the career specifiers nervous, truck builders prepared a set of pre-engineered vehicles for various vocations (dubbed "Work Ready," "EZ Spec,"

and other catchy names), and sweetened the deal with guaranteed quick deliveries and extended warranties. These vehicles still offer many choices of power train and other equipment, but eliminate many oddball combinations which, according to one builder, "add cost but no value to the customer.

Bucking the trend of merely being an assembler virtually since its founding in l903, Mack Trucks consistently designed, engineered, and built most of its own major components, including engines, transmissions, and axles. To meet competition, however, it will accept orders for trucks with components from outside suppliers, as specified by the customer. But in terms of dollars and cents, it usually is to the buyer's advantage to specify Mack components.

The push for further "vertical integration" of American truck building may gain momentum from the European, market, where it has been the practice for generations. Two European truck builders now own old-line U.S. companies: Daimler-Benz bought Freightliner, and Volvo purchased assets of the White Motor Company in 1981. Volvo is testing the waters by offering its own powertrain components in American-built White and GMC chassis. But given the history of North American manufacture, design, and buyer preference, a detectable trend to vertical integration could be long in coming.

The futuristic "Bison" truck of 1969 was co-sponsored by several firms for an exposition. It was aerodynamic, powerful, and wholly lacking in "machismo" associated with trucking. Courtesy, American Truck Historical Society

Partners
In Progress

The outlook for long-haul trucking is favorable, as the industry has experienced a changing business climate in the 1980s and has proven adaptable to change. Photo by Christopher Springman/The Photo File

127

Specialized Carriers

What's so special about specialized carriers? The name says it all: The materials they carry require special handling—from chemicals, petroleum products, and other hazardous materials, to steel, huge electrical transformers, heavy equipment, and perishable products, such as produce requiring refrigeration.

General freight usually rides the road in the classic tractor-trailer mode. Cargo requiring special handling, however, travels in or on such conveyances as tankers, refrigerated units, lowboys, drop frames, extendables, and flatbeds, depending on the needs of the shipper.

Among the more demanding special-handling assignments is the moving of nuclear reactor and power plant machinery, and various tasks for America's space and defense programs, such as moving the space shuttle, missiles, and rockets.

The key factor in this trucking category, obviously, is safety—in pickup, movement, and delivery. The materials carried by specialized haulers have to be considered, in most cases, as perilous cargo—things that can be a menace on the highways of America, both to those who share the roads with truckers and to the general countryside.

Consequently, successful specialized carriers are known for their cargo care as well as for their more obvious attributes of on-time delivery and extensive customer service. On the mission of specialized carriers, one official makes this point: "They (customers) don't want a carrier that's out there dumping its chemicals on the ground all the time. They want someone who's safe, who can perform for them, and who can get it there on time."

Maintenance and cleanup go hand in hand with safety in this portion of the trucking industry, the latter being of major importance on the chemical-hauling side. Sound maintenance, of course, helps to ensure that the trucks are prime movers when they hit the road.

Most major carriers can point to excellent safety records, but that doesn't mean they're willing to let the past carry the present and future. They seem always to be pursuing new avenues to safety along the open road. Of special interest to many are opportunities to test new equipment, something that's becoming more pronounced as manufacturers are continually trying to design and produce a finer, safer piece of equipment for use by these carriers.

Above: The Mack C series was introduced in 1963 with a short bumper-to-back of cab dimension of only 89 inches. Servicing was made easy by the hinged fender design. Courtesy, Mack Truck Corporation

Facing page: Threatening skies do little to impede a trucker's progress; only the most inclement weather will stop the haul. Photo by Jack Williams/The Photo File

SCHILLI TRANSPORTATION SERVICES, INC.

In recent times the highest praise of an athlete's ability is usually wrapped up in one phrase: "He can do it all." Carrying that idea out of the sports world and into the business world—in this case the trucking world—it certainly can be said of Schilli Transportation Services of Remington, Indiana, that "they can do it all."

The Motor Carrier Act of 1980 attributed to a major rework of an industry that had been pretty much status quo for almost 50 years. With the new, highly competitive market that was created, Thomas R. Schilli immediately initiated a planning process to ensure the survival of his company, at that time Schilli Motor Lines. Thomas R. Schilli, who grew up in the trucking business, has been active in both state and national trucking organizations; his latest venture has been as president of the Interstate Truckload Carrier Conference.

Right: Schilli is first with leading-edge transport technology, developing in-house a lightweight flatbed unit with a load capacity of 60,000 pounds.

Below: Affiliated Schilli trucking companies through which Schilli serves its broad customer base.

As a result of the planning, Schilli Transportation Services, Inc., was formed in February 1987 and serves as a centralization of the many services that have been offered by the Schilli organization for more than two decades. The company offers custom-designed services: executive administration, rating and billing, sales and marketing, tariff compiling and issuing, data processing, driver training, free consulting services, personnel and recruiting, accounting and finance, permits and licensing, and insurance and safety.

Schilli Transportation Services, Inc., via the mode of a broker, serves its broad customer base through its various affiliated trucking companies. Each of those companies— Atlantic Inland Carriers, Wabash Valley Transportation, Schilli Specialized, Inc., and Schilli Leasing— are designed around specific services and are staffed with professionals with many years of experience in that particular segment of the motor carrier industry. Schilli's massive operation, even though it provides service throughout the continental

United States, is most prominent in the area east of the Mississippi River. The total equipment fleet consists of more than 450 tractors and 700 trailers of various types with numerous terminals located in key areas of service.

Here is the way the trucking operations hit the road:

Atlantic Inland Carriers Inc. of Indianapolis—dry van truckload service throughout the continental United States;

Wabash Valley Transportation Inc. of Wolcott, Indiana—specialized flatbed truckload service throughout the continental United States;

Schilli Specialized, Inc., of Remington, Indiana—liquid and dry bulk truckload shipments originating from or destined to Indiana, Ohio, Northern Kentucky, Illinois, Michigan, and Southern Wisconsin. From a Lafayette, Indiana, location—expedited door-to-door package and LTL delivery service throughout central Indiana with daily delivery service between Lafayette and Indianapolis. Industrial waste removal service is also performed from the Lafayette location.

Schilli Leasing Inc. of Remington, Indiana—specializes in property management and in the design, development, and leasing of transportation equipment. (Integrated equipment management systems, volume purchasing, and maintenance promote safety, efficiency, and productivity.)

Though the latest Schilli trucking effort began in 1967 with Thomas, the Schilli name goes back almost another 40 years from there when Bernard Schilli, Thomas' father, and his brother Al started Schilli Brothers Truck Service in Missouri. Schilli's death in 1965 meant rerouting the business for a while before Thomas R. Schilli, a Marine Corps veteran, bought the company's assets and put the family's name back on the road, though only in first gear.

Following a move to the northwestern Indiana town of Yeoman,

the focus of the business, which had previously been based in Jeffersonville, Indiana, changed from hauling grain to Louisville, Kentucky, and fertilizer back to hauling grain to Chicago and building materials on the return trip. U.S. Gypsum and GAF provided the freight that put the company into high gear, and in 1971 the rejuvenated Schilli firm picked Chicago for its first terminal, serving 30 trailers and 20 owner-operators.

From there, in a stretch of little more than 10 years, Schilli terminals opened in Mount Vernon, Indiana, to serve a new GAF plant there; Shoals, Indiana, where U.S. Gypsum was the prime customer; Cincinnati, Ohio, serving Celotex of Lockand; Remington, which in the interim has become the site of corporate headquarters; Colfax, Indiana, serving such customers as Formica Corporation, Division of American Cyanamid of Frankfort, Indiana; Memphis and Knoxville in Tennessee; and Philadelphia, Pennsylvania; Detroit, Michigan; St. Louis, Missouri; and Champaign, Illinois.

In little more than 20 years Schilli has geared up from just six trailers to a near King of the Road status with revenues exceeding $38.5 million; some 600 employees, including drivers and support personnel; and 1,150 pieces of equipment. Schilli expects the growth and expansion to keep on rolling, carrying the company on down the road to greater responsiveness, service, and a place of continued leadership in America's trucking industry.

A piece of Schilli literature relates: "We were one of the first carriers in America to add 102-inch by 48-foot vans to our fleet; we were on the leading edge of computerized dispatching; first with a new lightweight, 60,000-pound payload flatbed tractor-trailer combination; and today we are taking the lead in providing services to both carriers and shippers to develop a higher level of professional, flexible, and cost-effective transportation service to American industry.

"We learned long ago that leading our own industry was the best way to keep up with the needs of yours."

Schilli Transportation Services, Inc., is most prominent in the area east of the Mississippi River. The total equipment fleet consists of more than 450 tractors and 700 trailers of various types with numerous terminals located in key areas of service.

RUDOLF EXPRESS

During its more than 50 years Rudolf Express of Bourbonnais, Illinois, has not always traveled a smooth road.

The bumps included the Great Depression, then World War II, and finally the untimely death in 1964 of Emil Rudolf, who ran the company through the 1950s and purchased it in 1962. However, even in death, the spirit and the toughness of Emil Rudolf persisted through his wife as she kept the business intact, deter-

This tractor-trailer is one of the modern, new units Rudolf uses in its over-the-road operation. Nearly half of the fleet has been updated in the past two years.

mined to keep it on a roll until her sons, then 17 and nine, could take their place at the company helm.

Rudolf's death thrust his wife, Marie, into a delicate and seemingly dangerous position that called for an immense amount of experience, which she didn't have. Though predictions of doom came from others in the industry, a fierce determination and a family atmosphere, which included—and still does—everyone from company executives to dock workers and office staff to mechanics and drivers, kept the wheels turning in high gear.

And now, a quarter-century later, Rudolf Express is thriving under the direction of sons Richard and Robert Rudolf. Richard is president and active head of the company, and Robert is vice-president/operations and secretary/treasurer.

In addition to her two sons, Marie Rudolf had several strong al-

In this picture, taken in the corporate boardroom, are some of Rudolf Express' key management people. Standing (from left) are Lori Hosier, Dick Johnson, Walt Zungailo, Joe Rudolf, Daryl Clark, Herb Gibson, Sue Rudolf, and Pat Prince. Seated (from left) are Robert Rudolf, Marie Rudolf, and Richard Rudolf.

lies through the years in her quest to not only keep Rudolf Express alive but drive it to a preeminent position in the industry in the Midwest, for instance, Emil's two younger brothers, George and Joe. The former was a vice-president until his death in 1980, and the latter still is terminal manager in Chicago. Other employees in important executive positions have added stability to the business. Daryl Clark, vice-president/traffic, joined the firm in 1950.

Rudolf Express, which began as Roosevelt Cartage in Kankakee, Illinois, under Emil's uncle, Tony, serves all of Illinois and parts of Wisconsin, Indiana, Iowa, Michigan, and Missouri as a regional LTL carrier. Its list of customers covers the spectrum of general commodities in American industry—chemicals, appliances,

Some of the people in the Rudolf family of employees pose for a group picture at the firm's corporate headquarters. Rudolf Express has nearly 200 employees working together to service its customers.

batteries, pharmaceuticals, food, and paper, for starters.

The firm reaches beyond regional boundaries with its red-nose Reindeer Division trucks, in which it handles truckloads throughout states east of the Mississippi River as well as Texas. To get the cargo to destination, the company has a fleet of approximately 135 power units and nearly 300 trailers for its own over-the-road drivers, and also hires a select number of owner-operators.

The firm's main terminal is on a fenced, 12-acre site in Bourbonnais, located, strategically, less than one mile from Interstate 57, 15 miles east of Interstate 55, and 25 miles south of Interstate 80. The land was bought and the modern buildings erected in 1974. With an eye toward expansion, Rudolf Express also has six acres adjoining the site.

The 71-door cross dock includes 32,000 square feet, and the company's maintenance building totals 15,000 square feet. The office complex has 7,250 square feet. Additional Rudolf terminals are located in Chicago, Milwaukee, Kewanee, and Springfield, and the firm works cargo out of agency terminals in 12 states.

Pictured here is Rudolf's corporate office in Bourbonnais, Illinois.

Buildings and trucks notwithstanding, Rudolf Express relies heavily on its tradition of outstanding service and the people who give that service. "We have good, sincere people at every level in the company," says Rich Rudolf. "They believe in the company and work hard for its success. I consider every one a member of our family.

"We continually hear from our customers, not just traffic people but supervisors and office personnel as well, commenting on the courteous treatment they receive from our drivers, traffic people, and just about everyone from Rudolf with whom they come in contact. This is a service business, and giving good, courteous service is the key to our success."

That key was cast through long and arduous work on the part of Emil Rudolf, a fact not lost on his succeeding generation. His policies and

personality became the cornerstone on which to build Rudolf Express' industry position of today.

The life of the German immigrant boy who came to America with his parents when he was three, grew up in the Kankakee area, and began driving for his uncle, Tony, almost as soon as his feet could reach the pedals, has always been a road sign to follow. Even in those days, when the run was from Kankakee to Chicago and back, there never seemed to be any limits to the firm's potential. The toughness that Emil Rudolf exhibited in his drive to fulfill that potential left an indelible impression on his wife and sons. And their perseverence, along with that of the long list of loyal employees, has served the company and his memory to the fullest.

SWEENEY BROS. INC.

It seems that from its very beginnings, Sweeney Brothers Inc. has been on a roll. There has been no need for double-clutching, and certainly no need for gearing down.

Sweeney's, which has grown steadily over the years while serving as the foundation for the much broader Sweeney Industries Inc., was founded at Chicopee, Massachusetts, in 1967 by Richard M. and Martin G. Sweeney, after the brothers began their transportation careers with a local manufacturing company.

Originally their trucking company, which had the Fisk Tire Co. (later Uniroyal) plant in Chicopee as one of its first prime accounts, specialized in handling less-than-truckload freight for other carriers. But the firm's growth was propelled forward in the early 1970s, when it shifted its workload gears and put itself on the road to becoming a reliable local carrier, providing overnight service to metropolitan New York and New Jersey.

"Service you never dreamed possible" became the company's motto, and its reputation as a first-class regional carrier was recognized by both local and national accounts. The reputation was well founded; many of

those firms are still, 20 years later, doing business with Sweeney, which has routes covering Vermont, New Hampshire, Rhode Island, Connecticut, New York, New Jersey, the Philadelphia area, and, of course, its home state of Massachusetts.

According to Richard Sweeney, the company president who oversees operations and maintenance, the firm is a dedicated common carrier with no commodity as its primary business, preferring, instead, to be firmly based in consolidation and dis-

Sweeney Bros. rigs are lined up for action at their terminal at the former Westover Air Force Base in Chicopee, Massachusetts.

tribution.

In the late 1970s, in recognition of a need for change inspired by the company's growth, Richard Sweeney and brother Martin, treasurer, added Kevin B. Vann, who was to become executive vice-president/finance, to the company's administration team, and plans were made to diversify the operation and prepare for the advent of deregulation.

As a first step the company proceeded to develop a warehouse and distribution facility at the former

Westover Air Force Base. The Sweeney administration team realized quickly that the location was at the Crossroads of New England, and shortly thereafter the entire trucking operation was expanded and moved to the company's seven-acre Westover site that has since then served as headquarters for the entire Sweeney operation.

Rapid growth in sales followed, and the company continued to diversify by offering an outside fleet-maintenance program to other carriers, and a fleet- and equipment-leasing company was developed to accommodate the company's growing fleet needs.

In the early 1980s, shortly after deregulation, a fourth person joined the Sweeney administration organization. Thomas W. Dufault, who in the interim has become the company's controller, came aboard to begin implementing computerized financial and reporting systems that have enabled the organization to expand even further. Included in this expansion has been management systems for major air freight carriers and ground-support carriers; the company services all of the major airports in its region on a daily basis.

The Sweeney logo, a diamond border around the letter "S," is visible on all of the company's vehicles and trailers. The diamond's four points represent the firm's past, present, and future philosophy that image, self-reliance, service, and market share are the business plans that the company believes are the most important points needed to continue into the years ahead.

Today Sweeney Industries Inc., the overall corporation, operates several transportation companies in the Northeast and Mid-Atlantic regions of the United States. Through internal growth acquisitions Sweeney has become a major force in the Northeast. In addition to Sweeney Brothers Inc., the corporation operates Sweeney Nationwide Inc., Knickerbocker East-West Inc., Allied Freight Systems Inc., and Chicopee

Air Cargo Inc.

Aside from the location of corporate offices and main terminal in Chicopee, the company has terminals that range from 10 to 23 doors at additional locations: Hackensack, New York; Albany, New York; and Windsor, Burlington International Airport, and South Burlington, all in Vermont.

Throughout its system Sweeney

Industries employs 250 people, including its own drivers except for 40 owner/operators working for the 48-state-authority, Sweeney Nationwide. There are approximately 130 tractors and straight jobs in the company fleet, along with roughly 170 trailers. The people and the fleet handle LTL and truckload freight in what they consider the most efficient and professional manner possible.

Richard Sweeney and the rest of the management team believe the one thing that sets Sweeney Bros. Inc. apart from many carriers is that, although the Sweeney system has grown larger through the years, "we're still small enough that a customer can go right to the top and say 'This is what I need,' and we'll do it."

And he expects that attitude to prevail as Sweeney Bros. Inc. rolls into the 1990s. Continued growth—without expecting any dramatic expansion—and a dedication to becoming an even stronger regional carrier with a niche for the Northeast and Middle Atlantic regions is the road the company expects to take through the 1990s and right into the twenty-first century.

Left: This sign introduces visitors to corporate headquarters for Sweeney Bros. Inc. in Chicopee, Massachusetts.

Below: A Sweeney Bros. tractor-trailer rolls out of the Chicopee terminal on its way to another important destination.

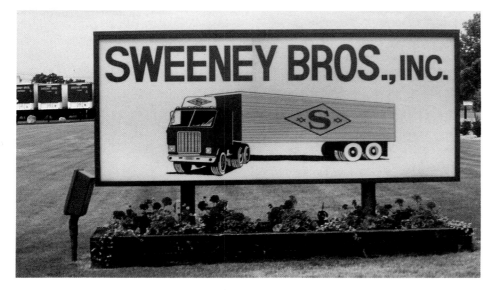

GULLY TRANSPORTATION, INC.

Gully Transportation, a trucking operation that was begun in 1947 by Bill Gully, an enterprising 19-year-old, has always been driven by a commitment to quality.

It runs into every corner of the organization—from service to equipment to drivers to all the others in the supporting cast—and it has been the cornerstone on which a spotless image has been built through more than 40 years.

From that day when owner/operator Bill Gully first turned the key in his truck to go on the road as a leased operator for Healzer Cartage of Kansas City on a relay run from Pittsfield, Illinois, to Chicago, Gully's has grown steadily and carefully into an operation that serves 16 states and runs more than 150 tractors and 400 trailers.

That's Gully Transportation of Quincy, Illinois, and points east, west, north and south.

Using Illinois, Missouri and Iowa as its central base of operations, Gully serves the country's Midlands, Southwest, Southeast, and North-central regions as a general commodities carrier of items from auto parts to cosmetics and on through the alphabet.

The firm's broad sweep of delivery capability means that if a customer needs something shipped between Texas and Minnesota or Minnesota and Georgia or Nebraska and North Carolina or to any number of destinations in between, Gully can get the goods there. In addition, Gully expects that its shipping lanes will expand as the company pursues more avenues to other growing metropolitan areas.

Bill Gully's early successes helped him build a leasing business that grew stronger each year and eventually led to a partnership in 1958 in Hannibal-Quincy Truck Lines of Hannibal, Missouri. Gully became sole owner in 1966 of the less-than-truckload carrier, and two years later the family and its leasing business moved a few miles up and across the Mississippi River to Quincy. In 1973 Gully Transportation Inc. was born as a truckload, general-commodities carrier with 12 trucks.

Throughout that time, Gully wasn't alone in his family-oriented business. Active from the start has been his wife, Barbara, who did all the bookkeeping and a good bit of the dispatching from an office in the basement of the family home until 1970. That's when a full-time helper was added and the office was moved to the company's main shop site. To-

Gully Transportation, Inc., serves the country's Midlands, Southwest, Southeast, and North-central regions as a general commodities carrier of everything from auto parts to cosmetics. Photo by Ginny Gully

day Barbara supervises an office staff of 11 people and serves as corporate secretary.

How does a company go from 12 trucks to 150 tractors and 400 trailers in fewer than 20 years? Service is the answer, say Gully officials, service that has always been top drawer and available around the clock. The fact that Gully's is a family owned business—with Bill Gully as president; his wife, Barbara, as corporate secretary; and his son, Michael, as vice-president—enhances that push for quality service because there always seems to be a family member available at the end of a telephone line.

Beyond that, Gully's has dispatchers on the job seven days a week, and that helps to keep cargo rolling to destinations regularly. In addition, Gully has a sophisticated telephone system that selectively routes calls to the right dispatcher, and the company safety department runs regular road patrols as a way of checking the status of deliveries.

In this just-in-time trucking world, Gully stands out particularly in its association with automobile manufacturers, for whom it seems to be constantly hauling parts from the Detroit area into assembly plants in St. Louis and Kansas City. Those parts go directly onto assembly lines, thus eliminating any need for huge stocks of inventory in the plants.

But that's only a part of the story, because Gully has an array of customers that matches its fleet of equipment and its terminals in Burlington, Iowa; Quincy, Illinois; Kansas City, Hannibal, Macon, and St. Louis, Missouri, and the company's approximately 250 employees are dedicated to giving quality, always on-time service to all customers. For example, the firm integrates sleeper teams with its relay operation, thus cutting "down" time and allowing the company to ensure on-time delivery. The use of the relay system sets Gully apart from most of its peers, since it is uncommon among truckload carriers.

Gully trucks that are hauling delicate cargo such as uncrated new furniture travel on air-ride suspensions, promising smoother rides for these

As a family-owned business, quality is the cornerstone of Gully Transportation, Inc. As the company's slogan says Gully is "Pulling for America with Professional Pride." Courtesy, Larry Block Photography, St. Louis, Missouri

items. To keep itself in the forefront of service, Gully counts 60 percent of its trailers as 53-footers as against 40 percent 48-footers, the latter size usually being in the majority in fleets throughout the industry.

In Gully's eyes, a major part of the firm's service is putting forth a spotless image. And that covers both men and machines. Company officials believe the trucking industry should be represented by the cream of the crop of over-the-road drivers and vehicles. That view calls for the company's blue and white equipment to be modern, well-maintained, and glistening clean as it makes its way across millions of miles of American landscape each year.

And in every Gully cab is a beardless, neatly shorn driver in an immaculate, crisp company uniform of dark blue trousers and light blue shirt with the Gully logo, an indication that Gully believes in the days when truck drivers were regarded as "knights of the road." A further expression of pride both in the firm and in the trucking industry is Gully's slogan of "Pulling For America With Professional Pride."

All of this goes toward helping to keep Gully Transportation's sales approach in high gear. Michael Gully, who is given much of the credit for company growth over the past several years, heads a sales staff that includes three regional representatives who are telling the Gully story to potential clients across the firm's business expanse.

In the future, Gully Transportation doesn't expect to shift too many gears in its service-solid business, but it doesn't expect to sit in neutral, either. There'll be no time for idling the company's motor if growth and expansion goals for the first part of the 1990s, which include expanding the fleet to 200 power units, are to be met. And, though respect and profitability have come fairly quickly to Gully, company officials are ever-watchful for new ways to keep Gully Transportation on the high road.

NATIONWIDE TRUCK BROKERS INC.

It seems that Dan Koster, the founder of Nationwide Truck Brokers Inc. with corporate offices in Grand Rapids, Michigan, was geared to the trucking life right from the start. Farming played an important role in his younger years.

He was born May 19, 1937, to parents Albert and Margaret Koster, and raised on a farm in Hudsonville, Michigan. While he; his brother, Bob; two sisters, Rose and Betty; and his mother took care of the farm, raising onions, his father was trucking produce to Ohio and West Virginia for VanderBunte Brothers in Hudsonville.

At this time Albert Koster had to sell the produce as well as truck it. From his father, Dan Koster learned to be honest and to work hard. Albert also instilled in Dan a love for trucks. The first truck he drove, at age 16, was an LJ Mack with a 707-cubic-inch engine.

Koster attended Hudsonville High School and spent the next two years in the U.S. Army's Second In-

Dan and Ardith Koster have been a partnership from the start of Koster's Grand Rapids, Michigan, trucking business.

This is one of the earliest tractors—a late 1950s Diamond T—that helped put Dan Koster on the road to success.

fantry Division in Fairbanks, Alaska. After an honorable discharge, he returned home, met Ardith Flagel, and married her October 17, 1958. Ardith, a homemaker, has supported Dan in all his decisions.

After an unsuccessful one-year ownership of a Gulf Oil station in Hudsonville, Koster began to pursue trucking. Bob Meeuusen of Zeeland, Michigan, gave him his first break, and Koster drove for him for the next two years. Clarence Gingrich, the Diamond T dealer in Grand Rapids, sold Koster his first truck and trailer.

For the next 14 years Koster was an owner-operator for Superior Brand Produce, hauling produce from Florida to Michigan. Al Blaukamp, a friend, became something of a second father to Koster at this time.

At age 37 Koster decided that it was important for him to spend more time with his wife and three sons. Roger VerLee, owner of Berghorst Poultry, was asked to back Koster with money and to provide a place from which to work. When that was accomplished they became partners, and that partnership grew and thrived for several years.

Through the years Koster has

gained experience with truckers, shippers, and receivers nationwide. At first he became a truck broker, but good truckers were hard to find, and some were not dependable. So he decided to start buying his own trailers and eventually tractors.

Today Nationwide Truck Brokers Inc. is a trucking company with more than 100 trailers and 44 tractors that travel the highways and byways of the nation under 48-state common-carrier authority. Never one to slight his home state, Koster has also obtained intrastate-contract authority for NTB.

In 1984 Koster took sole ownership of the corporation by buying Roger VerLee's shares of NTB. Koster says, "I have to say he was a very good partner. Without him, I do not think we would have been a success."

Each of his sons is now a partner in the company. Rick Koster is vice-president/operations; Greg

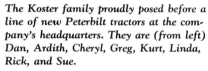

Dan Koster (right) is joined by his sons (from left) Greg, Rick, and Kurt, and one of the company's tractor-trailers on the grounds of Nationwide Truck Brokers Inc. in Grand Rapids, Michigan.

Koster is secretary of the board and a dispatcher in the company's Lansing, Michigan, terminal; and Kurt Koster is treasurer of the board and dispatcher in the Grand Rapids office.

The future for Nationwide Truck Brokers Inc. shines brightly. The new, 17,820-square-foot office-terminal complex at 7350 Clyde Park in Grand Rapids was occupied early in the summer of 1988. Con-

The Koster family proudly posed before a line of new Peterbilt tractors at the company's headquarters. They are (from left) Dan, Ardith, Cheryl, Greg, Kurt, Linda, Rick, and Sue.

struction of a new office-terminal in Lansing on the 2930 Creyts Road site is scheduled for completion in the winter of 1988. With property already purchased, another terminal—in Newport, Michigan—is in the planning stages. Eleven new conventional Peterbilt tractors with 400 Caterpillar engines and double-bunk sleepers have been added to the fleet recently.

Dan Koster comments: "I have to give all the glory for this success to the Lord Jesus Christ, because everything I have belongs to Him, and He is just allowing me to use it while I am here on this earth. I also would like to give credit to the many faithful, dependable employees I have had over the years."

The three sons will eventually be given control of National Truck Brokers Inc., as Dan Koster plans to retire and serve only as chairman of the NTB board. He is a member of Grandville Bible Church and a board member of the Independent Bible Mission of Michigan.

A special verse to Dan is: "Whosover shall call upon the name of the Lord shall be saved." Romans 10:13

L. NEILL CARTAGE CO. INC.

What started as something of a mom-and-pop Chicago-area trucking company operation in the mid-1940s has become one of the Midwest's most reliable full-service trucking and warehousing operations. That's L. Neill Cartage Co. Inc., headquartered in Berkeley, Illinois, with current operations serving a five-state area.

Starting as a one-truck delivery service in 1946 under the guidance and hard work of Lewis "Lew" Neill and his wife, Jean, the company grew into a truck and warehouse operation by 1966. General hauling of chemicals and plastic materials in

Delivering a substantial share of the paper that goes to the printing industry in Illinois, Indiana, Wisconsin, Iowa, and Michigan, L. Neill Cartage Co. Inc. provides local and short-haul trucking, in addition to other distribution and storage services.

that industry's early days got the firm rolling in the right way, and happenstance provided a later mile marker along the road to success.

According to the organization's president, Thomas Neill, who, with his brother, Rory, has been with the family business since the early 1970s, that milestone was created in

1967 when a call from a paper-products company meant for another trucking firm came to Neill by mistake. But, "as long as they had Dad on the line," Tom Neill says, "they decided to give us a shot at the business."

As a result, paper has become the firm's specialty, its trucks delivering a substantial share of the paper that goes to the printing industry in Illinois, Indiana, Wisconsin, Iowa, and Michigan.

L. Neill Cartage, with approximately 60 employees, provides local and short-haul trucking, public warehousing, rail and truck distribution, and consolidation, giving a customer the advantage of dealing with a single source from pick-up to delivery.

In a way short-haul trucking has always been a part of the Neill family. Since there was no family car in those days when the business was just getting started, Jean Neill had to learn to drive the tandem-axle straight truck in order to do the family shopping and take their four children to church on Sunday.

Rory Neill, now serving as executive vice-president, says the company continues to be dedicated to providing customers with quality service that's both reliable and cost effective. As a means of doing that, the firm has invested millions of dollars in modern physical distribution equipment and systems, including state-of-the-art computer technology, properly maintained equipment that's right for the job, and comprehensive warehouse facilities.

In the firm's pursuit of excellence, Lew Neill gives a large part of the credit to its employees, whose dedication to the business has ensured the success of L. Neill Cartage Co. Inc. "Whether it's making a routine shipment, an urgent less-than-a-load delivery, or processing an immediate warehouse release," says Lew Neill, "our people believe in doing the job right the first time."

The L. Neill Cartage Co. Inc. headquarters in Berkeley, Illinois.

BOSCH TRUCKING COMPANY, INC.

The dedication and integrity central to the onetime one-truck business started more than 30 years ago by Conrad W. Bosch still hits the road every time a piece of cargo-laden Bosch Trucking Company, Inc., equipment heads for its destination.

The promise of fast, efficient, and economical delivery still drives the business, and that's a fitting memorial to Bosch, whose untimely death in 1979 was a blow to both his young family and his business. So dedicated was Bosch to the aforementioned principles that when he started his business in 1956, fresh from an Army stint in Germany, with one tractor and trailer used for hauling steel from Peoria to Chicago, he not only drove but also handled all the mechanical and body work.

That same dedication has persisted as his widow, Sally A. Bosch, and Steve Wright, a close friend of the founder serving as company president, have given the firm the careful management and direction that have moved it into the elite circle of the 100 finest small trucking operations in the country.

Bosch Trucking Company, Inc., counts more than 110 company-

owned and employee-operated tractors, 220 vans, and 120 flatbeds, traveling 10 million miles annually across 48 states. Under the just-in-time shipping philosophy, Bosch has become an integral part of its customers' operations with efficient, effective delivery dates that guarantee steady production output.

Flexibility is credited by Sally Bosch for the success that has seen the firm not only fulfill but surpass

Bosch Trucking Company, Inc., counts more than 110 company-owned and employee-operated tractors, 220 vans, and 120 flatbeds, traveling 10 million miles annually across 48 states.

Safety and driver performance are integral parts of the company's fulfilling its mission of delivering its customers' products safely and on time at the lowest-possible cost.

the goals set by her husband. This flexibility, she believes, allows Bosch Trucking, Inc., to be responsive—a company hallmark—to increased demands dictated by the growth and changing needs of the industries served.

Looking to the future, chief executive Wright sees continued promise for Bosch because the demand for efficient transportation is expanding. That demand seems more and more to be calling on the trucking industry for safe and on-time delivery. The firm is committed, Wright says, to using high technology in the quest for better routing, load control, and prevention of lost time.

Wright believes that safety and driver performance are integral parts of the company's fulfilling its mission of delivering its customers' products safely and on time at the lowest-possible cost. In this respect, the firm regularly conducts safety programs and briefs its drivers and dispatchers on ever-changing safety rules and regulations.

All employees, on the road or off, get high grades from Wright. They have made a critical difference throughout the life of the firm thus far, he says, and he's confident they will make that same difference as Bosch Trucking Company, Inc., rolls into the future.

WAYNE W. SELL CORPORATION

For more than a century western Pennsylvania has meant raw materials and products, such as limestone, coal, pig iron, and cement. Hauling such products takes big men, big trucks, and a company like the Wayne W. Sell Corporation of Sarver, Pennsylvania.

"Service is my Business," is the Sarver motto. Top-quality service and efficient equipment is the combination that has brought the firm from a small, one-truck operation to today's 50-tractor fleet.

"We have always strived to provide the best service possible," says Jane Sell. "This cannot be done without the help of our great drivers. The drivers are number one at Sell. We never forget that." The Sells also credit company vice-president James Beechey for much of their success.

In 1954 Wayne W. Sell was only 23 years old and fresh out of service in the U.S. Army motor pool. He had been driving since he was 16, delivering pickles from Sarver to Pittsburgh. He had a good job driving a tractor and trailer throughout western Pennsylvania, but his dream was to own his own rig.

In 1955 he and his wife, Jane, took the plunge and invested their life savings in a used GMC tractor and a 24-foot Trailmobile flat trailer. Their first contracts called for local hauling of cement and steel. The work was hard and the hours were long, but eventually the rewards proved great, for it was the beginning of what has become an outstanding family-owned company.

In 1955 Wayne W. Sell and his wife, Jane, bought their first (used GMC) tractor and 24-foot trailer. The company grew, with the Sells acquiring new rigs and servicing an extended area, and in 1962 they incorporated their company.

Sell's first steps included the purchase of Public Utility Commission (PUC) authority to extend his service area. To meet the needs of new customers, he purchased new rigs, including dump trailers for hauling asphalt and bulk milk tankers. Later additions to the Sell fleet included pneumatic tanks, more flats, and additional dump trucks.

Wayne and Jane Sell incorporated their growing company in 1962 as the Wayne W. Sell Corporation. The growth that had been an early hallmark of their style of business continued. Today the firm has a 4-person office staff, 4 dispatchers, a crew of 13 mechanics, and 50 full-time drivers. The company's PUC and Interstate Commerce Commission authorities cover 48 states, and its fleet includes 50 tractors, 78 trailers, and 5 triaxles.

The firm has a wide range of devoted and loyal customers, including Union Carbide, Armco Steel, Allegheny Ludlum, Warner Lime, Dravo Lime, Bethlehem Mines, Freeport Terminals, Allegheny Minerals, and Armstrong Cement. The company's cargoes include such regional staples as coal, lime, pig iron, cottonseed, fertilizer, boxite, steel, graphite, and cement.

The Wayne W. Sell Corporation continues to be a family firm, and it looks like that tradition will continue for many years to come. Company employees now include sons Wayne Jr. and John, as well as the Sell's two daughters, two sons-in-law, brother, and brother-in-law. Altogether, it makes a proud family that has created a proud business in a crucial American enterprise.

Top-quality service and efficient equipment is the combination that has brought the Wayne W. Sell Corporation from a small one-truck operation to today's 50-tractor fleet.

COAST DISPATCH, INC.

Publishers, printers, and other users of bulky, time-sensitive materials nationwide know that their one-call answer to shipping needs is the New York-based Coast Dispatch, Inc. Originally conceived as a sales and operating agent for another carrier, Coast Dispatch has become a widely admired 48-state Irregular Route Common Carrier and full-service transportation company.

New white GMC Aero ES with 48-foot by 102-inch-high Cube Trailer.

New fleet modernization program.

Coast Dispatch was established in June 1982 by John Lewis Udell and Jesse Dobrinsky. Their new firm was designed to market the transportation services of a major national hauler while providing shippers with customized transportation management services. Within months the new company became the national distributor for several prominent publishers and printers.

Quick success almost destroyed both the new company and its affiliated truck operator. The midwestern carrier that originally contracted through Coast Dispatch proved unable to continue to ensure the high-quality service that had already become the hallmark of Coast. To fill its own needs, the agent purchased equipment needed to supplement the existing fleet.

In December 1983 Udell and Dobrinsky moved to develop their own full-fledged operation. They obtained 48-state authority from the Interstate Commerce Commission (ICC); leased a 5,000-square-foot terminal in Valley Stream, New York; and purchased warehousing equipment. Under the leadership of Howard Schulman, director of special services, Coast Dispatch began purchasing and operating its own fleet of tractor trailers.

It took less than 30 days for the company to take full advantage of its ICC Brokerage Authority and create a countrywide network of more than 400 trucks. Early in 1984 Coast Dispatch contracted with a major airline to operate and develop its New York-area road feeder system. The result proved phenomenally successful, and Coast Dispatch, Inc., has been growing rapidly ever since.

The company's outstanding reputation is built on excellent service and competitive prices. In just six years it has achieved a solid relationship with a group of loyal customers that includes Aer Lingus Irish Airlines, Agvar Chemicals, Airborne Express, Airmax/Direct Air Airlines, American Family Publishers, Publishers Clearing House, and *Readers Digest*.

Coast Dispatch is an ICC-approved property brokerage and uses that authority to accommodate the needs of all customers, providing everything required by its shippers, including equipment, transportation, management, and warehousing. The firm is fully computerized with a unique, custom-designed system that allows it to constantly track and monitor all equipment and freight movements. Jay Finkelstein is director of operations.

New white GMC AERO ES tractor.

Headquarters and the national dispatch center for Coast Dispatch, Inc., are in Valley Stream, New York. The company is currently growing at a rate of 5 percent per quarter and is now in the midst of a major fleet modernization program that will outfit it with new tractors, trailers, and local delivery equipment.

BRUCE W. TRENT TRUCKING COMPANY

The farms of Somerset County, Pennsylvania, may be an unlikely birthplace for a major heavy-industry trucking company, but that's exactly where the Bruce W. Trent Trucking Company of Friedens, Pennsylvania, got its start. Bruce Trent began driving for his father, Mervin Trent, in 1942. The Trents hauled hay, potatoes, and other products—first from the family farm and then from the neighbors'—to markets in surrounding areas.

To keep their truck busy year round, they began hauling coal from local strip mines to nearby rail sidings for shipment to the steel mills of Johnstown and Pittsburgh.

Bruce Trent Trucking now operates a fleet of 20 vehicles of its own and leases an additional 20 or more trucks to haul coal, lime, fertilizer, and other bulk products throughout Pennsylvania and the surrounding states. The company also operates a Goodyear Tire dealership. The other family corporation, Trent Coal, Inc., mines coal and sells it to power plants throughout the region.

Bruce Trent bought his first

Bruce Trent started his trucking company on the farms of Somerset County, Pennsylvania, hauling hay, potatoes, and other products to markets in surrounding areas. Pictured here is Trent's first truck, an Army surplus GMC 6x6 dump truck, circa 1946.

truck, an Army surplus GMC 6x6 dump truck, in 1946. No longer interested in hauling farm products, he used it exclusively to and from area strip mines. In 1948 he replaced it with a new International single-axle dump. This too saw duty hauling coal from the strip mines—until they closed.

For Bruce Trent, the suspension of one activity became the beginning of another. He removed the dump body from his truck, added a fifth wheel, and bought a Fruehauf open-top van trailer. He leased the new rig, with a driver, first to Schreiber Trucking Company and then to Interstate, and it was the beginning of a 30-year relationship between the two firms.

In 1950 he bought a small mine of his own on his father's land and founded Trent Coal.

While his truck was on the road, Bruce Trent was down in the mines digging coal. On the day in 1952 when his daughter was born, Bruce's right arm became entangled in some mining equipment. To free him, the arm had to be amputated above the elbow. Trent was back at work two weeks later.

Bruce Trent Trucking began expanding in the mid-1960s, first adding two tractors (leased to Cooper-Jarrett), then a coal and stone hauling tractor and dump

Today Bruce W. Trent Trucking operates a fleet of 20 vehicles of its own and leases an additional 20 or more trucks to haul coal, lime, fertilizer, and other bulk products throughout Pennsylvania and the surrounding states. Bruce Trent stands next to the latest addition to his fleet, a 1988 International tractor.

trailer rig.

In 1971 the company added a tri-axle dump to haul coal from Somerset County to plants in the surrounding regions. The firm also added a garage and maintenance operation. The coal boom of 1974 brought not only a surge in demand for coal, but also rapid expansion of the truck fleet. In 1980 Trent purchased Maust Brothers Trucking of Berlin, Pennsylvania. With the acquisition came ICC and Pennsylvania Public Utility Commission authorities that enabled the company to expand its territory.

Bruce and Bessie Trent are preparing to retire now, and Robert Trent will be taking over the business. His brother, Blaine Trent, is a commercial pilot. Their sister, Beverly, and her husband are both engineers with Westinghouse. The Trent family, like its companies, has driven a long way from the farm.

INTERSTATE TRUCKLOAD CARRIERS CONFERENCE

Left: Thomas R. Schilli, president of Schilli Transportation.

Right: Lloyd B. Clark, ICC president.

"It's not just the truck itself that matters," says J. Terry Turner, executive director of the Interstate TruckLoad Carriers Conference, an affiliate of the American Trucking Associations. "It's what's in the truck, on it, under it, and where it's going that makes all the difference."

The Interstate TruckLoad Carriers Conference was formed in 1941 as the Common Carrier Conference—Irregular Route. It merged with Contract Carriers Conference in 1983 and became the Interstate Carriers Conference. The organization adopted its current name in 1988.

Throughout its history, however, its responsibility has remained the same: representing the interests of its members—a group of largely nonunionized, family-owned companies.

Interstate truckload operators work by individual contract or tariffs with shippers, delivering whatever needs to be carried, wherever in the United States (except Hawaii) or Canada it is needed. With their tractors and dry vans, flat-beds, refrigerated trailers, or other vehicles, truckload operators carry almost 75 percent of the freight that is moved in the United States.

The Interstate TruckLoad Carriers Conference collaborates with shippers and receivers to improve industrial practices, and advises Congress and the regulatory agencies as it seeks a more productive and uniform working environment.

"One of our biggest problems today is the patchwork quilt of laws regarding access to state and local highways and streets," says Lloyd B. Clark, chairman of C-Line, Inc., Warwick, Rhode Island, and a past president and chairman of the conference. "It's a problem for shippers and receivers as well as for carriers. It's everybody's problem. After all, the whole American economy moves by truck."

Deregulation of long-haul trucking and the introduction of such recent changes in industrial practices as just-in-time manufacturing systems have brought about extraordinary changes in the trucking business. Rapid increases in the numbers of trucks on the road and individually contracted rates and contracts have added to the stress.

"Truckload carriers only make money when their trucks are loaded and moving," says Turner. "The new competition and changing profes-

sional practices have put a lot of pressure on us.

"Our whole business is market driven," says Turner, "with shippers and receivers insisting on critically tight schedules. Manufacturers don't want to tie up their money in inventory, so trucks have become the warehouses of the nation."

Another big problem is the shortage of trained drivers. "This is a difficult, demanding profession with a lot of solitude and a lot of critical, instant decision making," says Rocque Dameo, Sr., president of Dameo Trucking, Bridgeport, New Jersey. Truckers are a highly skilled, special breed, and there just are not enough of them."

Here too, the conference and its 600 trucking members are working to make things better. Their efforts are directed toward improving the curriculum and standards of truck driver training schools, and toward lowering age restrictions on drivers. "We've got to get them young," says Dameo. "We've got to make good drivers out of them and keep them in trucking."

Thomas R. Schilli, president of Schilli Transportation Services, Remington, Indiana, is the current president of the Interstate TruckLoad Carriers Conference.

General Carriers

Americans in all walks of life can thank general-freight carriers for most of the things that keep them going through each day. From the wake-up alarm to the bedclothes they pull up around them on cold, winter nights, as well as a fleet of things in between, Americans are touched in numerous ways each day by the truckers who haul those things to all corners of the country. Think about it. That alarm starts your day. Your coffee pot gets you going and readies your system for a breakfast item that almost assuredly traveled by general-freight truck to the supermarket. Soap, washcloths, towels, shaving cream and accessories, toothpaste and brushes, cosmetics, and clothing all have seen the inside of a truck before they find their way into your home. Your car runs on parts trucked to the assembly line. Travel plans for typewriters, computers, and an array of other office equipment, as well as plants that bring a homey touch to the work place, included a trip by truck. Billboards, street signs, paint to stripe parking lots and roads, shingles and siding for homes, and appliances from can openers to stereo systems—the list goes on and on, but you get the picture, in living color.

Any trip to the supermarket, the drugstore, the department store, or the furniture and appliance store is vivid testimony to the presence and importance of general-freight carriers.

Many of these carriers were begun as small, one-man operations by people who have lived the American dream that says hard work, integrity, and keeping the customer satisfied will be rewarded with success. Most often they carried freight that was indiginous to their area—coal, building stone, and farm products, thus becoming a prime factor in the economy of their home basae. These original solo operations, in many cases, have become family affairs, with second- and third-generation leadership coming to the fore as these businesses roll toward the twenty-first century.

While many of these enterprises have become massive in both stature and service, there are others that have chosen to follow the business philosophy that big isn't necessarily best for everybody. Maintaining a smaller, tighter operation is a way to more closely customize service, they believe. Whether large or small, these companies most often remain in the region, if not the city, of their origin, continuing to make an impressive contribution to the stability of that area.

So it remains for all of us to remember that before we hit the road each morning, a great number of things that already have touched our lives have been on the road long before with the truckers of America.

The organizations whose stories are detailed in the following chapters have chosen to support this important literary project. They dramatically illustrate the variety of ways in which individuals and their businesses have contributed to the growth and development of the trucking industry.

Above: This 1926 Chevrolet utility truck was restored by Winross Restorations. Courtesy, American Truck Historical Society

Facing page: Independent owner-operators are represented by several organizations, adding to the extensive alphabet soup of trucking organizations. Photo Kent Knudson/The Photo File

EDWARD J. MEYERS CO.

Safety is the preeminent factor in attaining success in the increasingly important and demanding field of liquid bulk transportation.

Few trucking companies are more aware of or practice safety better than Edward J. Meyers Co., a leading transporter of chemicals and other hazardous materials based in Summit, Illinois, a near-western suburb of Chicago. In fact, the Meyers company's safety record is one of the major factors that has kept it rolling to success.

According to one of the firm's executives, the size of Meyers' contracts with large chemical producers are in direct relation to its ability to

The entrance to the maintenance washing facility of the Edward J. Meyers Co. home terminal, located in Summit, Illinois.

deliver the goods in a safe and sound manner. In his words, "Meyers' loss record is carefully watched by its customers. Shippers will not use a carrier that may dump its chemicals on the ground. Shippers want a carrier that's safe, that can perform, and who can get it there on time."

Such producers as Union Carbide, Amoco, Shell, and Dow Chemical are extremely aware of the advantages of safety and "make sure their carriers are good, viable companies," the executive says. But safety isn't just something that happens in programs and posters, it has to be in everything a company does—an ongoing state of mind and state of readiness that includes everyone in a trucking operation, most importantly the drivers.

Edward J. Meyers Co.'s current fleet of liquid bulk transporters.

The Meyers company, a division of Wright Industries, became a prominent transporter of gasoline and diesel fuel in the 1960s. A major change in emphasis came in the early 1970s as Meyers, under the leadership of Mark Wright as president, decided to move into chemical-transportation. Success was followed by major expansion as Meyers went from being a local hauler with 23 drivers in 1973 to a national transporter rolling into the 1990s with approximately 125 drivers.

The company continues to be a transporter of fuels and other petroleum products. But chemicals that reach into practically every corner of American society have become the catalyst for its major growth in the 1980s, and hold the greatest promise for the future. The chemicals transported by Meyers include naphthas, alcohol, liquid plastic materials, and a variety of other liquid products that go into such consumer goods as cough syrup, other pharmaceuticals, perfume, anti-freeze, and windshield washer fluid.

Edward J. Meyers commenced op-

eration in 1911 and is authorized to transport commodities to and from all states except Alaska and Hawaii from its home terminal in Summit and branch terminals in West Virginia and New Jersey. Approximately 83 power units and 163 trailers carry the company banner across much of the country, with special emphasis on the 26 midwestern and mid-Atlantic states.

The highly specialized field of handling hazardous materials calls for proper training, precision in transporting and delivery, and a public image that's unblemished by lapses in safety and enhanced by internal and external vehicle cleanliness. The company allows no compromise in any of these factors.

Although Edward J. Meyers' reputation with its shippers is important, the company's professional obligation goes far beyond business to its belief in ensuring the safety of those who share the highways of America with the trucking industry. In this regard the Meyers company offers not only the image but the reality of safety and cleanliness.

A clean tank interior and the high-caliber maintenance of a tank, are musts for liquid bulk transporters. These commandments help ensure both safety against spills and the integrity of the materials being carried. They also reflect favorably on the carrier and the shipper.

Additionally, the demand for meeting tough national transportation and safety standards is not only taken in stride, but is welcomed by Edward J. Meyers Co. as a way of helping it stay on its best business behavior and by aiding in weeding out unsafe operators. Tougher regulations, more frequent inspections, and heavier fines for offenders assure that a company will meet and surpass prescribed standards a Meyers official says. No matter how well a company thinks it's doing in meeting standards, there always seems to be room for improvement.

Those are words and actions the Meyers Company lives by.

A view of the modern tank cleaning facility, ensuring internal and external vehicle cleanliness—part of Edward J. Meyers Co.'s rigid standards for safety.

KANEY TRANSPORTATION INC.

One of the most familiar sights on the highways of seven midwestern states is the gleaming tank trucks of Kaney Transportation Inc. flashing their crisp blue striping and block letters KTI across the landscape as they travel toward another safe delivery of petroleum products.

KTI has been doing that for more than 40 years. Even so, the company still approaches each delivery with the same care and earnestness it demonstrated with that first truckload back in 1945, when it began as a regional petroleum carrier. From that beginning, Kaney, headquartered in Rockford, Illinois, has expanded to 48-state authority for carrying liquid bulk, though it only seldom travels outside the Midwest.

Most of its petroleum activity, which makes up about half of the company's hauling, is still centered in Illinois, Indiana, Iowa, and Wisconsin. About 70 percent of the petroleum loads originate in Chicago.

KTI's growing fleet of more than

Kaney Transportation uses several light-weight tractor-trailer tandems to haul gasoline and fuel oil throughout the seven-state area it serves in the Midwest.

70 tractors and nearly 100 tank trailers is divided almost entirely among the company's terminals in Janesville, Wisconsin, and in Rockford, Huntley, Hazel Crest, Peoria, and Kankakee, Illinois. A few rigs are based separately in cities within the firm's operating area.

Only a small number of the fleet's tractors are owned by KTI. The rest belong to owner-operators, who often adopt KTI specifications

for their tractors and carry the KTI colors. The company also assists some of its first-time owner-operators in buying tractors.

Trying something new is not foreign to KTI. In fact, the contrary is true, and the testing and evaluating of new equipment is a major case in

This pressure trailer is used for transporting propane gas.

point. President Bell points out that there is an apparent convoy of new equipment coming into the transportation scene, and manufacturers make it extremely attractive for companies to test that equipment. KTI, of course, is always looking for new equipment that will let it increase its payloads or in some other way put it ahead of its industry competition.

Among its various testing encounters to find products that work best in its operation, KTI tested a tank trailer constructed of composite mate-

rials, and compared several makes of aluminum-tank trailers. The judgment on the composite tank (fiber-reinforced plastics) was that it had many outstanding features, but weight was a problem. Weight reduction was one of the many factors under scrutiny in the aluminum-tank testing.

In contrast to its pioneering attitude toward equipment, KTI doesn't experiment with safety. The company's long list of safety awards from the National Tank Truck Carriers group is testimony to that. KTI's dedication to safety begins with its careful attention to the drivers it hires. They must be at least 25 years old and have a minimum of four years' truck-driving experience with a record that indicates attention to safety.

KTI, which also drug tests its drivers, has a full-time safety and training director who oversees the company's two-week orientation and

training of new drivers. Among the things they learn during that period is the company's insistence on drivers' pre- and post-trip inspections and reports on equipment. Any problems are required to be reported to maintenance at that time, and drivers are told they face disciplinary action or dismissal for failure to

This safety and on-site maintenance vehicle is an integral part of the regional petroleum-products carrier's dedication to the safe arrival of cargo.

All the action starts for Kaney Transportation Inc. at its corporate headquarters in Rockford, Illinois.

comply with the paperwork and inspections.

KTI's drivers are rewarded for pursuing safety and complying with the company's rules; one reward is being named driver of the month, a distinction that entitles its recipient to a jacket with the honor's emblem emblazoned on it. Selection is based on customer service, conscientious handling of paperwork, and safety.

Extended safety records are rewarded through the years with special recognition at the company's annual banquets. Such things as belt buckles, rings, watches, lighters, cuff links, and other similar items that usually are adorned with gems signifying special accomplishments are awarded at this function.

KTI's own special accomplishments through the years have included setting high standards for customer service; its safety record; and its innovative approach to testing, analyzing, and evaluating new offerings in equipment. Because of these things and countless others, Kaney Transportation Inc. has enjoyed continuous growth and has earned high regard in the bulk liquid field—traits that will keep KTI on the high road to the twenty-first century.

J. SUPOR & SON TRUCKING, RIGGING, AND CRANE SERVICE

J. Supor & Son Trucking, Rigging, and Crane Service supplies trucking, crane, and warehousing service to companies throughout the United States, providing customers with a single source for diversified services that few other businesses can match.

Located in the centralized hub of the major state and federal highway systems, J.Supor & Son is minutes away from Routes 1, 9, 3, 21, 22, 46, 78, 80, 278, 287, and the New Jersey Turnpike (95). Nearby are the Port of New York, Port Newark, Newark International Airport, and the major railroad systems.

The firm's yard and warehouse are served by a pier on the Passaic River and a railroad yard with Conrail tie-ins. This location is excellent for any mode of transport, be it land, sea, or air, and permits fast, efficient service no matter what the transport condition or load size.

Supor's warehouse facility, offering more than 175,000 square feet of storage space, features a computer inventory system. The specially designed facility houses all types of industrial machinery and is equipped with special cranes capable of handling equipment weighing as much as 50 tons.

J. Supor & Son Trucking, Rigging, and Crane Service can find the proper solution to any transport or rigging problem. The firm has the engineering staff, skill, and the tractors and/or trailers to meet all its customers' hauling requirements.

J. Supor & Son provides complete turnkey service—whether it be rigging out one piece of machinery or an entire plant. It can dismantle, rig out, transport, and reassemble articles quickly, smoothly, and safely.

Each move poses many different problems, and each calls on the skill and inventiveness of years of accumulated experience gained through many and various hauling situations. Each move requires the proper vehicles, modification of the vehicles if necessary, and a qualified, skillful rigging crew.

Bridges, roads, tunnels, and other structures must be checked to determine their capacities and clearances. The grades existing on each route must be checked, as are the utility poles and lines, highway signs (being removed if necessary), and state and local restrictions. Permission must be obtained for each passage.

Each of Supor's vehicles have the best-qualified drivers in the heavy hauling industry to ensure a safe and rapid passage.

The company as a specialized carrier must meet shipper requirements, no matter what size, weight, or shape. The firm's trucking fleet consists of flatbed trailers, double gooseneck units, double-drop well, expandable lowboy, and triaxle and multiple-axle arrangements specially designed to distribute heavy loads. To protect against road shock, trailers are equipped with air-ride suspension units, special fixtures, and tiedowns to guarantee the safe transportation of materials.

Supor & Sons is limited only by state restrictions and man-made obstacles. Other than those, the operation's vehicles are capable of hauling any load, whatever the demand.

Among the firm's most challenging jobs was hauling a 100-ton U.S. government-owned piece of equipment that required negotiating arrangements with 15 municipalities. When the Three Mile Island disaster occurred, Supor was called on to deliver special stainless-steel tanks, stored in its warehouse, to be used as part of recovery operations. Su-

J. Supor & Son's trucking fleet consists of flatbed trailers, double gooseneck units, double-drop well, expandable lowboy, and triaxle and multiple-axle arrangements specially designed to distribute heavy loads.

por trucks were on the road within minutes after the call. Whether it's removing an overturned truck containing toxic materials or removing a crashed helicopter, Supor has the equipment and people to do the job.

A wide range of cranes is available in various capacities and configurations: truck-mounted and crawler cranes, hydraulic and lattice boomed, with capacities from five to 500 tons. They can be contracted, rented, or leased.

Founded in 1963, the company started as a two-truck operation pri-

"We believe it's important to have a diverse operation, which is why we expanded from strictly a trucking operation to handling rigging, heavy hauling, and warehousing."

The business has grown through the acquisition of the Wm. Tuma Rigging Company, Rahway Motor Freight, and Harrison Warehouse Corp. Each acquisition resulted in more equipment and expanded facilities to benefit the firm's customers. Despite its tremendous growth, the corporation retains a family atmosphere with Joe's son and his three nephews all involved in the operation. Supor credits Paul Lofberg & Co. Insurance and Alan Bindeglass Accountants with helping him build his business.

Reflecting its financial strength, the company also has expanded to owning and operating commercial properties, including the Julia Gardens Apartments in Harrison, New Jersey, and the Supor Industrial Park warehouse facility in Kearny, New Jersey.

Supor is a collector of antique cars. His vehicles have been featured in the films *Annie, Without a Trace,* and *The Godfather.* According to Joe Supor, "We have served many large and small corporations throughout the United States, and each one of our clients has become a satisified regular user of our services. Our clients' heavy hauling requirements can be met and exceeded by our trained staff of hauling experts—whether it's one piece or an entire plant—across town or country—we can haul it."

Above: J. Supor & Son Trucking, Rigging, and Crane Service has the engineering staff, skill, and the tractors to meet all of its customers hauling requirements.

Left: J. Supor & Son Trucking, Rigging, and Crane Service has all types of industrial machinery and is equipped with special cranes capable of handling equipment weighing as much as 50 tons.

marily hauling steel. Some of its earliest rigging customers include Westinghouse, Belyea Company, and G&S Motor Equipment. Supor has built long-term relationships as the exclusive hauler for many of its clients, including the Lindy*Griffith Construction Company.

Supor, a member of the Heavy Hauling Association of the United States, began his career working for an engineering company, which gave him early experience in handling rigging jobs. After he bought that business from its previous owner, Supor decided to expand the firm's services.

According to Joe Supor, Sr.,

DON FRAME TRUCKING, INC.

A Peterbilt triaxle under Jamestown Macadam's Block top number four in Cossadoga, New York.

Don Frame Trucking, Inc., is among the largest carriers of construction aggregates in western New York. Its fleet of heavy-duty trucks includes 17 tractors, 30 trailers, and 8 triaxle straight trucks. At the peak of the construction season, Don Frame Trucking adds as many as 40 owner-operators to its own full-time staff.

Don Frame first entered the trucking business in 1963, when he purchased a used 1958 Brockway tractor-trailer rig to provide local service to a group of local customers. His cargoes included sand, stone, salt, and coal.

It took several years of long hours and hard work to get the business fully established, but, starting in 1965, Frame was able gradually to expand his fleet. By 1968 Don Frame Trucking had become an important part of the Chautauqua County, New York, transportation scene.

Jamestown Macadam, the region's largest producer of asphalt paving materials, became one of the company's loyal customers. James-

town not only contracted with the firm for local hauling of its construction aggregates, it also hired it for long-distance hauling of special materials.

In 1983 Jamestown purchased a portable asphalt concrete plant and hired Don Frame Trucking to haul it back to New York. One of the trailers was more than 100 feet long, requiring a specially escorted convoy of oversized trucks to bring it home.

When Jamestown had to move a gravel plant from the Philadelphia area, Don Frame Trucking again got the call. For about 10 days a steady stream of oversized and overweight trucks moved between Pennsylvania and New York to complete the job.

Such professionalism and willingness to provide whatever services are needed by its customers are special hallmarks of Don Frame Trucking. Its dedication is appreciated—about 90 percent of its contracts come from loyal, repeat customers.

Throughout most of its history, Don Frame Trucking has been a regional business, concentrated

A 1971 Brockway and 1986 Peterbilt along the shore of Lake Erie in Dunkirk, New York.

largely in the scenic and historic Chautauqua County region of western New York State. In 1988, however, the firm received 48-state bulk and general commodity authority from the Interstate Commerce Commission and expects gradually to expand its business on a national scale.

"Actually," says Larry Frame, son of the founder and vice-president/treasurer of the corporation, "our main intent is to be able to meet the cross-country hauling needs of our regular customers. These people have been very loyal to us, and we want to be able to provide them with all of the trucking services that they need." Larry Frame has been working for the family-owned company since 1970.

Don Frame started his business in the backyard and garage of his Fredonia, New York, home. In 1979 the firm built its own maintenance garage, but Don continued to use his house as his office. By 1986, however, Don Frame Trucking had finally outgrown its shared facilities, and the company built a new headquarters complex. It is still based in Fredonia.

Today the operation's trucks haul the full range of construction aggregates, and his list of loyal customers includes most of the region's leading construction companies and contractors. The firm also hauls and disposes of fly ash and bottom ash for the Niagara Mohawk Power Steam Station in Dunkirk, New York. Another special contract calls for Don Frame Trucking to haul malt beverages and wine coolers within the state of New York.

Don Frame Trucking, Inc., anticipates substantial continued growth, gradually taking full advantage of its expanded ICC authority. The company is also expanding its parts and service department, now open to outside customers, to cover all of western New York. The enterprise is especially proud of its highly qualified drivers and supervisory personnel, top-quality service, and highly competitive pricing structure. It specializes in just-in-time delivery contracts.

Arlene Jamieson heads the five-person office staff. Formerly an executive with Norstar Bank, she joined the firm as corporate secretary in 1982. Company founder Donald L. Frame continues to serve as president.

W.J. CASEY TRUCKING & RIGGING CO., INC.

If you think that gold-and-red W.J. Casey logo on the side of the company trucks has a slightly old-fashioned look, you're right. Tradition is cherished at W.J. Casey, and it has been using the same distinctive design since its earliest days. The company also prizes its vintage 1922 A B Mack, crank-start, four-cylinder, 60-horsepower antique tractor. "Special Hauling" reads the sign on the antique; today's fleet of high-powered tractors still lead the way in "special hauling."

A dryer, 18 feet in diameter and 30 feet long, weighs 139 tons and is held by a 150-ton-capacity Fontaine Cometto steerable hydraulic.

Whether the job calls for delivering a 150-ton boiler section, moving nuclear reactor and power plant machinery, or carrying one of the gigantic vessels used in the chemical and pharmaceuticals industries, transportation engineers throughout the Northeast know that W.J. Casey Trucking & Rigging Co., Inc., has been the company to call for more than 80 years.

W.J. Casey was founded in 1900 in Brooklyn, New York, by William J. Casey. His son, W.J. Casey, Jr., ran the company until 1949. The firm was a pioneer in heavy and specialized hauling and carried much of the structural steel that built the landmarks of Lower Manhattan, including the Federal Reserve Bank Building on Liberty Street. But hard times set in after the death of W.J. Casey, Jr., and the company suspended operations in 1952.

Nicholas J. and James P. Biondi,

Sr., purchased W.J. Casey in 1954 and relocated the company to Newark, New Jersey, where the revitalized firm not only attracted many of its older clients, but many new ones as well. In 1975 the expanded, renovated W.J. Casey moved to Union, New Jersey, where its five-acre headquarters complex is located.

Despite the massive size of many of its rigging and hauling projects, W.J. Casey remains a relatively small organization. "We've kept the company small so that we can continue the W.J. Casey tradition of personalized service," says Nicholas J. Biondi. That tradition will be maintained by the next generation as well. Two sons of the owners, Jay C. and James V. Biondi, are already active participants in the business.

Casey operates a fleet of primarily Mack trucks, with a large assortment of highly specialized trailers, including lowboys, drop frames, extendables, and flatbeds. The firm

This picture shows a cold box that is being handled by a book end fixture. The weight of the box is 130 tons.

Pictured here is the rear of a cold box, weighing 130 tons, being moved on haul road. The rear assembly is a Cometto steerable hydraulic four-axle transporter.

also owns such specialized transporting equipment as hydraulically steerable dollies, removable hydraulic goosenecks, and a variety of suspensions. Much of its equipment was custom built to the company's specifications. "Only the right piece of equipment will get the job done," says James P. Biondi, Sr.

The organization is also involved in export shipping and handling. W.J. Casey operations include ship or barge loading, roll-on and roll-off operations, storage, and crane and railroad services.

W.J. Casey Trucking & Rigging Co., Inc., is a member of the New Jersey Motor Truck Association and the Specialized Carriers and Rigging Association. The firm has won several national industry awards, including recognition for fleet safety improvement, overall safety, and the On-Road Hauling Job of the Year in 1985.

Top: Although many early experiments were made using multiple truck trailers, John Keeshin was one of the first to use the concept successfully in 1930. However, many states soon passed laws against these "truck trains." The rig pictured is an A-series International. Courtesy, Navistar International

Above: This 1925 Model OL Kenworth was equipped with pneumatic tires, which were becoming increasingly popular. Courtesy, PACCAR, Inc.

Suppliers and Manufacturers 11

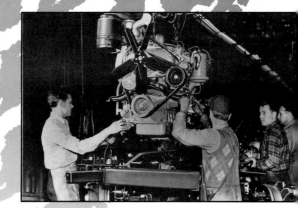

P utting trucking equipment on the road and keeping it there is a team effort. The players, however, vary dramatically in their approach and in their offerings to the industry.

The players include those who manufacture original equipment, those who build replacement parts, those who specialize in driver comforts, those who offer special ways to protect equipment from the vagaries of winter and wear, those who bring another kind of protection—insurance—and those who keep the public and potential customers aware of a company's presence. It takes all of these players to keep a trucking organization on a roll.

Being a component-driven industry, truck manufacturing calls on specialists—as in so many areas of our society—to ensure that the highest-quality product results from its efforts. From huge and time-tested builders of engines to smaller and often much younger makers of such prime features as drivetrains, suspensions, brakes, clutches, seats, and sleepers, these specialists blend their skills to create a road-running machine that has few, if any, peers worldwide.

But that's only the part that puts the trucker on the road; keeping him there is another matter. And that's where those involved in reducing wear and tear on primary parts and replacing those parts when they finally give way to old age or some other kink of the road come in. Special lubricants, fuel additives, and a truckload of similar products go toward extending a tractor-trailer's life and, in so doing, help to ensure profitability for a company or an independent trucker.

The replacement-parts market has become huge as trucking has steadily expanded in the United States. Seldom do original equipment manufacturers want to bother themselves with the aftermarket, and that has created a lucrative niche for a number of firms that provide a strong link in the life chain of a trucking company. These companies aren't just tailgating original manufacturers, looking for a free ride with inferior products just because the market's there. Instead, pride in their products pushes most of these operations to manufacture parts that are at least as good as the original.

Trucking companies may not fall into the household-name category, but name recognition doesn't take a backseat in the trucking industry. As a result, graphics, which are sometimes rather sophisticated instead of just plain block letters, are becoming increasingly important to the transportation industry. After all, if you have a truck traveling the highways and byways of America, it makes sense to let the public know just who you are. Graphics help put a company's name in the eye of a beholder. Industry officials have come to realize that the kind of commercial artistry that travels by truck can be just as important to a company as any art by the masters in a gallery.

Above: GMC workers install a diesel at a Detroit plant in the 1950s. Courtesy, American Truck Historical Society

Facing page: Logging trucks are required to negotiate difficult terrain, such as this narrow, unpaved mountain road. Photo by Roger Tully/After Image

CATERPILLAR INC. ENGINE DIVISION

Caterpillar Inc. is global enterprise with engine manufacturing and assembly facilities stretching around the world and nearly 60,000 employees, ranking it as a major force in the design and manufacture of diesel engines.

Today the company offers seven diesel engine families ranging from 40 to 7,300 horsepower. Among the nearly 200 engine configurations available are 35 truck engines ranging from 165 to 425 horsepower. Caterpillar truck engine shipments have increased the past five years in a row, and 1989 looks to be another record year due to excellent acceptance of 3306B and 3406B ATAAC and PEEC engines. Currently about half the 14-liter truck engines sold in North America are Cat 3406B engines. Considering all size engines sold into this heavy-duty market, Caterpillar is currently getting about 27 percent of the business.

The company's diesel engines come in power ranges to meet the demanding challenges facing today's on-highway trucks. Other uses include electrical and mechanical power for water and sewage treatment; construction; mining; petroleum exploration, production, and distribution; irrigation; and agricultural equipment. In addition, more than 1,000 original equipment manufacturers offer Caterpillar engines as standard or optional power for mid-range and heavy-duty trucks, marine vessels, locomotives, materials-handling equipment, and agricultural machinery.

Caterpillar's interest in its engines doesn't stop with delivery. There are more than 200 independent dealers worldwide with more than 1,000 sales, service, and parts facilities in about 140 countries. In North America alone, there are nearly 2,000 authorized parts and service locations supporting a working population of around a half-million Caterpillar-powered trucks.

The firm's long history of innovation and development in engine technology began in 1931 with the manufacture of its first diesel engine designed for mobile applications. That engine, dubbed the D9900, weighed 5,175 pounds (2,349 kilograms), had a displacement of 1,090

cubic inches (17.8 liters), and developed 87 horsepower at 700 r.p.m. That contrasts with the present-day heavy-duty 3176 Truck Engine that weighs 1,945 pounds (883 kilograms), has a displacement of 629 cubic inches (10.3 liters), develops up to 325 horsepower at 2100 r.p.m., and utilizes a powerful microprocessor as its operating brain.

The prototype for that first engine, nicknamed Old Betsy, is displayed as part of America's industrial heritage at the Smithsonian Institution in Washington, D.C. The D9900 signaled a new era in diesel engine acceptance and production. In 1932, for instance, the first Caterpillar diesel for use by another manufacturer was sold to Thew

Premium quality products, supported by a host of services, add up to the highest total value during the life of the vehicle—Economy Plus—that's Caterpillar's total engine value promise.

At Caterpillar power has purpose. Power lies in the resource, capabilities, and dedication of the Engine Division and its employees. The purpose of that power is to build technologically advanced, reliable engines.

Shovel Co. of Lorain, Ohio, for a huge power shovel. Other original equipment manufacturers soon began adapting diesel power for their uses. As a result, Caterpillar's 1933 production of diesel horsepower exceeded that of the entire United States for the preceding year.

In 1935 the firm developed its first engine designed for use in applications other than construction and materials handling. This eight-cylinder D17000 was tailor-made for industrial and marine applications and was so successful that it was manufactured for the next 20 years.

From there, Caterpillar moved to its first truck engine in 1939, followed by a second in 1940. However, both were discontinued as Caterpillar focused itself on World War II—designing and building rotary engines for American tanks and construction equipment for roads

and runways.

In the postwar years Caterpillar resumed building diesel engines, and in the 1950s became a pioneer in both turbocharging and aftercooling. The 1960s brought engines with such features as hardened crankshafts, dual overhead camshafts, two-ring pistons, and direct-injection fuel systems.

The truck engines kept coming on into the 1970s with updated features and such new items as the Caterpillar BrakeSaver hydraulic retarder, Jake Brake compatibility, a 1,600-r.p.m. heavy-duty economy truck engine (the 3406), and a truck engine for intercity use (the 3208) that ran at 2,600 r.p.m. The 1980s brought a mid-range economy engine (the 3208 T) that ran at 2,000 r.p.m., air-to-air aftercooling (ATAAC), Programmable Electronic Engine Control (PEEC), and an integrated-electronics heavy-duty truck engine (the 3176) that rivals the world's best.

In 1987, nearly 50 years after that first successful effort, sales of engines and related parts totaled $2.2 billion—more than the company's total sales volume as recently as nine years earlier.

During its 50 years in the truck engine business, the firm designed engines that improved efficiencies; increased performance in a lighter, more compact package; and created improved reliability and durability without sacrificing performance. In 1988 Caterpillar spent nearly $300 million on research and development, about 4 percent of sales. A little over one-third was spent on engine research to further develop new product and features aimed at maintaining Caterpillar leadership.

For all its global impact, Caterpillar has a special relationship with its home, Peoria, Illinois, which gained

Caterpillar's new heavy-duty diesel packs up to 325 horsepower into an in-line six-cylinder engine. Electronics, sophisticated manufacturing techniques, and an advanced design contribute to light weight, performance, and durability.

most of its early notoriety from the show business query, "Will it play in Peoria?" Caterpillar has for many years and there's little sign that the run will end any time in the near, or even distant, future.

Consider that Caterpillar, the area's largest employer, has a majority of its engine-producing sites in the immediate Peoria area, and a picture of stability for the firm and the community become clear. Nestled in the Central Illinois community of about 125,000 is Caterpillar's worldwide corporate headquarters, built in 1967.

Top left: The 3406B builds on Caterpillar's more than 20 years of experience manufacturing reliable, job-proven, heavy-duty diesels in the 300- to 400-horsepower class.

Bottom left: Whether it's peak fuel efficiency in a line-haul operation or high torque for construction, mining, bulk material transport, or refuse hauling, the CAT 3306B is accepted as the time-proven performer.

Below: Durability and low cost of operation, longtime Caterpillar standards, start with the design and development of engines and engine systems at the Caterpillar Technical Center.

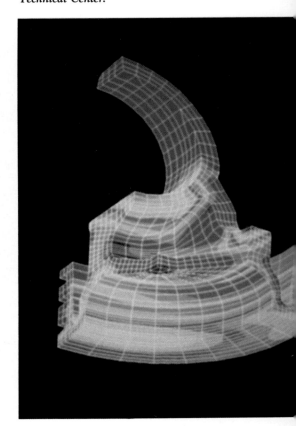

The Peoria-area Caterpillar sites with engine responsibility are the Technical Research Center, the Mapleton Foundry, the Mossville Engine Complex, the Pontiac Fuel System Plant, and the Morton Parts Distribution Center. The Lafayette, Indiana, plant, home to Caterpillar's two largest engine families, is only a few hours away. Each facility has a special function, not only for Peoria, but also for Caterpillar's worldwide presence.

The Technical Research Center, located near the Mossville Engine Complex just minutes north of Peoria, provides office, laboratory, computer, and experimental manufacturing areas totaling more than 27 acres. The engineers, scientists, technicians, and support people at the Technical Research Center pursue new product and component development; basic research in materials, combustion, heat transfer, and acoustics; and development of new engineering and scientific techniques. Nearly one-third of the center's facilities is devoted to engine development.

In the manufacturing area, Mapleton Foundry workers produce castings, from patternmaking to the finished, tested product; Pontiac

Caterpillar's standard of excellence continues long after product purchase. Access to a worldwide parts and service support network come standard with all CAT engines and engine systems.

Plant employees manufacture and assemble fuel systems; and Mossville Plant employees machine, assemble, and test Caterpillar engines and engine systems. The Mossville Engine Complex is one of the largest engine-manufacturing sites in the world. In each case, these plants operate on the most advanced technological level, using robotics where possible, specialized tooling—including lasers—where called for, and computerized testing.

The Morton Parts Distribution Center is the heartbeat of Caterpillar's major service function, providing replacement parts in the shortest time possible. The Morton, Illinois, facility is headquarters for Caterpillar's worldwide parts distribution network, which consists of 13 major parts distribution departments, 9 depots, and more than 1,000 parts, service, and sales facilities in about 140 countries. When customers place parts orders at Cat dealerships, almost 96 percent are filled immediately, nearly 98 percent are filled within 24 hours, and 99.6 percent are filled within 48 hours of placement. This far-flung network is tied together by master computer systems that control distribution, forecast demand, order inventory, and give the information that helps keep inventories at desired levels.

While pride in its past is strong and warranted, Caterpillar does not dwell on history. Instead, it has contin-

ued to go forward, looking to the next century when the world's population is expected to reach 6 billion. Such a world will require massive efforts toward sustaining basic needs such as food, housing, transportation, and energy. Caterpillar Inc.'s Engine Division is up to any task required and will continue to set standards for its engines and engine systems.

Caterpillar assures product quality through extensive product monitoring and process controls, taking extra measures to ensure that quality, energy efficiency, and investment payback are integral with any product that bears Caterpillar trademarks.

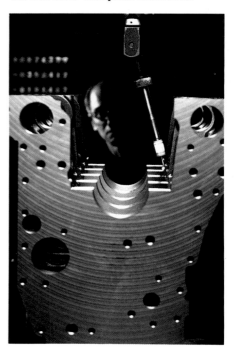

MACK TRUCKS, INC.

The name "Mack" across the cab of a commercial motor vehicle and the powerful bulldog perched proudly atop the grille are readily recognized everywhere. Throughout the world they symbolize Mack Trucks, Inc., and call to mind the company's international reputation for quality, dependability, and reliability.

Today the company John M. "Jack" Mack founded in 1900 has become one of America's largest producers of heavy-duty diesel trucks and major product components. Mack Trucks, Inc., also markets a line of medium-duty diesel trucks throughout North America, parts of Central America, Australia, and New Zealand. Mack vehicles are sold and serviced in more than 65 countries worldwide.

The world headquarters for Mack Trucks and the company's Engineering Development and Test Center are located in Allentown, Pennsylvania. Mack Trucks also has facilities in Macungie and Middletown, Pennsylvania; Somerset, New Jersey; Hagerstown, Maryland; New Bern, North Carolina; Brisbane, Australia; and Oakville, Ontario, Canada.

The company's newest facility, Winnsboro Assembly Operations, opened in Winnsboro, South Carolina, in 1987. It is the first heavy-duty truck plant in the industry to employ the "modular" concept of assembly.

Mack/Winnsboro combines simultaneous subassembly and assembly functions supported by just-in-time parts and component delivery, all driven by computer integration and statistical process control. The plant can produce 70 trucks per day and has the capacity to build all models in the Mack product line.

The history of Mack Trucks, Inc., starts with Gus Mack, the youngest of the five Mack brothers. Gus Mack left his native Pennsylvania in 1889 and took a clerical job with a Brooklyn, New York, builder of horse-drawn wagons and carriages.

Jack Mack joined Gus at the carriage factory in 1890. Jack was a

widely traveled engineer, thoroughly experienced operating and maintaining steam-powered construction machinery. The brothers purchased the factory in 1893. Their oldest brother, Willie, joined them a year later.

The Mack Brothers Company was chartered in 1901 "for the manufacture of carriages, wagons, and harnesses . . . and for the purpose of doing a general wheelwright and blacksmith's business." Their popular line of Mack-designed horse-drawn milk wagons made The Mack Brothers Company an immediate success.

The transformation from wagon maker to truck and bus manufacturer required ingenuity, inventiveness, and daring. There was no easy path to follow, and for this infant industry there were no reliable suppliers of components. Of necessity the brothers hand crafted chassis of

their own design and mated them with Mack-built engines. Thus the famed Mack/Mack combination, a Mack engine and a Mack chassis, dates back to the earliest days of the company.

Its most successful product, the Manhattan sight-seeing buses, became often-seen sights on the streets of New York, New Orleans, Boston, and Havana, Cuba.

A fourth brother, Joseph Mack, receives the credit for bringing the young company to Allentown, Pennsylvania. At Allentown Mack was able to bring its manufacturing operations under a single roof. There the firm made the four-cylinder engine that became the basis for the Mack motto: "Simplicity, Strength, Durability, and Plenty of Reserve Horsepower."

The fifth Mack brother, Charles, joined the company in 1910. The

same year the firm dropped its Manhattan trade name and began painting the name "MACK" on the side of the cabs.

But the company that we now know as Mack Trucks only emerged after a long period of corporate mergers and reorganizations. Mack withstood challenges from several powerful truck and automobile manufacturers and combined with others.

In 1912 the Mack brothers sold their operation to the International Motor Company, a firm backed by a group of American financiers including J.P. Morgan. The International Motor Company nearly failed during the economic crisis of 1913, but revived in time to help supply the Allies with trucks during World War I.

The AC Mack model truck that the company sent to the front had a newly designed and highly distinc-

The CH600 is a new dimension in heavy-duty highway hauling. It combines a spacious new cab with integral sleepers, unified aerodynamics, and exceptional comfort and convenience features. The all-new chassis incorporates a unique, air-suspended cab/sleeper subframe and a standard axleback configuration.

tive, short, rounded hood. "In appearance these Macks, with their pugnacious front and resolute lines, suggest the tenacious quality of the British Bull Dog," wrote one reporter. The trucks became known as Bull Dog Macks. Their reputation for durability, literally won in the trenches, brought a new phrase to the English language: "Built Like a Mack Truck."

Mack underwent a technological revolution as well, as the trusty Bulldog engine was phased out and, starting in 1938, diesel technology

moved in. While diesels produced by other manufacturers were available for installation in Mack chassis, Mack became the first independent truck manufacturer to produce its own engines.

The Mack reputation for dependability was again tested in World War II, as the new diesels found service in Europe and North Africa. Many tanks built after 1941 used Mack-built transmissions.

At the end of the war, International Motor Company changed its name to Mack-International Motor Truck Corporation. The company later acquired several other firms, including Brockway Motor Trucks, Radio Sonic Corporation, White Industries, the French truck manufacturer Bernard, and the Ohio-based C.D. Beck Company (inter-city buses and custom fire apparatus).

John B. Curcio was elected president and chief operating officer of Mack Trucks, Inc., in 1980. (Curcio is now chairman and chief executive officer of the corporation.) Under Curcio's leadership Mack has embarked on a program to replace and expand its entire product line.

With its new truck models—Ultra-Liner, Mid-Liner, CM-400-Baby 8, and the CH600—along with a line of Mack heavy-duty T200 transmissions and E-7 engines, the company is positioned to meet the competitive environment of the future.

Mack Truck's marketing organization was consolidated in 1987, bringing about a streamlined, worldwide approach that integrates sales efforts wherever Mack sells trucks, while establishing a leasing network that will permit all Mack branches and distributors to enter the leasing market.

Today's Mack Trucks, Inc., is a company that reflects its roots. It features a clear, crisp organizational structure. It is efficient and smooth running. It demonstrates "simplicity, strength, durability, and plenty of reserve horsepower." What else would one expect? This company is built like a Mack Truck.

MIDLAND HEAVY DUTY SYSTEMS

Midland Heavy Duty Systems believes it can put the brakes on rising insurance and maintenance costs with quality products accompanied with a high level of technical service.

Backed by its parent company, Echlin of Branford, Connecticut, Midland is a five-way stop for those in transportation. Its products are Midland air brake and wheel end products; Berg electrical products; Grey-Rock brake blocks, linings and pads; Lipe clutches; and Like-Nu remanufactured products.

In each case immense pride is

Heavy-duty brake components are manufactured with state-of-the-art robotic machinery by Midland.

Kansas City, Missouri. In addition, it has a production network that spans North America and includes plants in the United States, Canada, and Mexico. Midland serves both the manufacturing and the aftermarket replacement fields.

The origins of Midland Brake are rooted in the beginnings of air brake technology in the 1890s, which began with the development of the first railway air brake. From that first stop through today's sophisticated heavy-duty air brake systems, Midland continues as the leader in both product development and innovation and stands as the number-two brake manufacturer in the United States.

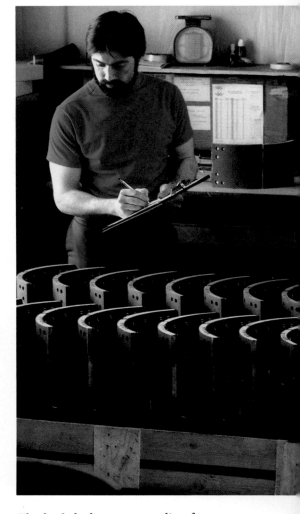

The final check to assure quality of a brake block is made just prior to shipment.

taken in quality work paired with quality materials, research, and development that puts Midland in the vanguard of new technology. Product reliability and durability also warrants long-term consideration from manufacturers of trucks, tractors, trailers, buses, and off-highway vehicles.

Midland, a vital link since the turn of the century in keeping the transportation industry safely on the road to progress and profit, is headquartered in Owosso, Michigan, and

Midland's combination of engineers, designers, researchers, and technical specialists brings quality and dependability to each of its products. Midland believes that from its computer-aided design to finite elemental analysis and comprehensive environmental, vibration, and life testing, the products meet or exceed industry standards for durability and performance.

In the brake field, Midland compressors set the standard for quality

and performance and are backed by an extended warranty. Multifunction valves are designed and tested to comply with the most stringent of safety standards. Double-diaphragm spring brakes are designed and built to eliminate the corrosion found in other aluminum housings. Slack adjusters are designed to perform high-torque brake applications, resulting in lower cost and a higher level of safety.

Midland's dryers deliver air to the brake system that is up to 99.4 percent pure, protecting components from corrosion, deterioration, sludge buildup, and freeze-up.

In friction materials, Grey-Rock has meant quality in the transportation industry for more than 60 years and has a distinguished string of firsts in the industry. That string winds all the way back to 1926, when Grey-Rock developed the first woven lining with a ground friction surface. Soon after came a lining woven with zinc alloy wire instead of brass wire. This eliminated drum scoring in 1934. Later Grey-Rock introduced balanced brake block sets to equalize the work done between the two shoes within truck brakes.

The emphasis on research and development has, in more recent years, helped to refine the performance of non-asbestos brake blocks. Responding to poor wear in non-asbestos brake blocks offered by other manufacturers, Grey-Rock developed a formula for its block that outperforms other materials in the combination of braking power and drum wear.

In the remanufactured-products arena, Like-Nu pledges original performance and original equipment warranty for its remanufactured compressors and valves. The remanufacturing process includes thermal cleaning of parts in temperatures that reduce paint and grease to powdered residue. It also encompasses "roto-blasting" in a rotating barrel where the residue is blasted away, and the cast iron or aluminum is returned to a like-new condition. Continual inspection and testing are the keynotes for keeping Like-Nu's quality the highest in the industry. In addition, parts and components must meet 100 percent of the original specifications or they're discarded. In doing this the company believes it creates the quality that assures origi-

made the Franklin automobile run smoother. In 1932 Lipe developed a multiple-lever clutch that revolutionized performance in large trucks and off-highway vehicles.

The efficiency of Lipe clutches is based on a simple but powerful concept. Lipe's springs are perpendicular to the pressure plate, not on an angle to it. Therefore, springs push directly against disc facings ensuring even, constant pressure throughout the clutch life. The result is durable, reliable performance, the signature of all Midland Heavy Duty Systems products.

This cutaway view illustrates Lipe's patented direct-pressure design.

The assembly of remanufactured valves with new rubber and brass components ensures longer life and original-equipment performance.

nal performance and durability in all remanufactured products.

The Berg product line is a descendant of the first electrical connector that was designed and sold by Joseph Berg in 1939. It has grown into a full offering of wire, cable, switches, noseboxes, and intervehicular connectors.

Coming through in the clutch is not new to Lipe; it goes back to 1902, when the Lipe equalizing clutch, later called a differential,

The true difference between Midland Heavy Duty Systems and other manufacturers is a high level of technical service. It offers distributor and fleet training sessions, diagnostic brake clinics, and fleet engineering work in diagnosing brake problems and recommending corrective action. The result to the consumer is lower brake maintenance costs and an increased level of safety. That's the Midland difference—quality products accompanied with quality service.

MODAGRAFICS CORPORATION

Seeing is believing, so the saying goes.

A company name emblazoned across the body of a truck's trailer says that business is rolling and the message is being transported across the landscape of America.

Making a company's name go farther is the business of Modagrafics Corporation, a leader in high-speed, high-volume screen printing and complex decal constructions. Today's 18-wheelers can feature innovative and creative movable graphic feasts for a leader in the fast-food industry, or an attractive invitation beckoning customers to a retail outlet, or can designate the location of a major corporation's headquarters or branch offices. Produced by Modagrafics, these are all signs for the times.

But there's more to graphics than meets the eye. Modagrafics believes, in fact, that a strong visual identity says who you are, what you do, and where you're going. The firm's mobile billboards register millions of impressions on potential customers each year, adding exposure to a company's advertising program—over the

For some customers, such as this one, the company maintains inventory and supplies promotional decals for truck rears.

long haul.

Survivors of the troublesome days of deregulation in the trucking industry seem to be far more conscious of those impressions than ever before. A clean, identifiable message on a truck with stylish graphics, together with a courteous and safety-conscious driver, go a long way toward enhancing the pride of the modern image-aware trucker. The combination makes an impact on prospective customers as well as the traveling public.

Sometimes the work for Modagrafics' stylists requires the removal of existing decals, painting of trailers, and the application of new graphics—as in the case of the Ace Hardware job.

"There's no reason to think this won't continue and expand," says John Koepke, Modagrafics' president and chief operating officer. "I see graphics getting larger, bolder, and more stylish, and, after all, a truck serves as its company's calling card on the nation's highways."

Headquartered in Chicago's northwest suburb of Rolling Meadows, Modagrafics has made its mark nationally with a variety of companies, including such well-known names as Bekins, Greyhound, Santa Fe, United Technologies, and GTE. In its short 15-year history the firm has acquired a second facility at Wichita, Kansas, and the two sites employ more than 150 people. The company's operations cover marketing analysis, design, processing, and application from the drawing board to the road, targeted to communicating an image that has impact, continuity, and class.

Modagrafics believes it can make the first impression a lasting one. Its graphics experts are confident they can provide clients with impact and excitement designing visuals ranging from simple, informational emblems

to the most exotic promotional decal systems.

When a company signs with the firm, Modagrafics Marketing Center specialists assess the client's objectives, style, and scope of operations. As the research is completed, the team sets out to graphically portray the client's corporate personality. The task of presenting the personality is delegated to the Design Center, where skilled art directors evaluate every aspect of the client's advertising and marketing needs. Developing a program can follow several roads: careful and exacting reproduction of trademarks already in use, development of bright, new graphics tailor-made to the client's preference, or coordination with outside design firms or consultants determined by the client.

But that's only the beginning. The next step is to analyze the size and types of vehicles in a client's fleet. This information serves as a guide to the dimensions and working surface of the medium—painted or plain; corrugated, riveted, or smooth; straight or curved.

For Thurston, Modagrafics designed, manufactured, and applied a new corporate image to the client's fleet.

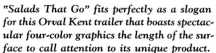

"Salads That Go" fits perfectly as a slogan for this Orval Kent trailer that boasts spectacular four-color graphics the length of the surface to call attention to its unique product.

The hostile environment in which a fleet operates requires special attention as well. The service life of any graphic system is affected by weather extremes and exposure to chemicals and abrasion and cleaning methods. Meeting these demands means a careful selection of films, inks, and adhesives that will perform to expectations while delivering maximum punch and ensuring maximum durability.

Borrowing from an old saw, the proof of all this preliminary work is in the processing. Through state-of-the-art equipment and technology, and the right combination of men and machines, Modagrafics' screen-

ing and fabricating plant skillfully executes four-color printing that demands precise registration of screened colors and die-cut parts. The firm easily manages large-size decals—or Super Graphics—and accomplishes complex decal configurations.

The process also includes the use of vacuum applicators, which guarantees better bonding for die-cut letters, and a final baking process, which assures maximum color stability. Both of these steps are important factors in generating a longer life span and giving extra value to graphic markings.

Application of the pressure-sensitive decals, which have a durability of seven years, marks the final milepost on the road to designer trucking. The Modagrafics team of professionals can install the completed graphics at the Rolling Meadows headquarters, at a regional center established specifically for the purpose, or at the client's location. In addition, Modagrafics offers the option of instructing a client's own personnel in the necessary installation skills.

By making a name for others, Modagrafics Corporation continues to make a name for itself in the graphics field and the signage industry by putting its clients on the road to success.

LUBRIZOL CORPORATION

Webster's defines an additive as "a substance added to another in relatively small amounts to impart or improve desirable properties or suppress undesirable properties."

Users the world over of Lubrizol Corporation products will buy that—and they do to such an extent as to make Lubrizol the world's leading independent producer of specialty chemicals—additives, that is—for lubricants, fuels, and functional fluids.

These additives, which can be either a single compound or a blend of many components, are sold to petroleum companies worldwide to enhance performance of their motor oils, automatic transmission fluids, gear oils and farm-tractor fluids, as well as gasoline and diesel fuels.

Although the firm, which was founded in Cleveland in 1928 as the Graphite Oil Products Company, also develops specialty chemicals for industry in the form of additives for industrial oils and fluids and corrosion-control coatings, its work

in the transportation field—and consequently trucking—outweighs its other efforts.

From its beginning the firm, which moved in 1932 to its permanent base in the Cleveland suburb of Wickliffe and took on its present name, has maintained a strong liaison with the transportation industry. Its major products in those early days were Lubri-Zol Concentrate, an oil additive that reduced friction in automobile engines of the era, and a gasoline additive that dissolved carbon deposits. It wasn't long before Lubrizol expanded its base beyond the four-wheel vehicles to their multiwheel big brothers—trucks.

By enhancing the performance of fuels and lubricants for the trucking industry, Lubrizol plays a prime role in enhancing the performance and the durability of vehicles. Though lubricants make up only about one percent of the overall cost of operating a vehicle, they have a massive impact on the highest costs in the industry—maintenance and fuel

costs.

In the maintenance arena, the blending of Lubrizol products with basic lubricants can extend the life of a truck engine lengthening the time between major overhauls. In the fuel category, Lubrizol products can increase the time between fuel-system maintenance stops, keep injector systems cleaner, protect the fuel system against corrosion, and just generally improve fuel efficiency.

Research and development has always been a major factor at Lubrizol as evidenced by the fact that more than 1,000 of its approximately 4,800 employees worldwide are involved in such activities. Three major laboratories are maintained in the United States, Great Britain, and Japan, and Lubrizol operates manufacturing plants in several locations worldwide, along with sales and tech-

The Lubrizol Corporation administration building.

nical service offices in principal cities. Aside from the United States, Great Britain, and Japan, Lubrizol operates sites in Canada, Mexico, Brazil, France, Italy, the Netherlands, Spain, Sweden, South Africa, India, Singapore, Australia, and New Zealand.

Lubrizol counts at least 20 major technological achievements in the area of fuel and lubricants over the past 50 years, with the first major breakthroughs occurring during World War II, when the United States' need for higher levels of performance in military equipment made it possible to demonstrate the value of high-quality lubricants. Lubrizol developed the additives to meet those needs.

After the war Lubrizol applied its technology to new lubricant quality standards for civilian markets. Growth, technical advances and extensive testing, and a continuing elevated standing in the industry followed. As a result, Lubrizol supplies additives to more than 1,600 companies in the United States and more than 5,500 businesses worldwide. The North American market accounts for about 40 percent of Lubrizol's business, and the remaining 60 percent is done in international commerce.

Lubrizol enjoys about one-third of the lubricant-additive business worldwide. Some of the company's major competitors are chemical company affiliates of major oil companies that supply much of their own captive need, so Lubrizol has an even larger percentage of the noncaptive business.

Lubrizol prides itself on being an independent producer—not being affiliated with any oil company—and turns this to its advantage with customers by pointing out that its independence allows it to focus its attention on each of its customers equally.

Because Lubrizol recognizes that meeting the needs of individual customers worldwide is a complex commitment, the firm has created a

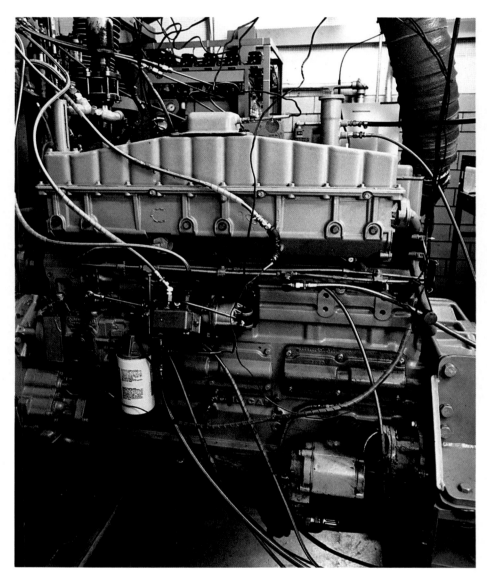

working environment it believes recognizes the value of experimentation —the implementation of novel approaches to customers' problems and the development of new quality products. The focus is on finding solutions that call for the cooperation of skilled professionals in all parts of the organization.

One might say that the working environment—acting as the firm's motor oil—uses additives from all corners of its operation, and those additives—like Lubrizol Corporation's products—enhance overall performance and keep the engine running smoothly toward its goal of continuing to set high-quality standards for its industry throughout the world.

Cummins NTC-400 test installation at Lubrizol.

TRUCK-LITE COMPANY, INC.

Truck and automobile drivers worldwide depend on Truck-Lite products. From the driving lights up front to the tail lights on the back of the trailer, Truck-Lite Company, Inc., of Falconer, New York, is among the largest independent lighting suppliers to the transportation industry.

To the uninitiated, the engineering for lights on trucks may appear simple and basic. Transportation professionals, however, know that lighting system failure is a major fleet maintenance problem, and every driver on the road knows that lighting system failure is a major safety threat. Solving that problem with sealed lighting systems and electrical harnesses has become the mission of Truck-Lite.

The firm's sealed lighting systems, fully sealed to prevent damage from corrosion and vibration, have established outstanding records for long-haul reliability. In the process, they have transformed the company from a cottage industry to its current status as an international leader.

Truck-Lite traces its origins to a

manufacturing operation that saw plastic lenses and lamp housing parts manufactured by outside contractors, assembled at home by individuals, and distributed to the customers by a new and ambitious company. In 1956 the firm developed the first completely sealed safety light for the heavy-duty trucking industry. The Model 10 established Truck-Lite's reputation as a top-quality supplier.

The firm soon outgrew its cottage-industry style of operation and built an assembly and distribution plant in Jamestown, New York. In 1964 the Quaker State Oil Refining Corporation of Oil City, Pennsylvania (now known as Quaker State Corp.), acquired Truck-Lite. The following year Quaker State purchased United Precision Plastics, thereby bringing the entire light-manufacturing process under Truck-Lite control. Truck-Lite is a wholly owned subsidiary of Quaker State.

The corporation's history includes a startling number of technological firsts. Truck-Lite was the first company to use lens grade LEXAN® in its products and the first to offer

A wide assortment of both sealed and bulb-replaceable products manufactured by Truck-Lite.

sealed safety lighting products. It was the first to use shock mounting systems for bulbs and to offer sealed wiring harnesses for truck trailers.

The firm's comprehensive warranty policies were also an industry innovation. Limited warranties cover many of Truck-Lite's sealed shock-mounted lamps. And Truck-Lite's Super 40 Stop/Turn/Tail lamps have proven to last 10 to 20 times longer than conventional type lamps, allowing fleets around the country to experience more than 500,000 miles of trouble-free lighting.

The company experienced tremendous growth from 1970 to 1980. During that decade investment in plant equipment quintupled, employment increased 100 percent, and sales increased more than sevenfold. Truck-Lite now supplies more than 4 million stop/turn/tail lamps and more than 8 million clearance marker lamps annually. That's enough to illuminate more than 2 mil-

Aerodynamic styling of safety lighting products is evident in this ATL (all-terrain light) suitable for snowplows, construction equipment, farm machinery, and many off-road applications.

lion vehicles

Today's Truck-Lite Company, Inc., manufactures lights not only for trucks, but for automobiles as well. Ford, Chrysler, GM, and Volkswagen all use such Truck-Lite components as interior courtesy lights, reading lights, side marker lights, and rear light assemblies.

Among the international truck and heavy equipment manufacturers that rely on Truck-Lite systems are Ford, Navistar, Kenworth, Caterpillar, Deere, Case International, Mack, Freightliner, Volvo, GM, M.A.N., Neoplan, and countless others. The firm's leading trailer-manufacturer customers include Fruehauf, Trailmobile, Strick, Utility, and Monon.

For the marine and boat trailer industry, Truck-Lite manufactures a complete line of both bulb replaceable and sealed lamps, which are fully submersible.

Truck-Lite senior management credits the company's employees for its success. From engineering to in-house prototype and preproduction facilities, and from testing and evaluation through manufacturing and quality control, Truck-Lite employees aspire to maintain the highest-quality standards. The firm has maintained a consistent work force throughout its history. Along with its low turnover in personnel has come a corporate pride in workmanship and accomplishment.

The company's research and development facilities are located in Falconer, New York, where Truck-Lite has more than 30 employees involved in product engineering, engineering services, manufacturing engineering, and laboratory and quality control. The goal of all these people is to ensure that Truck-Lite products not only meet the requirements of the Society of Automotive Engineers and the Department of Transportation, but also exceed the ex-

pectations of their customers.

Truck-Lite is proud of its Continuous Improvement Program, QUEST (Quality Every Single Time). Among the components of this program are the DIRTFT (Do It Right The First Time) and the Just-In-Time concepts of manufacturing. This companywide dedication to quality control is keyed to offering all Truck-Lite customers the benefits of higher-quality products at lower costs.

Truck-Lite remains alert to the ever-changing needs of the vehicular lighting industry. Some of the newer products from Truck-Lite include Easy Seal®, a modular component wiring harness system that simply plugs and snaps together, yet, like other Truck-Lite products, is fully sealed

against the harsh road environment. Super Flash, Truck-Lite's heavy-duty electronic flasher, is guaranteed to give heavy trucks with trailers all the flashing power they need. Truck-Lite's newest product is a sealed shock-mounted headlamp for light-, medium-, and heavy-duty trucks that offers longer life and better visibility. And there's more just down the road. The firm's engineers are already working with light-emitting diodes, multiplex systems to control safety lighting, and electroluminescence

Truck-Lite Company, Inc., continues to light the way to the future for the transportation industry.

Truck-Lite's safety lighting products are found on all types and sizes of vehicles.

DANA CORPORATION

Dana Corporation, founded in 1904 as Spicer Manufacturing and headquartered in Toledo, Ohio, grew up with America's automobile- and truck-manufacturing industry. Today Dana is North America's largest independent supplier of vehicular components, with annual sales near $5 billion—80 percent of which is to the vehicular original-equipment and replacement-parts markets.

Dana is a decentralized global operation, with more than 39,000 people working at approximately 700 facilities representing 25 countries. At the heart of the organization are four regional operating groups, each with a president and operating committee: North America, South America, Europe, and Asia/Pacific.

Though this structure means decision making is diffused, the Dana commitment to excellence remains constant. The commitment that for years has guided supply relationships with Ford, General Motors, Chrysler, Mack, and Navistar/International today also serves Nissan, Hino, Isuzu, Volvo, Renault/RVI, and Daimler-Benz.

Through more than 80 years Dana has developed an impressive lineup of products and services the world over. These include drivetrain systems, engine parts, chassis products, industrial power transmission products, fluid power systems, and parts distribution and service.

The global growth of the firm, which ranks among the 100 largest industrial corporations in the United States and the 250 largest in the world, is just the latest chapter in a story that began with the birth of the automotive/truck industry.

Clarence Spicer, whose name continues in Dana's many Spicer-brand drivetrain components, was the early inventive genius behind the corporation's growth. He developed the first practical automotive industry universal joint and driveshaft in 1904.

Spicer's early customer list was a who's who of passenger-car makers. But his patented universal joint and driveshaft arrangement was also a

prominent fixture with such pioneering truck manufacturers as Mack (first order placed in 1906), Diamond T (1907), Autocar (1910), Brockway (1912), and International Harvester (1914).

In 1914 Charles A. Dana, an attorney and businessman, joined Spicer's company to provide needed financial support and business guidance—

A view of a Dana drivetrain system.

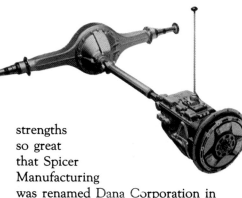

strengths so great that Spicer Manufacturing was renamed Dana Corporation in 1946. Dana broadened the firm's coverage to include the basics of the Dana product lineup that now serves truck manufacturers worldwide.

In 1919 came the addition of Parish Pressed Steel, still a top-quality manufacturer of truck side rails and frames. That same year came the purchase of the Sheldon Axle Co., forerunner of today's Spicer Heavy Axle. In 1929 the Brown-Lipe Gear Company, predecessor of Spicer Transmission, joined the Dana lineup, and in 1947 Dana acquired

Spicer universal joints and driveshafts began replacing chain and sprocket drives in 1904.

the Auburn Clutch Co., which today is known as Spicer Clutch.

With more recent acquisitions, such as Perfect Circle engine parts (1963), Victor gaskets (1966), Weatherhead hydraulics (1978), and Wix filters (1980), Dana Coporation has grown to be a full-line automotive and truck industry supplier.

Dana's products and services meet the needs of customers in five key markets: highway vehicle (original-equipment manufacturers of trucks, trailers, and cars); automotive and truck parts distribution (distributors, dealers, and other outlets); mobile off-highway (heavy-equipment manufacturers and distributors); and industrial equipment (specialized distributors supplying non-vehicular power equipment to manufacturers and users).

Dana serves customers with this unmatched range of vehicular products and product systems:

Drivetrain systems—Dana offers the world's most complete line of drivetrain components. Of particular importance are the Spicer System medium and heavy truck complete drivetrain packages, unique in their precision-engineered combination of clutch, transmission, driveshaft, and axle configurations. Dana is a leading supplier of Chelsea power takeoffs, which provide auxiliary power for trucks and heavy-duty equipment.

Engine parts—This coverage includes Perfect Circle piston rings, pistons, camshafts, cylinder sleeves, and valve seals; Victor gaskets and sealing products; and Wix oil, air, and fuel filters. The Precision Controls Division also develops electronic engine speed controls for light and heavy-duty applications.

Chassis parts—Parish frames and heat-treated side rails remain the standard structural support of the truck industry. Dana is a leader in heavy-duty applications with Spicer trailer axles and C&M truck and trailer springs and suspensions.

Fluid power systems—Dana prod-

uct coverage for truck and off-highway applications includes Tyrone pumps, Gresen control valves, Hyco hydraulic cylinders, and Weatherhead hoses and fittings.

No less important is the Dana "extra" in quality and service. Heavy-truck manufacturers in particular benefit from two special Dana strengths.

The company's assembly concept places small, flexible, just-in-time delivery centers close to truck manufacturers worldwide. Dana regional assembly plants can build individual products or complete product systems, add non-Dana components, and ship them just in time, according to customer assembly schedules. Across North America and in Europe, South America, and Asia/Pacific, Dana has more than 40 regional assembly plants, with plans to further increase that number in the coming years.

Dana's "Excellence in Manufactur-

Top: A sampling of Dana's engine parts includes Perfect Circle, Victor, Wix, Williams, and Speedostat products.

Above: Products that serve fluid power systems include these well-known names: Tyrone, Gresen, Chelsea, Hyco, Weatherhead, and Boston.

ing" program is achieving world-class standards of performance. EIM techniques such as machining cells for flexible operation and statistical process control for built-in quality give customers the highest quality at the lowest cost—helping Dana operations earn more than 80 quality awards from its 10 largest customers.

Dana people put all these things together in what is known as the Dana Style, a management system emphasizing self-management by the people who know the job. The Dana Style also emphasizes on-the-job experience as the best way to learn, promotion from within, encouragement to own company stock, and training programs. As Charles A. Dana said more than a half-century ago: "There is only one thing really worthwhile about a business and that is its men and women. Brick and mortar can be replaced; people and their contributions cannot." Dana Corporation people have been proving him right ever since.

Below: Parts distribution and service are sales targets for all Dana operating units. The backbone of the corporation's global distribution network is a system of 250 distribution facilities.

Bottom: Chassis products include those carrying the names of Parish, Perfect Circle, Spicer, C&M, Victor, and Weatherhead.

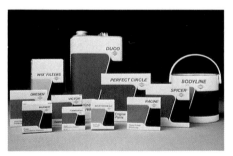

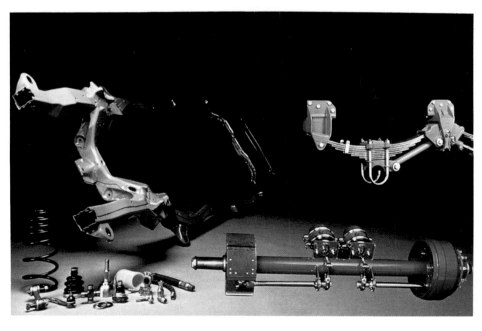

SENTINEL AGENCY, INC.

It took Frank M. Sedlacek, Jr., only two years in the insurance business to get his own agency show on the road—a road that has carried him and his associates to impressive policy destinations with numerous clients in the transportation industry for nearly 30 years.

Since its founding in 1960, his Sentinel Agency, Inc., with headquarters in Crystal Lake, Illinois, has been a force in the transportation field throughout the upper Midwest. While it is a full-service insurance firm, Sentinel, the first office of which was in Cary, a neighbor of Crystal Lake, finds 85 to 90 percent of its business among trucking companies that are local, intermediate, or long haulers. Its expertise in the field is reflected in a client loyalty factor that registers an average of 18 years.

Just a little more than two years out of Northwestern University with a business degree and having just completed a two-year tour of duty with the U.S. Army, Sedlacek got his first taste of transportation insurance when he joined an insurance company in Crystal Lake that specialized in the field.

After only two years he left the firm and hit the road on his own, hooking up with five top-rated insurers. It didn't take long for Sentinel to become a specialist in the transportation field, though it did take a full load of dedication and hard work on the young man's part.

Quick prosperity that saw the firm outgrow three offices in little more than four years, earnest attention to service, and extreme client loyalty served Sedlacek's company in its beginning. That early growth meant an eventual move to Crystal Lake, where the firm rented office space for eight years before buying its own building and where it did business for 22 years. Continued growth meant a move to its present location, known as Sentinel Complex, where Sedlacek's son, Frank R., serves as vice-president.

Sedlacek considers his agency's

Frank M. Sedlacek, Jr., president of Sentinel Agency, Inc.

ability to call on years of specialized experience in giving professional guidance as a major asset when a prospective client looks at the array of services Sentinel has to offer, including guaranteed cost, retrospective, large deductible, and self-insurance plans.

Sentinel's basic truckers' service package includes detailed accident reporting packets, safety award programs, meeting participation, detailed loss runs for all lines of coverage, and premium-payment programs that aid cash flow.

Sentinel is an independent agency, so its objectivity is a selling point. The firm believes it can give a client an eagle-eyed approach to rate shopping because it deals with a full spectrum of top insurance companies rather than just a few. With that in mind, Sentinel hopes to take some of the bumps and curves out of the insurance road traveled by the trucking industry.

LEAR SIEGLER TRUCK PRODUCTS CORP.

For the Lear Siegler Truck Products Corp., it's a stop-and-go world. The company's premier products are Anchorlok spring brakes and Neway air suspension systems, both of which have kept the trucking industry rolling comfortably and safely along the highways for more than three decades.

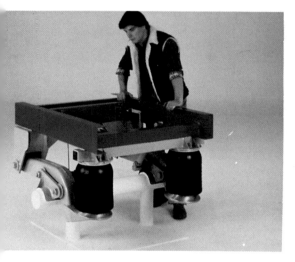

The new AR-90 trailer air suspension. This topmount, on-highway suspension is light in weight, economically priced, and has design features to keep maintenance costs low.

"Pushing performance to new levels" is the message Anchorlok sends out to the transportation industry. The implication is that when push comes to shove, pushing on an Anchorlok brake doesn't give shove much of a chance. It's been that way since Anchorlok introduced the double-diaphragm design and has continued through a long list of innovations and technological advances that include the first release tool pocket on the side of the brake, the first safety chamber hooks, the first double lip seal in the flange, and the first Arctic (minus 60 degrees Fahrenheit) diaphragm.

The most recent of those advances is Anchorlok's Gold Seal spring brake, a system that includes an integral crimped seal of the chamber and adapter. This new innovation continues the Anchorlok dedication to safety without using

traditional clamp bands and bolts. The Gold Seal also incorporates a dust shield and tethered end plug to reduce internal contamination. A double O-ring seal provides longer service life. And finally, the Gold Seal incorporates Anchorlok's "orange alert" stroke indicator to help take guesswork out of spring brake adjustments.

The new height control valve offers significant performance and durability improvements.

Neway has been taking the suspense out of air suspension systems for about 30 years, during which time it has become the world's leading supplier of specialty air suspensions for trucks, tractors, and trailers.

The new Anchorlok Gold Seal spring brake continues Anchorlok's tradition of safety and reliability.

Neway's smooth ride offers increased payload profit through reduced cargo damage, as well as savings on tire costs, general operating costs, maintenance, parts inventory, and fuel costs when using lift

axle suspension models.

Never one to rest on its laurels, Neway is now producing what it calls the next generation in suspension systems—Air-Beam.™ It is light in weight and is less expensive to install and maintain. Nevertheless the system, in the works since 1983 and counting 12,000 engineering manhours in development, offers the durability and performance that have marked all Neway products.

This development is only the latest in Neway's never-ending quest for excellence, a quest that is born in a commitment that is a state of mind with Neway employees, who average well in excess of 10 years with the company. That state of mind is not so rigid that it doesn't allow recognition of the fact that user acceptance just happens. Product integrity and dependability are the factors that bring success and continued growth.

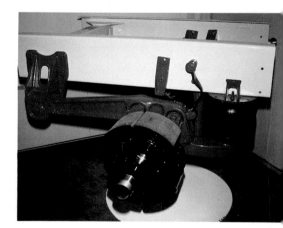

Air-Beam™ suspension.

Neway's preeminence in its field goes beyond engineering, research and development, and manufacturing to a sales and service organization that stands ready to serve an individual customer or a major fleet account or anything in between. The largest parts and service network in the specialty suspension industry backs up more than 500 Neway distributors. All of that, obviously, takes the suspense out of dealing with Neway.

DeCAROLIS TRUCK RENTAL, INC.

DeCarolis Truck Rental, Inc., has become the largest independent, full-service truck rental and leasing company in Upstate New York. Service, convenience, and dependability are three characteristics of this second-generation, family-owned business that recently celebrated its 50th year of service to transportation in the Rochester community.

The organization began operating as DeCarolis Trucking Company in 1938, primarily carting goods and produce from one destination to another. In the early days the DeCarolis family was involved in just about every segment of the trucking industry. Paul's father, Louis, started with the cartage company, added a truck terminal, and expanded into warehousing in the 1950s. Then came the truck stop, a truck dealership, a Thermo-King franchise, and a leasing company. Following the death of his father and brother, Paul DeCarolis was thrust into the presidency at the age of 25. He carefully surveyed the many phases of his truck-related operations and ultimately focused his concentration on truck rental and leasing with a special emphasis on customer service.

Today the DeCarolis fleet exceeds 1,900 vehicles. In the past five

DeCarolis Truck Rental, Inc., provides a host of services to the transportation industry, including truck, tractor, and trailer leasing; trailer and van parts and service; driver safety programs; daily rentals; and storage trailers.

years five new facilities have opened in western and central New York to accommodate the businesses that have come to depend on DeCarolis Truck Rental for all or part of their transportation needs. The main office is at 333 Colfax Street on Rochester's west side. Branch locations include Buffalo, Geneva, Henrietta, Perry, and Syracuse. From 21 employees in 1975, the company has grown to a staff of more than 125. In the past two years DeCarolis has been rated among Rochester's top 100 by the chamber of commerce.

As a member of Amtralease—a nationwide network of independent truck leasing companies—DeCarolis can offer its customers local attention with coast-to-coast coverage. Amtralease affiliates provide reciprocal fuel emergency service, and even replacement vehicles if necessary. More than 200 independently owned service facilities are backed by more than 3,000 approved service and fuel locations across the United States.

DeCarolis Truck Rental now offers a host of services to the transportation industry, including truck, tractor, and trailer leasing; trailer and van parts and service; storage trailers (warehouses on wheels); daily rentals; and driver safety programs. Films on safety and operating techniques are available for viewing on Colfax Street or for customers at their own location. Fully equipped facilities, yielding modern, thorough, and efficient operation, reflect Paul's

Paul DeCarolis is president of DeCarolis Truck Rental, Inc., the largest independently owned truck leasing company in Upstate New York.

solid, progressive thinking and determination to stay ahead. Leases and service contracts are specifically designed for each customer. A full-service lease includes vehicle maintenance, licenses and permits, repairs, as well as custom painting and lettering, including company logos. Leasing a vehicle from DeCarolis Truck Rental can provide the means to better manage any company's transportation budget.

From vice-presidents to fuel island attendants, DeCarolis' employees are schooled to meet the needs of the customers, large and small. Their commitment and hard work ensure the company's stability as well as customer satisfaction. In fact, the growth and success of DeCarolis Truck Rental is directly related to the confidence its customers have placed in its highly skilled and productive staff. Paul DeCarolis recently complimented his co-workers: "We all can take pride in our accomplishments in the past and anticipate the future with confidence."

DeCarolis Truck Rental, Inc., continues to be a growth-oriented, high-quality service company with an uncompromising emphasis on quality as its highest priority.

KOLD-BAN INTERNATIONAL LTD.

Fact: Diesel engines often leave you cold.

But Kold-Ban International Ltd. believes it can warm your heart as well as your diesel engine. For starters, it puts the heat on cold engines with its product, KBI Dieselmatic and Dieselmatic Kompac, technically advanced ether-injection systems.

KBI has been in the starting-fluid-injection business since 1970 and has been on the high road to research and development for most of its life. As a result, the company has developed several prominent changes in the way ether-injection systems work, resulting in its holding a number of patents in the field.

The key to its research and development is in a cold room that the 40-employee company, located in Algonquin, Illinois, has operated since the mid-1970s. It is in this room that those conditions that will test the effectiveness of engine-starting fluids are created and where each reaction to conditions by a product is monitored and graded.

"The change that most sets the Dieselmatic apart from other such products," says J.O. "Jim" Burke, vice-president/marketing and son of president and chief executive officer James W. Burke, "is the valving and flow-control mechanisms used. They are unique in that they use a much smaller amount of starting fluid and use it in a much more refined and controlled method."

The Dieselmatic system is wired into a truck's starting circuit so that it functions only when the cranking motor is engaged and the engine is cold enough to require the starting fluid, Burke says. In older systems, some of which Kold-Ban still makes, it was up to the operator to decide when and how much ether was to be used, which often led to system abuse. For instance, it was not uncommon for a driver to use the ether to give his truck an extra boost going uphill or when he might be racing a buddy along the interstate. Both situations could damage an engine and therefore lead to costly, time-

KBI's complete line of engine-starting fluid-injection systems—the KBI Diesel Start and Dieselmatic Kompac.

consuming repairs.

Burke sees a future filled with many more technical advances, most of which he hopes will result from KBI's research and development efforts. In addition to new technology, Burke believes some old-fashioned educating of the trucking community will help KBI overcome the common "if-you've-started-one-you've-started-

them all" view of engine-starting systems.

Kold-Ban International Ltd., a worldwide sales company, must warm to that challenge, Burke believes, and in so doing should be able to convince the industry that it has the ultimate among engine-starting systems. Once that is accomplished, there should be open road ahead for Kold-Ban and its products.

KBI maintains its own cold test room complete with state-of-the-art data acquisition.

DOUBLE EAGLE INDUSTRIES

When it is time to hit the road, thousands of truckers take a little bit of home with them in the form of a Double Eagle Industries custom-made sleeper in their trucks.

Double Eagle is respected for the innovative designs and industry standards the company, located in Shipshewana, Indiana, has developed since its first sleeper was built in 1967 by Amish craftsmen in the small northern Indiana community.

The roomy, well-appointed sleepers, containing a luggage compartment, at least four flush-mounted doors, lighting, chrome two-way

Roominess and the comforts of home go along with this plush-looking sleeper by Double Eagle Industries of Shipshewana, Indiana.

vents, and a variety of other features, offer truck owners comforts that a typical factory-built truck does not provide. With kitchen, bath, and entertainment facilities, the owners can realize savings on motels and restaurants, and, chances are, be better-rested and safer operators, too.

Among specific items offered for Double Eagle's "homes on the road," which have been inspired in part by a growing number of husband/wife driving teams, are a refrigerator with ice tray, color television, videocassette recorder, fluorescent lighting, AM/FM cassette stereo system, lavatory, roof-mounted air conditioner with a heat strip, microwave oven, hot and cold running water, and a central vacuum system.

Another one of the many trucks leaving Double Eagle with a new custom-built sleeper featuring a custom paint pattern on the sleeper, beautiful exterior lighting, and attractive stainless-steel finishing, setting it apart from other trucks on the road.

And if all those possibilities still do not cover a trucker's needs, Double Eagle will set out to customize the sleeper even further to satisfy the customer's desires. That kind of tailoring can make it seem as if the driver never left home.

In addition, the company produces a large number of smaller, sleeper-quarters-only sleepers. Many of these are bought by fleet owners, since the price on these basic sleepers is competitive with those of other sleeper manufacturers.

Double Eagle was the first sleeper manufacturer to design and patent a boot opening for a cabover application, a major industry innovation. The firm now produces its own generator system, called the Gen-Pac. It is diesel powered and water cooled, circulating hot water through the truck's heaters and engine on winter nights and creating plenty of AC power with which to operate all those home conveniences. Among the latest additions to Double Eagle's list of extras are custom tool boxes, custom deck plating, and further additions to the interiors that will satisfy even the most discriminating of drivers.

But even though Double Eagle sleepers have all those conveniences, they are still road tough and durable. Double Eagle Industries' craftsmen are dedicated to making sure that comfort has a sturdy foundation and maximum safety factors.

EUCLID INDUSTRIES INC.

For 50 years Euclid Industries has worked relentlessly to provide the heavy-duty truck parts market with parts and customer service of the highest quality, thereby, earning the reputation as "The Most Trusted Name in Truck Parts."

Euclid Industries was founded in 1939 by Zygmunt Zukowski as Ohio Screw Machine Products. Following the World War II years in defense production, Euclid specialized in the manufacture of heavy-duty truck wheel attaching studs and nuts for such original equipment manufacturers as Alcoa, White, Mack, Shuler, and Rockwell.

Euclid entered the aftermarket when Alcoa referred its distributors

Nearly 5,000 parts comprise the Euclid line of foundation air brake, hydraulic brake, wheel attaching, suspension and front end parts, and friction material for domestic and import trucks, tractors, trailers, and school buses.

directly to Euclid as another source for its replacement parts. Continued inquiries from warehouse distributors for Euclid to provide them additional parts led the firm to make the decision in the late 1960s to no longer service the OEM market, but rather to dedicate all efforts solely to serving the aftermarket. Concurrently, the company name was changed to Euclid Industries Inc. in order to more accurately reflect its focus.

Euclid is committed to providing its distributors with as wide a range of parts as possible. Thus, product line growth continues at an aggressive pace. The Euclid line includes nearly 5,000 parts, ranging from air and hydraulic brake, to wheel attaching, suspension, and front end parts and friction materials for medium- and heavy-duty domestic and import Class 4-8 trucks.

Euclid's engineering, manufacturing, product development, and quality-control teams are constantly researching products that will provide longer product life and improved performance. For example, Euclid's diamond-knurled brake shoe roller and hard chrome anchor pin designs have become industry

Euclid corporate headquarters in Cleveland, Ohio, includes manufacturing and distribution facilities serving more than 800 independent heavy-duty truck parts warehouse locations in the United States.

standards for excellence.

Euclid operates with the belief that a wide range of products alone does not adequately serve the aftermarket. The combination of parts availability, 95-percent-plus order fill, fast shipping, and technically trained salesmen who assist distributors and fleets with any maintenance problems add up to an unmatched level of customer service and satisfaction. Furthermore, Euclid catalogs have set the industry standard for convenient and comprehensive parts selection.

As its product line has grown so, too, has Euclid's facilities. In its early years Euclid Industries was located in Euclid, Ohio—hence the company name. Outgrowing that facility, it built a new one that now encompasses more than 115,000 square feet on 11 acres. In addition, Euclid entered the Canadian market in 1984 with the establishment of Euclid Industries Canada Ltd. With locations in Mississauga, Montreal, Edmonton, and Vancouver, Euclid serves the Canadian aftermarket with a full product line that parallels that in the United States.

Euclid Industries Inc. customers have learned that when they see the familiar yellow box, they know they are getting much more than just replacement parts from the industry leader that has earned their trust.

MARVIN JOHNSON AND ASSOCIATES, INC.

In the years since the founding of Marvin Johnson and Associates, the company has concentrated on excelling in the field of truck and truckers' insurance. During those years both the truck insurance business and the company itself have experienced notable change. What hasn't changed, however, is the trucking industry's need for an all-encompassing range of insurance coverage. Nor has there been a change in the firm's dedication to providing that coverage.

The company, located in Columbus, Indiana, just 35 miles south of Indianapolis, started as a modest two-person operation, consisting of founder Marvin Johnson and his wife, Frances, in 1970. In the decade that followed, sales volume rose from "just enough to keep the doors open" to $3.3 million in 1979. During that decade the Johnsons were joined in the business by their sons Steve, now chairman of the board; Mike, now the firm's president; and Roger, secretary/treasurer. Together, the family forged remarkable growth through the early 1980s—to $6.1 million in 1983.

By 1987 annual premium volume had reached $18 million, and the staff had expanded to more than 40. That surge through the 1980s has made Marvin Johnson and Associates Indiana's largest truck insurance agency and one of the top 100 in the United States.

The brothers are quick to point out that the basis for the company's rapid growth is the stable foundation on which their father started the firm. Before he established the company, Marvin Johnson spent the late 1960s specializing in truck insurance, actually operating his business out of a friend's trucking terminal. This provided him with actual hands-on experience on a daily basis and a greater understanding of the truckers' very unique needs. Because of that practical background, the company has always been extraordinarily service oriented and an innovator in the truck insurance business.

As a recognized and respected independent agency, Marvin Johnson and Associates is able to offer clients programs tailored to fit their individual needs—whether a small owner-operator or a larger fleet. The company offers full-line truck insurance service that includes fleet physical damage and bobtail programs; primary liability, collision, fire, and theft; cargo; bobtail/deadhead; workers' compensation; umbrella; bonding and permitting; premium financing; health and life plans; and building and premises coverage.

Marvin Johnson and Associates also offers its clients an in-house claims department to provide the prompt, personal service that is so critical to professional truckers, accelerating the processing of claims. In addition, clients have access to free WATS lines and a 24-hour answer-

Marvin Johnson and Associates, Inc., headquarters at 305 Washington Street in Columbus, Indiana.

ing service, with claims personnel on call 24 hours a day to facilitate claims handling.

The company's state-of-the-art computer and communications equip-

The claim department of Marvin Johnson and Associates is very knowledgeable on all aspects of trucking and truck claims. One of the main responsibilities is to work with a client in setting up a Client Protection Plan. This includes safety meetings, safety films, and any other information which will help its clients keep losses to a minimum.

ment is an extension of the services provided. Complete computerization affords the ability to call up programs and policies in moments. That, combined with its facsimile and telex equipment, permits immediate transmission of such documents as certificates, binders, motor vehicle reports, and other driver and company information.

The firm also provides what it calls a Client Protection Program, which includes on-site safety audits

One of the main assets of Marvin Johnson and Associates is the number of backup personnel available to its customers. Each customer has at least two people assigned to his or her account to assure them of proper service.

of clients' equipment, special safety presentations, and careful monitoring of clients' claims experience to hold rates down.

In order to maintain the firm's leadership position, management and staff personnel serve on national and state truck association committees and maintain regular contact with industry and regulatory sources.

The company has witnessed almost two decades of phenomenal growth that has come on the basis of long-term client relationships, built on its reputation for fairness, innovation, and integrity. The organization's management and staff is focused on a commitment to continue to offer the kinds of programs and services that the trucking industry has come to expect from Marvin Johnson and Associates.

Marvin Johnson and Associates' underwriting department works hard to offer its clients programs that are tailored to fit their individual needs. In addition, the company's clients have access to free WATS lines and a 24-hour answering service.

NATIONAL SEATING COMPANY

Doing things behind one's back isn't always the nicest thing to do, but for National Seating Company it's what it does best—and makes you like it.

In fact, the company's slogan for its Cush-N-Aire seat is simple: "Our truck seats do some nice things behind your back." National Seating, located in Vonore, Tennessee, just southwest of Knoxville, in one way or another and under one name or another, has been working behind the public's back since early in this century, providing seating for the transportation industry for more than 60 years.

It serves the intercity bus industry with bus-driver seats and deluxe recliner products. In addition, it provides manufacturers of large trucks with its Cush-N-Aire seat, making National the major producer of air-ride seating in the trucking industry.

In 1987 a second generation of air-ride seating came down the pike from National Seating—a self-contained air ride known as Easy-Air. This seat needs no air, electric lines, or special attachments for its operation and is a simple matter to install—whether it's in a truck, a motor home or recreational vehicle, farm equipment, construction equipment, van, off-road vehicles, or industrial vehicles.

Easy-Air has fore and aft seat movement, seat back-angle adjustment, and several height options that are accomplished through the use of a hand pump at the side of the seat that raises the seat gradually, leaving the driver riding on a cushion of air that absorbs practically all road shock and vibration. The seat, which is available in red, blue, brown, tan, black, or gray and in either vinyl or velour, has nearly all the comfort features of the time-tested Cush-N-Aire seat. Among those comfort features are contoured cushions that cradle the body, a knob that rotates to adjust the lumbar support to give extra lower back comfort and lessen the fa-

Located in Vonore, Tennessee, just southwest of Knoxville, National Seating is the major producer of air-ride seating in the trucking industry.

tigue factor, and the so-called Chugger Snubber that minimizes back slap.

In addition to these regular amenities, National Seating's Cush-N-Aire offers such special features as back recline, folding arm rest, bellows, and an off-road heavy-duty shock absorber. For back recline, the driver has only to turn a knob and the seat reclines up to 12 degrees, with an infinite number of adjustments so that the driver can achieve just the right spot for maximum operating comfort. The folding arm rest can be added to either or both sides of the seat, swings up and out of the way for easy exit from the cab, and can be installed either by the vehicle manufacturer or in the field.

The bellows provide a protective covering for the base of the seat and enhances the appearance of the truck cab. The shock absorber merely gives extra support and comfort to what is already an airy ride, and stiffens flotation ever so slightly.

For National Seating it all started with a company that built railroad and streetcar seating in metal and rattan. Between 1920 and 1935, in an effort to establish itself in the bus-seat manufacturing industry, part

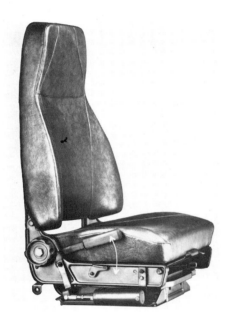

of the company, under the name Art Rattan Works, moved first to Cleveland and then to Mansfield, Ohio. As the firm advanced into intracity and intercity bus seating, it replaced the rattan with rubber cushioning and fabric covering.

In 1948, because of a breakup of the Art Rattan Company, National Seating Company was formed. This firm produced seating for all of the nation's major bus manufacturers, who at that time were concentrated in the Great Lakes region.

Recognizing a need to expand its product line and stabilize its business cycles, National Seating in 1965 received its first patent on an air-operated seat for truck drivers and started to produce that seat under the tradename of Cush-N-Aire. To the surprise of a truckload of skeptics, the emerging air-operated truck seat, riding the wave created by National Seating's Cush-N-Aire prod-

National Seating has been providing seating for the transportation industry for more than 60 years. Famous for its Cush-N-Aire seat, the firm has just recently produced the Easy-Air seat—a self-contained air ride seat.

uct, has revolutionized the truck-seating industry.

During the years there have been a variety of owners of National Seating Company, the latest of which is Chromalloy American Corporation. That purchase came in 1976 and made National Seating a subsidiary of American Transit Company. Prior

National Seating serves the intercity bus industry with bus-driver seats and deluxe recliner products and provides manufacturers of large trucks with its Cush-N-Aire seat. As the company slogan states: "Our truck seats do some nice things behind your back."

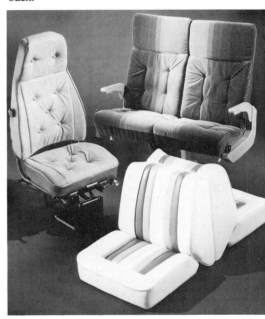

to National Seating's move from Ohio to Tennessee in 1985, the firm had opened an additional truck-seat assembly plant in Horse Cave, Kentucky, in an effort to better accommodate its customers.

Serving customers and producing a quality product continue to be major factors in National Seating Company's business attitude as it looks toward the twenty-first century. A prime example of that attitude and of National's confidence in its product is the firm's 500,000-mile limited warranty on air-suspension seats, and the knowledge that more drivers choose Cush-N-Aire than any other air-suspension seat. And that's not a bad combination to take into the 1990s.

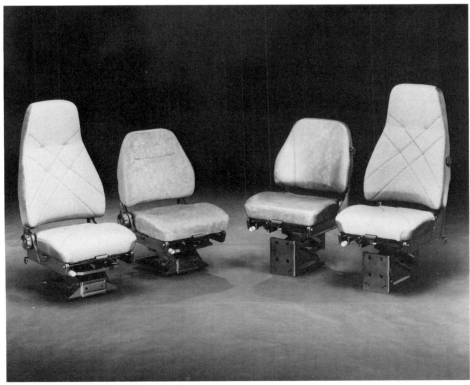

ILLINOIS TRUCKING ASSOCIATIONS, INC.

Now in its second half-century of service to the state's highway transportation industry, Illinois Trucking Associations, Inc., continues to be the voice of the Illinois trucking industry within both the state's borders and across the land. It also remains a source of dedicated and progressive leadership in the field.

It is committed to keeping the wheels rolling for trucking organizations in Illinois through a number of stated responsibilities, through an annual business-oriented convention, through emphasis on safety, and through various workshops on such subjects as the handling of hazardous materials and the Department of Transportation's annual safety audit that keeps industry executives in tune with the times. Equally important, though on a different level, are the association's social and charitable functions that help form a stronger bond among members and between the association and worthy state and national causes, thus enhancing the industry's image.

A major function of the organization, which is headed by an executive director and a general manager, is to be the industry's watchdog at the semiannual sessions of the state

The PR trailer for the Illinois Professional Truck Driving Championships was formerly known as the Illinois Truck Rodeo.

legislature in Springfield, downstate from the association's home office in Western Springs, a Chicago suburb. The legislative responsibility falls to the general manager, with the executive director behind the wheel of the rest of the load for the organiza-

Pictured (from left) are Vernon Schrof, chairman of the board of Illinois Trucking Associations, Inc., Neil Hartigan, attorney general, and Ferdinand Serpe, executive director of Illinois Trucking Associations, Inc., at the Annual Central States Truck Show.

tion's approximately 600 (and growing) membership that stands at a ratio of three trucking members for every allied member.

The following is a list of the things the ITA does for its membership, which includes all categories of for-hire motor transportation, private carriers, allied industry, and intercity bus operators: In addition to representing the industry in the Illinois legislature, working for passage of beneficial laws while trying to put the brakes on legislation deemed detrimental to the industry, the ITA counsels members on labor problems; updates members on compliance with laws; provides group insurance at reasonable rates; provides an out-

Burness E. Melton, director of government affairs, Illinois Trucking Associations, Inc., loads film into the projector for TIP-AC's Derby Day. TIPAC is the Trucking Industry Political Action Committee.

time each year to participate in social activities that include a golf outing where they can show off their skills to a tee and a Kentucky Derby celebration that serves as a fund-raising event for the Trucking Industry Political Action Committee. The fund raiser is held each Derby Day, with attendees placing bets with play money. When the day is over, winners have the opportunity to choose gifts and pay for them with the play money.

In addition, the association is a sponsor of the Central Truck Show, held at McCormick Place in

A judge measures the distance at the Illinois Professional Truck Driving Championships, a yearly event sponsored by the Illinois Safety Management Council and Illinois Trucking Associations, Inc.

standing bail-bond program; participates in safety programs beneficial to the entire industry; keeps members informed through a bimonthly magazine, a semimonthly newsletter, and a number of bulletins; and provides liaison with state agencies such as the secretary of state, state police, the Illinois Commerce Commission, the Illinois Environmental Protection Agency, and the Illinois Department of Transportation.

Lobbying the legislature has become a prime activity among industry associations nationwide, especially in the years since deregulation and the heightened awareness of environmental problems—and Illinois is no exception.

How a state legislature—or on a larger scale Congress—handles such things as taxation; licenses; fuel or wheel taxes; safety regulations; labor laws; vehicle emissions, noise, size, and weight restrictions; and hazardous materials and waste rules can put a company on the road to either success or disaster. Recognizing that,

Illinois Trucking Associations, Inc., maintains a constant presence in Springfield in an effort to keep the interests of the state's truckers in high gear.

Among its recent accomplishments at the legislative level, the ITA numbers the defeat of a proposed 9.5-cent increase in the fuel tax and of a license-fee increase, as well as the repeal of a law calling for mud flaps on power units.

"All work and no play makes Jack a dull boy," so the saying goes. Believing that, ITA members take

Chicago. The show, one of the biggest in the region, usually draws nearly 25,000 people.

While many organizations hold Christmas parties, Illinois Trucking Associations, Inc., looks on Christmas as a time for sharing. That is why members organized a toy drive some years ago for the benefit of needy children, loading its own Santa Claus down with about 2,000 gifts a year for the children of the Parents Too Soon program, sponsored by the Illinois Department of Public Aid.

DYNEER-GRANNING DIVISION

"Life's a whole lot smoother" is Granning's way of saying it has a product that will put the trucking industry miles ahead in comfort and confidence. Little wonder, then, that Granning, a division of the Dyneer Corp., calls its ride AirGlide.

Granning designs, prototypes, tests, manufactures, and markets a family of primary and auxiliary (tag and pusher) air-suspension systems with and without axles. The company's customers include the original equipment manufacturers of specialty light and medium trucks, buses, recreational vehicles, Class 8 trucks, and heavy semitrailers.

Granning air suspensions, which have been marketed since 1949, are manufactured in the United States, Canada, and Great Britain. The firm promotes its suspension system as not only providing superior riding comfort but also helping to reduce wear associated with road vibration. It also positions its product as effective in minimizing vehicular roll on curves with what it labels as superior, long-life roll stability. Granning accomplishes this roll stability through a minimum use of rubber or flexible bushings at pivot points

and its unique spring-beam design.

Granning, which has its headquarters in Livonia, Michigan, and its manufacturing plant in Brookston, Indiana, adds to this the ability of its suspensions to reduce maintenance expense and cargo damage, and to minimize installation time, sometimes cutting it by 50 percent of what other systems take.

In this age of light beer and so-called light foods, the company offers the Granning L-Series, a line of low-weight, high-performance auxiliary air suspensions. Depending on

the model chosen, the Granning L-Series can weigh up to 100 pounds less than comparable suspensions. That means, among other things, that the Granning L-Series can carry a payload of up to 100 pounds more than others can. In addition, these suspensions have a less filling overall length that allows the spacing of axles closer together and the capability of being fit into spaces too small for comparable suspensions.

Among the vehicle types that Granning Trailer air suspensions can excel in roll stability are vans, tankers, lowboys, furniture vans, dry bulkers, car haulers, dry freight haulers, flatbeds, livestock vans, and practically any other heavy-duty semitrailer application. Granning is so sure of its ride that hangers, spring beams, bushings, and all other major structural components of its trailer-primary suspensions carry a three-year or 300,000-mile warranty.

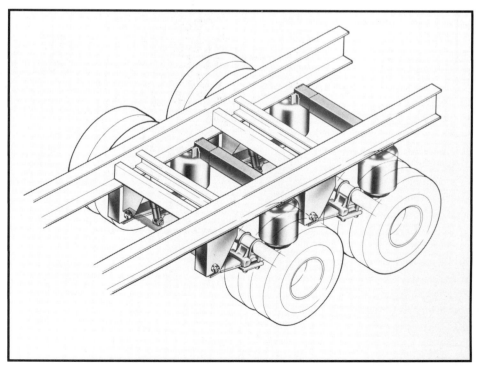

Gramm Trucks represent a quarter century of seasoned manufacturing experience

HAVING been "at it since 1901", the makers of Gramm Motor Trucks have accumulated an experience that is reflected in the vehicles they make and in the preference shown for them by motor-wise buyers of trucks.

This seasoned knowledge of truck operation has been applied in making constantly better, more easily serviced and efficient transportation units.

Co-operation between Gramm Motors, Inc., and Lycoming engineers was the culminating step which provided the 1½-, 2- and 2½-ton trucks with powerful, flexible, smooth-running and economical engines—Lycoming Motors—capable of insuring road speeds up to 45 miles per hour (depending upon the weight and model) and the acceleration to meet the requirements of all traffic and road conditions.

LYCOMING MANUFACTURING COMPANY
Makers of fine Fours, Sixes and Eights-in-Line
WILLIAMSPORT :: PENNSYLVANIA
Export Department — 44 Whitehall Street, New York City
MEMBER OF MOTOR TRUCK INDUSTRIES, INC., OF AMERICA

LYCOMING
Motors

Years Ahead in Automobile Motor Efficiency

"Gramm" trucks tried to capitalize on the connection with Lycoming Motors in this 1927 advertisement. Lycoming went on to make powerful warplane engines in World War II, but got out of trucking. Courtesy, American Truck Historical Society

Patrons

The following individuals, companies, and organizations have made a valuable commitment to the quality of this publication. Windsor Publications gratefully acknowledges their participation in *A Tribute to Trucking*.

Bosch Trucking Company, Inc.*
W.J. Casey Trucking & Rigging
    Co., Inc.*
Caterpillar, Inc. Engine Division*
Coast Dispatch, Inc.*
Dana Corporation*
DeCarolis Truck Rental, Inc.*
Double Eagle Industries*
Dyneer-Granning Division*
Euclid Industries Inc.*
Don Frame Trucking, Inc.*
Gully Transportation, Inc.*
Illinois Trucking Associations, Inc.*
Interstate Truckload Carriers
    Conference*
Marvin Johnson and Associates*
Kaney Transportation Inc.*

Kold-Ban International Ltd.*
Lear Siegler Truck Products Corp.*
Lubrizol Corporation*
Mack Trucks, Inc.*
Edward J. Meyers Co.*
Midland Heavy Duty Systems*
Modagrafics Corporation*
National Seating Company*
Nationwide Truck Brokers Inc.*
L. Neill Cartage Co. Inc.*
Rudolf Express*
Schilli Transportation Services,
    Inc.*
Wayne W. Sell Corporation*
Sentinel Agency, Inc.*
J. Supor & Son Trucking, Rigging,
    and Crane Service*
Sweeney Bros. Inc.*
Bruce W. Trent Trucking
    Company*
Truck-Lite Company, Inc.*

*Partners in Progress of *A Tribute to Trucking*. The histories of these companies and organizations appear in Part Two, beginning on page 127.

Barrett, N.S. *Trucks.* New York: Watts, 1984.

Behrens, June. *Truck Cargo.* Los Angeles: Elk Grove Press, 1970.

Cheng, Philip C. *Accounting and Financing for Motor Carriers.* Lexington, MA: Lexington Books, 1984.

Crews, Donald. *Truck.* New York: Greenwillow Books, 1980.

Glaskowsky, Nicholas A. *Effects of Deregulation on Motor Carriers.* Westport, Connecticut: Eno Foundation for Transportation, 1986.

Greene, Carla. *Truck Drivers: What do they do?* New York: Harper, 1967.

Hadad, Helen R. *Truck and Loader.* New York: Greenwillow Books, 1982.

Kautz, John Iden. *Trucking to the Trenches; Letters from France, June-November 1917.* Boston and New York: Houghton Mifflin Co., 1918.

McNaught, Harry. *The Truck Book.* New York: Random House, 1978.

Madsen, Axel. *Open Road: Truckin' on the Biting Edge.* San Diego, CA: Harcourt, Brace Janovich, 1982.

Moore, Thomas Gale. *Trucking Regulation: Lessons from Europe.* Washington, DC: American Enterprise Institute for Public Policy Research, 1976.

National Petroleum News. *Truck, Tractor, Trailer Study.* New York: McGraw-Hill, 1969.

Radlauer, Ed. *Truck Mania.* Chicago: Children's Press, 1982.

Siebert, Diane. *Truck Song.* New York: Crowell, 1984.

Stern, Jane. *Truckers: A Portrait of the Last American Cowboy.* New York: McGraw-Hill, 1975.

Tak, Montie. *Truck Talk; the Language of the Open Road.* Philadelphia: Chilton, 1971.

Talmadge, Marian. *Let's go to a Truck Terminal.* New York: Putnam, 1964.

Vreeland, Barrie. *Trucking From A to Z.* New York Shippers Conference of Greater New York, 1969.

Index

GENERAL INDEX
Italicized numbers indicate illustrations

About the Author

Jack Thiessen operates his own agency, PR Counselors, based in Toledo, Ohio where he does public relations work for several truck-related companies and associations. His clients have included Detroit Diesel Allison, Rockwell International's Automotive Products Group, and Whiteford Systems, Inc. Thiessen is also editor of *Truckers News*, a monthly truck trade magazine, and *Truckstop World*, a bimonthly trade magazine for truckstop management.

Thiessen and his wife, Marie Louise, currently make their home in a suburb of Toledo. They have four children and 10 grandchildren.

About the Business Historians

Gene Williams is a seasoned newsman, having spent 30 years as a writer and editor, the past 25 years with the Courier-Journal and the Louisville Times in Louisville.

In addition to hes work on the newspapers, Williams has been a member of the adjunct faculties of Indiana University Southeast and the University of Louisville. Currently a freelance writer, Williams lives in Louisville.

Mark H. Dorfman is an independent writer based in Washington, D.C. A distinguished finance journalist and economic historian, he has taught American studies and communications at Penn State and George Washington University. His publishing credits include numerous scholarly and popular articles as well as corporate histories in three previous Windsor books.

This book was set in Palatino and Goudy type
and printed on 70 lb. Mead enamel.
Printing and binding by Walsworth Publishing Company.
Book design and layout by Tom McTighe.